INGREDIENT CALLED LOVE

AUGUST 1997

The *Ingredient Called Love* is based on the true story of Vernon Cecil Fuller of Winters, Texas, born 31 January 1916 and died 10 January 1988. Vernon Fuller passed away in his daughter's arms, Reta Lee Fuller, in her home in Wisconsin, and surrounded by his granddaughters, Pamela and Kimberly, and friends, one year and two months following his massive stroke. Fulfilling a promise Reta made to her father, she flew his body back home and buried him next to the grave of her mother, Minnie Lee Merck Fuller, who had died when Reta was very young.

by

Reta Lee

THE
INGREDIENT
CALLED
LOVE

Library of Congress Catalog Card Number: 97-94242
ISBN 1-57502-578-7

Property of

Reta Lee Enterprises, Inc.
3957 South Euclid Avenue
Las Vegas, Nevada 89121
ph: 702-734-7406 fax: 702-734-7393

Printed in the USA by

MORRIS PUBLISHING
3212 East Highway 30 • Kearney, NE 68847 • 1-800-650-7888

DEDICATION

 I would like to dedicate my book to the good Lord above for giving me and my family the strength and endurance we needed to care for my daddy, and to the memories of my mother, Minnie Lee Merck Fuller and my father, Vernon Cecil Fuller.

 They were the best and most wonderful parents a child could have ever dreamed of having. They always encouraged me to be the best I could be. I am so grateful for the wonderful foundation on which they built my life, and for the values they instilled in me. I thank God for giving me such wonderful parents.

RETA LEE

was born of Irish and German descent and raised on a small farm and ranch near Abilene, Texas. She knows all about hard work, or what some might say, *"paying your dues."* She pulled cotton, milked cows and tended to the chickens. However, she loved barrel racing and working with her horses most of all. She, like so many other country entertainers, started singing in a small Baptist church. At a very tender age her mother, *Minnie Lee Merck Fuller,* lovingly coached her voice. Her father, *Vernon Cecil Fuller,* managed her singing career making sure she appeared in all the local talent and television shows.

She attended college in Abilene, Texas, did some modeling, married and gave birth to two daughters, *Pamela* and *Kimberly.* She and her family moved to Hastings, Minnesota where she opened her first dance studio. She taught ballet, tap, jazz and baton twirling. After a divorce, she organized her country band, *Pure Gold,* and performed all over the upper Midwest. Her television show, ***Country Side Roundup,*** was televised from Duluth, Minnesota. She later moved her daughters to Frederic, Wisconsin and continued to sing and teach dancing in the local areas. However, Amery, Wisconsin is where she made their home. *Pamela & Kimberly* graduated from Amery High School.

After her father's death, *Reta Lee* turned her dance studios over to her daughters and moved to Las Vegas to continue her singing career. Businessman, *Johnnie Milam,* heard her singing in a local club on the strip. He gave her the financial backing she needed to record her first album, **"Dare to Dream."** She named this album for her wonderful fans who had given her *hope* to *dare to dream* throughout the years.

Johnnie made all her **"Dreams Come True,"** also the title of her second album dedicated to him. *Reta Lee* received two **Number One Hits, "Hey Baby..Que Paso?"** and **"Ship of Fools."** (*C.M.A.A. Airplay International Chart* Nashville,Tennessee). *Reta* gives her grateful thanks to the air play given her songs by all the wonderful *C.M.A.A. **Independent Radio Stations in the United States, the Spanish and European Radio Station, but most of all to her wonderful friends who supported and embraced her.***

Johnnie bought *Reta Lee* a dinner theater in Branson, Missouri. She performed two shows per day six days per week. Unfortunately, *Johnnie* was forced to sell the club in Branson and return to Las Vegas in 1997 after his doctor told him the *stress* he was under in Branson could cause him to have a **heart attack** or a **stroke**. After you read **"The Ingredient Called Love"** you will understand why *Reta* totally supported *Johnnie's* decision to leave Branson and return to their home in Las Vegas. She did not want *Johnnie* to go through what her daddy went Through. **Reta Lee's Roots Run Deep.**

Acknowledgments

To my daughters, Pamela and Kimberly, for your love and support during this emotional time of our lives. You were always there for me, a shoulder if I needed one and the backbone of our studios. I thank God for giving me two such wonderful daughters.

To my Aunt Sissy, Marie Merck, for your love and support during daddy's illness and death. You've always been my friend and confidant throughout my life.

To my adopted mother, Louise LaCasse, for your love throughout the years, your guidance in my dance studios and for choosing me to be your adopted daughter. Thank you for inspiring me to write my life story.

To all the Medical Professionals who lovingly cared for Daddy at Abbott-Northwestern Hospital and Sister Kenny Rehabilitation Center in Minneapolis, Minnesota. A special "Thanks" to Dr. Charles Petersen and Dr. Jennine Speier.

To Nurse Joyce Schaefer who headed the most loyal and supportive home care team anyone could ask for. We could alway count on each of you to be there when we needed you. Thank you my friends.

To my dear friends, Brad Fougner and home care attendant, Fred Gulseth. Without your help and support we couldn't have endured. You will always own a very special part of my heart.

To Mike Meyer, Winters Funeral Home, for your assistance in bringing Daddy safely home and laying him to rest beside my mother. I will never forget your kindness.

Last, but not least, to my dearest friend, Johnnie Milam, for giving "THE INGREDIENT CALLED LOVE" a wonderful ending and for making all my Dreams Come True. I love you.

A Special Thanks To

Terry Dawson

and

THE**ABACUS**GROUP

Literary Agency

Ridgecrest, California

**For Their Invaluable Editorial Assistance
In Bringing This Project To Completion**

SYNOPSIS

The Ingredient Called Love is based on the true story of Vernon Cecil Fuller of Winters, Texas, born 31 January 1916 and died 10 January 1988.

This book was written by his youngest daughter, Reta Lee Fuller, who took her Daddy out of an Abilene Hospital near Winters, Texas, and put him in a hospital bed in the back of a van because the doctor advised he was too sick to fly home by air-ambulance. Reta was able to attain *Power of Attorney* to manage her father's affairs before the massive stroke took over three-fourths of Mr. Fuller's mind. Her brother, Cecil, was in harmony with Reta taking him to Wisconsin, but her sister, Loraine Shores (nicknamed Yane), wanted to put him into a care-facility in Texas. Just how that issue was resolved makes for an intriguing read.

The story demonstrates the love and caring that Reta and her daughters, Pamela and Kimberly, had for Vernon Fuller. It describes in detail, with pictures included, how far Vernon Fuller was brought back to a life of recovery following his massive stroke, a real-life testimony to proper rehabilitation and *The Ingredient Called Love*.

The story acknowledges the wonderful medical services provided by Abbott-Northwestern Hospital and Sister Kenny Rehabilitation Center in Minneapolis, Minnesota. Also the wonderful home care and support Reta received from the local caretakers in the Amery, Wisconsin area.

Vernon Fuller died in Reta's arms, surrounded by his granddaughters and friends, in Reta's home in Wisconsin, one year and two months after his massive stroke. At the end, he had progressed to a point where the stroke was not obvious, but died when his one remaining kidney finally failed. Reta had been advised to enter him into a nursing home in Minneapolis, but defied everyone as she had done in Texas, and took him to her home in Wisconsin to die with family. She then fulfilled a promise made to her father before the stroke: When the time came, he would be taken to Texas and buried next to Reta's mother.

The story tells of the love, hardships, financial problems and sheer joy she and her daughters shared while caring for the elder Mr. Fuller; the personal hardship Reta endured concerning her sister, Yane, as Reta went about the daily process of caring for their father; plus the turmoil of having to divorce a cheating husband which, in itself, bordered on the impossible. The story also tells of how financial aid was pulled from Vernon Fuller, and at a time when the family needed it most.

The ups and downs Reta endured with the bureaucratic system while trying to live by their rules is spared no barbs, a condition which would break any normal person into a heap of emotional rubble.

The story is, though, MORE THAN ANYTHING ELSE, about a daughter's love for her father. It's warm, tender, loving, humorous and jam-packed with everyday reality. Reta Lee wrote these words in the hope that others might learn from her mistakes and gain knowledge about this horrible sickness that touches so many families, and to recognize the warning signals of the treacherous mini-stroke which, often, is the danger signal to a massive stroke.

A final thought: Nothing is impossible if you try hard and want it bad enough. *The Ingredient Called Love* proves that human love and caring is stronger than the hardest steel.

1

This is the Vernon Fuller story, as written by his youngest daughter, Reta Lee Fuller, June 1, 1994. Reta began writing the account of how she and her family cared for her father, Vernon Fuller, after the elder Mr. Fuller suffered a stroke on December 19, 1986. What you are about to read is, at times, both gut-wrenching and wistfully poignant. BUT IT IS NOTHING IF NOT COMPLETELY TRUE...

AIRLINE TICKETS HAD BEEN PURCHASED FOR MY husband, Steve, and me to fly to Texas to visit my Daddy for Christmas, the holiday season of 1986, and I must say, tickets acquired with my own hard-earned money.   Beyond that, this opportunity was to provide an ulterior motive: The honeymoon we never had in our three years of marriage.

I suppose this would be the proper time to say that our marriage suffered desperately because of Steve's immaturity. To be fair, though, that wasn't the only reason. I was severely overworked, trying to keep the bills paid, and had very little energy remaining to fulfill the marriage bit—keeping the spouse happy, making the right meals at all the right times and, in general, being the bubbly, exciting, always mysterious little woman he had married.

One morning, about a week before we were supposed to leave, as I remember it, I awoke and poured myself the usual cup of coffee, sat down in the living room and—after staring blankly at the wall for some minutes, something I did a lot of during that time—started making an agenda for "another exciting day" of activities. I started in the usual manner and popped a piece of Nicorette gum into my mouth, as I had been off cigarettes for about six weeks but actually felt more addicted to the damned gum than to the cigarettes! I looked around the room, shook my head and said out loud with no one else around, "Will Steve ever finish this...this house?"

You see, Steve had started this masterful art of house construction after we had married—some three years before—but seldom, if ever, finished a project before bouncing to another. Therein lay the problem, of course. I should have known better, I told myself, over and again, and I must say it showed. Many times over those years, I wished I had bought the trailer house instead of getting caught up in this ain't-never-gonna-get-done project of his. Truly, I regretted not getting the trailer house—just like I was going to do before ever meeting Steve. Guess that says something about my internal constitution at the time. Of course, on this particular morning that issue was cause for deep, personal reflection, as it was most mornings, the kind of soul-searching that sometimes can leave you devastated and wishing you were someone else. To be fair, though, when I had first met Steve, it was a very low point in my life. Even still, for as long as the Good Lord lets me live, I will always wonder why I went through with the marriage in the first place. Sometimes we humans do things to ourselves and to others for which we are truly sorry, and sometimes we do things that we know beforehand will turn out a real tornado-disaster, and still, beyond that, we sometimes do things to ourselves that we know will drag us down to the lowest pit of emotional degradation. Why? I can only answer for myself. Did I do this to punish myself? To do a make-over on myself so that I could never, ever be the person I truly wanted to be? Was I afraid to be the happy, smiling, shining person God intended? Was I truly afraid, at the time, to step forward in an attempt to be successful within myself and for others, to be the person my father wanted me to be? I don't know. Only God knows. I would hate to think that I even unconsciously used Steve to drag myself into the depths of despair so that I could, eventually, emerge as a martyr. If that is so, when the time comes, I will have to answer to my God.

This particular morning, Daddy was on my mind more than usual, and I just couldn't shake it. I couldn't even concentrate on compiling the day's activity list, usually an exciting exercise! Throughout my life, I always had a really close bond with Daddy, and that commitment became even stronger after Mama died, which happened when I was very young.

After marrying Chuck Albrecht, the father of my daughters, Kim and Pam, we moved to his home state, Wisconsin. The actual distance away from Texas and Daddy never mattered. I always intuitively knew if he needed me or was thinking about me. Many times, I would call, and upon picking up the telephone, Daddy knew I was on the other end. This was the eerie feeling I was experiencing this morning, only worse. The mood was so strong that I knew the warning was from God, an actual wake-up call from Heaven, and He was telling me to get home and fast—that Daddy really needed me.

My daughters, Pam and Kim, came in with their usual bowls of cereal and joined me. They knew something was really wrong. Kim asked, "Mom, what's the matter?"

As best I could hide it, I said, "Something's really wrong with your Papa Texas, and I have to go home now. I can't wait until the 23rd. I know it's something bad."

They had known me to have these kinds of feelings before and knew they were for real. I said, "I'm gonna call Mary. I need her advice." Mary Casey was one of my friends from high school and I had asked her to keep an eye on Daddy for me when I left Texas in 1983.

I was able to reach Mary by telephone and explained my feelings to her. "This makes the hair on the back of my neck stand up," exclaimed Mary. "I was gonna call you today. Your Daddy has really been acting strange."

"Strange, how?" I quickly asked.

"Well...he called me this morning and said, "Mary, tell Reta to get on back over to the house. I got some mail from the government and I want her to explain it to me." I told him, "Vernon, Reta's in Wisconsin. She won't be here until the 23rd." He was always scared the government was going to cut his social security or disability checks.

"Mary, my ticket for the 23rd is paid for," I said, "and indicates there is no refund available. Do you think I should wait another week?"

"Reta, I think you should be here now! He really scares me."

"I'll be there as soon as possible, Mary." That was all I needed to hear. I told her goodbye, then turned to Pam and Kim and said, "That's it! I'm leaving today!"

"Mom, if you could just wait another day and teach the class in Spooner tonight, then Kim and I could handle the studios until Christmas Vacation," Pam said helpfully, as it was only one week away.

All three of us were teaching ballet, tap, jazz, and baton twirling in six different locations. My dance studios had always been my bread and butter jobs. I sang with my country band on the weekends and I was making a very decent living between the two careers. It had really been nice since Pam and Kim had gotten old enough to help me. They had become more like partners and could teach just as well as I could.

"Okay," I said, "but I'm leaving no later than tomorrow, even if I have to cancel classes." We were all in agreement.

Steve finally woke up and joined us in the kitchen, and then we filled him in on my change of plans. "Crap," he muttered grumpily, "I was looking forward to flying. Oh, well, I'll get the oil changed in the car and go with you." I would have rather gone alone, but Pam and Kim insisted that I take Steve with me.

I taught the classes in Spooner that night and, by the time I arrived back home to Amery, I had everything figured out so that all of us could spend Christmas with Daddy, in Texas.

"Girls," I explained, "I am really worried about Daddy and would like you both to be there for Christmas. I've decided— If you want, Kim can go with Steve and me in the car, and then, Pam, you and Brad can use our airplane tickets to fly down on the 23rd."

Both girls indicated that they were quite delighted with the changes I had suggested. "Sounds great to me, Mom," said Pam, "but let me call and talk with Brad before I decide."

Brad and Pam had been going together since she was sixteen. He only had one arm and wore a hook-type prosthesis, yet, I never thought of him as handicapped because he didn't see himself as handicapped.

I remember an incident that occurred back when Pam first started dating Brad. I was singing at one of the local clubs and needed a big speaker brought in. Without thinking, I asked Brad to bring it in for me. By golly, the door swung open and in came Brad with that big ol' speaker!. That's when I knew he wasn't handicapped. At that point, he became like a son to me.

Pam called Brad, and he said, "Yeah, that'll be fun." Brad had met Daddy in August when he had come up to visit me in Amery. They really got along well; therefore, he was in total harmony with our new plans.

Steve, Kim and I headed for Texas early the next morning, driving straight through. Thanks to the Good Lord, we had no car problems during the trip.

I HAD NOT CALLED TO TELL DADDY ABOUT OUR new plans because I wanted to surprise him. When we pulled into Daddy's driveway about sunset, the next day, he had just gotten home and was standing at his front door fiddling with the key. He turned around and said, "Piss Ant, help me get this damn door open." He had nicknamed me Piss Ant when I was just a little girl.

"Well, hello to you too," I said, as I gave him a big hug. He looked at me really confused. I think he still believed I was in Winters and must have just been coming home from Mary's house or something.

"Where have you been, Daddy?" I asked.

"Now, Piss Ant, you know I always go visit your Ma's grave on Sunday."

After helping him open the front door and we were in the house, I said, "But Daddy, this is Friday!"

"You're shittin' me!" he exclaimed with some irritation. "It can't be Friday 'cause I went to the Badlands dancin' last night!"

"Trust me, Daddy, it's Friday," I told him gently.

As he sat down, he muttered, "Well, hell, maybe that's why nobody was at the Badlands last night. It was Thursday night!"

I looked around his little house. It still looked the same. Even the curtains I had hung in 1983 (when Kim and I lived next door to him in our trailer house) were still in place.

Before Kim and I left to go back to Wisconsin later in 1983, as a surprise for Daddy, I had completely redecorated his little house and also gave him my furniture. I'll never forget how surprised and happy he had been back then, especially about the new carpet. He had taken his boots off and walked into each room digging his toes into the soft, deep pile. Looking at me he had said, "Hell, Piss Ant, I ain't never had carpet, afore."

As we stood in the living room, this week before Christmas, Daddy looked at me, and out of the clear blue, said, "Piss Ant, I'd give anything for a nanner puddin' and a chocolate cake."

"Boy, Daddy," I said, "You're easy. That's a pretty cheap Christmas gift." We all laughed, but he was really serious. I wondered if it had been awhile since he had last eaten.

Later, I called my Aunt Sissy. She was my mother's baby sister and, even though a small woman, she was as tough as an old boot. No one in the family wanted to get on the wrong side of her, not even my sister, Loraine Shores, whom everyone called, Yane.

"Hi Sissy, I'm here!" Since she wasn't expecting me to arrive until the 23rd, she was really taken by surprise to hear my voice.

"Baby, what in the world are you doing here this early! I thought you were not coming until the 23rd?" She sounded breathless and excited at the same time.

"Well, Sissy," I replied, "It's a long story, but if you will help me make Daddy a banana puddin', I'll tell you all about it."

Sissy was over in a flash after stopping by the store and picking up the items we needed to make the pudding. Daddy never baked, you see. He mostly lived on frozen Mexican dinners; therefore, there wasn't anything in the house with which to make a banana pudding.

Daddy visited with all of us for awhile and then said, "I don't feel too good. I'm gonna lay down while y'all make the nanner puddin'. Wake me up when it's ready."

"Okay, Brody," I answered, calling him by the nickname I had given him a few years back.

Sissy and I had a good visit. We hadn't seen each other since Kathy had died. I will always remember what a special lady my aunt was because she was there for me throughout my whole life. She was like a mother, sister, and my best friend all rolled up in one.

Sissy used to come and pick me up on a regular basis to spend the night at her house when I was a little girl. She let me dress up in her clothes, play in her makeup and wear her jewelry. I remember once, mother came in and caught me in one of Sissy's squaw dresses. She laid it on me, and said, "Reta, get out of your Aunt Sissy's clothes! And right now!"

She was going to spank me, but Sissy ran in, saved the day, and said, "Now, Minnie Lee, I gave her permission to play in my closet. She knows to put everything back the way she found it." She was my hero, and I love her very much.

Sissy had to get home after we got the pudding made. I woke Daddy up and said, "Hey, Brody, aren't you gonna get up and eat this great nanner puddin' Sissy and I made for you?"

Daddy opened his eyes and said in a drowsy tone, "You betcha."

He got up slowly and started for the kitchen. I noticed he was swinging his right arm. "I must'a slept on my hand wrong," he said. "I can't hold a cigarette with it and it feels asleep." That was the first sign that something was wrong.

Sitting down to eat his banana pudding, he took the spoon in his right hand as usual, but couldn't make it work correctly. When he tried to pick up a spoonful of the pudding, it just kept going across to the left side of the bowl. With help from his other hand he finally managed to get a bite into his mouth. Little did I know this would be the last bite of food my Dad would ever eat with his right hand. After that, he placed the spoon in his left hand and finished every bite. Then he went back to his bed.

I was very worried about him as he had lost two sisters and one brother to strokes. I only wished I had known then what I know now.

The next morning Daddy's hand was not worse, but it wasn't any better either. I said, "Daddy, I really think we should take you to see the doctor. This is the way strokes start sometimes, you know."

"Oh, hell, Piss Ant, I'll be okay," he assured me.

I fixed bacon and eggs for breakfast and Daddy grabbed his plate and started eating like a starved puppy. I said, "Daddy, slow down before you choke. When did you have a decent meal last?"

He thought for a moment, then said, "Hell, I don't 'member."

"Daddy, I'm not going to start ragging on you until after Christmas about going back to Wisconsin with me, but I will not leave you here." In a joking way I continued, "If I have to, I'll take you to court and get custody of you!"

With a big smile, he said, "Well, I got news for you. I'd already made my mind up to go back to Wisconsin with you after Christmas."

I gave him the biggest hug in the world and said, "Daddy, that's the best Christmas gift you have ever given me. Now, I want to call Sissy and have you tell her you've decided to go to Wisconsin. That way, if anything should come up in the future, she will know what your wishes were."

I called Sissy, and Daddy told her exactly what his plans were for the time after Christmas. She was really happy he had decided to go back with me; after all, she had been worrying about him, too.

Daddy sat there and continued to drink his coffee with a really far away look on his face. This bothered me, and I said, "Daddy, what are you thinking about?"

He said with a serious look on his face, "I was just thinking how far Wisconsin is from big ol' Texas."

"Oh, Daddy," I said, "You're worried about me bringing you back here if something should happen, aren't you?"

"How did you know that?" he responded, and in a serious way.

"'Cause I know you, Brody. I give you my word— If anything should happen to you, I will bring you back and plant you by Mama."

He laughed and said, "Do I have your word on that?"

"You got my word on that, Daddy." My father's word was always good. As a kid, if I could get him to give me his word about doing anything, it was as good as done. He instilled this value in me at a very young age, and to this day, I am a better person for it.

DADDY AND I PROCEEDED TO MAKE PLANS.   WE decided to close up his little house, possibly even rent it out. He said, "We'll go to the bank and talk to Bill Sneed, and first thing Monday morning. That way you can take care of my business affairs when we get up yonder."

"Daddy," I questioned, "Did you ever put your little nest egg in the bank after you had me take it out of the savings and loan in 1983, before I left to go back to Wisconsin?"

He looked at me like I had lost my mind. "What in the hell are you talking about, Piss Ant? I never had no nest egg." I thought he was joking, but he was serious.

"Daddy, don't you remember you gave me the key to your lock box in 1983 and told me to open an account at the savings and loan so you could draw interest? Remember, you had it stuck in your lock box and I was scared someone was going to break in and rob you? Then, when I left to go back to Wisconsin, you had me draw it all out in $100 bills and you stuck it right back in your lock box. You promised to take it to Bill Sneed." He just sat there looking at me like he had no idea what I was talking about.

Daddy got up and went to his room and came back with his lock box. Opening it as he had done so many times in the past, he went through all his paperwork, telling me what he wanted done with his belongings when he died. How he wanted his wedding ring, that Mama had given him, put back on his finger. He had worn it during their twenty-five years of marriage and also for some time after her death. There were also his insurance policies, and other papers.

"Daddy, believe me, I will make sure all your wishes are carried out at your death."

I then knew there was a big problem. "But, Daddy, you had $5,000 in $100 bills in that lock box when I left here in 1983!"

He just laughed, again. Sitting there for awhile in really deep thought, he then said, "Piss Ant, am I getting feeble or what?" Then he started crying. This almost broke my heart.

I put my arms around him and said, "No, Daddy, you're not getting feeble, you just need to retire and let me do all the worrying for a change. You took care of me all those years, now let me spoil you a little. Don't worry about anything, we'll go see Bill Monday morning and I'm sure we can get everything straightened out."

I was sure hoping that Bill Sneed could come up with some answers, but decided to drop the matter until Monday. First, I had to get Daddy to the doctor.

"Daddy, right now I'm gonna call the hospital and make an appointment for a doctor to check you." He didn't like it, but he knew he had to go. I called the Winters Hospital and they said to bring Daddy right over. Next, I called Sissy and asked her to come over and go with us. As usual, Sissy was there in a flash.

Unfortunately for daddy, the older Dr. Lee was the doctor on call. His attitude was so indifferent and non-caring. He acted as though he was upset we had called him in on the weekend.

He took Daddy's blood pressure and found it was ungodly high! Taking Daddy into the examination room, Dr. Lee told him to drop his pants, then gave him a shot of Lasix. Afterwards, he came out and said, "You can take your father home now. Call and make an appointment to bring him to my office, Monday morning."

"Dr. Lee, I believe my dad is having a stroke, is this all you're going to do?"

"Yes, at this time. I will see you on Monday."

I couldn't believe it! He acted as though my Dad had a cold or something really minor. I took Daddy home and Sissy stayed for a little while and visited. Dad seemed to be feeling a little better but went to bed unusually early, as he was very tired.

THE NEXT MORNING, WE ALL GOT UP FAIRLY EARLY. Daddy seemed to be doing better. He ate a good breakfast and said, "I'm gonna take a bath and wash my hair this mornin', then I wanna watch wrestling:"

"Okay," I said feeling much better about his condition, "I'll go visit Mary and bake that chocolate cake I promised you."

I sure was glad he was gonna take that bath because I had never seen my Dad look so shabby. Steve said, "I'll stay here with Vernon and watch wrestling, too." That was fine with me because I wanted to catch up on all the gossip with Mary.

"Daddy, when I get back, we can go down to the cafe and have some coffee like we used to. Sound good?"

"Okay," he answered.

Mary and I had a nice visit. We made the chocolate cake and, as soon as it cooled, I went back to Daddy's house. I figured the wrestling would be over and Daddy would be shaved and all cleaned up.

But when I walked in the front door, I couldn't believe my eyes! Daddy was sitting in his chair and all slumped over, white as a ghost and mumbling to himself! I yelled at Steve, "How long has he been like this?"

He looked up as though he wasn't playing with a full deck and said, "Oh, I guess about twenty or thirty minutes."

"For heaven sakes, Steve! Didn't it occur to you that something was wrong, and to call me?

"Or something," he murmured, not very interested. "Yeah, I guess I shudda called. He's been asking for you and Cecil."

I was so angry at him I could have killed him, but—first things first—my Dad needed help. Immediately, I called Dr. Lee, and he told me to bring Daddy in the following morning! At that point, I totally lost it.

"Dr. Lee," I said with as much sarcasm as possible, "I am so sorry my Dad picked the weekend to have a stroke! And how dare he interfere with your weekend! You don't have to worry about us anymore. I am getting my Daddy a real doctor before it's too late!"

In tears, I then called Sissy to come over as soon as possible. I felt so bad calling Sissy so often, but I have always respected her judgment and, besides, I needed some moral support.

Then, I called my sister, Yane. She was somewhere on the Gulf Coast getting ready for her family to come in for their Christmas festivities. Finally, I got through and told her what had happened, that I was going to call Abilene Hospital.

Yane said, "Oh, they won't take him there unless another doctor makes the appointment."

"I have never heard anything like that in my life!" I screamed. "Don't worry, I'll take care of him myself." It was at that point that I felt she was not going to be any help, so I quickly said, "Goodbye, I'll call you later."

Sissy arrived in record time and I told her what Yane had said. "I've never heard anything like that before, either," she said, sounding puzzled. "Just call the emergency room in Abilene and see what they say."

This we did, and the duty nurse was very nice. She said, "I agree with you. It sounds as though your dad might be having a stroke or has just suffered one. Bring him in as soon as possible and I will notify Dr. Mendenhall, the doctor-on-call, that you're on your way." I was delighted to hear Dr. Mendenhall would be the one looking after him as he had been Daddy's doctor in 1984.

IN A FLASH OF INSIGHT THAT ONE ONLY GETS EVERY SO OFTEN, USUALLY UNDER SEVERE STRESS, I INSTINCTIVELY KNEW WHY YANE DID NOT WANT ME TO TAKE DADDY TO ABILENE. IT WAS ALL SO CLEAR, NOW.

MY MIND SUDDENLY RELIVED A TERRIBLE INCIDENT that happened to Daddy back in 1984. This short story will clarify why I had accepted Daddy's memory loss when he visited my home that past August when, in fact, he was having mini-strokes.

This episode began when Uncle R. A. Long, Daddy's brother-in-law, also deceased now, came by Daddy's house to check on him as he usually did every morning. He found Daddy lying on the floor, and in a stupor, Daddy said upon seeing R. A., "Call Yane." Daddy later told me he had meant to say, "Call Reta."

He then told Uncle R. A. to take his lock box and not to give it to anyone but Yane." Daddy was always getting names mixed up, but this time he really did the big one!

Uncle R. A. was a little confused about this because he knew that I had handled Daddy's business for him during the time when I lived next to his house in 1983. He also knew Daddy had continued to call me in Wisconsin, after I had moved back, if he had a problem. Above all, he knew how close Daddy and I had always been. Nevertheless, he did as Daddy instructed, he called Yane.

She came immediately and took over. Days later, she called me and said, "Reta, Daddy has cancer and I am taking him back to Zapata. You don't need to come down here. I have everything under control." You see, and this point needs to be made, she was so hateful to me. She and I had never been close, in fact, she was not close to any of the family. She was a pretty lady, but very controlling, hateful, and extremely judgmental. She was quite a bit older than my brother Cecil and me. Never had she treated us as equals and, after the death of our mother, she became even worse in her attitude towards us.

She took control over Daddy's care at Winters Hospital and continued to try and control his treatment in the Abilene Hospital. In fact, Daddy had already been transferred to Abilene before she even bothered to call Cecil or me.

When she finally called me from the hospital, I said, "I want to talk to Daddy."

In a really hateful way, Yane said, "Okay, if you insist, but he won't know who you are." She put the telephone to Daddy's mouth and all I could hear were strange noises! I was fifteen hundred miles from my Daddy, and this scared the hell out of me. She came back on the telephone line and said, "Are you satisfied now?"

I was in tears, which seemed to please her, of course. I said, "Is Cecil there?"

"Yes," she answered in a really sarcastic voice.

"Then put him on the phone!" I said harshly, not really caring what she thought.

When Cecil came on the line, I was in a panic. "Cecil, what in the hell is wrong with Daddy and why is Yane being so hateful to me?"

"Daddy is really bad, Reta. I told Yane to call you now, because she was gonna wait till she got Daddy back to Zapata." I could tell he was scared to death for Daddy.

"Don't let her take Daddy anywhere," I quickly said. "I'll be there as soon as possible."

After hanging up the phone, I grabbed a few things and hit the road—literally. I arrived at Abilene the next evening totally exhausted as I had hardly slept during the past twenty-four hours and Yane knew it.

When I arrived on the floor where Daddy's room was located, the nurses looked at me with disapproving eyes. I couldn't imagine why they treated me with such little respect. I ran into Daddy's room and found Yane hovering over him while a nurse was standing helplessly at the end of the bed. It was quite obvious Yane didn't even want the nurses near him. I went to Daddy immediately and took his hand in mine. "Daddy," I said softly, "This is Reta. I'm here." He looked near dead, and I was terrified at the really pitiful situation.

Yane looked at me with a clear satisfaction in her eyes and said with a grin, "He isn't acknowledging your presence, and doesn't even know you."

We hadn't seen each other in years so I couldn't understand her obvious hate for me. I knew I hadn't done anything to deserve this treatment. It could only be that she knew how close Daddy and I were, and was jealous. That was the only answer. However, I knew she was wrong about Daddy not knowing that I was there because he was squeezing my hand. I knew, in my heart, that he did know.

"Well, I'm tired," Yane complained in a martyr's voice, "And since you're here, I'll just go get some rest." Then she proceeded to instruct me on how to change Daddy's diapers and how to properly powder his private areas. She said with a smirk, "I'll be back in a day or two." She threw her head back and marched out of the room as though she had just discovered penicillin for the world and had given final instructions for her doctoral dissertation on the matter!

I looked at her in total disbelief. She had been mean to me most of my life, but this was the ultimate insult. Then relief came to me as soon as she walked toward the door, even though she still had a satisfied look on her face. Turning to the nurse, she tightened her lips and rolled her eyes as if to say, "Keep an eye on him because my sister has no idea what she is doing," and then she was gone. Relief at last! I am sure Yane thought I was so irresponsible that I would call her to come back. Obviously, she didn't know me.

I asked the nurse, "What's the matter with my Dad and why is he in diapers?"

"Mr. Fuller was totally sedated when he arrived here and has not really been awake since. We were going to put a Texas Catheter *(not inserted but slipped over the penis, causing no discomfort to the patient)* on him but your sister demanded we put him in diapers," the nurse kindly explained.

In an authoritative voice, I said, "Well, she's gone now and I'm taking over. I want this diaper off and the Texas Catheter used. My Daddy would just die if he knew he was in diapers. Do we understand each other?"

The nurse looked at me with a totally different attitude now and, with a grin, she said, "You got it."

She started ripping those diapers off immediately and said, "Why in the world did she put all this powder on him? There is so much powder that it is sticking to itself. She once again began performing her hospital duties and got Daddy cleaned up nice and neat. "Your sister has really been hard to deal with. I am glad you're here, now." Daddy was still squeezing my hand and I knew he was glad I was there, too.

When Cecil came in and he said, "Boy, am I glad to see you." He then filled me in on Yane's activities.

I told him the way the staff had treated me upon my arrival. He laughed and said, "No wonder. After I arrived, one of the nurses asked us if we were the only children? Yane said, in her high and mighty way, 'No, we have a sister who might be coming, but she is the wild one and very irresponsible.'"

"That explains the reception I received from the nurses when I arrived," I said with a heavy heart. "No telling what she has them thinking of me, but I can imagine." I looked at Cecil hoping that he could shed some light on her hateful attitude towards me and asked, "Why is she so mean to me, Cecil? Has she been mean to you, too?"

"A little," he responded, "But not as mean as she is to you. I just don't understand her attitude, either."

The nurse brought me a cup of coffee which I greatly appreciated. While I gulped it down, Cecil continued to fill me in, "She doesn't want the nurses near him, or anyone else, for that matter, except when really necessary, and that includes me." He shook his head and said, "She even gives him some of his medications."

Hearing this last statement, I got really upset and said, "That doesn't sound right, Cecil. Something's wrong."

After Cecil left, I pulled a chair up next to Daddy and talked to him while holding his hand. "Daddy, I'm here, now, and you are going to be all right." I then placed my hand on his forehead and asked God to take away the demons that were hurting him. I truly felt God's presence or maybe it was Daddy's guardian angel.

Within twenty-four hours after my arrival and Yane's departure, Daddy woke up, looked around and said, "When did you get here, Piss Ant?"

"Yesterday. What in the hell is going on?" I grinned and said, "Well, you've been so lazy we couldn't wake you up."

He was definitely confused and asked, "What's going on with 'The Young and The Restless?'" This was his favorite soap opera. I gave him a big hug and thanked the Good Lord for answering my prayers.

Daddy's voice was like music to my ears and I looked up again and said, "Oh, yes, God, thank You for not letting him wake up to find himself in diapers. He would have wanted to kill someone."

After that, Cecil and I stuck together like glue. We were not going to let Yane get near him again or to control things, ever again. I hadn't felt this close to my big brother since we were kids.

CECIL AND I WERE JUST A FEW YEARS APART, so we grew up pretty close as kids. He was on the short side, but an extremely handsome man. He supported a few extra pounds, but they did not, at all, detract from his good looks. He reminded us a lot of our Uncle Virgil, Daddy's brother, who had died a few years back from—guess what—a stroke.

As kids, Mama used to say, "The Good Lord is raisin' you kids. I seem to have nothin' to do with it." This statement was so true.

It seems that Cecil and I were always doing things that were dangerous. One time, when I was about four years old, we decided to take our little red wagon up into the loft and then "bail out," but we needed something soft on which to land. We waited until Mama took her afternoon nap and then took her flour sifter and used it to sift the dirt. Of course, we had it back in the flour container before she got up. We must have sifted dirt for two weeks before we figured there was enough for the big landing from the loft.

The big day finally came. We waited for Mama to nap again, then we pulled the wagon up into the loft. Cecil, being the always alert engineer, figured I should go first and said, "You go first, then we'll pull it back up and then both go together." With that pronouncement, he put me in the wagon and told me to hold onto the tongue. (Yeah, sure!)

Very trustingly, I said, "Okay," and then I got into the wagon. We really thought the dirt would make a soft landing. Well, right before the count down, we heard Mama calling us. We knew we had better do double-time when she called or we would be in big trouble.

We decided to tell her about our big adventure since she was already awake. Excitedly, we grabbed her hands and led her to the barn, and when she saw what we were planning, she started crying and thanking God for waking her up. Cecil and I got a good talking to about the danger we almost got ourselves into and then, as usual, we got spanked for taking something without asking, this time, her sifter.

AFTER DADDY'S MIRACULOUS AWAKENING IN 1984, Cecil and I decided to have Daddy transferred to a private room. Shortly after the nurses got him settled in, Dr. Mendenhall arrived and gave my Daddy an examination. He then came out and told us he was going to run some tests to see if he could find out what exactly had happened. He did reassure us, however, that he felt fairly certain that Daddy did not have cancer. He could not imagine where Yane had got that idea.

Meanwhile, Yane had called the hospital and found out from the nurses that Daddy had been moved to another room. She also was notified that Dr. Mendenhall was going to run some tests the next morning. Immediately Yane called because she didn't seem to be overly thrilled about the wonderful change in Daddy.

"Why haven't you called?" I immediately asked Yane, in a very impatient tone.

"I have been calling every day," she said in her typical sarcastic tone, "and have been talking to the nurses." With great authority in her voice she continued, "I know exactly what has been going on." I realized that her pride would not let her call and ask either Cecil or me anything. After all, in her mind, we were incapable of accurately reporting Daddy's progress to her.

The next morning, Yane arrived at the hospital bright and early. When she walked into Daddy's room, she glared at me and said, "Well, Daddy, has Reta been taking good care of you?"

"Yeah, I feel good," Daddy responded to her.

"Did she brush your teeth this morning?" she continued her interrogation.

"Yes, Yane, I brushed his teeth, helped him shave and the nurses gave him his bath. Very good care has taken place here," I responded in a very angry voice. It was hard to understand her hateful accusations and attitude. Again I prayed for self-control as I was growing very tired of her.

Yane then grabbed Daddy's chin and made him open his mouth. She just shook her head and then got his toothbrush and started brushing his teeth so hard that Daddy was pulling back from her. She put the toothbrush away and then proceeded to check everything else. Daddy looked at me as if to say, "Get her the hell out of here!"

About then, Dr. Mendenhall came into Daddy's room and, as he passed Yane, glared at her. Turning towards me, he looked me right in the eye and asked, "Has your Daddy been on drugs or is he an alcoholic?" The good doctor was looking somewhat confused and puzzled as he spoke.

Before I could answer his question, Yane said with unmistakable authority, "Daddy is an alcoholic."

This really pissed me off and I said to Yane, "How dare you say something like that!"

Turning to Dr. Mendenhall, I responded to the question. "Daddy used to drink quite a bit, but since he has been on Lopressor, he hardly drinks at all." I looked back at Yane and said, "If you were around him more, you would know that."

"Then you explain why he has a twelve pack of beer in his refrigerator right now," she spat out at me.

"Is it Miller Lite?" I said laughing at Yane.

"I don't know that much about beer," she said with a judgmental attitude, "but I think that was the name."

"Well, Dr. Mendenhall, I guess I'm the big alcoholic in this family. I left that beer in Daddy's refrigerator when I was here for a visit this past summer. It's been there all this time, so that tells you what a big boozer Daddy is!" I confessed in my best theatric manner.

Dr. Mendenhall laughed and said, "If having a twelve pack in your refrigerator makes someone an alcoholic, then I guess I'm one, too." Yane actually shut up for once. Dr. Mendenhall then turned to me and said, "I'll talk to you later," and then he walked out of the room.

Yane stormed out of the room immediately after the doctor left without saying a word to Daddy or me.

"Boy, has she got her stinger out!" Daddy commented after Yane had so rudely left.

"Daddy, you don't know the half of it, but when you're better, we are going to have a serious talk." I fully intended to tell him everything, including the bit about the diapers.

Shortly after Yane had left, Dr. Mendenhall came back into Daddy's room. He asked me to have Cecil come to the hospital as soon as possible because he wanted to talk to both of us in private.

I immediately called Cecil and was very relieved he was home. After giving him Dr. Mendenhall's message, he agreed to come right away.

I notified Dr. Mendenhall when Cecil arrived. He then took us to a private room around the corner and asked us to please be seated. With a very serious look on his face, he said, "As you know, we ran a number of tests on your father this morning. We were surprised to find traces of a drug which was not administered by this hospital. It has been too long to identify the specific drug, but this drug along with what we were giving him had to be the problem." He sat down and continued, "Now it's been too long to prove it, but what concerns me is the fact that your father came around within twenty-four hours after your sister left. Again, we are unable to prove anything, however, I am not taking any chances. I am putting a note on Vernon's chart stating she cannot be in his room, unsupervised, anymore. In other words, he is not to be alone with her at any time! Do we understand each other?"

We both nodded. Cecil and I just sat there in total disbelief trying to absorb what the doctor had just told us. Cecil thought for a moment then said, "I saw her giving Daddy some little white pills but never once thought you had not prescribed them."

"If I had prescribed them, a registered nurse would have administered them, never your sister," Dr. Mendenhall said, clarifying the situation and the legality of the matter.

"Could this be the reason Daddy's mind keeps jumping from the present to the past and seems confused?" I asked. Then I told Dr. Mendenhall about the morning Daddy had insisted that I pour Mama Merck a cup of coffee and truly believed she was there to drink it with him. At the time, Mama Merck, my grandmother, had been dead for two years.

"He also thought I was still in high school playing basketball and dating Tommy Cumby, my first love," I explained.

"Definitely, his memory may never be the same and he most likely will remember the past better than the present," the good doctor explained.

"Dr. Mendenhall, would you please give this information to our Aunt Sissy? I would like for her to hear this from you instead of Cecil or me," I urged."

"By all means, ask her to come in. I'll be glad to talk to her."

When Aunt Sissy arrived at the hospital, after dropping her latest project, she looked very concerned, yet strong. Dr. Mendenhall showed her into the same private room and then proceeded to tell her exactly what he had told both Cecil and me.

I knew if what the doctor had told us were true, we would need Aunt Sissy as a staunch ally because there was going to be hell to pay with Yane—and soon.

Yane came back to the hospital the next morning to say goodbye to Daddy before she left for Zapata. I stayed in the room for awhile but she was so insulting I couldn't take it any longer. A friend of mine was there, so I asked him to stay in the room until she was gone. I believe if I had stayed one more second I would have physically attacked her.

I went down to the coffee shop to blow off some steam. When I thought she had plenty of time to say her goodbyes, I started back to the room. I pushed the elevator button and when the door opened, there stood Yane. She looked like Lucifer himself. Her eyes were wild and she looked half crazy. Glaring at me and with a growling voice, she said, "See ya around."

"Not if I can help it," I shot back with quite a bit of anger in my voice. I didn't care.

I went back to Daddy's room and we all rejoiced over her leaving...even the nurses. None of us wanted to be the one to tell Yane that her visits with Daddy would have to be supervised!

ALONE WITH DADDY WHILE HE WAS SLEEPING WAS A special time for me. This afforded some moments for quiet reflections of my own. Sitting in the big chair in his hospital room, I tried to relax and found my thoughts always focusing on Yane and trying to make some kind of sense out of her actions, and this entire current mess.

I remembered that when I had first arrived, Cecil and I had made a trip to Daddy's house in Winters. Looking around, it looked to us as though Daddy had been doctoring himself for a bad cold. We found an open bottle of Nyquil in his kitchen. He probably had taken even more over-the-counter drugs along with his Lopressor pills.

I had then gone into Daddy's closet to get his lock box. We needed the insurance papers and I also wanted to make sure Daddy had deposited the $5,000 I had drawn out of the savings & loan for him before I left for Wisconsin. I had given it to him in $100 bills.

Looking all around the closet, I could find no lock box. I yelled at Cecil, "Do you know where Daddy's lock box is?"

"As far as I know, he keeps it in the closet," he said, rolling into the bedroom.

"Well, it's not here," I told him. "Let's go over to Uncle R. A.'s house. Maybe he has it." I was so scared he had been robbed. I had told Daddy every time I called to make sure he put it with Bill Sneed, in the bank—where it belonged. He always assured me he would take care of it his next trip to Coleman.

I shared my fears with Cecil, "Who would steal that box just for some business papers and souvenirs? Maybe the money's still in it?"

We went directly over to Uncle R. A.'s house. Fortunately, he was home but I was puzzled why he seemed to have a really guilty look on his face. I gave him a hug and said, "Uncle R. A., do you have Daddy's lock box?"

He answered, "No, I don't."

Knowing Uncle R. A. pretty well, I had a suspicion something was wrong and asked, "Uncle R. A., are you sure?" He couldn't look me straight in the eye, so I knew he was lying for some reason. I continued, "Don't you remember, before I moved back to Wisconsin, Daddy had me take his money out of the savings & loan for him, and then he put it in that box? He promised me he would deposit it with Bill Sneed, but I don't think he ever did. Do you know if he ever deposited it?"

He just shook his head but still didn't look at me. He said in a low voice, "I just don't know, but I do remember you giving that money to him." He scratched his head in serious thought and continued, "I think I was there the morning you came back from the bank, or maybe Vernon just told me about it, but I don't know anything."

This was definitely wrong. Now, I began to panic, "That is all the money Daddy has left in this world! He's evidently been robbed! I better call L. C. Foster." L. C was our local sheriff and a very good friend of Daddy's.

I headed for the telephone but, before I reached it, Uncle R. A. said in a stronger voice, "Reta, wait a minute. I know Vernon made a mistake when he told me to give that lock box, car and house keys to Yane. I know he really meant you. Just a minute, I've got it in the house." He left us and then came back in a few moments with the lock box and, as he handed it to me, said, "I'm so sorry I worried you 'cause I knew Vernon really meant to say, 'Reta.'"

I was so relieved and said, "Uncle R. A., I totally understand. Daddy never gets his names right." Then, with some anxiety, I opened the lock box and to my delight the money was still there. All $100 bills, just like I had given it to him, and even in the same envelope. I was so happy that it was all there but knew I would need to have a talk with Daddy for not depositing it like he had promised.

"Uncle R. A., you just put Daddy's keys in his lock box and keep it all just where you had it until he gets home, then you can give it back to him," I said with a light heart, so much so that I couldn't stop smiling.

Uncle R. A. said, "Okay, but Yane has the keys to his car and house. She's really gonna be mad, Reta. She told me not to tell you and Cecil."

"Don't worry, Uncle R. A. We'll handle that witch," I reassured him.

Cecil and I went back to Daddy's house where I got his extra keys for his car and drove it back to the hospital. We had decided not to let Yane know anything about what had transpired in Winters. The last thing we wanted to see was a big fight at the hospital. A fight, okay, but not at the hospital.

Probably we will never know the truth regarding what really happened when Yane was in charge of Daddy. There was enough evidence that Cecil and I would never leave her alone with Daddy again. Everything now made sense. Why Yane had been so smug when I asked her if she had got Daddy's insurance papers out of his lock box for the hospital. She had just rolled her eyes and said with a grin, "Don't worry about that, I have everything under control." She must have believed that lock box contained thousands of dollars. No wonder she grinned when Cecil and I had told her we were going to Winters to take care of some of Daddy's business. She knew that she had Daddy's keys and must have thought that his lock box was in her control. Maybe she hoped we would look like a couple of fools when we had to come to her for all the answers. I just chuckled to myself because she didn't know about the extra keys that Daddy kept hidden, but I did.

When Daddy finally got home, he assured Uncle R. A. that he had made the right decision regarding his lock box. He thanked him, and said, "It's good you used your head since I ain't usin' mine very well lately."

A shiver ran up my spine as I thought of the wild stories she would probably tell her family about Daddy's lock box. It contained many important items including his will, which would be of special interest, also, to her would-be playwright son, Delferd.

I thought it a shame that her family didn't really know me, especially her sons. If they did, then they would understand that the character she portrays me to be is only created from her frustrations and fantasies.

Trying to make excuses for her, I thought, Maybe if she had lived a more exciting life she wouldn't have become so bitter. She really should be pitied. Yane was and always will be my only blood-sister, but she was quickly becoming a void in my life. I loved her but I didn't like her and had lost any respect I might have had for her. In fact, with a sibling like her, I certainly didn't need any enemies. For me, all there was left to do was to pray for her.

Just then my reverie was interrupted when Daddy woke up and said, "What the hell! You dreamin'?"

"Not actually," I smiled. "It was more like a nightmare." We laughed and I knew he would be ready to go home, and soon.

Before Daddy came home, there was another subject that we had to deal with and that was the medications we had found at Daddy's house along with his Lopressor pills. Cecil and I asked Dr. Mendenhall regarding the drugs and what had been found in Daddy's system. He told us that these drugs would have already cleared out of his system by the time the tests were run.

Until this day, only two entities know the real truth about what happened to Daddy in 1984. One is Yane and, of course, the other is God. However, I am totally convinced that if she did give Daddy drugs, she never meant to harm him. What I mean to say here is that I want to believe that, want to believe that with all my heart.

When Daddy got well enough to leave the hospital, he stayed at Cecil's house for awhile, until strong enough to journey home. However, his mind was never the same, not even close. Dr. Mendenhall was right, he couldn't remember things in the present very well, but we accepted it.

AFTER RELIVING THIS TERRIBLE NIGHTMARE OF 1984, I KNEW, WITHOUT A DOUBT, I HAD TO TAKE MATTERS INTO MY OWN HANDS, REGARDLESS OF WHAT YANE THOUGHT, AND GET MY DADDY TO THE ABILENE HOSPITAL WHERE HE WOULD RECEIVE PROPER MEDICAL ATTENTION.

PAMELA LEANN ALBRECHT
RETA LEE'S DAUGHTER

2

NOW BACK TO THE SITUATION AT HAND. I HELPED Daddy into the bathroom to try and clean him up. His hygiene was terrible. My Daddy had always kept himself so nice and clean, smelled good and was impeccably clean shaven. For him to let himself go like this, I knew there had to be something dreadfully wrong.

It nearly broke my heart to see him like this. I remembered so many times where he would be decked out in his white western shirt, black western pants, cowboy boots, and his white Stetson, standing in front of the little gold mirror I had given him twisting his butt saying, "It's Sadie Nite Gotta shake a leg, Piss Ant." And so we'd head down to the Badlands where he loved to dance. In my opinion, he was the best dancer in Texas.

The Lord knows I tried to wash his hair. He was supposed to have bathed that morning, but evidently just hadn't been able to do it right. If I had only known more about mini-strokes, I would have known immediately what the problem was and, therefore, what to do about it.

After cleaning him up as best I could, Steve and I helped him walk out to the car. I told Sissy to stay home and didn't want her to have to face that emergency room scene in Abilene. It hadn't been that long since Kathy had died there, and I thought it wouldn't be good for her to be there again, so soon anyway.

We got as far as Tuscola where Daddy said he wanted to take a pee. We stopped at a gas station and when he started to get out of the car his right leg went out and would not hold him up. Steve carried him into the restroom and helped him do his business then got him back into the car. This was certainly one time I was happy Steve was there (...Give every dog his dues—).

I was so glad when we finally got to Abilene and checked Daddy into the emergency room. They immediately gave him a Cat Scan and determined he was having a progressive stroke. If Dr. Lee would have made some attempt on Saturday to determine what was going on with Daddy, maybe something could have been done at that time to help him before it got to this point. Doctors like him should be tarred and feathered; Ask me after a few beers and I'll tell you what I really think.

Shortly after Daddy was taken to his room, Dr. Mendenhall came in and asked me if Daddy's face had become distorted at anytime. I told him no but as I turned around to look at him, just then his face began to distort on the right side. I was scared I was going to lose him right on the spot.

Dr. Mendenhall explained that there really wasn't much to do at this point but to start him on glucose and pray. I spent the longest night of my life in a chair by his bed doing just that.

His mind was gradually leaving him and I couldn't do anything to stop it; I tried to accept that. He was scared and I felt so helpless. His right arm was still strong and in his confusion he tried to pull the I.V. needles out of his left arm. The nurses finally had to restrain him for his own good, but he fought those damn restraints all night.

It was so hard to watch as his body and mind fought to be in control, again. My irrational mind toyed with the idea of just pulling the needles out, taking off the restraining cuffs, grabbing Daddy and running away with him to where I don't know. The rational mind knew this would not help and was only an escape for us both. I did the only thing logical and practical...I prayed that God would not take him from me.

While sitting by his bed that night, I found myself looking at him and remembering all the good times we had shared, and the bad times, too. We always stuck together, no matter what.

I thought back to the day mother was buried. We had all gathered at Sissy's house. Someone had brought a guitar and Daddy said to me, "Piss Ant, sing, *What A Friend We Have In Jesus*, just for me." It was a song my Mama had always loved and had taught it to me when I was just a little girl. It was so hard to do that, to sing without losing it, but I did it for my Daddy. He never knew how hard that was for me but I guess I would have done just about anything for him.

The next morning was hard, too, because the Daddy I knew and loved was just a memory. He seemed to know me but his memory was basically gone. It was like talking to a small child.

It is so hard to explain how I felt at this time. Daddy had always been a giant among men, and I had grown up thinking there was nothing he couldn't do. He always seemed to have the right answers whenever I needed advice. Now, in just a few, short hours, that Daddy was gone forever. His body was there, but the Daddy I had grown up knowing and loving was gone.

He was not in control of his bodily functions anymore and yet I just couldn't bear to see him put in diapers again like Yane had done to him in 1984. I vowed that, if at all possible, it would never happen. Going to his nurse, I explained and asked her to put a Texas Catheter in him as had been done back in 1984. The nurse asked the doctors and they said that it could be tried, at least for awhile, to see how he tolerated it.

ANOTHER THING THAT KEPT CROPPING UP IN MY thoughts while at the hospital with Daddy was the problem that Cecil and I had with Yane the last time he had been ill. I thought, Dear God, why didn't I get Daddy to sign a Power of Attorney to me or Cecil back then! I could just imagine the hell she was going to put us though this time.

If she knew that Dr. Mendenhall's orders stated, emphatically, that if Yane was there, her visits to our father were to be strictly supervised, she would probably raise Holy Terror around there, and especially with me. Only God knew what she would be like.

I knew one thing for sure: She wasn't taking my Daddy to her home, and she sure as hell was not going to put him in any nursing home! I planned to take him back to Wisconsin with me, just like we had originally planned. Thank God he had told Sissy his plans, and I knew Sissy would stand with me.

I would have given anything in this world if we could have all pulled together like most families do during a crisis. With Yane, Cecil and me, that was only a fantasy, of course, never a reality.

That next morning, after Daddy had been admitted, I could not put off calling Yane any longer. When I finally got through and told her the news, she responded in typical Yane fashion by telling me she was busy getting ready for her children and grandchildren to arrive. They were going to join her and Dub for their Christmas festivities at a rented condominium somewhere on the Gulf Coast. She instructed me to keep her informed of Daddy's progress. As far as it went, the nerves were still intact after interfacing with Yane.

After that, I then made a call to my brother, Cecil, told him how serious Daddy's condition was and how I was so scared, just as I had told Yane. I said that Daddy and I really needed him and that I would feel much better if he would come and visit, even though it was Christmas.

Cecil said, "Well, I'm heading this old pickup that way right now. I'll be there just as soon as it can get me there." Bless his heart he was there within a couple of hours. I was ever thankful to God that my brother was there with me.

Pam and Brad eventually arrived and I had asked Mary if she would pick them up at the airport. Kim had been staying at Mary's home since we arrived because she was visiting with her daughter, Michelle. I had told Mary how serious Daddy was but had asked her not to tell the kids. I needed time to pull myself together before I talked to them or they might freak.

It took about four days before that damn stroke totally took my Daddy from me. When Mary brought the chocolate cake to the hospital, I tried to give Daddy a bite and he just started grabbing it off the plate and shoving it into his mouth like a little, starved puppy. He had a terrible vitamin deficiency from improper eating and maybe his body was trying to help him out.

After we had cleaned the cake from Daddy, Dr. Mendenhall came in with a doctor from the Far East. I grew to have a lot of respect for that foreign doctor because he seemed to know what he was doing. At least he was trying to do something positive. He told us he wanted to administer a drug called Heparin. He didn't know how far the clot would go but if he didn't start the Heparin, to help dissolve it, he was worried that our Daddy would surely die. To this day, I wonder if that doctor had been there to treat him at Winters Hospital, instead of Dr. Lee, if he would have been able to help prevent this stoke from happening. I have also wondered if he had been there four days before the stroke took Daddy's mind, if he could have made a difference. These are questions I will always wonder about.

Cecil and I decided that what the doctor said made sense and wanted to go with the Heparin. I told Cecil we had better call Yane and get her vote, too. Cecil said, "If she really cared, she would be here with us." He was correct but we still needed to do what was right.

We then called Yane and explained what the doctor suggested about the Heparin and then asked her what she thought should be done. She said it was probably okay but she insisted on speaking directly to the doctor, as she didn't believe Cecil or I were qualified to give her a correct diagnosis.

After speaking with the doctor, she ordered us to keep her posted and then hung up. It always irked me that while Cecil and I kept vigil over Daddy, she and her family were all together in Galveston, Pasadena or somewhere on the Gulf Coast having their happy little family Christmas with turkey, gravy, and listening to Bing Crosby records.

CHRISTMAS DAY, 1986, WAS THE SADDEST HOLIDAY I had experienced since Mama died. Pam, Kim, Brad, Cecil, Chris (Cecil's son), Steve, Sissy and I were all with Daddy on Christmas Day. Daddy also had a lot of friends stop by to see him and wish him well.

This was an extra sad Christmas for Sissy, as it was her first without Kathy. We all missed Kathy, too. I had been especially close to her as she and I were together constantly when little girls, and this closeness had continued as we grew up.

While we were all visiting with Daddy, Sissy had been able to get him to laugh but it was not the same. It was so sad because Daddy was now like a child.

He was still on the Heparin but it was too soon, yet, to know what the outcome would be for Daddy. Only time would tell. It was hard to accept the fact that my Daddy would never be the same strong man I had loved and felt so safe with all my life. I determined, then and there, that I would take loving care of him and not let anyone ever hurt him.

Part of me had wished that Yane would have come, but in a way, I was glad she wasn't there. She had treated Cecil and me so bad, back in 1984 when Daddy was in the hospital, acting as though we did not exist.

I think nothing would have made her happier than if Cecil and I had never been born. She never treated us with love. When I was a little girl, I used to think she was the most beautiful woman in the world and looked up to her.. As time passed, I realized what my mother meant when she would say, "Pretty is as pretty does." Yane had ceased to be a pretty person to me for many years. She has hurt me more than anyone else during my lifetime with her hateful words and actions.

I thank God I have always had Sissy with me. She had always been my sister, mother and, basically, my best friend while growing up. She was always there for me whenever I needed her, and I pray I will always be there for her.

AFTER CHRISTMAS DAY, DADDY WAS MOVED   TO another room. They were shorthanded at the hospital because the big-wigs had decided to save money by not hiring any nurse's aids. That meant the poor nurses were totally overworked and unable to bathe Daddy until one or two o'clock in the afternoon and, then, it was just a quick sponge-bath.

Sissy came to the hospital one morning, took one look at me and said, "Baby, what's wrong?"

"Sissy, Daddy is not being bathed until late afternoon and then they don't have time to do it right. I want to start bathing him myself, but I just can't bathe his bottom yet," I said in such a discouraged tone.

"I'll take care of Vernon's bottom," she quickly assured me. With that decided, we got us a pan of warm water and gave Daddy the best bath he probably ever had.

After that morning, I decided I couldn't always wait for Sissy to be there to help me bathe Daddy. I came up with the idea to put a pillow on his chest so that he would not see that it was me washing him but a nurse that was bathing him. This was the hardest thing in the world for me to do. My Daddy had always been a very private person and I felt so out of place having to bathe his privates. I was able to put my own feelings aside when I rationalized that if I did not bathe him, then his private area would never be washed. Daddy, having been so fastidious in his personal hygiene, would have been very upset so that helped make my decision easier.

I had to feed Daddy every bite because he wouldn't eat anything unless I did. Knowing he loved buttermilk, I ordered a big glass and would then give him a sip of the buttermilk and then a spoonful of food. It would take me hours to feed him this way, but at least I was able to get some of the food down him.

Sometimes he would want a cigarette so bad. Dr. Mendenhall said to go ahead and let him smoke. I would light the cigarette then hold it in his mouth while Daddy took only two or three drags and then fall back asleep. After about a week of this, I found that I was finishing his cigarettes. Now I was off the gum and back on the cigarettes. I guess that this was just not the right time for me to give them up.

ABOUT A WEEK AFTER CHRISTMAS, YANE CALLED and said she and her family were coming to see Daddy, now that Christmas was over. I was staying at a little motel next to the hospital and asked her, "Do you want me to reserve you guys a room at the same motel where I'm staying?"

"I'll take care of that myself. I have to get rooms adjoining for my grandchildren," she replied in her most insulting voice.

"Isn't their mother coming?" I asked, choosing to ignore her ungrateful attitude.

"Yes," she replied, "but I want adjoining rooms so that I can see that they are taken care of, properly." I guess the motel I was staying at didn't measure up to her standards because she made reservations in one of the best hotels in Abilene.

They were all due to arrive a couple of days later. I can tell you I was not looking forward to seeing Yane, at all. Cecil and I knew she would come in and tell us how we had done everything wrong, then go to the nurses and doctors and try to make us look like total idiots.

I liked to be at the hospital by 7:00 a.m., every morning, so that I was there when Daddy opened his eyes and then would stay until he went to sleep at night. I would put on what little makeup I wore in Daddy's little bathroom and just let my hair dry naturally and used a banana clip to hold it in place.

As usual, I got up early the morning of her arrival. I thought Yane would probably be at the hospital fairly early, especially, knowing what had happened to Daddy and since she hadn't seen him for some time prior to his stroke. But she didn't come in until around 10:00 a.m.

Arriving dressed fit to kill, complete with every hair in place, her make up perfect, she came strutting down the hall in front of her family, just like she owned the whole hospital. As soon as she arrived in Daddy's room, she paused, looked me up and down with the usual, cold, judging eyes, as if to say, "For heaven's sake, Reta, can't you dress a little better and put on some makeup." Of course, Daddy and I got the traditional kiss and hug, but she didn't get too close for fear of catching something. I have always said that maybe, someday, she would catch the disease called "nice." Then she went over and checked Daddy over from stem to stern to make sure I had been caring for him properly.

I guess I did look pretty bad as I had been practically day and night at the hospital since Daddy had his stroke. Before that, I had driven straight through from Wisconsin, right before it had happened, and I was living in jeans, sweat shirts and tennis shoes. At least I was comfortable.

After visiting with Daddy for a while, Yane, commanded Cecil and me to meet her and Dub at the Country Kitchen Restaurant. We knew all too well she was fixing to break loose.

PRIOR TO HER ARRIVAL, CECIL AND I HAD MADE A trip to see Bill Sneed at Daddy's bank. We had told Bill about my plans to take Daddy back to Wisconsin and he was in total agreement with us.

It seems that Daddy had already told him of his plans to go to Wisconsin with me Bill also had Daddy's "lost" money He told us, "Vernon came in one day and had me put it in a safety deposit box. It's not that much and if you are planning to take Vernon back to Wisconsin with you, in the condition he is in, I know you are going to need all the financial help you can get. I will have the paper readied and if Cecil and your sister, Yane will sign their permission, I will give the money to you whenever you want."

"That sounds good to me," Cecil said. "Make up the paperwork and I'll sign it before I leave. Yane can come down and sign it later. You know, there might be some problems with her. I'm sure Daddy has told you a little about her."

"Yeah, he has talked to me about all you kids," Bill laughed

On the way over to the restaurant I said, "Now, Cecil, no matter what, don't blow your stack there."

"I'll try," he answered, "But I ain't gonna promise you nothin'."

We got to the restaurant and found Yane waiting for us. She sat there like she was some kind of a judge. We had hardly sat down before she said, "Now you both know we have to put Daddy in a nursing home."

I said, "Yane, it has already been decided that Daddy is going home with me. He had planned to go back with me after Christmas, anyway, and I am not going to change our plans now."

She really had a big laugh about that and said, "How do you think you can take care of Daddy?"

I said confidently, "We have built a new home in Wisconsin and can incorporate some extras into it to accommodate Daddy's handicap. The house is a split-level so I plan to have an elevator installed so that he can go into all areas of the house with his wheel chair."

She really blew a gasket over that and said "I guess you want to take all of Daddy's money to buy an elevator. Do you know how much that would cost?"

I said, "Yane, I'm not an idiot. The elevator would consist of a lift placed in a shaft built onto the house and, by the way, I am financially able to take care of Daddy." This really made her laugh.

Cecil then interjected, "Bill Sneed has prepared some paperwork for you and me to sign so Reta can take what little money Daddy has with her to help with the expenses."

Yane glared at him and said, "If you think I'm signing anything for her to be able to touch any of Daddy's money, you are crazy and so is Bill Sneed! She can submit invoices to me, and if I think she needs the money, then I will 'okay' it." Cecil and I knew it was time to get out of there. The she-devil was back.

Outside the restaurant, Cecil said, "Reta, I'm going back to Weatherford until she's gone. Call me and then I'll come back and help you figure things out. If I stay here, I don't know what I might do." He got Chris from the hospital and then left directly to go back home.

THAT NIGHT, I SAT UP ON THE BED WITH DADDY and told him he had to sign a Power of Attorney before he got any worse. The Heparin had reduced the swelling in his brain to where he could now understand what I was saying. I said, "Daddy, we have to get this done or Yane is putting you in a nursing home, or worse yet, she might try and take you back to her house."

Daddy came alive then, and said, "Hell, get an attorney up here and let's get it done!"

"Daddy, I want you to know that our plans have not changed at all. You're still going home with me," I reassured him with a smile and a gentle squeeze on his arm.

He looked at me with tears in his eyes and said, "Piss Ant, I'm gonna be a burden now and I don't want to be no burden."

I gave him a big hug and said, "Daddy, you may need a lot of help, but you won't ever be a burden, not to me. You know, when I was a little girl and got sick you never abandoned me, did you? Well, I'm not going to abandon you either. It's my turn to spoil you now. So get those silly notions out of your head... We're family, and families take care of each other."

I knew that I had to get the Power of Attorney signed before Yane returned. She was planning to take her family to breakfast before she came to the hospital so that she could make sure her grandchildren were cared for, "properly."

I called Cecil and told him what I had planned to do. He was with me one hundred per cent and said, "I'm sorry I bailed out on you, Reta, but I just can't be around her anymore."

I said, "I understand perfectly, Cecil. I wish she had never come down here."

I remembered back to when I was a little girl and how Daddy used to get mad at me for letting her run roughshod over me. He would say, "Reta, why don't you stand up to her? Don't let her talk to you like that, she's not your boss."

I'd answered, "Daddy, I don't wanna fight with her."

"One day, your gonna have to stand up for yourself," he had insisted.

Well, now was the time to stand up and fight. I knew what I had to do, and this time, as God is my witness, I wasn't going to let her stop me. I prayed that God would give me the strength to stand up for Daddy and me.

I called an attorney in Abilene, and made arrangements for us all to meet at the hospital early the next morning so we could get the paperwork done.

I arrived bright and early. Mike, Daddy's nurse, had him up and dressed in his housecoat waiting for us. He had helped him into his chair but Daddy was sound asleep when I arrived. I said, "My God, Mike! What is the matter with him? Why can't he wake up?"

Mike was also from Winters and he had known my family all his life. Therefore, he also knew my sister and understood how important it was to get the paperwork done—ASAP. Mike answered, "Last night, the doctor told them to cut back on his Heparin but instead of cutting back, they took him completely off it which threw his system into an electrolyte imbalance. I have been trying to feed him coffee for an hour."

We continued to give Daddy coffee, and to tell you true, it was a wonder he didn't float away.

The attorney walked in right on time, and said, "We need two witnesses for your father's signature. If you go down to the lobby, I am sure you can find some willing people to help us out."

I said, "Mike, keep pumping the coffee into him and I'll be back in a minute."

I went down to the lobby, actually I half ran, and found about fifteen people sitting there waiting, like we had done a few days before. I said to the group, "I need two people to witness a signature. My Daddy has had a stroke and I need to obtain Power of Attorney before it's too late. Unless I get this paper signed, right away, my sister will have him put into a nursing home, and I don't have the money to fight her. Will two of you please help me?"   Everyone, except a few, stood up and offered their assistance.

The two people I chose told me they were also from Winters and that they knew my father well.   They also seemed to know how close Daddy and I were and knew that he would rather be with me than with anyone else.

We went back up to Daddy's room.   Poor Mike was still pumping coffee into Daddy and holding the urinal.

The attorney explained all the details of a Power of Attorney to everyone and then turned to my daddy and said, "Mr. Fuller, do you understand everything I have just told you?"

"Hell yes," Daddy said, looking him right in the eye.

"Then place your mark right here," the attorney directed."

At that point, Daddy dozed off again and more coffee was administered by Mike.   I said, "Daddy, you better wake up and sign the paper or you might wind up at Yane's house!"

That was enough to wake him up.   He held the pen in his left hand and made his little mark.   The attorney looked at the witnesses and said, "Do you believe Vernon was in his right mind and knew what he was signing?"

They both said in unison, "Yes, we do."   Then they signed in the correct places.

The attorney looked at me, smiled, and said, "Well, little lady, he's all yours, now, and may God give you the strength you're going to need."

I cannot explain the feeling of relief that fell over my entire body. It was like thousands of pounds had been lifted off my shoulders.   Now, Yane couldn't tell Cecil and me what to do and what not to do any more, regarding Daddy.   Damn, but it felt good!

I looked at Daddy, and said, "Well, Brody, I now have custody of you."   I had teased him the past year that I was going to take him to court and get custody of him if he didn't start taking better care of himself.

Daddy smiled, and said, "Damn, I'm sleepy."   We all looked at each other and broke out laughing.

"Mike, let's get him back into his bed so he can rest now," I said. "It's all over, now, and thank you so much for everything."

I sat down in the chair watching him sleep and prayed that God would guide me and help me to do the best for my father that I possibly could.   He had always taken good care of me when I needed him, and now it was my turn.

I THOUGHT BACK TO WHEN I WAS ABOUT FIVE YEARS old.   Daddy would plow the fields and I would sit in the backyard and wait for him to let out a holler. That was my signal he had captured another little jack rabbit for me. I would run out to him to retrieve the little fellow and add him to my collection. Mama would say, "Vernon, she has twenty-seven rabbits now. Will you please stop giving them to her!" Daddy was as crazy about animals as I was and just couldn't leave those little, baby jacks out there to die after he had plowed over their holes.

When I was about six, Daddy bought me a horse who was sort of on her last leg, and we named her "Old Cricket." He hung an old saddle on a barrel between two trees and said, "Piss Ant, when you can ride that barrel, after I give it a push, then you can ride Old Cricket by yourself." Well, it took a few weeks for me to achieve this goal, but by golly I did. I was the best barrel rider in the county! Daddy held to his promise, and he put that saddle on her, gave me the reins, and said, "She's all yours, but remember all the things I've told you."

My mother was really upset with him about the horse, but he soothed her ruffled feathers just like he always did. Daddy always had a winning way with everyone, especially Mama.

A COUPLE OF DAYS PASSED BEFORE YANE AND HER family came back to the hospital. She really had her stinger out about something. She, Dub, Dexton and Delferd marched into Daddy's room and I was informed that Dub and the boys were taking me to breakfast and that she was going to talk to Daddy, ALONE! She looked like a real devil, she did.

It soon became quite obvious she not only knew about the Power of Attorney, but had also found out about the order for her supervised visits that Dr. Mendenhall had put on Daddy's chart.

"I'm not hungry," I told her.

"Reta," Dub, her husband, said in a demanding voice, "Loraine is going to be leaving tomorrow and she wants to spend some time with her Daddy, by herself. So let's go!" His eyes were fiery and full of uncontrollable anger.

Thank, God, Brad had come over to the hospital with me that morning. I guess Yane and her muscle men thought I would be there alone, and it would be easy for them to manhandle me.

Noticing that Brad was there, also, Dub glared at him and said, "You can go to breakfast with us, too."

"I'm not going anywhere," Brad said and glared back. He knew about the situation in 1984 and that the doctor, Cecil and I did not want her left alone with Daddy. He was looking at them as if to say, "Try to push me out of here and I'll break your face!"

Knowing that Brad would have Pam, Kim, and Steve back at the hospital before we had left the parking lot and that Pam and Kim knew to advise the nurses of the situation, I consented to go to breakfast.

Yane knew that she did not have much time so she quickly started her interrogation of Daddy immediately, Brad reported to me later. She put him through the paces to see if he knew what he was doing when he signed that Power of Attorney. Thank, God, for the Heparin, or maybe it was an answer to my prayers, but Daddy was able to keep his wits about him until she was done.

After leaving Daddy's room, she then proceeded to keep an appointment she had scheduled with Dr. Mendenhall. She wanted to know if he thought that I was capable of taking care of Daddy, and if he believed Daddy knew what he was doing when he signed the Power of Attorney.

Dr. Mendenhall was already a little put out with her, not only from the episode in 1984, but because she had the gall to give the nurses, and him, the third degree regarding my capabilities. They all knew my abilities, first hand, having witnessed my love, devotion, and personal care of my daddy since 1984. Also, they were quite aware of who had been there for him and who really cared about him. She had lost in that department a long time ago.

"Mrs. Shores, I believe your father belongs with no one else other than Reta: They have a very special and close bond. I can also assure you that Vernon knew exactly what he was doing when he signed the Power of Attorney so that Reta would have sole care and responsibility of him," Dr. Mendenhall said, responding to her impertinent questions. He was more than fed up with personalities like hers, and her crew just wasted his time. He found, I am sure, that he was becoming more and more intolerant with their self-centered stupidity.

Angrily, she whipped herself around and left the room in a typical Yane huff. She did not really want to take Daddy to her house, and to be the one to physically care for him. Also, she was quite aware that the nursing home situation was bad and that Daddy had a horror of being put in one. So, it was obvious, to all, that she really wasn't that concerned about his welfare.

Brad, Pam, Kim and Steve were in Daddy's room when I got back from a most stressful breakfast with my brother-in-law and his two sons. Yane had only visited with Daddy long enough to interrogate him and wanted to leave as soon as I returned. "Daddy," she said, "We are going home in the morning. But I will be back tonight to say goodbye." We all held our applause, but it was hard.

After she and her flock made their exit, I said, "Brody, I stood up for myself this time and for you too, and thank you Sweet Jesus, we won."

Thank you, darlin'," Daddy managed to say before slipping into an exhausted sleep. I was so proud of him, too. We both had triumphed over Yane.

Cecil and I figured that she must have thought Daddy had a great deal of money put away. After all, she was hardly ever around Daddy and she sure didn't know anything about his personal business. Maybe she thought she would get a nice little inheritance if she could keep him in Texas. However, if he went to Wisconsin, she wouldn't have a chance to exert any control over him, or his money. Just like in 1984, we found that we could not understand her, at all. We could only wonder at her reasons and actions.

The nurses talked to me, later, after she had left, and I found that Yane had made them quite upset also. In her imperious manner, she had grilled them about everything regarding Daddy's care and especially about what I really did all day and what they thought of my abilities. She really had made an ass of herself and I hoped that she knew it, too!

I WAS FEEDING DADDY USING MY BUTTERMILK method when Yane and her entire clan came marching into the room that evening. Without so much as a by-your-leave, she grabbed the spoon from me and said, "I'll feed Daddy."

"Yane, I have a method I've been using since the stroke which has worked very well," I tried to explain to her. As usual, I couldn't tell her anything. She started poking the food at him and Daddy wouldn't open his mouth. In a few minutes she gave the spoon back to me, and not in a nice way.

I then continued to successfully feed Daddy with the tried and true method. Glancing over at Pam, Kim, and Brad, I saw that they all looked like they were ready to attack her. Needless to say, the tension was so thick you could cut it with a knife.

"Give Daddy a cup of coffee and put three teaspoons of sugar in it like he likes," Yane instructed her son, Delferd.

"Delferd," I said kindly, "Daddy only takes one half teaspoon of sugar in his coffee." Delferd fixed the coffee like I had asked.

It was surprising to all of us how little she really knew about Daddy. I said to myself, Lady, you sure have missed a lot of precious time with him that you will never be able to recapture. At that point, I almost felt sorry for her. She was trying so hard to look so caring, strong and powerful in the eyes of her family, and wanting me to appear so inadequate.

She gave Daddy the traditional hug, but this time I didn't get mine, and I was glad. She just glared at my family and me, and sarcastically said, "Good luck," and with that she and her brood made their exit.

The relief and joy of her departure could only compare to my getting Daddy's signature on the Power of Attorney. It was such a wonderful and free feeling to know I didn't have to get her approval for anything. Now I could seriously get down to the important business of taking care of my Daddy.

I called Cecil, right after Yane's exit, to let him know that she would be gone the next morning. He said, "Good, Chris and I'll head my ol' pickup that way this weekend."

It was now time to get Daddy ready for bed. Pam, Kim, Brad and Steve had already gone back to the motel. After Daddy was tucked in, I sat down in my little chair and was able to relax for the first time since Yane's arrival.

I couldn't help thinking how sad it was that we three kids couldn't be close at a time like this. We should all be pulling together, for our father's sake, not wasting energy on family differences and personalities.

While relaxing in Daddy's room, I purposely tried to remember some fond memories of Yane from my childhood. Surely there were some, but sadly, I just couldn't recall any. I remembered the times she would comb my hair, and if I moved or cried out, she would hit me on the head with the brush or comb and warn, "Keep still!"

My thoughts then wandered to an incident that occurred when I was about nine. I had been singing on a variety show in Abilene and wanted to share my dreams with my sister. "When I grow up, Yane, I want to be a Super Star and sing on The Grand Ol' Opry."

She chuckled, then said, "I'm going to Abilene tomorrow. Maybe I can help you." I was so happy because I thought she really meant it.

The next day I put on my newest little Sunday Dress, slipped on my white patent leather shoes that Mama had bought for me, and with high hopes, I headed for Abilene with my big sister. Yane pulled up in front of the Windsor Hotel: The offices for the television station were located near the tenth floor. She opened the car door, glared at me and sarcastically said, "Now, go on up there and tell them you have come to be a Big Star."

"Aren't you coming with me?" I asked in a very puzzled and confused voice.

"No, you could probably do better alone," she replied.

"Yane," I started to whimper, "I can't go up there by myself."

She rolled her eyes, started the car and took off. I could tell that she was totally disgusted with me. "Don't you ever ask me to do anything for you again!" she snapped. I was miserable and felt like I must be the most ungrateful brat who had ever missed a wonderful opportunity.

When we got home, I was still in rears and told Mama what had happened. "Honey, didn't you know she was only trying to make a fool out of you?" she said. Believe me, later, Mama had more than just a few words with Yane about what she had done.

It seemed so sad that I just couldn't remember any really happy childhood memories with her, as I could with Cecil. A few days before, I had asked Aunt Sissy, "What did I ever do to make her hate me so?"

"Baby, I don't know. Maybe you couldn't do anything about it, one way or the other," she had sighed.

I HAD STAYED ALL NIGHT IN DADDY'S ROOM. THE next morning, since Dr. Mendenhall was off for a few days, the door opened and in walked a diminutive, foreign, woman doctor. She walked over to Daddy's bed and in her broken English began asking him a lot of questions that I thought were rather stupid. Daddy couldn't understand a word she was saying and just laid there with a confused look on his face and didn't say a word.

"Nursing home full of people like this. He not understand anything I say," she said looking at me, coldly.

I was standing by the bed holding Daddy's hand. I looked at her and yelled, "Hell, lady, I'm looking right at you and I can't understand a damned word you're saying, either, and I haven't even had a stroke!" She knew I was mad as hell and as I moved toward her I continued, "If you don't get out of this room and quit talking like that in front of my Daddy, I'm not going to be responsible for what I do to you!" I guess she believed me because she headed for the door and we didn't see her any more.

Mike, Daddy's nurse, had been standing behind the doctor and motioned to not leave until he talked to me.

Later, Mike came back and gave me the hope that I desperately needed. "Reta," he told me, "there is hope for your Daddy. Taking him to one of the many rehabilitation centers would greatly help him."

I needed reassurance so much, at this time, and what Mike told me made a lot of sense. I tearfully said, "How can I locate these centers? Where do I start?"

"There are several really good ones around the country. One, is the Patricia Neal Institute. I'll try to get you more information. There are probably some right in your area," he informed me.

"Thanks, Mike, I really appreciate your support and help." I gave him a hug and he left. I felt like there was something positive, now, that could be done for Daddy.

"Brody, don't you listen to what that stupid doctor said, you just listen to what I tell you. Like you always told me, 'there ain't nothin' that you, me and the Good Lord above can't do together,'" I said looking at

Daddy and gave his had a good squeeze. He looked as though he understood me.

Thinking about what Mike had told me, the only place I could remember was The Mayo Clinic. I called Steve's daddy, Andy, and asked him if he could check the Twin Cities for a good rehabilitation center. He assured me he would find out whatever he could and get back to me as soon as possible.

Andy was a big man with white hair and was very loud and boisterous. His wife, Isabelle was a very little woman, very meek and totally subordinate to him. They both had always been good to me and I knew I could count on them to do their best.

Andy called back the next morning. He said, "Reta, I've checked the entire state of Minnesota. I have been assured that the best facility for Vernon would be The Sister Kenny Rehabilitation Center in Minneapolis. It is also connected to Abbott-Northwestern Hospital which is also a wonderful facility. I already called them and told them about Vernon. They said to contact , Dr. Golden, who is a neurosurgeon on their staff."

"Oh, thank you so much, Andy. I am very grateful to you for all your help and will give this information to Dr. Mendenhall when he comes. You are really appreciated," I fervently told him

"No problem, Reta. If you need anything else just call," Andy replied in his usual robust way.

Even though Daddy had been improving and was getting stronger every day, Dr. Mendenhall wanted Daddy to be totally recovered from the electrolyte imbalance before I took him up north. He still hoped I might have second thoughts and put Daddy in a nursing home in Texas.

When Dr. Mendenhall came to check my Daddy, I told him about Dr. Golden and gave him his phone number. He finally believed I was serious and was really going to take Daddy home to Wisconsin.

I asked the good doctor, "Would it be okay for me to fly Daddy home in an air ambulance?"

"No, keep him on the ground. If something should happen, you would be better able to get him to a hospital," he replied.

He finished checking Daddy over real good and then said, "Well, Vernon, I've done all I can do for you. Are you ready to go to Wisconsin?"

"You betcha!" Daddy responded without any hesitation.

"Well, little lady he's all yours. You can leave whenever you're ready," Dr. Mendenhall reluctantly gave me his permission "I'll call Dr. Golden and get every thing lined up for you on that end."

At that moment I felt the same as when Pam and Kim were born, and the nurse had handed them to me when I left the hospital. To be totally responsible for another human life is quite a commitment, but for that life to belong to someone who had, in turn, been responsible for my own life in previous years, was an overwhelming concept. I just prayed to God that I could take as good care of him as he and mother had taken of me.

I TELEPHONED ANDY, AGAIN, AND SAID, "ANDY, YOU told me that if I needed anything else to just call."

"I meant that," Andy said in a very firm voice. "What can we do?"

"I can't fly Daddy by air ambulance. They feel it would be safer to keep him on the ground..."

He interrupted, and said, "Can we bring him home in my van?"

"Andy, would you really come down here and get Daddy and me?" I was so hopeful and excited as I could see things beginning to come together.

"You just tell me when you'll be ready, and Isabelle and I will be there," he responded, without any hesitation.

I just couldn't hold back the tears any longer. I said, "Andy, Daddy is ready now but I still have to make arrangements for his house and take care of some unfinished business here in Texas. I should be ready by the time you get here."

"We can leave early tomorrow morning," he said. "The only problem is money." I could tell he was embarrassed to have to mention the money.

"Don't you worry none about money, Andy. Daddy and I will absorb all the expenses. Just keep all your receipts and we will settle up with you when you get here and give you enough for the return trip home," I gladly promised him.

My next call was to Cecil and I made arrangements for him to meet me, the next day, at Daddy's little house in Winters.

Cecil arrived, as planned, with his pickup truck and a trailer. We packed up all of Daddy's things. I took care of all his personal things and Cecil took the furniture, air conditioner, etc., to his house for storage.. We didn't know if Daddy would ever return or not, but we had hoped he would be able to decide what he wanted done with his things at a later date.

My best friends, Mary and M. J. Casey, I called and arranged for them to take care of renting the house out to someone. M. J. said he would repaint and mend a few things, first.

My next order of business was to go to The Winters Funeral Home and talked to Mike. I told him of my plans. "Mike, if something should happen to my Daddy on the way up north, or at a later date, what should I do?"

"Reta, all you have to do is call me and I will take care of everything," he assured me with a big smile.

"Thank, God, for friends like you," I told him.

"I've known Vernon and the family all my life and I will help you anyway I can." Mike's offer and assurance certainly took a big load off my shoulders.

Cecil had already headed for Weatherford with his load of Daddy's possessions and I went back to the hospital to make final arrangements for Daddy's dismissal.

In the meantime, Pam, Kim, Brad and Steve had taken our car and already gone back to Wisconsin. They planned to get things ready for our arrival, plus, the studios were due to be back in session and the girls needed to be there to do the teaching and cover for me.

ANDY AND ISABELLE ARRIVED IN TWO DAYS, BLESS their hearts. I sure was happy to see them!

The arrangements for a hospital bed and potty chair to be put in the van had already been made. After visiting with Daddy for awhile, we then went over to the Abilene Medical Supply Company where they loaded the hospital bed and potty chair into the van for me.

One of their employees said, "I can't believe you are going to attempt this project."

I must have taken umbrage at his tone of voice because I immediately snapped at him. "This is not a project, this is my Daddy and it's the only way the doctor will permit him to travel other than by ambulance! Since Daddy and I don't have that kind of money, this will have to do." They quickly finished getting me everything I needed and we were soon on our way.

We then headed for Winters, where we loaded Daddy's personal things, such as pictures, his brown leather recliner, clothes and, of course, his lock box. Andy's van was almost totally loaded by then but I was able to make room for Mama's little sewing rocker for me to sit on.

Our next stop was at my Aunt Sissy's. We went over to say goodbye and when we arrived, she had coffee and a snack waiting for us. She looked at me and said, "Baby, do you know how much you're taking on your little shoulders?"

I said with a reassuring smile, "No, Sissy, I just know I have to take Daddy home. I can't leave him in a nursing home waiting to die."

We stayed awhile, glad for something to eat and a chance for a last visit with my beloved aunt. I gave Sissy a big hug and, of course, we had our tears, then we said our goodbyes. I have always thanked the Good Lord for her. If only my sister could have been more like Sissy.

Exhausted, Andy, Isabelle and I spent that night at a motel in Abilene. The next morning we got up bright and early, ate a good breakfast and gassed up the van. The only thing left to do was pick up Daddy.

Excitedly, I got Daddy dressed, packed his little suitcase and took care of his discharge papers. I helped him into a wheelchair and then waited for someone to help me take Daddy down to the van. After waiting quite awhile, no one came so I went to the nurse's desk and asked, "When will someone be here to help put my Daddy in the van?"

She looked at me as though she didn't understand the English language and said, "That is up to you, we are short handed."

Furious, I went back to Daddy's room. I thought, Andy and I could probably handle everything but I had forgotten about his bad back.

I then went back out to the desk and said in a very demanding voice, (reminding myself of Yane) "Look, I need some help getting my Daddy into the van downstairs so get someone up her to help me, NOW! He has been sitting in that wheel chair for over thirty minutes."

Knowing I now meant business, the nurse said, "Well, maybe I can get someone from Physical Therapy to help."

"Great!" I said. "I would certainly hope so! This is ridiculous!"

After another thirty minutes or so, two young girls came and announced they were from Physical Therapy. They took Daddy downstairs and right to the van, which was outside the front doors. Those poor girls proceeded to tug and pull at Daddy until they finally rolled him into the van. What a sight! His housecoat had come up and his privates were showing. Quickly, I put a blanket over him and said, "My God, where did you people get your training?"

I gingerly moved them out of the way and between Andy, Isabelle and me, we finally got Daddy into his bed. Dr. Mendenhall had the nurses place a Texas Catheter so I wouldn't have to worry about putting Daddy on the potty chair during our trip back to Wisconsin. Smart move.

After all the fooling around that was done, Daddy was now wide awake. He said "What the hell is goin' on, Piss Ant? Where's my hat?"

"Daddy, just you relax, now. We are on our way to my house in Wisconsin. Your hat is right here," I said, reaching back and retrieving his old Stetson. He grabbed it from me and tried to put it on. Calmly, I retrieved it back and said, "Daddy I'll just lay it at the foot of the bed until we get there."

He said, "Okay." I had no idea at this time what an important role that old Stetson would play in his therapy.

AS WE SAID OUR GOODBYES TO ABILENE, DADDY went right to sleep while I tried to think of something that I might have forgotten. I mentally checked off things that had to be done: The two most important were the filing of Daddy's Power of Attorney with the court house and making arrangements with Bill at Daddy's bank regarding his funds. Bill had assured me he would work closely with me on everything regarding Daddy's account.

Daddy had already made arrangements for his Social Security Check to be deposited directly into his bank account. The little savings that he did have were transferred into my name, in case Daddy were to need it.

I had bought a little book in which to keep accurate records of all expenses and transactions made on his behalf. The reason I had planned to do this was in case Yane were to ever question my use of Daddy's funds, or if she tried to cause problems for me. My records would show a correct accounting, and she wouldn't be able to accuse me of any dishonesty, including spending Daddy's money frivolously.

It was nice to know I had good supporters. Bill assured me that I didn't have to concern myself with Yane, anymore. He explained, "Reta, according to the world at this time, you are Vernon Fuller. I certainly can't understand why your sister would give you any trouble over this small amount of money. It will only be 'a drop in the bucket' compared to the financial burden you are undertaking."

"I know, Bill, but you just don't know her. Somehow, in her mind, she believes Daddy had a lot of money," I explained the best I could.

DADDY WASN'T REALLY AWARE OF THINGS WHEN WE left Abilene, nor did he seem to recognize anyone, or anything, except for me and that old Stetson hat. It's sure a blessing we don't know what the future holds for us. I knew it was not going to be easy, but I also knew, in my heart, that I was doing the right thing and that God would help me every step of the way. That made the difference.

I HAD PROMISED MY BROTHER, CECIL, AND HIS family that, before we headed for Minnesota, we would swing by his home in Weatherford, Texas, so that they could say their goodbyes to Daddy."

We arrived at his home around noon and found all his family waiting to see Daddy. Chris, Cecil's son, got into the van first. He had always been really close to his grandpa and kept in close contact. Having been with Daddy throughout this illness, it was hard for him because he was afraid he might not see him again.

Looking at me with tears in his eyes, he said, "Aunt Reta, does he know me?"

"Honey, he's no longer the grandpa you once knew, but I believe he does know you, yes."

He then dropped down on the bed, put his arms around his beloved grandpa and said, "Papa, I love you and I will be up to see you when school's out." He could not hold his tears back any longer and got out of the van.

Margaret, Cecil's wife, and Jennifer, his daughter, came into the van next. They had not seen Daddy since his stroke and were overwhelmed by the sight of Daddy's obvious deterioration. Tears came to their eyes and Margaret said, "Reta, I'll be praying for both you and Vernon."

She walked very close to God and I have always admired Margaret for her strength and moral courage. She, too, had her own cross to bear through the last few years. Her mother was in a nursing home at that time, plus the rest of her family counted on her for her support.

Knowing that she was not in good health herself, I said, "Margaret, you take care of that high blood pressure. You know Daddy's situation is the result of not doing so. I don't want you to wind up like Daddy." She quickly assured me she would take better care of herself.

We were ready to go and Cecil was still standing outside talking to Andy and Isabelle. I called to him, "Cecil, are you going to say goodbye to Daddy?"

"Okay—" I could tell he didn't want to get into the van and see Daddy in that condition. It was so hard knowing he couldn't do anything for him.

He gave Daddy a quick kiss and made his exit really fast, saying under his breath, "I just can't accept this!" He had tears in his eyes and I knew what he was feeling, believe me I knew. We were totally helpless.

Giving him a big hug, I promised, "I'll keep you posted." He had Daddy's furniture and belongings stacked nicely in his garage in the hopes that Daddy would return some day.

As we pulled out of Cecil's front yard and began, in earnest, our long trip to Wisconsin, I asked God to watch over his family and get us home safely.

WE HAD JUST CROSSED THE BORDER IN OKLAHOMA when Daddy woke up and said, "Damn, I'm hungry. I want a B.L.T!"

I said, "Okay, you got it."

No one, at the hospital in Abilene, had told me that a stroke patient should be fed a very strict diet. After all, they had let us leave without any medication or instructions whatsoever! We were strictly on our own.

Andy stopped at the next truckstop. I ran in and got Daddy his B.L.T. He was so hungry that he seemed to shove and push the entire sandwich down quite rapidly, almost wrapper and all...and then he started choking. I damn near lost him right there.

Somehow, I was able to get him out of the bed, bend him over and started pounding on his back. All this time I was yelling at Andy to stop and help me. Daddy had begun to turn blue and I was scared to death. All of a sudden, he coughed it all up, looked at me and said, "What the hell ya trying to do? Beat me to death or something!"

Those words were music to our ears and we all started to laugh. I said to Daddy in a joking way, "Are you trying to make me look incompetent or what? How in the hell would I have told Yane you choked to death on a B.L.T. in Oklahoma!"

He laughed and said, "Hell if I know!"

I determined that from then on I would hand feed him every bite, and very small bites they were going to be, too.

The next time we ate, I ordered him soup, a grilled cheese sandwich and a glass of iced tea with a straw. He grabbed the straw out of the glass and started "smoking" it like a cigarette. He seemed to really enjoy it and continued to "smoke" straws the entire trip. I cut one in half and he would use it for his "cigarette lighter." Until this episode, I hadn't realized just how far his mind had deteriorated.

He still recognized cattle trucks, cattle trailers and old ranchers going into the truckstops. He would look out the van windows and say, "That looks like Ol' Shorty or is it L.C.?"

I REMEMBERED BACK TO THE DAY HE AND MAMA decided to quit farming and start ranching full-time. They had taken all their savings to buy him a new stock trailer.

From that day forward, Daddy started making some really good money. I remember going to an auction with him one time when I was about eight years old. I couldn't believe how much he knew about cattle and horses. I would say, "Daddy, buy that one."

He'd say, "Now, Reta, look at that cut under the right leg. That could cause that animal to be crippled." Nothing ever got by him.

Daddy was always well respected because of his honesty in all his dealings. He had told me, several times, the story of how a man had skinned him on one of his cows when he was five years old. He would say, "I swore then, I would never skin anyone and by damn, no one would ever skin me again!"

WE MADE THE TRIP WITHOUT ANY CAR TROUBLE, Daddy did fine after the choking incident, and I truly believe the Good Lord was riding in Mama's little rocking chair with me.

We did have a few laughs along the way. Andy was a little reckless at times, driving I mean. One time, partly because he was so tired, he started down the wrong road, which was really rough with a lot of potholes. Daddy tried to get out of bed, saying, "Hell, let me drive this thing." But when we got into Iowa, the roads were really bad, a most unpleasant and rough part of our journey.

IT WAS TEN BELOW ZERO WHEN WE FINALLY ROLLED into Minneapolis. We were one tired crew as Daddy was the only one that had really gotten any sleep. It was very early in the morning, and we headed straight for Abbott-Northwestern Hospital. Andy stopped at the emergency entrance and waited, engine running, while I got out and went inside. Dr. Golden had not expected us until the following day, so the emergency staff had no idea what was going on.

I panicked because I was afraid there was going to be a repeat, of what had happened to us in Abilene. Quickly, I explained to the staff what had happened back there. They looked at me in total disbelief and assured me they would keep Daddy wrapped up and warm while things got straightened out.

They went out to the van to check the situation and could not believe I had attempted such a task and had actually accomplished it. One of the orderlies looked at me and said, "Lady, you are one brave soul to take on such a responsibility. My hat's off to you."

I said, "If you visited the nursing home in Winters, Texas, you would understand why I wouldn't leave my Daddy there. Besides, he belongs with me."

They were so professional. What a difference! They carefully slipped a stretcher under Daddy, wrapped him up nice and warm, and then transported him into the emergency room without hardly a disturbance.

In amazement, I turned to Andy and said, "Why couldn't they have done this in Abilene?" He just shook his head.

Daddy thought I had taken him to the North Pole. He said, "Damn, look at all that snow!"

The attendant said, "Welcome to Minnesota, Mr. Fuller."

A pretty little nurse came over to talk to us. Daddy looked at her and said, "Why, hello there, you pretty little thing." She, and all the staff, were overwhelmed by his charm.

He turned to me and said, "Where's my hat, Reta?"

This time I was ready for him and quickly responded., "Right here in my hand, Daddy."

He gave a big smile and felt his face. "Hell, I need a shave, Reta. Get my razor!"

"Daddy, let's wait until we get to your room. They are busy with you now." There was no getting around it. He insisted I give him that shave, right then. I placed his hat at the foot of the ER bed, asked Andy to bring his little suitcase which contained his razor, and I did it right there on the spot. Daddy would never leave the house without a clean shave, especially if he were going to meet some pretty ladies.

The staff was able to reach Dr. Golden and received his orders and instructions. Daddy was transferred to the fifth floor, right away. Upon our arrival, I could not believe how many nurses came to assist in getting Daddy checked in and settled in his official room. They were completely taking over his care by checking his temperature, blood pressure and getting other pertinent information. They took one look at me, standing there looking very bewildered, sat me in a chair, got me a cup of coffee and said, "Honey, I don't know who needs the most attention right now, you or your father."

I just sat there, watching in amazement, as they worked and made my Daddy as comfortable as possible. I started to cry and one of the nurses asked, "What is the matter?"

"I guess I'm just starting to relax because I feel like Daddy's finally in good hands," I said through my tears.

She smiled and said, "Why don't you get a room here at the Hospitality Hotel and get some rest. I promise we will take care of Vernon."

It was such a relief to know that I could leave him in such trusted hands. She even called the Hospitality Hotel for me but it was full. I thanked her and told her I would just stay at my in-law's house.

Andy and Isabelle lived right outside of Forest Lake, and besides, Steve had brought my Lincoln down so that I would have my own transportation.

As it turned out, I could only rest about four hours and then I hurried back to the hospital.

Arriving back at the hospital, I found that Daddy had already had his bath and was ready to have breakfast. After our experiences in Abilene, I felt like we had arrived in Heaven. No, I was sure of it: This was Heaven.

AFTER BREAKFAST, DR. GOLDEN CAME IN AND introduced himself, and said, "I am going to turn your father over to the care of Dr. Petersen, a specialist of internal medicine. First, we are going to run quite a few tests to help us determine what has gone on with your father, which will help us decide the best course of action."

Dr. Golden spent a few more minutes explaining some things to me, asked if I had any questions, answered them, and then excused himself.

It seemed like only a few minutes before Dr. Petersen arrived; he was a small man with black hair who seemed to know what he was doing. He closely questioned me regarding my Daddy's care and the prognosis given him in Abilene.

I said, "They told me they could not do any more for Daddy, that I should just put him into a nursing home."

Dr. Petersen looked at the records he had just received from Abilene and shook his head, and said, "According to these records, your Daddy has suffered such a massive stroke that I can't believe he survived. He must be a tough old bird."

Hearing that, Daddy spoke up and said, "You betcha."

Dr. Petersen then explained that he wanted to schedule Daddy for a Cat Scan plus many more tests. Before leaving, he said he would check on Daddy a little later and, in the meantime, had arranged for a Dr. Speier to come in and do an evaluation of Daddy's physical abilities.

It seemed that Dr. Petersen was gone but a few minutes, when a stout woman with short hair and a strong face came in and introduced herself to both Daddy and me, as Dr. Speier. I was impressed because she just looked like she knew her business. She had brought a physical therapist with her so I figured they intended to get started right away with what ever it was they came to do. I was becoming more and more impressed with this hospital by the minute. Daddy had not had this much attention and care shown him the whole time he had been in Abilene.

After asking some questions, she and her physical therapist then straight to work. Her therapist got Daddy out of the bed and sat him in a wheelchair without hardly any problem at all! I could hardly believe it. It was so good to see him sitting up even though he couldn't hold his head up and he wouldn't look to his right.

This was my first real understanding of what was going on with Daddy. Dr. Speier explained to me that a stroke patient will not accept his bad side but with rehabilitation, and only in time, will they learn to accept it. Also, she explained, my Daddy would probably cry a lot and that this was from his being so frustrated. There was an awful lot of work ahead, for all of us. This had to be a team effort, she explained. Then she looked right at Daddy and said, "Vernon, you have to do the most work of all."

I took Daddy's Stetson hat and placed it on his head and said, "Daddy, hold your head up or your hat is going to fall right off onto the floor! You don't look too much like a proud Texan, right now. Hold your head straight!"

Daddy started to try and straighten his head. Dr. Speier got a mirror so he could see what he looked like with his head all bent over. Daddy looked in the mirror and said, "Poor Ol' Vernon," and started to cry.

Dr. Speier said, "Now we begin the long road of therapy."

"Will he be able to get back to the way he used to be?" I asked, already suspecting the answer and even though I knew she couldn't know at this time.

"We will do our best to help him get back as far as possible. It's really up to him," she said, answering my question in her very positive way.

THAT FIRST DAY WAS REALLY A BUSY   ONE   FOR Daddy. They plum wore him out, but I felt better as the day progressed. His room was filled most of the day with doctors, therapists, nurses, technicians and I can't remember who else. I was so excited for him because I knew they were giving him the best care possible. They treated him like he was a young man with an entire life ahead of him. Nothing like he had been treated in Abilene; there, it was as though his life was over and a nursing home, or worse, was the only answer.

While Daddy was getting his treatments and being fussed over, everyone was treating me as though I had a little halo over my head for taking care of my own father! It made me feel a little uncomfortable and I just didn't know how to respond. I guess I was surprised at various reactions, as if they thought I was Joan of Arc or something. For me there was no question, I was doing this for him because this is what he needed and I loved him, not for any pats on the back or to be thought of as someone special.

One of the nurses summed it all up. She was giving Daddy a bath and said, "Mr. Fuller, you must have been one hell of a father to have a daughter who loves you this much."

"Thank you," I replied, cutting in. "He was, and is still, one hell of a father. Now I know what to say to anyone else that pats me on the back!"

The next morning, the X-ray people came early to have Daddy begin some of the tests that Dr. Petersen had ordered. Sometimes they took him on a stretcher, other times in a wheelchair. It didn't matter which mode of transportation, Daddy always had to have that ol' Stetson either on his head or close by where he could see it.

It wasn't many days before Daddy and I were well known around the hospital. I heard one of the staff comment to another, "If Vernon goes anywhere, don't forget his hat and kid." We enjoyed quite a reputation and were so delighted with how the staff did what they could to accommodate us.

I had a picture portrait of Daddy made about six months prior to his stroke, during his last visit to Wisconsin. It would be the last portrait ever made of him. He was seventy years old at the time, but looked fifty. Another picture, of him riding Brad's three-wheeler that summer, I liked so well that I had a blown-up poster made of it.

One day, soon after our arrival in Minnesota, I hung these pictures on his wall at the hospital and told him, "Daddy, you're gonna ride that three-wheeler again."

He looked at the pictures and started to cry. I really believed, at that time, I would get him back on that three-wheeler and have my Daddy back like he had been. An additional thought: Looking back, I often wonder if I had known more about mini-strokes, that last special summer, I might still have my Daddy here today. Only God knows the answer.

BY THE END OF THAT FIRST WEEK, DR. PETERSEN came to Daddy's room and gave us some of the test results that had recently been done. He said, "I cannot believe the extent of the massive stroke your Daddy suffered, and yet, he is still alive and slowly improving. Your father must have a very strong will to live."

"Yes, he does, and I'm not going to let him leave me," I told the doctor with much determination.

Dr. Petersen smiled and said, "Maybe that's the answer, THE INGREDIENT CALLED LOVE." I smiled, looked toward the window and knew in my heart he was right.

Continuing with his report, he told us, "We also have found that your Daddy only has one working kidney. When you look at the X-ray, it shows one good one and the other all dried up and useless. He may have been born this way or it could have happened almost at anytime in his life, possibly even from some accident. This is okay, though, and it just means you have to always keep plenty of fluids in him."

The doctors comments reminded me that in the past, many times Daddy would complain, "My ol' kidneys sure do hurt this mornin'." He always worried that he might have cancer in his kidneys. What amazed me, though, was that after all these years, no one had ever found the real reason for his discomfort.

Daddy was never a water drinker. He practically lived on coffee. I used to say, "Daddy, why in the world won't you drink more water instead of all that coffee?"

He would laugh and say, "Hell, Reta, that water'll kill ya!"

DR. PETERSEN CONTINUED TO FILL ME IN ON THE results of Daddy's tests, "It also appears that your Daddy has been suffering mini-strokes for some time." He took a pencil and paper and showed me how a mini-stroke would choose one part of the brain to attack. How a little piece of gristle, found in the main artery, would break off and travel into one of the little veins. It would then totally knock out that particular motor-function.

Continuing to explain, he said, "We only use a small portion of our brain, therefore, other parts of the brain can be trained to take over the functions of the damaged area."

By this time my mind was going a hundred miles per hour. All of a sudden, Daddy's past behavior became very clear. I had accepted these changes and assumed they were part of the problems he suffered in 1984 when Dr. Mendenhall had told Cecil and me that Daddy's memory would never be the same.

WARNING SIGNS? YES, THERE HAD BEEN PLENTY OF them that past summer, and I hadn't recognized one of them. One example was when I had taken Daddy to the Tac-Lo-Ban, a little night club in Amery, for a fish fry. After dinner, the band started playing and we went onto the floor to dance. As I have said many times in the past, Daddy was one of the best dancers in Texas, especially the Waltz.

The band started playing Waltz Across Texas, made famous by none other than the great Ernest Tubb, one of his favorite songs and singers. Daddy said, "Come on Piss Ant, let's dance."

We walked out onto the dance floor and Daddy just stood there and looked totally confused. He said, "I don't know what to do with my feet." I thought he was joking, but he wasn't.

I remembered also that many times Daddy would become confused as to where his room was, and in my home! Also he didn't seem to be able to remember what we had done just the night before.

Understanding more and more, now, I realize there had been many little warnings. As long ago as six months, they had been there, but I just hadn't recognized them for what they really were. I totally accepted any behavior changes as a result of the damage to his mind, suffered in 1984.

Had I been more up to date on strokes, I would have immediately taken my Daddy to a doctor, like Dr. Petersen, and he might possibly been able to clean out that clogged, main artery. I wanted to shout to the world, "Get...More...Knowledge...About...This...H-o-r-r-i-b-l-e...Illness!"

AFTER TALKING WITH DR. PETERSEN, I FELT AS though I now had two years of medical school crammed into me in twenty minutes! Now I better understood the reason why everyone was so astonished at the way I had taken my Daddy out of Texas.

It just goes to show that, in my case, the saying, "Ignorance is bliss," is sure true. If I had known and understood the true facts regarding my Daddy's health, I probably would have had second thoughts back in Abilene. I can only believe that God surely was my copilot.

I TURNED MY THOUGHTS ONCE AGAIN TO THE ISSUE at hand and concentrated on Dr. Petersen's concluding statements. "I am, at this time, turning Vernon over to Dr. Speier and her staff at Sister Kenny. They will start him on a rigid schedule. If she decides he can be rehabilitated, she will place him in their center. If not, she will advise me and we will take over his care at that point."

Dr. Speier came in later that day with one of her own special physical therapists! She was a very small, young woman about twenty-one or so. Dr. Speier told us, "We will be working with Vernon on walking, pushing himself in the wheelchair, shaving himself, combing his hair, and brushing his teeth. Basically, teaching him to take care of himself all over again. It will be like working with a young child.

Daddy took careful note of all that Dr. Speier outlined for him. He broke the ice by saying, "Hell, I'm already tired." We all had a good laugh.

Dr. Speier then checked Daddy's wardrobe and shook her head saying, "He can't wear these cowboy boots. They would be too hard for him to stand in. Could you please get him some tennis shoes?"

I said, "Okay," but with a smile, as I knew the job that was cut out for me in an attempt to make that one stick. To put those tennis shoes on Daddy was going to be quite a battle as he never wore anything but his boots.

They further said, "Also, could you pick him up some jogging suits? They would be much more comfortable for him. We stand and sit him so many times, he would be getting a lot of snuggies."

Again, I said, "Okay," even as I was trying to figure out how we were going to change some of the old habits which had become a part of my Daddy for as long as I could remember.

"Dr. Speier, can he still wear his Stetson hat?" I asked cautiously, knowing how attached he was to that old hat.

She laughed and said, "I've heard about that Stetson and I would never try to take that from him."

At Dr. Speier's nod, the young therapist proceeded to get Daddy up on the side of the bed and helped him work with his balance. He kept tipping over. She was so positive and cheerful that I am sure it helped Daddy from getting as discouraged, as I was expecting him to be. To help him, she put a transfer belt on him and stood him up. I couldn't believe how this little girl was able to handle him.

I couldn't help but ask Dr. Speier, "Shouldn't we be helping her before she hurts her back?"

She responded with a smile, "Oh, no, she knows just what she's doing."

I couldn't help but remember back to Abilene when one nurse would get on one side of Daddy and another on the other. They then would both pull at him. This looked so much more safe for the patient and this young lady made it look so easy.

Dr. Speier continued, "I have a very rigid program lined up for Vernon. Someone will be working with him just about all day long."

DR. SPEIER SURE MEANT WHAT SHE SAID. BEGINNING with that very day, Daddy was only given enough time to nap between sessions. Someone seemed to be there most of the time, even for his meals and baths.

I have never been so impressed with a group of professionals in all my life. I knew if Daddy could be helped and his physical dexterity improved, these fine folks would do it.

Knowing I was leaving Daddy in very capable hands, I left him for awhile so that I could go downtown and purchase him the jogging suits and tennis shoes.

I found just what he needed. One jogging suit was black and the other blue, and both had accents of white. They both were lined, so I knew they would keep him nice and warm.

I then purchased a new pair of Nike tennis shoes. I tried them on because I knew if they fit me, they would fit him. Daddy had a very short, wide foot, just like me. It was fortunate that we wore the same size.

That night I didn't get much sleep because I kept thinking how in the world I was going to convince him to wear this new style of clothes—but especially the tennis shoes.

SINCE I COULDN'T SLEEP, I FOUND MY MIND wandering, recalling many things from the past, especially memories once shared with Daddy.

My mind drifted back to when I was about thirteen and Daddy had taken me to just about every talent show in the area. He really believed someday, with the right break, I could be a big country singing star. I had been doing quite well on the local circuit, such as on KRBC Television with the *Slim Willet Show*, plus a few other small auditorium shows.

Anyway, Daddy had me scheduled to appear on a talent show in Odessa, Texas, and Mama had bought me a new dress plus a new pair of straw-like shoes with big flowers on the toes. I remember them being too tight and they hurt my feet.

When Daddy came home from the field, where he had been plowing cotton, Mama said, "Vernon, we are going to have to take Reta's shoes back before that show you have her scheduled to sing at. They are too narrow and hurt her feet."

Daddy said, "Let me look at them." He was still wearing his overalls, work shoes and straw hat. He sat down, pulled his work shoes off and placed one of my little shoes on his foot. He looked at my mother and said, "Hell, Lee, give me the other one, I can stretch these out to fit her."

I couldn't believe my eyes when I got home from school. There was my Daddy walking around in those little shoes with big flowers on the toes! He was really a sight! He stretched them out, though, and they no longer hurt my feet. I sometimes wonder how much they had hurt his feet before he was able to stretch them out. Just another act of love.

MOMMA HAD NEVER WANTED ME TO PURSUE   A singing career, even though she was one of the best singers in the area. Church was the only place where she sang though, and church was the only place she wanted me to sing. She was scared someone was going to discover me and take me away. Daddy and Mama, over the years, had more than just a few words concerning the matter.

Another time, when I was about nine, Daddy took me to another amateur show. I remember it was cold, and the roads icy. Mama said, "Vernon, you are out of your mind to attempt to take Reta to that show!"

He only replied, "Lee, this could be the one where she gets discovered. Needless to say, Daddy had his way and a few words later, we were on our way to the show.

Arriving in Midland, Texas, we went to the local television station. They were getting all the acts lined up for placement on the show.

One of the men asked my Daddy, "Who is accompanying your daughter?"

My Daddy gave him a harsh look and said, "Well, I am. Who do you think brought her?"

The man realized, immediately, that Daddy had thought he meant I had come alone to the show. He said, "Oh, no sir, I realize you're her Daddy and she came with you. I meant who was going to play the music for her when she sings."

Daddy was a little embarrassed over the misunderstanding. They shook hands and laughed. Daddy said, "Reta doesn't need anyone, she has a real strong voice and can hold her own."

A young man, by the name of Curtis Potter, had been standing near us waiting to get his placement and overheard the conversation. He was a few years older than me and I had seen him on some of the local television shows. He was good looking and had a really nice smile. He said to Daddy, "Sir, I play guitar and will be happy to accompany your daughter."

Daddy said, "Let's give it a whirl."

We were then ushered into one of the rooms. Curtis found the key I sang in and after a little practice we went out and he accompanied me on the show. Until then, I never knew I sang in a key.

Some tap dancers won first place, though, but I got second, and Curtis, third. A few years later, Curtis got his own fifteen minute show on KRBC Television in Abilene and he invited me, occasionally, to be his guest. We even dated some after I got old enough.

Back to that show. After the show, a man approached my Daddy and said, "Who is managing your little girl?"

Daddy answered, "Well, I am."

The man then said, "I would be interested in talking with you regarding her career."

He took our phone number and called about a week later. He said, "Mr. Fuller, I can get Reta a spot on the *Louisiana Hayride,* but I want to manage her, completely. I will take care of everything she needs, but I want a contract from you and your wife."

Daddy and I were really excited, but needless to say, there was no talking to Mama. She totally blew up and said, "No one is taking my little girl out of school and away from me!" That was the beginning and the end of my big break.

I was really hurt and angry at Mama for a long time after that. Now, I look back on it and say it was probably God's Will. That man could have been a real phony just like so many men I was "going" to meet in the future (Is "destined" a better word!).

After dragging all these past thoughts out to rethink and rehash, I finally cleared my mind and was able to get a little rest. Before I knew it, the alarm clock went off. Soon it would be time to face Daddy with his new clothes.

MY PRAYER WHILE GETTING READY TO VISIT Daddy's room was, "Sweet Jesus, please give me the right words to convince Daddy to wear those jogging outfits, especially these tennis shoes." What was in the back of my mind the whole time was a simple thought: No one ever Waltzed Across Texas in tennis shoes!

I walked into Daddy's room early and found the Occupational Therapist working with Daddy on how to feed himself, and this round dealt with his breakfast.

Next, she would help him bathe himself and, afterwards, work with him on shaving his own beard.

I had bought Daddy a new electric razor, which was also going to be new to him. He had always lathered his face and shaved the old fashioned way. Everything he was accustomed to doing all his seventy years was changing. Now, here I was to change his wardrobe.

It was my turn. He was ready to put his clothes on. I thought to myself, Maybe he won't remember how he used to dress since he has been in those gowns so long! WRONG! If looks could have killed, I would have dropped to the floor as soon as I pulled out that jogging suit.

Immediately, he snapped, "Hell, these ain't my clothes."

"Daddy," I said, "You're up in Minnesota, now, where it is really cold. I bought you these new clothes so you would be warmer."

"Okay, if you think so." I knew he wasn't completely convinced but at least we had got past the first hurdle without any terrible explosions.

I decided I wouldn't mention the tennis shoes, specifically. As soon as I managed to get him into his jogging suit, I just started putting on the shoes as though this was the natural thing to do.

Boy, did he get really upset with me and swore, and said, "I ain't wearin' those damn things on my feet! Now that's were I draw the line!"

I pleaded, "Daddy, you've got to wear these tennis shoes. You're going to be working on walking again and pushing yourself into your wheelchair."

He really came unglued then and yelled, "No, no, but hell no! Damnit, I ain't wearin' these damn shoes!" I knew I was in for a battle-royal, now. Every cuss word was enunciated perfectly. There was no misunderstanding as to what he was saying.

Still pleading, I tried again, "Daddy, you're up north now and these are what the Yankees wear for boots up here."

"Well, hell, they're crazy as hell, then," he grumbled. I finally convinced him to wear his new Yankee Boots, but he didn't liked them, and never once did I believe that he thought that tennis shoes were Yankee Boots! Not in this lifetime.

"Now, damnit, I ain't wearing nothing on my head but my Stetson!" he stated emphatically.

I would have probably agreed to anything, at that point, and made a deal with him, "Daddy, if you will wear the Yankee Boots, I will never let anyone take your Stetson from you. I promise." From that day forward, everyone referred to his tennis shoes as his Yankee Boots. True story—

Finally, exhausted, after all the mental energy used to get past the jogging suit and tennis shoes, we got him into the wheelchair. He looked right cute in his new outfit and that Stetson just set it off perfectly. I took the mirror and showed him how spiffy he looked. Seeing himself in the mirror, he worked hard to pull his head up so that Stetson wouldn't fall off. It was the best therapy in the world for him.

It was so nice to see my Daddy all dressed in something other than a hospital gown. I looked at the nurse and said, "Could I take him down to the coffee shop for lunch?"

She saw how much I wanted to do this and said, "It is totally against the rules to take him off the ward, but I am going back to the desk and if you and your Daddy disappear for awhile, I won't know anything about it. Now will I?" With that she gave Daddy a peck on the cheek and said, "Have fun you handsome ol' devil."

I must admit, Daddy really did look spiffy with his new northern look. We didn't waste anymore time and we took off like a bat out of hell. It was so nice to be mobile with him.

First, we went down to visit all the therapists, and they were very surprised to see us but didn't ask if we had permission to be there. Daddy had all of them charmed by the time we left, and had made dates with at least half the women.

We toured the entire hospital and wound up at the coffee shop. I was so proud of Daddy. He held his head up as straight as possible so that his hat would sit straight on his head. I gave him a real cigarette, and boy, did he enjoy it.

Looking at the clock, I was surprised to see that we had been gone almost two hours. I said, "Daddy, we better get our butts back or we are both going to be in big trouble." We took off for the elevator to the fifth floor, and as the doors opened, there were three nurses waiting for us. I apologized and claimed ignorance about leaving the floor. They knew that I knew better, but everyone sort of politely ignored it.

What a group. I knew then, Daddy and I were very special to all of them and they understood my feelings for Daddy. From then on, they would refer to us as the runaways. When they left his room, they would say, "Now, you two, still be here when I return." They would laugh and go on to the next lucky patient.

LET'S CALL IT THE WAY IT WAS: DADDY WASN'T cooperative at all with the Speech Therapy. He started crying when the speech therapist came into the room. I would ask, "Daddy, what's the matter?"

He looked at me and said, "Don't ya know that's your Mama?"

I took a real close look at the pretty lady siting there and couldn't believe my eyes. That I hadn't noticed the resemblance myself was even more surprising because she looked so much like my mother.

The earliest opportunity that I could, I explained the situation to Dr. Speier and she immediately changed therapists. She made sure that a blond came, since Mama had been a brunette like me.

When the new therapist arrived, she started talking with Daddy so she could understand where he was at, both mentally and emotionally.

She asked, "Who is the President of the United States? What month is it? What day is it?" Poor, Daddy, he didn't know any of the answers. She then said, "Look at your watch, Vernon, and tell me what time it is so I won't miss my next appointment."

Daddy looked closely at his watch. We knew he couldn't remember how to tell time. In a few seconds he looked at her and said, "It's day time." We couldn't believe our ears! He didn't know the time, but he knew enough to try and cover his inability.

The therapist continued, "Vernon, is it snowing in this room?"

He looked at her, then back at me, then cupped his hand up to his mouth and said, "Is she crazy or what?"

She said, "Vernon, I didn't understand you. What did you say?"

"I chew my tobaccy once and then spit it out," he responded.

She said with a really puzzled look on her face, "Excuse me?"

I decided to help her out and said, "He means, he answered the question once and he is not going to answer it again, even though he was talking to me when he answered the 'Is it snowing?' question."

I COULD TELL THAT DADDY WAS COMING TO   LIFE again and starting to notice things around him. Dr. Petersen said, "The swelling is going down in his brain, so this is allowing him to think a little clearer."

MY BEST FRIEND, KAREN, CAME TO SEE ME WHILE I was at the hospital with Daddy. Karen was a singer in the upper mid west, a pretty lady with blond hair, well, blonde sometimes. Other times, it might be red, just according to how Karen was feeling that day. She had been my very best friend for almost a year. Her husband had passed away the year before and she had taken an apartment in St. Paul with her daughter.

She said, "Reta, I have an extra bed in my room and you are welcome to stay with us. I know this motel must be eating away at your finances."

"Oh, Karen, you are God sent! My credit cards are about maxed out and I will gladly take you up on your offer." I packed my stuff and moved to Karen's apartment that evening.

It sure was nice to have a friend to talk to. She was so understanding and knew how much I loved my Daddy.

The next morning I got up early as usual. I had started down Highway 94 to Minneapolis, where Abott-Northwestern is located when I had a flat tire. Taking time to change my tire caused me to be a little late.

As I entered the hallway of Daddy's ward, everyone was in a turmoil. They told me, "Vernon is really upset this morning. He keeps looking for piss ants in his room and telling us to find them."

I laughed and explained, "Piss Ant is the nick name he has called me all my life. He is probably wondering why I'm not here." I hurried into his room and said, "Good morning, Brody!" He settled down—immediately.

STEVE (REMEMBER HIM? HE WAS MY HUSBAND AT the time!) very rarely came to the hospital. He had been trying to help Pam and Kim run the studios, and I think he was more of a liability to us than an asset (unless you assume the first three letters in the word "asset"). Every night I would call and talk to the girls and let them know how their Grandpa was doing Clearly, they were ready for me to come home.

One night, Pam said, "Mom, we are losing students right and left. I'm trying, and Kim helps whenever she can." Kim was still a senior in high school. "But, mom, a lot of students are quitting because of Steve, and they don't think you are going to come back to the studios. He also takes all the cash out of the cash box and only deposits the checks. He has really been acting strange."

I was aware that Steve's younger brother's wife, Cheryl, had been going up to my home quite a bit during my absences plus he had been spending a great deal of time at his Daddy's house, which was about a half mile from Rick and Cheryl's house. At the time, I had not put two and two together, not yet. I knew the only good quality Steve probably possessed was the fact that he didn't cheat: And even that was to change in the very near future.

Cheryl had come to the hospital and ridden up to my home, with me, on several occasions. I knew she had been having an affair with Steve's fifteen year old son, who lived in Amery with his mother, but I didn't know her plan was to sleep with all the men in the family!

I had told Pam and Kim, "I don't know how much longer it will be before I can bring Daddy home." I was sure proud of my girls. They were handling everything like little troopers and I knew I could always count on them. They were the two things I knew I had done really right in my life. Picking a husband, I had never been a whiz at, but I knew God had really blessed me when he chose me to be their mother.

DR. SPEIER AND HER GROUP HAD DONE EVERYTHING possible to rehabilitate Daddy. Now, they had given him all the final tests to see if he could qualify for admission into their facility.

When the tests were finished, it was like waiting for the jury to come in. We had been at the hospital for almost two months, now.

Dr. Speier called me and said, "We should have everything completed for evaluation by tomorrow morning."

That night, I gave Daddy a hug good night and left for Karen's apartment, as usual. I didn't feel good about the tests at this point. Daddy had not been cooperative and I knew he could have done better on some things.

After sharing my feelings and thoughts with Karen that night, she asked, "What if they don't admit him to Sister Kenny?"

I said, "Well, then I'll take him home and keep working with him and have them re-evaluate him at a future date."

I got up early the next morning and found Karen up also, breakfast waiting. Being nervous, I wasn't too hungry, but I did drink some coffee. I said, "Karen, I am so worried about their decision. Daddy has been so uncooperative."

She said, "Call me when you know."

When I arrived at the hospital, the minute I walked onto Daddy's ward, I knew my worst fear had already happened. Twyla, one of his nurses, said to me, with a real concerned look on her face, "Reta, come with me and let's have a cup of coffee. I need to talk to you." Twyla had been selected to talk to me because I had become very close to her throughout our entire stay.

I started to cry and said "Twyla, he didn't pass the testing, did he?"

She looked as though she couldn't make herself speak and finally said, "He passed some of them, but Dr. Speier and her group do not feel as though Vernon is ready to be admitted to Sister Kenny. They want to place him in our half-way house and continue to work with him."

I was aware that this facility was actually a nursing home. At this point, I really started to sob and was trying not to be angry because I knew that everyone had done their very best. I became almost hysterical and with some effort, Twyla got me calmed down, but only somewhat.

Then I made my decision, and told her, "Twyla, Daddy is going home with me. I have watched all the ways they have worked with him and I know, between me and my daughters, we can work with Daddy until they re-evaluate him again."

She couldn't believe what she was hearing. She said, "Reta, do you know what you are saying?"

"Twyla, I have never been more serious in my life. Daddy is going to Wisconsin just like he and I had planned before this damn stroke." I was in total denial and would not accept the fact that the Daddy I knew would probably never return.

I straightened my face up and said, "Okay, let's get the arrangements made."

I first called Pam and Kim and said, "Your Grandpa and I are coming home." They were so happy. I had missed them so much and knew they missed me. Their love, support and devotion had carried me through and given me the strength to keep going.

I went into Daddy's room and started packing his little suitcase. I said, "Daddy, it's time to go home to Wisconsin!" He got so excited about leaving and right then I knew I was doing the right thing.

All of a sudden, the door opened, and Dr. Speier walked in. She said, "Are you serious about taking Vernon to your home?"

Using some of Daddy's famous words I said, "You betcha!"

She smiled and said "After knowing you these past few weeks, I was half way expecting this. I have already made arrangements for you to go though some pretty ridged training. You will need to know how to use a transfer belt and all the other necessary equipment, plus how to properly continue your father's therapy."

"Dr. Speier, I would greatly appreciate anything you can do to help me. I have gotten a pretty good education by just being here from sunup til sundown and observing your staff. How long do you think this will take before we can go home?" I asked her.

"I think maybe three or four days," she quickly responded.

That was good enough for me.

I went back to the apartment and had a long talk with Karen. She said, "How are you going to work and take care of your Daddy at the same time? You are totally exhausted as it is now."

"I don't know, but I know God will give me the strength and wisdom to do it. He's taken pretty good care of us so far and I know I can't leave Daddy here in Minneapolis," I replied wearily.

Both of us sat there awhile, each absorbed in our own thoughts. Karen had given up singing some time back and wasn't really working at this time. This gave me an idea. "Karen, Daddy and I don't have much money, but do you think you could help me out for awhile until I can find some full-time help?

She gave me a serious look and said, "That's exactly what I've been sitting her thinking. I'm not sure if I could handle it, I still haven't gotten over all the care-taking I had to do for Curly." Curly had been her husband and had died just a few months before.

"I can understand, Karen. Don't make a decision just yet. Let's both think on it for awhile," I said, feeling there probably was light at the end of my present tunnel.

"Good idea, Reta," she quickly replied. "How about if I go with you to the hospital so that I can observe the training, in case I decide to go back and help you out?"

As we agreed, she went to the hospital with me the next day. After observing for awhile, she asked if she could go through the short training with me so that she could get a "hands-on" feeling for the actual procedures that would be involved...just in case. Of course, everyone agreed and thought it was a very good idea.

With Karen there, she soon had Daddy and me laughing most of the time. She was a very bubbly person and Daddy kept calling her Sissy. I had to agree she did remind me of my precious aunt and I think that really helped him accept her.

That day was actually fun as we learned how to use the transfer belt, the bath bench and a few more "tricks of the trade," designed to help the care-giver. Karen was only able to stay for the one day but I told her I could teach her later.

By the end of four grueling days, I felt like I was ready for the big time. Dr. Speier agreed, saying, "My staff has given you an A+. They feel you are ready and quite capable of taking care of your father. I have already written the order for the nurses to discharge Vernon—and you too!"

YOU WOULD THINK DADDY AND I WERE BIG celebrities the way everyone came to say "goodbye." His nurses said, "We have really gotten attached to you both. When you bring Vernon back for his check-ups, please bring him up for a visit." I promised them I would.

I had got them a really nice card expressing our appreciation for all the wonderful care we, both, had received. Everyone of them gave Daddy a little kiss on the cheek. Boy, did he love that! He felt really privileged and wanted to take them all home with us.

I placed Daddy's Stetson hat on his head or rather, I handed it to him and he placed it on his head. My training was already starting to pay off!

I told him I had to take care of some business and would see him in a few minutes. The discharge papers needed to be signed and then I brought my Lincoln around to the front. By the time I did this, he was waiting for me in his wheelchair at the entrance with Marlene, one of his nurses.

I put Daddy in the car, folded his wheelchair and placed it in the trunk like I was an old pro. Getting in the car, I fastened the seat belt around him and said, "Daddy, let's go home!"

Marlene clapped her hands and said, "I couldn't have done that better myself! Have a safe trip."

Giving a happy wave as I pulled from the curb, I called back, "We'll see you in one month."

I HEADED THAT OLD LINCOLN FOR WISCONSIN, starting down Highway 35, and by the time we got to Forest Lake, Daddy was sitting up as straight as a judge. He was looking at the countryside and talking a mile a minute, "Look at that snow! Look at that old house! Look at them cows!" and on and on he went. This was the first time he had been outside in quite some time.

After awhile, I said, "Daddy, we will be home in about an hour. Pam, Kim and Cheryl are really excited we are coming home."

"Who's Cheryl?" he asked.

I said, "She's that little red-head friend of Kim's that you met this summer." Cheryl had been living with us for almost two years. She had a bad home life, and I had taken her into my home. A really sweet little girl and I loved her very much: She was like another daughter to me.

"I don't know her," Daddy said.

"Well, you better be ready when we get there cause they are all going to be ready to talk," I said, reminding him and patting his arm.

He smiled his little crooked smile and said, "I can't wait to see 'em."

THE FEELINGS I HAD NOW WERE MUCH DIFFERENT from when we left Abilene. I better understood Daddy's illness, what had happened, and now felt confident, and very competent to care for him. Yes, I was scared, and at times almost was overwhelmed by the responsibility, but I knew I could handle it. I was so grateful to Dr. Speier and her fine staff for the time they had taken to train me.

DADDY DROPPED OFF TO SLEEP AFTER AWHILE SO I reclined his seat and let him rest. I knew he would need all his strength when we got home, as his grandchildren were eagerly waiting.

I didn't really know how Pam and Kim would react to this new Grandpa I was bringing home. They had not been with him that much, and I figured they still had not realized, nor accepted, the fact that he would be different—permanently different. I found that I was still dealing with the changes myself and at times was having trouble accepting my new Daddy. My prayer was that we would all be able to adjust and handle this new change in our lives.

It was a beautiful, March day in Wisconsin, and I was so thankful that the sun was shining so brightly. I looked at it as a good omen as I contemplated what lay ahead of us.

About a mile from home, I woke Daddy up. Groggily, he said, "What the hell's going on?"

Smiling at him and suppressing my excitement and anxiety, I told him "Welcome home, Daddy." Tears filled my eyes. I was totally exhausted and home had never looked so good.

Pulling into the driveway, I started blowing the horn. By the time we pulled up in front of my home, Pam, Kim and Cheryl came running out. Daddy just started to cry when he saw them.

I got the wheel chair out of the trunk while they were all hugging Grandpa and welcoming him home. To me, they looked so much more grownup than when they had been in Texas just a few months before. Daddy's illness was already taking a toll on his family, and we had only just begun.

Like an old pro, I got Daddy into the wheelchair. The girls couldn't believe how well I was able to handle him. I told them, "I will teach you the things I have learned, too, and that will make things easier for all of us."

When we got Daddy inside, I found that the girls had worked hard and the house was clean, neat and orderly. Daddy's hospital bed was in the living room and ready for him to crawl into. They had made a big sign and put it his bed. It said, Welcome Home, Grandpa. Pictures of them were on the wall by his bed, plus a picture of him and Mama. Daddy looked at my mother's picture, and he started to cry.

Pam and Kim felt terrible, they didn't understand why their Grandpa was crying. I explained, "This is just part of the effects of the stroke. Everything is just wonderful. You girls have done a great job holding down the fort." I gave each of them another hug and reassured them that I was very proud of them.

I turned the bed toward the wall so Daddy would have to look to his right to talk to us. In addition, I took all the pictures off the wall so that he didn't have anything to look at but the blank wall. To also encourage him, I told Pam, Kim and Cheryl not to approach him or get on his left side, so we had to encourage him to accept his right side.

After Daddy dropped off to sleep, I sat down with Pam, Kim and Cheryl and tried to fill them in on their Grandpa and how the stroke had changed his whole personality, physical dexterity and mental stability. Kim's reaction had been somewhat like Cecil's. She said, "Mom, will he ever be the same, like he was in Texas?"

"Honey, I don't know. I have to be honest with you—he won't, unless it's God's Will." She looked so confused and sad. Tears welled up in her eyes as she got up and walked over to Daddy's bed. She gave him a kiss on the forehead and then went to her room. Pam and I knew she needed to be alone for awhile. Cheryl followed her soon after. They were pretty much inseparable at this time being the same age and in the same grade in school.

Pam seemed to be able accept the changes in her Grandpa much easier. I had talked more to Pam on the telephone during the time I was in Minnesota, so I believe she was more aware of Daddy's real condition than Kim. She also understood my concern for her sister. She assured me, "Mom, everything will be okay with Kim. I'll talk to her."

I had relied so much on Pam throughout the past few weeks. She had graduated the year before and was working full time in the studios. She had been an extension of myself during my absence.

AFTER I HAD BEEN HOME AWHILE, STEVE SHOWED up. He was running true to form; whenever I needed him, he was nowhere to be found. Where he had been, I don't know, but he was running around in my new Firebird. Coming in for the first time, he said, "Oh, I see you got Vernon home okay."

"Good observation," I said, finding it hard to be civil.

Later, Pam filled me in on what was happening at the studios. How Steve had made a fool of himself in front of some of the parents by pretending to be a certified teacher. She told me, "Mom, a lot of our students have quit and I am scared more are going to."

"Pam, it's not your fault, I know you and Kim have done your best," I tried to reassure her while I was seething inside.

Steve came in on the tail-end of our conversation and started to whine, "It's not my fault, either."

I said in a harsh voice, "Did anyone say it was? You must have a guilty conscience or something."

I was becoming more and more bitter toward Steve. He had promised to have a screen built to go by Daddy's bed so he could have some privacy. This would help until we could get the shaft for the lift constructed. Then Daddy could have his own bedroom, upstairs and when he wanted to join us he could come down in his wheelchair.

Of course, I had arrived home to find that nothing had been done, not even started. I knew I should have hired someone to take care of this job. Brad had volunteered to do it, but Steve was so jealous of Brad he wouldn't allow him to do anything.

One thing about Brad, if he had a job to do, you knew it would be done right. On the other hand, if Steve had a job to do, he would only start it and never finish. This is the way it had been and now everywhere you looked there were areas of the house waiting for completion. Of course, at this time, I didn't know he had been too busy servicing his brother's wife, and only God knew how many others, to take care of these small details.

No wonder he had been so supportive of me staying with Daddy. He knew he could drive the new car I had just purchased before Christmas, steal all the money he needed out of the studios, and be free to bed whomever he could coerce.

WE HAD AGREED: WHEN WE GOT MARRIED, STEVE would quit his job to work full-time on the house. Yeah, okay! He had used some of his retirement money to buy the first load of lumber and have the basement dug. I agreed to support us during the project and even paid his child support from the day we married. He had five children by three different women. It always amazed me that he finished "those jobs." Of course, I don't look too intelligent for marrying someone like this, but like I mentioned before, I was at a very low-point in my life when I met and married him: Big mistake!

KAREN, MY BEST FRIEND, HAD AGREED TO COME help me with Daddy, and true to form, she arrived promptly early the next evening. She said straightway, "Reta, I'll stay as long as is emotionally possible for me to do, but I have decided I can't help you indefinitely. It is just too soon after Curly's death."

"Karen, I understand perfectly, but if you could help me just until I find someone else, I would really appreciate it," I said, almost begging.

"No, problem. I'll stay 'til then," she assured me. That really took a load off my mind because I had a lot to do now that I was home. I didn't need to be worrying about Daddy, above-and-beyond-the-call, as before.

Daddy was still sleeping good, so we sat down and had a cold, Miller Lite. It sure tasted good. I wished that Daddy could have joined us and had his favorite, Michelob, but until the doctor gave the okay, I would never give one to him—no matter how much he begged otherwise.

Daddy had always taken an Ex-Lax at bed time so he wouldn't have a problem the next day. I told Karen, "I am going to give Daddy an Ex-Lax just like he has taken all his life and he will have his movement around 1:00 p.m., tomorrow."

I had been really concerned about this function and had purchased a small box of Ex-Lax while Daddy had been here the past August. I got them out, fixed him a small snack and woke him up, saying, "Daddy, you better wake up and eat something. It's time for us to all go to bed."

He could hardly open his eyes, but when he looked around and spotted Karen, he got so excited and called out, "Dit?" his nickname for Sissy. "When did you get here?" he said, and began to cry.

"Now, Daddy, this isn't Sissy. This is my friend, Karen. Remember? You met her this summer? She's a country singer like me and she's going to stay here and help you, too." I wasn't sure if having Karen there would be a help or hindrance, with respect to his emotions, that is.

He was a little disappointed that it wasn't Sissy, of course, but said, "Hi, Karen," and extended his hand.

After I gave him his snack and he swallowed the two Ex-Lax, I tucked him in and said, "Good night, Brody. I love you." I gave him a kiss on the cheek like I had done so many times in the past.

I locked up the house and then took Karen down to the bedroom that would become Daddy's room after the shaft was built. She would use it until that time. Giving her a hug, I said, "See ya in the morning."

Once in the confines of my own bedroom and the door closed, I ran the water and took a hot bath and relaxed a bit. It sure felt good to be home and have all my family under the same roof.

Steve was already in bed when I got there and had the television blasting away, as usual. He couldn't sleep without it on. Does that tell you something?

Lying there, thinking, I couldn't get Kim off my mind. I felt so sorry for her. The situation with Daddy had really been a shock for her. I remembered back to 1983 when Kim and I lived next door to Daddy. We had bought a trailer house and had moved it next to his little house, on his second lot. Kim and Daddy really became close during the short time I stayed there, before we moved back to Wisconsin.

She spent most of her time at Grandpa's house, in fact. I would call them home for supper, and most of the time they were really hungry. But there were times they didn't eat much. I would say, "Kim, have you been cooking those rice crispy bars again?" She and Daddy would both look guilty and of course, Daddy would take all the blame. They loved to eat junk food, together!

That summer, I had bought Kim her first ten-speed bicycle for her birthday. She was so proud of it. Grandpa told her, "Kim, you can park it in my carport." He then took her down to the store and bought her a chain and lock for it. When they returned, he showed her how to chain it up to the post in his carport.

They were quite a sight to watch. He always talked to her and planned what they would do the next day, just like he used to do with me. I smiled and went back into the house, my heart overflowing with love for the tender care Daddy was giving Kim.

Late one night, about two days later, I heard Daddy's brakes squeal. I looked out the window just in time to see him miss Kim's bicycle. She had chained it up on the inside of the carport, instead of the outside as he had showed.

I went over to him. He was white as a sheet. He said, "Damn, Reta, I nearly ran right over the baby's bicycle."

"Well, it looks like you better have a talk with your little partner in the morning."

A couple of hours after sunup the next day I sent Kim over to Grandpa's house. It wasn't long before they were out in the carport and he was explaining, "Now, here is where you chain your bicycle, Kim. Don't ever put it on this side again or Papa might run over it."

You see, this was the Grandpa that Kim knew. Pam had never spent as much quality time with him as had Kim. Pam had gone back to Wisconsin that year and, therefore, Kim had spent even more time with Daddy.

This is why I could understand her reaction to Daddy. I prayed that God would help her accept this new Grandpa.

Before finally settling down to sleep, I got up and made a final check on Daddy. He was sleeping like a baby. I kissed him on the forehead and went back to bed. I knew tomorrow would be a very busy day. My first, without the nurses. I was so thankful that Karen was there to help.

I WOKE UP THE NEXT MORNING ABOUT SUNRISE, and went immediately in to see if Daddy was okay. With just a little bit of daylight shining into the living room, it looked as if he were bleeding to death! It appeared as if there was blood all over him and the bed!

My heart was in my mouth, as I quickly turned on the light, and to my relief, it was just the Ex-Lax! He had stool from one end of the bed to the other. I exclaimed, "Daddy, how in the world am I gonna get you clean?"

"Damned if I know," he replied. He looked so pitiful.

I said, "Brody, I don't remember them training me for this crisis at Sister Kenny I'll get some help and be right back." Knowing that Steve would be useless in this situation, as usual, I went down to wake up Karen.

Knocking on her bedroom door, I said, "Karen, are you awake?"

Still half asleep, she replied, "Oh, shit. What's wrong?"

I said, "Well, you just said it. That's the problem and it's everywhere!"

Karen threw on her robe and away we went. She took one look at Daddy and said, "Vernon, what in the hell have you done to yourself?"

He looked at her and said, "Damned if I know."

Looking at me, she asked, "Does the washer and dryer work?"

"I think Steve got them fixed," I told her hopefully. If he hadn't, there sure would be hell to pay.

She said, "Well, let's get started!"

I got a basin of warm water, plenty of wash clothes and towels while Karen began stripping Daddy down. She had had plenty of practice how to change beds and clean up such messes from taking care of Curly his last days.

Daddy didn't know what the heck was happening. He had not only pulled the Depends off that I had put on him for protection, but he had also pulled the Texas Catheter out. I said to Karen, "I think we should leave the catheter off. How is he going to know if he needs to pee if he can't feel 'what wet is?'"

She smiled and said, "Well, then, let's toss it, too."

Daddy was laying there agreeing with everything. Over the next few days we did a lot of Daddy-changing and the bed, but gradually Daddy started to tell me when he needed to urinate. Karen, however, spent most of the week in the laundry room.

After we got Daddy all cleaned up and he was having his morning cup of coffee, I heard a knock at the door. Karen looked at me and said, "Now, who in the hell could be here this time of morning?" It was around 7:30.

Opening the door, I found a very pretty nurse, standing on my porch. She was tall and slender with medium brown, short hair. She was dressed in her crisp, white uniform and with a nice smile, said, "Hello, my name is Joyce Schaefer. I have been contacted by Sister Kenny to head up Mr. Fuller's home care. Have I found the right place?"

"You sure have and you are a most welcome sight," I gratefully replied, bidding her into the house.

"One of my nurse's aids should be here anytime," she informed me.

I introduced her to Karen and then took her to meet Daddy. She was quite impressed with the setup we had for him. I explained our future plans were for him to have his own room but we had to wait until we could get the elevator shaft complete. Then we would be able to take him on all levels of the house. She said, "Well, Vernon, it looks like your daughter has plans to spoil you rotten."

In typical Vernon fashion, he smiled and said, "You betcha."

She proceeded to check Daddy over from stem to stern. Needless to say, Daddy was enjoying all this attention. I believe his hormones were still intact and were returning to life.

I told Joyce about our morning episode. She laughed and said, "Try Ducalax suppositories every other day. Some of my other patients with this same condition had pretty good success."

Just then, there was another knock at the door. Joyce said, "That will be Betty."

I opened the door and invited her in. She was a heavy-set woman, about forty-five and so bubbly and seemed really good-natured.

She and Daddy hit it off right away. She was a farm gal and started talking cattle and farming. Of course, Daddy was talking right back to her as though he understood every word. Sometimes, I think maybe he was understanding more than we thought.

Joyce filled me in on what Medicare would cover toward Daddy's home care services. She said, "You will have an aid who will come out two hours everyday. It will probably be Betty, but personnel will change occasionally. Once a week, I will come to check on Vernon, myself. In addition, he will also have a social worker, speech, physical and occupational therapists coming once a week to help him."

"It seems as though Dr. Speier has set up a wonderful program for him, but I have to find someone to live-in full-time so I can get back to my studios—while I still have them."

Nodding her understanding, she said, "Maybe Vernon's social worker can help you. I know that if he qualifies, there are state funded programs available. Ask his social worker about that, too, when she comes. Another suggestion would be to run an ad for help, in the newspaper. This type of help is really hard to find, unless you can afford to pay quite a good salary."

I told her, "Well, Daddy didn't have that much money and, with the student losses at the studios we've been suffering, I just don't know what I'm going to do. But I do know I have to get back to work."

"I will keep my ears open and will come back to see you, again, next Friday," she promised. She left her number and said, "If you need me for anything, day or night, just call." She smiled at Daddy, patted him on the hand and said, "See you, Friday, Vernon." He was so busy talking cows, pigs and horses with Betty, he hardly knew this pretty lady was leaving.

Karen was in the kitchen making Daddy some breakfast. I went out there and asked, "Karen, what am I going to do? I have to get back to work!" I was going to pay Karen $100 a week, plus room and board.

She said, "I wish I could help you, but I just can't, not for very long."

I understood where she was coming from and said, "Well, there has got to be someone out there who I can train to help me. I know I can't afford a full-time nurse, but with the medical force Dr. Speier has lined up to handle Daddy's home care, I feel really safe hiring someone other than a trained professional. As long as I can find a good person that will truly care about him."

She said, "After this morning, the way your Daddy's hormones have come alive, I think you should try to find a man."

This made me laugh, and so I said, "I agree."

About this time Betty completed her work with Daddy. She said, "I'll see you in the morning."

I said, "I hope you will continue, he really does get along well with you."

She smiled and chuckled, "I enjoy him, too."

Betty had barely left when there was another knock on the door. I went to the door and there stood another lady with a big smile. She was short and thin with blond hair. Introducing herself, she said, "Hi, I'm Kathy from Social Services. Am I—"

I interrupted her, saying, "Yes, you're at the right place. Please come in. I'm Reta, Vernon's daughter."

Laughing as she came in, she said, "I guess this has been a busy place this morning."

"Yes, it started early." Karen and I both looked at each other and laughed. I filled Kathy in on the morning's activities.

"Hello," she said, as she introduced herself to Daddy.

His eyes twinkled again and I said, "Daddy, what did you do to have all these pretty women coming to see you?"

He smiled and said, "Damned if I know."

About then, Kim and Cheryl came bouncing up the stairs, all ready to take off for school. They went over to Daddy and Kim said, "Good morning, Grandpa. You wanna go to school with me and Cheryl?"

I looked up and silently said, Thank you, God. I knew Kim had come to terms with some of her feelings.

They grabbed a little breakfast and headed out the door. Kim had her own car, so they drove to school each morning.

Kathy had met Kim and Cheryl before they left for school. She seemed impressed with them and said, "How do your daughters feel about having their Grandpa here?"

I said, "They support my decision one hundred per cent."

"That's good because you are going to need all the support you can get in the future."

Pam came up a few minutes later and said, "It sure feels good not having to get ready to go to school, but life was sure a lot easier just going to school."

"Honey, this is Kathy."

I explained to Kathy how Pam had been an extension of me for the past three months. Pam laughed and said, "Yeah, and I'm ready for my mom to be back!" I knew it had been extra hard on her trying to run the studios, while Steve was trying to be the big boss.

A few minutes later, when she could talk with me alone, she said in a very serious tone, "Mom, I hope you go over your accounts today because Steve has really taken a lot of the money."

"I will as soon as I can," I promised her. I knew I needed to check the books, but I also dreaded what I might find.

Pam then turned to go over and visit with her Grandpa, before she left for work. He sure was happy to have his grand daughters around him.

Kathy and I now had a chance to really talk. I explained my financial situation to her and how I needed someone full-time so I could get back to work. She told me, "If Vernon can qualify, financially, there is a program that Wisconsin has called, COP Assistance. That would help fund someone to live-in and care for Vernon."

"I don't know what I would have done if his SSI hadn't covered the 20 per cent not covered by Medicare at Sister Kenny and Abbott-Northwestern," I said, truly reflecting on a God-send. "I now understand, since he is living in Wisconsin, that the state of Texas will not continue to pay his SSI. Is that correct?"

"That's correct," she said, "and if he has more than $1,800 to his name, he will not be able to get SSI in Wisconsin."

"He has a little house in Texas that's worth maybe $5,000, a 1978 Pontiac worth about $1,500, plus a small savings account I have been keeping for hard times. I didn't want to use any of it, if possible," I told her truthfully.

She said, "Well, if you hope to get any assistance, you had better start making some quick adjustments." Smiling, she continued, "We won't have this discussion until my next visit, which will give you about one month."

I understood what she meant and thankfully said, "You will never know how much I appreciate this information. I will take care of everything."

Changing the subject, she said, "I am very pleased with the environment here in your home for Vernon. He's a very lucky father to have you and your wonderful family to care for him."

Daddy piped up and said, "You betcha."

AFTER KATHY HAD LEFT, I ASKED, "KAREN WOULD you and Pam take care of Daddy? I have some serious thinking to do and must call Cecil and try to work out this property problem in Texas."

I went up to my loft where I had my office set up. From there, I could see the entire lower level, and Daddy's bed was in plain view.

I needed to have another one of those serious talks with *The Man Upstairs*. He had become my only true confidant since the beginning of Daddy's horrible stroke. I had always been close to God, but now I was really leaning on Him and trusting Him to guide me.

A positive feeling came over me and I understood exactly what I had to do. I had always lived my life by the rules, but it was time now to break a few. I thanked God, again, for impressing me to get that Power of Attorney before Daddy completely lost his reasoning abilities. There was just no imagining what I would have done, at this time, if I had to contend with Yane and the budget she had wanted set up.

Once, again, I thought, "Why couldn't she be my friend? Someone I could count on at a time like this. Instead, I was worried about using any of the small savings Daddy had, which consisted of something under $7,000.

Next, I called Cecil and told him the situation. I said, "I am going to sign a Quick Claim Deed to you for Daddy's house and lot. Then would you put it up for sale? It has to get out of Daddy's name, ASAP."

He understood and said, "Does Daddy still have the $7,000?"

"Yes, but the way things are going we are going to need it plus the sale of the house for his care. My income, here, has been cut in half with the loss of students," I explained.

He said, "Well, I am behind three payments on my house and if I don't get them caught up, I'm gonna lose it. Do you think Daddy could loan me $1,500 which I would pay back in one year?"

"I will see what we can do," I promised him. Things were getting tighter for everyone it seemed.

At this time, I owed over $4,000 on my credit cards from the motels, clothing for Daddy, the expenses for Andy to come get us and other necessary items. I was still making my payments, but felt as though I could save the studios only if I could just get some help and get back to work.

I decided to help Cecil because I felt so sorry for him and Margaret. They had worked so hard and had fallen on some hard times.

Daddy would have wanted me to help them, I felt, and not just let the money sit in the bank. It was already in my name, so I just wrote Cecil a check for $1,500 and got it off right away.

Then, I contacted Mr. Norman, an attorney in Winters, who Daddy had dealt with for many years. The Quick Claim Deed needed to be arranged for Daddy's property. He said he would contact Cecil and take care of everything on that end. He was very nice and totally understood my situation.

One last thing I did: I arranged to put Daddy's car in my name. That would turn out to be important, too.

I wheeled 'n' dealed and by the time I saw Kathy, again, Daddy's total financial statement was now under $1,800. I had done it!

BECAUSE OF ALL THE DETAILS I NEEDED TO TAKE care of to get things arranged for this monumental change in Daddy's life and mine, I wasn't able to go back to the studios for approximately two more weeks.

I continued to rely heavily on Pam until I could get everything in order at home. Pam was doing a great job and Kim was helping when she could. Of course, Steve was still doing his thing, trying to be Mr. Entrepreneur. At times, Pam wanted to just knock him in the head and hide the shovel.

ONE DAY, KATHY CALLED AND SAID, "HELLO, HOW are you coming along?"

"Fine, I've taken care of a lot of things since you were last here."

She said, "Reta, guess what? Some good news for you. Help is on the way! I've arranged for a shift of aids to come in during the time when you will be working, but they have to leave as soon as you return home."

"Oh, thanks so much Kathy! What an answer to prayer! Now I can get back and relieve some of the burden from Pam," I said joyfully.

She told me about a program at Stout University, in Menomonie, regarding qualified personnel for positions like the person I needed. She continued, "These people are not trained for home care, Reta, but they have been checked out as to their characters so that you would feel safe with them living in your home." She gave me the number of Stout and I called right away to get my name on the list for help.

WHEN PAM AND STEVE GOT HOME THAT NIGHT, I said, "Guess what? I'll be able to start back to work, and next week!. Kathy has arranged for some help part-time help until I can find someone full-time."

Pam was almost hanging from the rafters she was so pleased. She had been trying to get recital routines arranged for the students, plus the choreographies. Steve, on the other hand, didn't seem too happy about my returning back to the studios—and for obvious reasons.

When Kim and Cheryl heard my news they quickly assured me they would help with Grandpa when they got home from school. They also agreed to clean house and do most of the cooking. The grocery shopping was also designated into their care. I could see a real team effort developing. I was so thankful to God for my little cheerleaders.

In the meantime, I ran an add in the local papers, the St. Paul Dispatch and on every bulletin board I could find. I thought $500 a month, plus room and board, would be enough to attract someone who might need a job and a good place to live.

ANDY AND ISABELLE CAME TO OUR PLACE THE following Sunday, after church. I told Andy, "I've just got to get this shaft done, so I can get Daddy out of the living room downstairs. Steve finally got around to making a screen for the exposed perimeter of Daddy's bed, but he still hasn't done anything downstairs for Daddy's bedroom or a room next to it for the home-care attendant, that is when I find one."

Isabelle said, "My brother, Jess, is a good carpenter, and he needs a place to stay after his divorce. If you want, I'll talk to him about helping you."

I had met Jess and liked him, so I said, "Okay, let me know because I've got to get someone in here as soon as possible that will finish the house." Andy and Isabelle knew their son, Steve, all too well and how he procrastinated in all his actions.

JESS CALLED THE NEXT MORNING, AND WE AGREED on $3.00 per hour, plus room and board. I was sure hoping he didn't eat like Steve or I'd have to open another studio to feed him.

He moved in immediately and started work. We got along with Jess very well and he did good work. What a joy to see the house starting to take shape.

That first week, he got the elevator shaft completed! He was not anything at all like his nephew, Steve. I was pleasantly surprised that he didn't eat like a horse and even loved to cook, so he took on some of the cooking chores as part of the team. Kim and Cheryl were delighted for his help.

Steve was really whining big time by now because his Uncle Jess got his butt out of bed every morning, early, and made him work with him until late, and every day. I just watched—and laughed to myself. He hadn't worked this hard in so long, his body probably had forgot what work really was. Anyway, with Steve's help, Jess was able to accomplish much more and faster than originally planned. I was delighted!

I WENT BACK TO WORK WITH PAM THE FOLLOWING week. My students were so happy to see me and said how much they had enjoyed Pam. They also really liked Kim, whenever she was there. NONE of them had any positive comments concerning Steve, however.

I was quite pleased with what my girls had accomplished, but not surprised. I knew they could handle the studios, but most important, now they knew it, too.

I told Steve to stick with Jess because he was needed more, at home, than at the studio.

Now I could not put off the inevitable, any longer. I began the task of checking my accounts and it didn't take long to realize that he had taken an unbelievable amount of money compared to the amount of deposits. I had opened an escrow account for costume payments as I had always done in the past because the costumes always came C.O.D. I couldn't believe it! He had even gotten into this fund, too! No wonder he wanted to continue running the business end of the studios!

THE NEXT MORNING IN MY LOFT, I WENT OVER EACH account and verified my checkbook to see how many checks he had written during my absence. To my disbelief, he had not been making the payments on anything! Looking around, I found all the unpaid bills stuffed in one of my desk drawers.

In a state of shock, I called him up to the loft. Confronting him with what I had discovered, I said, "Get your ass out of the house and find yourself a job. I am NOT going to support you or your kids any longer. You just take care of yourself and all those kids you bred, and I'll take care of everything else. Also, stay out of my check book, cash box, do not charge anything on my credit cards and keep away from my studios!"

In hindsight, I ask myself why I had waited so long. There is no easy answer, not today, not then. What is for sure is this: When I finally made the decision, it was the right one.

KIMBERLY MARIE ALBRECHT
RETA LEE'S DAUGHTER

3

HIDDEN CAMERAS WOULD SURELY HAVE WORKED wonders, but, of course, I didn't have any. I couldn't prove anything at this time, but I knew Steve had been cheating on me, too, even using money out of my studios to finance his "entertainment." My bed had been lonely for some time, so I knew he had been going elsewhere.

Our relationship had changed drastically right after my hysterectomy that past August. In his ignorance, he thought I had damaged my womanhood in some way, that I was less a desirable object of affection. I only wish I could have proved his infidelity at that time, which would have, of course, given me a Biblical way out. I had wanted this marriage to survive, but it was really looking hopeless. No, let's tell it the way it was: I would rather have pulled cotton all day than to have had to continually deal with Steve and his misdirection on most everything.

Often, I entertained the idea that there would never be a man with whom I could live and totally respect, twenty-four hours a day. Men all seemed so weak. To be fair, I had to always take care of my family.

Steve's usual rebuttal was always something like, "The Bible says I'm the man of the house!"

I usually responded by saying, "Great! Then start providing for your family, and I'll stay home and bake cookies! That's perfectly Biblical! Then and only then can you take that position!"

There was nothing, of course, I would have liked better, and usually finished off such squabbles with a last dig, something like, "I would just like to see you take care of yourself and all the children you have brought into this world. Now, that would really be something to behold!"

It was the same this time. His response to my telling him to go get a job was typical Steve. "Well, just wait and see. I am going to start a body shop in the garage, then you'll eat your words." We had already initiated work on a three-car garage or, at least, he had started it.

"That's great, Steve," I told him. "If you could just support this family for two months, June and July, I would be happy. I don't want to have to teach during the summer.   Whether you care or not, I am exhausted."

Forget about any logical response to my request, or for him to have said any kind words to me about my mental exhaustion. All he did, or would ever do, was snicker and head off somewhere to avoid any confrontation or attempts to resolve the problem. He took off downstairs to go back to work with Jess, and lose himself in his surrealistic diatribe of whatever irresponsibility of the moment took his fancy.

I became lost, in my own self-reverie and went back to the bills. I first started by calling the credit card companies and other concerns in an attempt to make arrangements to catch up with the bills

Toward this end I worked upstairs, every night.   After getting home from the studio and getting Daddy all settled and off to sleep for the night, I would then start my "third" job.   I was barely hanging on, financially, but didn't want to touch the remaining money in Daddy's account. That would have only been a temporary solution and would not have solved the biggest problem: Steve, himself. That's what drove me on.

ALMOST TWO MONTHS PASSED AND I STILL HAD NOT found anyone qualified to care for Daddy. Some came to the house and tried, but they just didn't work out. Being pulled in so many directions, at one time, I found I was going downhill, fast, totally exhausted. I would have given anything to just go to bed for an entire day and not have to think about anything.

During this time, in my mind, "Reta" ceased to exist any longer, at least not as I once had been. In her place was a mere robot, perhaps even less. She was daughter, mother, wife, banker, teacher, counselor. I knew I had to get some full-time help or blow a gasket in true medical terms. My entire family was starting to suffer and being so on edge, I found crying was my only release, sad but true.

Karen, sometimes, would come over and help out, but I needed someone full-time, someone who could be relied upon. Pam and Kim were wonderful, but they needed a mother, too, not simply a sad dishrag. I knew I had to find some help and fast!

IN THE MEANTIME, RECITAL WAS UPON US. WE HAD one scheduled at Cumberland and one at Rice Lake. Pam was my lifesaver and had done an excellent job getting the students ready for these productions. Everyone had worked extra hard for us and thankfully, most of my parents had been wonderful and extremely understanding. However, a few made my life miserable with their complaining about my absence, etc.

Kimberly's graduation was also coming up, soon and I had been busy making plans for her Open House. I ordered the horsd'oeurves, for her party from the Amery Locker Plant. There was no way that I would have the time to make them as I had for Pam's Open House last year.

I also had started another project. Needing to earn some extra money to pay Jess and for Kim's graduation expenses, I started teaching some Country Western Dance Classes. Daddy's Social Security and S.S.I. checks were taking care of his supplies from Chet's Pharmacy in Amery. They had extended credit to me personally which helped me in great measure to secure Daddy's medicines and other incidentals. In addition, the medical professionals in the area had done every thing possible to help us. I was so fortunate that most everyone was very understanding of our situation. But I still needed help!

ONE NIGHT THE PHONE RANG. AUNT SISSY TO THE rescue! I was so glad to hear from her. She had been gone for awhile working as a cook on a boat and so we had not talked for quite a few weeks. She was now home and called to get caught up on everyone and everything. When I heard her voice on the other end of the telephone, it was as if God had sent and Angel to call on me. And what did I do? I started crying!

She said, "Baby, what's wrong? Is your Daddy okay?

"Oh, yeah," I said, "Daddy's getting stronger and smarter every day. But I'm not doing so well."

Naturally, she wanted to know all about my difficulties. I explained my financial situation to her and the problems I had been having getting a full-time attendant. "The money is going so fast, Sissy. My credit cards are maxed and I am totally exhausted."

She said, "Baby, didn't Vernon have some money put back."

"Yes, he did, but I don't want to use it unless I have to. He had planned for that money to go to Cecil, Yane and me at his death," I explained

"Well, Vernon never counted on this happening, either," Sissy commented. "I know Vernon would not want you to be in this condition. You take what you need out of that account and pay some on your credit cards or wherever you need it."

"Oh, Sissy, I just hate to do that. You know how Yane has acted about *this money* in the past. She would just start her hateful accusations, again," I cried.

"Don't you worry about Yane. If she has a problem with it, I'll talk to her," promised my beloved Aunt.

"Sissy, I am sorry to be coming apart when you had hoped for some nice family news. It seems that I keep leaning on you, but I do thank God that I have you. Now, I don't feel so bad and will use some of Daddy's money."

Then I told her about the loan that I had made to Cecil. She said, "I know you want to help, but remember, you've got a long ol' ways ahead with your Daddy, so don't put yourself in a bind."

"Sissy, thank you so much. I feel much better about the situation. Now, maybe, I can get some good sleep tonight. After that, we discussed other family matters, especially Kim's coming graduation and the plans we were making for the "Open House." Needless to say, my heart was much lighter after we hung up.

I did just what Sissy had suggested. The next day, I pulled enough out of Daddy's account to make all the creditors happy. After mailing those bills, I felt relief for the first time since I had found the drawer full of all those unpaid bills. I was able to save my credit cards.

WHILE I WAS HAVING BREAKFAST WITH DADDY, THE next morning, an aid came at 7:00 a.m. This aid was paid by one of the funds Kathy had arranged. It was so nice not to have to get up early to give Daddy his medication and for changing him. The extra help I had been using had been costing me $5 per hour. We all agreed to pitch in and handle that time, as much as possible, ourselves, in order to save some money. .

I said, "Daddy, I don't know if you can understand but I want to tell you about our finances." I explained about the money I had sent to Cecil and also told him about the money I had used to help catch-up the credit cards. In simple terms, I tried to let Daddy know just where his money, as well as mine, was going. He looked at me as though he understood everything I was saying, but I was pretty sure that he didn't understand what I had been telling him.

I would have given anything in the entire WORLD if I could just have my old Daddy back. He would, then, have been able to help me figure things out. Instead, I had a new Daddy who kept pouring his buttermilk onto his plate while I was talking to him. I said, "Daddy, you're ruining this nice breakfast I've made for you."

He just shook his head and said, "What the hell am I doing?"

I continued with our financial meeting, even though I knew Daddy probably didn't understand what I was explaining. Just telling it to him, though, made me feel better that I was giving him the benefit of the doubt. I said, "Daddy, I've tried to keep your money separate from mine in case Yane would try and make trouble over it.

He looked at me with fire in his eyes and said, "She better not!"

I smiled at him because he did seem to grasp that point, about Yane. I continued to explain my feelings, "Even though I have power of attorney, it is important to me that both Yane and Cecil don't think I've misused your money. I talked to Sissy last night and she said you would want me to tap into your savings to help pay some of the expenses I incurred, while staying with you while you were at the hospitals. I hope this is okay with you, Daddy."

There was no hesitation, "You betcha, do whatyagotta do," he told me.

I said, "Well, Daddy, from now on I am going to throw our money together in one big pot and pray we have enough to go around. Like you've always said, to me, 'There ain't nothing me and you and the God Lord above can't do together."

He grinned and said, "Yep, that's what I always said."

I felt better after our little meeting. Daddy continued to eat his breakfast and kept the buttermilk in his glass. When Kim, Pam, and Cheryl came up from their downstairs bedroom to have their breakfast with Grandpa, I gave him a kiss on his forehead and headed back up to my office in the loft.

I had just sat down at my desk when the phone rang. Answering it, I was relieved, that it was Stout University. The lady calling, said, "I know it's been awhile since you called in for a home attendant, but I have been unable to find any one suitable, until now. I might have someone you would be interested in. He is a former football coach and social studies teacher."

In an excited voice, I said, "When would he be able to come for an interview?"

She answered, "Well, he is sitting right here in my office." We have made a thorough check on his character and he has a flawless reputation. He has never done this type of work, but he is willing to learn."

Immediately, I responded eagerly and said, "Please ask him if he could come for an interview today!"

"Just a minute, please." A couple of seconds later she said, "Yes, and he's on his way. He really needs the job and I think he would do a good job for you."

"Thank you so very much for remembering us," I gratefully told her.

I looked up, and out loud, said, "Please, God, let him be the one!"

I continued to just sit at my desk, musing over the possibility of having a male attendant to help us with Daddy. Downstairs, Betty had arrived, as she was on duty this morning. I could hear her getting Daddy cleaned up from breakfast. They had already started buying and selling cows as she got him prepared for his bath. She was so great with him and knew just how to keep his interest.

Kim and Cheryl were getting ready for school and Brad was over visiting with Pam. They had not been able to spend much time together since Daddy's stroke because Pam had been so busy running the studios for me. Brad was truly understanding, one in a million!

Going downstairs, I called everyone together and said, "Stout University just called. They may have found someone to help us with Grandpa. In fact, he is coming for an interview in just a little while. He sounds like he may be the answer to our prayers." We were all very excited and expectant.

While we had our family council, Betty had got Daddy into the bathroom for his tub bath. I had purchased a bath bench, snack tray, plus the potty chair out of my money. Medicare wouldn't pay for these supplies, in addition to quite a few other things I felt he needed.

It wasn't long before an old, blue Dodge Dart, with dents and rust all over, pulled into the driveway. Taking a closer look, I also noticed the front bumper and grill were missing. My heart went out to him and I thought, Dear God, this poor man needs us as much as we need him.

When he stepped out of the car I saw that he was a tall man. He did look like a football coach and as if he could handle Daddy, with the proper training. Wearing glasses and balding, in front, slightly, I noticed that he combed his hair across his head to try and hide the bald spot. The wind was blowing pretty strong, this morning and it blew his hair back over to the side. He kept trying to keep his hair, in place, over the bald spot. I couldn't help but chuckle. I liked him already!

He knocked on the door. I introduced myself and invited him into the living room. His name was Fred and he appeared more nervous than I. Sitting down, I offered him some coffee, which he readily accepted. A few seconds were spent sipping our coffee and observing each other. I found that I liked him, immediately, and I sensed the feeling was mutual. He spoke first, saying, "You look exhausted."

"I'm sure I do, but if you think I look bad from the outside, you should see what I look like in here," I said pointing to myself. We both laughed and this helped make us more at ease.

He told me about himself, saying, "I have recently gone through a divorce. My ex-wife caused so much trouble for me at the school where I was teaching, they replaced me."

"Well, I can understand about divorce. I've been through that myself," I shared.

He continued, "I've got three children and I am behind on my child support payments, right now. If I don't get caught up, I won't be able to see my children."

It was obvious his children were extremely important to him. It didn't take long for me to feel comfortable with Fred and to realize that I wouldn't worry about him sharing my home with my daughters. I could tell that he was a kind man, had a big heart and a very caring spirit. I said, "Fred, I want you to meet Daddy. If the two of you decide to give it a shot, then you certainly have my approval."

Excusing myself, I went to see how much longer Betty would be with Daddy's bath. I found that he was already bathed, shaved and smelled like a million dollars. All that therapy, had started to pay off. He could, now, shave himself, and comb his hair, but was still trying to master brushing his teeth.

Betty wheeled Daddy into the living room. Fred stood up and said, "Hi, Vernon, I'm Fred Gulseth. I hope I'm going to be working with you."

Daddy looked up at him with a surprised look on his face, extended his hand and said, "Well, you're one big sonofabitch."

We all laughed at Daddy's observation. I said, "Daddy, if it's okay with you, Fred is going to be staying here for a while to keep you company while I'm at work and the girls are gone. Is that okay with you?"

"Hell yeah, he's my ol' podner!" I was so glad Daddy seemed to take to him, right away. In the past, he had taken a quick dislike to many of the men that worked with him, especially, if they had a beard or mustache, Thank God, Fred was clean shaven.

Betty then took Daddy into the dining room for his medication and snack so I could continue talking with Fred. "Fred, our money is a little low. I can only pay you $500 per month plus room and board until the social worker can work out something more," I explained to him apologetically.

He said, "That's fine, I am so grateful. When can I start?"

Thinking quickly, I asked him, "What are you doing for the rest of the day?"

"Nothing, and I've got my clothes in the car."

"Well, go get them and I'll show you to your room," I replied.

He went to his car and was back in a flash with a suitcase and a few suits.

I took him downstairs to Daddy's room. Jess had put a wall in the large guest room, to divide it into two rooms. Daddy's hospital bed was on one side and the water bed I had bought for him during his last visit was on the other. I showed Fred where the downstairs bath was located, the laundry room and the recreational room which I had turned into Daddy's therapy room. Fred seemed really happy with his small room and I was so thankful for Jess being there to get things completed.

Next, I showed Fred the newly completed shaft Jess had built which made it possible to transport Daddy from down stairs to upstairs. It consisted of an addition built on to the house, with a winch installed at the top. It was the same kind of winch that was used for lifting heavy motors.

Jess had attached a pulley to an overhead hook. When turned on, the pulley would pull the "floor" up with Daddy's wheelchair on it.

This was not anywhere near the elaborate type of elevator my sister thought I was going to squander Daddy's money on, but it served the purpose. It had also been approved by the inspector from Stout University who was in charge of home care safety. It had cost approximately $800. I had paid for it with the extra money I had earned from teaching my Country Western Dance classes.

While Fred was getting settled in, I called Kathy, Daddy's social worker, to tell her my good news. She said, "That's great! I will let you keep the three aids until Fred has been trained. Then you will only need one for a backup and for Fred's days off."

I said, "Kathy, anyway you can help us financially, it will be greatly appreciated."

By this time, I needed to get ready to leave for the studio. I was glad all the girls and Brad had met and liked Fred. My prayer had been answered. I felt really good about Fred.

Betty took charge of Fred as soon as he had moved his things into his room and had come upstairs. "Well, I guess there's no time like the present to get to know your new podner." She then began to show Fred the ropes, immediately.

PAM AND I THEN LEFT FOR THE STUDIO. I TAUGHT the classes better that day than I had in a long time. Now, I felt such relief and hoped that I could get Daddy on the ridged schedule I had planned for him when we left Sister Kenny. With so many different attendants helping with Daddy's care, it was impossible to get him on a regular schedule.

When Pam and I got home late that night from Rice Lake, Daddy was in bed, Betty had gone home and Fred was sitting in a chair reading over the procedures given to me upon leaving Sister Kenny. He looked right at home and made me, once again, feel that he was sent by the Good Lord

Kim and Cheryl came running upstairs to greet our arrival home. They promptly gave me their full-hearted approval of Fred too. It seems that he had been helping them with their homework. Smiling to myself, I thought, This is going to work out better than I had hoped.

Before going to my bedroom, I went down to give Daddy a kiss on the forehead and see, for myself, that he was okay. He was sleeping like a baby.

Then I went to bed and slept soundly all night. I was surprised, the next morning, when I woke up to see how late it was. The kids had turned my alarm clock off per instructions from Fred.

I jumped out of bed, threw on my housecoat and came running into the living room. Fred had Daddy at the table working on some of the therapy that was described in the procedure manual. Looking up he smiled, "Do you feel better?"

Yes, I feel like a million bucks! Where's Betty?" I asked as my eyes scanned the room.

"She will be here about 11:00. She had some business to attend to this morning. Kim an Cheryl are at school and Pam is still asleep. Steve and Jess are out working on the garage."

You can't imagine my thoughts of joy. I knew right, then, that Fred was going to work out just great. I truly believed that God had looked down and smiled at me.

The next few days were really busy, for everyone, especially for Fred. When Betty would leave, Joyce came on duty and the following shift was Mary. All the woman jumped right in and helped training Fred. Daddy was beginning to really feel popular.

I TOOK THIS OPPORTUNITY TO TAKE CARE OF A LOT of unfinished business. Arrangements needed to made for auditoriums for the two up-coming recitals. I had costumes to give out to the students and I just prayed they would fit and that all the pieces were there. Then there were the pending preparations yet to do for Kim's graduation.

Kim had fallen a little behind on her assignments in school, due to the turmoil the family had been through. She had quite a few projects which had to be completed before she could be graduated. Our team went into action. I took the typewriter, Pam the book reports, Cheryl drew maps and Kim tried to complete her accounting project.

Cheryl was behind, herself. Her counselor had told her that she needed a few more credits before she could graduate. She had said, "Well, at least we can get Kim down the aisle." Cheryl did, however, get her GED (general education development) diploma a little later.

DURING THIS TIME, I HAD ANOTHER APPOINTMENT for Daddy at Sister Kenny with Dr. Speier. I usually took him down every two weeks. This time Fred went with me. He was really learning the procedures fast and was with Daddy every waking hour. He intently listened to and observed everything the therapist said and did so that he could continue the same kind of help at home.

Dr. Speier said, "Vernon is coming along so well that I will schedule him for his re-evaluations at the end of the month."

In my excitement I turned to Fred and said, "I've been waiting for this news ever since Daddy was dismissed. Now, we really have our work cut out for us."

I asked Dr. Speier for a copy of the type of schedule she would put Daddy on if he passed the evaluation tests. She gave me the schedule. It showed everything he would be doing from the time he would open his eyes, in the morning until he would close them at night.

Daddy always got really scared each time I would take him to Sister Kenny. I think he thought I was admitting him again. His blood pressure would shoot up and he would become extremely quite. I would always reassure him he would be going home after he saw the doctor.

On this visit, Dr. Speier said that she could not believe how Daddy was progressing. She said, "I can sure see you have been working hard with him."

I said, "Dr. Speier, we have been working hard, but most of the credit belongs to Fred. He has really been attentive."

She smiled at Fred and said, "Keep up the good work, it's paying off." Fred grew about four more inches high, I believe.

We took Daddy out to dinner after his appointment. I had been trying to socialize him. When he was out, he was usually on his best behavior. He would eat really nice, say thank you to the waitress, etc.

However, there were times he would really embarrass me. A really big woman had just come into the restaurant Fred and I looked at each other because we knew Daddy was about to say something. I said, "Daddy, don't say a word!"

He started laughing and said in a loud voice, "You thought I was gonna say something about that big fat woman, didn't you?" Well, there was nothing we could do now. She was very nice and gracious about the whole incident.

DADDY WAS SUPPOSED TO EAT ONLY BLENDED foods, but he had been on table food since about the second week at home. Since the day I had made a big hamburger hot dish. Every one was eating and poor little Daddy was eating his blended dinner. He spoke up saying, "Reta, I want some of that."

Karen had been there. I looked at her, burst out laughing and said, "Hell, I haven't gone by the rules yet, why should I start now."

I got Daddy a plate of hot dish and said to him, "Daddy, you're not supposed to be eating this kind of food so be sure and chew it real good. If you start choking, YOU'LL have to go back to the other food."

Grabbing the spoon he started eating very slowly. He did so well and from that day on, I let him have what he wanted to eat and he never had a problem.

Daddy continued to baffle the medical profession. He was turning his head totally to the right, now, and he could talk on the telephone really well. I was thrilled as I watched him beginning to bounce back.

WHEN FRED, DADDY AND I GOT HOME FROM Minneapolis, Daddy was really pooped out. He enjoyed his day out, but he was ready for his bed when we returned.

After Daddy was settled for the night, Fred and I sat down at the kitchen table for a cup of coffee. I said, "Fred, starting tomorrow morning, I want to begin Daddy on the Sister Kinney schedule. If he should get accepted, he will need to build stamina." Fred agreed 100 per cent. Right then I made out a schedule for Fred because I found that he worked best with an agenda to follow.

First thing, the next morning, he put Daddy on the schedule. Fred drilled him on everything.

One of the things I did was put a rod up in Daddy's room and hung all his clothes on it. Each morning Daddy was to select the color of shirt, pants, etc. that he wanted to wear that day. This was to improve his color awareness.

THE CUMBERLAND RECITAL WAS FINALLY OVER! THE students had done a beautiful job and I was so pleased for them as well as Pam and myself. Now we only had the one left in Rice Lake. I had scheduled the recitals for the end of April so that they would be finished and behind me before Kim's graduation. This was a special time for her and I wanted her to have her mother's full attention.

Even though Pam and Kim had not complained, I knew they needed more of my time than they had received since Daddy's stroke. It was so hard trying to make the time needed for everyone. Steve was never home. I was going to wait until after the recitals and graduation were over and then I was going to find out where he had been spending his time. I had a feeling, inside, that he was cheating on me but, there just hadn't been time for me to investigate. Also, I knew that I just didn't have the emotional energy, at this time, to deal with him. So I just ignored it all, for now, and let the little weasel run.

DADDY WAS DOING SO WELL AT THIS TIME THAT I thought maybe he would like an outing. I asked Fred his opinion, "Do you think Daddy would be okay if we took him to my Rice Lake recital?

"I think so and besides I would love to see it also," he readily replied.

Daddy, of course, was all for it and was sitting on "Go." He really enjoyed getting out and I had been taking Daddy to the clubs for the past few weeks. Country Music was his favorite and couldn't seem to get enough of it.

SINCE DADDY'S STROKE, I HAD GIVEN UP MY SINGING because there just wasn't time for it. My band, *Pure Gold,* had continued the scheduled engagements without me. I really missed them as they were a great bunch of guys. Some had been with me for four years.

Don Cords was my lead guitar player but he also played a good fiddle and banjo. Besides being my good friend and confidant, he was the one who really held the band together. A tall man with medium brown hair and quite good looking, he was quite a hit with the ladies. They were out of luck though, because he already had his lady. He had been happily married to Debbie for four years and they had two small children. I felt that he should have already been discovered, but it's not what you know, it's who you know in the business.

Rick Larson played bass. He was small in stature, dark hair, wore glasses and had a dynamite voice! At that time, he was a brand new husband too, he and Lynn had been married for only a few months. It was his plan to go into Gospel someday. I greatly appreciated his help with learning better projection on my vocals. He would say, "Reta, it's in there, just take a deep breath and let it go."

Donnie Corski was my drummer. He and his wife, Julie, were real health nuts. She was always sending alfalfa sandwiches with Donnie and, of course, he shared them with us. I could sit and talk with him for hours, such an interesting person. Once, he told me, "I have two very memorable days I shall never forget. One is the day I married Julie, and the other is the night you, Cords and me had band practice and killed a bottle of Chablis and talked all night." I, too, have remembered that night with fond memories. We must have covered every subject possible, nothing was sacred.

All the members of my band and I had a good rapport, we were all good friends and greatly respected each other both professionally and privately.

Another added bonus, for me, was that all their wives were also my dear friends. Each, was a very special person in her own right. As wives of husbands, who are musicians, they would have to be in order for their marriages to survive.

Unfortunately, I was not in the same situation, in my marriage. Steve had a real problem being married to an entertainer, his only claim to fame. He would dance with all the groupies and pretend he was some big star. Observing his behavior, my friends would say, "Reta, what in the hell did you ever see in him?" What could I say. Marrying Steve had been such a big mistake and I just didn't know what I was going to do regarding it. I kept putting off making any kind of decision, but that decision would have to be made, later.

I HAD SO MANY GOOD FRIENDS IN MUSIC, AND SINCE Daddy's stroke they had all been calling and letting me know that their prayers and thoughts were with me. Most of them, as well as Pure Gold, had known my dad before his stroke. It was common knowledge with all of them that Daddy's all time favorite song was *Waltz Across Texas*.

One Sunday afternoon, right after Daddy had been released from Sister Kenny, I took him to see two of my very best friends, Rex and Rex of the famed *Rex Cactus Show*.

Their real names were Gregg and Clarion Lane and were, in fact, first cousins. Their dad's had taught them to play music at a very young age. Gregg had been my bass player, in Pure Gold a few years back and we had been friends for almost twelve years. He and Clarion were very special people in my life.

It seemed only natural that when Daddy and I arrived, they started singing Waltz Across Texas for him. Daddy sat up extra straight in his wheel chair, held his head erect and did that Stetson hat proud as he grinned from ear to ear!

It was always such a release and a joy for me to get on the band stand and sing some country songs. That day, Gregg asked me to come up and I was more than ready. I asked his band, "Do you guys remember Loretta Lynn's song, *They Don't Make 'Em Like My Daddy Anymore?*"

They put their heads together and came up with a collective, "Yeah."

Clarion said, "Let's try the key of *G.*" He kicked it off and I started singing.

Daddy was sitting at the table with Pam, Kim, Brad and Cheryl and when I began singing, to him, he started crying. Pam put her arm around him and asked, "What's wrong Grandpa."

Tearfully, he told her, "That's my little girl singing up there."

When I saw what was happening, I lost it. I realized right then that his mind had come back even more than we had thought. I turned around to compose myself during the lead ride. Gregg turned around with me and with tears in his eyes, too, said, "Reta, you're a professional and you are going to turn around and finish that song for your Daddy, even if it kills us both."

He was right. I composed myself, turned around and said, "This is for my Daddy." I then sang that song better than I had ever sung it before, or since. There wasn't a dry eye in the house or on the bandstand when I was done. It was such a joy to know that he was able to understand the love I had for him.

I had hoped to be able to go back with my band that coming summer. It didn't pay that much money, but it was something I truly enjoyed. Everyone in the band had a day job, so we played for our own enjoyment. However, this summer the money was going to be counted on because it was much needed.

THE RICE LAKE RECITAL WAS SCHEDULED FOR A Sunday afternoon. The weather didn't look good and it was really hot for that time of year, but I thought we could sneak everything in. Fred got Daddy all dressed up in one of his suits. Boy did he look spiffy.

We all headed for Rice Lake. Pam and Kim had their parts down really well, but Pam was feeling more anxious for her students than for herself.

We arrived at the Rice Lake High School Auditorium, early, to get everything setup. The dress rehearsal went great, so I knew we would be okay.

Arriving in Rice Lake, the weather was a lot worse than it had been in Amery, and I remember thinking, "Guess you can't win 'em all." If I had known, I would have left Daddy home. The weather had kept a few people away, including some of my students. It was very hot and muggy and we were all a little worried about a tornado.

When I had first walked into the auditorium, there stood Louise Lacasse, my self adopted mom. I was so glad and pleased she was there. She had been my baton twirling instructor for years and it was from her that I learned how to be a good teacher. She had always come to my recitals and even though she never participated, just her presence always calmed me down. I really needed her this year.

She had been surprised to see Daddy with me as she hadn't seen him since Sister Kinney. His progress was really noticeable and she was quite impressed with the progress he had made. They had been friends for many years and she was delighted that he seemed to recognize her when he asked, "Hello, don't I know you?"

Daddy was in his element and was so gracious to everyone. Some of the parents came over and shook his hand and, of course, all the students stopped to say, "Hi, Grandpa." They all loved Daddy and he had become everyone's Grandpa. After all the greetings were finished, Fred took Daddy inside and sat down then they waited for the curtain to open.

I was so happy to have my Daddy there. In all the years I had taught, none of my family had ever seen any of my recitals. So, I guess I sort of felt like Daddy's little girl that afternoon.

I had arranged for Steve to run the spot light so he would not be backstage to upset any one, especially me.

It was almost time to begin. Back stage, we all took our positions. Louise was assuring me everything would be okay as she usually did. This year, however, I also was in that same situation. Pam was a nervous wreck and I kept assuring her that everything would be okay. Kim was busy in the dressing rooms getting the students calmed down and ready for their performance. The children all loved Kim and Pam and many had told me that they wanted to grow up to be just like them.

First, the national anthem was played, then the show was officially in progress. The little girls were all ready in their pretty little costumes to perform their routines. Everyone was doing a really good job and I was so proud of them all. I always say, It's not quantity it's quality. At last, it was time for the Grand Finale. After the students finished, and were off stage, it was now my turn to give a little speech and to hand out certificates and special awards, as I always did.

The curtain opened and I stepped up to the mike. Immediately, my eyes went to where Daddy was sitting and I saw that his head was resting on Fred's shoulder and he looked half dead. Panicking, I said over the microphone, "Fred, is he okay?" Fred nodded his head yes, but I could tell Daddy needed to be home. The air conditioning was not working properly and it was rather hot and humid inside.

Thank God for Louise. She could tell I was very concerned about my Daddy so she, Pam and Kim assisted with the awards. I thought we would never be finished!

As soon as the last award was given, I hurried to my Daddy. I felt so selfish for having brought him there. Obviously he really had not enjoyed the program nor did he actually know what was going on. I said, "Daddy, I'm so sorry. We will get you home as soon as possible."

He then began to wheeze and choke on his phlegm. Trying not to panic, I said, "Fred, we've got to get the phlegm out of his throat before he chokes to death on it!"

Fred said, "Before my dad died, we had a suction pump we used to get the phlegm out of his throat. Maybe we can get one."

"I will call Dr. Rimestad as soon as we get home. Let's get out of here, right now," I insisted in as calm a manner as I could. I didn't want Daddy to be worried or alarmed.

When we headed back to Amery, the wind was blowing, the clouds were dark and ominous looking. Originally, right after the recital, I had planned to take everyone out to the *Country Dam* for dinner. First, I had to get Daddy home and locate some kind of a suction machine. Fred said, "Don't worry about Vernon and me. I'll fix us something for dinner." Fred was one in a million!.

I couldn't believe my eyes when we finally pulled into the driveway. The wind was whipping like crazy, a big tree limb was laying on top of my Lincoln, and the pump house Steve had just finished building was blown all over the yard. Everything was just a mess. I was just thankful that the house was still there and seemed all right.

I think I was in a state of shock but we got Daddy inside and into the basement. Then, I called Dr. Rimestad, explained the situation, and he prescribed the suction machine needed for Daddy. Someone had to run to St. Croix Falls to pick it up. I asked, "Steve, will you please go get it? I don't want to leave Daddy."

Instead of immediately saying, Sure thing! He was thinking only of himself and started whining and said, "Well, when are we going to eat?"

Hardly able to control my furry with this man, I answered, "When I know for sure my Dad is not going to choke to death! What do you think?"

Before Steve could respond, Brad looked at him with total disgust and said, "Reta, Pam and I will go get it." They left immediately. Steve went to the kitchen and made himself a sandwich to hold himself over. Too bad he didn't choke on it.

Fred got Daddy into bed and we were all trying to get him to cough but he just couldn't cough hard enough to get the phlegm out. Louise, Kim, and Cheryl were trying to help with Grandpa, too. Everyone was concerned.

I said, "Why did I take him? I should have known better!"

Fred told me, "Quit beating up on yourself, I thought he would be okay, too, remember?"

Worried, scared, full of regret, drained from the recital, and thinking of the damage that I had found upon arriving home, I did what most women do when stressed to the max, I started to cry.

Kim put her arms around me and said, "Mom, Grandpa will be okay."

We had to wait only a little while before Brad and Pam came running down stairs with the suction pump. I thought, *Thank God Fred knows how to use it.*

He tried to put it in Daddy's mouth, but Daddy kept fighting him. I said, "Daddy, I'm going to give you this tube and you put it as far down in your throat as possible to get that junk out."

With a gargle, he said, "I'll try." We couldn't believe it. He took that tube, stuck it down his throat and started pulling phlegm out like a real pro. Everyone started cheering him on and finally, he got it all out. Before long, he was breathing real good.

Fred made him some soup and after he had eaten it all, got him tucked into bed. I was so thankful he was okay and Fred turned to me and said, "Now, why don't you and the kids go have your dinner. Vernon and I will be just fine."

Giving Fred a hug, I told him, "What would Daddy and I do without you?"

I called the Country Dam to ask if they would keep our reservations. They told me that their electricity was out and they would be unable to serve us. What else can go wrong, today, I thought to myself. Next, I called the Paradise Supper Club in Balsam Lake. They had power and were serving dinner, so I made reservations for my group. Feeling Daddy was in capable hands, we went over to Balsam Lake. Everyone was starved to death, especially Steve.

When shown to our table, Steve sat himself at the head of the table. It was obvious, that in his mind, he believed the day would not have been possible without his expert help and advice. He was truly his biggest, and only fan.

We all looked at the menu and began giving our orders. I had told everyone to order whatever they wanted. This had always been my custom; to treat my little crew to anything they wanted to eat for dinner after the recitals had ended. A little token of my appreciation for their help and support throughout the year. This dinner would really be an extra special appreciation treat from me, as well as Grandpa, for all the extra love we had received.

Of course, since he wasn't paying, Steve had to order the biggest steak on the menu. I ordered a steak and so did Louise. Kim asked me, "Mom, can I have a steak, too?"

Before I could answer, Wonder Boy said, "No, you can have a hamburger."

That did it. I said, "She can have whatever she wants."

"What's it to you, Steve, my Mom's paying for it?" Kim said, responding with a whole lot of suppressed anger and sarcasm.

This remark really pissed him off, and he then started a big fight with Kim. Naturally, Pam and I went to Kim's defense, and immediately. As if the day hadn't been stressful, enough, this guy had to start some trouble.

Kim started to cry and ran to the bathroom and Pam went in after her. I told him, "Steve, you just eat and shut your damn mouth for the rest of the day!"

Then I got up and went to Kim. She said, "Mom, I hate him so much. He doesn't do anything but spend the money we all work for. I'm sorry, but I'm going home. He's ruined everything!"

I understood how she felt, and didn't blame her one little bit. Kim took Pam's car and went home, while Pam and I went back to the table. If looks could have killed, Steve would have been dead. I knew his day in the sun was soon going to be over. We finished dinner with no one saying much of anything. He had ruined the evening for all of us. God, how I hated him, too!

THE NEXT DAY, WE ALL WORKED TOGETHER TO get the mess in the yard cleaned up as a result of the storm. My insurance company said that they would cover my car and the pump house. It could have been worse.

Things were going smoothly so far in the a.m., and Steve even apologized for ruining the rest of my day. Daddy was feeling better, and Fred was working hard with him on his therapy program because he knew how badly I wanted Daddy to qualify for rehabilitation. As it stood then, we only had a few weeks left before his appointment.

Steve came to me and said, "We have the garage finished, so Jess is planning on going back to St. Paul. I can take care of everything." There was more to it than that: I knew Jess was tired of trying to work with Steve. Also, I really could not afford to keep Jess on through the summer.

Steve continued by saying, "I am now ready to open my body shop out, and I can make enough money to support you and take care of all the bills this summer. You need some time off."

He seemed sincere and I did need some time off. But never trust what your eyes see, or think they see, and only believe half of what you hear. The fact: Steve was aware that I had money from the recitals, and the last month payments. Then he ruined it all by saying, "If you could just give me the money to buy a compressor, I can pay you back as soon as I get rolling." There it was, plain as day, I told myself.

I said, "Steve, if you could just contribute to this household, I wouldn't care if you didn't pay me back. But I can't give this to you and jeopardize this family unless I know your business will bring in the revenue you say."

He faithfully promised he would have the best body shop in town and, like a fool, I went for it. I gave him a check, and he went out and bought the compressor.

He kept coming back needing more and more money and finally I asked him point blank, "When are you going to start contributing instead of taking."

"Soon— We have one car just about ready," he told me anxiously.

He had hired Cheryl to help him, and he was paying her a lousy one dollar bill per hour, working her like a dog.

Fred was even promised that Steve would fix his poor old Dodge Dart if he would just help Steve on his weekend off.

Everyone was trying to help him succeed. I even pitched in and helped him with some sanding but before long he wanted me working every day, too. "Wait a minute, this is my vacation," I said, and went back into the house. The garage situation I wanted to be successful, but I was not going to do his job for him.

A few days later, Cheryl came running into the house. She was really upset because Steve had tried to put the make on her. Of course, when I confronted him with the goods, he denied it.

But the fact is, Cheryl did not go back "to work" in the garage, and from that day on, he worked alone. He had just pounded one more nail into his coffin.

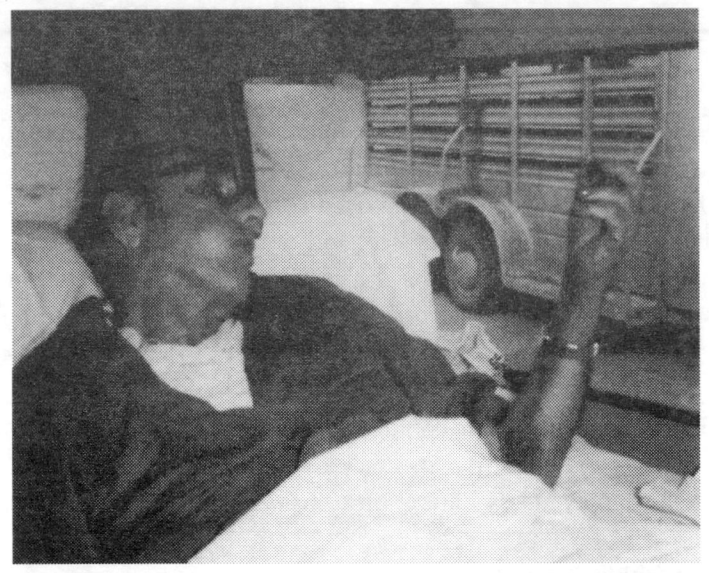

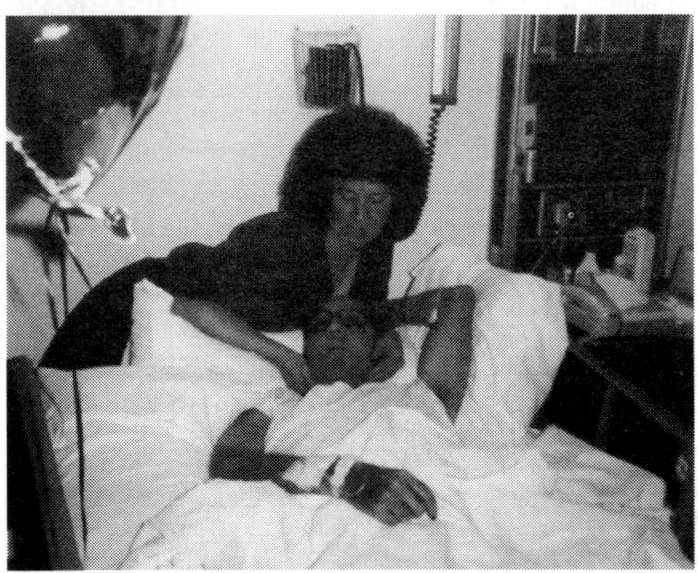

TOP: **VERNON** LEAVING ABILENE, TEXAS IN THE VAN. HE IS SMOKING A STRAW THINKING IT WAS A CIGARETTE. HE THOUGHT THE CATTLE TRAILER OUTSIDE THE WINDOW BELONGED TO HIM. HE WOULD NOT ACCEPT ANY PART OF HIS RIGHT SIDE. THIS IS HOW SICK HIS MIND AND BODY WAS WHEN WE LEFT ABILENE, TEXAS

BELOW: **VERNON & RETA** ARRIVES AT ABBOTT NORTHWESTERN HOSPITAL, MINNEAPOLIS, MINNESOTA. RETA IS COACHING HER DADDY TO ACCEPT HIS RIGHT SIDE

4

NEVER TAKE YOUR HEALTH FOR GRANTED. JUST AS important, when your vital signs tap you on the shoulder with little hints that you had better slow up and change what's bothering you, then, by all means, you had better listen or pay the piper.

There wasn't any doubt about it— I had not felt good for a number of weeks. At one point, I thought I was having a heart attack, but it was only a bad case of angina. It fooled me. My stomach would knot up and I would be in quite a bit of pain.

One Sunday morning the pain in my stomach was more severe than times before. Now, I've always had these problems, in one form or another. While growing up, doctors would tell me I had a nervous stomach and spastic bowels. Well, okay, I figured that was the problem. But later in the day, the pain continued to increase. Not sure of what to do, I solved it by doing what any normal person would do—I went to bed.

Before retiring that night, I had told Steve how I felt, but of course he just blew it off as more whining from the little lady. But in the back of his mind, I am sure he was always afraid that one day I might get really sick and he would have to take over the responsibilities of the home. Poor Steve.

When I finally turned the sheets down for the night (my side of the bed only), he was wearing little green workout shorts, no shirt, and kept admiring himself in the mirror. Without acknowledging my pain or the fact that I was tired, he said, "Cheryl and Kim are working out, so I'm going to show them some exercises for firming up." This trite incident shows clearly how much he was like a small child. And of course, my pain meant nothing to him—my comfort and well-being was totally a secondary issue.

After drowning my sorrows under the pillow for a few hours, I finally made it downstairs where Fred was working with Daddy on his therapy, and I let them know where I was in the event they needed me. I must say, Daddy was really doing well. I was so pleased with Fred and grateful beyond words.

Fred said, "Reta, you go back up stairs and lay down. Don't worry about Vernon." He patted Daddy on the back and then added, "We'll be okay, won't we, Vernon?"

Daddy looked up at me, shook his head and said, "Baby, you look so old and haggard!"

"Well, thank you, Daddy, I really needed that," I said laughing, then went back upstairs to go to bed.

As I walked to the stairs, I saw Steve was busy in the living room showing off for the girls. Kim saw me and asked a little worriedly, "Mom, are you okay?"

"Yeah, I'm going to lay down for a while and see if the pain in my stomach will go away," I said.

"If you need something, let me know," she offered, then looked at Steve with disgust. He chose to ignore us and continued demonstrating his moves to Cheryl.

As I lay in bed, the pain kept getting more intense. Finally, when Pam and Brad came home, Pam came in, took one look at me and announced in a voice that left no room for argument, "You're going to the hospital!"

I started crying and said, "I can't, I have too much to do!" Ignoring me, Pam picked up the telephone and called Karen. "Can you come out here and help me convince mother to go to the hospital?"

Twenty minutes later, Karen walked into my bedroom carrying a twelve pack of beer. She laughed and said, "I brought you some medicine! God, you look awful."

"Thanks. Daddy has already filled me in on how old and haggard I look," I retorted. At the sight of Karen, my tears turned to a smile. She just shook her head and laughed, "you can always count on Vernon to tell it like it is."

Karen is someone I consider to be a really true friend. I don't know what I would have done without her, and she was always there for me. She opened a beer, handed it to me and then asked with a laugh, "What in hell's *Boy Wonder* doing out there?"

Pam said with a derisive laugh, "Oh, he's demonstrating his wonderful knowledge of the body to Cheryl."

Karen had never liked Steve, and only barely tolerated being around him. With a motion that belied her anger, Karen snatched off two beer pull-tabs—one for herself and Pam. After a long swallow, she took another look into the living room then looked at me and asked, "Why don't you get rid of that little f-----? He's a worthless piece of s---, absolutely good for nothing!" She took another long pull, sip of beer.

We'd had this conversation a hundred times, but I wasn't up to arguing. "Karen, I can't drink this beer," I said weakly.

"Now, I know your sick!" she said with due concern, and got up and took a long look at me. Apparently she saw something that worried her, and then she said in a stern voice, "Okay, we're going to the hospital. And don't argue with me!"

With this decision made, Pam went into the living room and called Kim, Cheryl and Steve into the bedroom. "We're taking Mom to the hospital," she said slowly, expecting an argument, but none came.

All eyes watched Karen and Pam as they helped me get dressed. No one offered to help. I saw by the look in Kim's eyes that she was scared to death. She always had a terrible fear that Pam or I might die and leave her alone. In fact, she would often say, "Mom, if you or Pam die, I hope I die with you!"

Once I was dressed, Kim started crying and bawled, "Mom, are you going to be okay?"

I knew I had to be strong and gave her a hug and a wink then said, "You betcha!"

Then I looked at pathetic Steve, who stood there in his little green shorts. Then in his whinny, little voice, he said, "Are you sure you need to go to the hospital?"

I thought Pam was going through the roof and she almost attacked him. "Can't you see my mom is in pain? If you cared at all about her, you would have been in here trying to help her instead of trying to be some kind of exercise king and worrying about your own little self!"

Steve just looked sheepish and turned and stood there. For once, words failed him.

I was ready to go, bent over in pain and could hardly walk. Pam and Karen practically pushed Steve out of the way and helped me toward the door. As I walked by Steve asked lamely, "What can I do?" Karen yelled in his face, "Just stay the hell out of our way!"

Once outside of the door, I said, "Kim, you stay here with grandpa. Tell Fred what is going on, but don't let Daddy hear you. I don't want Daddy to know I'm sick. You know how it affects him."

DR. RIMESTAD WAS ON DUTY. HE CHECKED ME OVER and admitted the sickly one immediately. He said, "You are totally exhausted, Reta. I am keeping you in the hospital for at least three days on total rest." I didn't argue with him, for the pain was too much. Also, I knew it wouldn't do any good. Between Pam, Karen and the doctor, I knew I hadn't a prayer in winning any argument.

For the next three days all I had to eat was the intravenous feeding and some Jello now and then. The doctor made sure I got enough rest, and at the end of three days, I felt like a new person. The pain had gone away, and Dr. Rimestad dismissed me, but cautioned about taking better care of myself. He held my arm and said in a fatherly voice, "Reta, you have ulcers. That's what you're suffering from. I want to start you on some medication, a strict diet and please try to get more rest." I nodded my assent.

Steve had come to take me home, which he did. Apparently, he couldn't stand suffering the wrath of Pam anymore. When he picked me up, he pretended to be the caring, concerned husband. It made me sick. Actually, I'm sure he was happy to have me back home to take over all the responsibilities again, leaving him free to do nothing worthwhile.

KIM'S GRADUATION WAS COMING UP, AND NOW THAT the recitals were behind me, I could give her open house my full attention. Fred was doing such a good job with Daddy that I didn't have to worry so much about him. Daddy was getting stronger every day, and I felt good about it.

A few days later I came in as Fred was transferring Daddy to his brown recliner chair which I had brought from Texas. Daddy was complaining about it being hot, and I knew Daddy never liked that chair anyway. He always griped, "It's hot in the summer and cold in the winter."

I decided right then that Daddy was going to get a new chair. I would take some money out of our savings account and get one for him that day. I gave him a hug and said with a big smile, "Daddy, I'm going shopping for you, a big surprise."

I knew he loved surprises, and I had bought him some new shirts and pants when we got home during the winter. His clothes were not warm enough for Wisconsin, and he loved red, so I got him a red flannel western shirt, and a blue and yellow one. He was like a little kid when I got home. I had wrapped them all up, and he lit up like a candle when I gave them to him. I loved to bring him home something new, to see the joy on his face.

If I squandered any of Daddy's money, it would be so he could be happier and more comfortable.

I got into the car and drove to Amery to the Anderson-Mclaughlin furniture store. I must have sat in every Lazy Boy recliner they had. I felt like Goldilocks. Finally, I found the right chair. It was beige and so comfortable. "I want this one. How much is it?" I asked a salesman.

"On sale for $795 plus tax," he answered quickly.

"That doesn't sound like a sale to me, but I know my Daddy would love it," I commented.

"Should we scotchgaurd it?" the salesman asked, no doubt smelling a sale.

"No, not until you deliver it and my Daddy approves it," I said. "I am buying this out of his money and, therefore, I want his vote." For some reason, I felt I had to explain.

The salesman agreed to take the chance on him liking the chair, and went ahead and loaded it up. I knew he would like it, but just wanted to be sure. The money was coming out of our pot.

The delivery truck followed me home with Daddy's new chair. Suddenly, a dark cloud came over me because I knew Yane would probably think I was squandering Daddy's money on this luxury. Then the sun came back out, and I thought to myself, Quite frankly, honey, I don't give a damn! I smiled to myself as I thought of all the comfort this new chair would give Daddy. He would be spending a lot of time sitting and I didn't want him to have to sit in a wheel chair all day or a hot chair.

When we arrived at home, I went inside. Daddy was still in his brown leather chair, still complaining about it being hot. Just then the delivery men brought the chair in and Daddy's looked up and a look of confusion came over his face. He blurted out, "What the hell is going on?"

"Well, Daddy, I blew some of your money today and if you like it, we will keep it," I said as a way of explanation. I transferred him from his old chair into the new one, and he broke into a grin from ear to ear and snuggled right into it.

I asked unnecessarily, "Do you want it?" Daddy looked up at me with a huge grin on his face, then answered with his famous line, "You betcha!"

"Okay, I have to put you back in the old one for about twenty minutes while they scotchguard it and it dries," I explained lightly.

"Hell, no! I ain't gonna get up!" Daddy bellowed. It took a lot of persuasion, but I finally got him to cooperate. When I saw how much time he spent in the new chair and the enjoyment it gave him, I knew I had made his days a little more tolerable.

BUT I STILL NEEDED TO CONTINUE FINALIZING plans for Kim's open house. She had gotten all her work in, with a little help from her friends, so the graduation was still on.

I checked with the cheese store at the Amery Locker and they had everything written down exactly like I wanted for her trays. I then got Daddy's new suit out, the one Yane had given him some time ago, and had it cleaned and pressed for the big occasion. I ordered flowers for everyone. Daddy would have a carnation for his lapel, and so would Fred. I was so proud Kim had completed high school, especially with all the turmoil going on in our home. She and Pam had even completed modeling school that year, driving to Minneapolis every Saturday for their classes. I was very proud of my little girls. They were now women. I shed a few tears and continued on.

I still had Kim's picture frame to complete. I had taken pictures from the day she was born all the way through her graduation picture, and was going to put these special pictures on a 4' x 4' board, frame it and put Plexiglass over it. I had pictures of her with her Daddy, her grandparents, first haircut, first steps, dance recitals, etc. I had made one for Pam last year, and they had both been so very proud of the picture collage made by their Mama with tender loving care.

The way things had been going, I began to worry that I wouldn't get Kim's collage finished, but fortunately I did.

THE BIG DAY FINALLY CAME, AND DADDY WAS feeling really good. It turned out to be Fred's weekend off, so Betty took care of Daddy. She assured me she would have Daddy looking real spiffy when we returned from the school, and also helped get the food, drinks and various other party items ready. She was such a big help. And she made sure Daddy had a good nap so he would be in a joyful spirit!

Kim, Pam and Cheryl were so excited! I felt bad for Cheryl, though. I wish she could have graduated, too. But I knew she would later.

The graduation service was beautiful, and like every good Mama, I cried when my baby walked in. She looked so pretty! I couldn't believe the years had gone so fast. It seemed like yesterday she and Pam had been playing in their sandbox. Then my thoughts raced ahead. Kim planned to join Pam and me in the studio the next year. I thought, "What a lucky woman I am!" Then a million wonderful thoughts rushed and swirled through my head of Kim and Pam's childhood. How fast time had gone and how very proud I was of my daughters.

Snapping out of my reverie, I then turned and looked at Steve and a feeling of sadness came over me. I knew what my next project was to be.

Looking across the gymnasium, I saw Chuck, Kim and Pam's Daddy. He looked just as pleased as I was, and as proud! For a moment I thought of the good times.

He had remarried some years back to a woman who had caused me much pain and torment over the years. She was unable to have children and hated woman that could, especially the one who had given her husband two such beautiful daughters. They had adopted a little girl five years ago, and I knew her biological mother, Kara, very well.

With the adoption of Elizabeth, Shirley (Chuck's wife), had turned her venom on Pam and Kim. Instead of trying to replace me with herself in my daughter's lives, she tried to replace Pam and Kim with Elizabeth in Chuck's life. She was a very pathetic woman, and I pitied her.

Even though my feelings for Shirley were less than those of admiration, Chuck was still Kim's father and, therefore, he and his family were invited to my home for Kim's open house, just as he had also been invited to Pam's open house the past year.

I thought the speeches would last forever, but finally, the services ended. We went outside to watch the class toss their hats in the air then we took off for home to get everything prepared before the guest arrived.

Betty was busy in the kitchen and Daddy was sitting in his beautiful Lazy Boy chair. He was dressed in his black suit, compete with boutonniere and all. "Daddy, you look really spiffy!" I complimented him, and he grinned back. Then he said, "You betcha!" I then complimented Betty on a job well done.

THE FIRST TO ARRIVE WAS FRED AND HIS THREE children. He was all dressed up and also wearing his boutonniere. I met his children and was very impressed. They were well-mannered—two boys and one girl. Fred went over right away and greeted Daddy. "Hi, Vernon! Boy do you look great."

Daddy then leaned forward and whispered conspiratorially, "Fred, my boots are too tight." He had just bought those boots before the stroke, and they weren't broken in yet. He always wore them for dress, though, even if they killed him. I had asked Betty to put some baby powder in them before Daddy slipped them on, and she had done so.

Fred stood up and said, "Reta, should we put his old ones on?"

"No," I said, "not until later." Then I turned to Daddy and said, "Daddy, I know you wouldn't want to be seen in those old boots with your new suit, now would you?"

"Hell, no, I'll suffer baby, suffer!" Then he laughed. Thank god he had a good nap. He was sitting up straight and holding his head high. I was so proud of him.

The guest started to arrive, then Kim, Pam and Cheryl came bouncing in. Kim took over answering the door and welcoming her guest while Pam helped with the table. I had Kim's graduation cake proudly on display on a table, a one dozen red roses in the center—one for each year.

Then Chuck, Shirley and Elizabeth arrived. I took a deep breath and said to myself, "This is for Kim." Chuck was quite pleasant, and Shirley had her camcorder, taking pictures of the activities. She was really checking over my home, as usual.

Shirley was a very material person, with very little depth. She was short in stature, had short, straight black hair and wore no make-up—just a rather plain woman and seemingly insecure and frustrated.

Shirley continued to take her pictures and flutter around the other guests, and Chuck came over to the table where Kim, Pam and I were standing. I had asked him to pop the cork on the Champaign bottle and make a toast for Kim as he had done for Pam. This made Pam and Kim very happy to see their parents together for such a wonderful occasion.

Chuck made a nice toast, then I made mine. The tears were so hard to keep back. I looked at Chuck and said, "Well, we finally made it. They both graduated!" With a sarcastic look, he said, "Speak for yourself!" Then he glanced over at Elizabeth. I said, "I'm glad it's you and not me just starting over." Then Shirley had the camera in our face, and I wanted to assure her she wasn't missing anything, but I bit my tongue. Chuck excused himself and joined the men down stairs.

Elizabeth was sitting on the chair with Daddy. She was talking to him a mile a minute. She was very outgoing, just like Kara, her biological mother, and I thought how proud Kara would be of her. Elizabeth was a pretty little girl and was busy feeding grandpa junk food. Naturally, he was enjoying every bite of it.

I wondered around and made it a point to visit with a few of the guest, then I went down stairs to get more ice. Chuck was sitting on the sofa, and when he looked up and saw me, he jumped up and said, "Reta, I really admire you for taking care of your Daddy like this. I couldn't have done it." He was never good at taking care of people, and I remembered back when Kim and Pam were born. He wouldn't come into the delivery room. He had told me he just couldn't handle it.

Chuck was still a handsome man, even though he only had hair around the edge of his head now and sported a mustache. He was tall and still had a nice body. Kim had inherited his height, but Pam was short like me. I could see his features in both the girls. He was finally retiring from the Air National Guard. We had met and married while he was in the Air Force.

Before an awkward silence could settle, I asked lightly, "Chuck, do you want to say hello to Daddy? He probably won't know you after twelve years and you do look a little different." He rubbed his bald head and laughed. "I know, but I'd like to say hello anyway."

Together we went up stairs and over to Daddy. He and Elizabeth were still having a good time, and we realized later he must have thought she was me when I was a little girl. She had black hair and never stopped talking. Daddy use to call me "Polly Parrot" whenever I talked too much, and now he was referring to Elizabeth as "Polly Parrot."

Daddy looked up at Chuck and his smile quickly turned to tears. He said in a low voice, "That's your husband." Chuck didn't know what to say, nor did I. I couldn't believe he recognized him after all these years. He thought we were still married, and when we finally got him settled down, Chuck went over to the sofa and sat down. He was totally blown away by my Daddy's actions.

Immediately, I went over and sat down by Chuck and we continued our conversation. Shirley, of course, monitored every word and action. We talked about the past and exchanged some old pictures of the kids. I'm sure Chuck was reprehended severely when she got him home, but Pam and Kim were very happy to see their parents conduct themselves in a respectful manner toward each other. And I was glad it went so smoothly, too.

While I sat there on the sofa observing Steve and Shirley, I idly wondered if I should have taken that last chance with Chuck to save our marriage way back when. Neither one of us had done too well with our new partners. Then I abruptly brushed the thought away. Anyway, we will never know, I told myself.

Steve's family had also been invited to the open house, and Cheryl, Steve's sister-in-law, asked me, "Are you going to be home next week? I would like to come up for a visit with you now that your recitals and Kim's graduation is over. I have something I want to talk to you about." When I looked into her eyes, I realized she was very serious I told her, "Give me a call next week and we will set a day for you to come up."

Kim opened her gifts, then the day was finally over ended and all the guest were gone. Daddy was totally pooped, and eager to get those boots off. As soon as Daddy's head hit the pillow, he was asleep.

I was very pleased with the way the day went. Kim had a wonderful day. Then she, Pam, Cheryl, Brad and all her friends took off to join the other parties still in session.

Brad had videoed the entire day, and we sat down and admired how well Daddy looked and conducted himself. I said, "I am going to make a copy of this video and send it to Yane and Cecil so they can see how far Daddy has come back." The next day, Brad made the copies for me and I sent them off.

Fred returned after he took his children home, and we sat at the table and discussed the forthcoming appointment with Sister Kenny for Daddy's re-evaluation. Fred had really worked with Daddy and said, "I believe Vernon is going to do really well on his test." He knew how much I wanted Daddy to be admitted for total rehabilitation. I still believed at that time my Daddy could be brought totally back to his old self. I realize now, of course, I was in total denial.

THE NEXT MORNING I FELT LIKE A NEW WOMAN. The recitals were finally over, Kim's graduation had been a success and Steve was actually working on someone's car. I just prayed he would pay the bills through June and July. I would start taking enrollment again in August, so I needed some time off. I was totally exhausted and needed to go in for a complete examination myself. I decided to do so after Daddy's re-evaluation.

I decided to go into Amery to take care of some business. I had consolidated all of our bills and been approved for a loan for $7,000 through Thorpe Finance. I thought that if I could get the bills lowered, then Steve might be able to handle them. After loaning him some of our money to get the equipment he needed, the pot was getting low. With this consolidation, we could pretty much skip the June bills, and then the Thorpe bill wouldn't be due until July.

After I got home, Pam came up to me and said, "Mom, Steve came in awhile ago and went to the loft. You had better examine your checkbook."

Immediately, I did exactly that and, sure enough, the little weasel had taken a check out. When Steve returned from town, I was waiting for him. "What did you take a check for? Don't you have money from the car you finished last week?" I asked pointedly.

He looked really worried and lamely said, "I needed some bonding material and I don't have any money left."

"What did you spend the money on?" I asked surprised, for I had loaned him over $3,000 to get what he needed to start the garage business.

"Different things," he shrugged, and that was all he said. Now I was really upset. After loaning him the money, he was stealing money out of what I had left from recitals and May payments to buy supplies for his stupid garage. I realized again I was going to regret ever helping him. "Don't touch any of my checks again," I warned him.

When the check from Thorpe was ready, I went into town and picked it up. I also had a check for $1,200 from the insurance company for the pump house to be rebuilt. I deposited the $7,000, then went home and made checks out to pay off all my credit cards, the car and a few more bills. Now all we had was the house payment, utilities and Thorpe payment. God, it felt good to mail those bills! Some were way behind, and I had almost lost my car at one point. It took just about the full $7,000 to get caught up on everything.

Steve came in and immediately started whining about me paying all the bills off. I asked him incredulously, "What in the hell did you think I borrowed the money for? For you to blow?" I shook my head in disgust.

He had no mind whatsoever for business. When we married, he was so far in debt and had such bad credit it took me two years to straighten things out. I had added his name to my credit cards to help him build credit again. These proved to be some of the biggest mistakes I made.

Then Cheryl, Steve's sister-in-law, called and asked if she could come out Saturday and talk. I said, "Well, Louise is coming up, but it doesn't matter. I will have time to visit with you, too." Suddenly out of nowhere she asked, "Are you still looking for a biblical way out of your marriage?"

Stunned, I said, "Yes."

"Well, maybe I can supply you with what you need. Can you meet me somewhere other than you house?"

"How about the *Country Dam* supper club?" I suggested.

"Okay. I'll be there at ten a.m. Saturday," Cheryl said.

"I'll be there."

I hung up the telephone totally confused. Cheryl sounded as though she knew for a fact Steve was cheating and with whom he had been cheating.

Suddenly Steve came running into the house. Apparently, he had picked up the extension telephone in his garage and heard Cheryl say that she would see me Saturday. He was as white as a sheet, scared to death. He yelled, "Don't believe anything that little bitch tells you!"

"What is she going to tell me, Steve? I know she has been screwing your son, Jason, but this is not about Jason. I guess I'll find out Saturday!" I said, turning the knife a little. He was still white as a ghost.

FOR THE NEXT FEW DAYS, STEVE WAS A NERVOUS wreck. Then Saturday came.

Louise arrived bright and early. She was a great friend and I referred to her as "Ma." In many ways, she was like a mom to me. Louise had a little tape recorder with her and had been taking a journalism class. She wanted to start writing my life stories. I laughed and said, "Ma, I've got to meet with Cheryl this morning. If you want to go with me, you can. This might be a very interesting story." I told her about the incidents from the last few days. I finally pieced it together and, choosing to not hold back anymore, said in a burst of words, "Ma, I think she's screwing Steve, too."

Ma was in total shock. She was an older lady and had a lot of energy. She never stopped going here and there, and I could hardly keep up with her. She could put thirty-six hours into twenty-four and like the Ever Ready battery, she just kept going and going... She was short in stature and I was always after her to lose a little more weight. As a good catholic woman, and I never heard her say a cuss word in all the years I knew her. Nor did she take a drink or smoke a cigarette.

Lee, Ma's son, was going to come up later in the day. He was like a little brother to me, a small man with black hair like mine. Most people thought he was really my brother. He and his brother, Peter, were responsible for me getting back into music after my divorce from Chuck.

Ma and I went out to the car about 9:45 a.m. so we could meet Cheryl at 10:00. As I got into the car, Steve came running after me and said, "Don't go! She is just a bitch and I know she is going to tell you a bunch of lies!"

I just smiled coolly and said, "Well, we'll soon find out." I started the car and Ma and I headed down the driveway.

CHERYL WAS SITTING IN FRONT OF THE COUNTRY *Dam* supper club when we arrived. She had gotten there early, and was acting really nervous. She was a pretty girl with long, blond hair, and if she was an inch shorter, would have been a dwarf. She looked so scared I felt sorry for her.

We went inside, and sat next to her. She sat very quite while we ordered breakfast. Finally, I looked at her and asked softly, "Cheryl, are you screwing Steve?" She turned white and said, "Yeah." Well, ma almost choked on her bacon and I started laughing. I couldn't believe the little weasel, Steve, was screwing his own brother's wife. I got up and went to the bathroom and washed my hands. I suddenly felt extremely dirty.

When I returned, ma was still sitting at the table with bacon hanging out of her mouth and in total shock. I sat down and casually started to eat my breakfast. Cheryl asked tentatively, "Aren't you going to hit me or something?"

"No, Cheryl. I guess I would rather just say thanks. You seem to be beating up on yourself enough without me helping you. Anyway, I guess you're right. You have given me a way out."

As I spoke, she started to cry. Then she said in between sobs, "You're such a nice person and you've been through so much!"

"Did that occur to you as you slipped under the covers with my husband? Does Rick know about this mess?" I asked, suddenly getting angry.

"Yes, I confessed to him before I left."

"He must feel really popular. How many more men in his family have you..." I interrupted myself. Then a thought struck me. "My God, Cheryl, you haven't had Andy, too, have you?" I asked quickly. Again Ma choked on her bacon.

"No," she continued to sob. Ma then asked, "Reta, do you want me to get this on tape?"

"No, Ma. I think we can remember this story," I said dryly.

We finished breakfast as Cheryl went into details about how she had met Steve at a motel by her home after Rick went to work. She had been with him in my bed after the girls were gone to school. They had just had a great time. No wonder the money was gone, the bills not paid and he had been acting like an idiot.

"Well, Cheryl, I guess I should thank you for at least telling me," I said.

Cheryl then said, "I know Steve is going to deny this, but I will face him in front of you and Rick if you want."

"Well, you will probably have to do that before this is over," I responded. Then I collected Ma and we went home. Ma's first story was turning out to be a dandy. She had never liked Steve anyway, nor did Karen or any of my friends. Karen always used to say, "Reta, you can't make a silk purse out of a sow's ear." Right now, it was more like a sow's ass.

As we drove home, I told Ma, "I have to control myself until I get the check for the pump house. His name is on it and I have to get his endorsement to cash it. Without that, I don't know how I can make it until enrollment time in August." My mind was going ninety miles per hour. If I had had the money, I would have gone straight home and booted Steve's butt so far down the road he wouldn't have known how many miles it was to Flag Town!

"I know he is going to deny this, so if he does, I am loading him up and we are going to Rick's house. You stay here with Pam and Kim. Lee will be up this afternoon." Lee hadn't seen Daddy since the stroke.

However, he knew Daddy before because Daddy had always called him Jesse James.

As I pulled into the driveway, Steve came running out of his garage and I could see how worried he was. He yelled, "Whatever she told you is a damn lie!" before we even stopped and I looked at Ma and said, "Well, there's my answer." Very quietly, Ma went into the house.

As the car stopped, I said, "Steve, get in the car. We're going to Rick's house."

Steve froze in his tracks, and said, "Why?"

"Steve, don't even start. I know the entire nasty mess," I said with clenched teeth.

"What did that little bitch say?"

"Just get in the car!" I yelled.

THE TRIP TO RICK AND CHERYL'S HOUSE IN FRIDLEY, Minnesota, seemed to take forever even though it's only a forty-five minute drive. When we got there, Cheryl had just returned shortly before.

Rick answered the door. He was a handsome man and also a good person. He had converted to Jehovah's Witness just a few years before, and most of Steve's family belonged to the church as, well as Cheryl's family. Steve and I had even been studying with Rick and Cheryl during this affair. Needless to say, this mess certainly put a stop to my studying. However, I had met a few people in the church who lived what they preached and Rick was one of them.

He and Cheryl also had a baby boy just one year old, and I thought to myself as I looked at the baby, I wonder which one of the Anderson men sired the child. For Rick's sake, I hoped the baby was his. Lord knows Steve had enough kids running around the area, and five of them I had been paying support for up until two month's ago. Fine mess you've gotten yourself into this time, Reta. I could now see my own stupidity, and it amazed even me. Now, I could clearly see what my friends had been trying to tell me from the beginning of the relationship.

Rick invited us in. Cheryl was still crying, and I couldn't help but feel sorry for the poor little thing again.

Then I remembered back a few months before when her church, parents and the entire Anderson family, including Rick, had disowned and disfellowshipped her for the affair she had with Steve's fifteen-year-old son,

Jason. She was young, only about twenty-three, and had no one with whom to talk. Steve and I had gone to Andy's house during that time, and I couldn't believe how the entire family was ripping that poor, little, stupid girl apart, including Steve, the "concerned father." But unknown to the rest of us, he was also sleeping with her. He had even met with Jason and had one of those "father and son talks," and reprimanded him severely.

These hypocrites amazed me! They billboarded themselves as Christians, yet were judging and condemning her as if they were without blame! Cheryl had really done a bad thing, but my mother had always told me, "Don't kick a dog when he's down." I had told Andy, Rick and the entire clan, what a bunch of phonies I thought they were. "I don't understand this kind of religion. Whatever happened to 'Thou shalt not judge.' If this is your Christianity, then I'll stick with my own religion!" I had then stormed out of Andy's house, got into my car and went directly over to Cheryl's house. I had been worried she might harm herself in some way.

I now looked back at that time and understand why Steve had been so against my helping her—he was scared she might tell me about their disgusting affair.

But this time, the family and church was going to totally destroy her, especially for committing adultery with her husband's married brother. The thought brought shivers to my spine.

When Rick opened the door, I was glad to see he hadn't deserted her yet. Needless to say, I just wasn't ready yet to console her over the affair she was having with my husband, even though she seemed to still be clinging to me for help. Rick may have forgiven her for the Jason affair because of the baby, but I didn't know what he would do this time.

As we walked in, Rick looked at Steve with wrath in his eyes and said, "You better be happy I have God in my life now or you would be dead!" Steve was scared to death, for Rick was much bigger and could have probably killed him with one punch. Secretly, I would have given anything to see Rick knock him through the door! Instead, we all sat down at the table in an orderly fashion. I didn't know what to expect, and neither did anyone else.

Calmly, Rick opened the Bible and said, "I think we should open this discussion with a scripture and a prayer." I was tired of their sanctimonious religious crap and said, "Rick, forget the scripture and Steve.

You should be the one praying 'cause I'm here for one reason. I want to know if my husband is screwing your wife."

I was proud of Cheryl, for even in this uncomfortable situation, she stood up and admitted her wrong. She looked Steve straight in the eye and said, "Yes, we have been, and I'm so sorry!" Immediately, Steve started whining big-time, and in an accusing voice said to me, "Well, I needed someone. You're always so busy!"

I stood up, slammed my fist down on the table and shouted, "Don't you dare try to blame me for your animal activities! Our sex life has been next to nothing since my hysterectomy. Remember, in your stupidity you believed they had destroyed my womanhood and treated me as though I was not capable of having sex anymore!"

"But I was afraid I would hurt you!" he said in a manufactured, concerned voice. That really made me mad.

"That's a bunch of crap! When did you ever worry about hurting me? You sorry excuse for a man! Anyway, I've been just too busy trying to keep the bills paid, food on the table and a roof over our heads while you ran around the country pretending to be a big macho man! Don't forget, someone had to pay for your motel bills," then in a baby voice, "so you could have someone."

"But it didn't mean anything," Steve whined.

I sat down, looked him straight in the eye and said in a low monotone voice, "Don't you dare insult my intelligence by thinking I might believe that crap!" Then in a louder voice I continued, "No wonder you were so supportive for me to bring Daddy home. You knew I wouldn't have any spare time and you would be free to screw around all you wanted, while I continued to work and support you! You are the dirtiest, poorest excuse for a man I have ever known!" I took a breath, then Rick took his turn.

"If you needed someone, why did you have to pick my wife? Where in the hell are your morals?" Rick yelled angrily.

I said, "Rick, I have to get out of here. Let's go outside and talk." I knew if I didn't get Rick away from Steve, Rick was going to do something he would regret later. We got up and left Steve and Cheryl sitting at the table.

Outside, Rick and I sat on an old barrel by his garden. I said, "What are you going to do, Rick?"

"I don't know. I have just barely healed over her and Jason. I can't believe my own brother and nephew would do something like this. Whatever happened to family and trust?"

"I don't know, but I do know Steve will no longer live at my house. I am divorcing him just as soon as possible, but I have to be cool for awhile until I get the pump house insurance money. I loaned him most of my money to buy the equipment he needs for his garage, plus his supplies. I have put myself in a serious financial situation, and I figure with the money I get from singing, plus the twelve hundred from the insurance company, I can survive until enrollment time in August. I needed some time off this summer, more than anyone knows. I have some dental problems I need to take care of before enrollment starts. I hate him for what he has done to me and my family!" I started to cry.

Rick put his arm around me and said, "I would like to beat him unmerciful, but my religion won't let me."

I started laughing and crying at the same time and said, "Then change religions!"

Rick started laughing with me and said, "Maybe you're right. You should have let me continue inside. I was about ready to break his neck."

I thought for a second and said, "Maybe I should have let you." We were at least finding a little humor, even if it was sick humor. Steve and Cheryl must have been going crazy, wondering what we were laughing about. We sat and continued to talk for a while. Then I looked at my watch and said in mock horror, "My God, Rick, we've left them in there alone for one hour! They're probably in your bed by now!" Together we laughed and went back inside.

When we went back inside, they were still at the table and Cheryl was still crying. I said, "Cheryl, crying is not going to help. What is done can't be undone."

Steve, always concerned about himself, whined, "What are you going to do?"

I wanted to say, "After I throw up, I'm going to take a dull knife to you," but I knew I had to control myself until I got his name taken off my credit cards—which I had just paid off with the loan—and get his endorsement on the pump house check. Instead I said, "I don't know, Steve." I could hardly stand to look at the little dirty weasel. "I have Daddy's re-evaluation to go through yet at Sister Kinney, and Tuesday, in case you don't remember, I have my dental surgery. This time has been scheduled for six months and I have to get it taken care of during my time out of the studios.   I've already made arrangements with the band to continue without me.   When the surgery is over, I will know what I am going to do.   I need that time to think."   Of course, I knew already what I was going to do, but I had to buy time.

With nothing else to do, I said good-bye to Rick and even gave Cheryl a hug, which only made her cry harder.   I don't think I've ever seen anyone cry so much in my entire life.   I truly believe she was a nymphomaniac and couldn't help herself.   I was happy, though, she had a conscience, or *Steve the Parasite* would have continued to suck me dry at every turn.

STEVE AND I GOT INTO THE FIREBIRD AND STARTED back to Amery.   I knew I had better keep my mouth shut or I'd blow my plans.   I sat in silence as my mind slipped back to a couple of months after my hysterectomy in August...

I had met Yvonne, one of my long time friends, at the Country Dam Lounge. We sat at a table and had a drink when I was approached by a very handsome man. He said, "Hi! My name is Bob Marcum.   Could I buy you a drink?"   He was tall, had black hair and was just down right gorgeous.   I thought, "wow."

But before I could answer, Yvonne said, "You sure can, and bring your friend over, too."   He and his friend joined us and I really enjoyed talking to him.   I was impressed and felt like an attractive woman for the first time since my surgery.   I also knew my womanhood had not been destroyed as Steve had me believing.   After all, they had only removed my uterus, everything else was just fine.   My hormones were jumping all over the place, and I was so relieved to know I could still function.

Bob and his friend wanted Yvonne and me to join them the next day for boating in Balsam Lake.   Of course, I immediately told him I was married so that would be totally out of the question.   Yvonne said disgustedly, "Yeah, she's married all right, to a jerk that doesn't even make love to her any more."

In a very stern voice I said, "Yvonne, that's my business."   I knew that Yvonne was in total agreement with Karen, Louise and everyone else.   Her opinion of Steve was zero.

I really was attracted to Bob, more than I should have been, and wanted to explain.   "I do have some problems with my marriage, but as long as I am married, I will honor my vows."

"I don't believe I've ever met anyone like you. I really respect you for that," Bob said sincerely.

He made me feel good for voicing my values, and I said with a laugh, "Give me your telephone number and when I work my life out, you will be the first one I call."

"You promise?"

"You can count on it," I told him, and he seemed happy about that. Then we continued to talk and I told him about my children and he told me about his. I was having such a good time that I didn't want to go home that night, but I knew I had to in order to live with myself.

The next day I had felt so guilty about the feelings I was having. I couldn't get Bob off my mind and wanted very much to see him again. I finally called Steve out onto the deck and told him just what had happened the night before and about the way I felt. I said, "I know our marriage is falling apart. You don't want to make love to me anymore, and after last night, I know my hormones are still functioning. I was unfaithful to you only in my mind, but that really bothers me."

Steve had just stood there looking across the forest in the backyard. I could tell he was in really deep thought. Then I said, "Did you hear what I just said?"

Steve had turned and looked at me with sad eyes and asked, "You didn't do anything with him?"

"No, I didn't physically, but I sure did with my mind! That's why I know our marriage is in bigger trouble than I thought. I don't feel that way about you any more. Besides, I think you're having an affair. Are you?" I asked, looking closely at his eyes to see if he was lying.

Of course, he denied having any outside activities, and I wanted to believe him, but in my heart I knew he was seeing other women. After today, I understood why he looked so guilty back then. I had found out he had been screwing Cheryl plus lord knows who else, weeks before that conversation.

AS WE PULLED INTO THE DRIVEWAY, I CAME BACK TO reality. I smiled inside because I had decided to make that call to Bob as soon as I sued for divorce. I looked over at Steve and got sick to my stomach. What a waste! I wished it was all over.

The sun was going down and I still hadn't spoken a word to him since we left Rick's house. Steve got out of the car and said, "I've got to get that car finished." Now he was going to show me what a great provider he could be. I didn't say a word and went into the house. He went to his garage.

Everyone, including Daddy and Fred, was sitting in the living room, and when I walked in, you could have heard a pin drop. All eyes were on me, and I said, "Well, the little s--- has been getting it on with Cheryl."

Daddy said, "Well, that son of a bitch!" I don't know if he understood what had really happened, but he did know I was upset. I had to be very careful, for he still wanted to protect me from anyone hurting me. I went over to him and said, "Daddy, don't you worry. I'm okay. No one is going to hurt me," and he started to cry. "They damn sure better not!" I felt terrible for letting him see my anger and hurt.

Fortunately, Lee was there and came to my rescue. He started talking to Daddy and got his mind off me while I took the kids and ma downstairs to explain my plans. As we left the room, Lee had Daddy telling him all about ranching and Fred was adding his comments to the conversation. They knew I needed some private time with my family.

Once downstairs, I explained to Pam, Kim, Cheryl, Brad and ma what had happened at Rick's house. I told them we had to pretend as though I might give him another chance until I could take care of the financial situation. In a stern voice I said, "We've all got to stay calm until I get his endorsement on the pump house check and his name off my credit cards and checking account. They all understood our financial situation and agreed we had to buy time.

Pam said, "Mom, this is going to be so hard. I hate him more than I've ever hated anyone!"

Kim joined in as well and said, "We'll just have to stay totally clear of him or I'll probably blow it." Cheryl, Brad and ma also gave their opinion of him, but everyone agreed to cool it.

With that settled, I said, "I'm going up stairs and see how Daddy is doing. It's really important not to talk about any of these problems around Daddy. Just try to act as natural as you can." I received a big hug from everyone and was re-assured of their loyalty. Thank God for my little team!

As I started upstairs, I added as an afterthought, "Do you guys think you could handle me staying with Karen after I have my dental surgery done Tuesday? In fact, I would like to go to her house tomorrow. I could call the credit card places and everything from there and not worry about him listening on his telephone in the garage." They all decided that would be a good idea.

I went back up stairs and visited with Lee and ma before they left. I asked, "Well ma, has it been an interesting enough day for you?" All she could reply was, "Unbelievable!"

Lee was still in the dark, but ma assured him she would fill him in on the way home. I gave them both a hug and they left.

With everyone gone, I visited with Daddy until his bedtime. Fred came back up after he tucked him in, and I informed Fred of the situation at hand. He assured me Daddy would be all right and agreed, under the circumstances, it would be the best for me to stay at Karen's for a few days after my surgery. Karen was only twenty minutes away, and I knew if Daddy needed me I could be there in a flash.

Steve worked late in the garage, then. slithered in after everyone had gone to bed. He went straight to our bedroom and even took a shower before he went to bed. I could smell the cologne clear out in the living room and was dumbfounded that he thought I was going to sleep with him. I realized then it was going to be a horrible week if I didn't stay at Karen's house. I just prayed that the insurance check would be in the morning's mail.

About an hour later, Steve came into the living room. I was sitting in Daddy's Lazy Boy trying to make plans for the next day. I had to get his name off my credit cards and checking account, but couldn't let him know I was doing it. If he found out, he would realize I had no intentions of ever staying with him. The thought of him touching me made me want to throw up.

Steve approached the chair and knelt down. In his sexiest voice asked, "Are you coming to bed?" Then he tried to kiss me. I pulled away from him, amazed at the gall of the little weasel. He really expected me to make love to him! I prayed for God to give me the strength I was obviously going to need to get through this time.

I took a deep breath and got control of myself, then said, "No, Steve, I'm not coming to bed. I am sleeping with Pam and Kim tonight unless you want to sleep on the sofa."

With his usual pathetic whine, he said, "You're not going to forgive me, are you?"

To get away from him, I got up and went into the kitchen to get a glass of wine, the whole time continuing to pray for self-control. Finally I said, "I am going to Karen's house in the morning. My surgery is scheduled for Tuesday morning. I will need a couple of days to heal, so I'm just going to stay at her house. This will give me uninterrupted time to think of what I'm going to do. I will know what I am going to do when I get home Thursday." I could tell he wasn't keen on the idea.

With an angry look he stood up and said, "Well, if that's what you want, I guess I can't do nothing about it. It's gonna be a long four days!"

I realized I'd better be a little more convincing or I was going to blow my cover, so in a soothing voice I said, "Maybe that time will be just what I need to work through this mess. Who knows, maybe I can forgive you. Just leave me alone until Thursday. I guess I just need some space right now."

Apparently this satisfied him and he said, "Okay." Then, like a spoiled child, he stomped back into the bedroom.

As soon as he left, I thought, "You dirty little bastard! No sofa for you." Disgusted, I went down stairs and crawled in bed with the girls.

THE NEXT MORNING CAME TOO EARLY FOR ME, BUT I couldn't wait to get packed and out of there. I called Karen and asked, "How would you like to have company for a few days?"

"Are you finally leaving that little f-----?" she asked excitedly.

"Even you won't believe what he's done this time!" I said with disgust. "He finally did the ultimate. Put the coffee pot on. I want to wait until the mail runs, then I'll say goodbye to Daddy and come right over and bring you up to date."

Karen sighed and said, "Hurry up! My curiosity's killing me!"

Steve was already busy at work in the garage, really trying to impress me. Pam, Kim and Cheryl were still in bed, so I fixed Daddy and Fred some breakfast. I even made myself call out to the garage and ask Steve if he wanted to eat. Thank God, he had already eaten.

As we sat at the table and ate, I told Daddy I had to go on a business trip with the dance studios for a few days. "Now, while I'm gone, Daddy, can I count on you to watch over everything here at the house for me?" He nodded, and I continued, "Make sure Pam and Kim stay out of trouble." I looked at Fred, winked, then said, "Make sure you keep Fred in line, too."

Fred smiled and said, "I bet you can handle all that, can't you, Vernon?" Daddy sat up really tall and said with authority, "You damn betcha, it's as good as done!"

A long time ago I realized that it was important to make Daddy feel needed, so every time I left the house to go to work or whatever, I would always leave him in charge. This made him still feel like the man he was before. I thought to myself, Even in his condition, he was more of a man than that poor excuse I was married to.

Gathering my purse and keys, I yelled good-bye to the kids, grabbed my suitcase and headed for the door. I took the Firebird and left the Lincoln. Steve came out of the garage and said, "Why aren't you taking the Lincoln?"

In amazement I said, "Because some times I even like to drive the Firebird. Is that okay?" He mumbled, "I guess so," and I said, "I'll be back Thursday and we will have a long talk. I should know what I feel by then."

As I pulled out of the driveway, I looked at Daddy's little, red Grand Prix. I always left it there for Fred to use if Daddy needed something or wanted to take him somewhere.

Thinking back, I chuckled as I remembered Daddy's expression the day I made a Yankee car out of his pride and joy. I had taken him with me for a little outing to the Wisconsin Department Of Public Safety. After I changed the plates from Texas to Wisconsin, I had teased him saying, "Well, Daddy, your car is now a real Yankee car." He had roared, "Damn well better not be!" I had hushed up real quick and headed for the dinner club.

As I got to the end of the driveway, the mailman was stopping at the mailbox. I quickly uttered a prayer, "Please, God, let that insurance check be in there!" As soon as he drove away, I got out and ran to the mailbox. To my delight, the insurance check had finally arrived. I was so excited, I had to calm myself down.

Now I could get rid of Steve! I turned the car around and drove back to the house, thanking God all the way. But I still had to get Steve's endorsement. As I pulled up, Steve came out of the garage and asked, "What's wrong?"

"Well, good news," I said in a normal voice. "The insurance check is finally here. I need you to sign it so I can deposit it." I was trying to not show any emotion so he wouldn't get suspicious. But Steve never caught on, he just casually signed it.

Once the check was signed, I went into the house to get a deposit form. I was bursting with excitement, and told my team the good news. "Thursday is the day. I will get everything else handled today.   I can't cancel my surgery, I've waited too long already," I said excitedly. Everyone agreed to try and keep cool.

Quickly, I ran up stairs to my office and got a deposit ticket. I decided to hide my checkbook so he wouldn't start writing more checks since he knew I was going to deposit the $1,200 insurance check. It would probably never occur to him we might have to build another pump house with at least part of the money.

On my way out, I again told my little team good-bye. I also cautioned them to keep their enthusiasm under control until I had all the details worked out, and my surgery was over. Pam said, "Don't worry, Mom, we'll be okay. At least we know now when he will be gone."

Again I got into the Firebird and headed toward Amery. I went directly to the bank and opened another account in just my name with the $1,200. God, it felt good to know he couldn't write any checks on it! I knew the other account would have almost a zero balance after all the checks cleared from the $7,000 I had borrowed to consolidate the credit cards, car, etc.

From the bank, I went directly across the street to Don Novitzke, the local attorney's office, and filed for divorce. I told Don to give me the papers and I would present them to Steve when I returned home on Thursday. He said, "I will have everything ready for you to pick up Thursday morning." I had total confidence in Don, for I had been told he was the best attorney in the area. Plus, I knew him from singing. He was a country music fan, or at least liked the refreshments sold at the clubs. Anyway, I felt he would do a good job.

Additionally, Don had also handled the last divorce between Steve and one of his previous wives, either Ann or Bonnie. I'm sure he was well informed of the kind of free-loader he was dealing with.

Finished at the attorney's office, I headed for Karen's house. She came running out to the car, fit to be tied. She yelled, "Where in the hell have you been? I thought that little f----- might have tried to kill you or something!"

I realized she was genuinely worried and told her, "Don't worry, Karen, I can handle him. Let's have that cup of coffee and I'll tell you the entire nasty mess."

"Hell, I'm ready for a Windsor Water," she declared. "Make mine a Bacardi and Coke," I said. Laughing, I looked at my watch. "It is afternoon, isn't it?"

ONCE WE WERE INSIDE KAREN'S HOUSE, I BEGAN TO relate the whole sordid details, beginning with the visit from Cheryl up to filing for divorce. She gave a big sigh, shook her head in disbelief and said, "I'm ready for a double, and I think you need one, too." I shook my head and said, "No, I have some calls to make. But then I'll catch up!

Using her phone, I called the credit card companies and they assured me Steve's name would be removed from my cards. I also called the bank and talked to Ann, one of the tellers I had known for a long time, and explained what had happened. I gave her the numbers of the outstanding checks and asked, "As soon as these checks clear, if there is a balance left will you just transfer it over to my new account?"

Ann was more than willing to help and said, "I totally understand what you mean!" She also knew Steve through his ex-wife, and said, "If there are any problems, I will call you."

I then told her about my scheduled surgery the next day and said, "If you foresee any problems, don't call the house. He's still there until I get back Thursday. You can reach me here at Karen's house." Ann assured me she would keep an eye on the situation, and as I hung up, I felt a lot better.

As I looked up, I saw Karen and said, "Well, the little b------ is totally castrated now. If he spends any money, he is going to have to earn it!" With a bit of a slur she said, "That's impossible! He would have to have balls first," and we both started laughing. "You better start catching up," she said and handed me a double Bacardi and Coke. I gladly took a big gulp, and relaxed in the chair. Things were starting to look better.

In a better mood, I called home and talked to Fred. He said, "Pam, Kim, Brad and Cheryl left for the lake, Steve is still working in the garage and Vernon and I are playing some dominoes." He assured me everything at home was fine.

"Fred, just tell the kids everything is fine with me. They will understand. Also, tell Pam and Kim I will see them in the morning." They had planned to be with me for the surgery. I had to be very careful what I said because I knew Steve was listening on the garage telephone. I decided to use it to my advantage and said, "Well, Fred, if you need me for anything, just call. I am going to use this time to do some serious thinking." Fred said "Okay," and we hung up.

As I put down the phone, I breathed a sigh of relief. "Now, Karen, let's celebrate!" We sat there and got totally wasted. It felt so good to just sit with a friend and talk. For the first time in months, I felt as though I had reclaimed my life.

THE NEXT MORNING WE GOT UP EARLY. MY HEAD felt like three elephants had crossed over it and my mouth was so dry I couldn't spit. In other words, I was looking forward to getting fresh oxygen at the hospital.

Karen had the coffee ready this time, and the Windsor put way back in the cabinet. We looked at each other and laughed, even if it did hurt. I said, "Did we have fun?"

"The way I feel, I don't think there is any doubt!" Karen joked.

Pam and Kim were right on time, and got to Karen's just before we had to leave. Karen then made the supreme sacrifice and decided to go, too. We all headed for the city, and I had extensive dental surgery.

AFTER THE SURGERY, THE GIRLS TOOK ME BACK TO Karen's house. My face was pretty swollen by the time we there, and I laid down with ice packs on my face per doctor's instructions. I promised Pam and Kim I would do exactly what the doctor said. Karen also laid down with an ice pack, per her own instructions. She had us laughing most of the trip down and back, and was still at it.

Within a few minutes after getting comfortable, the telephone rang. Pam answered, and it was Steve. "I want to talk to your mother," he said, but Pam replied, "Mother cannot talk right now. The doctor wants her to stay down with an ice pack." Then he got really nasty, and Pam hung up.

Steve called right back. This time Kim answered. He said, "Don't hang up on me again! I want to talk to your mother!"

"I haven't hung up on you yet. Like Pam told you, mom cannot come to the telephone," Kim said sweetly. He started ranting and raving again, and she said, "Now I'm going to hang up!"

The next time Steve called back, Karen answered it. He was a little scared of her and she yelled into the phone, "Steve, this is my telephone and don't call back raising hell anymore or I'll call the police!" then slammed it down. Needless to say, he didn't call again.

We all felt pretty safe since I had everything worked out, and it was just a matter of getting well and serving him the divorce papers. Pam and Kim stayed over—I didn't want them to go home and listen to Steve's abuse even though I knew he wouldn't touch them.

Pam called Brad and told him to stay at the house until Thursday and to keep an eye on everything. She told him to fill Fred in on everything, including the divorce papers I was going to serve on Steve that Thursday. I didn't mind because by this time, Fred was like one of the family.

Steve was scared of Brad, so I knew with both him and Fred there he wouldn't do anything but whine. I said, "Steve must suspect something is up, or he wouldn't be acting like this."

Karen said, "Who knows what's in that little f-----'s mind." We all laughed, then went to sleep early. I was on some pretty relaxing medication, and had no problem sleeping.

EARLY THE NEXT MORNING, THE TELEPHONE RANG and woke me. It was Ann, from the bank, and she said in a worried voice, "I am sorry to bother you, Reta, but Steve is up to something. He just called to see what the balance was in your account, and I told him it was only forty-eight cents. You do still have over twenty-five hundred. I don't think he believed me and if he comes over here and writes a check for the balance, I will have to give it to him."

I totally panicked. I couldn't believe that little bastard would pull the money out and let the checks I had written for bills bounce. "Ann, what can I do?" I plead. I couldn't let him get the money and ruin everything, not with the divorce so close to becoming a reality.

Ann was totally sympathetic and said conspiratorially, "If you can come over here right now, I will pull the money out of this account and put it in your new one. Then I will make sure that when these two checks come in we will cover them out of the new account."

Almost in tears, I asked, "Are you sure you can do that?"

"No problem, but you have to sign some paperwork. Do you feel like coming over?" she asked, concern in her voice.

"I don't have a choice. I'm supposed to stay flat with an ice pack, but I can't let him do this. I will get dressed and be right there," I said.

As soon as I hung up the telephone, I informed Karen, Pam and Kim of the situation. Their first thought was to just go out and kill him. I felt the same way, but said instead, "We can handle him later. Right now I have to get to the bank."

"What about the swelling?" Pam asked.

"I'll just have to handle it," I said with a grimace.

"God, how I hate him!" hissed Kim.

I then asked Pam and Kim to stay there in the event he tried to call. "I know it's going to be hard, but don't piss him off. Just try to be civil until I get this taken care of," I coaxed. They nodded, and with a sigh said, "Okay, Mom."

Karen drove me to the bank, and Ann did just as she said. She transferred the balance into my new account and assured me she would take care of the outstanding checks. Then she said, "Now get back to Karen's house and try to get some rest. Your face is starting to swell more."

"I can't thank you enough," I said, wishing there was something I could do for her.

When we got back home, Pam and Kim panicked. My face was really swelling, and when I looked in the mirror, it scared me, too. I immediately laid down with the ice packs, feeling better in spite of my swollen face. "I think everything is covered now," I said to Karen. I didn't know what else he could do.

A while later Brad came by and said, "Steve has been tearing up the house looking for the checkbook. I thought I'd better come and tell you. He's been acting like a crazy man, and I think he knows his numbers up." Pam filled him in on the morning's activities, and he said in an angry voice, "I wish I could just have one shot at him!"

Just then the telephone rang. Karen answered it and it was the little weasel. He screamed, "You had better tell Reta to talk to me if she knows what's good for her!"

"Reta is not coming to the damned phone! What in the hell is your problem!" she screamed back.

"I want to know what she plans to do! I can't wait until Thursday!"

In a furious voice, Karen let him have it. "Look, you whinny little creep, leave her alone until Thursday, then, believe me, you will know everything! The swelling in her face has got to go down and the pain go away before she is going to be strong enough to deal with you!"

Steve went nuts. "Well, tell her that every check she has out is going to bounce! I'm taking what's left of the money she deposited from the Thorpe loan out of the bank. I know she didn't make that deposit of twelve hundred dollars because I called the bank and her buddy said we only had forty-eight cents in the bank, but I know she's lying! I am going over there and talk to someone else. And further more, if she don't want to come home and find her Daddy sitting out in the yard with his suitcase, she had better talk to me!"

"You dirty little f------!" Karen screamed back and slammed the phone down. Her face red, she repeated to me what he'd said.

Needless to say, I went crazy, but Brad assured me Steve wouldn't touch a hair on Daddy's head. He said, "Fred and I will take care of him."

"Thanks, Brad," I said feeling comforted and gave him a hug. "I am going to call the police department anyway and try to get a restraining order or something on him." Brad nodded and went directly home.

When Brad left, Pam and Kim wanted to go with him, but I knew that would be a big mistake. I knew they would go out there and try to beat him up themselves or something worse. Then, Brad and Fred would wind up in the middle and Daddy would really be upset. Instead, I had them stay with me.

Next I called the police department and spoke to the sheriff. I explained the situation, but they told me, "Until the divorce papers are served, he legally has as much right at your home as you do. Although I would like to help, unless he actually does something physical, our hands are tied. Would you like for us to go out and talk to him?" he asked, seeming to really want to help.

"No. Unless you can arrest him for something, just stay away until I can take the proper action. Thank-you," I said. They knew Steve. With his driving record, he was well known to the local police department. The sheriff took a deep breath then said, "Reta, I will look at his record and if there is anything we can legally do, we will." I thanked him again, said a silent prayer and laid back down. I knew if I didn't stay down with the ice pack for at least twenty-four more hours, I would be in big trouble.

Through out the rest of the day, I just laid back and kept ice packs on me. The swelling went way down, but I was still really sore.

About sundown, the phone rang, and I thought to myself, I hope it's not anything bad! Pam answered the phone and it turned out to be Brad. He was laughing hysterically and said, "Pam, tell Reta all her problems are over. The police just picked Steve up!"

Pam started jumping up and down as if she had won the lottery, and yelled, "Mom! Steve's in jail!" There was so much excitement in Karen's house! Everyone was laughing and yelling, and I just couldn't believe the wonderful news. I was afraid the medication had made me imagine it!

Immediately, I called the police department and managed to speak to the same sheriff. He told me, "Well, until you started paying his child support, he never did and the state wanted him for the tune of about thirty-two thousand dollars." He laughed, then continued, "We decided to pick him up for awhile until they decide what they want to do with him. I figured you wouldn't mind and can get your paperwork done while he is in here, then put that restraining order on him. We just bought you a little time."

"Well, another prayer has just been answered. Thank you so much for your help," I said.

"No problem. Glad to be of service."

I was so thankful for the good news that I took some medication and went back to bed for the tenth time that day. I didn't wake up until noon the next day, and fortunately the swelling had just about gone. I told Pam and Kim, "Let's go home." The nightmare was over. I gave Karen a hug and said, "Thanks, buddy. Come out soon. You won't have to look at him any more."

"That's a step in the right direction," she said with one of her famous laughs.

On the way home from Karen's, I stopped by the attorney's office and filled Don in on the latest. He said, "That's good news! I'll have the paperwork delivered to him in jail, then I'll call you as soon as he is served so you can go over to the courthouse and get the restraining order signed and put into effect." I didn't know how to thank him.

Pam drove back to the house, and it felt so good to get out and walk in without having to see the little weasel or hear his whiny voice. Daddy and Fred were sitting at the table having a snack. I ran in, put my arms around Daddy and said, "I love you!" He looked at me and said gruffly, "I love you, too. Where in the hell have you been? My ol' podner here has just about drove me crazy!" It sure was good to see he still had his spunk and none of this mess had affected him. I gave Brad and Fred a hug and said, "What would I have done without you guys?" Daddy quipped up, "Hell if I know!"

BRAD IMMEDIATELY WANTED TO TAKE CHARGE OF the house. He said, "I can't wait to get started! I can rebuild the pump house for about fifty dollars."

"Brad, you know what is needed and you know my financial situation," I said.

"Don't worry!" he patted my arm reassuringly. "I've found enough building material here that Steve's' thrown away to keep me busy all summer." Then, with a grin he said, "And I work cheap! I'm going to get that ramp built for grandpa off the back deck first." With that, he got his tools and happily went out the door.

Everyone, including Daddy, seemed to be in good spirits. I think it was because I was relaxed for the first time in months. I went up to my office in the loft and began trying to figure out my plan of attack on the bills. It felt so good knowing Steve could never write any more checks on my accounts or charge any more on my credit cards. It was wonderful to be free from him! I only wished the divorce was final!

AFTER I WAS COMPLETELY HEALED FROM THE surgery and my life was almost back to normal, I remembered a promise I had made to myself. I smiled as I looked up Bob Marcum's number. It felt strange to be back in the rat race of dating, but at least I knew who I wanted to see!

Nervously, I dialed the number he had given me, and was a little surprised when his secretary answered. "Mr. Marcum is not here at the present time, may I take a message?" At that moment I was so nervous, I almost hung up.

Am I making a fool of myself? Maybe he was only joking about me calling him. A thousand negative thoughts ran through my head, for after being married to someone like Steve Anderson, my self-esteem was pretty low.

Fortunately, I collected my thoughts and said in my best professional voice, "Yes, my name is Reta Lee. I don't know if Bob will remember me, but if he does, tell him I have my life straightened out now. If he remembers the conversation, then he will understand. And if he would like, he may call me." I gave my phone number and the secretary assured me she would give him the message when he called in.

I hung up the telephone thinking, You idiot! She must think you're a mental case or something. Besides, he won't even remember who you are.

Slightly embarrassed at what I'd just done, I went back to the bills. About fifteen minutes later, the telephone rang, and to my shock, surprise and delight, it was Bob. He said, "Hi! You finally got it together, huh?"

With that opening, we talked for almost an hour and I told him a little about the situation, but not all. He was so easy to talk to that words just poured out. As I listened to myself talk, I felt like such a fool to have let Steve get away with the things he had done. It didn't make me look too intelligent.

Finally, Bob said he would be in my part of the country again in a few weeks, and asked if I would like to get together with him. I gave him my band bookings and invited him to hear me perform. I had planned to go back full-time with the band immediately after Daddy's re-evaluation. Bob willingly agreed and said, "I'm looking forward to seeing you again, and hearing you sing!" Thank God he liked country music!

"Me, too," I said lamely, then we hung up. For the first time in years I felt warm inside. Things were looking up!

The telephone rang again and brought me back to reality. This time it was my attorney, Don. "Reta, the divorce papers have been served on Steve. Now you can proceed with the restraining order." I thanked him profusely, then called Pam and Kim. Together we went to the courthouse to take care of the restraining orders.

When we walked into the courthouse, my face was still swollen. The lady filling out the papers thought he had battered me, but I explained my situation with the dental surgery. I don't know if she believed me.

While she was filling out the paperwork, I saw Ann and Bonnie walk in, Steve's ex-wives. They were there to sign complaints for the state regarding back child support, and I thought to myself, Thank you God for not letting me have any ties like that with him! Chuck and I might have had our problems, but I had been lucky all those years, for he paid his child support, even though it was only $108.00 per child, per month.

By the same token, Chuck was lucky because I had never asked to increase the amount, even though I had been advised to many times through the years. I made enough money through those years that I really didn't want to do that to him. He had always helped with extra expenses I had with Pam and Kim.

We got the paperwork all finished and we left the courthouse. Then we stopped by the grocery store and got a new supply of buttermilk for Daddy. He was still drinking it like there would be none left in the world tomorrow, and I was glad he liked it. We took our groceries and went home.

AT HOME AGAIN, FRED AND I SAT DOWN AND began to discuss the forthcoming reevaluation for Daddy. It was Monday morning, and we lived about twelve hours away from Sister Kenny. "Let's go down Sunday evening and get a room at the hospitality hotel so Daddy can get a good night's rest before they start early the next morning," I suggested. Fred agreed, so I called and made reservation for us.

The hospitality hotel is part of Sister Kenny, and I told them of Daddy's condition. They assured me he would have a room ready to accommodate his situation. I also made arrangements for me to stay in the room with Daddy and got Fred a room by himself. I thought he would enjoy a good night's rest, too. Besides, I had been away from Daddy a few days and wanted to care for him myself.

Kim came up from her room and asked, "Mom, do you know where my television set is?" Before I could answer, Fred chuckled and said, "I do! Steve had the police wait for him to get a television before they took him to jail. He went downstairs and came back with a small, white portable one."

"That was the television my Daddy gave me when I was little!" she exclaimed, hurt in her voice.

"Don't worry, Kim, I'll get it back," I promised. I couldn't believe he had taken her television, even though I knew how important his television was to him. After all, he couldn't sleep at night unless he had it on. I had to laugh, though. At least he will have to watch regular television now. I'm sure they won't let him watch his porno flicks! I thought to myself.

That night I slept really good in my own bed, alone.

THE NEXT MORNING I WAS HAVING BREAKFAST WITH my Daddy when the telephone rang. It was Rick and he said, "Reta, you won't believe it, but Steve has the entire family, including Daddy and Mom, believing that you, me and Cheryl are making this terrible story up. Verlynn is even going to bail him out of jail!"

Verlynn was their older sister, extremely obese with long blond hair. She was a pretty lady and we had been good friends, but I couldn't imagine her being taken in by Steve again. I had just paid her back $1,700.00 he had owed her for years, and she had been so grateful.

"Rick, I didn't think he could get any lower, but I guess he can," I said.

"Well, Cheryl and I are going to the church today and maybe they can do something. I just wanted to warn you."

"Thanks," I said and we hung up.

Verlynn bailed him out that same day. Thank God I had the restraining order. Andy, Isabelle and Steve's other sister, Gwen—all came to the house later to get some of Steve's things. They were all so unfriendly, and Gwen even turned her back on me as she sat in the van. She was younger than Verlynn, but older than Steve. I had been giving her three children free dance lessons for the past two years, along with Steve's three daughters.

Finally, I had to ask. "Andy, do you really believe Rick, Cheryl and I made up such a hideous lie?"

"We intend to get to the bottom of this. I can't believe you had my son put in jail!" he snarled, anger in his voice.

"Wait a minute! I didn't have him picked up, the state did for all the back child support your lazy son owed from before he married me! I started paying it as soon as we were married. Believe me, I tried, but I couldn't legally do anything at the time!" I said disgustedly. Then I told him about Steve's threats about Daddy, but Andy continued to stand up for Steve. As the old saying goes, 'blood is thicker than water.' "Well, Andy, he is your son and you can't change that, but I certainly can change my relationship with him. Now, I'll get his clothes, and until you people come to your senses and start giving some support to Rick, the son you have that really needs you, then stay away from my home!" I was so angry! How ignorant they were to believe we would fabricate such a story.

I had always liked Steve's family, but I just wanted now to be free from the entire bunch. I would never forget what Andy and Isabelle had done for Daddy and me, but I was not going to condone their actions any more.

After they left, I called Rick and told him of the encounter with Andy and how his sister, Gwen, had acted.

"Did Mom say anything?" he asked.

"No, she just sat there almost in tears. I really felt sorry for her," I said.

"I think Mom knows the truth as well as Dad, but they are all scared of Verlynn," Rick said. For some reason, the entire family had always feared Verlynn, including Andy.

"Rick, I wish I could help you, but I have my hands full right now."

"I understand. I will handle this," Rick said, resignation in his voice.

"Let me know how it goes. As long as Steve stays away from here, there won't be any problems," I promised.

Rick was still with Cheryl and they were trying to work it out. However, I wanted only to wash my hands clean of the entire mess and concentrate totally on my family.

Karen came out to the house that night, and had told my band the good news. Everyone had been so happy I was rid of him. We had a few drinks to celebrate and then she left so I could get to bed early.

SUNDAY MORNING WE ALL GOT UP EARLY. DADDY looked great, and sat at the breakfast table talking a-mile-a-minute when I came in. I said, "Good morning, Daddy!" but he just answered, "Hush, Piss Ant, I'm talking."

"Well excuse me, I stand corrected!" I responded somewhat surprised, then kissed him on the forehead, grabbed a cup of coffee and sat down to listen to his most recent filibuster. He was jumping from one subject to the next, and if anyone said a word, they were told in no uncertain words, "Hush!"

When Pam and Kim came up from downstairs, I said, "Well, girls, he's all yours. Don't talk, just listen." Fred and I looked at each other and laughed, then gave them our chairs. We went down stairs to pack Daddy's things for the hospital. I just knew he would pass all the test and be admitted for total rehabilitation. I packed with that in mind.

About five o'clock we got Daddy into the car. We told Pam, Kim, Brad and Cheryl goodbye. They were all cheering Grandpa on as we left the house. We had all prayed Daddy would pass the tests. Brad had even assured me that he would stay at the house and if Steve should start anything, would call the police. I felt secure with him there, for I knew he would take care of my girls. I was so thankful to God for my little team.

Daddy continued to talk all the way to the hospital and clear through dinner. If Fred or I tried to talk, we were immediately told, "Hush." But when we got back to his room, Daddy got very quiet. Then he said, "I wanna go home!" Every time in the past when I had taken him in for an appointment, he got very nervous. I believe in his mind he thought I was putting him in the Winter's nursing home, otherwise known to the elderly in Winters-proper as "The Hell."

Later, after Daddy finally went to sleep, Fred and I were able to discuss the morning schedule. We were confident, especially after the long and talkative trip, that Daddy would pass all the test in flying colors. He had never been any brighter, his weight was just right, color good and the Lord knew, his speech was excellent! Just in case, I said a quick prayer anyway.

THE MORNING OF THE APPOINTMENT ARRIVED, AND we got Daddy up bright and early. His first appointment was at seven o'clock that morning, but we weren't worried—Fred had him on that same schedule for some time. We took him to breakfast, and I don't know who was the most nervous, me or Fred. I felt the same as I did the first time I took Pam and Kim to kindergarten. I wanted so much for him to pass all the test and be a good boy!

Daddy was taken from one test to another, and each time we sat and watched him fool the technicians. Questions he had answered accurately and completely for us, when asked by the technician, he would just drop his head as though he couldn't speak English. He wouldn't stand, push himself in his wheel chair or anything of the like. He wouldn't even talk to them or even to admonish all with a command, "Hush." I could have spanked him!

About lunch time, when we had taken him to get something to eat, I asked, exasperated, "Daddy, why are you doing this? You know how to do everything they've asked you to do!"

He said, "I wanna go home," then started to cry. I put my arms around him and tried to console as best I could. It was all very clear now. Fred and I were to be the only ones at Sister Kenny who would ever know how far Daddy had come back. I said, with a sigh of disappointment, "Well, Fred, you've done so good I guess you've got him spoiled!"

Daddy said, "Yeah! Let's get out of here!"

There were still more tests to complete, but we knew he was going to be as uncooperative in them as he had been all morning. Dr. Speier asked me to meet her at 3:00 p.m. in one of the conference rooms. We took Daddy for a cup of coffee and a big glass of buttermilk, then returned at exactly 3:00 p.m. We were ushered into a big conference room, and I sat Daddy at the head of the table and sat beside him. Fred took a chair on the other side of the room. I said, "Fred, you come over here and sit on the other side of Daddy. You know you're family now." He smiled from ear to ear and joined us, and Daddy patted his hand and said, "My ol' podner." If Fred was upset with him, it was all history now.

Dr. Speier came in and was followed by the heads of each department. I was so impressed to see how important my Daddy was to them. As they marched in and said, "Hello," Daddy looked at me, rolled his eyes and whispered, "Boy, Piss Ant, you're in big trouble now." I laughed out loud and said, "Don't you wish!"

But as they came in and sat down, I felt as though we were in court and Daddy was about to be found guilty. Then each department head gave their report and findings to Dr. Speier. Believe me, these reports were not favorable. Dr. Speier listened with total attention.

After all the reports had been given, Dr. Speier looked at Daddy and said, "Vernon, I believe you knew exactly what you were doing today. You could have done much better if you wanted to." Daddy put his head down like a child being scolded. She continued, "You would rather go home with your daughter and continue your therapy there, wouldn't you?"

Daddy's head popped up and he said with big eyes, "I damn sure would!"

"In that case, that is what I recommend we do," Dr. Speier concluded. She then looked at me and said, "Your Daddy has made remarkable progress. Even though he was uncooperative today, we could see the progress. You have done a wonderful job, young lady."

"Thank you, Dr. Speier, but most of the credit goes to this man sitting next to him, Fred." I told her how hard Fred had worked with Daddy and what a member of our family he had become. She then complimented Fred on a job well done also and he seemed to grow about four feet.

"I will make arrangements for him to have therapy at one of your local hospitals. Which one would you like?" Dr. Speier asked.

"Amery, Wisconsin, would be the best," I said quickly.

"We will also give you more material to work with at home. Vernon seems to be flourishing there, and I believe if we took him away from you, he would regress. The improvement we see in him has got to be the ingredient called 'love,'" concluded the doctor.

I thanked Dr. Speier and her wonderful staff for all they had done and especially for taking that kind of quality time for my Daddy. I was impressed with their facilities before, but never as much as I was at that moment. Appointments were set for the end of each month.

When the formalities were concluded, we got Daddy into the car and he was smiling from ear to ear. I looked at him and said with assurance, "We're going home now, Daddy, and from now on you can sleep as late as you want to."

Daddy looked back at Fred, and with a smirk said, "Did you hear that, ol' boy?"

Fred grinned back and said, "You betcha!"

To celebrate, we went to McDonald's and got Daddy a hamburger and fries. He loved junk food! I said, "Now, Brody, don't think you're gonna start eating like this every day, but some of the rules are going to be broken, and starting right now. We are going to get down to just plain livin'," but he was so busy eating that hamburger, I wasn't sure if he understood all I was saying.

AS WE HEADED DOWN HIGHWAY 35, ALL OF US WERE munching on our food, including Fred. The speed limit had just been changed to 65 miles per hour on this freeway, and I thought I was in the area where it had been changed. But as the little red lights started flashing behind me and in my rear view mirror, I knew something was wrong. I pulled over and the patrolman came up to the door. I said, "I was only going sixty-five miles per hour."

"I know, but that is one mile further up the road before the sixty-five mile per hour speed takes effect. Right here it is still fifty-five," the patrolman explained.

What a case of entrapment! I thought after he checked my driving record and found I had not had a ticket in over ten years, he would only give me a warning, but I was wrong. Instead, he presented me with a $45.00 ticket.

As I drove away, I was so angry I could have screamed. This was a total case of legal entrapment. I looked over at Daddy, and he was grinning and just munching away on his fries.

"What are you grinning about?" I asked, and Daddy just laughed.

"They gotcha, didn't they?"

I said in a teasing way, "If you think it's so funny, then maybe I'll just pay the fine out of your part of the money."

Instantly, Daddy's grin vanished. Now it wasn't near as funny. I said to Fred, "Can you believe this is the same man that didn't even know what a policeman was back at the hospital?" Then I looked back at Daddy and said, "Brody, you're dumb like a fox." He just grinned and kept eating those fries.

After some time, Daddy laid back and took a little nap. Before we got home, I had to pull into a filling station to gas up. I had put a cigarette out in the ash tray, or at least I thought I had. Daddy was still sleeping, so I got out to pay and Fred went in to get a soda.

As we started out the door towards the car, I looked toward the car and yelled, "My God, the car is on fire!" The whole inside of the car was so full of smoke Daddy couldn't even be seen. Fred and I ran to the car and I yanked the door open. To our surprise, there sat Daddy, happily puffing on that cigarette. He had pulled it out of the ash tray and got it going again. He looked up at me and said, "Now that was a good'un."

We were both so relieved the car wasn't on fire and that Daddy was okay, and at the same time realized how far he had come back. He had played possum until I got out of the car, then got that cigarette. He had come a long way from smoking straws!

Getting back into the car, we headed home, and after a long and grueling drive, capped by the ticket, we finally pulled into the driveway. The kids were all waiting for us, and when they saw us pull up, they all ran out to welcome Daddy back. They helped us get him into the house and unload the car. After we had gotten settled down, I filled them in on Daddy's activities. Pam shook her head and said, "Grandpa, were you naughty?" As innocently as he could he said, "You betcha!" Everyone laughed, glad to have him back home!

Before we all turned in, I said, "Fred, Daddy always sleeps till around nine, but from now on get him up for his medication at seven with a glass of buttermilk. Then he can have his breakfast when he wants to." Then I put my arms around Daddy's shoulder and said, "Well, Brody, you are now officially retired!" He looked at me and said, "Well, good. Is there a little boy's room in this place?" In unison we all said, "You betcha!"

Fred took Daddy to the bathroom, the kids took off in all directions and of course, I headed for the loft and the bills. I thought, "Now, maybe we can find some kind of norm in my home." And most of all, I was so proud of Daddy!

I STILL HAD MOST OF THE SUMMER LEFT, SO I CALLED Cords, my lead player, and asked, "Do I still have a job?"

"You bet you do!" he laughed. "When can you come back?"

"Where are we next week?"

After checking the schedule, he replied, *The Point,* in Grantsburg."

I promised, "Well, I'll be there," then we chatted for a while. Apparently Karen had kept them well up to date on the latest happenings and had even filled in for me singing a few times the last few months. Thank god for good friends!

By the time the news got around about Steve, I was got all kinds of calls of congratulations for finally coming to my senses. Even Cheryl called just about every day to fill me in on the latest gossip with the Anderson family. "Andy and them have almost decided to believe us, and even Verlynn is starting to wonder if she made a mistake with Steve. He has disappeared with one of their cousins who is married with two children! Rick attended a family gathering last Sunday after church—I wasn't allowed to go, but Steve came. The husband of the woman he was seeing said to the entire group, 'I would like all of you to say hello to the sorry sonofabitch who stole my wife.'"

Before she could continue, I interrupted and said, "Cheryl, I really don't care to hear about any of this anymore. It's not part of my life any longer." I excused myself and hung up the phone. I appreciated her telling me about Steve, but I was not interested in being her best friend and confidant any more. Enough was enough.

After I had hung up, I thought about Cheryl for awhile and decided to talk to Rick. I called him and said, "Rick, I don't want to be mean to Cheryl, but I would appreciate it if she would find someone else to cling to. I really don't want to be her friend anymore. It still hurts, and hurts too much."

"I totally understand," he said. Then he promised, "I'll take care of it."

A few days later, I was surprised when Andy and Isabelle pulled up in front of the house. They had come to ask my forgiveness. Andy said, "Steve has pulled the wool over all our eyes, but we know the truth now. We will support you one hundred per cent." They also informed me that Verlynn had seen the light, too. Apparently Steve had taken her to the tune of several hundred dollars which she now knew she would never see again. The church had even gotten behind Rick and now they were supporting him totally.

"Andy, I'm so happy you know the truth now. You and Isabelle are always welcome in my home. Thank you for coming out here to tell this to me." I then gave them a hug and they left. I truly felt sorry for them. They were good people and had been so wonderful to me and my Daddy.

DADDY WAS DOING SO GOOD. HE ADJUSTED quickly to his old routine, and we got him on a schedule for therapy twice a week at the Amery Hospital. Brad had put more mirrors and ballet bars up downstairs so Fred could work with him.

But Daddy fought Fred tooth and toenail about making him push himself in his wheelchair. Daddy refused to hold his right foot up with his left, as they taught him to do in Amery. I watched them work one day, unbeknownst to Fred. It was like watching the *Freck 'n' Frat Show*. Again,

Daddy wouldn't hold his right foot up. Fred said, "Vernon, if you don't hold that foot up with your left one, I'm gonna hogtie them together just like you used to do to those calves on the ranch!"

"Like hell you are!" Daddy said stubbornly.

"Like hell I'm not!" Fred replied as he took his belt off. He wrapped it around both feet, making good on his threat. Daddy was kicking and squirming, calling him every name in the book. I really admired Fred and appreciated everything he had done for Daddy. He just kept on working.

Finally, Daddy held his foot up and started cooperating. After that day, all Fred would have to say was, "Vernon, you want me to hogtie you?" and Daddy would immediately take his left leg and pick up his right leg. Fred was more stubborn than Daddy, and that's what it took, I guess.

But Fred needed rest, and I had him take a couple of days off. I could tell he was getting pretty burned out. He had already lasted longer at this job than is normal. "Fred, if you need more time, just let me know. I can get extra help or we can watch Daddy." He assured me two days would be enough.

While Fred was gone, I took Daddy out for dinner and a little socializing. He was also looking forward to going to The Point that weekend to hear me sing. Fred would be back in time for the weekend so he could take Daddy home after a couple of sets. We had a good meal and a great time.

When we got home that evening, I took Daddy downstairs to get him to bed. I looked at his waterbed which I had bought him that summer and recalled how much he had enjoyed it. I said, "Daddy, would you like to sleep in your waterbed tonight since Fred is gone?"

His eyes lit up and he said, "You betcha!" I transferred him into it, and he snuggled right down and groaned with pleasure, "This is the boss." He drifted off to sleep within minutes.

I smiled and knew Fred had just lost his bed. Also, I didn't know if we would be able to get him out of it the next morning. Oh, well, I thought, I'll worry about that situation tomorrow. Besides, Fred would be back before Daddy got up.

I set my clock for Daddy's medications at seven a.m. and went straight to bed myself. It was so nice to be able to turn on the radio to a good country music station and not have to listen to Steve's television moan and groan all night. Then I said a little prayer and asked God for guidance, and thanked him for bringing us this far. Like Daddy always said, "There ain't nothing me and you and the Good Lord can't do together!" I smiled and drifted off to sleep.

No sooner had I gone to sleep when the alarm went off. Groggily I climbed out of bed, got Daddy a glass of cold buttermilk and headed for his room. I whispered a quick prayer, "Please, God, let Daddy take his medications without a fight this morning." Sometimes he would take them without a fuss, but then there were the days he would spit them at us.

I blamed myself for him being that way, though. After the episode in 1984, I had really given him a stern talk about taking drugs he didn't know anything about and letting other people put pills in his mouth. I guess I did a better job than I thought. I believe that is why he fought us on taking his medications sometimes—he remembered that lecture back then.

As I walked into his bedroom, I saw he was still snuggled in the waterbed. I got him changed before he was really awake, as I usually did. Then I went out and came back in and said, "Good morning, Daddy, are you ready for a nice cold glass of buttermilk?" He never knew it was me that changed him.

The first time I had changed him he had looked at me and said, "Reta, what are you doing? You know that ain't descent." I had felt so bad that morning, so I devised this new method to change him. He would think it was Fred, Betty or one of the other aids. It was one of the hardest tasks I had to do for him, but it had to be done.

Thank God, Daddy took his medication without a fight. Otherwise, we had methods for camouflaging his pills. We would crush the ones we could and mix them with a spoon full of nanner puddin', which he dearly loved. The other ones we couldn't crush, we would punch a hole in the capsule and pour the liquid on to the spoon. If he were eating a meal, we would hide the pill some where in his food. Most of the times he would eat it. However, he was getting wise to us and sometimes he would hide the pills in his cheek then spit them out after we left the room. We were wise to him, though, for he only thought we left the room. We always managed to get them into him, although, sometimes it was a long procedure.

I handed the pills to him and Daddy put them in his mouth. This was the best method, especially after the lecture I had given him in 1984. He never liked any one stuffing something in his mouth, but then, neither would I. I tried to keep him as independent as possible and requested my aids to do the same.

I also had the aids let Daddy have a few drags off a cigarette if he got grumpy. If they did, there was not a problem, but if they didn't, they paid the fiddler. Daddy could get really hateful sometimes, although, I knew it was only frustration. Some times he just wanted people to leave him alone and they would finally learn that was the best policy.

Daddy and I were chatting while he drank his second glass of buttermilk. I asked, "How can you drink that stinky stuff?" He licked his lips and just smiled.

Just then I heard a car pull up and knew it was Fred returning right on time. He was still driving an old Dodge Dart and, of course, Steve never did any work on it as he had promised Fred he would in exchange for Fred helping him on his day's off. I said, "Daddy, one of these days you and I are going to do something really nice for your ol' podner." He took another sip of buttermilk and said, "You betcha! He's a good ol' boy!"

A few minutes later, Fred came bouncing down the stairs. He opened Daddy's door and walked in expecting to see Daddy in his hospital bed. Even though they were in the same area, each had a private entrance and could also close off the door between them. The look on Fred's face was priceless as he glanced at the empty hospital bed and then at the waterbed with Daddy all cozy, drinking his buttermilk. Fred bent over laughing.

After Fred collected himself he asked, "Is that your hospital bed now?" Daddy just laughed. Fred looked at me and said, "That bed nearly kills my back. I'll be glad to sleep in the hospital bed." Daddy quickly answered, "You can have that damn thing, I like it here!"

I said, "I know this would be great for him. Daddy has always loved his waterbed, and besides, we won't have to worry so much about bed sores!" Daddy had never had a bed sore yet, but we watched him constantly and made sure he was turned regularly. I also had purchased a pressurized mattress for his hospital bed which alternated air pressure every two minutes. "The only problem is getting him out of the water bed," I said.

"That won't be a problem for me," Fred said.

"Yeah, but you're over six feet tall. Let's see if I can get him out," I suggested. I looked at Daddy and said, "Okay, Brody, Fred is giving you back your waterbed, but you have to really help us get you out of there or we can't make the trade."

Daddy agreed to do anything to keep his waterbed. I sat him up, put the transfer belt around his waist and he pushed and tugged with me until we got him in the wheelchair. Actually, with his help, it was quite easy. I said, "Well, it looks like it can be done. I just hope Betty and the other aids are in harmony with us."

Then we took Daddy upstairs in his elevator. Fred put him in at the bottom level and I waited for him at the top. I fixed bacon, eggs and hot biscuits and gravy. Daddy got an egg twice a week, otherwise he loved oatmeal or french toast. Sometimes Fred would make Daddy his famous hole in toast breakfast. This consisted of cutting a hole in the middle of a piece of bread, dropping an egg in it and cooking it in butter. Needless to say, with all that fat, we didn't give him this treat very often.

After breakfast, Fred proceeded to get Daddy ready for his tub bath. I said, "Daddy, this weekend you and Fred are going honky-tonkin' with me, and I'm gonna sing you a song. Would you like that?" With a big grin he said, "Hell, yeah! You wanna go, boy?" Fred laughed and said, "You betcha!"

While Daddy had his bath, I poured another cup of coffee and called Don Cords. After some idle chat, I asked, "Do you think we could get together this week and go over a few songs and maybe finish working up that duet we started on before Daddy's stroke? It would be nice to be able to band stand it this weekend at the gig in Grantsburg."

"Just tell me when," Don said enthusiastically, so we set a time for the next day. He was going to try and get Donnie and Rick to join us, but if not, we could work things out on his flat top. I sang most of my duets with him anyway, and his voice was very compatible with mine.

When Pam and Kim got up, together we cleaned the house. I took the kitchen and they took everything else. They hated doing the dishes and would clean upstairs and down if I would take care of the kitchen. I said, "Heck of a deal. You got it." With in a couple of hours, the house was completely clean.

When we had finished cleaning, I decided to call and talk to Karen. She was glad to hear from me and I told her about my call to Bob Marcum. "I sort of look for him this weekend in Grantsburg," I said, "but I'm a little nervous. Sometimes I wish I hadn't called him."

Karen laughed and said, "If he's as cute as you said, and if you chicken out, let me know!"

It was so good to be back to some kind of a normal life, just like it was before Daddy's stroke when Karen and I got together almost every morning for coffee or we talked to each other on the telephone while we had our coffee.

"Do you hear from that sister of yours?" she asked.

"She calls about once a week and talks to Daddy, but very rarely talks to me," I said.

"Will Vernon talk to her now?"

"Sometimes he will until she's ready to hang up, but mostly he just hands the phone back to me while she is still talking. I know she thinks I tell him to do that, but you know I don't. I don't know why he won't talk to her. He finishes his conversations with every one else," I said.

"I just talked to her one tiny minute on the phone and that was enough to make me want to hang up. Has she always been so judgmental?"

"Karen, she has been the same toward me ever since I can remember," I said with disgust.

"Are you still reporting everything to her?"

"I call her if there is any change in Daddy. I wouldn't feel right about it if I didn't call her and Cecil. He's their Daddy, too."

"Well," she said with a sigh, "I give you credit. I wouldn't put up with her attitude more than two seconds!"

We talked a few more minutes, and Karen said she would try to make it to Grantsburg for my coming back party. Then we said "good bye" and hung up.

Glancing at my watch, I decided to go get the mail. I hated seeing it run because I knew it would bring me more bills to worry about, but I walked up to the mail box anyway and sure enough, a couple of my credit card statements were there.

As I walked back to the house, I opened them up—and almost fainted. I couldn't believe my eyes! Steve had taken six hundred dollars off one of them the day his child support payment was due. I had stopped paying his child support two month's ago, but he said he was paying it out of his garage money. The dirty little bastard had been stealing money to buy his supplies and now this! Evidently, he was taking what little money he made to entertain his sweat hogs. The transaction date was before I stopped him from charging, so there was nothing I could do.

Furious, I ripped open the next credit card, wondering what surprise I was in for next. This time Steve had taken a three thousand dollar cash advance! Horrified, I checked the date. It was the day he was having his fit and going to pull all the money out during my surgery—after I had called the credit card company!

I went straight home and called the credit card company, completely incensed. When I finally got one of their representatives on the telephone, I said, "I called you people and told you to remove my ex-husband's name from my credit cards. I even cut his cards in half, yet he has managed to draw three thousand dollars after this call!" The representative asked in a very unconcerned voice, "Did you write us a letter for your file stating this?"

"No! When I spoke to you, I was never told I had to write a letter. Instead, I was assured his name would be stricken that day and that I need not worry about it!" I said loudly, trying to control my temper.

In a sarcastic way she replied, "Do you know who you talked to?"

"Yes, someone with about as much intelligence as you!" I shouted as I lost my cool, then slammed the phone down. I was so upset I couldn't continue the conversation.   I didn't know what I was going to do. Murder was illegal or Steve would no longer be among the living—nor the idiot who was supposed to remove his name from my account.

Panicked, I called Don, my attorney, and told him my problem. He said, "Well, without proof of the conversation there isn't much we can do." He didn't seem to really give a damn either and I hung up and went to my room for a good cry.

After I realized that crying wouldn't help, I wiped my eyes, wrote a letter to the credit card company and tried to continue my day. I figured the only solution would be for me to keep making payments, and just hoped someday I could pay Steve back for all the hell he had caused me. God, how I hated him!

Gathering my emotions, I went downstairs to check on Fred and Daddy. They were getting ready to leave for the hospital for Daddy's therapy. After therapy, Fred was taking Daddy to the barber shop. He was bouncing back so well! Everyday, I thanked God that Daddy was okay and Fred was handling his activities for me.

"Daddy, after your therapy and haircut, would you like to take Fred out for a cup of coffee and pie at the bakery?" I knew how much Daddy loved to have his afternoon coffee and snack.

Daddy took his billfold out of his shirt pocket where I always had Fred put it and looked inside. Then with a very sad face he looked at me and said, "Reta, I can't do it 'cause I ain't got no money in my pocket."

I could have cried again. I said cheerfully, "Well, I betcha I can fix that! You have some money downstairs in your dresser drawer, and I'll get it." I ran upstairs and got a ten dollar bill and ten ones out of my petty cash drawer which I kept on hand for emergencies for Pam and Kim if I were gone.

I raced back down and said, "Here, Daddy, you put this money in your billfold and I promise, you will never be broke again! You'll always have money in your pocket." He looked at that wad of money, his eyes got big and asked in a serious voice, "Did I have that in my drawer?"

"You sure did, and there will be more if you need it," I said reassuringly. Then with a little help from me, Daddy got it all put into his billfold.

While Daddy happily opened and closed his billfold, no doubt checking the money, I took Fred aside and said, "After he gets his haircut, have him pay for it. Then, also give him the bill at the bakery and let him pay it, too. This will be good therapy for him to try and figure out the bill, plus count the correct amount of money needed." Then with tears in my eyes, I said, "Fred, please never let him be without money in his pocket. Let me know when he needs more!"

Fred promised me he would do all I asked, for he understood perfectly. He knew I wanted Daddy to feel like the man he used to be. Daddy had always been the first to have his billfold out in the past, to pay for entertainment or anything else. I couldn't believe I had overlooked this important detail, and felt so low for making Daddy feel like he had no money!

Pam and Kim went outside to help Brad build a wheelchair ramp off of the deck for Daddy, but he had already finished and was ready to come get us for the unveiling. We all went out together to see it and I said, "Daddy, look what Brad made just for you. You can try it out as soon as you and Fred are ready to go."

Daddy looked surprised and patted Brad's arm. In a husky whisper he said, "Thanks, boy," then looked at me with tears in his eyes and said,

"He's a good ol' boy, ain't he, Reta?" I gave Brad a hug and said, "One in a million!"

Brad shook Daddy's hand and said affectionately, "Well, you're a good ol' Grandpa!" Pam and Kim also gave their Grandpa a hug and said, "Grandpa, you're worth it!" then went off with Brad to start another project.

Brad was quite proud of himself, and rightfully so I think. He had done a great job on the ramp, but never received any compliments at his home for a job well done. In fact, his dad had called me once to tell me what a good-for-nothing Brad was. I had shut him up in a hurry. "Norm, you don't even know what kind of a man your son is! Don't ever call over here talking about Brad to me again! He is the son I never had and I am extremely proud of him and grateful for all he has done!" This ended the conversation and Norm never called again to put Brad down.

Brad's family wasn't a friendly bunch, and his mother, Carol, could have fit in very well with my sister, Yane, and the girls' stepmother, Shirley. I had often thought they should have started an organization called J.F.W.O.—Judgmental Frustrated Women's Organization! It certainly would fit.

Brad's sister, Barb, otherwise known in the area as "Barbie Doll" because she was so spoiled, worked for me a while with Daddy. She was a certified aid, but had such an attitude problem that I didn't keep her.

Shortly after showing Daddy the new wheelchair ramp, Fred and Daddy took off for their afternoon outing. I was so happy to think Daddy might start having some real fun now that he was improving daily. I still had high hopes of him getting out of that wheelchair and walking some day. My prayer had always been, "Please, God, give my real Daddy back."

After a while, the kids came in laughing. "Please tell me what's so funny," I said, "I need a good laugh, too." Brad explained, "You won't believe this, or maybe you will. No wonder the pump house blew away—Steve never anchored it to the ground in any way. It was just setting there, waiting for a puff of wind to blow it away. I'm surprised it stayed there as long as it did!"

I just shook my head. Kim said, "Mom, you wouldn't believe the stupid things he has done around here and the money he has wasted on materials he didn't even use." Pam jumped on the band wagon and said, "Yeah, that expensive wall paper he had you buy was laying under some of the deck material, all wet!"

Brad said, "Well, crew, let's get busy," and turned to leave. On his way out the door, he stopped and said, "I'm gonna have one of my friends who's an electrician come out and check over this cable Steve buried. Things don't look right the way he has wired this house, if that's okay with you."

"Thanks, Brad, I honestly don't know what I would do without you," I said, which was true. He hadn't stopped working since the day Steve was picked up. With only one arm and a hook, he had accomplished more in two weeks than Steve had in two months.

WITH EVERYONE GONE, ALL OF A   SUDDEN   THE house seemed so quite. I sat in Daddy's *Lazy Boy* for a few moments just to enjoy the infrequent silence.

Suddenly, the telephone rang, interrupting the peaceful silence, and it was Cords. He explained, "Rick and Donnie can't make it tomorrow, but I'll be there at three. The guys said to tell you 'hi' and they are really looking forward to having you back fronting the show!"

"You don't know how happy I am to be able to go back now, either! It will be the best therapy in the world for me," I answered.

After I hung up, I thought maybe I had better work a little on the songs I hadn't sung for so long. After all, I hadn't done an entire show since Daddy's stroke, only sat in sometimes with my band, Rex Cactus Band or Trigger Happy Band. All my friends had been so wonderful and supportive to Daddy and me.

I started working on the duet cords I planned to do that weekend. As I was listening to the music, I realized I was going to have to teach some country western dance classes along with singing in order to pay all the bills. Daddy didn't have that much left, and I had to keep his money to pay for the expenses of his needs.

Unable to concentrate anymore because of the money situation, I called a couple of the clubs we booked and made arrangements to teach country western dance classes in their clubs on the off-nights. I called the Inter-County Leader in Frederick and made arrangements for my ad to began immediately with classes starting in two weeks. A six-week course would take me up to the beginning of the fall dance sessions. I had wanted so much to not have to teach this summer, but thanks to that little weasel, I had to. What made me so angry was the fact that I would have to work to pay off the credit cards he had charged up again or risk ruining my credit. God, how I wished I had never loaned him the money for that joke of a garage!

My next problem was to find a cowboy to be my partner in the classes. Last August, when Daddy had come for his final visit before the stroke, I had talked to him about coming to live with us and working with me in the country western dance classes. He almost had, but changed his mind at the last minute. I wish he had stayed and took me up on it. Maybe he wouldn't be in this mess now. He would have been a wonderful dance partner, for after all, he had taught me most of my country western dancing years ago.

On its own, my mind drifted back to when I had turned twenty-one years old. Daddy had taken me to the Bad Lands in San Angelo to celebrate. I had never had a drink before in my life until then, and I ordered a malt liquor. The waitress wanted my identification to check my age. I guess I thought every one in the entire world knew I was of age because I had forgotten to bring it. She knew Daddy and said, "Can you vouch for her, Vernon?" Daddy had replied in a very serious voice, "Hell, Jerri, I picked her up on the road coming down here,. I've never seen her before in my life. You ain't gonna start me to lyin'!"

At my expense they had a little fun until I almost started to cry, then Daddy immediately told her the truth. Daddy said, "Now, baby, are you sure you want a malt liquor? It's like drinking three beers at one time," he warned.

"Sure, I'm twenty-one now and full grown. I can handle it," I insisted. Jerri laughed, then brought me my malt liquor and wished me a happy birthday on the house. I felt I had now reached total womanhood.

Daddy was so proud of me that night! When we walked in, all of his friends started looking our direction. One man came up and said, "Hey, Vernon, where did you get the little squeeze?" Daddy had looked at him with fire in his eyes and said, "She ain't no squeeze, she's my daughter and you best remember that!"

"I'm sorry, I didn't know," the man apologized.

"Now you know, so spread it around," Daddy growled and the man took off in a hurry. No one messed with my Daddy!

Before long, the band had played one of Daddy's favorite songs, other than Jody Blond, which was his very favorite to waltz to. He said, "Baby, let's do put your little foot," and started for the dance floor.

"Daddy, I don't know how to do that dance," I said reluctantly.

"Well, hell, come on out here and I'll teach you!"

I joined Daddy on the floor and within five minutes, I was dancing all over the place with him. During that night, he taught me the John Paul Jones dance plus a few others.

I was always so proud of my Daddy. He turned all the ladies heads and everyone loved him. He was always so kind to the elderly and would say, "Piss Ant, these old people have forgotten more than most of us will ever know. Listen to them and you will always learn something."

Daddy was still a handsome man, even in his condition. He still possessed that wonderful charm he always had, and I would give anything in this world if I could dance with him right then, or have a long, intelligent conversation with him. I sure could use his advice now!

The shrill ringing of the telephone interrupted my thoughts, and it was my attorney, Don. "Reta, you will need to be in family court next Tuesday morning at ten a.m. to meet with the judge. He will decide then if you keep the house until the final divorce or if Steve gets it."

I panicked. "Don, you do know about my Daddy, don't you?" He said, "yeah, and I'm sure it will go your way, but the judge has to make that decision."

I hung up the telephone. Surely the judge will give me the home under these circumstances, but the way things had been going, I don't know, I thought to myself. It seemed like Steve was coming out smelling like a rose on all angles. He had stolen money off my credit cards and his sister, Verlynn, had taken care of his fines. I wished I could just shut my eyes and he would be just a bad memory, wished I would never have to look at his face again or hear his whinny voice!

My mind switched back to my immediate problem—a dance partner. Unfortunately, none of my musician friends could dance that well, so I decided I would go to some of the country clubs in St. Paul that week and find a cowboy with potential. Then I could teach him the course and maybe work together for the remaining time left this summer. What a good idea!

With that problem on its way to being solved, I turned my attention to dinner. I made my famous hamburger hot dish for supper, the kid's favorite, then made Daddy a nanner puddin' with real whipped cream to keep his weight up. I really did enjoy my day alone in the house, even though the telephone kept ringing.

Sometime later, the electrician came and checked over "wonder boy's" electrical work. He said, "The way he has this wired, you are sitting on a fire hazard. The cable he has buried is not for under ground. The fuse box is a maize!" He just stood there in disbelief.

"How much will it cost to get things straightened out?" I asked, mentally preparing for the worst.

After he checked his figures and added everything up again, he replied, "Basically, it's like starting all over again from the pole. With materials, etc., I can do it for four hundred and thirty-five dollars."

I really had no choice, so I told him to do what he had to do. I knew with Brad supervising, he wouldn't take advantage of me. I sure was hoping the country western dance classes went well, because the money was getting lower and lower.

Thinking about money, I called Cecil and asked how the sale of Daddy's house was going.

"Marva Jean has been trying to find a buyer, but the market is so bad right now, we won't get much for it, maybe five thousand dollars."

"That is what Daddy paid for it in 1982, and I had it remodeled in 1983 plus you've added some improvements! This is terrible, but I know now, we are going to need the money. Daddy is improving daily and with each good report I get, I can get more assistance, but the supplies alone take his monthly checks," I told him. Cecil never mentioned the $1,500, nor did I. I knew he couldn't afford to pay Daddy back.

All we had left was the house, but with Daddy's improving like he was, I had high hopes of Kathy arranging for more grants to help us. She had said, "If Vernon keeps on the up swing I can do a lot for you, but if his health goes the other way, they will pull just about everything."

I couldn't understand how all these programs worked. I wondered Why does the government and state arrange for these benefits, then put them under a name where no one can find them? Some day I am going to investigate this and make public to all Americans what is available out there.

It is a shame some people are in the condition they're in and don't know of these programs. I just thank God for the guidance I had received, but felt bad for the many people out there that are still in the dark.

WHEN DADDY AND FRED CAME HOME, DADDY WAS completely pooped out. "Did you have fun? Your hair sure looks nice!" Daddy said with much concern, "My damned hair is too gray. I need to fix it!" Daddy always used Grecian Formula to keep the gray out, but when I was there I would put some color in it and dye his eyebrows, too. I said, "let me see what I can do about that, Daddy. Maybe I can fix it."

Fred said, "Everything went really good at the hospital. He's working well with the therapist. I had to help him with his payments at the barber shop and bakery, but he handled most of it, didn't you, Vernon?"

Daddy was not paying any attention. He looked at Fred and said, "hush," then asked me, "Is there a bed in this house?" Fred chuckled and said, "Let's find the little boy's room first, then I'll bet I know where a nice waterbed is." Before he went to bed, I reminded Daddy what a nice supper I had prepared for when he woke up.

I had planned to put a color in my hair before the weekend, but decided I would do it in the morning before Cords came over. Then I could do Daddy's at the same time.

When the kids came in, Daddy got up and we all had supper. I told them of my plans to color Daddy's hair the next morning. Everyone thought I was nuts, except Daddy. He was all for it!

THE NEXT MORNING, I GOT UP BRIGHT AND EARLY. I had everything out on the table when Daddy came up. I said, "Okay, Brody, do you want that damned gray taken out of your hair before we go honky-tonkin' this weekend?" He just grinned and said, "You betcha!"

Then I explained to him firmly, "Now, Daddy, you are going to have to sit real still. You can't put your hands in your hair at all. If you get this stuff in your eyes, we will both be in big trouble. The doctor would have a fit if he knew I was doing this. Do you give me your word of honor to be good?" He made a little cross over his heart and said, "You betcha!"

Then Fred sat down and folded his hands and said, "Vernon, you and your daughter are truly unique!"

I put the mirror up so Daddy could view everything I was doing, and the whole time he sat as straight as an arrow while I put the color on. He never touched his head once. I was so proud of him!

When I had finished his hair, I said, "Daddy, I will do your eyebrows if you will really be good." He promised, and I took a Q-tip and comb and colored his eyebrows. He didn't blink and eye.

Fred got his bath bench ready and took him in for his tub bath. We waited a little too long to get him in the tub, and his hair got a little darker than it should have been, but when he looked in the mirror he was so happy the gray was gone. He said, "Damn, that looks good!"

"I'm glad you like it," I said. I was quite proud of myself, for it had really lifted his spirits. Then I turned to Fred and said, "We'll have to wash it everyday until the weekend so it will lighten up." Fred agreed. He couldn't get over the difference in Daddy, either.

"Vernon, you look twenty years younger!" Confidently, Daddy said, "I know, ole podner!"

When Pam and Kim came in for breakfast, they marveled at their grandpa. Pam said, "How about a date with your granddaughters this weekend, grandpa?" Kim chimed in, "Yeah, we'll shake a leg!"

Daddy smiled and sat up extra high in his wheel chair and said, "If you're waiting on me, ya better wind up your clock!" Sometimes he would come back with the old sayings and it would really do my heart good. No one had the same slang as my Daddy, it was unique. Now he looked and sounded like my real Daddy. I was amazed.

"Daddy, you look plum spiffy," I said. He just grinned and said, "I know!" I decided then and there I would keep the gray out of his hair for the rest of his remaining days.

After breakfast, everyone went about their daily activities. I went up to the loft and got everything prepared for practice because Cords would be there pretty soon.

As always, Cords arrived right on time. Punctuality was one of the attributes he possessed, which was important to me and always necessary as a band member. I opened the door and there he stood with his old flat top guitar. The sight of him brought a tear to my eye, and he put his arm around me as we walked into the living room. "Are you okay?" he asked gently.

I said as I blew my nose, "Yeah, it just feels good to be able to get back to my music. I never realized how much I've missed it and you guys!" We had been together for almost four years.

Cords said, "I'm sorry we haven't been over to see you more or call, but none of us knew what to say. We didn't know how to make the hurt go away. All we could do was keep the bookings and wait for your return." I smiled and said, "You'll never know how much I have appreciated you guys," and gave him another hug. As I blew my nose the final time I said, "Enough of this mush, let's get busy!"

With a laugh, Cords pulled out his old flat top and started to tune it up as Fred wheeled Daddy in. Cords said, "Wow, you look good, Vernon." He hadn't seen him for a couple of months. Daddy looked at him and I could tell he was trying to figure out who he was. I said, "Daddy, do you remember Cords? He's my lead player in Pure Gold. You danced many times to his music in the past."

Daddy still looked confused and said, "I don't remember!" and started to cry.

"Hey, that's okay, Vernon, you haven't seen me for a while," Cords said, then he started strumming the guitar and singing. Daddy immediately reached for his harmonica which was setting on the end table.

I had placed his harmonica there when he first got home, but this was the first time he had decided to play himself. His oxygen level had gotten low a while back and Dr. Speier had given him a breathoscope. He was doing really well making the balls go to the top until one of the aids came to work one day and said, "Hi, Vernon, I see you're playing with your new toy." Needless to say, that was the end of the breathoscope—and her job. I had replaced it with his harmonica, trying to get the same effect, but had not had much luck—until now.

As Daddy picked up the harmonica, Cords smiled and said, "That's good, Vernon, let's jam a little!" All Daddy did was go "toot! toot!" but he was having a great time like he use to years ago.

Seeing Daddy play the harmonica sent me back to my childhood when I use to beg until Daddy would take it out and play some songs for me around the fireplace in our home back in Content, Texas... *Mother would sometimes sing while he played When The Role Is Called Up Yonder or one of the many other gospel songs she knew. He would play another tune and she would dance Put Your Little Foot, or dance a jig to Louisiana Gal, Won't You Come Out Tonight. She would often try to teach Cecil and Me the steps, but we were too little to do them right. However, we sure did a lot of jumping around. My Mama and Daddy were very affectionate and always let us know how much they loved each other. I had prayed to grow up someday and be happy like that, but unfortunately, this had not happened.*

Those where the happiest memories of my entire life. Since I became an adult, I've had to scratch just to survive and give Pam and Kim a good life.

My thoughts came back to the present, and Daddy had gotten so much oxygen into his lungs with all that playing that he put his harmonica down and asked, "Is there a bed in this house?" I laughed and said, "Sure is!" Cords shook hands with him and told him how much he had enjoyed jamming with him and that he planned to do it again real soon. Daddy just wanted the bed.

After Fred had taken Daddy to bed, I thanked Cords for taking the time out for Daddy. "Actually," he said, "I enjoyed it. I bet he was good at one time." With a smile I said, "If you could have read my thoughts during your jam session, you would have known just how good he was." Then we began to practice seriously.

We practiced until supper time, and felt real good about the duet. Additionally, we worked up a couple of new songs I had managed to learn during my absence. Cords said, "I'll fill Rick and Donnie in on the arrangements and we'll see you Friday night!" With that, he took his old flat top and went out the door.

I went into the kitchen, starved. Pam and Kim had made pork chops with biscuits and gravy for supper. Daddy was all refreshed from his jam session, and we all sat down to eat.

I always sat Daddy at the head of the table, and he had now started choosing the food he wanted. We would pass the food to him, hold the bowl or platter, and he would take what he wanted. I always poured the milk out of the carton into a glass pitcher for the table, while Daddy always chose to drink his buttermilk.

This time, the pitcher of milk was left by Daddy's left hand and I noticed him glancing over at the pitcher then back at his water glass. He also noticed us watching him. Fred started to move the pitcher, but didn't want Daddy to think we didn't trust him to pour. After all, we encouraged him to do everything by himself.

Suddenly I saw a little twinkle in his eyes, the kind I'd seen many times in my life when he was up to some kind of practical joke. He would reach for the pitcher, then pull his hand back. He teased us for two or three times this way. He knew we were all holding our breath.

Finally, Daddy finished drinking his water and ate a few more bites of food. We thought he had forgotten about the milk and went back eating ourselves. All of a sudden he reached over, took the pitcher and like a professional poured himself a glass of milk then sat it back.

All of us had sat very quite during this entire nerve-wracking time, and you could have heard a pin drop, for we just knew he was going to pour the entire pitcher into his plate.

After he poured it perfectly into his glass, he looked at us, laughed out loud and said, "Scared ya, didn't I!" I couldn't believe this was the same man who had been smoking straws a few months ago! Kim was sitting next to Fred, and she reached across and said with enthusiasm, "Okay, Grandpa, gimme a high-five!"

Daddy grinned, right proud of himself I might add, and gave her a big high-five. We all cheered him for a job well done, however, I hoped he wouldn't try that every day—I don't think my heart could take it.

After supper, we went into the living room and Daddy pulled out a cigarette, which I always let him keep in his shirt pocket like he used to. He took out the lighter I had given him without fluid in it, and instead of flicking it and thinking his cigarette was lit, he flicked it a couple of times and said, "Now give me a damn lighter that works!" I immediately got up and gave him a damn lighter that worked. For a moment, I thought he was going to tell me to get the belt, or just get up out of his wheelchair and get it himself. His mind seemed so much more alert since he had pulled in all that good oxygen! I told myself we had to keep it up.

BEFORE WE KNEW IT, FRIDAY WAS HERE. FRED AND I dressed Daddy in his black western pants, white western shirt, boots and, of course, topped the package with his white Stetson hat. His mind was so clear. I put cologne on a cotton ball and dabbed some under his shirt collar because he was allergic to most colognes. We could never put any on his skin. When he was dressed, I got his little gold mirror out that he used to twist his butt in front of back home before we headed for the Bad Lands. I said, "Daddy, look at yourself. You even have to admit that you look pretty spiffy!"

Daddy looked in the mirror for quite a while. He knew something was wrong, but I don't think he figured out it was the wheelchair. He finally said, "Damn, my hair sure looks better!" Thank God we had it lightened up some. I said, "Daddy, you visit with Fred while I finish dressing, then we will go honkey-tonkin'."

Pam, Kim, Brad and Cheryl had already headed for the club. They were helping with the Welcome Back Party the fans and Pure Gold had planned for Daddy and me. The party was supposed to be a surprise, but they never could keep a secret like that from me—I was too nosy.

Ready to go at last, we put Daddy in his little red Grand Prix. He looked at it and said, "Reta, this is my car, ain't it? How did it get here?" Another milestone was made! He not only recognized his car, but he knew his car wasn't where it should be.

"Daddy, I'm gonna have you playing that harmonica every day. The oxygen you get with all that puffing is sure making you smart!" I said. He laughed and said, "Reckon so."

On the way to the club, I was really feeling good. Not only was Daddy bouncing back day-by-day, but I was going to see some of my friends that I hadn't seen since I got back with Daddy. I looked over at him and he was checking the countryside out with every mile, idly chatting with Fred about the cattle they saw or anything else Daddy wanted to chat about. At least he hadn't told Fred to hush yet.

As they talked, I kept going over my songs in my mind. I was worried I wouldn't remember all the lyrics. After all, I really hadn't performed a full show for some time.

When we finally got to the club, I was really nervous. I just hoped and prayed I wouldn't hit any sour notes. We got Daddy out of the car and wheeled him inside.

As we walked in, we were greeted by a round of applause. Everyone was there—Karen, Rex Cactus, Louise (Ma), Lee, with my other little brother, Peter, the peanut gallery (the name I called all of Pam and Kim's friends,) my dear friend Joyce Ross, the Sanbergs, Arnie and Lila with their family, and last but not least, my dear friends Leon and Pat, plus so many of the wonderful friends who had supported me all through the years. The tears came and I headed for the bathroom to re-glue my eyelashes. The glue was not water proof.

When I came out, I visited with as many as I could before show time. Daddy was so popular, you would think he was the star of the show. I was so proud of him! He was shaking hands and talking to everyone just like nothing was wrong with him. I told Rex Cactus, Gregg and Clarion about the jam session with Cords and how much Daddy enjoyed tooting on his harmonica and about the improvement in his mind after sucking in all that oxygen.

Gregg said, "We are playing every Sunday afternoon now at the Straight Eight Bar which is just a few miles from your house. If you would like, we can stop by on our way to work and jam with him some of these Sundays."

"You guys are gonna make me cry again!   That would be wonderful of you," I said.

"We'll be there Sunday afternoon about two, since we don't start till four," Clarion said. I shook my head and said, "Thank God for friends!"

Then it was time for the band to start. Pure Gold took their positions on the band stand and Cords stepped up to the microphone. "Ladies and gentlemen! This first song is for our friend, Vernon Fuller, all the way from Texas!" and with that he immediately started singing, *Waltz Across Texas*. Daddy sat so proud with his Stetson totally straight on his head. How I wished we could dance, but I was thankful to God for what we had.   Like Dr. Speier had said about his unbelievable come back, *"The Ingredient Called Love,"* these words had to be the answer.

Then *Pure Gold* hit the take off to *They Don't Make 'Em Like My Daddy Anymore*, and the lead man said, "Let's please welcome back...Miss Reta Lee!"   At that moment, I never felt more loved in my entire life.   I grabbed the mike and said, "This is for my Daddy!" and everyone sang along.

Before the next song, I thanked everyone for their prayers, cards, love and support then proceeded to sing everyone's favorite song. For Pam and Kim, *I sang Bridge Over Troubled Water*. I could tell they were enjoying themselves, too.

After the first two sets, Daddy was getting tired.   I told him "Goodnight" along with the rest of the club.   He and Fred then left for home.

The night had been perfect with the exception that Bob had not showed up.   Karen asked, "Where is this Bob fellow?"   I said with disappointment, "I guess he didn't make it up this weekend."

Karen did not have a lot of admiration for any man, for she had been hurt too many times in the past.   She said, "You just got rid of one of those f-----s, give yourself a break!" she lectured.

"You're probably right," I said and we all went to *Wayne's Restaurant* on Highway 8 after we had packed up.   The party continued with our favorite waitress, Evie   The party finally broke up in the wee hours of the morning.   It had been a memorable night for me.

NEEDLESS TO SAY, THE NEXT MORNING EVERYONE slept in, including Daddy. Fred almost didn't get him awake enough to give him his medications.

At brunch, I said, "Daddy, did you have fun last night?" He looked at me totally confused and said, "I reckon." I knew he didn't remember anything about it, but it would be a memory for me the rest of my life.

That evening, the kids went to the *Tack Lo Ban Lounge* to hear a rock-and-roll group. They had been with me the entire night before, so I didn't feel slighted. They were my biggest fans, but all of their friends were not country and I wanted them to have a nice weekend, too, and be with their friends.

Daddy and Fred stayed home because I didn't want Daddy to get too pooped out, after all he had another jam session coming up tomorrow with Gregg and Clarion.

Fred reminded me that Betty would be there Sunday morning and that he was taking the day off to be with his children. He said, "Don't worry about getting up with Vernon in the morning. I will take care of him until Betty gets here at eight."

"Fred, some day I am going to pay you for what you are really worth, but I have to become a millionaire first!" I said. He smiled and said, "I'm just glad to see you smile more."

I got dressed, kissed Daddy good bye and told him to take care of the house and keep Fred out of trouble. I said, "Pam and Kim are out, so don't worry about them. They will be late getting in." He assured me he would handle things while I was gone.

I got in my car and headed for the *Country Dam* in Amery and talked to God all the way to the gig. "I know *You* are working things out for me. I am so thankful for the improvement in Daddy and for sending Fred to us and for giving me such caring daughters, but God, could you please help me get these bills caught up and stop Steve from taking any more from me?" I pleaded. And I must say I continued to fill God's ear all the way there, until I pulled up in front of the club.

As I got out of the car, I looked up and said, "Please watch over my family tonight and get us home safely, and please let me sing—on key." I walked in feeling much more relieved after our little chat.

I was glad I was alone tonight and didn't have to worry about anyone but myself. Somewhere, I had lost all individuality and needed to reclaim myself.

As I went on stage, said hello to everyone and took a quick glance around the club, I thought, *Maybe Karen's right. He would probably only hurt me if he showed up anyway, besides I'm not ready for any relationship other than friendship and something tells me he wouldn't be happy just being friends.* I put Bob out of my thoughts and concentrated totally on my performance.

Pure Gold kicked the show off as usual, then introduced me. We had a great audience, and it was so nice to be back singing again. The stage has always been my best therapy. I could totally get into what I was doing and let everything else, including Daddy, take a back burner. My mind needed the relaxation.

When we went back up on the third set, the audience was starting to feel no pain. I had only drank warm water and lemon during the show, but afterwards I would have a drink. But not too much since I had to drive home.

Right in the middle of singing Conway Twitty's, *It's Only Make Believe,* I looked down at the bar and there looking back at me was none other than Bob Marcum. I didn't remember him being that tall. He had black hair and that wonderful smile which had attracted me month's before. He was dressed very casual, wearing a red windbreaker. My mind went on auto-pilot to make it through the song, because I was trying to think what I was going to say to him. I felt like a silly little high school girl.

When the set finally ended, Uncle Bob, the manager at the Country Dam, handed me a Bacardi Coke as I came down from the bandstand and said, "It's on your friend down there." He pointed to Bob. I couldn't believe he remembered what I drank, and that impressed me. I said, "Well, hold the water and lemon, I need this one now!" He just laughed. I'd known Uncle Bob since I first came to this part of the country. He was well liked and respected by all the musicians.

After a swallow from the drink, I walked up to Bob. He said with a smile, "Hi, you sound great!" and squeezed my hand.

"I didn't know if you would be here or not," I said.

"Let's get a table," he suggested and he led the way to an open spot. We sat down and started filling each other in on the happenings since we had seen each other last.

Before I knew it, Cords said, "Let's put those hands together and welcome back our little China Doll...Miss Reta Lee!" Their break song was always China Doll and they used it sometimes to bring me up, unless I had given them the song I was going to start with. I had been so engrossed during the break that I had forgotten I had a band, much less what song I was going to sing.

As I got up to go sing, Bob asked quickly, "Could I buy you breakfast when you're done?" I looked back over my shoulder and said with a smile, "You betcha!" He jumped up and walked me to the stairs going up to the bandstand then took his place back at the bar right in front of me. I think that was one of the best shows I had ever done. For the first time in a long time, I felt attractive.

After the show ended, I introduced Bob to Cords, Rick and Donnie. They had told me that after I got rid of Steve, I had to let them meet anyone I decided to go out with. They wanted to meet him and make sure I wasn't picking another loser. After I had introduced Bob, I could tell they all liked him, as did all my other friends who met him later on.

We had a few drinks afterwards, then Uncle Bob announced, "The bus is leaving." Everyone knew that meant, "Get the hell out! It's time to go home!" I only lived about five miles from the Country Dam. I looked at Bob and offered, "If you want to come over to my house, I'll fix you breakfast there. I just want to make sure Daddy's okay." Bob understood and said, "Is there a grocery store open so I can pick up what you need?"

I laughed, "Welcome to Amery. The Country Dam was the last thing open in this area until morning. Don't worry, I have plenty of breakfast food. I hope you like bacon and eggs!" He smiled. "My favorite!"

BOB FOLLOWED ME BACK TO THE HOUSE, AND I thought, "What in the world is everyone going to think of me bringing someone home in the middle of the night, especially Fred?" Oh, well...

It turned out Bob really liked my home. He couldn't believe all the responsibilities I had with six studios, children, Daddy and the band. He asked in amazement, "When do you find time for yourself?"

"This is the first time I've taken time for me in a very long time," I admitted, then looked at my watch. "I guess between two-thirty and seven a.m." He laughed and replied, "You're quite a gal!"

I made our breakfast and he helped me clean up the kitchen, then we sat down in the living room and talked until sunup. Before I knew it, Fred came up to get Daddy's medication. He smiled and said with questioning eyes, "Good morning."

"Gosh, is it seven?" I asked surprised, looking at my watch to verify the time. Fred said, "Yep," and I introduced him to Bob. They shook hands and Fred continued with the medication.

"Bob, would you like to meet my family?" I asked. "They will all be up pretty soon."

"I'd love to," he said with a smile, and I made a pot of coffee which we both needed.

Out of the blue he asked, "Have you ever been up in a hot air balloon?"

"Not hardly. I've never had the time to do things like that," I answered.

"Well, it's high time you start taking some time for yourself. I'm going to Chicago next week. Do you think you could get away and go with me? I'll take you hot air ballooning plus many other fun things. I promise to have you back in time for your next performance," he said, and I could see the sincerity in his eyes.

I sighed. "Bob, that is so sweet and sounds absolutely great, but I can't leave Daddy that long. I would be worried to death!"

"Can't Fred handle everything," he asked, trying not to sound disappointed.

"I'm sure he could, he's quite capable, but I just couldn't leave like that," I said firmly. It wasn't long before my nosy daughters came up to see what was going on, and when they saw Bob, they were smiling with that look of, "We know what you're up to, Mom!" I introduced them to Bob and assured them we had been sitting on the sofa talking all night. They just smiled with approval and went in the kitchen to get some cereal.

"Hey, I'm gonna fix breakfast for everyone," I yelled out to them and Bob joined in, "And I'm gonna help!" That made Pam and Kim really smile. I said, "Why don't you guys go down and see how your grandpa is feeling this morning." They disappeared down the stairs, giggling like little girls.

Bob said, "They're beautiful, just like their mother," and I blushed. I tilted my head back and said, "Well thank you, kind sir, I needed that!"

Before long, Pam came running up to receive Grandpa on the second level. The elevator arrived with grandpa half-asleep in his wheelchair. He opened his eyes, looked at Bob and said, "Hi there, big boy!" We all laughed and Daddy started talking to Bob like he had known him forever.

As we talked, there was a knock on the door. I said, "That's Betty." Fred swallowed his breakfast and said, "I'm outta here. Vernon, I'll see you in the morning." He shook hands with Bob and said, "I hope we see you again soon. You look like you're good for Reta." With a wave, he ran out the door and took off for his old Dodge Dart.

Betty stood there totally confused. "What is the occasion," she asked as she checked Bob out. I'm sure she was shocked to find everyone up at 8:00 on Sunday morning having breakfast. All of us were usually sound asleep that time of morning, including Daddy.

I introduced her to Bob and she checked him over with a fine tooth comb. Finally she said, "Glad to meet you."

I reminded Daddy who she was and he invited, "Come on and have some vittles."

After breakfast, Bob said, "I better report in to my family over in Luck. They'll think I've been in an accident or something." I showed him the phone, and he called to assure them he was just fine.

The door swung open and in came Brad and his friend, Danny. He stopped dead in his tracks when he saw Bob. Quickly I said, "Brad, Danny, this is Bob. Pam will fill you in on all the details, I'm sure." Brad shook Bob's hand, grabbed his carpenter supplies and he and Danny headed outside to continue working on the house.

Bob laughed and asked, "Is it always this busy around here?" I jokingly said, "No, sometimes we really get busy!"

"What about that trip next week? You need a break even more than I thought," he asked again. My nosy daughters were still listening from the kitchen, and before I could say anything, Kim blurted out, "Are you going on a trip, Mom?"

"Not that it's any of your business, but Bob invited me to go with him to Chicago to hot air balloon next week." Pam joined in, "Mom, that would be great! We can take care of grandpa."

"I'll think about it," I said, then looked at Bob and asked, "Can I let you know later?" He could see I wanted some time to think about it and said, "Sure! Just call me whenever you decide."

Bob ended up staying until Gregg and Clarion came for Daddy's jam session. They met him and really liked him, too. He stayed and listened to their music and watched Daddy try to play his harmonica.

Finally, after what I am sure was an exhausting day, he shook hands with Daddy, Gregg and Clarion, then told Pam and Kim to look after me. I walked him to his four-wheel drive Blazer, and he took me in his arms, kissed me tenderly and said, "I don't know when I've had a more pleasurable time. You and your family are absolutely wonderful! If I don't hear from you about the trip, I'll plan to see you Halloween, if not sooner. I have business in De Moines and Dallas to take care of until then, but if you need me for anything, please call."

I hadn't felt so secure in a very long time and knew he meant what he said. I only wished this could be another time in my life where I would be free to go. I kissed him and said, "Thanks for being so understanding." He got in his Blazer, waved good bye and headed out the driveway.

As I watched Bob drive away, I stood there for a moment thinking how much I would like to take that trip, but in my heart I knew I wouldn't. I just wasn't ready for that kind of relationship yet. Somehow I knew Bob realized that, too. He was truly one in a million.

Back in the house, I joined in on the jam session. Clarion was picking guitar, Gregg was playing his banjo and Daddy was doing the best he could with that harmonica. Betty was sitting next to Daddy patting her foot, having a good time.

After about one hour, Gregg said, "Well, Vernon, we gotta go and get set up for the jig, but we will be back real soon." Daddy said, "You're damn good ol' boys."

Gregg and Clarion gave their approval of Bob. Neither of them ever liked Steve either. Clarion said, "Are you guys coming over later? You know we always like to have you join us."

"Well, I need to get a little sleep now, but we will see about later if Daddy wants...." Daddy interrupted and said, "Hell, yeah! We'll be there." I wondered why he couldn't want a bed this time. I thanked Gregg and Clarion for all they had done and assured them we'd be there if possible. Then I helped them put their equipment back in Gregg's old white van and they took off for the Straight Eight Bar.

Alone in the driveway, I looked up and said, "Thank you, God, for friends like them."

Back inside the house, to my delight, Daddy had changed his mind. He was now asking if there was a bed in this house. That reminded me that Betty didn't know about the waterbed and hospital bed swap. I said reluctantly, "Betty, there has been some changes since you were here last. Daddy put Fred in the hospital bed and he took back his waterbed." She started to laugh, "Vernon, did you do that?" "I damn sure did," he replied.

"If it's too hard for you to handle him in the waterbed, just let me know. We can put him in the hospital bed until Fred gets back," I said.

"I'll be all right," Betty said reassuringly. "Besides, I don't want to get on the bad side of Vernon." She patted Daddy's shoulder and asked, "Right, Vernon?" He very sleepily said, "Right."

Betty wheeled him out of the room and they went out the back door, down the ramp and in through the patio doors downstairs. Betty would not put Daddy in the elevator—the winch made a terrible noise and it frightened her. I felt the same way about it, and knew I had to get a different one before winter because using the ramp in the snow would be out of the question. I planned to change it to a quieter one with my enrollment money late in August. I sure wished I could afford the fancy one Yane thought I was going to buy.

Pam and Kim were busy outside working with Brad and Danny. I had told the kids I would have a house party when the house was finished—complete with Pure Gold set up and playing. I knew the guys would be happy to play and celebrate the completion of the house. They loved parties as much as I did.

Alone in the house again, I called Karen to tell her about my wonderful night. She was on her way to tend bar at *TJ's Lounge* on the lake, and asked, "Why don't you bring Vernon out for a while later and I'll make him a hamburger?"

"That sounds good, but the bed sounds better right now. I'll try to do that next Sunday," I promised. As I hung up the telephone, I just lay in my bed thinking about the past few hours. How I wished I could go on that trip, but I really didn't know Bob that well. I also knew I had better wait until after I went to the family court and got things more squared away with the little weasel before I left town. I could just see him finding out I was out of town and starting a bunch of trouble.

I was very tired, but before I could fall asleep, I decided to call Bob and make arrangements for Halloween. He was surprised and happy to hear from me so soon, and I thanked him again for the wonderful time.

THE INGREDIENT CALLED LOVE   169

Then I explained why I couldn't accept his offer to go with him on the trip. It wasn't that I didn't want to, it was just that I had unfinished business hear with the divorce and all, and he was very understanding. He assured me there would be other times, and I knew I had made the right decision in my mind, but not in my heart.

The weekend was over, and what a great weekend it was! I almost hated to get back to the weekly routine. With these thoughts, I fell into a deep and contented sleep.

I HAD MADE AN APPOINTMENT FOR DADDY WITH MY chiropractor, Dr. Gosso in Amery, to check his hip and back for an old injury. I had noticed Daddy rubbing his hip occasionally and remembered the fall he had taken back in 1983 when I was living next door to him.

That morning I had gone to get his laundry and found him sitting in the middle of his kitchen floor. I had asked in a panic, "Daddy, what's wrong?" He had replied with disgust, "Hell, I climbed up on the cabinet and was gonna get the curtains down for you to wash, but lost my balance and fell on my butt. I think I broke my hip." As I had run for the telephone to call Mike, the local ambulance attendant, I had asked, "Daddy, why do you do things like this? Do you think your a monkey or what?" He had laughed and said, "I feel like a pure idiot," then talked me out of calling Mike. He had said, "Oh, hell, I'll be okay. Just give me a few minutes." Daddy had finally gotten up and limped around a little until he decided it was okay and didn't need to go to the doctor. I had put up a argument, but as usual, he had won.

When I got Daddy to the chiropractors, Dr. Gosso checked him over thoroughly. He said, "I need to X-ray that hip, Mr. Fuller and see what we can do."

After the x-ray was read, Dr. Gosso concluded, "I can give him some relief, but I don't really see any injuries. I think it's just lack of activity." I was glad everything was all right. At least I now knew. He said, "What I would recommend is a good massage about once a week," and gave me the name and telephone number of a good masseuse in the area. He also recommended a variety of vitamins for Daddy. They cost over $100 to start, but I decided it would be worth it—I didn't want Daddy to have any vitamin deficiencies.

From Dr. Gosso's office we headed for Dr. Christopherson's office, the local eye doctor. I knew Daddy hadn't had an eye examination since Dr. Hale, his long time friend and optometrist, had died years ago.

I thought back to the last time we tried to get Daddy to a doctor or optometrist. During the last summer vacation Daddy had had at my home, he had stayed until I got home from the hospital after major surgery. Even though I tried to make him stay, he left for Texas when I got home. I had called Cecil and told him of my concern for Daddy, and we both agreed his memory loss was from the drugs taken in 1984. I then had asked Cecil to go to Winters and try to persuade Daddy to go back to Weatherford with him. I thought Daddy just might go and live with Cecil since he would still be in Texas.

I had also explained to Cecil how Daddy would skip his medication. I knew he hadn't seen a dentist, chiropractor or eye doctor in years, and hadn't had a general check up for years either. I had pleaded with Cecil to try and do something, if all possible. Cecil had said, "I'll try, but you know Daddy." I assured him if he had a problem with Daddy, he could call me collect from Daddy's house and I'd rag on him some more. I also assured him that Daddy wouldn't want to have another round with me like he had before he left Wisconsin. Cecil agreed with me, and told me he would leave for Winters the next morning.

The following day the telephone rung and an operator said, "Collect call from Cecil Fuller." I immediately accepted. "Well, I've been here five minutes and he's already mad at me. He says he's not gonna do all these things," Cecil said exasperated. I said, "Okay, you tell him if he don't take care of the things he promised me he would do before he left here, then I'm gonna let everyone know Vernon Fuller's word is no good." I knew that would make him think. He had never lied to me, and he prided himself on his word as being his bond.

Cecil had given Daddy the message, but Daddy didn't want to talk to me. He said in an angry voice, "Hell, write down Reta's 'want list' and I'll go today!" Cecil said, "Okay, I've got to get on back home. Now I'm going trust you to do what you said, and I'm gonna leave Reta's 'want list' on the table so you don't forget anything." Daddy had said, "Yeah, yeah," and Cecil left.

Cecil later called me, laughing like crazy. "Daddy thought I had gone back to Weatherford, but I went over to Marvin's house and waited awhile. Then I went back to his house, opened the door and there he was, still sitting in his chair and watching television. He jumped up and said, 'I thought you went home!' I told him, 'Okay, I'm calling Reta right now,' and he begged me not to. He jumped up and got himself ready to head for Coleman to see all his doctors!" Together we laughed, but never knew for sure if he had actually seen all of them. His excuse for not seeing his eye doctor was, "Dr. Hale died." I had told him then, "Daddy, there are more eye doctors in the area than Dr. Hale."

My mind snapped back to the present as we arrived at Dr. Christopherson's office. I laughed and said, "Now, Brody, you're gonna get the eye check up I don't think you ever had in Texas."

The doctor performed the test and Daddy couldn't read the letters, even with his glasses on. Dr. Christopherson made up new lenses, and I picked him out a new pair of frames. The ones he had were very old. With the new frames, he looked ten years younger. The Medicare only paid for the lenses, but the frames they would pay for looked terrible. So, for $75.00 I got the ones we wanted.

Daddy looked really spiffy in his new glasses. Everyone noticed them right away and complimented him on them. He would smile and say, "Well, thank ya, you must wear 'em sometime." I think he was pleased with them, too.

SUDDENLY, IT WAS TUESDAY MORNING, AND TIME TO appear before the judge and settle the house issue. I was glad we would finally get it settled.

I parked and went into the court house, and as I walked in I couldn't believe my eyes. There sat Steve with his new girl friend. He looked awful. He hadn't shaved or cut his hair in weeks, and his clothes were wrinkled as though he had just got out of bed. He probably had just risen for the day because his girlfriend didn't look too put together, either. She reminded me of Olive Oil, the girlfriend of Pop Eye. She was a skinny thing, with no make-up and hair just hanging where it fell. *How did I ever get tangled up with something like that? What a loser!* I told myself. Actually, I felt sorry for poor little Olive Oil, and said sarcastically to her, "I hope you have a good job. He's an expensive boy." She just looked at me with a stupid look on her face, and I wasn't sure if this wasn't his cousin! Actually, I didn't care. He was her expense now.

We went into family court, and the judge took his place. He asked who the woman was and Steve answered, "A friend of mine." Under my breath I said, "And she's an improvement over the rest of them." I was so embarrassed that Steve made me look like a loser, too, for having been married to him.

I told the judge about my family and how I needed the home to care for my father, and he seemed very sympathetic. Then it was Steve's turn.

Steve told the judge how very close he was to my Daddy and promised he would continue to keep my Daddy there and care for him if the judge would let him have the house. The judge looked at him quite confused and said, "Let me get this straight, Mr. Anderson. You want me to put Reta and her children out and leave her Daddy there on twenty-four hour care for you to take care of? Is that right?" Steve said with his famous whine, "Yeah!" The judge said, "I don't think so. I am awarding the house to Reta until the final divorce, then we will re-evaluate things then.

But Steve whined some more, "Can I go get some things?" The judge said, "You may go get some personal items as long as you make time arrangements with Reta." He looked at me and continued, "What day and time would be best for you?"

"Your Honor, he can follow me home right now and get his stuff. The sooner I'm done with him the better!" Steve agreed to come over immediately, and the judge reminded him of the restraining order and not to make any problems or he would visit the jail again.

Before I went home, I called to make sure Brad was there, just in case Steve got a little crazy. He was, and I warned him what was happening. Then I went straight home.

Brad was there and so was Danny, Rusty and Gator. I knew Steve wouldn't start any thing now. He pulled into the driveway and had Olive Oil still with him. They looked like they deserved each other. They got out and went into the garage. I followed them and said, "You have nothing personal in here. I have your clothes on the steps, and if there's something I don't have packed that you want, I'll get it."

Steve walked over to his clothes, followed closely by Olive Oil. He looked at his things and snarled, "I want to go inside and check for myself. I also want the luggage my sister gave us for a wedding gift!" I said, "Steve, you can have anything your family gave us or you, and just get the hell out of my sight."

The little weasel started in the house and Olive Oil started to follow him. I looked at her and said, "Look, lady, you're really pushing me. You get your skinny little butt in the car and stay the hell out of my way or I will call the police. You can have the useless bum totally as soon as he is out of my home!" She turned a little white and headed for the car.

In the house, Steve walked around like some peacock. He collected a few more items and took them out to the car. Then he stood out by the garage a while. He said, "I've got a couple of personal things out here to get. I'll go unload this and be back." I said, "You better get what you want today, 'cause this is the last time I want to see your face out here until the final divorce!"

A little while later, Steve was back with his big Indian friend and a pickup. They got out and headed for the garage and proceeded to start loading the $1000.00 air compressor I had loaned him money to buy. I ran out and said, "You sorry bastard! You're not taking that compressor or any of this equipment with you." He just ignored me and continued loading. Brad and his friends were ready to step in, but I said, "I don't want you guys to get into a fight. I'll call the police." I ran inside and called the police, then called Don, my attorney. I told him what Steve was doing, but he acted totally unconcerned. "We'll get it back at the divorce hearing," he said. I said, "That's not the issue! He is breaking the rules laid down by the judge!" He just continued to mumble and didn't seem to care if Steve stole everything or not. Maybe he had an important meeting to attend or maybe was late for cocktails. I hung up and went back outside.

The police arrived, and I told the officer what was happening. He said, "This is a domestic problem." Steve had him totally convinced I was keeping him from working. He whined, "I can't come out here and work 'cause she has a restraining order and now she won't let me take any of my equipment to work at my friend's garage. I have to work." I thought he was going to cry at any time. I knew his friend only wanted the compressor or whatever else he could get his hands on because he knew as well as me Steve had no intentions of working. He had already set up housekeeping with Olive Oil in the city where she had a good job.

The officer allowed him to take the equipment even though I told him the situation. Steve had him feeling so sorry for him. He loaded the compressor and few more expensive items he had purchased with my money. Then he looked sincerely at the officer and said, "Thank you so much for allowing me to get my stuff so I can continue the jobs I have contracted." I could have thrown up. I said turned to the officer and said, "Yeah, and on behalf of my family, thanks for allowing him to steal the equipment I paid for with my hard work!" I turned back to the weasel and said, "You better check your quality control. One of your customers called pretty pissed off! It seems you pinstriped one side of his truck and left the other untouched." I glanced back at the officer and said, "The next time you see this wonder boy, it will probably be to keep one of his customers from killing him. Believe me, they are all looking for him!"

The officer now looked a little confused. He didn't seem quite sure if he had done the right thing or not, but without my attorney doing anything, he only did what he thought was best. He looked at Steve and said, "Do you have what you need now to work?"

Steve whined, "I guess so."

"Good. Now I don't want to hear of you coming back out here. Get in your vehicle and go." The officer stood there until Steve and his buddy were down the road.

I looked at him, shook my head and said, "I don't understand the judicial system sometimes. Thanks for nothing." I walked back into the house, feeling like I had just been raped and no one gave a damn. If I could have afforded a new attorney, I would have changed gumshoes then and there. Unfortunately, I had loaned too much money to *Wonder Boy* for that damn garage.

Inside the house, I tried to lick my wounds. Brad said, "The sonofabitch, how can he keep getting by with screwing people like this?"

I said, "I don't know, Brad. Sometimes life seems so unfair, but it sure feels good to see the last of him. I only wish the divorce was over!"

A short while later, Pam, Kim and Cheryl drove up after the police left. They said, "What's going on?" I told them the entire story, and Pam said, "I wish I had been here! I would have killed him!"

"Actually, I'm glad you girls weren't." Brad and his friends had been enough to control Steve.

"I can't believe he wanted the judge to kick us out and let him take care of grandpa! What did he say about the credit cards he charged up?" Kim asked.

"Well, he couldn't do anything. I am still legally married to him. I have to continue to fight with the credit card company regarding this," I explained.

Fred and Daddy came up from downstairs. Fred had been working with him on some therapy after his nap. We all had supper together, then Fred put Daddy to bed.

After Daddy was in bed, I told Fred I planned to go into St. Paul the next evening for ladies night at one of the Country dance places and try to find a good dance partner to teach Country Western dance with me. I explained that I just didn't know of anyone in the area who could work with me. If they could qualify for a partner, they usually had a wife or girlfriend who wouldn't allow them to work with another female, especially an entertainer. Fred smiled and wished me luck. Then I reminded Fred that Daddy had a dental appointment the next morning.

THE NEXT MORNING, FRED GOT DADDY UP AND ready to go to the dentist office. Daddy was scheduled for a check up with Dr. Shootie, my dentist. When I had made the appointment, I had explained to him about Daddy's condition and also about the time he had bit my finger almost off when I tried to get a pill out of his cheek. Needless to say, Dr. Shootie was not too excited about that. "I will take a look and do what I can," he said with a chuckle, then continued "but I do value my fingers."

We brought Daddy in bright and early, and the doctor talked to Daddy for a while. When he asked Daddy to open his mouth, Daddy told him what he could do with all his instruments in no uncertain terms. Dr. Shootie said, "I don't think this is gonna work with him awake, and if he has a really bad problem then we would have to put him to sleep, but until then we will have to just let everything be." Daddy said in a grumpy manner, "Reta, get me the hell out of here before I kill 'em." I apologized for my Daddy's bad manners, but Dr. Shootie assured me this was not the first time he had been cussed out. Daddy finally did shake hands with him before we left for the hospital.

Next, we took Daddy to the hospital for his therapy. The therapist put him through all the paces and reported to me about the fine job he had been doing. We then took Daddy to lunch at Wayne's Cafe in Amery, then headed for home. Daddy was looking for a bed when we pulled into the driveway.

Once we had put Daddy down for a nap, I called the masseuse Dr. Gosso had given me the number for and asked her to come once a week to give Daddy a massage. She said she would start the following week.

Then I called Yane and Cecil to tell them of Daddy's progress. They had received their video of Kim's graduation showing Daddy's progress and were both extremely happy to see him look so good. I said, "He has improved so much more since the video. I will try to get a new video for you soon." I didn't have a video camera, but I did make duplicate photos to send to them periodically. Yane even seemed to care how I was doing, and it was a shame we couldn't be closer. I had needed her so many times throughout the years, but she had never been there for me. In fact, she always made things harder for me. With friends like her, I certainly never needed any enemies.

Cecil said, "Marva Jean has had a few good prospects for Daddy's house."

"Great! It looks like we are gonna need every penny we can get, especially if I don't get the enrollment I need for next year, due to the fact I was absent so much last year with Daddy."

After I hung up the phone, I went about cleaning up the kitchen then making supper. When Daddy got up from his nap, Fred brought him upstairs and we visited for a while. Then I served dinner.

Because of all the running around and the physical therapy, Daddy was still very tired, and after dinner, he went straight to bed. I thanked Fred for taking good care of him, then went to the bedroom to get dressed.

After I got dressed, I headed for St. Paul. I was looking forward to dancing, and wished Karen could have gone with me, but she had to tend bar again at *TJ's Lounge*.

On my way to St. Paul, I decided to stop at K-mart and get Daddy an electric toothbrush. Even though he tried brushing his own teeth, we still had to finish up for him, and I never felt as though we were doing the job good enough, either. Now that I knew the dentist couldn't work on his teeth unless he was put to sleep, I hoped the electric tooth brush would be the answer. He would only have to move it around in his mouth and it would do all the scrubbing!

Thinking about Daddy brushing his teeth made me go back in my memory to when I was a little girl standing out on the east porch at our farm house watching him brush his teeth. He always took extremely good care of his teeth all his life. He only brushed at night, but he would brush for thirty minutes. He used to say "Well, I gotta go brash my teeth and put these ol' bones to bed." Mother would correct him and say, "It's brush your teeth, not brash your teeth." He would laugh and say, "You brush your teeth and I'll brash mine!"

I found just the right electric toothbrush for him, and also picked him up some new underwear and tee-shirts. He had not been put in a diaper yet and, God willing, he never would. I would never forget how upset he had gotten over being put in diapers in 1984. Just in case, though, I bought some more depends then got some chocolate malt balls for Pam and Kim and headed for the check-out. I could hardly wait to see his reaction to the new tooth brush.

After purchasing my things, I got into the car and headed to the Country dance club. I got there just before the band started, and to my delight the band performing was none other than my friends, Trigger Happy, from the Amery area. They were surprised and happy to see me, too. Mike Murtha, the bass player and Eddie Schmidt, the lead steel and saxophone player, were studio musicians who had played on my demo record, cut live in 1986.

Right away, Eddie asked, "How's your Daddy?" They, like Rex Cactus and so many of my other friends, knew Daddy both before *and* after his stroke. I filled them in on his progress, and Mike asked, "Would you sing a song?"

"I'd love to," I said with a smile. Eddie requested, "Sing that one you did last time we were at the *Country Dam,* you know, the one you do for your Daddy." He hesitated as he tried to remember. I said, *They Don't Make 'Em Like My Daddy Anymore?*

"Yeah, that's the one! I like that."

"Call me up pretty soon, I'm just gonna be here for a couple of sets. I have to get up early in the morning and meet with Daddy's home care nurse," I said. Then I told them about looking for a dance partner. Mike said, "If we see a good dancer out there, we'll let you know."

I went and sat at a table close to the bandstand. Mike recognized me from the band stand right away and said, "We have a really good friend here tonight, Reta Lee! She is going to sing a song for you later." A few people stopped over to say hello, those who remembered me from

Countryside Magazine and when I had sang in the Twin Cities area. That really made me feel good.

Then Eddie went right into the steel guitar rag and kicked everything off. As I listened to their good country music, I remembered 1986 when I cut my demo record. We cut it live at one of the lake resorts. Eddie had come in, grabbed his saxophone, stood behind one of the speakers and played one of the nicest lead rides you ever heard. We took the recording back into the studio and decided to change the bass player. Mike Murtha came in and played the bass for both sides. After the session, I asked Mike, "How much do I owe you?" He had smiled and replied, "How about a beer and you get up and sing with us when you can." I had thanked him and promised I would always be there for his band stand.

I was happy I would be able to pay back that promise again tonight. I thanked God again for the wonderful friends I had, and have had through the years.

Then my mind wandered back to some of mine and Trigger Happy's dear friends who were no longer with us. Kay Kizer popped into my head first. He was probably one of the best musicians and singers I had ever had the privilege of knowing. He also produced my record in 1986. Unfortunately, Kay was killed in an automobile accident—hit by a drunk driver while on the way to a gig just a short time ago.

Next Curly Hastings came to mind, another wonderful friend and musician who had died of heart problems about a year before Kay was killed. He had been my manager and friend—and Karen's husband. I had met Karen through Curly.

The next friend I remembered was my husband, Ron Nicol who died from cancer a few years before Kay and Curly. He was the one who had brought me to Wisconsin and introduced me to all these wonderful musicians and friends. I have never found anyone else who could replace him on the band stand. We had our problems offstage, but up there we were unique.

The three of them are still playing music—only on a higher level. I had to chuckle as I thought of how God must have His hands full with the three of them. They were all such wonderful characters! My life was much more enriched from knowing them. Through losing our dear friends at such a young age, the bond between many of us had strengthened, such as Rex Cactus, the members of *Trigger Happy,* plus many more wonderful musicians in the area. When one of us had a problem, it became everyone's problem. This is the reason for the support I was receiving with Daddy.

My thoughts raced back as I heard Mike announce, "Let's put your hands together and welcome my friend and yours, Miss Reta Lee!" I stood up and went to the bandstand while Eddie kicked off *They Don't Make 'Em Like My Daddy Anymore.* I grabbed a mike and hit the band stand singing and followed with a couple more songs. Other than my friends, no one in the audience knew the true meaning of that song, and I thought, "One day I'm gonna thank Loretta Lynn for writing that wonderful song." She was, and still is, one of my biggest inspirations. Maybe someday, I can meet that super singer and thank her in person.

After I had finished my song, I danced a few songs with some of the men. The rat race was still the same, and most were still out there looking for a one night stand. The only one I talked to who was close enough to my area to work out for my partner was named Tim. I made arrangements for him to meet me at the *Country Dam* the following Wednesday to discus the classes.

Having accomplished what I had gone there for, I waved goodbye to *Trigger Happy* and headed back home.

IT WAS LATE WHEN I GOT HOME, AND I WENT straight to bed. I had had a nice evening, but was extremely tired.

I woke up to Daddy and Fred's chatting away at breakfast. I quickly got up, brushed my teeth—which reminded me of Daddy's new gift—then joined them. I gave Daddy a kiss on his forehead and said, "Good morning, Brody, how's my favorite Daddy this morning?" He grinned and said, "Fine, just fine, but this ol' boy is drivin' me crazy."

I then noticed Fred didn't have the sense of humor he used to, and asked, "Fred, are you okay?"

"Yeah, but I would like to talk to you later," he said.

"After Joyce and the masseuse leaves, and Daddy takes his nap, we'll have time to have a long talk." I knew in my heart he was going to give me notice. I was surprised he had lasted this long. I also knew school was getting ready to start again and Fred wanted more than anything to teach and coach again. Although I would miss him, I did want him to teach again. I just wished Daddy and I could afford to pay him more money. His child support took almost all his money each month, and his total social life consisted of the time he spent with his children.

Daddy finished his breakfast, and I said, "Now, Brody, I have a surprise for you," and wheeled him into the bathroom. There I gave him his electric razor and then pulled out the electric toothbrush. I said, "Look at this gadget! All you have to do is hold it in your mouth and it will do all the work."

Daddy looked at it with a suspicious eye, then took it. I showed him how to turn it on, just like his razor. He flipped it on and sat there and watched it wiggle. I said, "Daddy, put it in your mouth and move it around. It will do all the work." Quickly he put it in his mouth, but even quicker he pulled it out. "I ain't having that damn thing doing the jitterbug in my mouth," he declared determinedly. After that, he totally refused to use it—then or ever.

I was disappointed, but I gave him back his old, red toothbrush and continued with the tried and true method. I said, "Well, I've always wanted an electric toothbrush myself."

"Well, you can damn sure have that jitterbugging thing," he grumbled.

Later that morning, Fred answered the door and invited in Joyce Schaefer, Daddy's home care nurse, in for her weekly check up. She was such a nice person and was always there if I had a question. She laughed as Daddy filled her in on the jitterbugging toothbrush I tried to put in his mouth. You would think I was being mean to him. She checked his vitals and was really happy with his progress. I said as I patted Daddy's shoulder, "Is there anything we can give him for an attitude adjustment?"

She was more than pleased with the therapist report and our report of how Daddy enjoyed socializing. I said, "He would run the roads everyday if we would let him."

Just then the masseuse, Mary Christianson, arrived. She was young, had black, short hair and was a pretty little girl. She was going to school to be an Emergency Medical Technician along with her job as a masseuse.

Daddy and her hit it off right away, and as she gave him the massage of his life, he groaned with pleasure. Joyce said, "Well, it looks like he doesn't want to visit with me anymore," and said goodbye to Daddy. Then she reminded me she was just as near as the telephone if I needed her. I thanked her, and she left.

I then asked Mary how long she would be. "Oh, quite a while. I'm going to do some special things on his feet today." I looked at Fred and said, "Why don't we have our talk while Mary is here." He nodded and followed me out onto the deck.

When we had sat down, Fred sat there quietly for a moment. I realized he was having a hard time trying to give me notice, so I helped him out. I said "Fred, I know you're burning out on this job and need a change. I also know Daddy is hard to manage sometimes and tries your nerves. I am aware, too, you want to go back teaching this fall. How can I help you?"

He relaxed visibly and said, "God, I hate to leave you and Vernon, but I do need some time out. I want to start sending resumes to schools, maybe I can even get a part-time teaching job and help you part-time."

"Fred, I will run an ad immediately and try to find someone. I know I can't replace you, but I realize you need that time out. My copy machine is available for any copies you need to make of your resume or any of my other equipment." I gave him a hug and we went back in.

Mary was done with Daddy and he was passed out, as though she had been giving him whiskey. We walked out of the room, and I visited with Mary for a while and told her I was looking for a replacement for Fred.

"I would be happy to work part-time if you need me," Mary generously offered.

"Great! I'll see you next week and let you know my plans." Mary only charged $25 per visit, and I figured another $100 per month was worth Daddy having this type of pampering. Mary packed her things and left.

Upstairs, I told Pam and Kim about Fred's notice. They had noticed him losing some of his patience, too. We all loved Fred, but knew he had to take some time off.

"Mom, Lisa is coming back from California. Maybe she would be interested in helping us," Pam said.

"I don't know," I said. "I've never been able to depend on Lisa to continue doing anything very long." Lisa Clover had been one of my students since she was eight years old and her mother, Sandy, had been one of my best friends for a long time, too. Lisa had moved in with me two times during her twenty-two years because of problems at home, and each time it didn't work out. She was unable to live with my rules—which were very reasonable—such as going to school, getting home at a decent hour, etc.

"Mom, I know she would be good. Would you give her another chance?" Kim begged.

"I'll talk to her if she is interested, but I'm not promising anything as far as Lisa is concerned. I love her dearly, but I'm not sure if I would trust her with Daddy."

In the mean time, Pam, Kim, Cheryl and I tried to relieve Fred as much as possible with Daddy. He was going to stay until I found someone or made new arrangements.

In desperation, I called Kathy at social services and told her about Fred's leaving. I said, "I just don't know who I can hire for the kind of money we are paying Fred." Kathy said, "Let me do some checking, maybe with the progress Vernon is making, I can get a raise for his attendants. I'll get on that right now."

I started getting my enrollment forms addressed to be mailed out to my old students, and prayed to God all of them would return this year. I so needed the money. I was re-opening studios in Cumberland, Rice Lake, Clear Lake, Luck and Spooner. I had planned for Pam to run her own studio this year and Kim to work with me as Pam had last year. Hopefully, the following year, both Pam and Kim would have their own business.

The remainder of the day was spent upstairs in my office, while Pam and Kim were helping Fred with Daddy. When I came down, Fred was sitting in the dining room working on his resume. I asked, "Where is Daddy?" He said with a grin, "His granddaughters have him outside on the deck."

As I started for the patio door, Fred laughed and said, "I hope you're ready for this." I had no idea what was so funny until I got out side. There Daddy sat with headphones on, sunglasses and eating potato chips and dip. Pam and Kim were nearby, addressing envelopes for me.

Quickly I ran back inside, grabbed the camera and took a picture. Then I said, "Daddy, you're a sight for sore eyes. I hope that's country music you have on." Kim looked at me as though I was insulting their intelligence. "Mom, we know better than to try and get grandpa to listen to rock." I said, "Well, looks like yawl have everything under control. Just don't let him ruin his supper."

THE NEXT FEW DAYS WENT BY FAST, AND BEFORE I knew it, the weekend was there again. We were booked at the Foxhole Saloon in Lewis, and I had made arrangements with Betty to work the weekends for Fred until I found someone full time. I decided to let Daddy miss the gig Friday and Saturday, but planned to take him to *TJ's Lounge* Sunday afternoon for supper after we went to see Rex Cactus at the Straight Eight Bar. He had been sleeping quite a bit lately, and I was a little concerned about this and so was Fred. He said Daddy had not been as alert in therapy as he was before, and the therapist had told him, "If Vernon continues to be so lethargic, we may have to discontinue his therapy."

Before I left Friday for the gig, the telephone rang. I answered and was delighted to hear Bob's voice on the other end. He had just called to see how we were and wish me luck for the weekend. That call made my day!

Sunday finally came, and the weekend had been a success. I was feeling like the old Reta Lee again and was catching up with some of the happenings of my following.

Apparently, Daddy got up on the wrong side of the bed, and he was so hateful to Betty she put him back down for a nap as soon as he was done with breakfast. I said. "Let him sleep as long as he wants so he will be perky this afternoon and evening."

Daddy woke up about 2:00 p. m.   Betty was concerned about how sleepy he was too. I asked, "Daddy, do you want to go run the roads today? We'll go see Gregg and Clarion first, then Karen is gonna make you a hamburger."

"Hell, yeah! I'm ready." He was well-rested, but still a little grumpy.

We started to get ready, and Betty had Daddy's black pants, white shirt and boots on him, but he would take his belt off and throw it at her. She would put it back on him only to have him repeat the same thing. He was cussing her out and acting really ugly.

I walked in and said in an angry voice, "Daddy, what is the matter with you? Betty is only trying to get you ready so we can all go have a little fun this afternoon." I was standing to close to him and he lifted his left foot—complete with boot—and kicked me. I remembered what I had been told at Sister Kenny, if he does something to you, do the same thing back. Train him like you would train a child, so I kicked him back, but not anything like he had kicked me. He looked at me like he could kill me and kicked me again. I bent down and said, "Daddy, don't you ever kick me or anyone like that again!" At that moment, he slapped me as hard as he could across the face.

Stunned, I slapped him back actually harder than I intended to. I had lost my temper with him! He was acting like a spoiled child. He sat there for a moment and started to cry. He looked at me really pitiful and said "What are we doing?"

I started to cry, too, and said, "Damn, Daddy, if I know. All I wanted to do was take you out for a nice evening and you started being mean to Betty and kicking and slapping me."

"Well" he said, "let's straighten up and fly right," and then he started to laugh. We all joined in. I said, "I feel so bad slapping you, I'm sorry!"

"Me, too," he said, and we gave each other a hug and continued to get ready. Betty looked totally relieved after our dispute ended, and she put Daddy's belt on him. He was just as good as gold, totally over his temper tantrum—and so was I.

I felt so bad for getting that upset with him that I decided to see if I could find a support group for families under stress like I had been. I just felt awful for slapping my Daddy, even though he was out of control. I was still suppose to be the adult in this situation. I prayed for strength and patience. My relationship with my Daddy was so hard some times. Everything was totally reversed now.

After the incident, Daddy was in a great mood as we left for the Straight Eight Bar. We stayed for a while, and I sang Daddy's song, plus a few more. Gregg said, "We'll try to stop by and see you next week, Vernon." We stayed for one more song before we left and Daddy looked at me and said, "That old boy can damn sure sing, can't he?"

I said, "You betcha!" as we left for *TJ's Lounge.*

On the drive to the lounge, Daddy was just as alert as could be. He told Betty and me to "hush" if we tried to talk, and dominated the entire conversation.

Upon arrival, Karen opened the door for us. Daddy said, "Hi, Sissy, when did you get here?" He was so happy to see her. I said, "Daddy, don't you remember Karen? She only looks like sissy." He took a good look at her and said, "Hi, gal, gotta beer?" He knew he was in a beer joint.

I had checked with his doctor about him having a beer, and she had said, "One or two won't hurt, but not every day." I told Karen to get him a non-beer. He took one swallow and said, "What the hell is the matter with this beer?" I laughed, then said, "Okay, give him a Michelob." He was getting to where I couldn't fool him on anything. The only problem we were having was keeping him awake.

I sat at the bar with Karen while Daddy and Betty sat by the window looking at the lake. Daddy said, "Let's just buy this place, Betty. We could make a lot of money here." Betty played right along with him. "How much do you think we would have to pay for it?" Daddy looked around, evaluating the property and said, "Ah, hell we can buy this cheap." They continued for the next hour buying and opening their new beer joint. Everyone there was thoroughly entertained. He ate his hamburger and then asked, "Is there a bed around here?" I knew it was time to go home.

DADDY WENT TO THERAPY THE NEXT DAY, BUT HE could not wake up. The therapist said, "I hate to tell you this, but Medicare will not cover your Daddy's therapy any longer. He has to attain a certain grade in order for them to continue to pay. Unfortunately, he just can't seem to stay awake."

That news really upset me. I said, "He have an appointment at the end of the month at Sister Kenny. If they find out why he is so lethargic will Medicare cover him again?" She said, "In time, but it would be a few months and a great deal of paperwork."

"How much would it cost for me to pay it?" I asked.

"Twenty-five dollars per visit."

"Well, my studios start pretty soon. Daddy just has to continue this therapy. He didn't qualify to be admitted into rehabilitation." Tears formed in my eyes.

The therapist could see I was very upset and said, "I'll keep his time scheduled until you call me with your decision."

"Thank you," I said.

We took Daddy home and put him straight to bed, then I called Dr. Speier and told her Daddy was getting more lethargic every day, and about losing the therapy. She said, "Let's take Vernon off some of the medication, that could be the problem." She cut his Lopressor pills in half, which controlled his blood pressure.

The next day Daddy woke up and was back to his old self. The pills were just keeping his blood pressure so low, he didn't have any energy. I called the hospital and arranged for Daddy to continue with his therapy, at the cost of $200 per month.

Then I called Mary Christianson and explained why I would have to discontinue Daddy's massages until fall. She said, "Well, if you hire me part-time to help out, I can give him his massage as one of my duties." I said, "You got a deal. Betty doesn't want to work as many hours as she's been working." Mary agreed to start the next week.

Finally, I called Kathy to see how the financial help was coming. She said, "It's looking good. We can help you with the extra help until you get someone full time. However, we can't help you with the extra therapy."

Things were starting to get complicated like they were in the beginning. I just couldn't find good help for what we could afford. I knew I had to have everything worked out before classes started.

Lisa was coming home within the week, and I thought, "Maybe she has grown up enough to take a job which would require this type of responsibility." I hadn't seen her since she left my home the last time and headed for California. All I wanted her to do then was finish her senior year. She had been an assistant teacher at one of my studios, and therefore I knew she was a good worker—and a certified aid with experience.

Lisa had been working in California as an aid, and was a very sweet and loyal person, but I couldn't hire someone that might quit within a month or just leave me high and dry with no one—especially with classes starting.

I guess Lisa had confided to Pam and told her she wanted to talk to me about the job and would arrive the following week. I really had my fingers crossed that she would work out. After all, she was like family. But she just never could stick to anything for very long.

5

WEDNESDAY FINALLY ROLLED AROUND AND I decided to take Daddy, Pam, Kim, Cheryl, Brad, and of course, Fred, to the *Country Dam* for dinner. Afterward, they would take Daddy back home with them while I stayed and discussed the dance classes with Tim.

We got a big table in the dining room. Daddy took his place at the head of the table and was acting so normal that no one could tell he was a stroke patient. He took the menu and started looking it over with his new glasses. Brad said, "Grandpa, I really like your new glasses. You look great."

Of course, Brad's sentiments were echoed by the girls.

He beat his chest and said, "Well, thank ya. My daughter got 'em for me."

I just marveled at the progress he had made in the past few months. Things that were so hard before seemed easy for him, now. I had no doubt we could get him all the way back within the year. I looked around at my little team and thought to myself, *Daddy you're mighty lucky to have all this love and support.*

"Well now, Daddy, what do you want to eat? You can have anything you want."

As he sat there looking at the menu, you could have sworn he was really reading it. Finally, he said, "I wanna big ol' steak."

We all laughed, and I said, "You do realize that Dr. Speier only wanted you eating blended foods, which you haven't eaten since the first week anyway, and now you want to attempt to eat a big ol' steak?"

He looked at me like I was crazy to even question his ability and answered, "I damn sure do, and I want a some hot coffee, too!"

The waitress had heard about Daddy's stroke and knew the kids and me. She looked at me, then back at Daddy, shook her head and said, "I thought your Daddy had a stroke? He doesn't look sick at all, to me."

Very seriously, I said, "Well, we forgot to tell him and never allowed anyone else to tell him he was sick, so I guess he decided he wasn't."

Kim said, "Yeah, Grandpa, give me a high five!" He grinned and slapped her hand.

Then I looked at the waitress and said, "Would you please bring my Daddy the biggest steak you have, and if you burn it a little, he'd like it even better." Then, he finished his order with mashed potatoes and gravy. He had been eating so well, lately, I had taken him off all his weight gain foods and now his pants were starting to get a little snug but man he looked good!

Even though I told the kids and Fred to order what they wanted, they had all ordered the special. I know that they did that just to help keep the cost down. If Daddy had known how much that steak cost, he would have choked for sure, but again, we forgot to tell him. We had all decided, from the beginning, to spoil him rotten for what time the Good Lord gave him to us.

I remembered the many times I would go see Daddy and take him out to *Zeitner's Steak House* in San Angelo and buy him a big steak. He enjoyed steak so much. I would say, "Daddy, why in the world don't you treat yourself to a steak at least once a month?"

He would reply, "I just don't have that kind of money."

Then I would respond, saying, "Then take some of that money you've poked away for our inheritance and use my portion to enjoy your life more."

He would just say, "Now, I want to leave something to you kids from yor ma and me."

The total money he had saved for our inheritance, at that time, was about $5,000.00. This money could have given him a lot of steaks, but divided three ways, it wouldn't have been a great deal. We argued many times over this issue. Now, I'm happy he was able to put that back, plus add another $2,000.00 to it. We were sure gonna need everything we could put together to handle the load.

I made a toast to Fred and told him how much he was appreciated and how much we were gonna miss him. Daddy looked at him with sad eyes and said, "Are you going somewhere, ol' podner?"

Fred almost shed tears. I knew even if Daddy had been a handful some times, that he was really quite fond of him. I answered for Fred, "Daddy, he has some things he needs to take care of for a while, but he'll be back to see you often." Quickly, we changed the subject before we all got mushy. Fred had become part of our family.

Daddy ate every bite of his steak and never even burped. He pushed his plate back and said, "Larpenin' good!"

It was about time for Tim to arrive, so we adjourned to the lounge. Daddy took his medication and we had an after dinner drink while we waited for Tim. I had wanted the kids to meet Tim, but he was late getting there. At last I told them, "Well, Daddy needs to get home, you guys can meet him later."

EVERYONE HAD LEFT FOR HOME AND I SAT THERE talking to "Uncle Bob" while I waited for Tim to show. It wasn't long before the subject of Steve came up. Uncle Bob laughed and said, "Boy did he have it made. He would come in here and cash one of your business checks for fifty dollars once or twice a week while you were gone. I never even thought that you might not know about it."

I told him most of the nasty little story and he wasn't surprised at all. He had known Steve long before I had ever laid eyes on him. It seems that most everyone but me knew what a freeloader and loser he was.

Evidently he expected his ex-wives to live on welfare or some kind of government funds, that is if they could qualify for any. His first wife, Bonnie, worked and finally got rid of the parasite, just like I did.

After waiting for two hours, Tim hadn't shown so I called Karen and asked her to join me. I no more than hung up the telephone and Tim walked in. He had a good excuse, but I wasn't buying it. Punctuality was imperative when working with me.

In a conceited, cocky manner, he said, "I'm sorry I'm late for our date."

I sternly replied, "Let's get this straight right now, Tim. You're late for a job interview—not a date."

No way was I gonna get tangled up with another punk looking for a free ride. He ordered a drink, which he paid for, and I insisted on by the way.

Before long, Karen came bouncing in. She took a look at Tim and said for my ears only, "Not bad, but he's still a f---ing man." She laughed, ordered a Windsor Water and sat on the other side of the Neanderthal. After a few drinks, I must say, they were hitting it off pretty good.

I already knew there was no way, however, this man was going to be working with me. It was obvious that he was interested more in what he might get, instead of a job. Before long Karen told him off in her famous, well understood way. Turning to me he said, "Well, when do we start?"

I laughed and said, "When hell freezes over. You are definitely not what I am looking for in my studio. You would be trying to screw all the wives and girlfriends." Insulted, he stomped out the door.

Karen and I then ordered another drink and discussed what losers all men were. Uncle Bob teased, "I'm gonna stay clear of you gals."

Karen said, "Hell, Bob, we don't mean you, you're different. It's just all these dirty little f---ers we're talking about."

She took a sip of her drink, thought a minute and then continued, "You're not gonna hire that little f---er that just left, are you, Reta?"

I answered "No, I already told him to hit the road. If he acts like that in front of you and me, what would he be like with Pam, Kim, or my students. No, thank you."

JUST THEN, ONE OF OUR FRIENDS, GARY MILLER, walked through the door. He looked like he had lost his best friend. It turned out to be his wife. We had known Gary from some of the jam sessions, he played accordion and banjo. His wife would never allow him to stay too long at the sessions. He was a nice looking man, but not too street wise. He sat and had a Bacardi Coke with us and told us his problems. I sympathized with him and said, "If you need a friend to talk to don't hesitate to call me or Karen." They ordered another drink, Karen continued to listen and I headed for home.

THE NEXT FEW DAYS WENT BY PRETTY FAST FOR US. Fred took Daddy for his therapy and I was getting good reports again. The therapist applied again for Medicare to pay, and thought that they would for at least three more months. So it would be about three months before I would have to begin to pay for his sessions again. They wanted to be sure he wasn't going to regress.

We took Daddy down for his appointment with Dr. Speier. She was so impressed with Daddy's progress, but she actually never saw just how far he had really come back because, as soon as he entered the hospital, he turned into a very quite, scared and withdrawn person. I said, "I wish you could see him in action at the Country Dam." I told her about the steak and the way I was feeding him.

She just shook her head in disbelief and said, "As long as he doesn't aspirate, it's okay. He doesn't act anything like a normal stroke patient so it's got to be The Ingredient Called Love."

She was glad I was watching Daddy's calorie intake. After she weighed him she said, "Vernon, you're really porkin' out! You've put on fifteen pounds since I weighed you last."

I said, "It's from eating all that nanner puddin' with real whipped cream."

Sympathizing with him, I said, "Well, Daddy, looks like you're on 2 per cent now."

Dr. Speier agreed and made an appointment to see him again, in thirty days. She then decreased the dosage of his Lopressor, cut some more of his medications, and totally took him off other pills. She gave him a new prescription for a medication to calm him down during his temper tantrums, but after I started letting him have a cigarette every so often, we hadn't had a lot of problems. "Sounds like you have everything under control," she commented. Then she complimented Fred on a job well done and said she regretted losing him.

I told Dr. Speier how Daddy's attitude had become so rotten, lately and about the fight we had. She just laughed and said, "If that's the worse thing you've done, then don't concern yourself. However, we do have a wonderful support group for families of stroke patients if you are interested."

I said, "That's good to know 'cause sometimes I get as frustrated as Daddy."

"Vernon's attitude change could be from all the new aids working with him. He has gotten used to Fred and vice-versa, maybe he'll settle down when you find a full time replacement for Fred. This could just be his way of saying, leave me alone."

Daddy was quietly sitting and listening to every word we were saying. He looked at Fred and said, "Fred, you goin' some where?"

Fred patted his hand and said, "For awhile, Vernon, for awhile."

Next, we met with Dr. Petersen and he too, gave Daddy a clean bill of health. He was amazed, just like Dr. Speier, of the progress Daddy had made, and said, "You would never know by looking at him what a massive stroke he suffered. His Cat Scan doesn't look like it belongs to him.

Fred smiled and interjected, "The Ingredient Called Love."

Dr. Petersen agreed, "That's got to be the answer."

Before we left, he also made an appointment to see Daddy again in thirty days.

Leaving Dr. Petersen's office I asked, "Daddy, shall we go up to the fifth floor and see all your old girlfriends?"

I could tell his hormones were kicking in because his eyes got big and he said, "Okay with me." I knew he didn't know what in the world I was talking about, but I had promised his nurses on the fifth floor I would bring him for a visit, someday. We headed for the elevator.

I wheeled Daddy onto the ward and you would have thought a movie star had just arrived. Everyone gather around him and marveled at his progress. They all welcomed Fred to their little circle.

Marleen asked him, "Vernon, where are your Yankee Boots?"

He showed her his cowboy boots and said, "My Texas Boots, them damn sure ain't Yankee Boots."

Twila chimed in, "Boy, you sure do that Stetson proud these days." Daddy sat up even straighter after that compliment.

They all wanted to know everything, especially if he was still drinking buttermilk by the gallons. I assured them he was, but that he was going to have to cut down on his calories, because Dr. Speier had called him *Porky Pig*. Hearing this, Daddy said, "Yeah, I gotta watch my figure."

We had a really nice visit and, once again, told them how much Daddy and I appreciated the wonderful care they had extended to us last Winter. Marlene had a tear in her eye as she smiled and said, "None of us will ever forget the two of you."

Daddy also began to cry and said, "I'll never forget ya'll, either."

She and Twila gave Daddy a kiss on the cheek and Twila said, "Keep wearing that Stetson, proud."

Everyone had tears in their eyes, as we headed down the hallway. I turned Daddy around by the elevator and he gave his famous little wave. I told him, "Next time, you're gonna walk up here right."

He answered as usual, "You betcha." I will always love each and every one of people because of their kindness. All had taken that extra step.

We arrived back into Amery about 6:00 p.m. and as we were going through town, I asked, "Daddy, you want to have some dinner at the Country Dam?"

I knew he was tired, but also knew he probably was hungry. Answering me, he said, "It's okay with me, if it's okay with my ol' podner."

Fred said, "Fine, with me, I'm a little hungry too."

We got Daddy out of the car and entered through the door. As Fred wheeled Daddy in, I almost died. Jim Woodley, the owner of the Country Damn, had started strippers on Thursday nights. As we looked, there on the stage was a young girl wearing nothing but a smile. Daddy looked up and all of a sudden he wasn't tired at all! His hormones really started hopping. I don't think I have ever been so embarrassed in my life! I knew just about all the men at the club, they were usually there when my band played. I turned to Fred and said, "Fred, get him out of here." Fred was in shock along with Daddy. They were both staring with their mouth wide open. I think it had been just about as long for Fred, as it had been for Daddy, since seeing a girl in the buff.

All the guys in the club teased me saying, "Ah, come on Reta, let him stay." Daddy was certainly agreeable, Fred was still in shock but out that door we went.

Needless to say, the next time I saw Jim, I gave him an earful."

He assured me he was only going to have them on the weekdays, never on the weekend when the bands performed.

I said, "Well, that makes me feel better since we're booked here next weekend." He just laughed, thought I was overreacting, but then he wasn't a woman.

CORDS CALLED TO SEE IF I WANTED TO PRACTICE next week before the gig. I thought a moment, then said, "Great, when are you setting up?"

He said with a chuckle, "Oh, we thought we would go down there Thursday night!"

"Okay," I said, "I guess I'll never hear the end of taking my Daddy to see the strippers."

He laughed and said, "We heard about it at *Louis' Inn,* in Dresser. You're right! You are going to be teased a lot! Donnie and Rick can hardly wait to see you and start in!"

I said, "Well, I guess they can join the club. Pam, Kim, Cheryl and Brad haven't shut up since they heard about it. One of their friends was there when we came in, so they got a first hand report. Poor Grandpa and Fred will never live it down!

We decided to set up on Wednesday and practice. He was still laughing when he hung up the telephone. I had to even chuckle myself because I don't think I will ever forget the look on Daddy's or Fred's face.

I HAD ONLY RECEIVED TEN CALLS REGARDING THE Country Western Dance Classes. So many new couples were now teaching in the area that they had ruined it for the legitimate studios. They would go to the cities, take a few lessons, cut the class-time prices and take all the students. I decided to just forget it as I had already mailed out my enrollment forms and was starting to get enrollment money in the mail. We should be okay, I figured. The band had been kept working, steady, so I had made more money this summer than I expected.

ONE MORNING, I RECEIVED A TELEPHONE CALL from A man representing a medical magazine. He said, "I am interested in doing an article on your father and you. I have heard what progress he has been making through a man named, Rick, at the St. Croix Hospital."

Slowly, I answered, "Yes, Rick has been wonderful to help me with extra equipment for Daddy. He supplied me with a lift-out chair when Medicare wouldn't pay for it. Also, a pressurized mattress and suction pump at a reasonable rate."

He continued, "Why do you think your father has made such progress? What have you done different?"

I answered, "All we do is treat him as much like we used to as possible. I guess you could say it's *The Ingredient Called Love.*"

He then asked, "Would you be willing to start a journal, and I'll call again after the first of the year. Maybe we can get together and write an article for our magazine?"

"Sure, I have pictures from the beginning up to now of Daddy's progress," I assured him.

"That will be great. I'll call again after the first of the year," he promised.

I hung up the telephone and said out loud, "Well, Daddy, you're gonna be a star."

THE ENROLLMENT MONEY WAS COMING IN REALLY well from my Spooner, Luck and Clear Lake studios, but Rice Lake and Cumberland were very skimpy. I was beginning to worry.

Some of my parents had received calls from another studio in the area advising them I wouldn't be there this year. They had been told I was taking this year off to be with my Daddy. After having been absent so much last year, many believed this story. It looked as though they had hurt me more than I thought in these two areas.

PAM AND KIM CAME RUNNING INTO THE HOUSE yelling, "Mom, Lisa's here!" They had all been such wonderful friends for years. Even though Lisa was a few years older, she had been in the same dance classes with Pam and Kim when they were younger.

Lisa had been in touch with us off and on so she knew about Daddy's stroke. When it came time for Fred to leave, she had called and asked if maybe she could take over his job.

I came downstairs and gave her a hug. I was so pleased to see her and she was glad I had forgiven her for the way she had taken off, last time. She said, "I've really grown up a lot since I left here and I know I have to prove myself, but I will, you'll see. Her suitcase was with her, as usual, because she hoped to spend a few days with us. Also, she wanted some time to get to know the new Grandpa.

Lisa had known Daddy before the stroke, so she had an advantage over anyone else that might want Fred's position. She also knew what his personality had been like before the stroke and what kind of things he liked to do, plus some of his likes and dislikes.

Before we talked about the job, I wanted to feel more comfortable about her dependability. Another advantage that Lisa had over others, was that she knew, and understood, how time-consuming the studios were for me. When we had talked on the phone, she told me that she wanted to make sure she didn't mess me up, too.

FRED WAS BUSY GETTING HIS RESUMES OUT AND applying to different schools. Since he was busy doing that, we all were pretty much taking care of Daddy. Betty and Mary helped about eight hours a day and Lisa gradually began taking over a lot of the responsibilities. Pam was caring for him as well but Kim was still having a problem with the personal care. She had rather help by taking care of the house. The girls never changed Grandpa, I always took care of that because I knew how hard it was for me, much less his granddaughters.

AUGUST WAS ABOUT OVER AND I WAS STILL interviewing live-in help without any luck. If they qualified, I couldn't afford them. The ones I could afford, I wouldn't have. By now, I realized that I was hoping that Lisa would take the job. In fact, at the time, I didn't know what I was going to do if she didn't.

The weekend came and Friday night Lisa, Pam and Kim went to the gig with me. They were out dancing like they used to, resurrecting some of the old dance routines and were more entertaining than we were. They had a great time letting there hair down, so to speak.

Sunday arrived and since Fred was taking the day off and the girls all had plans in Amery, that left me alone with Daddy After Sunday dinner, I said, "Well, Daddy, it's just you and me. How about us havin' one of those father and daughter days out?"

"Hell, yeah! If you're waitin' on me, ya better run up your watch!" He was always sitting on Go.

I got him dressed in his usual attire and we headed out. First, I took him to the *Fon-Da-Rosa*, a petting zoo on Highway 8 near St. Croix. It would be interesting to see how smart he was at naming the animals.

I would say, "Daddy, what kind of an animal is that?"

He'd shoot right back and say, "Hell, Reta, are you stupid! That's a goat!" He named every animal there! In fact, we were looking at the bears and he exclaimed, "Dammit, look at that big ol' Grizzly Bear!" I was so surprised and pleased! He not only named all the animals, he named the genus families from where they came.

On our way out, a little donkey came over and tried to bite him. He slapped it on the nose like he used to correct the horses and said, "Get away from here you damn little burro." Well, he certainly passed his test with animals.

Next, we went inside the visitor shop. They had a Player Piano and Daddy insisted on playing it. I think he must have played every song on it and while the music played, he talked with many of the visitors. He seemed so normal, like his old self, almost anyway.

After that, we drove around for a while. You could smell Fall in the air. Fall was always my favorite time of the year in Wisconsin. I said, "Daddy, I'll take you to see the pretty leaves up north in a few weeks."

He said, "I'm ready when you are."

I really enjoyed the day with him. Even though he wasn't quite the same Daddy I had known before, I found that this new Daddy was also easy to love.

I had talked about things we used to do when I was a kid, but he really didn't understand most of what I was saying. It was easier, for me to pretended that he did because it made me feel better.

On the way home, we stopped at *Wayne's Cafe* on Highway 8 and had our coffee-time and a piece of pie like we used to in Texas. Then, we headed home. I got Daddy out of the car and into the house.

THE GIRLS HAD ALREADY RETURNED AND WERE in Daddy's room looking at some of his personal items I had brought back from Texas. They had his pictures out and were telling Lisa who the different people were. Some of the pictures were the last ones Yane and Cecil had given of their families. It was sad because they were of way back when their kids were babies. Daddy had many times asked for some recent ones, but evidently, they had not made any new ones. They had promised to send him some more up to date pictures but they never came.

I had put some of his smaller belongings in a cigar box. We then started going through it and Daddy spotted his little black knife that he used to always carry in his pocket. He said, "Hell, Reta, I want my knife back in my pocket!" It was closed, so I couldn't see any reason why he couldn't carry that knife in his pocket like he used to. After all, he couldn't possibly hurt himself with a closed pocketknife. It was fun as we continued to look through old memories. Daddy recognized many things when we went through his lock box. He started crying when he saw Mama's wedding band. He remembered so many things. At that moment, I was totally happily.

WHEN DADDY GOT TIRED, WE PUT EVERYTHING away and laid him down on his water bed for a nap, and then went upstairs.

Kim said with a twinkle in her eye, "Mom, Lisa has some really good news." Pam and Lisa were smiling from ear to ear, too. By this time, good news was a luxury. I knew by their looks that Lisa was going to take the job.

Lisa said, "Reta, if you'll trust me with the responsibility, I want to take care of Grandpa."

Right then and there, Heaven's Gates opened, and I was so relieved to hear her say that. "After watching you work with Grandpa the last few days, I know you can handle the job and I also know that Daddy likes you. Okay, let's do it!

"Thank you so much, Reta. I won't let you down." Lisa hugged me as she gave her promise.

Pam and Kim were happy, too. They immediately started planning all the therapy they were all going to do with Grandpa. Lisa would be doing even more things than we had been doing. I thought, Daddy will be in his glory with all this new, female attention. I once again looked up and said a silent, Thank you, God.

FRED CAME HOME LATER AND, WHEN TOLD THE news, was delighted to hear that Lisa was going to take over his job. I noticed how tired he was and said, "Fred, if you want Lisa to start sooner than the two week notice, just let me know. You are still welcome to keep your room for the remaining two weeks and Lisa can stay in the room with Pam and Kim like she has been."

With relief in his voice, he said, "Thanks, Reta. I appreciate that." I felt so bad for Fred, he still hadn't heard any good news back on a teaching job.

OVER THE INTERCOM, WE COULD HEAR DADDY talking to himself downstairs in his room. Fred went down to bring him up with us and I started supper. All of a sudden Fred came running up from the lower level screaming, "He's gonna kill me! He's gonna kill me!" He ran out the door and jumped in his car and locked the doors. I just stood there in shock, I couldn't figure out who in the hell was going to kill him. I collected myself and ran down stairs.

The girls had been in the recreation room and had heard the conversation between Daddy and Fred. They had already run in, assessed the situation, taken the knife away from Daddy and laid it on the dresser by the time I got there.

Daddy was sitting in his wheelchair with a totally confused look on his face. He knew that he must have done something dreadfully wrong to create all this commotion.

I yelled, "What is going on? What is Fred yelling about?"

Pam said, "Mom, you won't believe this, but Grandpa got that knife out of his pocket and opened it somehow with one hand. When Fred started to give him his medication, he got mad, pulled the knife on him and said, I'm gonna kill you, you son of a bitch, if you don't leave me alone!"

I was really upset now, but mostly with myself for having let him keep the knife. Never, would I have thought that Daddy could have opened that knife. In an angry voice I said, "Daddy, have you lost your mind or what?"

With sad eyes, he looked up and said, "I reckon I have," and started to cry.

Putting my hand over my mouth I said, "Damnit, Daddy! I didn't mean to say that." Feeling so terrible, I gave him a hug and said, "Daddy, it's not your fault. It's mine for giving that knife to you."

The kids all took over soothing Grandpa's hurt feelings and I went to find Fred. They made me feel like I was the Wicked Witch Of The North. When I left his room, Daddy was enjoying all the attention the girls were giving him.

FRED WAS STILL LOCKED IN HIS CAR AND SCARED TO death. Finally, he let me get inside to talk to him. He said, in all seriousness, "He was gonna kill me!"

I explained about the knife and how Daddy had got it in the first place. I said, "Fred, it's my fault. It never once crossed my mind that he would be able to get it open. In fact, I still don't know how he did it with one hand. That thing is hard to open with two."

Fred just sat there trembling. After a few seconds, he said, "If Lisa wants to start right now, she can." I hadn't realized, until then, how much this job was getting to Fred. His nerves were gone.

We sat in the car and talked for a while. Finally he settled down and I was able to convince him Daddy really wasn't going to kill him if he came back inside. He came in, had supper, and visited with us all for awhile. Then he finally went down, with me, to say good night to Daddy.

When he walked into the room, Daddy started crying. I said, "Daddy, it's okay, just tell Fred you're sorry and that you never really meant to kill him."

He blew his nose and made his apology, like a man. Fred smiled and said, "Vernon, I just need some time-out for a while. I promise I'll be back soon." He then packed his car and headed for his mother's home in northern Minnesota.

IMMEDIATELY, LISA TOOK OVER WITH GRANDPA. OF course, the girls all started calling him *Killer Grandpa*. Pretty soon, they had him laughing so hard and he had already forgotten about the knife and the incident with Fred.

Later, I put that knife so far back in the drawer he would never find it again, much less pull it on someone. I gave him a hug, kissed him good night and went up stairs to sit in Daddy's Lazy Boy Chair to try and relax a little. I just couldn't get Fred off my mind and how he had reacted. Even though this could have been a terrible tragedy, Fred had actually run as if Daddy were going to get out of the wheel chair and chase him. For a while, he had totally lost all reason.

I felt so sorry for Fred. He was one of the nicest persons I had ever known, and he almost wrecked his own health by trying to stay longer to help us out. I asked God to watch over him.

Later on the telephone rang. It was Fred and he was at his mother's home. He said, "Reta, I can't believe I acted like that, I'm so sorry. Is Vernon all right?."

I said, "Fred, you had every right to be frightened, Daddy very well could have hurt you bad, with that knife. If he had hurt you, I would have never forgiven myself. I still don't know how he opened it.

"That's okay," Fred said, "I can't believe he got it opened either. Under the same circumstances, I probably would have given it to him, too."

I said, with compassion and understanding, "You're just suffering from total burnout, Fred. They told me, when we left Sister Kenny, a job like this would burn a person out in about three months. You've been here twice that long. Don't you worry, I understand and so do the kids. You just get some rest and stay in touch, please"

Fred laughed and said, "I can't believe I actually thought Vernon was gonna chase me down and kill me."

I laughed too, "Quite frankly, you had me going when you ran up the stairs yelling, 'He's gonna kill me!' My first thought was that someone had broken into the house with a gun."

At least, now, we were able to find some humor in the incident and I said, "Fred, if you need a recommendation or anything, just let me know."

He thanked and assured me that he would if necessary. "Please let me know if anything should go wrong with Vernon, you know I care deeply about him." He choked up.

I said, "Fred, we love you, too. Now, call soon. You know you're part of our family."

I just prayed that someday I could do something really special for Fred because he was one of the most special people I had ever had the privilege of knowing and calling my friend. If he ever needed me, I knew that I would always be there for him, just like he had been there for us.

AFTER HANGING UP THE TELEPHONE, I WENT DOWN to make sure Daddy was okay before I went to bed. Pam and Lisa were sitting in the bed with him and Kim was sitting by the bed in his wheel chair. He was just talking a mile a minute. Since it was still quite early, I stayed to listen.

After awhile, I told them about Fred's call and of course by this time, Daddy had forgot all about the knife incident. He said, "Where's my ol' podner?"

I told him that Fred was away for awhile but would be back. Daddy asked me to tell him, "Hello," just smiled and started another story.

I said, "Well, it looks like you've got these kids under control, Daddy, so I'm going on up to bed."

Daddy paused long enough to say, "Good night, daughter."

It made me feel so good when he called me, daughter, I loved him so much. While I took a long bath, I had a good chat with God and really thanked Him for protecting Fred and for providing Lisa to take over the job. Next, I prayed that I would get a lot of students next week, on enrollment days.

I TURNED OUT MY LIGHT AND GOT INTO BED. A FEW hours later I heard a little knock on the door and Kim said, "Mom, are you awake?"

In a sleepy voice I answered, "I am now. What's the matter? Come in!" She and Cheryl came in as I turned on the light and said, "Did you guys just see a ghost? You're white as a sheet."

Very seriously, Cheryl answered, "We haven't, but Grandpa has."

Kim chimed in. "Mom, Grandpa just scared the crap out of us!"

I panicked and started getting out of bed when she quickly said, "Oh, Grandpa is okay. He's sound asleep, now, but Cheryl and I were lying in the waterbed listening to Grandpa talking in his sleep. He was having a conversation with some of his old friends in Texas. I went in to see if he was okay, and when I turned the light on, there he was, wide awake, looking around the room. I said, 'Grandpa, who are you talking to?' He said, 'Why, I'm talking to Ol' Shorty.' I then asked, 'Isn't Shorty dead?' He just grinned and said, 'Yeah.' I then sat down in the wheelchair next to the bed because I figured he was gonna start another filibuster. Then I asked, 'Grandpa, where is Ol' Shorty?' He smiled real big and said, 'You're sitting in his lap.' We were scared, so Cheryl and I both jumped in the bed with him. I told him, 'Grandpa, knock it off! You're scaring me! You know there's no such thing as ghosts.' He looked around the room and just started grinning in that mischievous way, you know, the way he grins when he's teasing, and said really slow and spooky, 'Oh yes there is, and when I die, I'm gonna haunt you, too!' Then I said, 'Now, that's enough,

Grandpa, you're scaring us!' He just laughed and went right back to sleep. Mom, do you think he was really talking to a ghost?"

Laughing, I answered, "Kim, Shorty's Daddy's old Domino partner down in Texas! He's as much alive as you and me! Daddy is just playing with you."

"But, Mom, he was so serious. Do you think that Grandpa will really haunt me when he dies?"

"Kim, if Grandpa haunts you, he'll only come back to tease you. Now you two get on back to bed before I haunt you." They just laughed and headed back downstairs.

I thought to myself, Daddy, you old rascal, you always did like ghost stories. I chuckled a little as I drifted off to sleep.

You see, I really didn't know for sure if Ol' Shorty was still alive or not, but I'll never tell Kim or Cheryl. I figured that Daddy was probably just paying them back for taking his water bed. Lisa didn't care to sleep in the hospital bed so Daddy had to go back to it. He hadn't really seemed to mind though.

I GOT UP THE NEXT MORNING AND BEGAN TO GET everything ready for enrollment days next week. It sure was gonna feel good to have money coming in again on a regular basis.

Lisa yelled out that she was sending Grandpa up in the elevator. I turned the winch on and as it started pulling Daddy up, I decided right then I was gonna order that new, quieter winch. Daddy arrived, and I said, "Well, good morning, Brody."

He smiled and said, "Well, where have you been?"

I said, "Oh, just here and there." I never knew what he was thinking, so I always gave him an answer that would satisfy him.

Pam, Kim and Lisa all came running upstairs to join Grandpa for pancakes. They were having such a good time and Daddy was in his glory with all this attention. He even seemed more relaxed. I looked at Pam and Kim and said, "Well, the kitchen is yours, I'm going up to my little hole and order that new winch." I figured it would be thirty days before I would have to pay for it on my credit card.

I called Stout University and talked with the inspector who had been in my home a few months back. He approved the new winch and said he didn't blame me for changing it, even though the old one was fine, just noisy.

I called the company where Steve had ordered the old winch and told them what I wanted to do. They said, "If you will send the old one back, we will refund your $405.00 and get the new one in the mail, today."

Since I had already paid off the old one, I asked them to mail the check directly to me. She said, "Well, it was ordered by Steve Anderson, so we will have to mail the check to him."

I explained the situation, by saying, "I am the sole owner of the credit card he used, I only added him to it when we married to help him establish credit again, so please send the refund to Reta Lee." She assured me she would make that notation.

After hanging up the phone, I went back to getting everything in order for the coming year. All of a sudden, Lisa screamed, "Reta, help me!"

I almost broke my neck getting downstairs. I ran over to the table, and there lying on the floor, still sitting in his wheelchair, head on the carpet with his hand propped under it and looking rather ridiculous, was my Daddy.

I knelt down by him, started checking him over and said in a rather stern voice, "Daddy, what in the hell are you doing?"

He looked up at me totally confused, shocked, possibly a little embarrassed and said, "Well, hell if I know!" He, then, just burst out laughing and we all joined in. He was a sight to behold! This was one time I should have gotten my camera, but I didn't.

We must have all laughed for ten minutes while we struggled to get him, and his wheelchair, back up in the right position and scooted back up to the table. Finally I asked Lisa, "What happened? How did he get on the floor in that position?"

She shook her head, looked at Daddy and said, "Grandpa was a really bad boy, he got mad at me 'cause I wanted him to take his medication. He got that left foot up to the table, some how, and gave himself a push. With the brakes set on the wheelchair, it could only turn over backwards."

I checked Daddy over really good. He seemed to be just fine so I scolded him, "Daddy, you could have really hurt yourself. If you had hit the corner of that end table or hit any harder on the floor..." I caught my breath and continued, "I'll be so glad when you quit having your temper tantrums. You're gonna hurt yourself or someone else."

He just sat there shaking his head, agreeing with me, as he plopped his pills in his mouth and swallowed them with buttermilk. I said, "Thank you. Now, wouldn't it have been easier to take them nice like that awhile ago instead of almost killing yourself and scaring the hell out of us?"

He was still agreeing as he asked, "Is there a little boy's room in this house?"

Laughing I answered, "I think we all need a little boy's room after that."

Lisa then took him to the bathroom. Pam said, "Mom, Grandpa could have really hurt himself if he had hit the corner of that end table."

"I know," I said. "His Guardian Angel has a full time job."

Kim teased Grandpa as she headed back to the kitchen to finish the chocolate chip cookies they were making for him. "I don't know about you Grandpa, I'm not ready yet to find out if you're really gonna haunt me, so will you cut this crap out, and be more careful?"

AFTER SUPPER, THE TELEPHONE RANG. IT WAS GARY Miller. He said, "Hi, you said to call if I needed a friend."

I said, "Yeah, what's up?"

"Well, I'm at the *Country Dam* and I sure could use a shoulder. I finally left Kathy."

I was tired, but he sounded so pitiful so I said, "I'll be down in about twenty minutes."

Lisa assured me everything would be fine with Grandpa. Between her and his granddaughters, they were spoiling him even more than he was before.

I threw on a clean pair of jeans, brushed my hair and took off. Gary was sitting drinking a Bacardi Coke when I got there. He said, "Well, the same thing happened to me that happened to you. Kathy is seeing another man."

I said, with a chuckle, "As far as I know, Steve was only seeing other women, but then, who knows."

Laughing, he said, "I didn't mean it that way."

"Well, It's food for thought, as Karen Dee would say. One just never knows, do they?"

Kathy was also a member of the Jehovah's Witnesses, so he, like me, would never have dreamed of this behavior from a devoted member. Needless to say, he was not going to study any more, either.

I said, "Well, maybe we better go to a good old Baptist Church this Sunday."

We talked for some time and then I said, "Why don't you come to the gig this weekend, bring your accordion and sit in with me and the guys."

"Maybe I'll do that. Could I take you to breakfast at Wayne's Cafe afterward?"

I said, "Sure, I'd love to." We had already decided that we were just going to be friends. That's all either one of us could handle at this time.

DADDY HAD THE SNIFFLES WHEN I LEFT FOR THE gig that weekend. I asked Lisa to keep a close watch over him and don't hesitate to call the ambulance and take him in if he got worse. My band was booked in the cities, so I would be two hours away. She assured me she would watch him closely. I told her I had planned to meet Gary at Wayne's after the gig, for breakfast, so I would be a little later than usual.

Lisa had started dating, Gator, one of the kid's good friends. I never knew his real name, we just called him, Gator. She asked, "Will it be all right if Gator comes out and visits with me? Pam and Kim are going with Brad to Somerset and Cheryl is visiting her mom?"

I said, "Lisa, that's fine as long as Daddy's taken care of."

BY SUNDAY, DADDY WAS WHEEZING, HIS CHEST HAD started filling up, and his mind wasn't sharp like it had been. He was also sleeping more and more. I called Dr. Rimestad and told him how Daddy was doing and he said, "Bring him in, immediately! We don't want pneumonia to set in." I knew pneumonia was a very dangerous thing for a stroke patient because they can't clear their passages like a normal person can.

I called the ambulance and they were there within twenty minutes. Mary was riding with the crew because she had to log a certain amount of hours on the job for her classes. She came running in, "What is the matter with Vernon?" she said, as she ran down stairs? I followed her closely and explained the problem.

They loaded Daddy into the ambulance and immediately started giving him that wonderful oxygen. By the time we got to the hospital, he was like a new person. He was alert and his mind was sharp as a tack.

They took him into the emergency room. where Dr. Rimestad examined him and decided to keep him a few days, just to be on the safe side.

Again, Dr. Rimestad, marveled at the way the diagnosis didn't match the patient. He said, "I have to admit, you're doing a great job with your Daddy, Reta."

I smiled and said, "Thank you, Dr. Rimestad."

As they got Daddy settled in his room, I remembered how Dr. Rimestad had acted toward me a few months ago when had I called him about a problem Daddy was having. He had said sarcastically, "Well, Reta, this is what happens when we try to play nurse."

I had given him an ear full then when he suggested I put my Dad in a nursing home, and he had never brought it up again. The confidence he obviously had in me, now, certainly made me feel good. I told Dr. Rimestad the amounts of medication Dr. Speier had cut Daddy down to. Then he gave these instructions to the head nurse.

When Daddy was comfortable, I went home, got Daddy some clean underwear, picked up Lisa and returned to the hospital.

I informed the nurses regarding his bathroom behavior and told them how hard we had worked with Daddy to tell us when he needed to go. Also, I told them, "Under no circumstances do I want him put in diapers." I had brought a box of Depends and showed them how we put them in his underwear in case he didn't tell us in time.

"Instead of saying, Is there a little boy's room around here?, sometimes he will say, I gotta go doors, I told the nurses so that it would help them in dealing with him. This went back to his childhood when they had to go outdoors to the bathroom.

I also brought him a carton of fresh buttermilk and advised them about his love for this stuff. Then I stayed until Daddy was tucked in. Before I left, I introduced Lisa to the nurses and said, "I have enrollment at my studios this week, so if my Daddy needs anything, call her first, before you call the studio."

They were very nice and assured me they would follow everything to the letter. Since there were only a few patients on the ward, I was sure Daddy would be well taken care of. After all, I was totally happy with the Therapy Department.

Early the next morning, I called the hospital to check on Daddy. They informed me Daddy had a good night and had eaten a good breakfast. I reminded them to give him his suppository about 9:30 a.m. We gave him one every other day and had not had any problems. The nurse assured me this would all be done according to my instructions.

Next I asked, "Were the changes in Daddy's medication dosages recorded correctly in his chart?"

As if I had insulted her, she said, "Well, I'm sure it has been."

With a bit sterner voice I asked, "Will you please check to make sure. This is very important."

She read back the dosages listed on Daddy's chart, and what they were giving him. In a panic I said, "Just what I thought, those are the old dosages!"

I quickly gave her the correct amounts, again. She said, with authority, "Well, I'm not allowed to change the chart. You will have to take that up with Dr. Rimestad."

Quickly, I hung up the telephone and called Dr. Rimestad office. He was not there, but at the hospital. His secretary assured me she would take care of this matter, immediately.

I finished getting ready to go to Rice Lake. As I went into the kitchen and poured another cup of coffee, Karen pulled up in front of the house. She was going with us to help with the measurement of shoes, batons, etc. She came in, grabbed a cup of coffee, which I had already poured, and said, "I want you to know this the supreme sacrifice on my part. Because you know how I feel about those damn little rug rats."

Laughing, I said, "But you don't know how much I appreciate your help."

She said with concern, "How is Vernon?"

I told her about the medication dosage problem I was having with them.

"I can believe that, you have to watch them like a hawk," she said.

"What is it with these hospitals? In Winters, Texas, Dr. Lee didn't seem to give a damn about my Daddy. Then, I took him to Abilene. There the nurses were very caring, but the big wigs had cut out their *Certified Aid Program* so that they didn't have the time to care for him properly." I got so mad thinking about these instances that I started to cry, saying, "If it wasn't for the wonderful care he received at Abbott-Northwestern, I would believe that all these damn hospitals are good for is to take people's money and could care less about the patient's needs, especially if they are elderly or incapable of telling anyone what's going on." I took a deep breath, blew my nose and continued my diatribe, "Florence Nightingale would turn over in her grave if she could see how some of these hospitals treat people."

Karen said in a joking way, "Correct me if I'm wrong, but I would say you're a little upset, right?"

We both started laughing and I said, "Thanks, buddy, I needed that."

Pam and Kim came upstairs ready for the big day. We were all going to Rice Lake, and then over to Cumberland for enrollment day. We started loading the car and Karen could see I was still very upset. She said, "Why don't I take everything in my car, you go check on your Daddy and meet us over there as soon as possible."

I looked at Pam and Kim and said, "Do you think you can handle it for awhile? I will be there before noon."

Pam said, "Mom, we're not babies. We'll be just fine."

Kim agreed and said, "Give Grandpa a hug for us and tell him to get his butt home."

I gave them all a hug, jumped in my car and took off for the hospital. I was sure everything would be okay and then I could leave right away for Rice Lake and not miss anything. I really needed to be there, especially with everyone questioning my attendance for the coming year.

I parked the car and ran into the hospital. The nurses hadn't expected to see me until evening because I had told them that I would be taking enrollment all day. As I walked down the hallway I saw at least six nurses standing around their station talking and laughing. Daddy's room was the first one by the station. They looked rather surprised when I walked by them and said, "Good morning, I just wanted to check with Daddy before I leave for Rice Lake."

I continued on into Daddy's room. They just looked at me like they had seen a ghost themselves. When I entered Daddy's room, I knew why they looked at me that way.

I stopped dead in my tracks. My Daddy was lying half out of the bed, wearing a diaper and had feces on his hands and body where he had tried to get his underwear down and then find the little boy's room. He could see the bathroom from his bed and knew where he had to go, but obviously, they had ignored everything I had told them and had decided to just put a diaper on him and change him later.

I totally lost control. I yelled at the nurses, as I grabbed Daddy's wheel chair, sat him up on the side of the bed and began putting my transfer belt around him, which I always carried in my purse. The head nurse came running in to see what I was yelling about and she was followed by another nurse pushing a potty chair .

They knew exactly what I was yelling about, that's why they had a portable potty chair in tow. "What in the hell is the matter with you people?" I screamed "Can't you see he needs help? What did you do, put the suppository in, throw on a diaper and then go take your coffee break?" I was so mad I started crying and yelling at the same time. "I told them, when he was admitted yesterday, exactly how to handle this and how hard we've worked to get him to tell us when he needs to go to the bathroom, and now you leave him in here like an animal or something." Daddy was dittoing about every word I was saying, only using some of his special adjectives.

By the time I got through with my speech, just about every nurse on the ward was in Daddy's room and Daddy was sitting on the potty chair completing his business. I didn't have time to get him to the bathroom where he could have some privacy.

The head nurse looked daggers at me and said, in her most authoritative voice, "You can't be handling your Daddy, we have to do that. Those are hospital rules."

I said, "Well, then get off your butts and start handling it."

She didn't say anything else, just looked at her nurses and said, "Take care of Mr. Fuller."

Between two of them, they got Daddy off the potty chair and started cleaning him up. Daddy looked so pitiful and said to me, "Reta, these people are crazy!"

"No Daddy," I said, "They're not crazy, just lax."

I looked at my watch and knew I had to leave immediately or I would have problems explaining my absence, again, to some of the parents. I gave Daddy a kiss on the forehead and said, loud enough for all to hear,

"I'll be back this evening, Daddy, you get some rest." He was all cleaned up and ready for a nap after this ordeal.

I DROVE TO RICE LAKE AS QUICK AS I COULD. Being so upset, I needed that time to cool down and get myself in a pleasant mood to face my students.

I arrived in time to see the students who had come to enroll. They were my loyal parents and students who had not listened to the rumors being spread about me closing the studio to take care of my Daddy full time. They were all very supportive and were very pleased with Pam and Kim as their child's teachers. They were, however, happy to hear Steve would not be around.

We stayed as long as we could before we had to leave to set up in the Cumberland Studio. I was just about in tears, I said, "My, God, where is everyone?." We only had about fifteen students enrolled. I expected the enrollment to be down, but this was horrible!.

We packed up and headed for Cumberland. The enrollment there was better, but down about half from last year.

Pam rode with me back to the Country Dam where we met Karen and Kim. Thank, God, Jim had stopped booking the strippers. Feeling so down and depressed, I said, "You guys, I don't know what I'm gonna do if the other studios turn out like this."

They were all trying to cheer me up. Karen said, "Don't worry, you'll just have to book more gigs."

Pam and Kim said, "Yeah, and we can take a part time job."

"Maybe, Daddy's house will sell," I said and felt a little better.

PAM AND KIM WENT WITH ME THAT NIGHT TO SEE Daddy. Seeing their faces always cheered him up, but I could tell he was confused and seemed really tired. I figured he was still pooped out from the morning activities.

While we were there, his supper tray was brought and just left on his rolling shelf. We didn't help him because I wanted to wait to see if anyone was going to help him with his meal. Since I had already been instructed I couldn't be handling Daddy, I didn't dare put him in his chair like he was accustomed. We waited until all the trays were out, still no one came to help him. After awhile, I cranked his bed up as high as I could, put his tray in front of him and Pam and Kim supervised his eating while I made another trip to the nurses station. He started grabbing food like he was starving to death.

There were at least four or five nurses standing around talking. I said in the most polite voice I could find, "Who is in charge of supervising my Daddy's meals?"

They looked at each other and one said, "No one has been designated, can't he feed himself?"

I blew up, again, "I just don't understand you people. It doesn't take a genius to see he is not capable of feeding himself, totally unsupervised." I paused, giving them time to answer. They just looked at each other as if to say, Well, the bitch is back.

My temper surfaced again, I said, "If you can find his chart, will you please note, He needs supervised meals!"

Now I understood why he grabbed the food so fast, he probably hadn't had anything to eat since he got there. One of the nurses said, "Do you want us to take over his feeding now?"

"No, I'm sure my daughters have taken care of it this time, but I certainly hope someone will be there in the morning for breakfast."

One of the nurses rolled her eyes and said, in a very insulting way, "We will add this Request to his chart along with all your other Requests."

I yelled, "Look, damnit, if my Daddy doesn't start getting some proper care, I am going to be your worst nightmare. Now do I make myself clear?"

I turned around and went back into Daddy's room. I told him, "Daddy, you get better really quick so I can break you out of this joint."

He answered, "Damn, I'm ready."

I CALLED LISA WHEN I GOT HOME. SHE WAS spending a few days with Gator while Daddy was in the hospital. I explained what had happened with the suppository medication and meals. I asked, "Could you spend some time at the hospital tomorrow and make sure they are taking care of him right, while we are at Spooner? We should be done pretty early, so try to be there at least for his meals."

She was upset about Daddy's care too, and although I could hear Gator complaining in the back ground, she said, "Sure I'll be there."

After I hung up, I told Pam and Kim after I hung up, "I don't know how much longer Lisa is going to last. She's starting to act restless, again, like she did in the past."

Pam said, "Everything was fine until Gator started bossing her around."

Kim continued, "Maybe we should start looking for someone else, just in case. What are we gonna do if she just ups and leaves?"

"I don't know," I said, "This is why I hesitated to hire her, remember?"

THE NEXT MORNING I CALLED DADDY'S ROOM before we left for Spooner. What a relief, Lisa answered Daddy's telephone. I said, "I am so glad you're there, Lisa, I didn't know if Gator would talk you out of going."

She said, "Reta, he is giving me a lot of crap, but don't worry, I can handle him."

I sighed and said, "Well, that sure makes me feel better. You know, it would really leave me in a mess if you quit right now."

With confidence, she said, "Don't worry, you know I wouldn't do that to you." That took a load off my mind, at least for now.

KAREN SHOWED UP AND WE ALL TOOK OFF FOR Spooner. I felt a lot more relaxed knowing Lisa was at the hospital watching over Daddy.

Karen told me all about Gary Miller coming into the Country Dam right after we had left for the hospital. She said, "He sat there and talked about that damn wife of his for hours, I almost fell asleep."

"I know," I said. "He was a good husband, he even worked and paid the bills. Plus, he didn't screw around with every sweat hog he could find like that thing I was married to did."

We arrived at the Spooner Studio. Thank, God, we had a good turnout for enrollment. I was still down quite a bit from last year but not like Rice Lake and Cumberland. Of course, here I wasn't being sabotaged by an unethical teacher in the Spooner area or the remaining two studios we had yet to enroll, Luck and Clear Lake.

I felt a lot better this time as I drove back home. I said, "Well, if Luck and Clear Lake can hold their own, maybe we'll be okay."

When we got back home, Brad said, "I got a surprise for you." The new winch had arrived and he had already installed it. He said, "The bad news is, it's gonna cost a lot to send the other one back."

I signed a check and gave it to him and said, "just let me know the damages, I'll get a refund of $405.00 as soon as they receive it. Of course, I'll have to send it directly to the credit card company.

He then turned it on and it purred like a kitten. I gave Brad a hug and said, "Well, I owe you another $100.00!"

He laughed and said, "I'll add it to my bill."

What would we have done without Brad's help, I don't know. He had already added a little gate across the entrance down stairs. Ever since Daddy had pushed his wheel chair over with his left foot, I had been concerned about him pushing himself back and being caught half in and half out of the shaft when the winch was engaged. I looked up and said, Thank you, God, for my little team.

I grabbed a quick sandwich and headed for the hospital. Lisa was still there when I walked in. It was such a relief to see that Daddy was clean and chatting away. I gave her a hug and said, "You'll never know how much I appreciate you coming, especially, today."

She said, "Well, I gotta tell you they still haven't got Grandpa's medication right. I made them give him the right dosage, but if I hadn't been here, they would have given him the old dosage."

My blood pressure went through the roof. I said, I'm gonna find Dr. Rimestad and have him take a baseball bat and get their attention."

I was ranting and raving to myself all the way down the hall, as I looked for him. His office had advised me he was in the building. Soon, I spotted him as he was going into the doctor's lounge. Running to catch him, I quickly opened the door and walked in. Not seeing him, I yelled, "Dr. Rimestad, are you in here?"

Hearing the commode flush, I knew he was in here and I was a little embarrassed as he walked out of the bathroom. He asked, "What's wrong?"

I settled down the best I could and told him about the medication. He took off for the nurse's station saying, "I'll take care of this right now."

I followed closely on his heels. I wasn't going to miss this for the world! He sure let them know in no uncertain terms just how unhappy he was with them.

While I had his attention, I filled him in on the meals, suppository and everything else I could think of. Then I asked, "When do you think I can take my Daddy home?"

He answered, "Probably, he can go home tomorrow."

I said, "That's good, 'cause if I don't get him out of here pretty soon, we'll have to start all over again."

Thank God, the Therapy Department had been doing their job. Therapy had been in every day to take care of Daddy's range of motion exercises. Actually, every department had been very caring and professional, with the exception of a few nurses.

One of the aids came in about then and helped Daddy with his supper. They still weren't putting him in the chair, but at least they were making sure he got the food in his mouth.

After Dr. Rimestad's visit, everyone was taking care of business. I gave Daddy a kiss good night and Lisa and I headed home. Lisa said, "Do you want me to go to the hospital tomorrow?"

"No, you go ahead and take the day off. If I need help, I'll call Betty."

"Oh, thank you, Reta. I really appreciate that."

She then called Gator to come and get her. Before you could blink an eye, he was there . I had always liked Gator, but he sure was acting different. I knew that he drank a lot, but he had always been well mannered, not like he was acting now.

Lisa came running up the stairs and said, "I'm ready."

He glared at me and said, "Well, it's about time."

I said, "Gator, there's no need to be so hateful, Lisa does have a job you know."

Under his breath I heard him say, "Yeah, well, with what you pay, she might as well not."

This was all I needed. I knew Lisa would not be able to work much longer if she continued to date him.

I CALLED BETTY AND TOLD HER ABOUT THE incidents at the hospital. Then I told her, "Betty, I am going up there bright and early in the morning, and if I see anything wrong, I am loading Daddy up and bringing him home. Can you come if I need you for tomorrow afternoon?

She said, "Sure, but what happened to Lisa?" I explained a little about Gator's effect on her. Bless her heart, she told me, "Well, if you need me to go back on a shift, just let me know."

I KNEW THAT BETTY WOULD BE THERE WITHIN thirty minutes, if I needed her. I had left the hospital letting them think I wouldn't be back until tomorrow evening, but I really planned a little surprise visit. I wanted to see if they took as good care of Daddy when I wasn't there as when I was.

I set my alarm and got up early so that I could be at the hospital about thirty minutes after Daddy got his breakfast tray. I just wanted to see, for myself, if they would be as attentive as I had seen the day before.

I walked down the hallway toward the nurses station. Just as before, there were about six of them standing around the nurse's station having their coffee, talking and laughing. Believe me, when they saw me, they quit talking or laughing.

I said, "Good morning, ladies, I just wanted to check on Daddy before I headed for work." You could have heard a pin drop.

Walking into Daddy's room, you can't possible know the anger I felt as I witnessed the condition my Daddy was in.

They had sat him in a chair, he was slouched down and almost falling out. His head was hanging over the chair's arm and he looked awful. Would you believe it, his breakfast was not only cold, but still sitting on the tray, across the room, where it had been delivered at least thirty minutes before.

In a voice that could have been heard a mile away, I said, "Well, Daddy, are you enjoying your breakfast?"

I promptly got him straightened out in the chair and about then, in came the same head nurse, followed closely by her clones. Immediately, they started getting Daddy's breakfast ready to feed him.

I yelled, "Get the hell out of my sight, he'll have breakfast at home!

I then got Daddy's robe and started getting him ready to go home. Daddy looked so pitiful. I believe he thought that I had abandoned him. I said, "Daddy, don't you worry, we're going home now."

The nurses all took off like bats out of hell and I proceeded to get Daddy seated in his wheel chair.

About then, the head nurse walked back in and said in a harsh voice, "You can't take him out of here unless Dr. Rimestad dismisses him."

I yelled, "Then get your ass out there and call him, because my Daddy is not staying here one more hour!" Stepping toward her, I think, by God, if she hadn't left I would have punched her.

During all this action, Daddy was echoing just about every word I was saying. He was the best cheerleader I ever had and wanted to get his two-cents in too.

Within a few minutes, Dr. Rimestad came rushing into Daddy's room. He asked, "What are you doing, Reta."

I said, as calmly as possible, "What the hell does it look like I'm doing? I'm taking my Daddy home before these nurses kill him!"

As though he was dealing with a hysterical woman, he said, "Now, Reta, aren't you over reacting?"

I yelled, "Don't you dare patronize me Dr. Rimestad. You know they haven't been taking care of Daddy properly. Even if you think I am just playing nurse, we take a hell of a lot better care of him, than they do here."

Now I had his full attention. He knew something was really wrong and that I wasn't kidding. Looking at the nurse he asked, "What has happened this morning?"

She rolled her eyes and said, "Well, we didn't get in here as soon as she thought we should, to assist Mr. Fuller with his breakfast."

I said in a slow monotone, "Don't you dare lie to him about assisting Daddy with breakfast. None of you had any intention of helping him, any more than you took him to the bathroom or took care of his medication changes on the chart."

I caught my breath again and said, "Dr. Rimestad, I'm taking Daddy home."

He said, "Well, you know if you take him out of here without me properly dismissing him, Medicare won't cover any of his stay."

"Then dismiss him or I'll have to deal with the bill later." With my most authoritative voice I said, "Because he's going home!"

Dr. Rimestad, said, "Okay, I'll dismiss him. I had planned to send him home today anyway."

"Well, I do appreciate your cooperation, doctor. I have no complaints with you. You've always been very caring and so has the Therapy Department. Believe me, Daddy will never darken the door of this hospital again! If you feel he needs to be hospitalized in the future, I will take him back to Abbott-Northwestern Hospital in Minneapolis where he will be properly cared for.

Dr. Rimestad stayed for a while and we talked. He had taken an oxygen level test on Daddy and found his oxygen to be low, that's why he became so alert in the ambulance when they administered some to him.

"Do you think I should have some oxygen at home, for him?"

"Maybe that is a good idea. If he gets sluggish, just give him a shot or two, otherwise give him some every morning for a while before he starts his day. It'll wake him up." He then gave me the information on ordering the oxygen by the tank."

I said, "Before you leave, I'll make you a little bet."

"What is that?" he said.

"I left a half gallon of buttermilk here for Daddy when he first came in, I'll bet it's never been opened."

He called the nurse back in and informed her he was, in fact, dismissing my Daddy.

Then, in a very calm voice, I asked, "I left a half gallon of buttermilk here when Daddy checked in, could I please get it?"

She soon came back with the buttermilk...unopened. I smiled sweetly at Dr. Rimestad and said, "See what I mean?"

All he could do was smile and shake his head as he wished us well and left Daddy's room.

I CALLED PAM FROM DADDY'S ROOM AND ASKED, "Would you please call Betty and tell her to meet us at the house. I'm bringing Daddy home." I could hear the cheers from Pam, Kim and Cheryl. Everyone was ready to have Grandpa home.

I got Daddy loaded in the car so fast he didn't know what hit him. On the way home, I stopped at *Chet's Pharmacy* and had Daddy's prescription filled. They also helped me make arrangements for the oxygen to be delivered. Daddy drank a good cup of hot coffee while he waited for me.

When we arrived home, he was greeted by all his little cheerleaders. Betty was already there and had his bed ready and his oxygen was due to arrive a little later. I finally sat down and had breakfast and coffee with Daddy. The girls had prepared a feast for him.

AFTER BREAKFAST, WE STARTED TO GET READY TO go to Luck and Clear Lake for our last day of enrollment.

Daddy was pooped so Betty got him ready for a nap. She was delighted over the new winch, but she still wasn't crazy about that elevator. She did promise to use it when the weather got too bad.

Just then the telephone rang, and it was Louise. "How's enrollment going?"

"Like crap," I replied. "Ma, I don't know what I'm gonna do if I don't get good enrollment today at Clear Lake and Luck, plus I've had nothing but hell with this hospital!"

She said in her calming voice, "Now, sweetie, the Good Lord is just testing you. Everything will be okay."

I snapped at her, "Ma, I'm tired of you telling me how 'The Good Lord' is testing me! Sometimes, I don't think He remembers who I am at all, so I just wish you would stop telling me such things. I've had enough!"

In her sad, little voice she said, "I'm sorry."

Now I felt awful, "Ma, I'm sorry. I didn't mean to snap at you like that, it's just been a bad day and I still have most of it to go."

"Would you like for me to come up this weekend for a shoulder to cry on?" she asked.

I said, "I have to play at the Foxhole, Saturday but Sunday would be good. We could go out for dinner, maybe take Daddy too, if he's up to it."

"I'll be there after church, and I'll say a special prayer for you, too. I've been playing your song every night on the organ as I pray for you, *Thank You, Ma, I Do Love You.*"

"Which song are you playing for me now?" I asked.

With a chuckle she replied, *"Blessed Assurance."*

"Well, Ma, you just keep that hot-line going up to God. I need all the communication lines I can get. Like you say, He's not done testing me, yet."

AS I CONTINUED GETTING READY, I THOUGHT WHAT a special lady Louise had been in my life.

I first met her when Kimberly was just a newborn. Just having started teaching dancing and baton twirling in Hastings, Minnesota, I knew

I needed to further my education. I called Kraskin Baton Company in Minneapolis and asked for a reference of a good baton teacher. They gave me Louise Lacasse's name, and she was located in White Bear Lake, Minnesota.

I called Louise and made an appointment. From that first meeting, we hit it off, and I have had a very successful career in teaching which I credit to her superb guidance.

We adopted each other a few years back. She never had a daughter and my mother was dead, so we have had a very close and rewarding relationship.

Louise has always prayed for me, and since she bought her new organ, she also plays a song to God while she prays. Once again, I thanked God for her as I slipped on my jogging suit.

BETTY KNOCKED ON MY DOOR AND SAID, "RETA, I'M so mad I could spit."

I opened the door and said, "What's wrong?"

She said, "We've worked so hard to keep Vernon from having any bedsores and now he has one, come and look."

I went down to Daddy's room. He looked so clean and *comfortable* lying in his bed. I asked, "Daddy, do you have an owie?"

He looked so pitiful and said, "Yeah, they hurt me."

Betty showed me the bedsore, actually just a small break in the skin. The way Betty had carried on, I thought it would have covered his entire butt. However, to be fair, if he had stayed in the hospital a day or two longer, it might have.

Betty mumbled as she brought in the Hot Light and medication to care for it. "This makes me so damn mad! Don't it you too Vernon?"

Of course, Daddy was eating up all this attention. I decided if I started feeling sorry for him too, he would really put on a pitiful show. Betty assured me she would take care of it and leave Lisa a report on what she was doing.

I always had a report sheet for all the aids to fill out at the end of a shift or on day's off. Upon coming to work, the aid would read the report and know exactly what the status was on Daddy's health and behavior. I might also add, new owies.

I gave Daddy a kiss and said, "Welcome home, Betty will take good care of you and I'll see you for supper."

He looked at me totally confused and said, "Where am I going?"

Laughing, I told him, "You've already been gone, so now you have to rest up so we can run *The Roads* this Sunday with Louise."

I figured that he had already forgotten about the hospital stay and was wondering who in the hell Louise was.

PAM AND KIM WERE READY SO WE JUMPED INTO THE car and headed for Clear Lake. Karen was gonna meet us over there. I sure was glad Karen had moved back to Amery, but at the same time, I was thankful she had lived in the St. Paul area during Daddy's long confinement at Abbott-Northwestern Hospital last winter.

We had a pretty good turn-out in Clear Lake and Luck, but nothing like it had been the previous year. I knew I was going to have to make some new arrangements.

AFTER WE GOT HOME, I ASKED PAM HOW SHE FELT about running the Luck studio, alone. She said, "Yeah, but you'll be available if I need help, won't you?"

"Well, that's what I've been thinking about. I've had so many calls from Ladysmith, I thought maybe I would try to open a studio there. The problem is that the only night I have left is the same night you're teaching at Luck."

She sat there for a little while then asked, "Mom, do you think I can handle it?"

I said with confidence, "Honey, I don't think. I know you can handle it! You're ready to go out on your own."

"But you'll handle the recital, won't you?"

I said, "Of course, I will handle your books, etc. You just teach this year and you can take over more responsibilities next year."

She smiled and said, "Well, if you think I'm ready, okay."

I called Karen and asked if she wanted to ride to Ladysmith with me the next day to find a studio location.

She said, "Okay. How many of those little rug rats do you need?"

"A hell of a lot more than I got now," I replied.

BETTY MADE HER FAMOUS PORCUPINE HAMBURGER dish for supper. Like Fred, she always went that extra step that made her so special. She never just sat around. If Daddy didn't need her, she would help with laundry and any other chore that needed attention.

We all sat down to eat and I said with total sympathy, "Daddy, does that sore you have on you behind feel any better?"

He looked at me, cocked his head and said, "What sore?"

I laughed and said, "Well, that answers my question."

Betty chuckled, "Yeah, he's already milked that problem to death, haven't ya Vernon?"

Daddy said with a confused look, "I reckon so."

"That's all right, Grandpa, we know those nurses at the hospital were naughty to you," Kim assured him.

We had just about finished eating when, Lisa and Gator pulled up in front of the house. Lisa came running in to greet Grandpa.

Pam asked, "Why didn't Gator come in?"

"Oh, he's just being a jerk, as usual," she answered.

Betty told Lisa about the bedsore and then left to go home.

Lisa said, "Okay, Grandpa, let's go down stairs so I can check that sore." I heard her mutter, "Them damn nurses!"

Kathy, from Social Services, called after supper. "Reta, I've got some good news for you and Vernon!"

"Please lay it on me, I need some good news," I told her

She said, "Well, I have gotten a raise for your Home Attendant since Vernon is improving so much. They are going to let me double the pay."

With excitement I said, "You mean Lisa's salary will be $1,000.00 per month?"

She said, "That's right, and if he keeps improving, it could go right on up to $1,500.00 maximum."

I was so excited, I ran right down and told Lisa the good news.

She really brightened up. "Boy, that's great, 'cause I didn't know how I was gonna make it on $500.00, and I really hated to take extra money from you. I know you're having a rough time."

She went back to caring for Daddy's owie. He had her sympathy, too.

I laughed and said, "Daddy, with the attention that sore is getting, you probably hope it never heals, huh?"

"It's better though," he said in a reassuring way.

I GOT UP EARLY THE NEXT MORNING AND MADE A fresh pot of coffee. I took a cup down to Lisa and Daddy. She was busy with his owie again so I gave him my greetings and went back up stairs and got dressed.

Karen came bouncing in and said, "I hope you got the coffee ready."

"It's ready and a waiting," I chirped.

She stopped dead in her tracks and said, "Well, what the hell are you so chirping about? I mean I like it, but what happened? Bob call or what?"

I filled her in on Daddy's little owie and how he had Lisa and Betty eating out of his hand.

She shook her head and said, "That ol' rascal."

WE HEADED FOR LADYSMITH AND GABBED ALL THE way. No one on this earth has a healthier laugh than Karen. She was the best medicine I could have. She kept me laughing the entire trip.

I found and rented a space at the *Ladysmith University*. In fact, I was able to rent their ballet room. Then we went to the local paper and started my ad.

We met Gary at the Country Dam for a drink after we got back to Amery. He bent our ears talking about his ex-wife, Kathy.

After awhile Karen said with disgust, "Gary, can't you talk about anything else? I'm sick of hearing about Kathy."

I chimed in and said, "Me too, Gary. I think you're great, but everyone is really getting tired of hearing about Kathy. If you can't get over her, then try to get her back, but dummy up."

He laughed and said, "Maybe you guys are right, I do talk about her a lot."

"Not a lot," Karen replied. "All the damn time."

He quickly changed the subject to music and said, "Where are you playing this weekend?"

I said, "At the Foxhole, you want to sit in again?."

"Yeah, and if I promise not to mention the word, Kathy, can I take you to breakfast again?"

"Only if I can have that written in blood," I replied with a smile. I did find myself attracted to Gary. He was really a cute guy, and fun to be around, if he could just shake the Kathy syndrome.

IT WAS AFTER SUPPER WHEN I GOT HOME. DADDY was laid back in his Lazy Boy. He didn't really care for the lift-out chair that, Rick, my friend from St. Croix Hospital had loaned him. We all liked it because it was so much easier to transfer Daddy from his wheelchair to an almost standing position, instead of having to pull him forward, and then up from his Lazy Boy. Most of the aids used the lift-out chair, but Betty, Fred and I always let him sit in his Lazy Boy. I was happy to see Lisa was letting him sit in it too. He loved it so much.

The one chair I never allowed Daddy to be left sitting in was his wheelchair. My group knew the wheelchair was only used for transportation or sitting at the table for his meals. I was very adamant about this.

When I had gone to see my Uncle R.A., in the nursing home in Winters, I saw all those poor old people sitting in different kinds of horrible positions in their wheelchairs, left alone and trying to sleep, I had vowed, then, my Daddy would never be treated like that. Also, he would damn sure be treated with dignity, not like he was treated at the Amery Hospital. I just prayed, at that time, that the Good Lord would allow me, someday, to make a difference for all the elderly.

I walked into the living room and said, "Hi, there, Brody, how you doing?"

He sleepily looked at me and said, in a harsh voice, "Piss Ant, where the hell you been?"

I quickly gave him an accounting of my whereabouts as though I was still sixteen years old.

He finished his buttermilk and said, "Is there a bed in this house?"

Lisa piped up, "There sure is, Grandpa!" The raise in pay had really made a difference in Lisa. She was more at ease now, and I knew that she was feeling a lot more secure. I just wished that I could have gotten a raise sooner, so Fred could have enjoyed it also.

I HAD DECIDED TO SKIP DADDY'S THERAPY UNTIL the next week so that he could get stronger after his hospital stay. Lisa had been working with him on standing, sitting, and he was always given range-of-motion on his bad side, twice per day. Regarding that schedule, I was a real stinker. If anyone was lax in not assisting Daddy in doing those exercises, I could tell just by lifting Daddy's arm or leg. They would bend naturally and without pain if he were properly exercising. Otherwise, the limbs would stiffen and hurt noticeably when lifted.

BEFORE I KNEW IT, THE WEEKEND WAS HERE.   I really looked forward to singing every weekend for obvious reasons, mainly because it took my mind off the many problems of just everyday living, let alone taking care of Daddy.   Cords, Rick and Donnie had everything set up by the time I got there.

Cords asked, "How did the enrollment go?"

"Don't ask," I said. "We're gonna have to book every weekend, if possible."

They all assured me they were sitting on Go. In that sense, I was so lucky to work with such a wonderful and talented group.   They had really been supportive.

Donnie said, "Are Gregg and Clarion still dropping by for the jam session?"

"Yeah. It's sure nice to have friends like that. Daddy feels like he's now part of the Rex Cactus Show!"

"When do you start your classes?" Rick asked.

With a sigh, I replied, "Next week, and I don't feel like I've even had a summer break."

Cords mumbled, "That damn, Steve. Someone should break his sorry neck."

They all wanted to know how Grandpa was doing. I said, "Well, his oxygen tank and supplies arrived today, so he should be full of it tomorrow."

They all said to be sure and tell him hello.

Cords said, "Be sure and tell Grandpa I'll be over as soon as you have time for another practice and we'll jam too. Also tell him not to join the Rex Cactus Show yet, we want a chance to get him."

I laughed and said, "I'll tell him, he'll get a kick out if that."

GARY SHOWED UP DURING THE THIRD SET AND played some banjo. Gary and Brenda (owners of the *Foxhole* where we were playing) were two of our biggest fans. They were also two of the nicest club owners we had worked for, so kind and supportive about my absences because of Daddy's illness.

Before the evening was over, Rex Cactus and Karen Dee showed up. Together, they had played a wedding dance and got done early.

We closed our show with everyone on bandstand backing Clarion and singing, *Will The Circle Be Unbroken.*   Our fans really enjoyed themselves, almost as much as we did.

We packed up and headed for *The Ranch Restaurant* in Luck. The whole gang joined us, along with about half of the club.

Gary followed me back to my house for a nightcap.   After I checked on Daddy, we sat in the living room and visited.   I was really proud of him, he never mentioned the K word once.   When he left, he gave me a kiss good night and headed back to his little cottage in Amery.   I thought, What a fool his wife is, he really is a sweetheart.

We both knew our relationship was only for the moment because there were just too many obstacles in the way for it to be otherwise.   He understood my situation and knew I wouldn't have much time for any kind of a social life for quite awhile.   But that was what made it comfortable for both of us.

I wanted him to meet my family, including Ma, so I made another date with him for the next day.   He was a very family-oriented person and said he was looking forward to meeting my entire family.   Well, so far so good, right?

I got up early the next morning because I had things to do before Ma got there.   She had promised to come right after her church let out.   I went down and had my usual coffee with Daddy.   He was brighter than a new penny.   I teased him and said, "Whatcha been doing?   Sniffing on that Kick-A-Poo-Joy-Juice?"

He pouted, "I don't like her to put that thing in my nose."

I said, "But Daddy, that stuff really clears your mind and makes you smart."

He looked at me like I was crazy and said, "Really?   You ain't shittin' me now, are ya?"

We discussed his   intelligence level until   it was time to go up stairs.   Lisa had made him some French toast, her specialty.

I put him in his elevator, strapped the guard across and yelled, "Take him up!"

Daddy already had that foot up trying to push the chair back. Thank, God, for the safety belt Brad had installed.

BEFORE BREAKFAST WAS OVER, BRAD CAME IN, followed closely by Ma. She had come sooner that I had expected because she had gone to early Church. I gave her a hug and took over making the

French toast. Before long, Pam, Kim and Cheryl came up. I opened another loaf of bread and kept cooking.

After breakfast the girls cleaned up the kitchen while Lisa got Daddy ready for his tub bath. Daddy had already decided to Run The Roads with us today.

Ma and I sat in the living room and discussed the opening of our respective studios next week. She and Lee were opening in Forest Lake, White Bear Lake and Cambridge. She thoughtfully had brought some paperwork for me to add to my classroom work.

I then told her about Gary and that he would be coming over later. She was delighted to hear I was dating, but said with confusion, "I thought his name was Bob?"

"No, actually I haven't heard from Bob for awhile and I haven't called him either. He'll be here around Halloween time. The way my schedule looks though, I won't have time for a social life anyway."

Just then Lisa interrupted us by calling me to come help her with Daddy's bath. She was so little that I didn't want her to try and get him in and out of the tub without help.

Daddy was really good about his bath and when we got Daddy on the bath bench Lisa started scrubbing. While she was doing that, I got things ready for his shave.

Since I was helping with Daddy, Ma was busy visiting with Pam, Kim and Cheryl in the kitchen.

About then I heard old Max, Kim's German Shepherd, barking. Knowing it must be Gary, I yelled at Pam to let him in and introduce him to herself and everyone else. I sure was glad Gary was family oriented, 'cause he was fixin' to get initiated.

Daddy was now ready to get out of the tub. Lisa had her female problems and didn't feel good. I told her to go visit with Gary and that I would handle Daddy's shave. She was really happy to be able to sit down. I remembered how bad I use to feel before my surgery last year. I sure was glad I didn't have to go through that any more.

After getting Daddy dressed and in his wheelchair, I wheeled him up to the sink. I gave him his electric shaver and then got his tooth brush ready. The one that didn't do the jitterbug. I turned around and he was just sitting there looking at his razor.

I said, "Daddy, why aren't you turning it on to shave.

He said, "Hell, Reta, this ain't my razor, this is one of them ol' electric things. I want my razor."

I laughed and said, "Boy, that Kick-A-Poo-Joy-Juice is really doing its thing!" He totally refused to shave with the electric razor.

"Okay, Daddy, I'll shave you with your real razor, but you better sit real still 'cause I've never shaved anyone before and I'd hate to cut your throat."

His eyes got big and he said, "Me, too." He sat still as a little mouse, just like when I had colored his hair.

I was the one that was nervous! Remembering back to when I was a little girl watching him shave, I followed each step, just as I remembered it.

First he wet a towel with as hot water as he could stand and placed it over his face. Then he would hold his head back until it cooled off and then repeat the same procedure. I must have been doing it right because Daddy was putting his head back just like I remembered.

As a kid I used to say, "Daddy, why do you make it so hot?"

He'd say, "Well Piss Ant, my beard is so tough, I have to soften it up with hot water." Then he would always give me the towel when he applied the shaving cream. I would then, put it on my face, and lean my head back too.

Continuing as I had remembered, I then put the lather on his face and took the razor I used for shaving my legs. (His was packed away down stairs with the knife.) I put a new blade in it and said, "Daddy, if your therapist knew I was doing this, she would probably have a fit. Just sit really still."

Then picturing the direction of the strokes in my mind, I followed that mental picture to the letter. Daddy was so cooperative, you would think he was handling the razor. He would move his face exactly the way he did when he was shaving.

I did great until I got to his upper lip. He pulled his lip down, just like he always did, but I couldn't get in the right position to shave above it.

He said, "Hell, Reta, give me the razor." I reluctantly handed it to him and he finished his face just like he had done for at least fifty-five years without even a nick. In fact, neither one of us nicked him.

He handed the razor back to me, rubbed his hand over his face and said, "Ah, soft as a baby's butt." I knew from then on he was gonna get lots of whiffs of Kick-A-Poo-Joy-Juice, otherwise known as good old oxygen!

I put some Old Spice Shaving Lotion in his hand and he splashed it on his face. He then combed his hair and said, "Let me brash m' teeth."

I looked up, shook my head and said, "Mama, he's still brushing his teeth."

Lisa couldn't believe I had actually shaved him with a real razor and said, "Well Grandpa, if that's how you want to shave, that's how we'll do it from now on."

"Well that's damn sure the way I want to do it," he replied with authority.

I went into the living room to greet Gary while Lisa finished dressing Daddy in his running the roads attire. Gary was getting to know the kids and Ma really well. I could tell by the way everyone was acting he had passed their inspection.

I grabbed a cup of coffee and joined them, still in my jogging suit. I said, "All I lack is combing my hair, changing clothes and I'll be ready to go."

The door opened and in came Daddy and Lisa. The cheers all went out from the girls, complete with whistles and wolf calls. I said, "Daddy, you look plum spiffy."

He beat his chest and said, "Why thank you." Then he shook hands with Gary and said hello to Louise.

They were both totally amazed at the way Daddy conducted himself and sat straight in that wheelchair wearing that Stetson hat.

Gary asked him, "Where did you get that cowboy hat?"

Daddy gave him a dirty look and said, "This ain't no cowboy hat, boy. This is a Texas Stetson." With that, Gary stood corrected.

I excused myself and said, "Now, Daddy, you entertain everyone while I get dressed."

It didn't take long for him to get on a talking streak. He even told the girls to "hush" if they tried to interrupt.

I got dressed and came out. Daddy checked me over really good. I saw that twinkle in his eye and knew what he was gonna say so I beat him to the punch. Quickly I said, "Daddy, before you tell me how old and haggard I look, you better think twice.

He burst out laughing and said, "Hell, Piss Ant, I wuz just gonna tell ya how perty you looked."

I smiled and said, "Well, thank you kind sir. Guess I was wrong about your intentions." Giving him a kiss on the forehead I then explained to Gary and Ma about the old and haggard compliments he had been giving me lately.

EVERYONE WAS IN SUCH A GOOD MOOD THAT DAY that I found myself wishing this mirage could last forever. Ma said, "It sure feels different around here with that darn Steve gone."

Kim said, "Yeah, we're all glad to be rid of that parasite."

Daddy then echoed, "Yeah. Are we going somewhere?"

As I pushed him toward the patio door, I answered, "You betcha! Hungry?"

"Starved to death," he said.

I took him down the ramp and met Ma and Gary out front. I didn't have to use the transfer belt much any more for simple transfers because Daddy had gotten so strong and had become very cooperative.

I said, "Now, Daddy, are you gonna stand and help me get you in the car so I don't have to use that damned old belt?"

He hated us putting it on him and said, "I damn sure will." He stood right up and I pivoted him right into the car. He said, "Now, Reta, I don't like you liftin' on me like that. You're gonna hurt your little back."

"Not when you help me like that. There was no strain at all on my little back," I told him.

I buckled the seat belt and started around the car to get in. Gary said, "Well, I had planned to help you, but looks like you have everything under control."

I smiled and said, "Yeah, they trained me real well at Sister Kenny."

"Obviously," he answered as he headed for his car.

"Louise, do you want to ride with me and meet them at the Country Dam?" Gary asked.

"Sure," she said, "It will give us a chance to get to know each other better." I knew Ma wanted a crack at him, so that she would feel safe in her own mind that I wasn't going out with another creep. She had become very protective of me because of some prior relationships.

I knew that Gary was going to pick up his children for awhile later on, so I had decided to take Daddy and Ma to the Country Dam for lunch, since it was closer.

We had a nice lunch and Daddy ate every bit of his hot roast beef sandwich and drank two cups of coffee. He chatted with Gary and Ma just as normal as anyone. Once again I was amazed at how he conducted himself in public, compared to at home. It was like he knew he had to be good.

GARY LEFT FOR OSCEOLA TO VISIT HIS CHILDREN, and Daddy, Ma and I headed for the *Straight 8* to hear Gregg and Clarion. They were happy to see us and invited me to sing Daddy's song plus a few more. I always loved to watch Ma from the bandstand and could tell if everything sounded right. She would clap her hands together like I've seen her do so many times in her baby classes, counting out the beats. But, if there was a problem up there, she just sat there with panic written all over her face. Thank, God, she was clapping today.

We didn't stay very long because Ma and I wanted to work on some steps before she left. Lee had told Ma that he was gonna try and be at my house by the time we got back. The three of us always got together several times throughout the year to work on new steps.

Ma specialized in ballet and baton, Lee in tap and me in jazz. When we got together, we had a blast.

We said our goodbyes to Gregg and Clarion then headed back home. Daddy was already looking for a bed and it was getting late. As we pulled into the driveway, Ma said, "There's Lee's car, so he got away."

We were so much alike and I was always so happy to see him. I don't know who gave Ma the most gray hair between Lee, Peter and me. Peter never came up very often because he had chosen not to stick with the dancing, like Lee had.

When we got Daddy into the house, Lisa took him down to take a nap while the rest of us took out our batons and tap shoes, and whatever else we could get our hands on. Lee started out teaching us some new time-steps, then Ma continued with the ballet terminology and steps plus a few new tricks with the baton. Then I demonstrated some new bar exercises and body isolations.

I asked, "Ma, can you do the pelvis isolation yet?"

She smiled and said, "Just watch this." She went into the best pelvis rotation I have seen yet. Lee and I just cracked up laughing.

I had been working with her on this one move for six months. She would always say, "I don't know how you make your body wiggle like that."

I gave her a hug and said, "Ma, I'm right proud of you." We continued to work for awhile, then they took off for home. I was starting classes the next day and so were they.

I WENT TO BED EARLY THAT NIGHT SO THAT I COULD get up and go with Lisa and Daddy for his therapy session. I dreaded going back to that hospital but as long as I didn't have to leave him any more, it was okay.

Lisa had Daddy up by the time I brought coffee down and was busy whiffing his oxygen. We got him dressed and headed for the therapy session. Daddy was going through his paces with no problem and the therapist said, "With the reports I'm sending in on Vernon, Medicare should start picking up the tab soon."

I sighed and said, "That sure would be nice."

She had heard about the explosion I had caused by taking my Dad out of the hospital. She said, "Good for you. We work our butts off to get our people back on their feet and productive. Then they wind up in there and those nurses ruin everything we have accomplished. I hope you are going to write a letter to the administrator."

"Do you really think that would do any good?" I said.

She answered, "Well, it sure can't hurt. Someone needs to bring this to their attention. Maybe it will help the next person coming in."

I said, "Well, if you think the administrator will take any action, I'll do it."

We took Daddy home immediately after his session. He worked so hard and now he needed a nap.

Kim was all ready when we got back to go to Rice Lake with me. Pam was lounging, she smiled and said, "Well, Kim, I'm sure glad I don't have to go today. I've already put in my O.J.T."

Kim rolled her eyes and said, "Oh, shut up, Paml."

They started cat-fightin', so I said in my best "mother's voice," I said, "Do you two want to start writing?"

Laughing, they said, "No, Mom, we'll shut up." They gave each other a hug because they knew that would be the next thing I would make them do. They were right.

Smiling, I remembered back when Pam and Kim were little girls just learning to write. If they would fuss and fight I would sit them at the table and make them write five nice things about each other. When they talked back to me, then I would make them write five more good things. In the past, they had written up to fifty nice things about each other until they realized I was serious.

After they had completed their papers, I would take them and correct the spelling and then make them write the misspelled words ten times each. I would keep these papers for thirty days and they were not allowed to repeat any "good things" until that time was up. Needless to say, usually by the time they would leave the table, they were the best of friends.

Hearing the commotion, Lisa came up from downstairs and teased, "Are you two gonna have to write?" They all started laughing and remembering how I would make the three of them write when they would start fussin'. Lisa looked at me and said, "Yeah, well, those were the good old days."

Pam and Kim knew about the bad relationship I had with my sister and, therefore, they understood how much it hurt me to see them be mean or spiteful to each other. I always prayed they would be close and take care of each other and never be like Yane and me. Many times as the years rolled by, I watched them interact with each other and was usually very proud of the way they loved and cared for each other. Maybe I was even a little jealous because I never had a sister love me nor care about me in any way.

Shortly, Kim and I took off for Rice Lake. I couldn't believe how small the classes were. The other studio and her parents had even stolen some of my two year students.

I told Kim, "Well, we'll give it a month, if the classes don't grow, then I'll combine them with Cumberland. Maybe between the two areas, we can have one decent studio." Kim agreed.

We drug ourselves home and told Pam the bad news. She said, "Well, Mom, I've got some good news, the calls are coming in from Ladysmith like crazy." She gave me the list of call-backs.

I gave her a hug and shouted, "Thank you, God!"

GRABBING THE TELEPHONE, I STARTED CALLING THE people back, immediately. I was elated that just about everyone signed up.

One call was from the Ladysmith local radio station. They wanted to interview me on one of their talk shows, play my record and discuss my experiences with Daddy. They had heard about me through WXCE Radio out of Amery, and after seeing my ad in the local paper, decided I would be an interesting guest.

I made a date for the interview, knowing that it would really help my enrollment in the area.

AFTER TAKING A HOT BATH, I CAME BACK OUT INTO the living room. Daddy was still up and going strong. Pam said, "Grandpa, tell Mom what we did today."

He looked at her totally confused. "You ain't gonna start me to lyin'," he said with a grin.

I knew that was his way of saying, "I don't know what the hell you're talking about." He was fast-thinking and could always come up with some kind of an answer to cover himself.

Pam said, "Grandpa, don't you remember playing Dominoes with me?"

He thought for a moment and said, "Oh, yeah, now I 'member."

Pam was so proud of herself as she told how she made Grandpa sit for three hours with her until they had finished the entire game. She said, "Mom, I really believe he knew some of what we were doing because he would place the Dominoes where they should be."

"That's great!" I said. "Daddy played so many games of Dominoes in his life that I think he could play them in his sleep."

Daddy echoed, "You, betcha!"

Pam and Lisa continued to fill me in on Daddy's escapades until we went to bed.

PAM FOLLOWED ME INTO THE BEDROOM AND SAID, "Mom, I need to tell you something."

I knew I was about to hear something I didn't want to hear at this late hour, or any other hour, but said, anyway, "Okay, let's have it."

She sat down on the bed and said, "Mom, Gator is really making Lisa have second thoughts about helping us with Grandpa. He wants her to be able to date on weekends, and with the holidays coming up soon, well, I just know we're gonna have problems. He was out here today and I took care of Grandpa while they necked and stuff. I don't mind helping, but I'm not gonna do her job."

I said, "I'll talk to Lisa in the morning, after she has Daddy taken care of. Thanks for telling me honey."

"I hate to narc on her, but you need to know what's going on."

I got up the next morning and first thing got the letter written to the Hospital Administrator.

Lisa and Pam got Daddy dressed and fed. After I got the letter addressed and stamped, I came down from my little roost and had a cup of coffee with him.

After breakfast, we got Daddy settled in his Lazy Boy. He was looking out the big bay windows watching the horses graze in the pasture across the way. It appeared that he was dreaming about the Good Old Days when he used to break and ride horses.

I left him there with his thoughts and joined Lisa in the kitchen for another cup of coffee. I asked, "How are you and Gator getting along these days? Is he happier now that you've gotten a raise?"

"I don't know, Reta, he gripes at me all the time."

"Do you think he is going to interfere with your job?" I questioned.

"No, I'll make sure of that," she replied.

"I understand that he was out here all afternoon, yesterday," I stated.

She glared at Pam and said, "Yeah, but Pam said she would take care of Grandpa!"

Pam spoke up, "Not for the entire afternoon while you and Gator necked."

"Well, maybe you should find someone else if I can't have company," she snapped.

Taking a deep breath, I said, "Well, I've seen this attitude before, haven't I, Lisa? I had thought maybe you had changed but you are still going to do exactly what you want to, aren't you?" I walked into the kitchen and poured another cup of coffee saying. "Okay, Lisa," I said, "I will start looking for someone else, if that's what you want. But if you stay, I don't want Gator out here during the time you're on duty."

She settled down a little and said, "Okay, I'll talk to him."

I went back up to my loft and called Joyce Shaffer, the home care nurse, plus, Kathy and the rest of my support group. I asked them to start looking for a replacement.

I have known Lisa since she was eight years old, so I knew her pretty well. She was a follower, not a leader so if Gator told her to walk, she would. I couldn't take a chance and had to be ready for the worst.

Lisa mellowed-out before we left for work. She assured me Gator wouldn't be out today but I was still concerned because Pam started her classes in Luck today.

Knowing that Brad would be at the house, working today, made me feel a little better. I knew that he would let me know if, in fact, Gator did show up. Lisa had pulled too much crap on me in the past so I really didn't trust her now.

CLASSES WERE SKIMPY IN CUMBERLAND, ALSO, SO I knew I could easily combine Cumberland with Rice Lake if Rice didn't increase in enrollment within the next few weeks. Funny how that works. Here I was giving myself ultimatums.

We came home immediately after class and Pam was already there. "How'd it go, Pam?"

She gave me the okay sign, saying, "No problem. Two more students enrolled today, but I still need a lot more for it to be like it was last year. The rumors about us quitting is all over the place there, too. I had at least four mothers ask if we plan to continue."

"We'll see how it goes by the end of the month," I told her. "We might all have to get part-time jobs."

I WAS GLAD TO NOTE THAT LISA APPEARED TO BE back to normal and Daddy was sitting in his Lazy Boy. Daddy didn't have his usual glass of liquid sitting by him and I reminded Lisa of his need to have plenty of liquid because of his one kidney.

She said, "Oh, I have it ready. I just forgot to give it to him."

Privately, I told Pam and Kim to keep a check on her about the liquid. If Daddy didn't get enough, he would go into kidney failure. They said, "We'll watch her like a hawk."

At times like this, I sure missed Fred. When he was here, I never had to worry about Daddy. He took care of Daddy the same when I was gone as when I was there. This problem reminded me of the time when Pam and Kim were small, and the headache of finding a baby-sitter, the trusting, loyal kind.

After Lisa had put Daddy to bed, I went downstairs and checked his arm and leg. They were loose, so I knew she had been taking care of his range-of-motion exercises. *Maybe I was becoming paranoid,* I told myself, kissing Daddy goodnight and going straight to bed.

THE NEXT DAY I CHECKED OVER THE MAIL AS I STILL hadn't received the refund check on Daddy's winch. I called the company to see when they planned to send it out. The girl told me, "Why, that was sent out last week as soon as we received the unit back."

I said, "Well, I haven't received it yet, will you check and see for sure when it was sent?"

She checked again and said, "Yes, here it is. It was sent last Tuesday to Steve Anderson."

I screamed, "I told you people to send the refund check to me, not Steve Anderson!"

"Well, according to our records, Mr. Anderson ordered the winch."

"Yeah, on my credit card!" I yelled. "Your stupidity just cost me $405.00 plus the money it cost to ship the damn winch back to you."

I slammed the telephone down and started crying. I knew the post office would forward Wonder Boy's mail to him and he would cash that check and spend it on one of his sweat hogs. I yelled at God, "Why, don't you quit testing me, can't you see I can't take much more?"

I got in my car and went for a drive for two reasons. First, because I didn't want Daddy to see me crying and second, I knew I had a lot of apologizing to do to God.

I kept remembering my favorite poem, Footsteps. I said, "God, if you are carrying me, I wish you would drop me a time or two so I would know you haven't abandoned me. All I wanted to do was make things nice for my Daddy and now I'm losing everything. My Mother always told me You had a reason for everything that happens. She would say, Now, it might take a few years to see why God allows things to happen but he always has a reason for every thing He does. Well, God, all these years later, I still don't know why you took Mother from me and now I don't understand why my life is falling apart since I made the promise to care for Daddy. I'm so tired of fighting just to survive and give my family a decent life. I know I'm not a bad person like Yane would like for me to believe but sometimes I wonder what I did so bad for my life to be such a mess. The only thing I've done right is being Pam and Kim's mother."

All of a sudden I snapped back to reality, wiped my tears and started counting my blessings as my mother told me to do years ago whenever I started feeling down. I said, in a calmer voice, "I'm sorry, God. Please help me deal with it all, and thank You for giving me my wonderful little girls and my health." Before I knew it, the thank you list had outgrown my bitch list. I turned my car around and went back home knowing that God was gonna help me find the way. I drove back to the house feeling like a new woman. When I stepped out of the car and looked up at the big bay window, staring back at me was Grandpa with Kim, Pam and Lisa.

Boy, did I get and earful when I got inside for taking off like that without letting anyone know where I was going.

Quickly I told them what had happened. Daddy said, "That son-of-a-bitch."

"You got that right, Grandpa. He is a sonofabitch," Pam echoed.

"What are you gonna do, Mom?" Kim asked

"There is not anything I can do, until the divorce is final. It looks like he can get away with murder."

The insurance! All of a sudden I remembered. His name was on the policy as a beneficiary if the house should burn.

I thought, My, God, I wouldn't put it past him to burn the house with all of us in it. I knew how much he loved insurance claims.

I quickly called John Volgren, my insurance man, and told him to take Steve's name off the house immediately, I also asked him to send Steve a letter to that effect If he did have any ideas along those lines, he would bury them in a hurry, instead of figuring a way to bury me. John assured me he would get on it immediately.

IT SEEMED LIKE WE HAD JUST GOT HOME AND HERE we were ready to take off for the studio again. I hoped my health would last because we had only been in session for about a month, but I felt like it had already been six.

I finally had decided to cancel the Rice Lake classes and rearrange the students to go into the Cumberland studio. With the exception of a few, everyone was very understanding. Cumberland was only fifteen miles from Rice Lake, which didn't present an unusual problem for those students who really cared about what they were doing. At least, this is what I would have hoped they would think.

I gave them the times available and told them if they could start this week we could give them the lesson free. Most of them changed over, but some said, "Well, we'll go to Penny. Sorry—"

To which I responded, "That's fine, go to Penny. Maybe your child can teach her something new."

THAT NIGHT WE GOT HOME JUST IN TIME TO SAY goodnight to Daddy. I felt so bad that I didn't have enough time or energy to spend with him or Pam.

Kim and I became very close as a result of working together. She was even able to have me all to herself on the way to work and back, like Pam had the previous year. I so wished I could have had more time to spend with Daddy and Pam. It just seemed like my life was totally out of control.

When I went back upstairs to the living room, Pam said, "Mom, you have a lot of calls from Ladysmith! Looks like that studio is gonna fly!"

I said, "That's great 'cause I canceled classes in Rice Lake tonight and transferred the students to Cumberland. Guess now I'm going to teach classes in Ladysmith on their night."

Kim cheered, "Great! Now you'll be available if I need you in Luck."

With a sigh I said, "Yeah, but please don't need me. I would give anything for just one day to stay in bed and not think about anything." Sometimes I thought my mind was just going to snap from all the activity.

THE BAND WAS BOOKED AT THE *COUNTRY DAM* FOR Friday and Saturday nights. Lisa asked, "Do you think Vernon and I could go?"

I said, "Yeah, but you know Daddy can't stay out late."

"Don't worry," she said, "I'll take him home when he gets tired."

"Oh, Mom, I forgot to tell you," Pam said, "I'm sorry, Bob called."

My heart skipped a beat, "When?" I asked.

"About 8:00 p.m. and he's calling back about 10:30 p.m."

I looked at my watch and it was 10:15 p.m.. I said, "Gee, thanks for the warning."

I grabbed a quick sandwich and a Miller Lite, sat down and proceeded to watch the telephone as though it was gonna jump up and get me.

At exactly 10:30 p.m. it rang. I answered, "Hello."

"Hi, there," he said, "Where are you playing this weekend?"

Quickly I said, "The Country Dam."

"Can I take you to breakfast, I didn't want to wait until Halloween to see you again, so I made arrangements to be there this weekend. If it's okay with you?"

I tried to not be over excited, "It's more than okay with me. I've really missed you, it seems like I've known you forever."

"Me, too. I can't seem to get you off my mind, but at the same time, I don't know what I can do with you, with all the responsibilities you have, it doesn't leave much time for me."

With understanding I said, "I know, Bob, sometimes I would like to just wake up and be a normal woman like some of my parents in the studio."

"I'll be there Friday evening at the Dam. I'm not sure what time, but I will be there, he promised.

"Well, you know where to find me, I'll be singing my little songs," I explained.

He laughed and said, "Honey, I'll be there!"

My heart jumped about three beats. No one had called me honey for many years. He really made me feel special as we talked for over an hour. By the time I hung up the telephone, it was time to go to bed.

I went down stairs and Daddy was sleeping like a baby. Going to my room, I took a hot bath and climbed into my king size waterbed, alone.

I wondered if I would ever have time for any kind of relationship again and found my mind was on Friday night already Daddy and Lisa would be going Saturday instead of Friday and I was glad. Friday would be to just enjoy the evening with Bob and my friends. I knew Karen would be there to meet him this time.

BEFORE I DRIFTED OFF, MY MIND WENT BACK TO the studios. I was so disappointed with the terrible enrollment numbers. Spooner was the only studio with good attendance. Who could blame the student's parents for being skeptical with the way I had missed last year.

I had talked to some of the parents throughout the past month and couldn't get over the rumors going around about my personal life. These rumors were the direct cause for the decline in studio enrollment.

One parent said, "Oh, we heard Pam and Kim were going off to college, Steve and you were divorcing and that you were gonna devote your entire time to your dad."

With total disgust, I said, "With none of us working, did they suggest how I was gonna pay the bills? It's too bad they didn't figure that out while they were telling all these lies?" I was so hurt and angry. I wanted to cut their tongues out.

I suddenly remembered something Daddy had told me years before when I was worried about someone gossiping about me. He said, "Reta, there's three things you can't stop in this world—death, taxes, and wagging tongues. But remember, when they're talking about you, they're letting someone else rest."

I had my usual chat with God and said, "I know I've bent your ear a lot lately Dear God, but please let the Ladysmith Studio keep growing, you know our needs." I was so tired, I don't remember saying, Amen.

THE NEXT MORNING I GOT UP AND STARTED arranging class times in Ladysmith to start the next week, two days after enrollment.

The radio interview was scheduled the same day as enrollment, which would really help get parents over to the college to secure their child's class time. I was limited to only one day in the Ladysmith area due to the fact I only had one day left in my week.

I was overwhelmed at the responses. By the time Kim and I left for Clear Lake, I had already confirmed forty-five students. Between Kim and I, we could handle eighty but that would mean teaching seven classes. That would be a killer of a day, but we had to do it though, thanks to all the rumors and bad attendance at the other locations. I looked up and said, "Thanks, God, for hearing my special prayer last night."

BEFORE I NEW IT, FRIDAY WAS HERE AGAIN BUT THIS time I was looking forward to the gig more than usual. As I got ready to go, I kept having all these negative thoughts about meeting Bob. Rational thought told me I didn't want another relationship, nor did I have time for one. Then I would think about how I really liked him and then became so scared I was going to like him too much and get hurt again. My thoughts were all mixed up. I was excited and yet, scared at the same time.

I knew now how Aunt Sissy viewed relationships. One time I remember talking to her a few years back after her last abusive marriage. She said, "I'll never marry again. In fact, I don't intend to ever date again so that way I know I'll never marry again and give someone else a chance to hurt me."

I didn't understand at that time how she could be so bitter and she had totally given up on any kind of a relationship.

Then I remembered Karen's words, "I'll never give another f---ing man a chance to hurt me. I've had enough."

I hoped and prayed then, that I would never become that bitter, but now, I don't know. If Bob turned out to be a dud, then I believe, I would build the strongest wall around me in the world, even stronger than Sissy's and Karen's walls. Believe me, they built a strong one.

I FINISHED PUTTING THE LAST TOUCHES OF MY makeup on and thought as I looked in the mirror, *Reta, you need some rest! The only days I have off for the next eight months are Sundays, unless I don't have a gig!* This didn't leave much time for anything, of course, other than work or to make Daddy's appointments. Thank, God, Kim and Pam were out of school and I didn't have to worry about attending school activities.

Daddy was in his Lazy Boy drinking a glass of buttermilk. Kim, Pam, Brad and Cheryl had headed for a party in Amery, with the following night's schedule to include the *Country Dam* with Daddy and Lisa. They were also looking forward to seeing Bob again, but they decided to let me meet with him by myself on Friday night. Wasn't that thoughtful of them? Of course, we wouldn't be too alone with *Pure Gold* around and the entire club crowd thriving on every anxious moment. At least, I could spend my breaks with whomever I would choose.

I GAVE DADDY A KISS ON THE FOREHEAD AND TOOK off for the *Dam*. By the time I got there, Cords, Rick and Donnie had everything hauled in and lifted onto the stage. All the bands hated setting up at this particular club because of the height. The stage was located above the bar.

When I came bouncing in Cords said, "What are you so cheerful about? Did you win the lottery or what?"

Donnie interrupted, "Or is your boyfriend coming again this weekend?"

I said, "Well, as a matter of fact, Bob is gonna be here this weekend, hopefully tonight. I would like to see him by myself the first night. Lisa is bringing Daddy tomorrow night and, of course, the kids are all gonna be here to check him out again. I don't want him to feel on display the first night he's back. Besides, I don't think he's ready yet for the entire package. I scared the hell out of him last time with all my responsibilities." I laughed," I'll shock him again tomorrow night with the whole gang."

Cords sighed, "Boy, a girl like you would scare the hell out of me too, if I didn't know you." He shook his head and continued, "I don't think I could do what you're doing, but I damn sure admire you for taking care of your Daddy."

"Well, I can't take all the credit," I answered. "I have one heck of a little team at home. Pam and Kim have been great, I can count on them whether I need them at the studio or at home. I worry sometimes that I ask too much of them."

Rick said, "Ah, they're tough, like their mom—and pretty, too."

"Well, thank you, kind sir," I said with a smile.

LOOKING UP AT THE OLD CLOCK ON THE WALL, IT said it was time to hit the bandstand and play some good old country music. The guys went up first as usual.

Some of the bar owners wanted me on the bandstand the entire time, but others wanted a show. I liked doing a show because it gave me time to visit with the audience and gain a better following. It was nice that most of the club owners left it all up to me. They knew they would always get their money's worth whether I was on the bandstand or not.

My friend, Leroy Becker, was there, so I sat at the bar and visited with him. He was a big man, but gentle as a bear. I never dated Leroy, but he was one of the best friends I ever had.

Before long, in came my buddies, Wendy and Jeannie Howell. I had rented their beautiful home on the island in Amery in 1983. This was after I had returned from Texas and had just opened at the *Country Dam*.

Wendy was a tall man with salt and pepper hair. A handsome old devil and a retired airline pilot from Northwest. I might have been very attracted to him if he hadn't been married to a very sweet and pretty lady. Besides, I never dated married men. After being married to a cheater, I was best friends to all the wives.

Jeannie, Wendy's wife, was a former airline stewardess with Northwest and one of my best friends. If I ever needed a friend, I could always count on Wendy and Jeannie.

I still have a beautiful red gown that Jeannie gave me to wear for New Year's Eve, 1984.

That night I had started into my bedroom to get dressed for the show when Jeannie said, "Wait a minute, I have something special for you to wear tonight."

She smiled and hurried into her bedroom and came out with a beautiful off-the-shoulder red gown that was split up the side.

When I put on the dress, Jeannie said, "Well, that dress was made for you! I've never worn it and now I know why. I guess I was keeping it for you."

I gave her a hug and said, "Jeannie, I'll always think of you when I wear it."

When I went on stage that night, everyone flipped. That red dress was the center of attraction that New Year's Eve in 1984

Another time I wore that special dress was for a show I did with Marvin Rainwater, Brenda Lee's father. His song, *Gonna Find Me A Bluebird,* had been a big hit back when I was a little girl, in the summer of 1957. I had walked into the club wearing my red gown, and Marvin was shootin' pool. He looked up and said, "Well, howdy little, Reta— Whatcha tryin' to do? Upstage me in that perty red dress?"

I smiled and said, "Marv, no one could upstage you, but thanks. A dear friend gave it to me."

He said," Well, I guess I better change into something more compatible." Smiling, he left and went out to his van. In a few minutes he returned wearing a knock-out, dress Western suit, with beads and the whole bit. Still smiling, he said, "How's this?"

I whistled and drawled, "Now, Marv, whatcha tryin' to do, upstage me?" We all broke up laughing, especially his wife, Charee, who was taking tickets at the door and, from her angle, had been able to see us bustin' up.

Charee was a few years younger than Marvin and a very pretty lady with blonde hair. Since she had come into Marvin's life a few years before, he had done a complete turnaround. Now, he hardly drank any more and was very dependable. The new Marvin. A great transformation.

I really enjoyed working with Marvin. It always amazed me, the crowds he drew in the upper Midwest, even at some of the outlaw bars. Every show would be packed because Marvin was still as good as ever, and a great entertainer. People just loved him. My name was getting well-known from the exposure I received by being billed with him. We sang *Jackson*, plus a few more well-known duets together. Some referred to us as the *Johnny Cash and June Carter of The North*.

We had a show coming up again in the fall at the *Country Dam*. I was thinking about how much fun I have working with Marvin Rainwater and wondering how the next show would go, when I heard Cords say, "Now, let's put you're hands together and welcome please, Miss Reta Lee!"

The fans really made me feel welcome. I hit the bandstand singing an old Hank Williams tune, *Jambalaya*. Before my show was over, Bob walked in and stood right in front of me at the bar. My heart did a couple of flips, and, of course, the guys really teased me as I tried to sing while maintaining a semblance of composure.

Since I had told Jeannie about Bob coming, she, too, was trying to get my attention to confirm he was the one. Poor, Bob, he didn't know he was on-stage more than me.

Everyone wanted to see me have a nice relationship with a good man for a change but it was like having a club-full checking you out instead of just one's family, Buy the way, they too, would be checking him out again tomorrow night. I thought to myself, That poor guy is gonna take off before we really have a chance.

Most men would be gone if they found out a woman had two babies, let alone an invalid father, a band, a club-full of fans and was the *Kool-Aid Mother* to most of her daughter's friends.

The last time I saw Bob, he had asked, "With all your responsibilities, where do you have room for me?" Sad, but true. Maybe it just wasn't our turn this time, but he sure was good for me.

I could see Jeannie and Wendy were dying to know if the man in front of me was Bob, so I said with a smile, "I'd like to sing this next song for a good friend of mine. This one's for you, Bob." Jeannie gave me a nod of approval.

I finished singing, *Help Me Make It Through The Night*, introduced the guys in the band and said, "That brings us up to a small pause. We'll be back in fifteen minutes so don't go away now. It's people like you who make people like us."

As I left the stage, Cords said, "Let's hear those hands clapping for, Miss Reta Lee! We'll be right back." They then played, *Steel Guitar Rag* and took a break.

Uncle Bob smiled as I came down, and he handed me a Bacardi Diet. I said, "I gotta talk to him about me not drinking until the show is done but I'll drink this one to steady my nerves." Uncle Bob continued to smile in his teasing way.

I walked up to Bob then he leaned down and gave me gave me a peck on the lips and said, "Hi! Damn you look good and sound great, too!"

I just smiled and said, "Ditto."

He looked around and said, "Don't look now but every eye is on us."

"Sorry," I said, "They just don't want to see me get hurt any more, but believe me, I have gotten the thumbs up on you from the band and everyone else."

He said, as he glanced toward the end of the bar, "Well, that guy down there doesn't look to happy with me."

I looked at the other end of the bar and next to the door, there stood Gary. "Is he a boyfriend, or what? He's been throwing daggers at me since you sent that song out to me."

"He's just a very good friend of mine, Gary Miller," I answered. "He, too, is going through a divorce and he's probably like everyone else, very suspicious of anyone I might get involved with."

He shook his head and said, "Boy, I sure hope they all approve of me, you're one protected species!"

"Yeah, I gotta a lot of friends." Then I said, "Let's get a table."

Before we could sit down, I had to introduced him to Wendy, Jeannie, Gary, Leroy and about everyone else in the club. Finally, we made it over to the table, just in time for the band to start. Bob said, "We've got to go on that hot-air balloon ride. Maybe then I can be alone with you!"

I went back on bandstand while Bob visited with Wendy and Jeannie. Before the night was over, he was a very popular fellow.

After the last set, Mary Christianson and one of her girlfriends, Monie Christianson, came in. Although they had the same last name, they

THE INGREDIENT CALLED LOVE   241

were not related but were in a mood to party, and clearly Bob's friends were in a mood to do the same. They all decided to join us for breakfast. Bob shook his head and said, "Will we ever have any time alone?"

I smiled and replied with some wisdom for the moment, "This was not my idea. Talk to your friends."

We all went to the ranch restaurant in Luck, and after breakfast, we went out to Balsam Lake where Bob had his lake home. We partied and talked until the wee hours when Bob brought me home just before sunup.

I made us some coffee and we had just sat down in the living room when Lisa came up for Daddy's medication. She looked at Bob, smiled, and said, "You must be Bob. I've heard a lot about you." She looked at me with an approving eye.

Bob said, "Well, I've heard some good things about you, too."

Before I knew it, Daddy, Pam, Kim, Brad, Cheryl and Lisa were all at the breakfast table. Bob put his arm around me and said, "You're one helluva a woman, but..."

I interrupted, "But, I don't have any time for myself, right?"

He squeezed my shoulder and sighed, "Yeah, you took the words right out of my mouth,"

Daddy was his usual talkative self and I could tell everyone liked Bob. After breakfast he said, "You better get some sleep and I'll see you tonight."

I reminded him my family was going to be there tonight he smiled, shook his head and said, "Great, we'll get a big table." He gave me a kiss, shook hands with Daddy, told the kids he'd see them tonight and headed for his Blazer. I walked him out and he put his arms around me, picked me up and he gave me a nice, long kiss good bye. He was so big and strong, and I felt so secure and safe, that I just wanted to stay right there. I came back to reality and knew that was only a fantasy, we may never have our turn.

When I came back into the house every eye was on me. I smiled and said, "I don't want to hear anything out of any of you, I'm going to bed." They were still teasing and wolf calling when I went to my bedroom. I took a hot bath and hit the water bed. Before I closed my eyes I looked up and said, "Thank you, God," and drifted off to sleep.

I WOKE UP EARLY IN THE AFTERNOON AND WENT into the living room. Daddy was sitting in his Lazy Boy looking out the big bay window at the horses and Pam and Kim were in the kitchen working on dance exercises. I asked, "Where is Lisa?"

Kim rolled her eyes and said, "Down stairs with Gator."

"I thought we had that straight about his visits during working hours," I mumbled.

Pam said, "She asked us if we would watch Grandpa for awhile so she could visit with him."

"Will you girls please take Grandpa out on the deck for some fresh air while I get this straightened out?"

"Sure." Kim answered as Pam went over to get Grandpa.

I went down stairs and found them in her bedroom making out. I asked, "What the hell is going on here?"

Lisa jumped up and said, "Pam and Kim are watching Grandpa."

I said, "You don't work for Pam and Kim, you work for me. I thought we had all this straightened out about Gator's visits during working hours."

Gator raised up and said, "She's going out with me, tonight."

"Is this true, Lisa?" She just stood there. I said, "Get yourself together and come upstairs. We are going to get this straightened out once and for all."

In a few minutes Lisa came upstairs. I asked her, "Are you giving notice, now?"

"No." she said quietly.

"Lisa, Gator is costing you your job. Now is this what you want?"

Before she could answer, Gator walked in. It was obvious he'd had a few beers, and said in a hateful way, "Maybe you should stay home and take care of your Dad more often."

I lunged toward him and said, "You bastard! Because I took one night out in two months for myself, doesn't mean I've abandoned my Dad. How dare you talk to me like that! Get out of my house, now!."

He glared at Lisa and said, "Are you coming?"

She started crying and said, "I don't know what to do."

"Lisa," I said, "I don't need this crap and Daddy sure doesn't. If you don't have the guts to stand up to this drunk, then go with him, but if you stay, he will not be welcomed in my home ever again."

She looked at Gator and said, "Let me call you later."

"Okay, bitch," he said, and headed for the door.

I yelled, "Don't you ever bring your sorry butt out here again!"

Lisa continued to cry and I said, "Lisa, that man is going to do nothing but ruin your life. Besides putting me in a terrible position without help, this is why I hesitated hiring you. You're a good aid and a good person, but you never have or probably ever will stick to anything, especially, if you don't take charge of your own life."

She sat there awhile then said, "Maybe it's best if you find someone else. I'll stay until you do."

"Okay, Lisa," I sighed, "But this is the last time I will ever trust you or be there for you. Don't ever ask me for help again. I feel so bad, you are one of my biggest disappointments. You could have been so much and you sold out for so little."

Pam walked in and said, "What's happening? Gator squealed out and almost hit Max."

I said, "Well, Lisa, why don't you tell Pam and Kim what you've decided to do, since you've dumped on them too."

I got a cup of coffee and went out on the deck to visit with Daddy so Kim could join in on the conversation. I heard Kim say, "I knew it, Lisa. You screwed us over again! We talked Mom into taking another chance with you, why?" She just cried harder.

Daddy had finished his snack and was looking for a bed. I put him down for a nap, then I called my entire home-crew-team and told them the situation.

Betty said, "If Vernon needs me, just let me know."

I knew I could go back to the three aids if I had to, but with so many people working with Daddy at the same time had not proven to be good for his personality, in the past. Thank, God, I could count on them though.

I then went back up stairs. Pam, Kim and Lisa were still discussing the situation. I calmly looked at Lisa and said, "I know it doesn't matter to you what kind of a spot you put me in, but can I count on you to take care of Daddy tonight since I have to work? Don't worry about me going out with Bob, I'll just come back home as soon as the gig is over.

Pam glared at Lisa and said, "Mom, don't worry, if there is a problem, Kim, Brad, Cheryl and I will make sure Grandpa's all right."

I gave Pam and Kim a hug and said, "What would I do without you?"

"We love Grandpa, too, you know, Mom," Kim answered with reassurance.

I called Bob and told him the problem. He was so nice about the forth-coming date and said, "Well, maybe things can level out in your life before my next visit on Halloween. Don't worry, we'll still have a good time tonight."

When Daddy woke up Lisa was very attentive but I felt sad because I knew things were not going to work out with her. She had already proved to me she couldn't be trusted. I loved her so much and had tried so hard to help her throughout her little life, but she kept choosing not to help herself. The sad part was that I knew Gator would use her and just throw her away. But my Dad's welfare was the most important thing. I just hoped I could find some one soon.

That night we all got dressed and loaded Daddy into the car. Pam and Kim were spoiling him rotten and Lisa seemed like she was back to normal. If Gator should show up at the *Country Dam*, who knows what she would do. Her mind certainly wouldn't be on Daddy.

THERE WAS A GOOD CROWD THAT NIGHT AND, OF course, Daddy was the center of attraction. He was looking good and seemed to be having a great time. Pam was on one side and Lisa on the other.

Bob came in by the second set with his friends, pulled up a chair and joined my family. His buddies had made arrangements to meet Mary and Monie at the club too.

Mary assured me she would be there for me if I needed her. I was thankful for the support I had.

Daddy got tired before the third set started and wanted to find a bed. Brad said, "Grandpa, I'm tired too, let's go home."

"Daddy yawned and said, well, if you're waiting on me, you better run up your watch."

Lisa got him ready and the three of them took off for home. She always did such a nice job when Gator wasn't around. If Gator decided to show up, I knew Brad would be there and he had assured me he would handle everything. He had been the man of the house for some time and did a great job. It wasn't his choice to stay out late, but he never complained if Pam did.

After the third set ended, I joined Bob, Pam, Kim and Cheryl at our table. Bob had been so nice and the girls really liked him. For me, he had a hot water and lemon drink waiting. He now knew now about my not drinking until the show was over.

Bob excused himself and went to the men's room and came back laughing. I asked, "What's so funny? Tell me, I need a laugh, too."

He said, "There was a guy in there who came up to me and said, Who the hell are you and how come you get to sit with Reta and her girls? None of us ever get a chance to go out with any of them. I looked him straight in the eye and said, "That's my family, mister, and if you mess with them, you'll answer to me."

The guy was sitting at the bar, still looking at us at the end of the evening. He didn't make any moves, though, just looked.

Again, I felt so secure with Bob. He was the kind of man that would take care of his family, but I knew our relationship didn't have a chance, at this time.

We packed up and headed back to my house. The kids stayed up and visited with Bob until late and Bob's friends, with Mary and Monie stopped by also. Everyone was very compassionate and caring about my Dad's rest and kept the noise down. Mary spent the evening talking about what a neat guy Grandpa was. Another thing I found out was that Monie was also a Certified Aid. I didn't know if I would be interested in her though. She was a big gal with bleached, blonde hair and rougher than nails.

Everyone, including Bob, left in a couple of hours. He gave me a kiss goodbye and said, "I'll see you Halloween. Sure wish you could meet me in Chicago for that Hot-air Balloon Ride. I understand that you just don't have time for a social life, right now We'll see how things are next visit." He held me real close and continued, "Reta, I really care about you and your family. If you need anything, and I mean anything, just call my office."

I assured him I would and thanked him for the nice weekend. He then, reluctantly, climbed into his Blazer and left. Watching his car leave, I felt so sad inside, and once again wished we could have had some time alone...maybe Halloween.

The next day, Sunday, Gregg and Clarion stopped by for their jam session with Daddy. After awhile, they talked us into going to the *Straight 8*. Daddy was sitting on GO.

Pam said, "Mom, why don't you go on out and we'll take Grandpa to the grocery store, first, and meet you out there."

I laughed and said, "Take Grandpa to the grocery store! Whatcha gonna do Daddy, buy all the junk food?."

He licked his lips and said, "Hell, yeah! I wov dat stuff."

"Okay, Brody," I said as I gave him a hug. "I'll see you guys out there." I was so thankful I could count on Pam and Kim to keep an eye on Lisa. So far, Gator hadn't showed up, so she was doing fine.

I left for the club with Gregg and Clarion while the kids took off for the grocery store with Daddy.

When I walked into the club, there stood Cords grinning from ear to ear. He said, "Take a look at what I got." So saying he pulled out a brand new Fender lead guitar in baby blue.   He'd been talking about buying a new lead guitar for some time and had finally done it.

Gregg said, "Well, I hope you're planning on sitting in with us and breaking it in today."

Cords smiled and said, "I already have my equipment up there and I thought you would never ask. If I can't play it, at least it'll match my eyes." They all laughed and started setting up the bandstand. I was a very lucky lady to have so many good friends.

We were having a good country jam session going when the door opened and in came Daddy with his cheerleaders. They were laughing so hard, I thought they had been at a bar instead of the grocery store. Lisa was carrying the rubber that went around one of Daddy's wheels on his wheelchair. I shook my head, looked at Daddy and said, "Well, Brody, look what you've done. You've been running the roads so hard, you've run the rubber right off your wheelchair."

He started laughing, looked at Clarion and Gregg and said, "Hell, these ol' boys can fix it, can'tcha."

Gregg smiled and said, "You betcha, Vernon."

We transferred Daddy into a chair while they overhauled his wheel chair. The rubber slipped back on, it just took a little muscle. Clarion said when it was back on, "Better have Brad put a little glue on this when you get home, Vernon."

"Okay," Daddy answered.

The kids put Daddy back in his chair and wheeled him over to a table. Everyone who came in was shaking hands with him and talking. One lady said, "I can't believe he's the same man I saw a few months ago. What did you guys do to bring him back so far?"

Pam, Kim, and Lisa all chimed together, *"The Ingredient Called Love."*

She smiled and said, "Well, sure looks like you have enough love, Vernon. You're a mighty lucky guy."

Daddy beat his chest and said, "Yeah, you're right."

I asked, "How did the grocery shopping go?"

The girls all started laughing. Kim said, "Mom, I wish we had some pictures of our shopping trip. Lisa was sitting on Grandpa's lap so he could help her push the grocery cart and Pam was pushing them in the wheelchair and we were all grabbing groceries. Everyone in the store was laughing at us."

"Daddy was grabbing groceries, too, I bet," I replied.

"Yeah, but we put some of it back though," Kim said.

"That's nice," I said. "How much did this little shopping tour come to?"

They all looked at each other and Pam said, "About $150.00, but you know we needed laundry soap and just about everything else."

"That's okay," I said, "I know you guys don't get any more than we need."

Then I looked at Daddy and said, "Did you have a good time shopping, Daddy?" I could tell he didn't know what I was talking about but I knew that shopping trip would always be a wonderful memory for Pam and Kim.

He'd forgotten all about it but he knew just how to cover himself, as usual, and said, "You betcha." He hardly ever said, I don't remember." Instead, he would always come back with some kind of a clever answer.

WE STAYED ANOTHER HOUR AND THEN I TOLD THE guys goodbye and we headed for home. We had enrollment and the interview at Ladysmith the next day, so I had to get everything ready. Daddy said goodbye to everyone and promised to be back soon.

Before I left, Cords said, "Since we're not booked next weekend, why don't we have that house-party you've been talking about?"

"That's a good idea," I replied. "Why don't we plan for Saturday night. Is that okay with you girls?"

They were delighted and Pam said, "Brad will have the outside totally done by then." They started making their plans immediately for the weekend.

Lisa hadn't seen Gator since he squealed out of my driveway, and I hoped she would continue not to see him. Also, I was hoping he didn't get drunk and try to come to the party next Saturday night I certainly didn't want any trouble.

Gator had always been one of the peanut gallery before Lisa came. I always liked him and had never seen this ugly side of him. He had helped Brad with the house and I considered him a friend, therefore, I just couldn't understand why he turned into such a hateful person, but then, it was probably the booze talking. In any event, I didn't need his problems laid on me, I had enough of my own.

We got home, put the groceries away, had a bite to eat and by then Daddy was ready for bed.

Brad and I were talking about the up-coming party when Pam and Kim came running up stairs laughing. I said, "What is so funny?"

"You know that plastic hose Steve stuck into Grandpa's room for the heat to come in?" Kim said.

"Yeah," I said.

"Well, Grandpa thinks it's a cannon fixin' to shoot him. We had to turn his bed around before he would go to sleep."

"What is he gonna come up with next," I replied with a smile. "Do you girls remember the last time we turned Grandpa's bed around?"

"No, I can't remember," Pam said.

I continued, "It was back in 1982 when Daddy came for a visit. He walked into his bedroom and said, Now, Piss Ant, I ain't sleeping in this bed facing the east."

"What's wrong with facing the east?" I questioned.

"'Cause only dead people lay down facing the east so they can be ready to see the Almighty when He comes, and I ain't ready to see him yet," he answered, just as serious as could be.

Then I said, "Daddy, you and your superstitions!" I knew there was no arguing with him, so we turned the bed facing the west and he was just as happy as he could be for the entire visit."

WE ALL WENT TO BED EARLY. KIM AND I HAD TO GO to Ladysmith the next day, and the whole day promised to be rather hectic. Pam was staying home and helping with Grandpa.

I went to the interview first. We talked, first, about my band and then about my taking care of Daddy.

Tim, the interviewer, told his listening audience about enrollment and said, "Reta will be at the college right after the interview so get on out there and enroll. In fact, I've enrolled in her adult tap class." Tim was about twenty-eight and had always wanted to dance, so he had already enrolled and paid for his tap shoes.

After the interview, I joined Kim and Karen at the college. We enrolled over sixty-five students before we left that day. Everyone showed up that had enrolled over the telephone, plus brought a friend. The radio show had brought in even more. I was sure wishing I had another day to fill, but I didn't.

I was so happy on the way home and said, "Our prayers have really been answered. This studio will pull us though."

We were beat, but happy, when we got home. I gave Daddy a big kiss on the forehead and said, "Well, Brody, we can take a deep breath now, cause we'll have the money to handle our needs." We visited for awhile before he got tired and wanted to go to bed.

Pam and Lisa then filled Kim and I in on the party they had planned for Saturday night. I said, "Well, that's great! I'm gonna let you kids handle it. Now, I'm tired and going to bed. Goodnight."

I soaked in the tub awhile then went to bed and had my chat with God. I thanked Him for the good enrollment and for helping Daddy do so good. Then I asked him to keep Lisa away from Gator. Not just so she could continue to take care of Daddy, but for her own good. He was not a good influence on her.

Before closing my eyes I thought how Lisa and Pam worked really well together. Daddy really liked Lisa and of course, he loved all the special time with his granddaughter.

Then my mind wandered to the other studios. All had gone well this week but hardly any new students. Most of my Rice Lake students had transferred to Cumberland, so that made me happy.

I ended my thoughts and said, "Well, Lord, I've bent your ear long enough. Thanks for my daughters and for all my wonderful friends. Please help me keep my health. Amen." I was asleep within minutes.

THE NEXT DAY, PAM AND LISA TOOK DADDY TO therapy and afterward shopped for the party. Daddy was right with them every step of the way. I think he really had fun going places with them.

When I got home from work Pam said, "Good news, Mom! The therapist said to tell you Medicare will start picking up the tab for Grandpa's therapy again, and starting November 15th."

I smiled and said, "Boy, all this good news is too much, maybe it's gonna all work out."

SATURDAY AFTERNOON, THE GUYS SHOWED UP WITH all the equipment. While they set up downstairs, Daddy was taking in every move. He didn't want to miss a thing. Especially, he was fascinated when Brad brought in a big garbage can and filled it with ice for the Keg.

The girls were busy in the kitchen getting the snacks made. Everyone was busy doing their jobs. I said, "Well, Daddy, looks like it's just you and me. The kids have everything under control. Let's go out on the deck. "I wheeled him outside for awhile. The back yard was beautiful.

Noticing that the leaves were starting to peak out. I said, "Daddy, next Sunday would you like to take that ride up north that I promised you and see the pretty leaves, they should be totally peaked out by then." Hugging him, I said, "How about a date with your daughter?"

He grinned and said, "It's a date, baby!"

Pam and Kim came out for a break and joined us. Pam said, "Mom, we are closing off the upstairs. No one will be allowed up there, so when Grandpa gets tired, we'll just put him to bed in your waterbed."

Daddy interrupted and said, "That's fine with me."

I laughed and said, "But remember, Daddy, I get my water bed back."

He grinned, "Okay, I reckon so."

We heard the band strike up. Daddy's eyes got big and said, "Who's that."

"Well, you're such a popular fellow my band decided to come and play for you."

He started crying and said, "Damn, them are some nice ol' boys."

"Now don'tcha cry now, Daddy, we're gonna get your harmonica and have a little jam session with all of them," I assured him.

I brought Daddy back in, grabbed his harmonica, put him in the elevator and yelled at Cords to receive him downstairs. When he saw the band totally set up in his therapy room (my rec room) he just about flipped.

They were all having a beer so he said to me, "Gimmie a beer, Reta." I handed him a Kingsbury, which is a non-alcohol beer.

He sat there and drank his beer and listened to the guys and me play for awhile. He would occasionally toot his harmonica. Then he asked, "Reta, when did you get another guitar?"

"Just a few years ago, Daddy, but this is a bass," I answered. "Do you remember the guitar you bought me when I was a kid?"

He sat there in deep thought, then said, Can't say as I do.

I remembered the guitar Mother and he had bought at a pawn shop in Abilene for $5.00. It was for my birthday when I was about twelve.

One of Daddy's old friends, Carl Parker, was going to teach me to play. Mother had ordered me Chet Atkin's *Guitar Course* and I was actually doing pretty well.

One Sunday, after church, Yane and her family came, as they usually did every Sunday for dinner. I took my guitar and went out on the front porch, sat in the red porch swing and started singing and playing *Jambalaya*. Her oldest boy, Dexton, then about four years old, came out and wanted me to play with him. I said, "Leave me alone now. I gotta practice. Yane came out and told me I should play with him.

She had it made on Sunday's. Mother fixed her family dinner, Cecil and I washed dishes and she expected me to baby-sit her kids.

Well, this time Mama told me I could play with my guitar. After awhile, I laid my guitar down on the porch swing and went to the bathroom.

I came back in time just to see Dexton break it over the pillar on the front porch. I screamed, "Mama, come here!" The entire family ran out to find me crying and holding my broken guitar.

Mama said, "What happened?."

Dexton piped up and said, "Well, she wouldn't play with me."

Yane started laughing and picked him up. "Now, Dexton," she cooed, "That wasn't very nice of you."

Mama put her arms around me and comforted me as best she could. I said, "I hate him, and I hate her! She didn't even spank him! Will I ever get another one?"

She said, "I'll talk to your Daddy, baby. I just don't know.

Five-dollar guitars were hard to come by, so I never got another one. Till this day, I have never forgiven that little brat. He should have had his spoiled butt spanked off. Oh, well, I have a nice bass guitar now—and he'll never get his hands on this one!

I then asked, "Daddy, what would you like to hear?"

He thought a minute and said, *"Jodie Blonde."* We did *Tennessee Waltz* instead, as none of the guys knew *Jodie Blonde* and, anyway, I didn't know the words to the song.

Before long, the guests started arriving. We had especially invited everyone who had been on Daddy's home care team. All the pretty aids started showing up and giving him a hug and telling him what a handsome ol' devil he was. Daddy was just eating all this attention up. They were spoiling him rotten.

Daddy was still nursing the Kingsbury beer. Mary got up and set her glass down to get something. Daddy just reached over and took a drink out of it. He smacked his lips and said, as he pushed his Kingsbury aside, "I want one like she's drinking."

I poured a Kingsbury into a plastic glass, like Mary had, but he knew the difference. It was getting harder and harder to fool him. I said, "Daddy, before long you're gonna get out of that chair and get your own beer."

"I damn sure are," he replied as he took a little swig.

Just about everyone stopped by and marveled at the work Brad had done. So many of the kids, including Gator, had helped complete the house. Too bad things had to turn out the way they did with him.

About 10:00 p.m., Daddy said, "I'm tired, is there a bed around here?"

I said, "Daddy, I'm gonna put you upstairs in my waterbed where it will be quieter. Is that okay?"

"Fine with me," he said.

Everyone told him goodnight, the band played Waltz Across Texas, we put him in the elevator and took him up stairs to bed. He looked and acted so normal, I truly believed I would have my real Dad back before long.

We had a few uninvited guests but the guys quickly got rid of them. All in all the party was a success with Daddy and Brad as the two stars.

I told Lisa to enjoy herself and sleep in. I would sleep on the sofa and take care of Daddy's medication in the morning.

The next morning I gave Daddy his buttermilk, medication, and changed him. He went right back to sleep.

We all got up for a late breakfast. I asked, "Daddy, did that racket keep you awake last night?"

He looked and me and said, "What racket? I slept like a baby."

We just stayed home all day and got the house back to normal. Daddy was rested and in good spirits. I reminded him about our Father and Daughter day out alone next Sunday and was sure that he would enjoy the ride.

I told Lisa she could take next Sunday off and do whatever she wanted to. Everything had been going well and with all of us pitching in and helping with Daddy, she was getting quite a bit of time off. Also, he was not as much of a problem as he had been. He was getting more normal everyday. If he was hungry, needed a little boy's room, etc., he would tell us. Another thing I noticed was that he had been sleeping more lately. But I really wasn't too concerned about that, he had been getting great check ups at the doctor.

SUNDAY AFTERNOON THE TELEPHONE RANG. LISA answered it, handed it to her Grandpa and said, "It's for you."

I could tell the way Daddy acted it was Yane. She never wanted to talk to me, which I could never understand. Maybe she still didn't think I was capable of taking care of Daddy or advising her "properly" of his condition. Only she knows.

At the time, I even wished she could see our Daddy because I was sure that she would be so surprised and wouldn't believe he was the same person with whom I had left Abilene almost a year before.

Daddy sat there holding the telephone, but wasn't talking. I said, "Daddy, it's Yane. Talk to her." He just handed the telephone to me.

I said, "Yane, he doesn't want to talk any more."

In an accusing voice she said, "I just don't understand why he won't talk to me."

In a stern voice I replied, "Well, I don't either because I certainly encourage him to do so. He talks to everyone else, so your guess is as good as mine."

She asked, "Well, how is he doing?"

I replied, as nice as I could, "Great! He's getting good checkups and, like I promised, if there is any change, I will call you immediately, like I always have in the past."

"Okay," she said tersely, and hung up.

Talking to my only blood-sister was hard because she was so cold, and purposely so. She never said, "How are you doing, Reta?" or, "How is your family?" Nothing to make me feel like a sister.

In order to handle it, I made her a total void in my life and, as much as possible, in my thoughts. I had to remind myself that she was still Daddy's daughter, as much as I was, and I would keep her in that position even if it killed me. More than anything, I never wanted her to be able to say that I took Daddy away from her and never let her know about his condition.

I made Daddy's favorite Sunday dinner, Southern Fried Chicken, mashed potatoes, gravy, corn and homemade baking powder biscuits.

We all sat down to eat and Pam and Kim both, asked the Blessing. Afterwards, Daddy just kept looking at his chicken and finally asked, "Reta, what ever happened to Ol' Bitsey?"

I started laughing because Ol' Bitsey was my pet chicken when I was a little girl. I said, "Daddy, what ever made you think of Ol' Bitsey?"

"I don't know," he said as he began to eat.

I sat there for awhile and tried to think what had reminded him of Ol' Bitsey. Finally it dawned on me. I said, "Daddy, are you thinking about when you and Mama were culling the old hens and you thought you had accidentally killed Ol' Bitsey?"

He said, "I jest don't know."

Kim asked, "What is *culling* and did Grandpa and Nana kill your chicken?"

"No," I said, "they just thought they did. I don't know HOW exactly they could tell if the old hen was not laying eggs, but that's what *culling the hens* meant, sorting the productive from the non-productive ones.

"Anyway, one day I came home from school and Mama and Daddy were busy butchering the hens that didn't produce."

Kim interrupted, "You mean, if they didn't lay an egg everyday, they were killed?"

"That's right. Back on the farm, everyone, and I mean everyone, every animal had to carry its own weight."

Daddy chimed in, "Damn right—"

Pam said, "Go ahead with the story, Mom."

"Well, every day after school I would come home, grab a piece of bread and soak it with milk or water and head down to the barn to find Ol' Bitsey and feed her. But this time, I began as usual with my soaked bread and Mama started crying, saying, 'Where are you going baby?'

"I'm going to find Ol' Bitsey, Mama, like I always do. What's wrong?

"Daddy put his arm around Mama and I saw that he had tears in his eyes, too. She said, 'Vernon, what are we going to do?'

"I figured they had a problem with one of the cows, or the Bole Weavils were eating the cotton again. I went to the barn and called, 'Here, Bitsey! Here, Bitsey!'

"Before long Ol' Bitsey came limping out, just a squawkin' to beat anything. She was a pitiful looking thing. A big old white Legern. Her toes were all crooked on one foot from the time when Daddy had accidentally stepped on her when she was a baby. Also she had some paralysis from me carrying her so much. All in all, she was ugly, but to me she was beautiful.

"I fed her the bread and went back to the house. Mama and Daddy were still standing on the back porch looking pitiful. Mama said, 'Where have you been?'"

"I thought she was really losing it because she knew where I had been. I asked her, instead, 'Mama, what's the matter with you and Daddy? I was down at the barn feeding Ol' Bitsey her bread.'

"She said, 'You mean, you just fed Ol' Bitsey?'

"I replied, 'Yes, Mama.'

"She looked at Daddy, then back at me, and said, 'Go get Ol' Bitsey and bring her up here, and I'll feed her the whole loaf of bread.'

"She soaked another piece of bread and handed it to me. I knew she had really lost her mind then 'cause she never let me feed Ol' Bitsey more than one piece of store-bought bread a day.

"I took off for the barn calling Ol' Bitsey again. She had eaten every bite. I headed back to the house with Ol' Bitsey squawking close behind.

"Mama picked her up, hugged her, then hugged me. I asked, 'What's goin' on?'

"She said, 'Baby, we were cutting up the hens and found one with a crooked foot and we just knew we had killed Ol' Bitsey.'

"Mama started crying again, and I said, 'Don't cry. Ol' Bitsey is just fine.'

"I turned to that old chicken and said, 'Aren't 'cha Ol' Bitsey?' Bitsey confirmed she was okay by proceeding to poop a rather hefty prideful on the front porch. Instead of taking the broom to her, Mama and Daddy celebrated by just laughing."

Daddy had been listening to me tell the story with his full attention.

I asked him, "Do you remember that story Daddy?"

"Hell, Reta, I can't remember nothin' anymore. I think I'm goin' crazy or somethin'."

I laughed and said, "Daddy, you're not crazy, just retired, and you don't have to think about all these things anymore." I smiled and patted his hand, continuing, "But I have some wonderful memories."

We all continued to eat when all of a sudden Kim asked, "Well, what ever happened to Ol' Bitsey?"

"She lived to be fourteen years old and died in my arms on Christmas Day from old age."

Brad said, "She was a mighty lucky chicken. Where did you get her?"

"The skunks ate her mother and all of the babies except for her and another little black one. When we found them, they were full of lice. Daddy gave me the white one and Cecil the black one. Cecil's died also, but Ol' Bitsey pulled through."

"I always said, "Me and Tommy Smothers have one thing in common—a pet chicken!"

Kim asked, "Who's Tommy Smothers?"

I said, "Eat your dinner, Kim. No more questions for awhile."

Daddy said, "Yeah, Polly Parrot. Hush awhile, now."

WE HAD SUCH A NICE DAY AND BEFORE LONG IT WAS time to go to bed and start another full week. I was glad the band was not booked the next Saturday night because I was looking forward to Daddy's and my trip up north on Sunday.

Before I went to bed, Bob called to see how I was and to remind me he would see me in a couple of weeks for Halloween. He said, "Do you think we could find some time to be alone during my visit?"

"I sure hope so," I replied. I knew I didn't have time in my life for a relationship at this time, and I also knew if I couldn't make time, I was going to loose him.

I turned all my problems and needs over to God and went to sleep. I had a big week ahead of me.

Ladysmith studio was in session now, and it was by far my best. Pam was doing well with her studio in Luck. Spooner, Clear Lake and Cumberland studios were still hanging on but the enrollment was about one half of what they had been last year. Kimberly was turning out to be a really good little teacher and the students all loved her. I sure was proud of my girls, they were tough just like Sissy and me.

I wish my mother could have lived long enough for my girls to have known her. I know she knows them though, because I feel her watching over us every day of my life, especially now. I sometimes feel she is my Guardian Angel.

THE WEEK PASSED RATHER FAST. SOMETIMES I FELT as though my life was spinning out of control and I treasured every moment I could steal for myself. I was so happy to have Saturday off because I had so much book work to take care of for the studios. Thank, God, the girls took care of the house and grocery shopping.

I made bread and some pies to put in the freezer when I had time. I liked to cook up as many treats, hot dishes and so on, whenever I could. The Crock Pot became my best friend.

We always had a good nourishing meal and kept Daddy on schedule as much as possible. If he was hungry, he wasn't bashful, and he would certainly let us know.

Although my home was getting somewhat into a normal routine, there was still never any time left for me. I prayed that God would continue to give me my health. Sometimes I felt like I was headed for a nervous breakdown but a good cry, along with my regular conversations with Jesus, were always my best medicine. Somehow I was making it financially and emotionally. A testimony to Him, not to me.

SUNDAY MORNING WAS A NICE DAY FOR OUR outing. I was so happy and felt almost lighthearted. After getting on my housecoat, I went down with Daddy's coffee and walked into his room and there in the middle of his bed were Pam, Kim and Lisa. They were planning their day and Daddy was right in the middle of it all. I sat on the end of the bed. After all it was a hospital bed and there was not a whole lot of room left.

Daddy looked at me and asked, "Well, Reta, where have you been?" He acted like he hadn't seen me for weeks. I didn't get to see him as much now as I had been, many times he was already asleep when I got home from the studio.

I said, "Well, good morning to you too! I've been working trying to keep us all going."

He said, "That's good. Are we making much money?"

"We're okay. You don't have anything to worry about," I answered.

We drank our coffee and Lisa said, "Grandpa, let's get you shaved so you will look all spiffy for your outing with your daughter."

"Where are we going?" he questioned.

I said, "Don't you remember? You made a firm date with me last week to go up north and see the pretty leaves before they all blow away?"

"I don't 'member," he said, "but I'm ready."

Lisa said, "I'll give Grandpa a bed bath so that he can save all his energy for the trip."

"That sounds good." I looked at Daddy and said, "I'll fix you a bowl of oatmeal before we leave and we'll eat lunch on the road."

I went up stairs and started getting ready, then ran down stairs to see how much Daddy lacked being ready for breakfast.

I could hear the girls all laughing as I got to the bottom of the stairs. I walked into Daddy's room and there Lisa and Daddy were with shaving cream all over their faces. I started laughing too. "What in the world are you two doing?"

Lisa said, "Well, Grandpa wouldn't let me put lather on his face unless he could put some on mine."

I shook my head and said, "Daddy, you're spoiled rotten!"

He grinned and said, "Yeah, I suppose so."

"Well, when you guys are done playing, come on up for breakfast." I smiled and then ran upstairs. I was so happy the girls had accepted their new Grandpa and were having fun with him. My old Dad would have a fit if he knew the situation he was in, but my new Dad was enjoying what moments he was having with his family. Tears came to my eyes as I thought of the kind of man he was, and thanked God he didn't realize the kind of man he had become.

I went back upstairs to the kitchen and got Daddy's oatmeal ready. About the time Pam ran upstairs to receive him in the elevator, Lisa and Kim came up and they all proceeded to have breakfast with Grandpa and he was in his glory.

Lisa had dressed him in his jogging suit and Yankee Tennis Shoes. Dressed like that, he would be more comfortable riding in the car and also much easier for me to handle him, especially when he had to go to the bathroom.

While they were all eating, I went downstairs to pack his little bag for our road-trip. It reminded me of packing Pam and Kim's diaper bag when they were babies. The difference being these were different items. I put in Depends, medications, blood pressure cuff and a change of clothes.

With Daddy's things all ready to go, I then went up to my bedroom and finished dressing. I usually wore jeans, sweat shirt and tennis shoes so I could handle Daddy with ease. I sat down at the table and drank another cup of coffee with them before we took off.

While Lisa took Daddy to the bathroom, Pam and Kim got his things loaded in the car for me. You would think we were leaving for a week or two instead of an afternoon.

I took the Lincoln so that if he got tired, I could lay his seat back and he could sleep. We got him in the car, gave him his Stetson, loaded his wheelchair in the trunk, and waved good bye as we headed out.

THE SUN WAS SHINING AND I COULDN'T HAVE asked for a nicer day. Daddy was already talking a mile a minute as I headed out on County Road H.

He was looking at the big dairy herds along the way when I mentioned, "Daddy, those cattle look different from the ones you raised, don't they?"

He gave them a good checking over and said, "Yeah, that's them ol' Holsteins."

"What kind did you have?" I asked.

He looked at me in deep thought and said, "Now, Reta, you know what kind I had."

I laughed and said, "Daddy, you did it again. You've always got an answer, don'tcha?"

He grinned and answered "You ain't gonna start me to lying."

After a few more miles I said, "Now, I remember. Your cattle were Herefords, red with white faces, right?"

His eyes twinkled as he answered, "That's right."

THE LEAVES WERE ABSOLUTELY BEAUTIFUL AS WE
headed out of Luck toward Frederick. I showed him the little school Pam
and Kim had attended in Frederick and Daddy commented, "That's a little
thing, ain't it?"

"It sure is," I agreed. "It's kind of like the little schools they used
to have back in your days. Do you remember all the stories you told me
about when you were a little boy and how mean you were in school?"

He laughed and said, "Yeah, I gave 'em hell."

Laughing, also I told him, "I remember I was about ten when you
and Mama took Cecil and me to Buffalo Gap to go swimming. You saw
an older woman sitting at one of the picnic tables and you started laughing
and said, 'Reta, go over there and ask that woman who was the meanest kid
in Harmony School.'

"Since I never was shy, I walked right up to her and said, 'Hi,
Maam, my Daddy wanted me to ask you who was the meanest boy in
Harmony School.'

"She burst out laughing and said, 'Dear God, is Vernon Fuller your
Daddy?'

"I immediately smiled and said, 'Yes, Mam, he is.' By that time,
you walked up and it was quite a reunion. Do you remember that Daddy?"

"No, hell I can't remember nothin' anymore. Why is that, Reta?"

"I guess you just got too much to remember. I can't remember
things like I used to, either. Guess I take after you." We both laughed as
we continued on our drive.

Daddy was really enjoying himself I could tell, and that went
double for me. I loved that man so much and was thankful I could take
care of him and didn't have to put him in a nursing home. My daily prayer
was that I could continue with my pace of living. At times, I felt that my
energy was going downhill fast, what with the pace I was keeping and all.

We finally arrived in Siren and turned onto Highway 70 heading
toward Grantsburg. "Are you getting hungry, Daddy?" I asked.

"Hell," he said, "I could eat a skunk."

I laughed and said, "Well, we'll stop and have dinner at *The Point
Supper Club* in Grantsburg, if that is okay with you?"

"If it suits you, it jest tickles me to death," he replied with a grin.

We pulled into *The Point.* I got out Daddy's wheelchair and helped
him inside. A few people were there that knew me from the band. They
acted excited to see me as a normal person. It always surprises me that
people think that somehow a performer is not as normal as the ordinary
person. They have a preconceived vision of the performer on the
bandstand and don't realize that the singer has a life after the microphone.

Some of my former students were there also. They all came over
and met Daddy and were delighted at what a nice man he was. They

couldn't believe he'd had a stroke because Daddy handled himself so well. Even I forgot he was bluffing half the time.

Many times I wondered just how much he actually knew, but he was an amazing man even with three-fourths of his brain damaged. He certainly put the one-fourth the Good Lord left him with to work. I was very proud of my Daddy.

After a delicious and enjoyable meal, one of the waitresses watched the door while I took Daddy into the Men's Room before leaving. We said goodbye to everyone and headed the car toward St. Croix Falls. I had put Daddy's seat back when we first got into the car and he took a little nap on the way to St. Croix Falls.

When I pulled off at the St. Croix Overlook I woke him up. His eyes got big as he looked at all the beauty seen from that spot. "Ain't that perdy," he said in amazement.

"Yeah, if someone didn't believe in God, one look at all this beauty and they would have to know that only God could draw this picture," I said. He shook his head in agreement and continued to just look his fill. I was so happy that I had brought him today, This would be a memory I would always treasure.

On the way home, we stopped at *Wayne's Restaurant* on Highway 8 for a cup of coffee and a piece of pecan pie. Once again, Daddy was the center of attraction in his Stetson hat.

I was so proud of him He drank his coffee and ate his pie without spilling a drop while he held his head high and straight. When he was finished he placed his hat back on his head and asked, "Is there a bed any where around here?"

I told him, "I'll bet you I know where to find one."

I got him in the car, put his seat back and he slept all the way home. He woke up at the end of the driveway and said, "Is there a little boy's room anywhere around here?"

"Just hang on Daddy," I said, "We'll be home in a couple of minutes."

Everyone was gone when we got home. I took Daddy into the house, took him to the bathroom and he went down for a very long nap. Being exhausted, too, I lay down on Lisa's water bed and napped a little myself. It had been a very nice and memorable day.

THE KIDS ALL GOT HOME IN TIME TO TAKE CARE OF Daddy's supper, medication and getting him ready for bed. I asked Lisa if he had been sleeping more than usual. She replied, "Yeah, but I don't think there's anything wrong."

"Is he still drinking plenty of fluids?" I questioned.

She said, "Yeah."

Something in the back of my head was telling me she didn't watch his fluid intake like she should. I wish I had more time to really keep an eye on everything but with my responsibilities I just had to trust her.

LISA, PAM AND KIM HAD BEEN ACTING A LITTLE funny ever since they got home. After they got Daddy to bed they came back up to the living room. I said, "Okay, what's going on? All three of you look like the cat that swallowed the canary."

Pam said, "Mom, don't get mad until you hear everything."

"Just lay it on me," I said.

Lisa continued, "We saw Gator today, and he really feels bad about what he did and wants to apologize to you and see if he can start over again."

"Are you dating him again, Lisa?" I asked

"Yeah, I want to."

I shook my head and said, "You know it's gonna be nothing but trouble, but if he and you can live by my rules and he doesn't interfere with your job, I guess I will give him another chance."

They all started squealing and hugging me all at the same time. Lisa called Gator and told him to come out.

Within fifteen minutes he drove up. He came in, gave me a hug and said, "Reta, I don't know what the hell is the matter with me. I'm so sorry to have talked to you that way, you've been through so much, then I had to act like that."

I hugged him and said, "Let's start all over again, Gator. But the beer is your problem, you're gonna have to handle it or it will keep getting you in trouble." He nodded his head in agreement.

THE NEXT TWO WEEKS PASSED QUICKLY AND before I knew it the kids were planning their Halloween costumes. Even at their age, they were still kids when it came to Halloween.

We were booked at the *Country Dam*, again, for Halloween. The guys got everything set up Thursday night and we rehearsed some after I got done at the studio. I had the studios running Monday through Thursday which left Friday, Saturday and Sunday nights for the band.

I was a nervous wreck as I got dressed to go Friday night. Bob would be there by the second set.

Betty was working so Lisa could have the weekend off. I dreaded having to tell Bob I had to go home and relieve Betty as soon as I got off the bandstand. I wouldn't blame him if he found someone else to date because ours was not the best arrangement for a single guy.

When I arrived at the club it was already packed. Everyone was getting ready for Halloween the next night and some were already dressed up and making the rounds.

The bars always gave away big prizes and just about everyone dressed up and competed. The bands had a hard time picking the winners but I always disqualified myself as a judge because of the kids.

I kept my eye peeled on the door and about 10:00 p.m., Bob walked in with several of his friends. They were hooting and hollering like crazy. Mary and Monie met them there before break time. I was still dreading telling Bob that I couldn't drink and party after work because I had to go home and relieve Betty.

When I came down from the bandstand at the break, Bob picked me up and gave me a big kiss. My heart was pounding and I knew that I really liked him.

I sat at the table with him and his friends, they were in a mood to party. Bob put his arm around me and asked, "Can you go with me to Balsam Lake tonight?"

Looking at him with tears in my eyes, I explained. "Bob, I don't blame you if you find someone else to go out with that has time for a personal life. All I'm doing is messing up your time off. I know you work hard and would like to have some fun when you come up here, but I just don't know what to do." Then the tears really came in earnest.

He put his arms around me and said, "Hey, I understand, we'll go to your house like we did before. I'll go pick up the party stuff and it will all be okay." He gave me a peck on the cheek for reassurance.

I said, "You're one in a million."

Before I knew it, I heard Cords say, "Let's put your hands together for Miss Reta Lee!"

Bob smiled and said, ""Give 'em hell!"

I hit the bandstand and belted out a few old standards and of course, sang, *Help Me Make It Through The Night,* for Bob.

Bob left a little before the show was over so that he could get to the *Holiday Grocery Store* before it closed. He wanted to pick up the party items we needed.

I closed the show with *One Day At A Time, Sweet Jesus,* and as soon as Uncle Bob yelled, "It's hotel-motel time! The bus is leaving!" We all headed for my house.

Everyone was very quiet and considerate of Daddy and he never knew that anyone had come in.

When I got home I asked Betty, "How is Daddy?"

She said, "He's fine, but all he wants to do is sleep."

"I know," I said, "If this continues I'm gonna call Dr. Speier. Maybe she needs to cut back more on his medication again."

Before leaving, Betty said to me, "I'll be back about 7:00 p.m. tomorrow night. Is that what time you want me?"

"Yeah, that's fine. I have to leave about 7:30 p.m.

She volunteered, "If it will help, I can come earlier."

I said, "If you could come to give Daddy his supper I would greatly appreciate it. How about 6:00 p.m.?"

"Fine," Betty said with a big smile. "You kids have fun. She visited for a few minutes and then said goodnight to everyone and took off for home. Betty and her husband ran a farm so she had to get up early the next morning.

Bob said, "You really have some wonderful people working for you. Where is Fred?"

"He is living up on the Iron Range with his mother, and I sure do miss him."

THE PARTY HAD STARTED AT MY HOUSE BUT AFTER awhile everyone, except Bob, headed for Balsam Lake where they could make some noise and crank the stereo. I didn't blame them.

I turned to Bob and said, "If you want to join them, I will understand. Just because I can't go, doesn't mean you can't."

He hugged me and said, "Don't you worry. I'm happy just sitting right here on the sofa with you and helping you watch over your Daddy. You don't know how proud I am of you. I've never met anyone like you before and I'd rather sit and talk with you than party any day."

"Well, you sure know how to make me feel better," I replied. "I just wish things could be different."

"Maybe someday they will," he answered.

Before long the kids came home. They felt terrible because I couldn't have some time alone with Bob.

Lisa was spending the weekend at Gator's house which worried me. She was already starting to change back to the way it was before. The job was too confining for someone so young.

Pam said, "Mom, Gator treats her awful when he's drinking. He had her crying tonight."

Bob asked, "What's going on with Lisa?"

I told him the situation and then said, "I had better continue to find a replacement for Lisa, the writing is on the wall."

The girls were telling Bob all about their costumes for tomorrow night and then they all went to bed.

Pam and Kim checked on Grandpa and reported he was sleeping like a baby.

Bob said, "It's late and you need some rest, I'll be back about mid morning." He gave me a very frustrated kiss good night and headed home for Balsam Lake. I knew this was not going to work out much longer. There were plenty of woman, out there, who would love to latch onto him. It just wasn't our turn.

ABOUT 8:00 A.M. THE NEXT MORNING, BOB KNOCKED on my door. He took me in his arms and said, "I gotta talk to you." He looked so serious. I just stood there for a moment enjoying being held, it had been so long since I had been close to a real man.

I said, "How about some coffee?"

"That sounds good." He said, "I haven't had any sleep. All I can think about is you and I just don't know what to do with you. I care about you so much, but there is no time in your life for me."

"I feel the same way, Bob. You have been such a rock for me, but I can't expect you to only get leftovers."

He smiled and said, "Honey, you don't even have any leftovers! Have you thought about putting your Dad in a nursing home?"

I pulled away and said in a very firm, almost angry voice, "No, I will never put him in a nursing home!"

"Then you plan to devote your entire life to caring for him?," he asked.

"I guess I will, if I have to. All I know is he's not going to a nursing home."

"That's okay," he said. "I'm just trying to see if we have anything ahead for us."

I got us a cup of coffee and we continued to talk. Our relationship seemed so hopeless.

Before long the kids were up and so was Daddy. Brad came over just in time to visit with Bob while I took care of Daddy.

Pam and Kim made bacon and eggs with all the trimmings while I brought Daddy up. That left me some time so that I could visit with Bob.

He shook hands with Daddy and stood in the kitchen watching our activities. He didn't say hardly anything, I knew he was in deep thought and went over to him, put my arms around him and asked, "Are you okay?"

He just held me real tight and answered, "I wish things could be different, maybe some day. I need to get back over to Luck, so I'll see you at the *Country Dam* about 8:00 p.m., okay?"

I knew he was upset and that he had planned on a much nicer weekend than this but I didn't know what else I could do.

I walked him out to his Blazer. He took me in his arms and kissed me tenderly and said, "You are, and always will be, a very special person in my life. I'm caring too much for you."

I kissed him back and said, "I wish things could be different. I care too much for you."

He got in his Blazer, waved goodbye and said, "I'll see you tonight."

I watched him drive away and feeling as though I would never see him again.

Everyone was still eating when I got back in the house. Cheryl said, "Reta, I haven't made any plans for tonight and I didn't plan on dressing up like Pam and Kim. After Betty leaves, I'll stay with Grandpa so you can have some private time with Bob after the show."

I gave her a hug and said, "Cheryl, you'll never know how much I appreciate that.

Cheryl was a sweet and considerate young lady with fiery red hair and had been part of my family since Kim had met her in school their freshman year.

As soon as the breakfast dishes were cleared, the girls started working on costumes. I laughed and said, "You guys will never change. You always wait until the last minute to start any project."

AFTER BREAKFAST, I GOT DADDY DRESSED AND shaved. We were still razor shaving him, and I might add, I had gotten rather good at it. He still helped me with his upper lip but I handle the rest just like a pro. I then brought him out to the living room and let him sit in front of the big bay window, drinking his coffee and looking at the horses. He loved watching them and I wondered what memories he might recall as he watched them graze. Horses had always been such a big part of his life.

I poured me another cup of coffee and sat and watched him for a while. My thoughts went back to my childhood as they do quite often, now. We had ridden many a mile, together, on horseback when I was a kid. He would put me on behind him and I would hang on for dear life. He would say, "Now, Piss Ant, if ya start bawling I'll take you back to yor ma. I don't have time to mess with you." I would ride back there and never even whimper.

Another memory I had was of an old roan horse he bought, one time. She was a wild one. He saddled her up in the mountain pasture and was going to ride her down to the corral at our home so he could work with her on a daily basis. I cried and cried to go with him and against mother's wishes, he said, "Okay but you better not start bawling."

I promised that I would be very quite. Mama said, "Vernon, your gonna get her killed with that horse!"

He put his arms around her and said, "She'll be okay. I'll meet you down at the fishing tank and drop her off." Mother always loved to fish. As usual, he had charmed her into letting me go.

We headed down the mountain at a fast gallop. I was straddled behind the saddle hanging on to Daddy, but some how my little private part was rubbing between the horse and the saddle. By the time Daddy dropped me off with mother, I was totally black and blue, but I never cried.

Mother bathed me that night and when she saw my owie, all hell broke loose. Daddy felt so bad and asked me, "Baby, why didn't you tell me?"

I sniffled, "cause you wouldn't let me go no more."

He picked me up and hugged me and said, "Next time, you let me know. We can't have something like this ever happen again."

Mother was very unhappy with Daddy for a few days but by the end of the week everything was back to normal and I was still riding behind him. He was just a lot more careful of my placement behind the saddle.

THE RINGING TELEPHONE SNAPPED ME OUT OF MY reverie and back to the present. It was Lisa. "How's Grandpa?" she asked.

"Oh, he's just fine. He's watching the horses."

"Great," she answered. "Tell Pam and Kim we'll be there in about an hour to help with the costumes."

I couldn't get Bob off my mind and I kept having a really funny feeling that I wasn't going to see him again. When he had said *goodbye*, it had sounded almost final, not like someone who would be seeing me in a few hours. Whatever happened though, I couldn't blame him.

Lisa and Gator came in and Lisa said, "Reta, you said once that you didn't care what happened to your wedding dress. If you still feel that way, I sure would like to use it."

I sat down, "Lisa, you're not getting married, are you?"

She and Gator both started laughing, "No, I would like to wear it tonight for Halloween."

I was certainly relieved to know that's all she wanted it for. After thinking for a moment, said, "Well, I think Halloween would be appropriate for that dress. It certainly hasn't been a good memory for me."

I went up and got it, complete with veil and handed it to her. She and Gator took off downstairs with my $400.00 wedding dress. I chuckled to myself, Maybe now that dress will find it's true destiny. I didn't know what any of the kids had planned, just knew it was going to be a surprise for me.

I took Daddy outside for some fresh air and after a few minutes he started looking for a bed. I said, "Daddy, you haven't been up that long, how can you be so sleepy?"

"I don't know," he replied. "But I damn sure am."

I decided right then and there I was going to take him to see Dr. Speier this next week. I put him down for a nap and gave him oxygen. I thought maybe that would help wake him up .

Betty arrived about 5:30 p.m. and said, "I decided to get here a little earlier than we planned in case you needed me."

I gave her a hug and said, "Betty, if I haven't told you lately, I really do appreciate you."

She said, "I know. Where's Vernon?"

I said, "He got up about 2:00 p.m., ate some dinner and then went back to bed. I'm really getting concerned about all this sleeping he's doing. Come Monday, morning, I'm gonna talk to Dr. Speier."

BETTY TOOK OFF FOR DADDY'S ROOM AND I started to get dressed. The kids had been hiding out downstairs and I had heard my sewing machine a few times. I wondered what they were going to be.

Betty brought Daddy up for supper. She had made her famous Porcupine Hot Dish. I just finished getting dressed and was about ready to go when Kim yelled, "Are you guys ready?"

I looked at Daddy and said, "Well, Brody, get ready. It's Halloween and there is no telling what your granddaughters are gonna look like."

I yelled back, "We're ready!"

They were a sight for sore eyes. Daddy didn't know what the heck was happening.

Brad was dressed as *Count Dracula*, complete with cape and all, and Pam was *Dracula's Wife*, dressed in a black slinky dress made out of a dyed sheet.

Next came Lisa. My wedding dress had finally found it's true niche. She was going as the *Bride of Frankenstein*. I laughed and said, "That's the kind of bride I was in that dress, except, compared to the Weasel, *Frankenstein* would have been an improvement."

Everyone laughed as Kim came running up the stairs being chased by Gator. She was dressed in one of Daddy's hospital gowns and her hair fried out. She was dressed up as a crazy woman.

Gator was dressed all in white, like a doctor, with Daddy's stethoscope hanging around his neck. He was carrying my meat basting syringe and when he finally caught Kim, pretended to give her a shot which calmed her down.

By this time, all of us were practically on the floor from laughing so hard. Their makeup was perfect for the characters they were portraying. They all looked so real and I said, "If you guys don't win first place tonight, I'll be surprised. You've done great for not spending any money.

Daddy was still laughing, even though he didn't really understand what was going on. But believe me, he was wide awake.

They were anxious to take off for all the bars, hoping to collect some First-place Money. Pam said, "We'll be at the *Country Dam* before the last set." They gave me a hug and off they went.

Cheryl and Betty were spoiling Daddy as I gave him a kiss on the forehead and headed for the gig.

THE PLACE WAS PRETTY WELL PACKED BY THE TIME I got there. *Pure Gold* and I had decided to just go as our selves. We had tried dressing up in the past and it was just too constrictive to try and work in costumes.

Bob's friends came in during our first set but Bob wasn't with them. I was disappointed, but actually not surprised because of the way he had acted when he left my house.

At the break, I came down and asked his friends where he was. They avoided the subject and when the third show started and he hadn't arrived, I knew I had been stood up. Feeling like such a fool made me both angry and hurt. The least he could have done was be honest.

Gary Miller came in during the third show. He was happy to know Bob hadn't shown. I told him, "He picked a good time to stand me up 'cause I could have had some time tonight. Cheryl's watching Daddy so I don't have to go directly home."

Gary smiled and said, "Well, my name's not Bob, but I'll be happy to hit a few house-parties with you after you're done."

"Sounds great!" I told him.

A few minutes later, in came the kids. Gator was chasing Kim with the syringe. Brad and Pam looked like something out of a horror movie.

Pam said, "Everyone thinks we've rented Brad's cape. No one can believe we made it."

It did look professional, black outside with a fiery red lining and a collar that stood straight up with the help of a clothes hanger sewed into it.

Pam's dress was slit up the side and low necked. Her hair and make up, like Brad's, was perfect.

Lisa had white powder in her hair, white make up on and she looked totally dead. There were even a few drops of red coloring on my wedding dress for blood.

Kim, of course, had white powder in her hair, white make up and black rings around her eyes. They had used black eye liner to paint suicide scares on her arms. She totally looked the part of a crazy woman.

They had won first place at two of the local bars, but at the *Country Dam,* they took second. They had won enough money to take care of their evening's entertainment. The judges always had a hard time choosing the winners because everyone in the area was very competitive and creative.

After Uncle Bob yelled, "Hotel-motel time! The bus is leaving!" Gary and me, along with *Pure Gold* and their wives headed for a party at Wendy and Jeannie's house. The kids headed for another party somewhere in the area.

GARY HAD BEEN RENTING WENDY AND JEANNIE'S little cabin on their property. It was a cute one bedroom and I had almost rented it back in 1983, before I decided to rent their home.

Just about everyone showed up. Dave Swanson, who used to play with *Trigger Happy,* showed up with them. Before you knew it, the guitars came out and we were having another show. At least three different bands showed up, including Karen, Gregg and Clarion. All were friends of mine.

Upon arriving, I called home and talked to Cheryl. She assured me that Grandpa was fine and that I should just enjoy myself. She said, "I'll call you if I need you, but all is fine."

I wished that Bob could have been there but his friends had joined us. They were all having quite a good time.

Before the evening ended, one of Bob's friends got pretty drunk and was trying to hit on me and I set him straight, immediately. He knew if he didn't shape up, about half the party would be on his neck. My friends watched over me very well and were rather protective.

Jeannie fixed *Sloppy Joes* and chips for everyone to eat and then I went home before the sun came up.

Gary and I had made plans for that afternoon if Daddy felt like Running The Roads. Daddy and I would meet him at the *Straight 8* for Gregg and Clarion's show.

I MADE COFFEE WHEN I GOT HOME AND GOT Daddy's medication ready. Until time for his meds, I just sat on the sofa thinking about the weekend. I was feeling so bad about Bob but at the same time, I couldn't believe he would just stand me up.

I got Daddy a cup of coffee, grabbed his medication, poured him a glass of buttermilk and headed down stairs. Daddy was talking to someone, I could hear, when I got to his door. I said, "Good morning, Mr. Fuller. What are you chirping about this morning?"

He grinned and said, "I was just talking to Ol' Shorty."

I said, "Well, how about having some coffee with your daughter?"

"Suits me," he said. I gave him the pillow to hold while I changed his Depends and washed him.

Cheryl came in and said, "Why don't you go get some sleep and I'll visit with Grandpa until he goes back to sleep."

I gave her a hug and said, "You'll never know how much I appreciate you watching Daddy last night for me. Even though Bob stood me up."

"He what!" she almost yelled in her surprise.

"You heard me right. The jerk stood me up. Did he call here or anything?"

"I haven't heard a word from him," she replied.

Lisa came in then and was still wearing part of her make up. "Is everything okay?" she asked.

"Yeah, Daddy's just fine," I told her. "Will you fill Cheryl in on Bob's standing me up last night? I need to get some sleep."

"Sure," she said.

I kissed Daddy and said, "Are you ready to Run The Roads with me today?"

"You betcha," he replied.

Lisa patted Daddy's hand and said, "We better give you plenty of your Kick-A-Poo-Joy-Juice so that you can stay awake."

As I went up to my bedroom, I found myself wondering if Old Shorty was still alive

I took a hot shower and hit the bed. Before falling asleep, I had a little chat with God and then went sound asleep.

The kids fixed Italian spaghetti for dinner and I got up in time to join them. Daddy was in high spirits and Lisa had him dressed and everything ready to go. They were busy telling him all about their Halloween night.

I said, "Sure looks like that oxygen does the trick. Maybe I should go inhale some of it myself."

I got dressed and we met Gary at the Straight 8. Daddy was wide awake, feeling really good and he was in the mood to party so we left there and went to the *Country Dam* for supper.

He still wanted to party and I asked, "Daddy, you need to get home. Aren't you tired?"

"Hell, no," he said.

We stopped at the *Tac-Lo-Ban Club* on the way home. They had a hypnotist's show going on. I couldn't believe what this man was having people do under hypnosis. Afterwards I talked to him about working with my Dad.

He said, "I don't work with patients other than for smoking, dieting or just plain entertainment, but I will call you with a telephone number of someone who does. It might be possible to get through to his sub-conscience, if he can just be put under."

I gave him my number and said, "Please don't forget to call. This could be a total new breakthrough."

Daddy was still going strong at 11:00 p.m. and I finally said, "Now, Daddy, you've got to go home."

He yawned and said, "Well, if you think so. I'm a little tired."

Gary couldn't get over how outgoing Daddy was and his mind seemed so clear. He helped me get Daddy to bed because Lisa was out with Gator.

She was wanting more and more nights off now and I knew I had to find someone soon. Gator was already starting to interfere with her work. It was just a matter of time, if she continued to see him.

Gary and I went back up stairs and had a nightcap. Before long Lisa and Gator pulled up. She came in and apologized for being late, saying "Gator is being a jerk."

I could tell she had been crying and asked, "How long are you going to put up with this, Lisa?"

"I don't know because I love him," she whimpered. She took off downstairs, checked on Daddy and went to bed.

Gary stayed for quite awhile and we talked. I asked his opinion about the hypnotherapists and he agreed it might just be worth a try.

I said, "If they can reach his sub-conscience, it could start helping other parts of his brain to take over for the damage parts. That means, if it tells him to walk, he will. Do you see the concept, Gary, or am I just dreaming?"

"No," he said, "I think you might-be on to something."

Gary was such a nice person and like me, he just needed a friend to talk with and who understood. I could tell we were going to have a good relationship and he seemed to fit right in with the family. He wasn't scared off by them.

THE NEXT MORNING DADDY TOOK HIS MEDICATION, ate some oatmeal and slept until noon. He was plain pooped out. Lisa gave him some oxygen, later, but all he wanted to do was sleep.

I called Dr. Speier and told her about Daddy's sleeping problem and also about his night out and not wanting to go home. She said, "Bring him in this Friday and I'll check him over."

This would work out great as we were only booked at the Foxhole for Saturday night, so Friday was the only free day I had.

Looking in the mirror when I started getting ready to go to the studio, I noticed the black circles around my eyes were not painted like Kim's and knew I couldn't have another weekend like the past one. I had to start coming straight home after the gigs, no matter what. We couldn't afford for me to get sick.

Maybe I was lucky Bob left because I didn't really have time for any kind of a serious relationship right now. Just the kind Gary offered. He was very understanding about my responsibilities and actually helped me more than complain.

Kim and I got back from the Spooner Studio about 9:30 p.m. Daddy was already asleep and Lisa had been crying again, she and Gator were fighting.

I said, "Lisa, what are you going to do because I don't have time to worry about your problems. They could hinder your caring for Daddy."

She snapped back, "I'm doing my job, Reta."

I said, "Don't get huffy with me, little lady, that's my Daddy you're taking care of and I need to know your mind is totally on him."

She whipped down to her room and I looked at Pam and Kim and said, "We're gonna have problems again. I've got to get someone lined up, and soon."

THE NEXT MORNING AFTER DADDY'S THERAPY, Mary came out for his massage. He really liked her and the massage was wonderful for him and enjoyed it so much. I mentioned to Mary my concerns regarding Lisa.

She said, "If you need any extra help, just let me know. I'll put the word out at work you're needing someone and I'll also put a notice on the bulletin board at school."

"Thanks, Mary," I said. "That would be appreciated."

Daddy did pretty good the next couple of days. When Joyce Schaefer, the Home Care Nurse, made her weekly checkup, she, too, was a little concerned about Daddy sleeping so much. She was glad I was taking him in to see Dr. Speier that Friday. He was bright when he was awake but the amount of time he spent sleeping kept increasing more and more.

Friday came and I took him to see Dr. Speier, as planned. She ran some tests on him and said, "Make sure he is getting plenty of liquids. Remember, he only has one kidney and the tests show it is not working as well as it was the last visit."

"Is this what is making him sleepy?" I asked her.

"Oh, yes," she said, "If the remaining kidney does not function properly, he will become extremely lethargic"

On the way home I stopped and got Daddy his hamburger and French fries. He just didn't seem up to par so we went straight home afterwards and when I put him to bed, he was fast asleep within minutes.

Lisa was gone again with Gator, but she did get home at the time she had promised.

It was time for a family council. I sat everyone down and told them the problem with Daddy.

Lisa assured me she was giving Daddy plenty of liquid. I said, "Well, if you don't, his kidney will quit functioning and we will lose him. I can't tell you how important this is."

Pam assured me, "Mom—Brad, Kim and I will really watch this, too."

THANKSGIVING WAS JUST AROUND THE CORNER. WE were struggling to obtain more students but, other than that, things were going all right. I was getting more rest and had given up any kind of social life. Sometimes I would meet Gary and Karen for periods of time but, basically, just taught classes, sang my songs, and cared for my family.

One morning, about a week before Thanksgiving, I got up and went downstairs for Daddy's medication. Lisa was over at Gator's house again, and Pam, Kim and Cheryl were sleeping in her bed next to Daddy's room, to be able to hear him if he woke up, take care of him or wake me up if there was a problem.

When I opened his door and went over to his bed, I found him lying there with his eyes wide open, and his skin was pasty and cold. I dropped the coffee, medications and started screaming and crying, "Daddy wake up! Wake up Daddy! Don't die on me! Please don't be dead. Oh, God, don't let him be dead—"

Daddy shook his head, blinked his eyes and said, "What in the hell is the matter with you, Reta? You gone crazy or what?"

I grabbed him and started hugging him and crying, "Daddy, don't you ever scare me like that again!"

Naturally, this all woke the girls up and they came running into his room. They stayed with Daddy and cleaned up the mess and entertained him while I went upstairs and got more coffee, medication and buttermilk.

I was shaking so bad I had to sit down for a few minutes and collect myself. My nerves were shot and I felt myself crumbling inside but didn't know what to do. I was carrying too big of a load. Looking up I said, "God, please help me, give me the strength I need."

After a little while, when I had my emotions somewhat under control, I went back downstairs with new coffee, medication and buttermilk. I was so thankful for my girls, they were my lifelines.

Lisa came home about 9:00 a.m. and said, "I'm sorry."

With the experience I had just been through, I couldn't handle her excuses any longer. Interrupting her, I said, "Don't sorry me any more Lisa. This can't continue. I never know when you're gonna be here. You can't expect Pam, Kim and Cheryl to do your job for you."

She snapped, "I guess ya better find someone else." I just shook my head and went upstairs and wondered how much more I could take.

Pam came up and said, "Mom, I'll keep an eye on Grandpa, today, but let's find someone else. I agree, Lisa can't be trusted anymore now that she's back with Gator. He tells her what to do and she does it."

Kim and I got dressed and headed for the Cumberland studio. Right in the middle of one of my classes, the telephone rang. Lisa said, "Reta, I've sent for an ambulance because Grandpa just had a seizure!."

"Had a seizure!" I screamed. "I don't understand, he's never had seizures. I'll meet you at the hospital."

Kim said, "Mom, go ahead, I'll finish the classes and Cheryl will watch the front. Don't worry about us, we'll get a ride home." I hugged her and took off.

I was totally baffled. On that frantic drive back to Amery, I tried to understand why he'd had a seizure. Another thing I decided, he was not going to be admitted to that hospital, again, I would have him transfer him to Abbott-Northwestern if he had to be hospitalized.

Running into the emergency room I found they had Daddy on one of the examining tables. I hurried to him and took his hand in mine. He held on so tight the circulation was almost cut off in my hand. I assured him he would be okay.

Dr. Rimestad said, "I don't know what's going on here, but Vernon is not looking good at all. He called and talked with Dr. Speier and she had him put him on Delantin.

He came back and said, "You can take your Daddy home, but be sure and make an appointment for next week for a check up with me. If he has any more seizures, call me immediately."

I got Daddy dressed and took him home. My heart was just breaking, because he looked really bad. I couldn't understand what was happening, we had fought so hard. I prayed for God to watch over him and to give me strength because I was so scared. When we arrived home, I tried to get him to eat, but he only wanted to go to bed.

I called Cords and told him what had happened with Daddy. I asked, "Can you guys take over the shows again like you did last year? I have to find a replacement for Lisa."

He said, "What is the matter with her?"

"She's in love and she's letting the fire in her pants burn a hole in her brain, but I can't wait for her to dummy up. My Dad's life is at stake. I've got to get someone I can depend on. Damn, I miss Fred."

Cords said, "Reta, don't worry about the show. We'll handle it and if there is anything else we can do, don't hesitate to call. You know how much we care about you and your family."

I started to cry, "Thanks, buddy, and tell Rick and Donnie thanks too."

Everything was a little rocky for the next couple of weeks but we started planning Thanksgiving Dinner anyway. Daddy seemed to keep going down hill instead of bouncing back. Dr. Rimestad had checked him at his last appointment and said, "Reta, I think you're Daddy needs to get down to see Dr. Speier before his scheduled appointment."

I agreed and called Dr. Speier and set up an appointment with her for the Friday the week after Thanksgiving.

THE GIRLS PLANNED A BIG THANKSGIVING DINNER. They made arrangements for Gary to pick me up about mid morning to get me out of the house so I could relax some. They wanted to fix the entire dinner for their Mom and Grandpa. Gary took me to the *Country Dam* for a Bloody Mary or two. I felt really special not having to cook that big dinner. About noon they called and told Gary to bring me home.

I walked in and couldn't believe my eyes. The dinner table was set complete with my new china and silverware, which I had never used. The turkey was perfect along with all the trimmings. I started to cry and said, "This is so nice, you girls are the best." Lots of hugs were exchanged and of course, Grandpa got his share.

Lisa had picked up her Grandmother from the *St. Croix Nursing Home* and brought her over for dinner. We teased Daddy about having a date, but he was just not the same. He didn't seem to have any interest in anything but his bed. He did spend a lot of time in the bathroom, though, because we fed him so much liquid.

It was a beautiful dinner and the girls took care of the dishes while Daddy, Gary and I sat in the living room and visited. Gary said, "Vernon, can't you stay awake and visit with us?"

Daddy yawned and said, "Damn, boy, I don't know what's the matter with me.

I said, "Daddy, do you want to go back down for a nap?"

"Yeah, that sounds good." I was so worried about his kidney and Dr. Speier would be running more tests, I was sure, when she saw him tomorrow. Daddy just hadn't been the same since the seizure.

Lisa, Pam and Kim took her Grandmother back to the nursing home shortly after dinner. She was ready for a nap too, a real sweetheart of a lady. After thanking me for having her over, she then praised the girls for the beautiful dinner.

While the girls were off to St. Croix, Gary and I sat in the living room contemplated the meaning of life. We were going to meet Karen later after Lisa got back. After awhile Gary said, "You're really worried about your Dad, aren't you?"

"Yes," I replied, "The sleeping is related to his kidney, but he is not alert when he's awake like he was before the seizure. I'm so worried about mini-strokes. They told me when I left Sister Kenny, that it was possible he could suffer a mini-stroke at any time and that it could wipe out all the progress we've made."

Gary put his arm around me and said, "Now, don't start buying trouble. He'll come out of this."

I started to cry, "I just don't know, Gary. It feels like something is terribly wrong and I'm gonna lose him. This sounds so selfish, I know, because Daddy wouldn't want to live as he is."

"When he was at his best, I kept remembering him and me visiting Uncle R.A. in the nursing home. Daddy had looked at some of those old people and said, My, God, Reta, I hope and pray I'm never in that condition. Look at that poor old man in that wheelchair. I blew my nose and continued, "My mother always said, God had a reason for everything.

"There is a purpose for my Daddy going through this and maybe someday I'll understand but right now I'm scared to death of losing him. I just can't let go, yet."

Gary put both arms around me and held me for awhile. He said, "You need to fix your face, pull yourself together. When Lisa gets back we'll go over to Karen's house, she knows how to make you laugh."

I kissed him and said, "Thanks for being here. I don't know what I would do without you and Karen. I can be weak with you, but I feel like I have to always be brave for Pam and Kim or they would freak."

Pam called and said, "Mom, Kim and I are with Brad. Lisa took off with Gator but she said she would be home by 6:00 p.m.."

"Okay," I said, "I hope she shows up. It's been a nice day so far."

Over the intercom I could hear Daddy stirring so Gary and I went down to get him up. He was wet, lying very still and looking at the ceiling. I gave him the pillow to hold while I changed him and Gary helped me.

I said, "Daddy, are you okay?"

In a very quiet voice he said, "Reta, what's happened to me, am I crazy or what?"

I gave him a hug and said, "Daddy, you're not crazy, you're just tired. We are going to see Dr. Speier, next week and she'll fix you up brand new."

I gave him his medication and he drank a big glass of buttermilk. Then I asked, "Daddy, are you hungry? You hardly ate anything for dinner and Pam and Kim fixed you a big plate of leftover turkey and dressing."

His eyes got big. "Turkey and dressing?"

"Yeah," I answered, "don't you remember? This is Thanksgiving Day!"

He started to cry, "I didn't know that."

"I said, "Now, don't you cry, Daddy. Let's just go upstairs and have a bite to eat."

"Okay," he sniffled.

I warmed up his dinner while Gary chatted with him. He ate only a few bites and then said, "I'm jest not hungry."

I said, "Daddy, you've got to eat, you've already lost some weight." He took a few more bites and pushed his plate back.

"Okay, I'll make you some of your high calorie pudding with real whipped cream, that'll keep the weight on."

I put Daddy in his Lazy Boy and noticed that he seemed disorientated. Within minutes, he was back asleep.

I turned on the radio to my favorite local radio station, WXCE and heard Gregg Marrs playing some good old country music. I always kept Daddy's little radio on in his room tuned to country. They had told me at Sister Kenny to always keep some soothing music playing, as it made Daddy's condition easier on him. It did create a calming effect and, in Daddy's case, country music was always the answer.

The clock stuck 7:00 p.m. and Lisa hadn't showed up yet, nor called. I called Karen to let her know Gary and I would be late.

She said, "You've got to do something different. That little twit is so undependable."

"I know," I said, "It's a shame, because she is such a good person and aid when she is not involved with Gator. I've put out the word and I'm looking though."

She laughed and said, "Well, let me know if Lisa's gonna give you the night off!"

Daddy didn't want to eat any supper, but I did get him to eat a glass of nanner puddin' and drink a big glass of buttermilk. Then I washed him up and got him back to bed about 8:00 p.m.

Gary and I went back up stairs and I was sure getting madder by the minute. Gary said, "She sure takes advantage of your friendship, doesn't she?"

"Yeah, "I said, "And she's getting paid twice again what Fred got and I could always depend on Fred."

In a few minutes Lisa and Gator showed up. They walked in, and I knew right off that Gator had been drinking, but wasn't sure about Lisa.

She said, "Gator and I are going to a party, is that okay?"

I said, "No, Lisa, that's not okay. I gave you Halloween Night off and you're getting Christmas and New Year's Eve off and you promised to work Thanksgiving so that I could go out for a change."

Gator piped up, "Well she's going and you can watch your dad for a change."

I blew, "Get out of my house you ignorant idiot, and don't you ever come back apologizing again!"

"Don't worry," he snapped. Then he glared at Lisa and said, "Are you coming?"

Lisa didn't answer, just turned and ran downstairs. I yelled, "Get your butt out of here!"

Gator then yelled down at Lisa, "I'll be outside waiting for you!"

Lisa came back up carrying her suitcase and I said, "Lisa, if you walk out of here, don't you ever call me to come back into my life. This will be the third time you've pulled this crap, but this time you've really done it."

She started toward the door and said, "Well, I'm too young for a job like this."

"No, you're not too young, you're too immature and weak. You just blew off one of the best friends you will ever have."

She opened the door and walked out, got in the car with Gator and they peeled out of our yard.

I looked at Gary and said, "Well, good riddance. Now I don't have to worry about whether she is going to be here or not. One thing though, she will someday regret what she just did."

I looked at Gary and said, "I'm sorry, but I've got to start calling aids and lining up help for tomorrow. You just go on over to Karen's house and tell her what happened and I'll talk to you tomorrow night when I get home from the studio."

He gave me a hug and said, "Hang in there kid. It will all work out and don't forget, if you need me, just holler."

Immediately I called Betty and arranged for her to take a 7:00 a.m. to 3:00 p.m. shift. Then I was able to get Mary to take the 3:00 p.m. To 11:00 p.m. shift for the next week. I would be home to relieve Mary by 11:00 p.m. Also I knew that I could count on Pam, Kim or Cheryl to stay from 11:00 p.m. to 7:00 a. m. if I had to.

Pam, Kim and Brad came home. They were so mad at Lisa for what she had done, plus they felt responsible for talking me into hiring her.

I told them, "It's not your fault. I, too believed she had changed, but as soon as a man comes into the picture, she totally loses all perspective. Just never ask me to take her back in again. From now on she is a void.

I TOOK A HOT BATH, WENT TO BED AND READ MY favorite poem *Footsteps* again and wondered if God was truly carrying me now.

Before going to sleep, I had a really long talk with God. He knew all my needs and I just prayed he would give me the help, strength and patience needed to make it through each day. As I drifted off to sleep, the song I usually closed with, "One Day At A Time, Sweet Jesus" kept floating through my head.

About 6:30 a.m. I woke up and got coffee going so that I could visit awhile with Betty and fill her in on Daddy's condition before he got up.

Betty said, "I hope he's not having mini-strokes. I will be sure and fill Mary in on everything when she takes over."

I gave her a hug and said, "Betty, I really appreciate your willingness to help me out, full-time, until I can find someone, 'cause I know you don't want to work full-time."

"That's okay," she answered with a smile, "Don't you worry one bit about Vernon, we'll take good care of him."

It was such a relief knowing that Betty and Mary were going to be in charge because I totally trusted them with my Dad.

Looking up I said, "Thank you, God, for answering my prayers. Just please let me find a good live-in aid who's dependable and caring like Fred."

Then I called Kathy and told her about Lisa.

She said, "I'll make all the necessary payroll arrangements. We can carry Mary and Betty for awhile. As long as Vernon continues to improve, I can get you quite a bit of help with Vernon's expenses."

I didn't dare tell her about the problems Daddy was having because I just prayed they would all go away and he would start back improving like he was.

Later Kim and I went to the studio and realized that I actually felt better today. My mind was more at ease with Betty and Mary taking care of Daddy.

I Hadn't realized, until now, how much I had worried about Lisa. She was a good aid, but Gator ruled her. Probably I hadn't trusted her for some time. Daddy had been doing so good when she took over and now he was going downhill. Maybe she had done everything exactly right. Only she and God will know the answer to that question. All I knew now, was that I was totally relieved about the situation and Lisa had what she wanted...Gator.

The snow was coming down pretty heavy by the time we left the studio that night. Kim and I got home about 10:00 p.m.

When we walked in, Mary was folding Daddy's laundry. Bless their hearts, she and Betty had taken care of everything.

Brad had bought a plow to go on the front of his truck, and he and Pam were out plowing snow. Pam was keeping his books and appointments plus teaching her classes in Luck.

Going down to check on Daddy, I found him sound asleep and looking so peaceful and content. Mary had gone with me and she smiled and said, "It's good to see you guys again. I'll start spreading the word about an aid for you and my notice is still up on the bulletin board at school."

"Anything you can do would be so appreciated," I replied.

I was so exhausted, that I took a shower, called Gary, let him know I was okay and went straight to bed. The next morning I heard Betty sneak downstairs. I rolled over and went back to sleep because I knew she had everything under control.

I got up about 9:00 a.m., grabbed a cup of coffee and visited with Daddy and Betty. While she went in to get his bath ready, I poured Daddy another cup of coffee. He just sat there looking at it and had hardly eaten any breakfast.

I said, "Daddy, you've got to start eating or Dr. Speier will put you in the hospital and start feeding you through your veins."

"I'm just not hungry," he weakly replied.

LATER, THAT MORNING, THE TELEPHONE RANG AND the lady on the other end asked, "Is this Reta Lee?"

"Yes, who is this?" I questioned.

She answered, "Well, you know me, but I'm afraid to tell you who I am because I am calling about the job with your Dad and you may not be interested. You've only seen the wild side of me but I am a Certified Aid with a lot of experience."

I said, "I am looking for someone to start immediately but where do I know you from?"

She paused for a moment and said, "Well, do you remember a blond named Monie that came to your house one night after your show with one of Bob's friends?" She nervously laughed, "And I was feeling no pain."

A little slowly and disappointed I said, "Oh, yes."

She quickly continued, "I would like to come out and talk to you. I never drink on the job and I am very dependable. Mary told me the problems you've had with Lisa and believe me, you won't have any problems like that with me. The men in my life are history, besides, my job would always come first."

I laughed and said, "I'm not one to judge. Too many people in my life have judged me. Could you come out now for an interview and meet Daddy before I leave for work?"

"I'll be there in fifteen minutes." She was so eager, but I did remember what a party girl she was so I was gonna proceed with caution.

I went in and helped Betty finish up with Daddy's bath and told her about Monie coming out.

She said, "I sure hope she's what you're looking for, but take your time, I will help you until you find the right one."

I smiled and said, "Thanks, Betty, I appreciate that."

Daddy was sitting so quite, almost asleep and I said, "Daddy, can you stay awake long enough to interview a young lady to replace Lisa."

"Who's Lisa?" he questioned, then shut his eyes.

I just patted his hand and said, "That's okay Daddy. I'll interview her, you just rest."

Betty brought him in and sat him in his Lazy Boy. I noticed that he was losing weight. She tried to coax him into eating, but with no luck. All she could get down him was the faithful buttermilk. He was beginning to act like he had in the beginning.

In a few minutes Monie knocked on the door. I invited her in and she went directly over to Daddy. I could see love and concern in her face. She said, "How long has it been since the stroke?"

I explained how Daddy had progressed for quite some time. Then when I told her about the seizure and the way he had regressed, she shook her head and said, "Sounds like he might be having mini-strokes. When is his next appointment?"

"Friday," I replied.

"If you were to decide to hire me, I would like to go with you so I can see exactly what they are doing." I was impressed already and I could tell that Betty was also. She just seemed to have that certain something.

Daddy looked at her, smiled and said, "Hi, gal, get yourself a cup of coffee."

She said, "Okay, how about some more for you?"

"Reckon I will," he answered.

Shall we go to the table and have some of that nanner puddin' Reta told me she had made just for you?" Monie asked.

"I reckon so," he said.

She picked up the transfer belt, looked at Betty and me and said, "May I?"

"Go right ahead," I told her.

We watched as she slipped it around Daddy like an old pro and transferred him to his wheelchair. She then patted his hand, lifted his arm and moved it around. I could tell she was checking to see if range-of-motion had been properly administered.   This really impressed me and I could tell it impressed Betty too.

Monie wheeled him over to the table and had him eating a little nanner puddin', along with drinking his coffee and buttermilk. It was hard to believe she hadn't been working with him for months.

Betty looked at me and nodded her approval. Monie gave me a few references then she and Betty took Daddy downstairs for his nap.

I made a few calls and got nothing but good references on her. She had lived in the Twin Cities and had given up her job to relocate after her divorce.

When Monie came back up she said, "If you want me, I sure would like to work with Vernon."

I said, "When can you start?"

Smiling she replied, "Yesterday, but I do have two small problems."

Too good to be true passed through my mind as I asked, "What's that?"

I have two little girls. Could they stay here with me until I can make arrangements with my Mother and Dad to care for them? They could sleep with me and I would put money in for their food. They really are good kids and mind really well...

I interrupted, "Monie, I know what it is to be a single parent with two little girls. Yes, you can bring your daughters out her until you make arrangements with your mother."

She gave me a hug and said, "You're so understanding and you won't be disappointed, I promise."

I smiled and said, "Monie, you remind me so much of myself a few years back. We'll work out your personal problems if you will just give 100 per cent to my dad."

She said, "I'll give a hundred and fifty percent."   Somehow I believed she would.

Pam and Kim came upstairs. I introduced them to Monie and they liked her right away and started making plans for her to move in immediately.

Pam said, "I just teach one day a week and help Brad with his snow plowing business, so I will be here if you need any help."

"Thanks," Monie said, "I'll sure need help until I learn where everything is. As she was talking, she was busy checking over Daddy's medication list which I always had posted on the refrigerator. She also scanned through the range of motion procedures and other information regarding Daddy's care on the list from Sister Kinney.

She told me, "I'll read all this from beginning to end tonight after we get Vernon to bed. Right now, I need to make arrangements made for my kids. Maybe they can stay at Mom and Dad's house, immediately and then I have to go down to St. Paul and get my belongings.

She said good bye to Kim and me, told Pam and Betty she would be back before they knew it, then out the door she flew.

"Betty said, "I guess you won't need me in the morning. She seems to already have everything under control."

"You can say that again," I said in amazement, "She seems to know exactly what she's doing."

Betty agreed but said, "If for some reason, she doesn't work out, don't hesitate to call. Also, will I still be working on her days off?"

"Sure thing, we'll stay with the same schedule as we did with Fred. Every other weekend off, plus one day per week. I don't think it will be as crazy as it was with Lisa."

She laughed and replied, "Yeah, I never knew when you were gonna call while she was here."

"Me, either. Those few weeks she was here turned out to be a nightmare. She was okay until Gator, but she sure went to pot after she started going with him."

I looked at my watch and said, "Kim, we better start getting ready for work."

"Okay," she whined, "but I wish Pam would go so I could stay here and get to know Monie better. I sure like her!"

Pam piped up, "No way Kim, besides I've worked more with Grandpa than you have so I can help Monie more."

"You cannot!" Kim yelled. "I know just as much about Grandpa as you do."

I spoke up, "Do you girls want to start writing?"

They laughed, and Kim conceded, "Okay, but she always gets her way." She then stomped downstairs to get dressed.

Before I left for work, I called Karen to tell her the good news. She said, "Well I hope you can depend on her. What you went through with that other little twit was ridiculous. How is your dad?"

I paused, "I'm afraid he's having some mini-strokes and we have poured so much liquid down him to keep his kidney flushed out that it seems he lives in the bathroom. I will be so happy when Dr. Speier checks him over this Friday."

She said, "I'll stop out for coffee in the morning and meet Monie and then I'll give you my opinion."

I laughed and said, "Okay, but I'll give poor Monie fair warning that she's under fire."

Kim came up all ready to go, but I knew she really wanted to stay and get to know Monie. I said, "Honey, I would like to stay too but we have to bring home the bacon."

She looked at Pam and said, "Yeah, ya hear that Pam? We gotta bring home the bacon."

Pam laughed and said, "Well, I'll eat it so just keep that bacon coming."

"That's enough out of you two." I gave Pam a hug and out the door we went.

I REALLY FELT AT EASE WITH MONIE, JUST AS I DID with Betty, Mary, and of course, Fred. It still bothered me about Lisa and I felt she would live to regret what she had done. Especially if she knew in her heart that Daddy's regression was because of her mind being on Gator instead of his welfare. I will always love her, but she had finally given me the ultimate hurt when she walked out on us when we were counting on her.

Classes went really well that day and Kim said on the way home, "Mom, I really have a good feeling about Monie. She just seemed to fit with our family, right off the bat."

"I know," I answered." It's obvious, she knows her job. but I still can't believe she's the same girl I met with Bob's friend."

"Me either," Kim said, "But I sure do like her."

When we got home, late, Daddy was already back in bed and Monie was busy getting her room in order.

Mary was delighted I had hired Monie too. She had said to me, "She was so scared you would think she was a slut or something."

Laughing, I said, "Well, we've all had our times and I learned a long time ago not to Believe anything I heard and half of what I see. I always vowed I would never judge anyone until I got to know them." Chuckling, I continued, "If people had believed all the ugly things my sister and Shirley had said about me during my life, I would be a total outcast from society."

Pam said, "Oh, yeah, Mom, speaking of your sister, she called tonight. I told her Grandpa was asleep, but I don't think she believed me."

"That's okay, Pam. She's gonna think what she wants anyway.

Mary asked, "Who is Shirley?"

I laughed and said, "Oh, that's Chuck's wife, Pam and Kim's stepmother. If she calls, you'll know who she is immediately, because she never says hello to anyone. She'll just say in an authoritative voice, Are Pam and Kim there?"

Monie and Kim came up from down stairs and they were talking a mile a minute. I asked Monie, "Did you get everything put away?"

"Yeah," she said, "I like my room and I really like the waterbed."

"Were you able to get everything squared away with your children?" I questioned.

She answered, "Mom and Dad are going to take care of the girls, immediately, and will enroll them in school at Clear Lake. They are excited to have them live with them and I can see them as often as I want to." Clear lake was only a few miles away.

"I'm glad to hear that cause it will be best for them and Daddy but if you need to have them over, it's okay."

She said, "I really appreciate your understanding."

"If anyone can understand, Mom can," Pam piped up.

I WENT DOWN AND CHECKED ON DADDY. HE WAS sleeping like a baby. Mary said he had slept just about all day and wouldn't eat anything but his nanner puddin' and buttermilk. I kissed him on the forehead and said, "I love you, Brody, we're gonna find out what's going on with you Friday."

Putting my hand on his head, I prayed, "Dear God, please wrap my Daddy in Your Arms and take care of him. I don't know what to do to make him better..."

Daddy woke up in the middle of my prayer and murmured, "Hi, Piss Ant, who are you talking to?"

I smiled and said, "Well, it sure ain't Shorty. I'm just talking to God. Like you always told me, There ain't nothing me, you and the Good Lord can't do together. Right now I'm counting on just Him."

He said, "Me too," as he tried to pull the oxygen away from his face.

I said, "Daddy, let's keep that Kick-A-Poo-Joy-Juice going through the night, then maybe you will be more awake tomorrow to get to know your new friend, Monie." By the time I got the oxygen back in place, he was already asleep.

The next morning Karen was there bright and early just as she had promised. Monie already had the coffee on and was taking care of Daddy. She impressed even Karen. She said, "I think you got a winner this time, Reta!"

She then proceeded to fill me in on the latest gossip and told me *Pure Gold* was doing just fine.

I said, "Well, I hope they don't start doing so good they forget about me."

"Little chance of that. They really miss you and so does everyone else. Have you had any second thoughts about the nursing home?"

"Karen," I said, "You know how I feel about that. As long as I can possibly do it, I'm keeping Daddy at home."

She looked at me with concern, "Have you looked in the mirror lately? You are starting to look like hell."

I laughed, "Daddy told me I only look old and haggard."

She laughed even though she was very serious, "Reta, you have got to get more rest before you wind up in the hospital yourself."

I ran up stairs to get some more items to take to the studio and she asked, "Do you realize how many times you've run up to that loft and back since I've been here? I have got to go home and take a nap, you've made me tired just watching you."

I laughed, "Karen, you're a nut, but I love ya. I'll be fine, don't worry." We finished our coffee and she left for home.

Monie brought Daddy up for his breakfast and I made him a bowl of oatmeal. I fed it to him one bite at a time and chased it down with his buttermilk, just like I did in the beginning. I really liked Monie, there was no doubt she knew her business and I found I was wishing I had found her sooner.

I told Monie, "We'll need to leave about 9:00 a.m. in the morning so we can get Daddy there in time for his appointment."

She said, "Don't worry, we'll be ready. I'll give Vernon a bed bath so he won't get so tired out."

"I just hope we don't get any more snow tonight but if we do, at least Brad will get me plowed out of the driveway, and the county roads and Highway 8 will all be plowed by the time we leave."

Monie looked at me with concern and said, "You're really worried about Vernon, aren't you?"

"I sure am," I replied. "If you could have seen him a few weeks ago, you would understand why. He was Running The Roads, visiting with people and talking on the telephone. You would hardly think anything was wrong."

I grabbed Daddy's glass just before he poured his buttermilk into his oatmeal. He looked at me and said, "What are you doing?"

I said, "Daddy, I just didn't want you to ruin your oatmeal."

"Well, I like it that way," he replied in self defense. I knew he was still trying to cover himself. Tears weld up and I went into my room. I was feeling so defeated.

THE TELEPHONE RANG AND MONIE KNOCKED ON my door and said, "Reta, it's for you."

I picked up my extension and said in a low voice, "Hello." There was a long silence on the other end. I repeated, "Hello?"

"Hi, will you still talk to me?"

I got a head-rush and asked, "Bob, is that you?"

"Yes," he answered, "I finally got enough nerve to call. I am so sorry for just leaving like I did, but I'd started caring too much for you and I just didn't know what to do. I guess I took the cowards way out and ran."

"Well, if you cared so much about me, you sure have a strange way of showing it. Do you know how embarrassed I was?" I asked."

"According to my friend, you weren't too lonely because you replaced me with the snap of a finger," he sarcastically replied.

"What the hell are you talking about?" I snapped.

He continued, "Oh, he told me about being with you that night at the party."

"I would like for him to face me and tell me what we did because the only thing that happened that night was he almost got his butt kicked by some of my real friends for hitting on me."

Bob could tell I was really upset and angry and coed, "That's okay, I had already decided to forgive you."

"Don't you dare patronize me, Bob. First of all he never touched me then nor will he ever touch me, and second of all, it's none of your concern what I do. I don't belong to you or anyone else...."

He interrupted, "Truce, I didn't call to upset you. I called to explain why I left."

"Why did you wait so long, was it because of your friend's lie?" I questioned.

Very calmly he said, "I guess that did play a part, but I just wanted to let you know how much I do care for you, but like you said, It's just not our turn. I could never handle your situation. I want someone who can travel and have time for a relationship." I just let him continue, "I am sure you know you are not the only woman in my life and the other one is free to be with me."

"That's nice," I said. "Then you are better off to just stay with her. I don't know how long it will be before I have that kind of time but my family is the most important thing in my life and comes first."

He said, "I realize that but I want you to know I do care a great deal for you and also I want you to let me know if you need anything in the future, By the way, how is your Dad?"

I told him about Daddy's regression and he said, "I'm sorry to hear that. Will you please call me if there is any change. I do care you know."

I promised him I would let him know if something should happen to my Dad or if I needed him in any way. We talked for a little while longer and said goodbye.

AFTER WE HUNG UP, I WENT BACK INTO THE kitchen. Daddy was still trying to eat his breakfast and I gave him a hug and said, "Daddy, I love you and don't you ever worry about anything. I'll always be here for you. We are going to jump this hurdle, too."

In a very weak voice he said. "You betcha."

Brad came around to the patio doors and knocked on the glass. He had been out plowing driveways since early morning so he had snow from one end to the other. Daddy looked up, his eyes opened wide and he said very clearly, "Who in the hell is that, Reta, he looks plum scary?"

"That's just Brad, Daddy, he's been out plowing snow all morning," I assured him.

He cocked his head, shifted his eyes and motioned for me to come closer. Brad was taking his boots off and shaking snow off himself before he came in. Daddy whispered, "He don't look like no farmer, he looks like a monster."

I laughed, "Daddy, he's plowing snow out of the driveways, not cotton. I'll sit you in front of the window after you're done with breakfast so you can see his rig and watch the snow fall. Would you like that?"

"Yeah I would," he replied.

Brad came in about then and said, "Good morning, Grandpa, how ya feeling?"

"Fine, boy," Daddy responded with caution. He still wasn't taking any chances.

He kept watching Brad very closely and after Brad's hair, eye brows and lashes thawed out, Daddy realized it really was Brad. He laughed and said, "Boy, you scared the hell out of me!"

Brad laughed, "I'm sorry, Grandpa. You wanna go help me today?"

Daddy shivered, "Not no, but hell no!"

Pam came running upstairs to greet Brad. She gave him a hug and said, "You want some coffee and a bowl of cereal?"

"Sure do," he replied with a grin.

She then said, "Good morning Mom, and how is my favorite Grandpa?"

I said, "What are you in such a good mood about? Mind ya, I'm not complaining though, I love it when you and Kim are bubbling."

She smiled and said, "Christmas is coming and guess what, Grandpa?" Before Daddy could get a word in, she continued, "Me, Brad, Kim and Cheryl are gonna have the biggest and prettiest Christmas tree you ever saw standing, and decorated, when you, Mom and Monie get back tomorrow night from the cities. Plus, when Brad gets done plowing his driveways, we're going to Rice Lake to do some Christmas shopping for you and Mom."

Tears came into my eyes as I gave her and Brad a hug. "I love you guys. That'll be wonderful!"

Daddy then motioned me back over, he was too weak to speak very loud. He started crying and said, "I didn't know it was Christmas, do I have them any gifts?"

I said with all the assurance in the world, "You sure do. You will have a gift on the tree for everyone, just like you always did."

He grinned, "Good, I don't wanna look cheap."

"Daddy, you could never look cheap. Besides, me and you have plenty of money left in our pot, we're loaded." I would have never let him known how low the pot was really getting.

In the past, he always gave me the money to get Pam and Kim a Gift. I always made sure, even then, he had gifts for everyone so why should this year be different.

Kim and Cheryl came bouncing up the stairs. "Good morning," they chirped in unison.

"Well, I can see you two have the Christmas spirit too."

Kim glared at Pam and said, "I guess you told Mom and Grandpa about our surprise for tomorrow night?"

Pam said, "Yeah, but not everything. Besides, Mom needed some cheering up."

Kim then looked at Grandpa and said, "Just wait till you get home. We have lots of surprises for you." Daddy grinned, he loved surprises.

Monie said, "Since the whole family is accounted for, how about some hot chocolate with whipped cream? She received great reviews from everyone, including Daddy. Kim and Cheryl had already made some waffles and joined Daddy at the table.

I watched as my little family sat together for breakfast. Daddy was at the head of the table, just like he always was. As Monie poured the hot chocolate and pushed the button on the whipped cream can, my mind floated back to a time when I was about eight years old.

Daddy loved hot chocolate with fresh whipped cream when he would sit by the fireplace in our home in Texas and listening to the Louisiana Hay Ride (broadcast out of Shreveport). Mother had taught me how to whip the cream and how much of each ingredient had to be added to make the whipped cream and hot chocolate from scratch, starting with real cocoa and real cow's cream. I would make this treat about two or three times a week, but especially every Saturday night. Sometimes I would add a little blue, red or some other cake coloring to the cream to make it pretty then pour it into Daddy's big goblet, top it off and serve it piping hot. He would brag and brag on how great it was. Of course, all that bragging just kept the hot chocolate coming. Daddy and Mama always gave us nice compliments on a job well done.

THE RINGING TELEPHONE SNAPPED ME OUT OF IT. I found out real quick that it was the hypnotist. We made arrangements to talk at a later date when Daddy was stronger.

Daddy was getting tired, but I knew he had enjoyed visiting with his granddaughters and talking about all they were going to do for Christmas and how much ham and beans he was gonna eat.

I said, "Daddy, do you want to sit in your chair for awhile and watch Brad push some more snow around?"

Kim piped up, "Yeah, Grandpa, me, Pam and Cheryl are gonna build a snowman. You can watch."

In a very weak voice he whispered, "Okay."

Brad said, "I'll move your Lazy Boy over by the big window, so you can be comfortable." Daddy smiled and nodded.

Monie was right on the job. She said, "Well, Vernon, you've already had your bed bath and shave, so let's just get you over to that big ol' chair." Within a few minutes Daddy was sitting peacefully in his Lazy Boy directly in front of the window. Then she went directly to the kitchen and brought back a glass of buttermilk, orange juice and water and set them on the end table next to his chair, saying, "Vernon, you have a choice. Just help yourself."

I felt so good inside because I knew that now I didn't have to worry about him being taken care of properly. Also, he responded so well to Monie and I knew he liked her.

I went up in my loft and worked on books. Every so often I would glance down at Daddy. He tried to stay awake and watch the kids build their snowman and Brad push some snow around for his entertainment.

Before long, though, he was fast asleep. This would be a mental picture I would always treasure. I wondered if he really knew just how much he was loved.

Saying a prayer for God to watch over my family, I then returned to figuring out the bills. I wanted Daddy and I to buy a few gifts even though the Kids had said, "Mom, just you and Grandpa being here is all the Christmas we need."

PAM, KIM AND I HAD BEEN THROUGH A FEW LEAN Christmases during those years, so another one wouldn't be much of a shock. The girls always quoted me if I started feeling bad, "As long as we have each other, we are the richest people in the world."

Once, I had asked them, "Which Christmas was the best memory for you?" I couldn't believe their answer. Both cherished the same memory, and it was the leanest Christmas we ever had!

I had knitted both of them little caps, scarves and sweaters for their big gift. Then I had cut dolls, bicycles, and all kinds of neat things out of the catalog, glued them to a piece of typing paper and wrote, "This is what Mommy wanted to get you, but didn't have the money." Also I had gift-wrapped oranges, apples and even a potato or two for Kim, her favorite food.

All I really could afford then, had been the yarn and some Barbie Doll perfume they had wanted really bad.

The tree had been very small and we decorated it with all home made ornaments. We strung popcorn, made loops out of different colored crepe paper, cut tinsel out of Reynolds Wrap and the girls drew and colored a beautiful star for the top of the tree.

Of course, I had made the usual birthday cake for Jesus so that they would always remember what Christmas represented. Then we always sang happy birthday to Jesus and had a small party for Him.

I always tried to instill the right values in Pam and Kim, as my Mom and Dad did for me. As I stood there looking at Daddy, I understood why Pam and Kim loved that Christmas. It was because even though we had no money, we had, The Ingredient Called Love!

I WIPED THE TEARS FORM MY EYES AND CONTINUED to get the books in order. It seemed like I always ran about $1,000.00 short every month—after I had paid the bills. Sometimes I would dream of someone coming to my door with a million dollars check just like the television show Cecil and I used to watch called, "The Millionaire."

Another concern for me was that I didn't know what I was going to do if Daddy had to go back into the hospital. With the enrollment so low I could lose all my students if I had to stay away again.

Christmas vacation was always a hard time on dance studios because if a student was going to drop, it usually was over the holidays. I knew if they got wind of Daddy's setback, I could be in real trouble.

Just then the girls came running in yelling for me to come and look at their snowman. I came downstairs and they were ganged around Grandpa and teasing him about going out and helping them.

At this time none of us had any idea how sick Daddy really was. He was still covering up his problems as best he could.

Monie took Daddy down for a nap while Kim and I started getting ready to go to the studio. Pam started cleaning house and Brad took off in his pickup to plow more driveways. Before he had left, he came in to let me know the roads were clear for us to travel.

Classes went well that day but my mind was on the next day when we would be taking Daddy to Sister Kenny. I tried to not let Kim see how worried I was but she saw right through me. On the way home she said, "Mom, you're really worried about Grandpa, aren't you?"

"Yeah, honey, I just have this terrible feeling that we're losing him and I just don't know what to do."

She suggested, "Let's stop at the Country Dam for a nightcap and talk. Monie has everything under control and you need to Chill Out, a little."

Smiling, I said, "Good idea, maybe Cords and them are there setting up."

We pulled into the Country Dam's parking lot and sure enough, the guys were hauling in equipment. They gave me a hug and Cords asked, "How's Vernon?"

"Not good," I replied. "I'm taking him down to see Dr. Speier in the morning for the verdict."

Uncle Bob handed me a Bacardi Diet and said, "This is on the house. Do you think you will be here tomorrow night?"

"I honestly don't know, Uncle Bob. I'm gonna try and I sure do appreciate your patience with me through all of this."

"That's the least we can do for you. The guys are doing a good job, but everyone asks about you."

"Give them my love and hopefully I'll see you this weekend," I answered.

I called Monie to let her know where we were and she said, "Vernon is already in bed and I have everything ready for tomorrow. You just take a little time for yourself. Pam and I are finishing up the housecleaning and getting the Christmas decorations organized for the tree tomorrow. We even made some popcorn balls."

"That sounds good. Well, you know where I'm at if you need me. We won't be long as morning will be here too soon."

"By the way," she blurted, "Karen called and wants you to call her as soon as you land somewhere."

"Okay, I'll call her from here," I answered.

Hanging up the telephone, I then gave Karen a call. She said, "How long are you gonna be there?"

"Long enough for you to have a drink with me," I answered.

"Tell Uncle Bob to make me a *Windsor Water.* I'm on my way," she said.

I called Gary to come on over for a drink, too.

In a few minutes, Karen came in, followed right behind by Gary. We had a drink, and after the guys got set up, we played a few songs. Gary had his faithful squeeze box in his trunk and so he hauled it out, and before we knew it, we were having a good ol' fashion jam session.

Kim called home and told Pam and Brad to come over and join us. Before long, the entire peanut gallery was there, including Bryan, Bammer, May, Judy, Mark, Deon, Cheryl, Sandy, Chris, Thad and many more. It turned out to be a really fun night.

I called home several times and Monie assured me she had everything under control. Kim was right: I did need to Chill Out, and I did. We got home about 12:00 a.m. Daddy was sound asleep and so was Monie. We all quietly went to bed.

MY ALARM WENT OFF AT 7:00 A.M. ABOUT THEN I WAS wishing we had come home a little earlier the night before, as my hangover was a killer and the cobwebs in my head were everywhere, but I'd had such a good time with everyone that I didn't mind. Besides, it had been good for me to have done just that.

Monie already had coffee brewing by the time I came down. I poured myself a cup and joined her and Daddy. Already she had given him his bed-bath and shaved him. She said, "I wanted to get his bath done early so his pores will be closed before we hit that cold weather. I sure don't want him to take a cold."

"Good idea," I told her.

Then I turned to Daddy, he looked so weak and frail. I gave him a kiss and said, "Daddy, we are going to find out what the problem is today and get you all fixed up."

He whispered, "I sure hope so."

Monie said, "Vernon, I want you to sniff a little of this Kick-A-Poo-Joy-Juice and maybe it will give you more energy."

He didn't complain or anything. How I wished he felt like telling her to take the damn thing off or tell me to hush or anything like he used to. I was so angry, scared and puzzled all at the same time. What had happened? Why couldn't he keep progressing and get well? I felt as though my little world was crumbling right before my eyes and that there was nothing I could do to stop it.

Pretty soon Pam and Kim came in to sit with Grandpa. I said, "Boy, are you girls up early?"

Pam said, "We wanted to say goodbye to Grandpa before he went to the doctor and wish him good luck." Daddy just lay there and smiled.

Kim said, "Grandpa, we are gonna have the biggest and prettiest Christmas tree you ever seen, up and ready when you get back. There'll be lots and lots of gifts on it, too."

He glanced at me. By this time I could almost tell what he wanted by looking into his eyes. I smiled and said, "Yes, Daddy, you have gifts on there for everyone. We are all going to have a wonderful Christmas, but the best gift you can give us is to get better."

I went upstairs to get dressed. Pam and Kim visited with Grandpa and Monie went upstairs with me to get Daddy his bowl of oatmeal. She said to me, "I don't want to get him out of bed until we are ready to go. He needs all the strength he can muster just for the trip." Once again I sure wished I had found Monie at the time Fred had left. She was so efficient and had a heart as big as all Dallas!

By the time I got dressed and went downstairs, Daddy was all dressed in his white Western shirt, black Western pants, cowboy boots and, of course, wearing that white Stetson hat. Even as weak as he was he held his head straight to do that hat proud. That Stetson had become synonymous with the man, you never saw one without the other and, what it had done for him in therapy was unbelievable.

"Daddy, you sure look spiffy," I told him. "How about a date?"

He smiled, but he didn't rub or beat his chest and he didn't even say, "You betcha." He just sat there really still and weak. My heart was breaking and I was so scared.

Pam and Kim could see I was almost in tears. They both put their arms around me and Pam said, "Mom, Grandpa will be okay."

Kim said, "Yeah, Mom, don't cry. We are gonna have a pretty tree for you and Grandpa when you get home, that will make you happy."

I gave them a hug and said, "You girls are the two things in life that I know I did completely right. Only God knows how much I love you."

Monie then put Daddy in the elevator and we received him upstairs. As Monie took him out on the deck and down his ramp, I went out to the car and had everything ready for him to get in. Brad had already started the car so it was nice and warm inside. Monie brought Daddy into the garage and we quickly transferred him to the car. She put his wheelchair in the trunk as I fastened his seat belt. Pam, Kim and Brad all waved goodbye as we drove out of the driveway.

THE RIDE TO MINNEAPOLIS WAS VERY QUIET. Daddy dozed most of the way. Unlike the other trips, he hardly said a word.

Monie and I talked about her children and she told me a little more about herself. She had gone through quite a lot for as young as she was. I admired her strength and convictions. "Monie," I said, "You should go to school and become a registered nurse. The medical world needs more people like you."

She smiled and said, "Thanks. That's what I want to do when I have the money."

I thought to myself, I wish that millionaire would hurry up and bring my check to the door, I sure would know how to use it.

The roads were cleared but I still drove extra slow in my old Lincoln. I kept Daddy's seat reclined so he could sleep most of the way. It took us almost two hours before we arrived at Sister Kenny.

Monie got Daddy awake as I pulled up in front of the entrance, popped the trunk and Monie jumped out to retrieve the wheelchair. She quickly transferred Daddy into it and had him inside the building before you could blink an eye. Then I parked the car and joined them inside.

We went directly to Dr. Speier's office. Daddy napped while we waited for his turn, which was not very long. Unlike most doctors offices, we were never kept waiting more than fifteen minutes.

The nurse came out and took Daddy into an examining room. Within a few minutes Dr. Speier walked in. She shook hands with me then I introduced her to Monie and I said, "Dr. Speier, Daddy is not well at all."

Immediately she began checking him over and asked, "Has he been like this very long?"

I said, "He has been steadily going down hill since the seizure. I've had him in to see Dr. Rimestad two times, but he just keeps telling me how bad Daddy looks. That's why I wanted you to check him over.

She said, "I want to admit him to the hospital immediately and run some tests on his kidney and do another cat scan. He might be having more mini strokes along with the kidney failure. At any rate, he's got some serious problems." My heart just sank but I knew they would now get to the bottom of his setback.

She called Abbott-Northwestern and arranged his admittance. We took him directly over to the hospital, which adjoins Sister Kenny so we didn't have to take him out into the cold weather.

Daddy didn't seem to be up set at all. He was just too happy to find a bed. I wanted to have him put back on the fifth floor, but they put him on another floor instead. The tests were scheduled for the next morning so I got Monie and me a room at the little hotel in Sister Kenny and called Pam and Kim. They were devastated just like we were.

Kim said, "But, Mom, the tree is so pretty. We wanted to surprise you and Grandpa."

"I know, honey, but we'll be home soon," I assured her.

Pam said, "Mom, what about the studios?"

"Let's see how the weekend goes. We'll cross that bridge when we get to it. Just say a special prayer for Grandpa," I answered.

I knew in my heart we were headed for some bad roads ahead. All I could do was pray for God to direct me. If I had to be absent again like I was last year, I knew I would lose many more students. We only had one week to go before we had Christmas vacation, maybe we could get Daddy well and back home before anyone found out.

Before going back to Daddy's room, I had two more telephone calls to make, one to Cecil and the other to Yane. I dreaded calling them and telling them the bad news but I had to.

They both felt bad, and told me if I needed them to just let them know. I assured them I would keep them posted on the results of tests, etc.

After I had hung up from talking with Yane, I looked at Monie and said, "Gee, she was almost nice to me. She even told me to take care of myself and seemed to be sincere. I guess Dub gave her a nice pill or something."

Monie laughed, "It's too bad he doesn't give her one everyday. To go through something like this and have a sister that only finds fault instead of supporting you, must be terrible!"

"It's always been that way with her," I sighed "I just pray Pam and Kim can always be close, lookout for each other but most of all, be a support for each other."

We had dinner in the hospital cafeteria, then we went back to Daddy's room. He was sleeping like a baby.

The nurse gave me the schedule for his test times the next morning. I gave them our room number and she assured me I would be called if Daddy needed me.

Monie and I then left to go to a discount store where we picked up a few items for our overnight stay. I couldn't stand not having a toothbrush and toothpaste. We went to bed early so we would be bright-eyed for the 8:00 a.m. tests.

WE GOT UP EARLY, DRESSED AND WENT DIRECTLY to Daddy's room. He was awake, but was so weak I tried to get him to eat but no luck. I said, "Daddy, you haven't eaten since the oatmeal Monie gave you yesterday morning.

He whispered, "I'm jest not hungry, Reta." He was receiving Glucose by intravenous so I knew he would be okay, but he still looked like somethin' else.

The technicians came in to take him for his tests. Usually he had wanted his Stetson, first thing, but this time he didn't even ask for it. Being so weak, they used a gurney instead of his wheelchair. As they picked him up, I noticed how frail and almost lifeless he looked. He looked over at me and I knew what he wanted. I asked, "Can I go with him?"

The technician answered, "Sure you can." I held his hand all the way to the X-ray room.

They ran several kinds of tests and by the time we got back to his room he was totally pooped. Once he was in his bed, he went to sleep, immediately.

It was now about noon so Monie and I had a little lunch, then went back to Daddy's room. He was still sleeping.

A few minutes later Dr. Speier came in accompanied by Dr. Petersen. She said, "Until Vernon is better, Dr. Petersen will be back taking care of him. She said goodbye and left the room.

Dr. Petersen said, "Reta, could I talk to you in one of the conference rooms?"

I said, "Of course," as I followed him out of the room. Monie stayed in the room with Daddy.

He looked very serious and concerned. As we sat down I said, "Dr. Petersen, how serious is it?"

He took a deep breath and said, "It's not good. Your Dad has suffered several more mini-strokes and on a scale from one to ten, his kidney is over eight. In other words, his kidney has almost shut down. That is why he is so weak and lethargic"

Tears came to my eyes as I said, "What can we do?"

He shook his head and said, "We are going to do everything possible to get him back on the right track, If we can get his kidney to even five, we might have a chance. As far as the mini-strokes, we won't know until he's stronger just what motors have been affected. We do know he has suffered more brain damage and that your Dad would have died in a few more days if you hadn't realized he was in big trouble and brought him in."

"Quite frankly, I don't know how he does it, but then, he has amazed me since the first day I met him. He has the strongest will of anyone I've ever met." Smiling, he handed me a Kleenex, saying, "But love can do wonders." He assured me they would do everything medically possible to turn Daddy around but he couldn't promise me anything. I knew Daddy's life was in God's Hands.

I went back to his room and quietly told Monie what Dr. Petersen had told me. I said, "Will you stay with him? I need to go call Pam, Kim, Cecil and Yane."

"Of course. I'll be right here if he needs anything." She gave me a hug and I went back to our hotel room.

After I had myself a good cry and a long talk with God, I felt better. Then, I called Pam and Kim. They started crying, and Kim said, "Mom, it's not fair!"

I then remembered my Mama's words, and said, "I know honey, but God has a reason for everything he does. We might not see it now, but someday we will."

She said, "Isn't that what your Mom used to tell you?"

"Yes," I answered, "And someday you'll probably tell your little girl or boy the same thing."

Pam said, "Mom, don't worry about the studios, Kim and I will handle them next week, and maybe by the time Christmas Vacation is over, Grandpa will be okay and no one will know the difference."

"I knew I could count on you girls to handle things. Someday, maybe things will get easier," I sighed. "Until then, we'll just do what we have to do."

Next I called Yane and Cecil and told them exactly what Dr. Petersen had reported to me and assured them I would keep them informed about Daddy's progress.

Yane asked, "What does Daddy need for Christmas?"

I said, "Well, his old Stetson hat has really been through the mill. He could sure use a new one if you want to get him that, or he can always use shirts."

She said, "Well, I will send him a new hat for Christmas and some Western shirts for
his birthday."

"Great!" I replied. "He'll like that."

She closed with, "Make sure, now, you let him know it's from me."

I snapped, "Yane, Daddy is always informed as to where all of his gifts come from, whether you believe it or not." She just always had to close a conversation with some type of degrading comment."

Daddy wouldn't eat but a few bites for supper. He was having trouble swallowing, so they were only giving him Jello, ice cream and the old faithful, buttermilk.

After he was settled in for the night, Monie and I had some dinner and went to bed early. I was so glad she was there with me. Her support really helped to pull me through. With, Monie, I didn't feel like I had to be brave for her, as I did with Pam and Kim. I didn't cover up any of my feelings. I was able to get a lot of things off my chest and it did me good to talk and cry.

I was so angry and I just didn't understand why this had to happen. We had all worked so hard. I was even mad at God. I looked up and yelled, "Why, God? All I want to do is help my Dad, and now I'm losing him, losing my studios, and if you don't help me, and I'll probably lose my home..." I interrupted myself, "I'm sorry God, please forgive me for yelling at You. I know you haven't forsaken us, but sometimes I don't understand why everything has to be so hard all the time."

Monie put her arms around me and said, "Why don't you get some rest. You'll feel better tomorrow."

I calmed down and said, "Monie, sometimes I feel like I am going off the deep end."

"There's only so much a person can take, Reta, and you are pushing your limit. I am going to do everything possible to take some of this strain off you. And I know Pam, Kim and Brad will continue to be there for you. Just get some sleep."

Before I went to sleep, I asked God, again, to forgive my outburst and to give me the strength I needed.

The next morning we went directly to Daddy's room. I couldn't see much change in Daddy. He was so weak he could hardly talk.

I gave Daddy a kiss on the forehead and told him my plans. I assured him that Monie would be there until I got back. He was so lethargic and hardly responsive so I didn't know just how much he understood.

Monie stayed with him while I went back home to get what we needed for an indefinite stay. Another reason I was going to Amery was that I also needed to sit down with Pam and Kim to fill them in on everything. Also, I felt that they needed to know that I was okay.

I wasn't worried about them handling the studios. They could teach just as good as I could and I knew Brad would be there to take care of them if anything might need to be done at the house. I was so lucky to have such wonderful, responsible children.

When I took off for Wisconsin, the snow was lightly falling. I just prayed I could get home and back before too much fell. Even though I had been up north for quite a few years, I still was scared to drive in the snow.

I MADE THE TRIP, SAFELY, AND AS I PULLED UP TO the garage, I could see the pretty Christmas tree lights shining through the big bay window. Pam and Kim were looking out the window and Brad came out and opened the garage door and got me inside. The snow was really blowing by now.

I walked into the house and stopped dead in my tracks. The kids had the most beautiful tree that I have ever seen in my entire life standing and decorated in the living room. It almost touched the top of my Cathedral ceilings. I said in amazement, "Where in this world did you find that perfect tree?"

Pam said, "Well, you know Brad. We looked high and low until we found the biggest and straightest tree in the forest. Hell, this thing's as straight as a nail!" I gave them all a big hug and kiss.

Kim said, "Mom, do you recognize some of the ornaments on the tree?"

I looked very closely and said, "Those were mine and your Dad's when we were married." Then decided to add, "How'd you get them?"

"Shirley didn't want them, so she gave them to us."

They had the house nicely decorated and a few gifts already under the tree.

Pam asked, "Mom, do you think Grandpa will be home for Christmas?"

I got a *Miller Lite* and said, "Why don't you guys sit down. I want to tell you exactly what problems your Grandpa has."

They all sat down, you could have heard a pin drop as I told them the bad news. Since Pam and Kim were babies, I had always leveled with them. I was sure thankful I had an opportunity to get my feelings out the night before because they needed to see me brave and confident. It was worse than I had pictured. They took it really hard. If they had seen the way I fell apart the night before, they would have really been scared. Even Brad had tears in his eyes. I said, "all we can do is pray."

I got my suitcase packed while Pam and Kim packed one for Monie. Then I went down to Daddy's room and got some of the items he would need for shaving, etc. It was so hard for me to be leaving my little girls, again. They were trying to be so brave, but I knew they were scared to death inside. I felt so bad to lay such responsibilities on them at such a young age but I also know, now, that it only made them stronger.

We were all crying when I left. I knew they were remembering the last time I had to leave to be with Daddy and I was gone so long. Before I left I made sure that I had signed several checks for them to use for groceries or any expenses they might have. Boy, was I thankful Steve was no longer there. It wouldn't have taken him long to go through what money I had. I was so thankful to have children I could trust!

I DROVE VERY SLOWLY BACK TO MINNEAPOLIS, AS the snow was coming down pretty heavy. I know the Good Lord watched over me and saw to it that I had a safe trip. I was anxious to see Daddy.

When I walked into his room, Monie was there keeping a silent vigil over him. I again sent God a quick thanks for sending her to us. She looked up and said, "He's still not eating and really no change."

I went over to the bed and kissed his forehead. He opened his eyes and I could tell he was relieved I was there. Monie looked tired so I told her to take some time out and get some rest. She took her suitcase with her and headed for our room.

I sat and held Daddy's hand for a long time. It reminded me of that horrible night about this same time last year when my real Daddy was taken away. Now, one year later, I wondered if this new Daddy I had come to love so much was going to be taken from me, too. As I looked at him, I knew my real Daddy would never want to live like this and would have wanted God to just take him home, right then and there.

TOP: **FRED HELPS VERNON** FROM THE LIFT-OUT CHAIR SUPPLIED BY **RICK ROBL** (BACKGROUND) FROM THE ST. CROIX VALLEY MEMORIAL HOSPITAL, ST. CROIX FALLS, WISCONSIN.

BELOW: **VERNON & BRAD** ON THE DECK AT RETA'S HOME IN WISCONSIN. AT THIS TIME, HE WAS BEGINNING TO ACCEPT THE RIGHT SIDE OF HIS BODY

I HAD CHANGED THE WAY I PRAYED. I HAD become so selfish and obsessed with keeping Daddy with me that I had truly forgotten what his wishes might have been. From the beginning my real Daddy would have never wanted to live like he had been, much less continue in the frail and pitiful little body I was seeing before me.

I felt like God had slapped me on the head (or maybe it was my Mother) and said, "Dummy-up, Reta, and start looking at things from Vernon's point of view."

I put my hand on Daddy's head and placed him totally in God's hands. I believe, at that moment, I started to, Let go and let God steer the ship.

Monie and I kept vigilance over him for the next few days. Sometimes I just knew he was going to get better, but then the next day he would take a turn for the worse. Dr. Peterson and his fine group were doing all they could, but Daddy was in God's hands.

I called Pam and Kim every day. They were handling the studios just fine and without any problems from parents about my absence.

Pam said, "Mom, everyone has been pretty understanding, but I sure hope you are back after the holidays or we could run into problems with some of them." I was so proud of Pam and Kim, they had become the backbone of the studios.

By the weekend, the studios would be closed until after New Year's Day. The girls needed a break as much as I did. I said, "What have I gotten in the mail?"

Pam answered, "Mostly bills, but one letter is from your attorney."

"That damn, Steve," I muttered, "I'll be so glad when I am totally done with him. Open it and see what he wants."

It was a letter telling me my final divorce hearing was set for January 21. I was also scheduled to see a counselor prior to that date so they could tell me whether or not they believed I was doing the right thing to divorce the parasite. I figured that meeting wouldn't take long.

The divorce hearing had been put off several times in the past eight months because Steve had given his attorney two bad checks. It seems that he was having trouble coming up with the funds he needed. I sure was glad he was now totally off my credit cards or he would probably have me paying for that too. He was about the lowest form of human with the morals of a Tomcat in heat.

Pam continued to look through the bills. I was getting worried because my credit cards were getting close to being maxed with the incurred expenses. Pam said, "Here's a letter from *Underwood Reality* in Winters."

"Open it quick," I blurted, "Maybe Daddy's house sold."

She screamed, "Mom, it's a check for $3,500.00 made out to you and Grandpa."

I started crying from pure relief and at the same time thanking God. He knew our needs and had supplied the money we needed to see us through.

I said, "I will be home this weekend, and Monie is coming home with me, too. She will be staying with you girls."

Kim was on the extension and said, "Mom, I miss you so much! Can Monie stay with Grandpa and you come home?"

Pam jumped in, "Kim, quit being a baby. We're just fine, Mom, but it will be nice to have Monie here if you can't be here." Once again, I told them how much I loved and appreciated them, but I knew they needed their Mom.

I didn't say anything to Daddy about his little house. As I looked at him I thought, "Daddy, even in your condition, you're still contributing your share to the money pot." He would never know how much I needed that $3,500.00. I was already behind on bills and the credit cards were climbing fast with motel, food and fuel for the car.

Daddy was doing about the same, Saturday, so I explained to the nurses my decision to take Monie back to Wisconsin so that she could help out at home. I told them that I planned to return tomorrow, Sunday. They assured me they would call if there was any change at all.

I gave Daddy a kiss goodbye and told him I'd be back tomorrow. He just lay there and looked at me with those big, sad eyes. It just broke my heart to see him too weak to even talk, he could only whisper.

I was learning to read his eyes more and more every day. He squeezed my hand, just like in did in Texas back in 1984, and so many times throughout the past year, so I knew he understood.

WHEN MONIE AND I ARRIVED HOME, THE KIDS HAD dinner ready and a big Welcome Home Christmas party planned. They were trying so hard to cheer me up. The house was decorated beautifully and I still could only marvel at the beautiful Christmas tree.

Monie just stood and shook her head with tears in her eyes. She said, "You guys are something else." She gave Pam, Kim, Brad and Cheryl a big hug and told them how proud she was of them.

I knew I was doing the right thing by leaving Monie home. She was such a rock, and if Pam and Kim couldn't have their Mom, right now, at least they would have a wise and caring friend, like Monie.

After I visited awhile, I went up to my little office in the loft. I was so happy over that check Daddy got for his little house. It was a shame Marva Jean couldn't have gotten more for it, but with the price of real estate being so low, right now, I guess she did good to get the $5,000.00. I just wished we hadn't had to pay out so much of it for expenses incurred with the sale.

I was able to catch up on the bills to where I could breathe. If Daddy could just come home next week, for Christmas, the road and motel expenses would stop. Then if I didn't lose any students over the holidays, we might just be okay.

I looked up and said, "Thank you God for helping me, and please keep carrying me. Only you know how scared I am and how many are depending on me to make the right decisions. You, also know, I'm not as strong as I was. Please give me the strength you know I will need to continue to fight. Thank you for my little team."

"I wish I could ask my sister and brother for help, both financially and emotionally."

"Cecil can't afford to help me at this time and is unable to pay any of the $1,500.00 back that he borrowed."

"Of course, Yane believes Daddy had thousands stuck away that I am just squandering. She has not offered any type of financial help and I'm certainly not going to ask her. After all, You did let me inherit my Daddy's pride."

"I just place myself, my Daddy and my children in your hands, Dear God. I know You won't forsake me. Again, thanks for the $3,500.00. Amen."

I always felt like a new person after I had unloaded all of my problems on God. He had become my very Best Friend and Confident. Like Daddy used to say, "There's nothing me and you and the Good Lord above can't do together." Again I looked up and said, "But now, God, it's just You and me."

Sunday morning I got up and had coffee with my little family. Monie was the extra strength Pam and Kim needed, right now. They didn't seem so scared about my going away again.

I called the hospital and Daddy was about the same. A snow storm was forecast for later, so I wanted to be safe at the hospital before it hit. I hugged and kissed everyone and, at about 3:00 p.m., headed back to Minneapolis.

WHEN I WALKED INTO DADDY'S ROOM, HE WAS JUST lying there staring at the ceiling. As I gave him a kiss and squeezed his hand, I noticed his eyes were a deeper hazel than usual.

He looked at me with sad eyes and whispered, "What happened to your little ear?" I was highly allergic to ear rings and I had forgotten and left a pair in too long. Now my ear had a little infection in it and was red.

I laughed and said, "Oh, I just tried to wear those cheap earrings again. One day, when we get our million dollar check, I'm gonna buy me diamonds and you can have anything you want."

He grinned, "That's nice," he whispered.

I told him about the pretty Christmas tree plus all the good wishes and love his granddaughters sent back with me for him. I also told him that Yane and Cecil sent their love.

Next, I shared with him the conversation that I'd had with Sissy on her last trip home from the boat.

He started crying. "Is Sissy here?" he whispered.

I said, "No Daddy, but she sends you her love, too. Everyone loves you so much." He continued to listen to my reports as I filled him in on everything that was positive, not the negative.

After I had described the beautiful Christmas tree, I was sure to mention the Christmas gifts that I had bought for him to give everyone. God would forgive me, I knew, for some of the little white lies and it was so good to see him awake and more alert.

For awhile, I found myself wishing that maybe he could get well, then, I remembered I had Let go and let God.

Noticing that Daddy was getting tired, I said, "Daddy, you get some sleep and I'm gonna grab a bite to eat."

He smiled and whispered, "Okay." He shut his eyes and was asleep almost immediately. How I wished he could have said, Hush, Polly Parrot, Is there a bed in this house? or any of his favorite expressions. Instead, he just lay there so frail and weak.

I talked to Dr. Peterson the next morning and he said, "There is not much change in your Daddy. I am concerned about the weight loss, we can't seem to get anything down him."

I said, "I know because I've tried the buttermilk feeding routine that worked last year but he doesn't even want that."

"We'll try a while longer, but we might have to consider a feeding tube being placed in his stomach."

With tears in my eyes I said, "Whatever you need to do, just do it." He patted my shoulder and left the conference room. I sat down, cried for awhile, then blew my nose and went back to Daddy's room.

I tried to get Daddy to eat a little food, but he would whisper, "I jest don't wanna."

Later, I went back to my room and called Yane and Cecil. Even though my phone bill was getting ridiculously high, I felt they should know the latest regarding our Daddy. I kept hoping they would tell me to call collect but they didn't. I knew Cecil really couldn't afford it. Yane would never help because in her own sick mind she believed Daddy had all those thousands put away. Another reason she would not offer to help was that I had gotten Power of Attorney without her permission. I surely wasn't going to give her the satisfaction of asking her for help so that she could tell me, No.

THE NEXT WEEKEND I NEEDED TO GO HOME AND see my family—and to keep an appointment I had made with the counselor for Friday afternoon.

She was very nice, and told me, "After talking with you, I believe you are doing the right thing. The only problem, I see, is that if you should someday meet someone who could take care of you, you might not know how to handle it. You know all men are not like your Steve."

I laughed and said, "Well, this puppy has been broke from sucking eggs. I don't even want to try again with any man because I've been hurt too many times. I seem to always become the work horse, and they start playing with all the fillies and then expect me to support their habit."

She didn't have much to say after that but did wish me good luck as I left for home.

I VISITED WITH THE KIDS AND TOLD THEM THAT IT didn't look like Daddy would be coming home for Christmas. They were devastated because they had their hopes so high for Grandpa to have a wonderful Christmas with us.

Yane had sent Daddy's new Stetson hat for Christmas and a separate package with his Western shirts for his birthday which was January 31st. Pam and Kim had her gifts placed under the tree for Grandpa along with their gifts.

They had shopped some for me and had bought Daddy a bright red night shirt, 'cause his favorite color was red.

I said, "Well, Mohammed can't come to the mountain, so the mountain'll come to Mohammed."

Kim asked, "What do you mean, Mom?"

I smiled and said, "If Daddy can't come home Christmas, we'll have Christmas at the hospital with him. Brad, could you find me a really little Christmas tree to take down there."

He smiled and said, "I sure can."

Monie said, "I've got a little tree at home, but we need a fresh one because it's getting awful dry. The decorations on it would be perfect for your little tree as they are all miniatures."

"That's perfect," I said.

Within minutes everyone was excited about surprising Grandpa at the hospital on Christmas day. As they made their plans for the festivities, I went to my little loft to try to figure out my next strategy for making more money.

A few students had already called in and quit. I knew if that continued I was going to be in big trouble.

I went downstairs to get some things to take back with me. Pam and Kim were going to let me borrow a couple of things. As I went in their room to look into their clothes drawer, I looked up at the mirror and couldn't believe my eyes. Around the mirror, they had placed their payroll checks I had given them...untouched. That was really too much, and I sat down on their bed and started crying. Seems like I couldn't stop crying during moments like that, moments which were beginning to happen a lot.

Pam and Kim came down and I asked, "What are you guys using for money?"

Pam said, "We're okay, Mom. We can help, too.

"Kim piped up, "We're family and families stick together." I don't think I could ever be as proud of my daughters as I was at that moment.

Before long, Brad, Monie and Cheryl had joined us in the girl's room. They had me laughing by the time we went back up stairs and a smile on my face.

I took off for the hospital and the kids started making their plans for Christmas, which was the next weekend.

ARRIVING BACK AT THE HOSPITAL, I HEADED straight for Daddy's room. As soon as I walked in, I saw blue safeguard pads all around his bed. Panicking, I ran up to the nurses station, "What are the blue pads for? What happened to my Daddy?"

After they calmed me down, a nurse told me that Daddy had experienced a grand-mall seizure that morning, and they had placed the pads around for his safety.

I snapped, "Why wasn't I called?"

Very nicely, she said, "We talked about it but knew you would be back this afternoon and didn't want you to drive too fast in this weather. There was nothing you could have done."

I apologized for snapping at her. I was totally devastated and hit the tears again. Sometimes I wondered where all those tears came from.

I went back to Daddy's room feeling so helpless. He looked so small and frail lying in that big hospital bed, he was just wasting away. I gave him a kiss, squeezed his hand and went down to the cafeteria for some coffee.

On my way back to Daddy's room, I ran into Marlene, one of the nurses from the fifth floor who cared for him when we first arrived in Minnesota last year. She gave me a hug and asked, "Are you okay? We heard about Vernon's setback and we all feel so bad.

We have put in a request to have him transferred to our floor because we would like to have you two back with us. You're like family. The nurses on this floor understand because they feel the same about some of their previous patients."

There I went to crying again. "That would really be wonderful if you could do that. The nurses here are excellent, too but like you said, you are family." She gave me another hug and took off for her station.

I WENT BACK INTO DADDY'S ROOM AND TOLD HIM ALL about what Marlene and the others were trying to do. I don't think he understood anything I said. He had suffered more mini-strokes along with the Grand-Mall Seizure.

Monday morning Dr. Petersen came in. He checked Daddy over and said, "I would like to speak with you in one of the conference rooms." I followed him out of the room. I felt totally defeated and helpless.

He gave me a chair and pulled one up for himself. Sitting down next to me I could tell, from his expression, he had nothing good to tell me here this Christmas week.

"I don't know how to tell you this because I know how much you've fought for your Dad." He hesitated, "But, Reta, your Dad is dying. We can't do anymore for him."

After I regained some of my composure, he continued. "I want to ask you a very serious question, Reta, and I want you to think about this very carefully before you answer. Do you want life support systems given to your Dad?"

"You mean like Kidney Dialysis?" I asked.

"Yes, or anything else to help him live. Your Dad's arteries are so hardened, he could go with a heart attack, his kidney or many other complications. Do you want to have any of these lifesaving procedures performed if your Daddy needs them? He must also have a feeding tube put into his stomach as he is starving for food at this point. We have to get nourishment into him and the feeding tube is the only solution."

"Dr. Petersen, could you give me a few minutes to digest all this and to call my brother and sister. I need their opinion too."

He said, "I totally understand. You let the nurse know when you've made your decision and I will meet back here with you." He left the room.

I sat there for a few minutes, feeling like my whole world had just collapsed. Then I went back to my room and called Yane and Cecil. They both told me to do whatever I felt was best and they would support my decision 100 per cent. For once, I was glad my sister didn't find any fault or insult me. She was actually very nice.

More tears. After it seemed like I had cried all the tears out of my system I turned to my Friend again.

By the time I went back to Daddy's room, I knew what I had to do. I kissed his forehead and squeezed his hand. He opened his eyes and looked at me. I knew I had made the right decision. Leaving Daddy I went out to the nurses station and told them to please advise Dr. Petersen I was ready for our meeting.

WITHIN A FEW MINUTES A NURSE CAME AND TOLD me that Dr. Petersen was waiting in the conference room. I walked in and sat down.

He asked, "What have you decided, Reta?"

Very calmly, I answered, "Dr. Petersen, this has been the hardest thing I've ever had to do. I had to think what my real Daddy would want. Even though I know he wouldn't want to live another hour like this, I can't just let him starve to death either. Please, place the feeding tube in his stomach."

He patted my hand and said, "If you had said anything different I would have really counseled you. We can't let him starve to death, I agree. You do realize, with the feeding tube, your dad could hang on for a very long time until he should have a heart attack or his kidney completely fails?"

Yes, I know, Dr. Petersen but I can't let my Daddy starve to death," I said through my tears.

He said, "I will schedule his surgery for Thursday morning."

I told him about the Christmas party planned for Sunday, if Daddy couldn't come home.

He said, "That's fine and we will talk about him going home after the surgery." As he started out the door he turned back and said, "Now, when I write, No Life Support on his chart, you do understand his life is placed totally in the hands of God, and he could be taken at any time."

I swallowed and fought back the tears, "Yes, Dr. Petersen, I understand."

Going back to Daddy's room I watched him sleep. I knew I had made the right decision. Also, I knew that now, I had to get everything ready for his trip back to Texas.

GOING BACK TO MY ROOM, I KNEW I NEEDED TO call Pam and Kim. There was no way I could tell them on the telephone that their Grandpa was dying. I wanted them to have Christmas with him first, but I knew I had to get a few things taken care of.

I tried to be brave when I called home. Kim wasn't home, just Pam and Monie. I said, "Pam, could you take Grandpa's black suit, white shirt and tie into the cleaners and have them put a rush on it?."

She said, "Sure, Mom, is Grandpa gonna wear it for Christmas?"

"No," I answered, "But I did get him a new pair of pajamas to wear Christmas."

Then, I talked to Monie and asked her to explain the surgery to the kids that Daddy was going to have on Thursday. She asked, "Reta, are you okay?"

"No, but I'll be home tomorrow evening to talk to everyone and plan the party for Sunday. I'll explain what's happening, then"

Before I hung up the telephone Pam got back on. In a sad, little voice she said, "Mom, why do you want Grandpa's suit cleaned right now?" She started to cry.

I said, "Honey, just take it in and I'll talk to you when I get home tomorrow afternoon. Please don't mention anything to Kim right now, I love you." She was crying when she hung up the telephone.

I sure was glad Kim and Cheryl were gone, but Monie was there with Pam. I wasn't sure how Kim was going to take the news. She had just recently started to accept her new Grandpa. How was I going to tell her or Pam they were going to lose him, too.

RELAXING ON THE BED AWHILE BEFORE GOING back over to Daddy's room, I found my thoughts going over many details. That was easier than just dwelling on his condition and the probable outcome.

I was glad Pam was taking Daddy's suit to be cleaned. Ever since Yane had given him that suit, he had told me that he wanted to be buried in it. He really did look quite spiffy in it.

I still couldn't keep my mind from remembering what Yane had told me when she gave it to him. She'd said, "Poor old Daddy wears that same old gray suit to every wedding or funeral. You know, that same old suit he wore to Mama's funeral." She had rolled her eyes and continued, "It is so embarrassing, that's why I got him the new one."

Like the true coward I had always been around Yane, I didn't say a word, but I thought to myself, Heaven forbid, Yane, that Daddy might bring any embarrassment to you.

I never told Daddy what she had said. I just let him believe she only got it for him because she loved him.

He was so proud of it, I would have never had him know the truth. I had planned to follow his wishes down to the letter for his funeral, which would include him being buried in that black suit.

AFTER I HAD RESTED AWHILE, I WENT BACK TO Daddy's room. The nurse was standing by his bed. I asked, "Is everything okay?"

She said, "Vernon had another seizure a few minutes ago but he's okay now."

He was sound asleep. I said, "How long do you think he will sleep?"

She said, "Probably until morning."

"I need to go back to Wisconsin and make some arrangements for Christmas. I thought to go first thing in the morning."

She said, "Honey, why don't you go home now and spend some time with your daughters. We will take good care of Vernon and call you if there is any change. Your dad would want you to."

"Maybe you're right," I said, "I would like to be with my family right now." I took her advice and headed for Wisconsin and thought how surprised my little family would be when I just walked in on them.

The snow was lightly falling as I drove home. I needed that two hour drive to try and clear my mind before I saw the kids. I asked God to guide me and give me the strength I was going to need for the next few months.

The kids saw me drive up. Brad came running out to get the garage door for me while Pam and Kim held the door open. You would think I had been gone for a year. It certainly felt good to be loved and welcomed home. We all needed each other but I needed them more at this time than they knew.

I noticed that Pam had Daddy's suit laying out on the table so she wouldn't forget to put it in the cleaners.

After all the hugs and the kisses, Monie brought me a *Miller Lite*. We sat down in the living room and I started to tell the kids about Daddy's forthcoming surgery that was scheduled for Thursday. Kim and Pam were both sitting on the floor directly in front of me looking up at me with those big blue eyes. I knew they were looking for some truthful answers, not a lot of double talk like I had planned to give them.

Swallowing and looking them straight in the eye I asked, "Do you think you kids can handle the entire truth?"

Pam spoke up with all the assurance in the world, "Mom, tell us the truth, no matter what it is."

Kim started crying, "Grandpa is gonna die, isn't he, Mom?"

I was fighting back the tears. Brad and Monie came over and sat on each side of me, I was totally surrounded with love. I knew I had to tell them the truth, and I did.

Pam said, "I knew when you asked me to take Grandpa's suit into the cleaners, he was gonna die."

After we all had a big cry, I said, "Now, let's plan the nicest Christmas we can for Grandpa. When Daddy has surgery on Thursday, I will stay with him until Saturday. Then I'll come home for Christmas Eve. We can open our tree then and take Grandpa's gifts down for him to open Sunday."

Brad started laughing, "I still don't know how to open a tree." He definitely broke the gloomy session.

They had all teased me about my expression of, Opening the tree, for a very long time.

I said, "Okay, smarty, Grandpa could tell you all about *Opening* the tree." Every since I was a kid, we didn't open the gifts on Christmas Eve, we always said, *Open* the tree. My kids always got a kick out of the expression, and Brad was no different.

Monie said, "What do you mean, *Open* the tree?"

I said, "Oh, my gosh! Not you too!" Before long we were having a nice time.

Pam said, "Mom, do you think we could open one gift tonight like we normally do on Christmas Eve?"

"Sure," I said, "I think that would be a great idea." Since Pam and Kim were little girls, I had always let them open one gift before Christmas. I thought after all the bad news, they could use a little cheering.

Kim brought the first gift for me to open, then each opened one of theirs after that. It was a sad night but at least we were together and trying to make the best of it, as I knew Daddy would want us to.

I called the hospital before I went to bed and they said Daddy was still sleeping. Boy, was I glad that I had come home tonight. We all really needed each other.

The next morning we all got up early. I said, "I sure miss seeing Daddy sitting in that Lazy Boy."

Kim mumbled, "Yeah, we miss Grandpa in the Lazy Boy and miss you all over the house."

Giving her a big hug, I said, "I know it's been hard, but it won't be long until I'm home. Just hang in there for me."

She smiled and said, "I will Mom, but sometimes I miss you so much that I go in and lay down on your bed and then I feel closer to you." I took her in my arms and held her tight.

Then, I went down to Daddy's room and got his lock box. I couldn't stand to stay in his room and seeing his empty hospital bed. Taking the lock box, I went back up to my own room. I opened his lock box and went through everything just like we had done so many times in the past. I pulled out his little gold wedding band that he had saved all these years from his marriage to Mother. I remembered how many times he would tell me, "Now, Reta, when I die, I want ya ta put yor Ma's ring on my finger before you bury me."

I would say, "Daddy, for the hundredth time, I promise." I never really thought my Daddy would ever, ever die, but all of a sudden, it was happening. Really happening.

I took the wedding band, the blue plastic case which contained all his important papers, his will, insurance, and so on, and put them into a little travel bag. Also I put a clean pair of underwear, socks and tee shirt in the case. Then I went down and brought up his new boots and the black belt he wore with his black suit.

Pam knocked on my door and said, "Mom, can I come in?"

"Sure, honey," I answered.

She walked in and sat down on the bed and picked up Mama's wedding ring. With tears in her eyes she said, "Mom, isn't this the wedding ring Grandpa wore when Nana was alive?" I nodded my head. She looked at the other items and said, "Mom, what are you doing?"

I put my arms around her and said, "Honey, while my mind is still clear, I'm getting Daddy's things packed for his trip back to Texas. If I got him home without Mama's ring, I would just die. Long ago, I promised him I would make sure all his wishes are carried out, so I wanted to have his little case packed."

"When you pick up his suit, place it in my room along with this case, then I know I will have everything ready." We put our arms around each other and I let her cry. My tears were just about all gone. Numbness was beginning to enfold me.

Kim came in and said, "What's going on?" Between Pam and me, we filled her in on what I was doing. Kim said, "Mom, please don't ever die. I couldn't take it."

I remembered saying the same words to my mother when I was about twelve, and she gave me some good advice, which I used to answer Kim. I said, "Honey, God never puts anymore on you than you can stand, so if something should ever happen to me, you would be able to handle it. Just like I handled my Mother's death, and now, I'm gonna have to handle my Daddy's death."

She said, "But I'm not as strong as you."

I told her, "I didn't think I was as strong as my Mom either, but I found out I was. You just have to ask God to give you the strength you need, and you know what? He will. Besides, you and Pam are made out of the same stuff that me, your Nana, and Aunt Sissy are. The women in our family are strong."

We talked for a while longer, then I said, "I've got to head back to the hospital and if everything goes okay with Daddy's surgery, I'll be back home for Christmas Eve." Then I gathered my little girls in my arms and held them both real tight for a few minutes.

THE SNOW WAS STILL LIGHTLY FALLING AS I DROVE back to the hospital. I wasn't feeling well and could tell that the strain was getting to me. There just wasn't enough of me to go around. As I headed back to Minnesota, I prayed once again that God would give me the strength needed to make it through each day.

Daddy was sleeping when I arrived at the hospital. He was so gaunt and white and it was hard to believe that he hadn't eaten anything for three weeks, no wonder he was so weak. It was a relief to know the feeding tube would be placed in his stomach, tomorrow morning. At least then he would be getting some type of nourishment, even if it was only liquid.

I gave him a kiss on the forehead and squeezed his hand. He opened his eyes, weakly squeezed my hand and whispered, "Hi Piss Ant."

Fighting back the tears I managed to say, "Hi there, yourself. How's my favorite Daddy?" He tried to smile and then went back to sleep.

I sat by his bed for almost two hours, wishing there was some way I could bring him back the way he used to be, but I knew his life was over. I didn't want him to live like this, never to eat another steak, hamburger or any of his junk foods. I prayed that God would help me let go.

I remembered all the times throughout my life when he would say, "I hope and pray I never have to get old and suffer. I hope God will just take me."

For the last three years, he had said, "I'm ready to join ya, Ma, I get so lonely." I hadn't known what to do because he wouldn't come live with me, and I couldn't move back to Winters to make a living. I had felt so helpless to assist him.

Finally I gave him a kiss and went to my room. I wanted to be back bright and early the next morning so I could talk to Dr. Petersen before Daddy's surgery. I called Cecil and Yane to keep them posted, had my little chat with God and went to sleep.

Waking up about 6:00 a.m., I was really restless about Daddy's surgery and couldn't get back to sleep. Since I couldn't get him off my mind, I decided to get dressed and head for Daddy's room.

The nurses were in his room when I arrived and were obviously surprised to see me that early. I said, "What's wrong?" as I rushed over to Daddy's bed.

One nurse told me, "He just had another seizure."

"I knew something was wrong." They just kind of looked at each other in surprise as they didn't know about Daddy's and my silent signals.

His eyes were soft and he didn't look so scared any more. I squeezed his hand and said, "Hi, Brody, I love you."

He was too weak to whisper, but he formed the words, "I love you, too."

The nurse brought me some coffee and I sat by his bed until Dr. Petersen came in. He said, "Good morning, how are you feeling?"

"I'm tired, but okay."

He smiled and checked Daddy over but he didn't get much of a response. He said, "We'll get some food into you, Vernon, then you will gain some strength."

Before long the orderlies came with the gurney to take him to surgery. I picked up his Stetson in hopes he would ask for it like he always did, but he was too weak to even care about it. I carried it with me to the surgery waiting room just in case he wanted it. Actually holding it made me feel closer to him. Now, I knew how Kim felt when she would sleep in my bed to feel closer to me.

DR. PETERSEN CAME OUT OF SURGERY AND SAID, "Your Dad is just fine, he's in the recovery room and the tube is in place so he will be getting some nourishment shortly."

"Thank, God," I answered.

I took Daddy's Stetson and headed back to his room. I called Pam and Kim to let them know Grandpa had made it through the surgery okay. Then, I called Cecil and Yane. Everyone was relieved.

Before long, they brought Daddy back to his room. The nurse came in and started feeding him a liquid called Ensure through the tube. She said, "He will get all the nourishment he needs now because this is a perfect and complete food. It contains all the vitamins and minerals he needs to survive, plus it's high in calories."

"Well, it's sure not a big steak, but I'm so happy to see him getting some kind of nourishment," I replied.

I went to the cafeteria and had some lunch, myself. When I got back to the room, my adopted Mom, Louise was there. She put her arms around me and said, "Are you okay, baby?"

I started to cry, "I'm okay, but it sure is good to see you, I could use a little support this morning." Daddy was still sleeping, so we went back to the cafeteria to visit and have some coffee. She was just who I needed to see. Ma always had that special calming effect on me and it was good to know, it still worked. She was glad to hear I was going to spend Christmas Eve with the kids and then we were all coming down here to spend Christmas with Daddy.

We visited for a while, then she gave me a hug and said, "I better get home before the weather gets any worse."

I said, "Give Lee, Peter and Dick a big hug for me and wish them a Merry Christmas."

"I will, honey, and I'll be praying for you."

I hugged her again, "Those prayers are mighty appreciated," I replied. She waved goodbye and headed for the parking lot.

I SCOOTED MY CHAIR UP TO DADDY'S BED AND continued to watch over him. He was still sleeping peacefully. Every thirty minutes the nurses were in to check his feeding tube, and to make sure his stomach was accepting it. With not having eaten for so long, there could be several different side effects, such as diarrhea.

All of a sudden, Ma appeared at the door looking rather pitiful. I said, "Did you forget something?"

She sighed, "No, my car won't start. I think my battery is dead."

I thought, Boy, this is all I need! Instead, I told her, "Well, let's go see what we can do."

I followed her back up to the roof where she had parked her car. Immediately, I saw her problem, "Ma, you forgot to turn your lights off."

"Oh," she said, looking rather embarrassed, "The snow was still falling when I came over and it was so dark, I turned the lights on and forgot to turn them off." Tears were welling up in her eyes, "And I feel so..."

"That's okay, Ma," I interrupted, "Don't get upset. We can fix it." I gave her a hug of assurance and said, "I'll call Security, I'm sure they have a jumper cable and will help us. I'll bet you probably are not the first person to do this and I'm sure you won't be the last."

She followed me back into the building at her normal slow pace. I was trying to hustle her along, but Ma never rushed doing anything, especially eating.

Lee and I used to tease her when we would go out to dinner by saying, "Ma, you go on ahead and start eating, we'll finish the last class and join you later and still finish before you get to dessert."

She would laugh and say, "Well, I promised my mother I would chew my food twenty-one times each bite, so I wouldn't get a stomach ache." In all the years I have known Ma, she always kept that promise.

I called Security and they assured me they would meet me, immediately, up on the roof. I took off in a hurry to meet them but Ma was a dawdling behind. Finally, I said, "Come on Ma, I'm taking you to the cafeteria where you can sit down and have a cup of coffee while I take care of this." She very obediently followed me to the cafeteria and sat down with her cup of coffee. She was quite aware that my nerves were about shot and this episode was not helping them any.

I met the Security guards and we got Ma's car running. Then, I drove it around to the entrance and had one of the Security guards watch it while I retrieved Ma.

She was still sitting very obediently at the table with her cup of coffee. I smiled and said, "Your chariot awaits you, kind lady."

Looking relieved, she said, "I feel like such an idiot."

"That's okay Ma. I'm sorry I got up-tight with you, it's just been a rough day and it started early. I'm glad you came, and besides that, I got all that fresh air running around on the roof and it was good for me."

She finally laughed and felt a little better. I walked her to her car, hugged her, wished her a Merry Christmas and told her to call when she got home. The weather was increasingly getting worse.

I FINALLY WENT BACK UP TO DADDY'S ROOM.   HE was actually awake and said, "My stomach hurts."

"I know Daddy," I sympathized, "But you are getting some food in that ol' belly for a change."

I rang for the nurse. She came in and checked Daddy over and said, "We need to dilute the Ensure a little more. It still appears to be too rich for his stomach."

I asked, "How long will it have to be diluted?"

"Normally, just a few days. It's like getting the formula right for a new born baby. We have to get it just right or he will have stomach problems or diarrhea."

She could tell I was very concerned about this. Smiling, she said, "Don't worry, we'll have it all figured out before Dr. Petersen releases him."

"How long do you think that will take?" I inquired.

"Maybe another week," she replied. "He'll probably be here through New Years, but you'll have to talk to Dr. Petersen about that." She finished up with Daddy and left the room. He was already back sound asleep.

His feeding tube really concerned me. Everything was starting to get so complicated and I was scared that I would be forced, now, to put Daddy in that half-way house so he could be cared for properly. It was just starting to sink in what a traumatic thing this feeding tube was going to be.

Calling home, I talked to Monie. She said, "Reta, don't worry, I know how to handle this problem, I've worked with patients with feeding tubes before."

I sighed, "Monie, you just don't know what a load that takes off me. I would like for you to come down next week and spend some time with the nurses so you will know exactly what they are doing."

"That is a good idea," Monie said, "and I would feel a lot more secure about bringing him home after spending some time with his nurses 'cause, you know, all patients are different."

Feeling less worried, now, I settled back in my little chair and waited for Dr. Petersen to come before I went to back to my room.

The telephone rang in Daddy's room and I answered it. A little voice on the other end said, "Hi, I'm home."

I said, "Ma, is that you?"

"Yeah," she said, "I'm calling like you told me too."

"That's good Ma, now you just stay there and don't get out in this weather, okay?"

"Okay," she answered, "I'm gonna take a nap, this has been a nerve wracking day for me, too."

Laughing, I said, "Well, we made it though, didn't we?"

"Yeah," she replied, "Now you be careful going home tomorrow, and give Pam and Kim a big hug and kiss for Grandma."

"I will. Now you get some rest, I love you, Ma."

"I love you, too, Baby," she answered.

It wasn't too long before Dr. Petersen came in and checked Daddy over. He said, "He's doing just fine. All his vitals are normal."

"That's great," I replied, "But do you think he will be here until after New Years?"

"We should have him on a steady formula by then. That sounds about right." He looked at me with great concern, "Are you still taking your Daddy home?"

"Yes I am. The nurse I've hired at home has had experience caring for patients with feeding tubes."

Shaking his head, he said, "Little lady, you're taking on a lot more this time than you did when your Daddy went home before. You look like you need to get more rest yourself."

We walked out into the hall and he continued, "I wish you would consider the half-way house here."

"Thank you, Dr. Petersen," I replied, "But until I feel I can't handle him any more, I am taking him home." Tears welled up, "If God will give me the strength, my Daddy is going to die at home with his family."

He patted my shoulder and said, "You're a tough little gal, I admire your courage. I'll see you in the morning." He then headed back to the nurses' station.

I was just getting ready to go back to my room and get a little rest when Marlene walked in. She gave me a hug and asked, "How's Vernon?"

"Fine," I answered, "He just sleeps most of the time."

She went over and checked him and said, "We were unable to get him transferred to the fifth floor, but all of us wanted to wish you and Vernon a Merry Christmas, and let you know we are thinking about you."

Tears came into my eyes as I said, "You girls are all so special. Give Twila and everyone else a hug for me and wish them a Merry Christmas from that Ol' Rascal and me."

As she left, I could see the tears of helplessness in her eyes. She knew my Daddy was dying, and neither she, nor any of the other nurses on the fifth floor could stop it. No more than we could.

The nurses assured me they would call if Daddy needed me. I went straight to my room and took a hot bath before going to bed. Of course, before closing my eyes, I asked God to give me strength, take care of my Daddy and to watch over my little girls. I also gave a special thanks to Him for sending Monie to us. She had become my lifeline. Still bending His ear, I drifted off to sleep.

The next morning I got up early feeling starved. I had slept right through and hadn't taken time to eat any supper the night before.

After getting dressed, I went over to the cafeteria. I could hear people talking about the weather and how much snow was forecast for later in the day. Now I was really in a dilemma. If I didn't leave soon, I might not be able to get home for Christmas Eve. Then, if I did leave, there was the chance that I would be unable to get back to Daddy for Christmas. I asked God to help me make the right decisions as I walked up to Daddy's room.

Daddy was awake when I entered his room. I smiled and said, "Good mornin', sunshine! Nice to see those peepers open for a change."

He gave me a little grin and whispered, "Mornin'."

I gave him a kiss on his forehead and squeezed his hand, his grip was a little stronger. The Ensure was definitely making him stronger, and his color was so much better. I said, "Won't be long until we go home, are you ready?" His eyes got a little brighter with the thought of going home.

"Daddy, you know tomorrow is Christmas Eve. I am going back home and spend Christmas Eve with Pam and Kim, then we are all coming back here Christmas morning to spend the day with you."

"Dr. Petersen said you wouldn't be able to go home until after New Years, so this way we can all still be together for Christmas."

"The weather is really getting bad, so if you are okay, I'd like to leave for home as soon as possible. Will you be okay?"

He very weakly said, "Yeah, I'm okay."

"I'm gonna wait until I talk to Dr. Petersen before I leave, so I'll be here for awhile."

I didn't know how much he understood, but I knew I had to spend some time with Pam and Kim. Daddy was in good hands and I needed to go home, as soon as possible, to my little family.

Dr. Petersen came in around noon. He checked Daddy over and said, "Vernon, you're doing fine. In about one more week, you'll be able to break out of here."

I told the doctor that I was leaving for Wisconsin and would be back Christmas Day.

"I think that's a good idea, Reta. You need a break from here and you really should leave as soon as possible. The weather forecast doesn't sound favorable, especially toward Wisconsin."

By the time Dr. Petersen left, Daddy was back asleep. I went back to my room, gathered my stuff together and checked out. On my way back to Daddy's room, I stopped by the nurses' station and told them my plans. They, too, were glad I was going to take a break and spend Christmas Eve at home with my daughters.

When I went into Daddy's room, to say goodbye, he was just lying there looking at the ceiling. His eyes were so soft, relaxed looking, not scared. That made me feel better about leaving.

Giving him a kiss and squeezing his hand, I said, "Daddy, I'm gonna take off for home, now. I'll be back Christmas morning with your granddaughters. They are bringing the gifts that you got them, so that they can open them here with you. Now, you just rest so you'll be ready for your family to attack you on Sunday."

He just grinned and didn't utter a word. There was no need because I could read what he wanted to say by looking in his eyes. Knowing he would be okay, I kissed him, checked out with the nurses and hit the road for Wisconsin.

THE GIRLS WERE REALLY SURPRISED WHEN I PULLED into the garage. They had been watching the weather reports and were worried about me getting home for Christmas Eve.

Brad had the house warm and toasty and it felt so good to be home. Monie made me a Bacardi Diet, first thing, and then we all sat down to relax and catch up on Daddy's progress.

It wasn't long before Pam said, "Mom, why don't you go on to bed and we can visit more in the morning."

"Okay," I answered, "I really am beat." We all said good night and I headed for my room.

My heart stood still as I opened my closet to grab my housecoat. There, hanging on the rack, was Daddy's black suit, complete with white shirt and tie. Sitting on the floor, right under it was the little bag that I had packed for Daddy's trip back to Texas.

Not wanting to deal with that now, I went and took a hot bath, chatted with God and cried myself to sleep.

Early the next morning, I woke up to the smell of bacon frying. I called the hospital immediately and the nurse assured me that Daddy was just fine. In a few minutes, the door swung open and in came Pam, Kim and Monie with coffee and a breakfast fit for a queen. To avoid hitting tears again, I yelled, "Christmas Eve Gift!" and caught all three of them off guard.

Pam said, "Well, Mom you caught us again."

Puzzled, Monie asked, "What do you mean by, Christmas Eve Gift?"

We all laughed and I explained, "It's just a family tradition from my childhood back in Texas. Daddy used to hide in the closets, under the bed or where ever he could to catch all of us on Christmas Eve. The tradition was, if you said, Christmas Eve Gift, first, then everyone you catch has to give you an extra special gift. I don't know if all the families down there had this tradition, but we sure did."

Kim smiled at Monie and said, "Grandpa did a lot of things different, but they were always fun."

I took my plate and joined them at the table. We had a wonderful Christmas Eve breakfast, my girls made me feel so very special.

Pam said, "Mom, I hung Grandpa's suit in your closet."

"I know honey, I saw it last night and really appreciate your taking care of it for me."

Tears came into her eyes as she said, "Mom, I can't believe we are gonna lose Grandpa."

"Oh, honey, I know, but after you see Grandpa on Christmas, you'll know that he would never want to live like that."

"Does he look really bad mom?" Kim asked rather hesitantly.

"Well, he is very weak and that feeding tube is really spooky. Boy, I'm so glad you know how to take care of it, Monie."

"Don't worry," she assured me, "We'll be just fine."

Just then Brad came in grinning and said, "Go look out the window, I got something for Grandpa."

I went to Daddy's favorite big bay window to check it out, and there lying on the front lawn was a perfect, tiny, Christmas tree all ready for the trip to the hospital. I started crying again, "Brad, thanks so much, you are one-in-a-million."

He laughed and said, "I know," as he strutted back outside.

Monie came up from her room carrying a small box and said, "Here's my contribution."

I opened it and there were the tiny ornaments she had taken off her little Christmas tree at home, complete with a star for the top. The tears just kept flowing. Monie put her arms around me and said, "Reta, you really need some rest, I'm getting a little worried about you."

I tried to joke it off by saying with a nervous laugh, "I'm okay, the women in our, family cry over everything."

Pam and Kim were busy getting everything ready for our Christmas Eve party and all of us were trying to make it as happy a day as possible.

Later, Cheryl came home from visiting her mother then they all were busy with the festivities. The tree looked absolutely beautiful and they had all the gifts in order. They took care of everything and made me just take it easy.

While they were busy, I went through the mail and decided to just wait until Daddy got home to really put my mind to it. I answered just what were necessary and mailed a few bills that were due, now. The rest I just slid aside.

Pam and Kim showed me some of the new routines they had put together for the studios. We always did our choreography during the Christmas Holidays so we could start recital work immediately after classes resume after New Years.

I said, "You guys have done great, but remember, you can use some of the routines we've used in the past years too."

Kim said, "Yeah, we've been reviewing the recital video you had at Rice Lake two years ago and I'm gonna use some of those routines at Ladysmith."

"Sounds like you two have everything under control."

Reluctantly, Kim said, "Yeah, we're okay." I knew they were just trying to make me feel better, and they were, but I knew they really needed me.

About 5:00 p.m., Cords, Rick and Donnie pulled up. They were a welcome sight, but of course, I hit tears again. I said, "I don't know what's the matter with me, I seem to cry over anything."

"Your nerves are shot, Reta, that's the problem," Cords surmised.

Naturally, they wanted to know about Daddy so I filled them in on his condition and then they filled me in on the shows. I was glad everything was going well but told them I didn't know how long it would be before I could join them again.

Cords said, "Well, Karen Dee stops by occasionally and pinch hits for you. She said to tell you Hi and she would see you next week because tonight she had to work."

We had a Christmas drink, exchanged some gifts and then they headed home to their own families. I was sure lucky to have so many wonderful, caring friends.

By the time they had all left, the kids were sitting on "GO" to open their gifts. I said, "Are ya'll ready to open the tree?"

Brad immediately goes up to the tree and starts trying to figure out how to open it.

I said, "Okay, smart aleck, let's open the gifts."

Kim was already at the tree ready to start handing them out. First, she placed all of Grandpa's over by his Lazy Boy, to be taken to the hospital in the morning.

We all tried really hard to enjoy ourselves, but we were not having much luck. Pam looked over at the Lazy Boy with all those gifts sitting in it and started to cry. "Mom, it's not fair that Grandpa couldn't be here for this last Christmas. We worked so hard to have everything just perfect."

Putting my arms around her, I said, "Honey, believe me, Grandpa knows how much he is loved. You can tell him in the morning about how beautiful the tree is here. We'll keep it up until he gets home so he can see it."

"Yeah," Kim said, "Quit being a baby Pam, before you get Mom and all of us crying again."

Brad tried to change the tide, saying, "Yeah, Grandpa would kick all of your butts if he knew you were home bawling on Christmas Eve. Let's make the best of it." He took off for the kitchen to pour another glass of eggnog.

We all dried our tears and had a toast for Grandpa. As we drank our eggnog, I told the kids some of the stories about Daddy and his traditional eggnog every Christmas.

"DADDY AND MAMA MERCK, MY MOTHER'S MOTHER, always got together every Christmas and she would make the best eggnog from scratch. Mama Merck would never use that store bought stuff. She and Daddy might not see each other for months, but come Christmas, he would always pick her up and take her to his house for their traditional eggnog. Then she would beat up a batch and Daddy would add the booze...sometimes a little too much."

"They would sit, talk about old times and drink that eggnog down to the last drop. Then sometimes, they'd make another batch. All of Daddy's old friends would stop by to wish them a Merry Christmas, everyone knew they'd have the eggnog ready."

"Another Christmas, I remember, was when I was still married to Pam's and Kim's Dad, Chuck. They made the traditional eggnog and Daddy spiked it, but Chuck didn't see him do it, so he spiked it too. By the time we realized the mistake, everyone was feeling no pain."

"Believe me, that was a wicked morning. Mama Merck went home early and Daddy went to bed for a little nap. I was making dinner along with my Aunt Lois, Daddy's sister. Thank God we hadn't been nipping quite as much."

"I heard a knock on the door and lo-and-be hold, it was none other than Yane and her family. Daddy was gonna be in big trouble, I just knew, 'cause he was asleep and quite obviously, he had nipped a little too much."

"Yane came in with her family following close behind her. She marched into the bedroom and tried to wake Daddy. I brought him a wash cloth, hoping that would help him wake up, but no luck."

"She looked at him, then said with her holier-than-thou attitude, 'Daddy, you're drunk!' Quickly, she hustled Dexton and Delferd out of the room before they were exposed to such *ungodliness.*"

"I tried to explain to her what happened, but she had her mind made up, as usual We were all a bunch of drunks and totally beneath her and hers. She rolled her eyes and summoned Dub and the boys to leave. It was almost funny as she went still gasping for breath, all the way to the car."

This last story triggered another Christmas memory for me. "Back when I was about eighteen, Daddy and Mama Merck were having their eggnog when Uncle Albo, Mama's brother, called. He invited us to his house for a glass of eggnog."

I laughed and said, "If you haven't guessed by now, eggnog is the traditional Christmas drink in Texas. Anyway, I decided to go over and see Uncle Albo ahead of everyone else. I really didn't know Uncle Albo very well, because I was always much closer to Mama's younger brother, Elton, whom everyone called Humpty. Sissy and Humpty were always my favorite aunt and uncle and were always very close to my Daddy."

" Anyway, when I got over to Uncle Albo's house, he was feelin' no pain. His wife, Teenie was busy getting things ready for their two daughters to come home. I was feeling really out of place and I think Uncle Albo sensed that. His family was a lot like Yane, and they turned their noses up to most of Mother's family."

"Well, Uncle Albo said," Reta, let's have some fun. Let's call Yane, over at brother James's house and invite her over. Then you talk with her and act like I've been giving you eggnog with booze in it. Act smashed and let's see what she does.

"I said, Okay, that would serve her right for always judging people.

"We made the telephone call and I talked to her with a slur and she was over in a flash condemning me for drinking and Uncle Albo for giving it to me. She felt a little foolish when she found out that I was only drinking plain eggnog. That was about the only fun memory I ever had with Uncle Albo."

WHEN I FINISHED THE KIDS WERE ALL GLUED TO their seats and laughing. Brad said, "Did Grandpa ever get mad and let Yane have it for acting the way she did."

"Yeah," I laughed, "One time she was telling him just how bad he was for swearing and he said, Well, Yane, I couldn't be too bad, I raised one saint, didn't I?

"She shut up and left him alone after that. It seems she had learned who she could bully and who she couldn't. There's gonna be a real big surprise when she gets to heaven and finds the rest of us there, too. Maybe then, she will have learned how to treat family and appreciate them."

Pam said, "Mom, don't even think about her anymore. I know you wish she could have been a real sister, but she's not. She never will be and besides, you've got us!."

I put my arms around her and Kim and said, "You betcha!"

The rest of the evening went very well. We exchanged stories about Grandpa when he was at his best. When I looked at the clock I said, "My gosh, it's almost midnight. Let's get to bed so we can get up early and head for the hospital."

We were all determined that Christmas Day was gonna be a good one for Grandpa, no matter what.

I looked out the big bay window and said, "Boy, this weather is getting bad. I hope we can get out of here in the morning."

"Don't worry," Brad assured. "I'll get you out of here if I have to plow the snow all the way to the hospital."

I gave him a hug and he said, "By the way, I made a little wooden stand for the little tree and have put it in the car. I won't get to go with you in the morning, I'll have to plow driveways so everyone can get to where they're going. Just tell Grandpa Hi and I'll see him when he gets home."

I said, "Brad, why don't you stay here tonight instead of getting out in this. Besides, I'd feel much more secure if you were here."

He smiled and said, "You betcha."

I DIDN'T SLEEP VERY WELL BECAUSE ALL I DID WAS think about Daddy. I placed him in God's arms, once again, and asked Him to guide me in making the right decisions. I thanked Him for my little family, prayed for strength and cried myself to sleep.

I got up early the next morning and saw that the snow had almost stopped but we were really snowed in. Brad was ready to take off plowing and he had the coffee made. He was heading for the door and assured me as he went out the door, "Don't worry, I'll get you guys out of here as soon as possible."

I was so thankful for Brad and sometimes I don't tell him enough. I feel that sometimes I took him for granted. Looking up I said, "Thank you, God, for my little ol' boy."

The tears started again and I couldn't understand why I cried so much. Maybe it was my way of dealing with all the tension. It did help, but my eyes looked awful. Looking in the mirror, I thought, "Reta, you better put some tea bags on those eyes or Daddy's gonna tell you how old and haggard you look."

I would give anything if only he could feel like telling me that again. I boiled some tea bags, flopped them on my eyes and laid down for a little longer until I heard the entire family in the kitchen hustling around.

Walking into the living room, Monie greeted me with a "Merry Christmas."

Pam and Kim echoed "Merry Christmas," then came over and gave me a big hug.

Cheryl then came dragging herself up from down stairs. We all yelled, "Merry Christmas, sunshine!"

She grinned and said, "Merry Christmas to all of you, too."

Kim said, "We've got all of Grandpa's gifts ready to go, including Yane's."

I said, "Let's go ahead and give Daddy his birthday gift she sent him, too."

"Okay," Kim said, "You don't think Grandpa is gonna be here for his birthday, do you?"

"Honey, I don't know. Grandpa is totally in God's hands now. I don't want to keep him on this earth any longer than possible, in his condition."

While the girls finished getting everything ready for the trip, I called the hospital. The nurse said, "Vernon had a good night and when he woke up this morning, he asked about you. We told him you would be here as soon as possible with his granddaughters. He smiled and said, That's good."

"Will you please keep reassuring him that we will be there? We are trying to get dug out up here as we got a lot of snow in the last twenty-four hours."

"Sure," she said, "Just take it easy and we'll take good care of the guest of honor."

Pam, Kim, Cheryl and Monie got everything loaded into the car. They had really gone all out to make this a special day for Grandpa. There was a big, red, "Happy Face" balloon with *Lot's of Love For The Holidays* printed on it. Also a little tray of goodies wrapped up to take.

They had forgotten their Grandpa couldn't eat any more of his favorite junk food, and they had made all his favorites. Monie saw me looking at it and said, "They wanted to take the little platter down there and I told them it would be okay. If Grandpa can't eat it, we can. They really don't understand how bad Grandpa is, but after they get there, we will explain the feeding tube and everything. I think then it will be easier for them to understand."

"Maybe you're right, Monie. I don't want to say anything to them now, they're having too much fun planning the party." Pam and Kim hadn't seen Daddy since he had left almost a month ago. I knew they were going to be upset when they did see him, but it had to be.

Brad came in around 10:00 a.m. and said, "Okay, the road is clear all the way to Highway 8, so you should be fine all the way to the cities." We all gave him a hug of gratitude, piled in the old Lincoln and headed for the hospital.

IT TOOK US ALMOST THREE HOURS TO GET TO THE hospital because the roads were really slick. When we arrived, the girls all piled out of the car and took the gifts, tree and ornaments. I parked the car and met them in the entrance. We were quite a sight carrying a Christmas tree and all those gifts, but everyone was smiling and wishing us a "Merry Christmas."

We took the elevator up to Daddy's floor and the girls made a mad dash into Daddy's room. They came to a screeching halt when they saw Grandpa. He was asleep and looked so small and frail. I walked in and kissed Daddy on his forehead and squeezed his hand.

He woke up and whispered, "Hi."

I said, "Merry Christmas, Brody. I have some people here that can't wait to see you."

His eyes got big as he looked at the end of the bed to see Pam, Kim, Cheryl and Monie. Tears came into his eyes and within a few minutes the girls were up in the bed with him just like they used to be, telling him all about their plans for him when he got home and about the Christmas tree.

Monie and I started decorating the little tree and Cheryl started getting the gifts out. One of the nurses came in and said, "I hate to tell you this, but I can't allow you to put up that Christmas tree. We can only allow artificial ones in here."

We all looked at her with total devastation. I asked, "Can't you break the rules just for awhile. This is a very special Christmas and we have driven for three hours in this weather so his granddaughters can give him his Christmas tree and gifts."

She looked around at all the big eyes starring at her and said, "I'll be right back." We continued to decorate in the hopes she could work something out.

In a couple of minutes she came back in with a big smile on her face, "We talked it over at the nurses' station and decided to turn our backs for the next couple of hours, but, then you'll have to take it down."

We all said, "Thank you" at the same time. She walked out and closed the door behind her.

I raised Daddy's bed and said, "Look at your Christmas tree, Daddy. Brad cut it for you and Pam, Kim and Cheryl wrapped all the gifts. Are you ready to start opening?"

His eyes were brighter, but he was so weak. I said, "I'll help you." As the girls handed me the gifts, I sat on the bed by him.

I opened his gift from them first, a beautiful Cashmere sweater. Pam took the bow off and placed it on Grandpa's head, she said, "You're our best Christmas gift, but the gifts you got us are on the tree, too. We'll open ours after you get yours open."

Daddy looked at me, I knew what he was asking me. "Yes, Daddy, you got everyone a gift." He relaxed and continued to look at his gifts as I opened them one by one.

He loved his bright red night shirt and I had bought him a new pair of pajamas to wear today. After the surgery, they said it would be best to keep him in a hospital gown, so I wrapped them for his tree.

I saved Yane's gift until last. I knew he would really be excited over that new Stetson. The girls opened their gifts I had bought for them from Grandpa and they gave him a big hug.

I said, "Well, Daddy, I have two more gifts for you to open. They are from Yane. He looked at me with really questioning eyes. I opened the hat first, he grabbed it and starting trying to put it on his head. I said, "Daddy, you can't put it on while you're lying down."

He placed it on his chest and took a long, hard look at it, then he said, "This ain't my hat."

I said, "I know Daddy, but this is a brand new one Yane got for you because your old one is about worn out. It is different, the brim is a lot more narrow than your old one, but it's white and it's a Stetson."

"Yeah," he answered, "But it ain't mine."

I said, "I'll put it back in the box and you will get used to it later." Next, I opened the Western shirts she sent him and told him, "Yane sent you some pretty Western shirts to go with that hat, aren't they pretty?"

"They damn sure am," he whispered.

"Well, I'll take these home and you can wear 'em next time we go honky tonkin'." He just grinned.

The telephone rang and it was Sissy. I said, "What a perfect time to hear from you."

She said, "Baby, I just got in from the boat and I wanted to see how Vernon was and to wish you all a Merry Christmas."

She started to cry and said, "I called your house first and Brad told me everything. Baby, are you okay?"

I fought the tears back, "I'm fine Sissy. It's been hard, but the Good Lord is giving me the strength I need. Do you want to talk to Daddy?"

"I'd love to if he can."

I put the telephone to Daddy's ear and said, "Daddy, it's Sissy." His eyes got really big and I could tell he remembered who Sissy was. He was too weak to talk, but I could tell by looking in his eyes, he was very happy to hear from Sissy.

She and Humpty were just kids when he and Mama got married, and he loved them so much. I was so happy she called and assured her we would be okay. I said, "Sissy, if you can make it through the many trials and tribulations you've been through, I know I'll be able to survive this. Just pray for God to give me the strength I need."

Still crying she said, "I will, Baby, I love you."

"I love you too," I echoed.

I had brought Daddy's picture album and had climbed upon the bed and showed him all the pictures while the girls took down the tree and packed up the gifts. Even though I was trying to encourage Daddy, I knew I was only fooling myself. He would never ride that three wheeler again or go to listen to me sing.

The telephone rang again, it was Cecil and Margaret wishing Daddy a Merry Christmas. They no more than hung up when Yane called to wish him a Merry Christmas, too. He was too weak to talk to anyone but I put the telephone to his ear and let them talk to him.

The kids took the tree out and put everything back in the car, including the tray of junk food. They realized, right away, that Grandpa couldn't enjoy it. Monie had showed them Daddy's feeding tube insert and explained how it worked. They just stood there almost in shock, it was so hard to see them hurting.

I took a few minutes and walked out into the hallway to regain my composure. Pam and Kim came out and put their arms around me. Pam said, "I knew it was bad, but not this bad."

Kim said, "Now I understand, Mom. Grandpa wouldn't want to live like this."

Daddy was so tired, I said, "I think maybe we should let Daddy rest now and head on back to Wisconsin. Everyone gave Daddy a big kiss goodbye, he was sleeping like a baby.

I talked to the nurses and told them I would be back the next day, and thanked them again for letting us keep the tree. One of the nurses laughed and said, "I don't think he'll be awake until tomorrow. He had a big Christmas."

Everyone was really quiet on the way home. Now, we all knew that Daddy was dying and we couldn't do a damn thing to change it. We all agreed he wouldn't want to live like he was. We all felt so helpless.

Kim asked, "Mom, when will Grandpa come home?"

"Dr. Peterson said right after New Years," I answered.

Pam said, "Mom, Grandpa is coming home to die, isn't he?"

I was fighting back the tears, "Yes, honey, he is. Then we are going to take him back to Texas. I promised him if something should happen to him up here, I would take him home."

Cheryl sighed, "It's just so sad. We've all worked so hard to bring him back."

"We just have to turn him over to God, that's all we can do," I answered.

WE GOT HOME AROUND DUSK AND FOUND BRAD was home, totally pooped out from plowing snow all day. Pam filled him in on Grandpa's condition. All of us sat in the living room feeling rather numb. For the first time in my life, I was glad a Christmas was finally over.

Monie said, "Reta, are you okay?"

"I guess so Monie, I will just be glad when we get Daddy home."

She asked, "When do you want me there?"

"Just as soon as I know what day Daddy is coming home, then I will come and get you. Do you think two or three days would be long enough?"

"Sure," she answered, "Just let me know and I'll be ready."

The kids put on some videos and I went to bed. I was so tired that I think I would have given almost anything if I could just have one day where I didn't have to do anything, not even think.

The next morning I got up fairly early. The Christmas tree still looked pretty, but it was getting awfully dry. I didn't know if we could keep it up until Daddy came home or not.

Karen called about 9:00 a.m. and asked, "How ya doing, Babe?"

I started crying again, "Can you come out for a cup of coffee?"

"Sure," she answered, "I'll be there in twenty minutes."

The kids came up for breakfast and looking around at us, I thought we all looked like warmed over death.

I couldn't ignore it any longer, we needed to discuss what the agenda would be for the studios the next week.

Pam said, "Mom, don't worry, we will handle it."

At this point my mind was so far from the studios I didn't want to even talk about it. I just wanted to crawl in a hole and pull the hole in over me. What was going on with me? I didn't understand why I was feeling so strange. I just wanted to hide from everyone.

Karen arrived, gave me a hug and said, "You look like hell."

There I was crying again. "I know Karen and I don't know what's going on with me. It's like I feel so out of control."

"Simple," she said, "You are bottoming out. You've got to make some changes or you're gonna wind up in a straight-jacket."

"I know, Karen, but what am I going to do?"

She sat there for a moment then said, "You know what you are going to have to do, don't you?"

I sighed, "Yeah, but Karen, my Daddy is dying and I can't let him die in a nursing home." I started to cry even harder.

She put her arms around me and said, "Why don't you spend some time at my house after your Daddy comes home, at least the nights?"

Pam said, "Mom, I think that's a great idea. We can move Grandpa's bed up into your room and then, Monie can sleep in your bed. She will be closer to the kitchen for Grandpa's medicines and food."

Monie chimed in, "That would be a great idea and it sure would make things easier taking care of him."

I thought for awhile then said, "I'll think about it, but you're right, we will move Daddy's hospital bed into my room. Monie can bunk with me, that way I can be there to help her if she needs me."

"Yeah, Mom," Kim said, "Then you will be totally pooped out for the studios. I think you should stay the nights at Karen's house, then come home during the day, we'll be okay."

I said, "Well, it looks like all of you are ganging up on me. I'll wait and decide after Daddy gets home, okay?"

Pam said, "I'm gonna get Brad and we can start getting Grandpa moved up here."

"He won't be coming home for another week, honey, "I said.

"Well, we will have everything ready," she answered as she took off for the garage to tell Brad.

Karen and I visited while I got my suitcase packed again to head back to the hospital. I gave her a hug and said, "Thanks buddy for being there for me." I started to cry again.

Brad had my car warmed up, I got my things loaded, kissed them all and then headed for Minneapolis. The weather was much better and the drive not so dangerous.

I had plenty to think about those two hours or so. One thing that was weighing heavily on my mind was that I would be bringing Daddy home within the week. That was so scary for me. Another was that I would be strong enough to let him go home to Texas. I just couldn't imagine losing my Dad, but I knew I was. This was one of the saddest Christmases ever.

Arriving at the hospital I first checked into my room. Immediately I then went to Daddy's room. He was just lying there looking up at the ceiling. I gave him a kiss and squeezed his hand. He gave me a little grin and whispered, "Hi."

I said, "Hi there, yourself. I'm back. The kids are gettin' everything ready at home for your homecoming next week." He just smiled and drifted off to sleep.

Later, I talked to Dr. Petersen and he told me, "Your Dad's kidney is not improving and I just don't know how much longer it will last. We should have him stabilized with the formula in a few more days." He paused for a moment, "Are you still taking him to your home?"

"Yes I am," I replied, "I've come this far. My family and I have decided to bring Daddy home."

He said, "You do realize, if anything should happen, you won't be able to call the ambulance, doctors or anyone any more. It is going to be very hard for you waiting for your Dad to go?"

Tears weld up, "I know Dr. Petersen, but I'm taking Daddy home. My home care nurse is coming in for a couple of days before Daddy is released so she can get all the instructions firsthand from his nurses."

"Good idea," he said. "Let's plan on releasing him January 2, as he should be stabilized by then."

"Okay," I replied, "I'll make arrangements for that date."

I called Monie and told her to make plans to come on Wednesday.

She said, "Brad said he would take me down and save you from having to come back up here."

"That's great," I replied. "I can just settle in until I take him home."

"Aren't you coming home for New Year's Eve? We're planning to go to Louis' Inn?"

"I don't know, Monie, I'll have to think about that later. Two days down here would be enough for you, don't you think? Then you can celebrate New Year's before Daddy gets home and we really go to work."

"That's more than enough time, and don't worry, we already have Vernon's hospital bed in your room." She laughed, "You know your daughters, they have been busy rearranging the entire house for his homecoming."

"Yeah," I said with a chuckle, "they always loved to have a cause to get things rolling."

The next couple of days were about the same. Daddy just slept most of the time, and I was happy that he even knew me. He was still having mini-strokes, and I never knew when that motor would really be knocked out, perhaps the next time for good. That's the way it was. We lived with the fear that the very next minute would be his last, and God helped me prepare for that moment. I just prayed my Daddy would know me right up until the end.

9

WEDNESDAY WAS HERE BEFORE I KNEW IT, AND Brad brought Monie down. He hadn't seen Daddy since he left home and as he looked at Daddy, I saw tears well up, "Oh, God," he said. "I gotta go." I gave him a hug and thanked him for bringing Monie down.

He said, "No problem. I'll see you when you get home." He then headed down the hallway. I knew he was overwhelmed to see how far Daddy had gone downhill since Thanksgiving.

Immediately, Monie took over. I was amazed at her efficiency when she got with the nurses and started taking notes. During the next couple of days, she had everything down pat. What a relief! I now knew she would be able to care for Daddy, as well at home, as he was in the hospital.

Brad, Pam and Kim came down to pick her up Friday night. They assured me everything was ready for Daddy's homecoming.

Kim said, "Mom, please come home tomorrow night and be with us for New Year's Eve."

"Yeah, Mom," Pam echoed. "Let's have that night together before Grandpa comes home."

"Maybe I will. Let's see how Daddy is tomorrow." They gave Grandpa a hug, and I was glad to see that he still knew them. Even though he was too weak to visit, his eyes told me he knew his granddaughters and Brad. The kids, and Monie all gave me a hug and kiss and then headed for home.

The next morning, Dr. Petersen came and released Daddy to go home, Monday morning, January 2, 1988.

Daddy was just too weak to ride in the car, I knew, so an ambulance was the only way to get him there. I called an ambulance service about taking him home and couldn't believe the price. They wanted over $300 for the trip to Wisconsin!

Dr. Petersen didn't offer to try and assist me in getting him home, either. I believe he was trying to make me reconsider and move Daddy to the half- way house there at Abbott-Northwestern. He was right, I knew, but I was not going to let my Daddy die with strangers.

I called Monie and told her the problem. She said, "Let me talk to some of my friends in Clear Lake who have an ambulance service and see what they would charge."

I said, "Ask them if Medicare will cover the trip or at least part of it?"

A few minutes later she called back and said, "Yeah, they will come and get Vernon, Monday morning. They also said Medicare would probably cover all of it, but if not, you could cover them later."

"Thanks Monie," I sighed. "That takes a load off my mind."

THE NEXT MORNING WAS NEW YEAR'S EVE DAY. I wanted to go home and be with Pam and Kim, but I just didn't know what to do. Being so exhausted, the thought of making that long trip, again, almost defeated me. Looking back I realize that exhaustion was causing my brain to not function on all cylinders.

One of the nurses came in and asked, "Are you doing anything special tonight?"

"I don't know," I replied. Then I told her about the kid's plans for *Louis' Inn*.

She said, "I think you should go and be with your daughters, tonight. You know we will take good care of your Daddy and I don't think that he would want you to sit here and just watch him sleep. Besides, this will probably be the last time, for awhile, your family can all be together. It's going to be a little rough after you get home with your Dad."

"Maybe you're right. Thank you for your re-assurances," I told her before she left the room.

Daddy was sleeping like a baby as I sat there and thought about whether to go home or not. Finally I made my decision; I would go home and surprise everyone. Squeezing Daddy's hand and giving him a kiss, I told him I would be back the next day and we would both be going home in two days. He smiled and whispered, "Okay."

THE KIDS WERE TOTALLY SURPRISED AND ALMOST overwhelmed when I drove into the driveway. After the usual hugs, kisses and everyone talking at once we, finally settled down to firm up the plans for the evening. We all decided to get dressed-up and head for Louis's Inn.

I decided to wear a new, white suit I had bought a few months back and never had the chance to wear. The kids got a big table and we started celebrating.

My mind was still at the hospital, I realized, so I went up to the bar to visit with some friends. Before long, Louie came in. I had been his house-singer a few years back and considered him a good friend.

Naturally, we talked about Daddy. I told Louie how great he had been doing just before this last setback.

He said, "Reta, they always do the best right before the end." I didn't want to hear this, I guess I was still struggling with letting go and admitting I couldn't save my Dad.

I had a few Bacardi Diets, and since I had not eaten much and was so exhausted, it didn't take many before I was ready to go home. Even though I really didn't have that much fun, I was glad I had come home to be with the kids. I think that, just my being there, helped them to be able to "have a blast."

Before we knew it the band started singing *Auld Lang Syne* and announced the beginning of 1988. We all gave each other a big hug, blew the noise makers and decided to head back to Amery.

We headed out to the car and with my high heels, a few drinks and the ice, I fell flat on my behind in the parking lot. I had tried to catch myself, but only made things worse and when I fell, all my weight landed on my left thumb.

We finally made it home and I sure didn't have any problem going right to sleep. The next morning I woke up and my thumb was throbbing something awful. Looking at it, I found it was swollen, black, blue and green. I washed my face, brushed my teeth and headed for the smell of coffee. Everyone was up and looking like warmed over death, too. I think all of us had at least one too many, except Brad. He looked great because he had been the designated driver.

Monie saw my thumb and almost had a fit. She said, "Reta, you've got to go to the doctor. Looks broken!"

I laughed, "No, I think it's just a bad sprain, or the ligaments are pulled. It'll be okay, besides, I've got to get back to the hospital. Everyone gave me an argument, but I had no intentions of going to the doctor.

Monie wrapped it and said, "At least let them check it down at the hospital."

"Okay," I told her. Of course I had no intentions of doing so, but it made everyone feel better. I really didn't think it was broken. By, now, my entire body was beginning to feel like it didn't really belong to me anyway. I knew I must be falling apart, but I figured I would worry about me, later.

Before long, the entire peanut gallery was up in the kitchen. I told them they would all have to get used to a brand new schedule when Daddy got home. They would have to really be quiet and remember Daddy was upstairs, instead of down. They assured me they would be on their best behavior. Pam and Brad went to Wayne's Restaurant and brought home hot roast beef sandwiches for everyone so we wouldn't have to cook.

I opened my can of black eyed peas and made everyone eat a little bowl. Monie had never heard of this tradition. I said, "Well, where I come from, we always eat a bowl of black eyed peas for New Year's. This is to assure you of a prosperous year to come."

Everyone laughed at me, but they ate the peas. I felt sad knowing my Daddy wouldn't be able to eat his bowl this year. It would probably be the first year of his life he didn't have a bowl.

Remembering back to when I was a kid, I shared with my kids how Mama used to make a great big cooker full of black eyed peas. "As soon as the clock stuck midnight, we would all eat a bowl with corn bread. Her peas were always fresh, not canned. I think that most people in the South probably still follow this custom. I know Sissy and Humpty still do, plus most everyone else in our family."

After awhile, I got myself together and headed back to Minneapolis. I was so relieved to know this running back and forth would all be over soon and Daddy would be home.

As usual, I went immediately to Daddy's room and was delighted that he was awake. I gave him a kiss on the forehead, squeezed his hand and said, "Happy New Year's, Brody."

He very weakly tried to squeeze my hand back, "You too," he whispered.

"Are you ready to go home in the morning?" I chirped, trying to be as cheerful as possible.

His eyes got big and tears trickled down his cheeks, "Really?" he whispered.

"You betcha," I said. "We're gonna blow this joint."

He smiled but his eyes told me he was happy, yet confused. All I wanted to do was get him home.

THE NEXT MORNING I WAS UP BRIGHT AND EARLY. Dr. Petersen came in to give me the final instructions and to check Daddy over thoroughly before the ambulance came.

I followed him out into the hallway and said, "Dr. Petersen, how do I know when the time is near?"

He said, "Your Dad will just keep sleeping more and more of the time. Check his toenails and fingernails, if they start to turn blue, then you know it's just a day or so. Probably, he will just drift off without any pain."

"Thank God for that," I said with tears running down my face. "I'm so thankful he won't have to suffer."

He shook my hand, wished me luck and said, "Please, Reta, let me know when everything is over." I was just empty inside, everything was going to be so final.

Marlene and Twila, the nurses from the fifth floor came down to say good bye. Everyone was being so wonderful, all trying to make me feel better, but what could they really say. My Daddy was going home for the last time and we all knew it.

About 10:00 a.m., the ambulance arrived. The young couple that owned the ambulance service out of Clear Lake, Wisconsin, was so nice. They wrapped Daddy up and had him in the ambulance in a flash. The wife stayed in the back with Daddy and I rode up front to show them where to go.

Daddy was doing fine, his eyes were big. I said, "Daddy, you're going home in style, you can just be lazy and sleep all the way." He smiled and drifted back to sleep.

We pulled into the driveway about two hours later. My little team was all at their posts, waiting for instructions.

The young couple had Daddy out of the ambulance and into his hospital bed within minutes. Before leaving, they assured me Medicare would cover the trip and not to worry about it.

I said, "I can't thank you enough for what you've done."

The wife said, "Good luck, we're glad to have been able to help you. If you need us again, please call."

Sadly I watched them leave because I knew the next time I saw an ambulance pull up, it would be from the funeral home in Amery. Monie got Daddy settled and began checking him over for bed sores. She said, "His skin looks good, but we need to keep it that way. Do you mind if I cut up one of those blue hospital crate mattresses? I can use parts of it for relieving pressure on his skin."

"Monie," I said, "You can cut up anything you need to, and just let me know if you need anything else." Pam took off down stairs to retrieve the mattress for her.

Monie was like an old mother hen looking after her chick. She had such a warm and caring way of handling Daddy and was so gentle with him. She checked over the feeding tube and was so adamant about everything being sterile. It was a relief to know that he was in such good hands.

Since I didn't know how long Daddy would last, I worried about how long Monie's stamina would hold out. What would I do if I had to replace her? I just didn't know.

Going into the living room, I sat down in Daddy's Lazy Boy. I knew I had to make some important calls, but I was putting them off as long as possible.

First, I called Rick Robl at the St. Croix Valley Memorial Hospital and asked him to bring Daddy a *Geri Chair*. I knew he would no longer be able to sit in his Lazy Boy or the lift-out chair that we had used, before.

Bless his heart, he said, "I'll have it over there this afternoon and exchange it for the lift-out. Do you still want the pressurized mattress?"

"Yes," I quickly replied, "but we won't be needing the lift-out chair, any more." I explained my Dad's condition to him. Then I asked Rick to speak to his friend with the Medical Journal and tell him that there would be no need for an interview, my Daddy was dying.

He said, "I'm so sorry to hear that, Reta, I know how hard you guys have worked to get him back."

My next call was to Mike at the Winters Funeral Home in Texas. I said, "Mike, the time has come to call you. My Daddy is dying and I need to make arrangements to get him home. What do I do?"

He was so comforting, and said, "Reta, just give me the name of the nearest funeral home there and I will take care of everything. We'll get your Daddy home." I gave him the number of the funeral home in Amery then he said, "I'll call you back after I talk to them."

Then, I wandered back into the room to see how Daddy was doing. He was sleeping like a baby. Monie was busy hovering over him placing the little pieces of egg crate under different parts of his anatomy.

It didn't seem like very long before Mike called back and said, "Reta, I have everything arranged. When the time comes, all you have to do is call the *Williamson Mortuary*. They will come and pick up Vernon, get him ready for the trip, take him to the airport and fly him to Dallas where my ambulance will be waiting to transport him home."

I started crying, "Mike, thanks so much. Do you have any idea how much all this is going to cost?"

"Don't you worry, we'll work everything out when you get home. I will take care of all the expenses, so you will just owe me. We can work out a payment plan later."

"Thanks, Mike, you'll never know how much I appreciate you."

After I hung up the telephone, I had myself a good cry. It just didn't seem right to be making these plans. Daddy was still with us! Pam and Kim tried to comfort me, but I just couldn't stop crying. I guess the reality of the situation was finally hitting me.

Pam said, "Mom, why don't you go to Karen's house and we'll call you if we need you."

I FELT LIKE I WAS RUNNING OUT ON EVERYONE AND dumping my responsibilities, but I also knew I had to get out of there for awhile. I said, "Okay, after Rick delivers the *Geri Chair,* I'll go to Karen's house."

Kim said, "Good, I'm gonna call Karen and let her know you're coming."

I slumped back down in Daddy's Lazy Boy, my thumb was still throbbing. Pam said, "Mom, did you ever get that thumb checked?"

"No," I answered, "but maybe I will this week, if it doesn't get better."

In a few minutes, *Williamson Mortuary,* the funeral home in Amery, called to find out my address. They assured me they would be there as soon as they were needed.

Reluctantly, I asked, "Do I give you the clothes my dad will wear for the funeral?"

"It would be better to take those to Texas with you and let them dress him. If you have something else for us to put him in for transporting, just send it with him, otherwise, we will put a blanket over him."

I quickly assured them I would send something for him to wear home. They were very nice, but everything was becoming and sounding so final.

Once again, I went in and looked at my little Daddy. Maybe I had to keep reassuring myself he was still with me. I just couldn't believe his time was finally here. God, I felt so helpless.

He woke up and looked at me with those soft, hazel eyes and whispered, "Hi."

I fought back the tears as I kissed his forehead and said, "Welcome home, Daddy. I love you." He just squeezed my hand and I knew what he wanted to say, which was *I love you, too.* He looked so peaceful, and I knew he wasn't in any pain. That helped me feel a little better.

I decided to unpack Daddy's suitcase and placed his things in one of my dresser drawers. His new pajamas were still in the wrapper. Seeing them, I knew immediately what I would send for him to wear to Texas.

Then, I got another little bag out and placed the new pajamas I had bought for him to wear at Christmas, a clean pair of underwear, tee-shirt, his robe and house shoes in it. I then set it in the closet alongside the little bag containing his wedding ring from Mama and the other items I was going to take to Texas.

Then, I picked out a dress for me to wear and got my suitcase packed. I knew I had better get this all taken care of now, while I still had my thoughts straight.

Before long, Rick came with the *Geri Chair.* He was so nice, he picked up the lift-out chair and put it in his truck. Then he patted my shoulder and said, "I wish I could say something to make it easier, but I just don't know what to say."

I know," I replied, "but your kindness has been enough, because I know you really care. I'll call you when we no longer need the *Geri Chair."*

He looked at Pam and Kim and said, "Take care of her."

"We will," they promised.

Pam said, "Now, Mom, why don't you go to Karen's house, as she's expecting you."

"Okay," I sighed. "It would be nice to have somewhere to go and relax." I packed my other suitcase, again, and headed for Amery.

I was so proud of Pam and Kim, they were sure handling everything, including me, so well. It made me feel bad that I was dumping on them, but I knew if I didn't get some rest, I was going to be more of a burden to them than a help.

I talked to God all the way into Amery. "Dear, God, you know my body is not as strong as it once was and my mind is so tired. I just don't know how much more I can handle. Please give me strength and give my little girls and Monie the strength they need to see everything through."

I paused for a moment, then said, "Dear, God, please take my little Daddy home, he's ready and my family can't take much more of this tension." I never thought I would hear myself say it, but I was actually praying for the Good Lord to take my Daddy home.

WHEN I GOT TO KAREN'S HOUSE, SHE WAS WAITING with a Bacardi Coke for me. "Your room is ready, just throw your stuff in there and let's catch up on some of the gossip."

I said, "Okay, but I've got to call Yane and Cecil first and let them know that Daddy's home."

Cecil was really quiet when I talked to him. He'd had trouble and never really accepted his new Daddy. I assured him I would call him of any change, and that I knew it wasn't going to be long.

I just wasn't ready to talk to Yane so I decided to wait a few minutes before I called her. Karen said, "Is she still giving you crap?"

"No, actually, the last couple of times I talked to her she's been rather nice." I laughed, "I guess Dub is giving her some more of those nice pills." I finished my drink, then with a sigh I said, "I better call her before it gets any later."

Yane answered the telephone. I told her exactly what was happening with Daddy and that I didn't expect him to last more than another week.

She said, "Well, I want to talk to him."

"Yane, Daddy is too weak to talk to anyone right now," I told her. "I have his hospital bed in my room and the telephone won't reach over there for you to talk to him. But I promise you, if he gets strong enough to sit up close to the telephone, I will call you so you can say goodbye."

She choked up, "I would appreciate that." I almost felt sorry for her, after all he was her Daddy, too. In her way, I knew she loved him.

I remembered how helpless I felt back in 1984 when I was fifteen hundred miles away. She had been so uncaring of my feelings but I was not going to make her feel that way. I wouldn't do that to my worst enemy.

Before we hung up, she asked, "Did Daddy get his Stetson?"

"Yes," I said, "and I went ahead and gave him his shirts, too. I didn't know if he would still be with us for his birthday."

"Well, just bring them back down here with you when you come. I can take them back for a refund."

I couldn't believe my ears, but I assured her I would bring her property back to Texas with Daddy, unused and in good condition.

To help divert my mind from my conversation with Yane, Karen filled me in on *Pure Gold's* activities. She said, "They sure do miss you, but they are doing great."

"I don't know if I'll ever be singing with them full-time again. Right now, I don't care if I ever sing again."

She looked at my thumb and said, "What in the hell did you do?"

I told her of my fall at Louis' Inn New Year's Eve. She said, "Well, you better get your butt in to see Dr. Rimestad tomorrow."

"Maybe I will, it doesn't seem to be getting any better." We gossiped until about 10:00 p.m. then I hit the bed. I slept like a baby so I knew I had done the right thing to move over to Karen's for the time being.

I got up early the next morning and Karen already had the coffee ready. She said, "I'll see you tonight, I got to get to work." She was bartending at one of the local bars in Amery. As she went out the door she yelled back, "Call Dr. Rimestad!"

I decided that wouldn't be a bad idea. My stomach had been giving me trouble and I was feeling like a total wreck. I called home first and Monie assured me Daddy was just fine. She said, "Go on in and see the doctor before you come out."

I called Dr. Rimestad's office, they told me to come right in. Dr. Rimestad almost flipped when he saw my thumb. He sent me over to the hospital for x-rays, immediately.

After he read them, he shook his head and said, "Reta, you have been walking around all this time with a broken thumb, you have got to start taking better care of yourself! Also, I want you to come in for some tests. Your ulcers are probably acting up again."

"I will," I answered, "but I can't right now."

I told him about Daddy and he understood, but he said, "I want you in here as soon as possible." He set my thumb and put a little brace on it.

I stopped by *Chet Johnson & Son's Pharmacy* in Amery to get a supply of *Ensure* for Daddy.

Bruce said, "It comes in chocolate or vanilla."

"Daddy loves chocolate," I said, "so I'll take that."

Bruce hesitated for a moment, then said, "Reta, think about what you just said. Your Daddy won't be able to taste it, and the vanilla is less money."

I felt so stupid, "Of course," I replied, "it's just so hard to realize he'll never taste anything again."

Bruce figured the supply would cost me almost $500.00 per month. I said, "My gosh! Won't Medicare pay for this, it is his only survival?"

"You would think so," he replied. "If he was in a nursing home, I know they would, but not if he's at home."

"That doesn't make any sense. Why is everyone trying to force me into putting my Daddy in a nursing home?" I started to cry again.

He said, "Let me do some checking. Maybe I can work out a way for Medicare to pay."

"I really would appreciate that, cause I can't afford that kind of money on top of everything else." I took the case of Ensure and headed for home!

I WALKED INTO THE HOUSE AND GOT THE SURPRISE of life. The Kids all started singing Happy Birthday, and Monie rolled Daddy into the living room in his *Geri Chair* wearing his bright, red, night shirt we had gotten him for Christmas.

The tears really came now, but they were happy tears. It was the first time I had seen Daddy sitting up in weeks. He tried to grin, but he was so weak.

Monie put him in front of his big window so he could see the horses. The sun was shining bright through the window and for a split second, I thought we might be able to save him.

We had coffee and I blew out the candles on the birthday cake the kids had bought for me, but we didn't eat any. I said, "We'll have it later after Daddy is back in bed." We didn't dare eat something good in front of him. God, I felt so bad because he couldn't eat any more.

While we had some coffee, I noticed Daddy kept looking at Monie's cigarettes lying on the coffee table. I said, "Daddy, do you want a cigarette?" His eyes brightened up and he tried to reach for one. I lit one and he tried to take a drag off it, but he couldn't because he was just too weak.

I remembered my promise to Yane and said, "Daddy, let's give Yane and Cecil a call. I know you're too weak to talk, but you could just listen.

I called Cecil first. Margaret answered and she talked to Daddy for a while because Cecil was at work. I held the telephone to his ear. He just set there listening. Sometimes he would show some reaction to something said, but not much.

After we hung up from talking with Margaret, I called Yane. I explained the situation to her, saying, "I'll hold the telephone to Daddy's ear and you say whatever you want to, but don't expect him to talk, he's too weak." I know Daddy knew who she was. His eyes lit up and he tried to take the telephone but he was too weak to hold it, so I took it back. I don't know what Yane said to him but, she did get her opportunity to say goodbye, as I had promised.

After that, Daddy was so tired, I told Monie to go ahead and put him back to bed.

She said, "I thought this would be the best birthday gift you could have, to see your Daddy sitting up for the party."

I gave her a hug, "You're one in a million, Monie. I thank God everyday for you."

She smiled and wheeled Daddy back into the bedroom. Little did we know, that would be the last time my Daddy would ever sit in a chair. He was asleep by the time Monie got him back into bed.

When Monie came back out, we all had some birthday cake, then I worked on the books. I just didn't know how in the world I was going to pay all the bills with what we had coming in. Also, I noticed that we had lost more students over the holidays.

LOOKING AROUND AT MY HOME AND FAMILY, I WAS so glad to be here so I could keep an eye on everything. I told Pam and Kim that I would be teaching with them next week, no matter what. If I wasn't there, I might lose even more students.

Some of these parents I just couldn't understand. Pam and Kim could teach as well as me, and probably their minds would be more on classes, but some parents were having a fit because I was missing again.

Some of them were wonderful, but others I would like to punch in their big mouth. Every time the telephone would ring, I would cringe, hoping it wasn't another parent bitching about something. I was getting to where I absolutely hated some of those people, they were so rude and selfish.

The news kept getting worse. Kathy called and said, "Reta, I hate to tell you this, but they have cut your budget. Home Care has totally been pulled away, and your home attendant's wages will be cut in half."

"Those bastards," I yelled, "what are they trying to do? My Daddy is not dead yet, so why are they doing this?"

She explained, "Because his health has deteriorated. As long as he was improving, they would give you the moon, but if that turns around, which it has, then they start cutting everything. I'm so sorry, Reta, I really tried to save it for you."

"I know, Kathy, you've been wonderful. I guess the damn government is too busy taking care of all the other countries to care about their own, especially the elderly. I hope someday I can be in a position to make a difference, believe me, the elderly will be the ones I carry a flag for." I started crying and said goodbye.

I couldn't believe it! I just didn't know what I was going to do. Monie was working harder now than ever and the bastards cut her wages in half! Daddy and I couldn't afford to pay any more, our pot was empty. The house money was about gone, my students were quitting, my health was going to hell and sometimes I felt like I was losing my mind. I put my head down on my desk and cried so hard I thought my eyes were gonna fall out. This was one birthday I would never forget!

After composing myself, I went downstairs and told Monie the bad news. She said, "What can we do? I'm not leaving you and Vernon, I'm seeing this through if I have to work free." She put her arms around me and said, "Don't worry, we'll be okay, we're family. Why don't you take a hot bath and get relaxed."

I filled the tub and soaked awhile. After getting out, I put on my new, blue pajamas that Pam and Kim had given me for Christmas. I had practically lived in them since I got them, only taking them off to wash, bathe, and put them back on.

Daddy appeared to be getting weaker so I went in and checked his toenails. They were still okay, so I knew we had a little more time left.

As I went into the living room to drink a cup of coffee, I heard a knock on the door. Opening it, I couldn't believe my eyes. Gregg and Clarion had come to wish me a Happy Birthday. In all the years I've known Gregg, he never once has missed wishing me a Happy Birthday. He put his arms around me and, of course, the tears started flowing.

I asked them if they would like to see Daddy and Gregg said, "I'd rather just remember Vernon the way he was the last time I saw him." Clarion felt the same way.

They visited for a little while, then left for home. I always marveled at how nice Gregg and Clarion were, they are truly two of the best friends I have, or ever will have.

They hadn't been gone very long until Cords, Rick and Donnie knocked on the door. Tears flowed again, especially when I told them not to count on me coming back and if they wanted, they could get someone else to take my place.

They assured me they didn't want to do that and that they preferred just to stay the three of them and hope I would be back one day. The clubs had been very understanding, and rightfully so, the guys were great by themselves. I only wished some of my parents were as understanding.

They wished me a Happy Birthday, again, and let me know my family and I were in their thoughts and prayers. When they left for home, I thought, I am so lucky to have such wonderful friends.

KAREN CALLED AND SAID, "WHEN ARE YOU COMING to town?"

"Soon," I answered.

"Fine. Stop by *T.J.'s* first, my car wouldn't start and I need a ride. Besides, I want to buy you a birthday drink."

"Okay," I said, "I sure could use one. This has really been a memorable birthday. The damn government has cut off all our funds and I just don't know what I'm going to do. I might be forced into putting Daddy in the nursing home before it's over."

"Well, get yourself on down here, you need to get your mind off all these problems for awhile," she squawked.

I knew she was right because I could tell I was headed for a nervous breakdown, full speed ahead, if I didn't put the brakes on and soon. I changed into my jeans and sweat shirt, redid my hair in a Banana Clip, dabbed on a little lipstick, gave Daddy a kiss goodbye, let Monie know where I would be and headed for Amery.

While driving into town, I had my usual chat with God on the way. It seemed like driving in my car was the only space I had left in the entire world.

I stopped by Karen's house first to pick up my winter coat. I looked around the little room she had given to me in her trailer house, and it looked so good. It tempted me to just lie down and go to sleep, but, I couldn't leave Karen without a ride home. Besides she would kill me if I stood her up for that birthday drink. Now that I remembered, it was my birthday!

I walked into *T.J.'s Lounge,* and the tears really started to flow. All my friends, including Gary Miller, Leroy Becker, Dick, Ynonne Owllette, Diane and Jerry Crook, plus many of my fans were there that I hadn't seen for sometime.

Karen yelled over the mike, "Happy Birthday you little s___." Gregg, Clarion, Cords, Rick and Donnie had the bandstand all set up, too. Everyone all started singing Happy Birthday. Karen had a birthday cake and the whole works.

In a few minutes, in trooped Pam, Kim, Brad, Cheryl and the entire peanut gallery. I smiled and said, "I'm surrounded by sneaks! How did all of you keep this a secret?"

"It wasn't easy," Karen snickered. "I've been working pretty close with Pam and Kim."

Pam said, "Yeah, Mom, before you start, Monie is in full harmony with us. We all decided you needed to Chill Out and enjoy your birthday. Grandpa is okay and if there is any change, Monie will call, immediately."

"Yeah, Mom, just Chill and get your mind off bills, Grandpa and everything. Let's have some fun!" Kim echoed.

"Okay, okay, you guys win. I do need a break," I said with tears still streaming down my face.

Cheryl said, "Now, Reta, no more tears tonight."

I blew my nose, dried my eyes and said, "Okay, let's celebrate!" I laughed, "But this is going to be my last birthday, I start backward from here!" Gregg started singing *Backside Of Thirty*.

That was a really nice evening. I called Monie a few times and she assured me Daddy was sleeping just fine. I hit tears a few times throughout the evening, especially when one fan asked me to sing, *They Don't Make 'Em Like My Daddy Anymore*. It had been written and made famous by my favorite singer, Loretta Lynn, and had become synonymous with Daddy and me since Daddy's stroke.

Ted and Sue, the owners of *T.J.'s* made some snacks for everyone. They had helped me out once when all my equipment had been stolen, so I was glad the party was held there so that they could benefit from the business.

The party broke up fairly early, or at least, Karen and I went home. Of course, her car started just fine.

By the time we arrived at Karen's trailer, I was so tired I could hardly put one foot in front of the other. I gave Karen a hug and said, "Thanks, buddy, I really did need this."

She smiled and said, "You betcha," then headed for her bedroom.

I slept a little later the next morning and so I jumped up and called Monie immediately. "Is Daddy okay?"

"Yes," she laughed. "How did the party go?"

"Oh, it was great! I really did need that time-out with my friends. I only wish that you and Daddy could have been there."

"Well," she chuckled, "Vernon and I had our own party here. He was awake more last night than usual."

"Did he say anything?" I questioned.

"Just mumbled, like he was talking to someone else," she answered.

I laughed, "Ol' Shorty must have returned. Tell him I'll be there in a few minutes."

"Don't drive too fast," she cautioned. "I promise, Vernon is okay."

"Did the kids make it home okay?" I questioned.

"Oh, yeah," she laughed, "they're already fixing some breakfast, and moaning about starting back to work. Are you planning on going with them today?"

I answered, "Yes, but don't tell them, I want it to be a surprise."

I chuckled to myself as I drove out to the house, I've got to ask Sissy if she knows anything about the status of Ol' Shorty.

I COULDN'T BELIEVE THE HOLIDAYS WERE OVER already, and that we had to start back at the studio today. The reason I dreaded it was that I had no idea how many students would show up, and I could just hear the complaints about my absence. Thank, God, for the parents who had been understanding and supportive to Pam and Kim.

Pam, Kim and Cheryl were sitting at the table eating their pancakes when I arrived. They sure didn't look like any bundles of joy. I said, "Good morning! What time did you guys get in?"

"You don't want to know," Cheryl replied with her eyes still half shut.

I went in and checked on Daddy. He was sleeping and Monie was hovering over him. Giving him a kiss, I said, "Monie, you look really tired. I think you need some rest, too."

"I am tired, but I'm okay," she answered.

I got a cup of coffee and joined Pam and Kim. I could see the question in their eyes about me going with them this week.

Very calmly I said, "By the way, would you guys like for me to start back at the studios with you this week?"

Their eyes got big and their faces brightened up, "Really, Mom?" Kim said.

"You betcha! I have to start back before some of those she-devils eat you alive," I answered. All of a sudden, everyone found the energy they needed to go to work.

I went up to my office and just prayed God would give me the strength I needed to go on. I knew that the time-out I had staying at Karen's house would be a blessing. I stacked the bills on one side of the desk and decided to just wait and see how many students continued, then I would know which lucky creditor would be paid this month.

Going to my room, I got dressed in one of my leotards and tried to pump myself up to go back, but my heart just wasn't in it.

Pam and Kim came up and were ready to go. Before leaving, I checked Daddy's toenails, and they were still fine. I gave him a kiss and headed for Ladysmith.

This was our biggest studio, and the one that was paying my bills. Kim had been handling this studio just fine, and the parents had been very supportive, but she had to have help, therefore, Pam had been helping her.

They were not worried about taking the other studios. The enrollment was low in all of them, so Kim was able to handle them, with a little help from Cheryl. Pam was still running her studio in Luck and had been taking over the Clear Lake studio too. I was so proud of my daughters, they had worked everything out.

- Many parents throughout the evening told me what a great job Kim and Pam had been doing during my absence. Of course, Kim and Pam's head got a little bigger, and rightfully so. This was the shot they both needed to help them to gain more confidence.

We completed classes, and actually, it was good for me. I really did love my little students, they were all so sweet and happy to see me. Then, we packed up and drove the fifty miles back home.

When we got home, I crashed in my bed and bunked with Monie. Daddy was asleep and the house was very quiet.

The next morning, Monie came in with coffee. I said, "Monie, you look like warmed over death, too. I've got to get you some relief."

"You can't afford that, and the damn government won't pay for Betty or anyone else to help you."

"That's true," I sighed, "but I've got to do something. You can't continue like this."

"I'll be okay. Cheryl helps me a lot when you guys are gone, we'll be okay."

I went up to my office and asked God to help me figure out a solution. I had to get more help or I was gonna be forced into putting Daddy in the Constant Care Nursing Home in Amery.

I started working on bills, and it was just like God tapped me on the head and said, "Dummy up, Reta, call your friend Fred."

I looked up, smiled and said, "Thank you, God, I will."

I looked up Fred's mother's telephone number and dialed it. The last thing Fred had said to me was, to let him know if anything should go wrong with Daddy. Well, things sure had gone wrong.

Fred answered the telephone. I heard his voice and started crying, "Fred, Daddy's dying and I really need your help."

He got me calmed down to where I could tell him the entire problem. He said, "I'll be down there in a few hours to help you, don't worry."

I said, "Fred, they've cut just about all the financial aid and I can't pay you right now."

"Don't worry about that," he assured me. "I want to be with my Ol' Podner right now, and help you guys." I hung up the telephone and cried some more.

I went down and told Monie she had relief on the way. She said, "Well, I hope he knows what he's doing, cause I'm not letting anyone touch Vernon if they don't."

Smiling, I said, "Monie, you have got to let someone help you. I know they can't take your place but you can't continue this twenty-four hour vigilance, either."

She sighed, "I know, but I've come to love him so much," she started to cry.

I put my arms around her and said, "I know, Monie, you've become family to us, too, but I don't want you to become a basket-case like me, or Daddy's gonna have to start taking care of us."

We both started laughing and crying together. She said, "Are we both nuts or what?"

"No, we're just on our last leg."

She said, "It's time for Grandpa's feeding and headed for the kitchen.

I WENT OVER KISSED DADDY AND SQUEEZED HIS hand. He opened his eyes and looked at me with such softness. He didn't look scared or confused any more, he looked ready for his trip back home to Mama.

Pam and Kim took the studio in Spooner, so that I could get some rest. I took a hot bath, put on my blue pajamas and called Karen to let her know I was staying at my house, tonight. I sat down in Daddy's Lazy Boy and dozed off.

I was awakened by someone knocking on the door. It was Fred.

I gave him a big hug and through my tears, I said, "You look like an angel."

He said, "I'm just glad I can help."

I took him immediately into my room. Tears welled up in his eyes as he looked at Daddy. "How's my Ol' Podner?" he asked. Daddy just looked at him. I didn't know if he remembered Fred or not. He just looked at him, grinned and went back to sleep.

Monie started filling him in on all the procedures. She was a little sharp with him because he didn't understand some of them. I took her aside and told her Fred was not a certified aid and she would have to show him the procedures instead of just telling him.

She said, "I'd rather just take care of Grandpa myself," as she went back to Daddy and Fred.

I was really concerned about Monie. It seemed she was becoming obsessed with caring for Daddy, and although I loved her for caring so much, I knew she couldn't continue this unrelenting grind.

She started Fred cutting little strips of egg crate mattress and showing him how to place them under certain areas on Daddy's body. Fred was listening and trying as hard as he could. I knew Daddy had two people caring for him that truly loved him.

The kids got home from the studio and were filling me in on the student loss and attendance when Gary Miller came by. He came in and put his arms around me and said, "Are you okay?"

Through the tears, I said, "Not really, Gary. I'm just a basket case." He joined us in the living room while Pam and Kim finished telling me how many more students had dropped from the classes. After a bit, they excused themselves and went to bed.

Gary and I talked for awhile. I said, "Gary, I honestly don't know what I'm going to do. Daddy's and my money pot is just about empty. He has no more to contribute and with the loss of students, and my not singing, I'm in a mess. Plus I feel like I'm falling apart." By this time the tears were flowing but I tried to continue. "Dr. Rimestad wants me to check in for tests..."

Gary interrupted and held me really tight, "It'll be okay. Just go ahead and cry, that's good medicine." He was right, I sobbed for about five minutes then I did feel better.

I made us a Bacardi Coke and tried to be a little more cheerful. Gary said, "I hate to bring this up, but when is your final hearing with that creep you're married to?"

"I've tried to put him out of my mind, but Don Novitzke called a couple days ago and confirmed the hearing for January 21. I'll be so glad to be rid of that little weasel."

"Are you keeping the house?"

"Yeah, why?" I questioned.

He got a really serious look on his face, "Well, I was out here the other day with Brad, and we checked everything over. Brad showed me some of the problems he had found that he hadn't told you about."

He paused, "Reta, this house has really got some problems. It's obvious that the idiot you married didn't know what the hell he was doing when he built it. Brad told me about the pump house, electric, and all the other problems you've had.

I took a look at that deck he put up and he has it held up with four two by fours, it could collapse at any time. Your roof is starting to sway because the rafters were not put up properly, plus the leak you have in the basement is from him building the frost wall out of wood. This house is nowhere near code and you would have a hell of a time selling it. If you keep it, your gonna be paying out at least $50,000 on repairs to straighten out the mess he's made."

My mouth was wide open by this time, "But, Gary, I've got everything I've made for the last four years, in this house. Everything was purchased new at *Menards.*"

"I know," he answered, "but that stupid ass didn't know what he was doing. The house is beautiful, but five years from now, you're gonna have big troubles."

I was so angry by this time, that I swear I could have shot that weasel, and never blinked an eye. "What would you recommend I do, Gary?" I asked.

He sat there for a moment then said, "If it's just you and the girls by the twenty-first, I would let that bastard have this house, lick my wounds and walk away. You can't continue to fight to maintain it with the financial situation you are facing, now. Plus, you need to take care of your health. Frankly, I don't think it is worth it for you to keep it."

"He would lose it within three months, unless he finds a woman who can afford to pay the overhead," I snapped. "Damn him to hell for what he has done to us!"

"He built the problems, let him solve them. You better start thinking of yourself, or Pam and Kim will be caring for you like you're caring for your Daddy."

Gary was a professional carpenter, so I trusted he knew what he was talking about. We talked awhile longer, then he said, "I'll talk to Leroy Becker and Dick Crain, and see if they will come out and give you their opinion, that is, if you want me to?"

I was totally in shock, I knew Steve made a lot of mistakes, but I didn't know he was this bad. I assured Gary I would really appreciate anything he could do to assist me in making the right decision before the divorce hearing.

He gave me a kiss goodnight and said, "I hated like anything to drop this on you, but I am your friend. Karen and I also talked about this and she told me that I had to talk to you. Now dry those eyes and get some rest, I'll call you when Leroy and Dick can come out."

I went in to check on Daddy. Fred was busy caring for him and Monie was sound asleep in my bed. Fred assured me Daddy was just fine.

I went downstairs and crawled into Daddy's waterbed and went sound asleep. Fred was just going to nap in the chair if he needed to. He and Monie had decided to keep a twenty-four hour vigil over Daddy because he was getting so week and listless. We all knew his time was drawing closer.

I went to the studio with Kim the next day. I was totally numb, but, I made it through the night. On the way home I told her what Gary had told me.

She said, "Mom, do whatever you have to do, let's just rent a place or buy that trailer house you planned to buy before that jerk came into our lives. Anything, to get back to a normal life. I just want you to be okay." She started to cry, "Things have just got to change, Mom, all of us are falling apart. I wish God would just take Grandpa even though I love him so much and I never thought I would pray for God to take him, but I do!"

I stopped the car and put my arms around her and we both cried. I said, "Honey, don't feel guilty about praying for God to take Grandpa home. That has been my prayer for the last few nights, also."

"Really, Mom," she said, "because Pam's prayer has been the same."

"I felt guilty the first time I prayed that way too, but I know, that if Grandpa can still pray, his prayer would be the same, too. I know he's ready to go home to Mama." We dried our eyes and headed on home.

After we got home, Monie said, "Gary called and said to tell you that Leroy, Dick and he would be out tomorrow about 4:00 p.m. He said to call him if that time wasn't okay."

I explained the house situation to her and then went in to see my little Daddy. His body was just getting smaller and smaller. I felt so bad because I just didn't know what more we could do, except keep him comfortable.

Fred was feeding him and Monie snapped, "That's not the right way, Fred,." and immediately took over. I took Fred into the kitchen for a cup of coffee and apologized for Monie's attitude.

"Don't worry, I understand," he chuckled. "Remember how I reacted over the knife? She's suffering burn-out like I did. We'll be okay." He was so assuring, and that made me feel better. I wouldn't have Fred's feelings hurt for anything. He had been as good to us as Monie. I was so thankful for both of them.

I gave Daddy a kiss, checked his toenails and headed for Karen's house so Fred could sleep in Daddy's waterbed and Monie could sleep in mine.

Karen was already asleep when I got to her home, but she had the coffee going early the next morning. I told her about Gary's visit, and about the guys all coming out today.

"Good," she said, "I think you would be better off to let that little bastard have that house and all the payments that go with it.

Just get you and the girls a trailer-house like mine. That's all you need, and quit trying to carry the world on your shoulders. Let Cheryl's mother take care of her, and you just take care of yours.

Pam and Kim can help you with expenses, and maybe you could have some kind of a life before you wind up six foot under." She took a breath, "Now I've said it."

I sat there for a few minutes thinking then said, "All of you are making a lot of sense, Karen. Believe me, I'm doing some heavy thinking. I would like to just chuck the entire mess. Maybe then, I would have the energy to help Pam and Kim save the studios and get back with my band. My life is so out of control, I feel like I'm running downhill and can't stop."

I finished my coffee and headed for home. Arriving home, I went directly in and checked Daddy's toenails almost praying the blue would be there. Then I thought, What a horrible person I was to think this way, even though I knew Daddy would feel the same.

I went down stairs to talk to the kids, they were all sitting up in their bed having a really serious talk. "Hi, is this private or can your Mom join in?"

Pam laughed and said, "Come on in Mom, you know you can always join us."

Setting my coffee on the dresser I then flopped down on the bed with them. "Now, what is everyone so serious about?" I asked.

They just looked at each other and Kim finally said, "Go ahead, Pam, tell Mom what we were talking about."

She looked at me and said, "Mom, Kim told me about the conversation you guys had coming home the other night. Have you really prayed for God to take Grandpa?"

"Yes, honey, I have, and like I told Kim, if Grandpa is still able to pray, he is praying for God to let him go home, too. You know Grandpa, he wouldn't want to live like the way he is now." I paused for a moment, "And if he had any idea of what we were going through, he wouldn't be able to stand it. I know he would tell me to put him in the nursing home, but I just can't. I don't want him to die with strangers." We all put our arms around each other and cried.

-         I reminded them about Gary, Leroy and Dick coming later to advise me on the house. Pam said, "Mom, you stay here and take care of that. Kim and I will take Cumberland, and if any one has a problem with you not being there, then we will handle it. Everyone but a couple of ladies over there have really been supportive, but there are two women who have really made life miserable. They are still complaining about one makeup class we missed during a blizzard. I told them we would schedule our makeups during Spring, but they just keep griping."

"If that five dollars is so important to them, just give it to them, that's better than putting up with their complaining all the time," I replied.

"Well, don't worry, we'll handle it," Kim replied.

We went upstairs and had a bite to eat. Later I got our small deposit ready and took it to the bank, sent off some lucky creditors a payment, not all, but some.

When I came back, I sat at my desk and really thought about what Gary and Karen had said. I knew they were right, and with the student loss, I could not continue to make all the payments. Another thing, if Daddy kept hanging on, I would have to put him in the nursing home, especially if Medicare wouldn't pay for the Ensure. That, alone, would take more than Daddy's little Social Security check plus his S.S.I. I just hated the bureaucrats that made all those rules to cut the American people off at a time they needed them the most.

I asked God to direct me and help me to make the right decisions for my family.

Pam and Kim took off for Cumberland, they only had two classes left to teach over there. The studio had just about folded.

All we really had left was Ladysmith, Spooner and Clear lake. The Luck studio had not been very big to start with and had dropped off about 25 per cent after the holidays. Sometimes, I wished I just had a day job and didn't have to deal with another parent or stage mother.

BEFORE I KNEW IT, GARY KNOCKED AT THE DOOR. Fred let him in. They were having a long chat when I came down and said, "Hi, I'm ready for the jury to come in and give me a verdict."

I told Fred what was going on and he agreed with Gary and Karen. He said, "It's none of my business, but you can't continue like you are, this house is not worth it."

"I know," I said, "at least I had a nice place to bring my Dad for his last days."

"That's right," Gary replied, "just chalk it up to that, and let that little bastard have it."

Leroy and Dick didn't get out to the house until a couple of hours later. They both gave me a hug and their condolences.

I said, "I really appreciate you guys taking the time to come out and give me your honest opinions."

Leroy said, "Hey, what are friends for? From what Gary has told us, it doesn't sound too good."

"Yeah," Dick replied, "and I know that idiot you were married to, he's just a big blowhard."

They each took their yellow pads and started checking their specialty areas. Dick was a plumber and Leroy was a sheet metal expert. It didn't take them long to come back and give me their assessment of the situation.

Dick said, "The way he has the plumbing hooked up is a real joke. The holding tank for the toilet is connected into the faucet for the bathtub in your room."

I shook my head, "That explains why the water is always blue when I first turn the faucet on. The damn Tidy Bowl, from the holding tank is draining into the faucet."

"Yeah," Dick answered, "once the holding tank is empty, then it's okay."

He continued to tell me the entire horror story on the plumbing. The vent pipe for the sewer gases, that should have been vented out the top of the house, was vented out of my closet and on to the back deck.

Dick just shook his head, "Reta, this entire system would have to be redone from scratch, because the idiot used plastic throughout instead of copper. None of this would ever pass code. In all my years of plumbing, I've never seen such a mess." I was getting so angry, I was having trouble controlling myself.

Leroy came up from the basement shaking his head, too. He said, "I cannot believe the heating system he has put in. It's the biggest Mickey Mouse mess I've ever seen. He has heating ducts put together from cardboard, and that old furnace, well, I'm surprised it kept going as long as it has."

I screamed, "That bastard, he must have been spending most of the money he took on his women. I know he told me he bought everything he needed for the heating system and I gave him a check to cover it."

"What he's got down there, Reta, looks like he got from the dump. I can patch that old furnace up for you, to make it through this winter, but if you keep this house, you will need to have a new one installed plus all the heating ducts replaced."

They both completely agreed with Gary. They advised me to give it to Steve, lick my wounds and walk away.

Gary said, "If you do keep it, and decided to sell it later, a buyer could sue you for selling them something like this. Nothing is code."

I just went all to pieces. I sat down on the sofa, and Pam and Kim came running up with Brad. They had just returned from Cumberland. I said, "Brad, did you know the house was in this kind of mess?"

He put his head down and said, "Yeah, I did, that's why I talked to Gary. I didn't want to have to tell you because I know how much money you gave Steve to build it, and I just didn't know how to tell you."

By this time I was crying uncontrollably. Monie came running out of my room and said, "Reta, Vernon is really upset! He's trying to get out of the bed to see who's hurting you."

"Oh my ,God," I cried as I ran to Daddy.

His eyes were opened wide and with all the strength he had he said, "I'll kill the bastards!"

I sat down by him on the bed and calmed him down. I said, "Daddy, I'm okay. I was just having a bad dream, no one is hurting me. Don't you worry, you just go back to sleep. I promise I'm okay."

He was squeezing my hand with all the strength he could muster and finally relaxed and drifted back to sleep. It hurt me that he had to hear my racket but at the same time, somehow, I still felt protected by my Daddy. If he could, I knew he would beat the living hell out of Steve or anyone else who might try to hurt me. I sat with him for awhile until I was sure he was sound asleep. Even in his condition, I was still so proud of him. He always did protect us, and made me feel so safe with him.

I went back into the living room and apologized to the guys for losing my temper. Assuring them how I really appreciated them for telling the truth, I said, "Thanks to you, I now know what I have to do." Leroy and Dick gave me a hug and took off for Amery.

After they left Gary sat down on the sofa with me. He put his arms around me, and between him, Pam, Kim and Brad, they soon had me feeling better. We all decided that I would let the little weasel have his stupid house, and all the payments that go with it. The decision had been made. I think that down deep I was really relieved.

FRED GOT BACK FROM RHINLANDER, WHERE HE HAD gone to visit his children. He went right in to relieve Monie. She came out into the living room and sat down, she was very quiet. I said, "Monie, are you okay?"

"Yeah," she answered, "but I really want to talk to you about something, and I don't know how to do it."

"You're not quitting are you?" I cried.

"Oh no, you'll have to throw me out, I'm a staying kind of person."

I said, "Would you like to talk privately?"

"Maybe that would be best," she answered.

Gary said, "Well, I need to be going anyway." He gave me a kiss on the cheek and headed for the door. I thanked him, again, for his efforts and assured him I would be okay. Pam and Kim took off with Brad to see some of their friends.

Monie sat there for a moment, then said, "Reta, you might not believe me, but after that outburst from your Dad tonight, I realized why he is still hanging on. He's not sure you can handle him leaving you.

I truly believe, if you would give him permission to go, he would. He's hanging on because you won't let him go. You've got to talk to him, and I think you should do so, as soon as possible."

I was just numb. What Monie was saying made sense. Thinking back I remembered how I had told Daddy, repeatedly throughout the last year, that I wouldn't let him leave me. I said, "My God, Monie, do you really think it's my fault he keeps hanging on?"

"Yes I do," she replied. "Many times you have mentioned the strong bond you and your Daddy have always had, and I think it's still there. Reta, he's waiting on you to tell him it's okay for him to die. I'm going to take a bath, you think it over and make your own decision."

She left the room and I just sat there in Daddy's Lazy Boy. I felt like the world had just crashed totally down on me, but somehow I knew Monie was right. What she said certainly made sense.

I prayed for God to give me the right words to say to Daddy, if what Monie had told me was true. I prayed for strength, what and how to say what needed to be said. and to be able to talk to him without crying. I knew tears would only upset him, and possibly defeat my purpose.

I got up and slowly walked to my bedroom door. Fred was sitting by Daddy's bed. I walked over to the bed and saw that Daddy was awake and had calmed down. I kissed his forehead, sat down on the bed beside him and held his hand.

"Fred, I would like to talk privately to my Daddy, if it's okay with you?"

He got up and said, "You sure can," as he started for the door.

HE WAS SO WEAK. I KNEW MY EARLIER OUTBURST didn't do him any good. I smiled and said, "Hi, Brody, I love you." His eyes were different from before. They were a soft hazel, but they looked at me with more love than ever before. It was almost like he knew what I was going to say, and he was trying to help me.

I fought the tears back and said, "Daddy, do you remember back in Texas when we decided you would come and live with me?" He didn't answer, he just continued to look straight into my eyes. I slowly continued, trying to chose my words the best way possible. "I gave you my word, that if anything should go wrong up here, I would take you back home to Texas, and to Mama."

I paused for a moment fighting back the tears. This was the hardest thing I had ever done in my entire life. I continued, "Me and you fought a good battle to get everything back like it was, but it looks like God had other ideas." He just continued to look me straight in the eyes. "Daddy, I want you to know, I'm okay, and if you are ready to make that trip back to Texas, and be with Mama, it's okay with me."

Tears filled his eyes, and he weakly squeezed my hand. I knew, now, he understood what I had said. Giving him a kiss on his forehead I said, "Daddy, I love you enough to let you go. Please don't stay just for me. I know how much you've missed Mama all these years." I nodded okay to him and squeezed his hand really tight. "Let's go home Daddy. The battle's over." He squeezed my hand again, like he had done so many times in the past. This had become our way of communicating, so I knew in my heart he understood.

Looking at him I saw that he had such a peaceful look in his eyes, almost a look of relief. Now I knew that Monie had been right. I put my head down on his chest and thanked God for giving me the strength to let go. Again, I placed my Daddy in His Loving Arms, only this time it was different. I didn't ask God to heal him, I truly asked God to just take my Daddy home to Mama.

Staying where I was for a few moments, I listened to his heart beat like I had done so many times when I was a little girl. I wished I could just go to sleep and when I woke up, Daddy would be back to the strong man I once knew.

I must have dozed off, because, the next thing I knew Monie was saying, "Reta, are you okay?"

I raised up in a daze, looked at Daddy and saw he was fast asleep. Smiling I said, "Yeah, Monie, I'm okay, and so is Daddy. You were right, thanks for telling me the truth."

She smiled and said, "You betcha."

Getting some things together, I then headed for Karen's house. I really needed some time to be alone, right now.

Karen was gone when I got to her home. Actually, I was glad because I didn't want to talk to anyone. I just wanted to take a hot bath and go to bed.

There were no dance classes tomorrow for which I was very glad. Since shifting classes around, I now had Fridays off, and I really needed the time. Tomorrow, I had a thousand things to do. Most of the day would be spent working on books.

THE NEXT MORNING I GOT UP EARLY WITH KAREN. She always had been a morning person, no matter how late she stayed out. Dragging myself into the kitchen, pulled by the smell of coffee, I was delighted to see her smiling face She said, "Good morning, you sure look better!" She chuckled, "The circles around your eyes are a little, lighter shade of blue, today. You must have gotten a couple more hours of sleep."

I laughed, "You sure know how to make me feel better, but I do appreciate your honesty."

"How did things go last night?" she asked.

"Well, I'm gonna let that little bastard have the house and all the payments that go with it. He'll have to find himself another idiot to take care of him," I replied. "There's no way he can afford all those payments. Hell, he can't even afford his child support. Least ways he doesn't pay it."

I filled her in on the Tidy Bowl plumbing, the cardboard ducts and the four boards holding up my deck. She just shook her head in disbelief and said, "Someone should just take him out and castrate him so he can never mess up another woman again."

I laughed, "Yeah, and use a dull knife."

"Where are you going to move?" she questioned.

"I lay in bed last night and really did some soul-searching about that," I answered. "The kids have talked about getting a house, and all of them live together and share the rent. I think that would be a good idea. It's time they strike out on their own and not have to live under my rules. If they want to do that, and your offer of me being your roommate and sharing the bills with you is still open..." I stuck out my hand and said, "Hi, roommate! We've always talked about being the Golden Girls and getting a camper, traveling and singing our way around the world."

She let out one of her belly-busting laughs and grabbed my hand, "Hell, we'll be the Bell Sisters just like we talked about so many times, Ding and Dong."

We started making our plans of all the things we were going to do and I started feeling like a new person. I wanted more than anything to just have some time for me.

Before long, I came back to reality and said, "Well, at least I have a plan." I gave her a hug and said, "Thanks, Karen, for being my friend."

She hugged me back, "You know, you're the best friend I ever had, too. We've been down a lot of rough roads together, and we'll make it down this one too," she said with assurance.

While I headed for home, I thought back to all the hard times Karen had endured with her husband, Curly, before he passed away. Since then, she had lost one brother, and another brother was dying from cancer. She had certainly had her crosses to bear, too. She was right, we had been down some rough roads together.

WHEN I ARRIVED HOME, PAM AND KIM WERE SITTING in the living room busy making their plans for the day. I said, "Hi, kids," and immediately went to check on Daddy. His toenails were still okay, and he was resting peacefully.

Looking around, I asked, "Where's Fred? I noticed his car was gone."

Monie continued working with Daddy, as if to avoid the question. I repeated the question. She turned around and said, "Reta, he was getting on my nerves. I had rather take care of Grandpa by myself, so I told him I didn't need him any more."

"You what!" I yelled. "You had no right to dismiss Fred! Did you hurt his feelings? I know he's not qualified like you, but God knows, he does his best."

She could tell I was really upset because she knew Fred was also like family. She said, "I'm really sorry. I didn't yell at him or anything, just told him he could go home if he wanted to. I have everything under control and I really am okay."

"When did he leave?" I questioned.

"Last night after you left. He was just getting in my way," she replied as she busily continued taking care of Daddy.

Going up to my loft, I called Fred. He was home and assured me he understood how Monie felt. I thanked him for coming down and helping us for the few days he was here. I said, "At least, it gave her some time to get a second wind. She seems to be obsessed with caring for Daddy. God knows I appreciate her, but you know, Fred, that she can't continue like this."

"I know," he said. "You have my number, just call if you need me." He paused, "And please call me when Vernon goes back to Texas."

I assured him I would. None of us could mention the word "die." We just referred to it as Daddy's going home.

I WORKED ON MY BOOKS FOR AWHILE, THEN CAME down and visited with Pam and Kim. Pam said, "Mom, do you think it will be okay for us to go to Dad's house Sunday for the Albrecht Christmas party?"

"Sure," I quickly answered, "in fact, I think it would be good for you and Kim to spend the entire weekend with Chuck and get away from all the pressures here."

"That's okay, Mom," Kim quickly responded, "We don't want to be gone too long because we want to be here if Grandpa..."

"Goes home," I interjected.

"Yeah," Kim sadly said.

"We'll just go up there Sunday morning and come home that night," Pam assured me.

Brad came bouncing in and asked, "Have you decided what you're gonna do with the house?"

"Yeah," I replied, "I'm gonna let that ignorant bastard have it and all the problems and bills that go with it."

He gave me a high five, "I know a house that can be rented for $250.00 a month and it's ready to move into."

Pam and Kim jumped in on the conversation. I told them of my plans to move in permanently with Karen. They thought that would be a good idea and I would only be about five miles from them. As they were excitedly making plans, I told them they could take all the household goods and furniture. Suddenly, everyone was bouncing around making all their big plans for their own home.

Actually, it made me feel a little sad, almost like I was being kicked out of the nest, but I really did understand their enthusiasm. They felt the same about this house as I did, not a lot of good memories.

THE EVERLASTING BILLS WERE BECKONING SO I went back upstairs to continue working on the books.

The savings was all gone, and the money Daddy and I got on his house was down to the bare ending. Deposits from the studios were way low but somehow I wasn't letting it get me down like it had. Maybe it was because I was seeing, a light at the end of the tunnel.

I now had everything figured out for the kids and me for after my divorce was final on the twenty-first. The unknown situation with Daddy brought tears to my eyes.

Pam, Kim, Cheryl, Brad and Monie came upstairs and took a seat on the little sofa I had up there. "Okay, you guys look like the cat that swallowed the canary. What's going on?"

They all looked at each other. Monie said, "Well, I guess everyone wants me talk. We all have decided to take that house Brad was talking about and we think you should plan on being Karen's full-time roommate. If Grandpa hasn't gone home by the time we move, and if you can still afford to keep him out of the nursing home, then we will move him over to the new house and continue taking care of him."

I couldn't believe my ears! This was the most unselfish act from my wonderful little team. Beginning to cry again, I said, "I couldn't do that to you guys, and besides, if Daddy hangs on, there is no way I can afford your salary, Ensure or all the other supplies we need for him."

"The damn bureaucrats will win and I will have to put him in the nursing home. I will just put him in with Dean and Flo at *Constant Care* here in Amery where I would be just minutes away at Karen's house."

Pam said, "That would be good, Mom, 'cause Monie is gonna have to take another job to take care of her bills. She can't make it on what she's getting now."

Kim chirped, "I know! Monie could get a job at *Constant Care* and still be there with Grandpa."

"That's not a bad idea," Monie answered.

"If it comes to that, I know I can talk to Dean and Flo and they would give you a job," Kim assured her.

"That's a great idea, Kim," I praised.

WE ADJOURNED OUR LITTLE MEETING. I FELT SO much better, now, that we had everything settled and I could tell that the kids did too.

Brad was even excited about the move. He had worked so hard trying to make everything work at the house, but like Gary had said, If you could tear the house down and start over again, there would be a chance, but everything was so screwed up."

Bless Brads heart! He had worked so hard and really done his best to help us out in so many ways. I would never forget all the efforts on his part.

He was truly a remarkable young man, but somehow, I didn't really think that he and Pam would ever be married. At least I hoped they could always remain friends.

I knew Pam loved Brad, but not the way she should love a husband. They were more like best friends. One thing I knew in my heart, even though Brad may never be related, he would always own a special part of my heart.

I made a few more telephone calls to creditors and made arrangements on past due bills. About ready to wind it all up and go downstairs, the phone rang and it was Ma calling to wish me a belated, Happy Birthday.

She asked, "How are you, Baby?" Just the sound of her voice threw me into tears.

I brought her up to date on all the current happenings. She was glad I had decided to give the house to the weasel and move in with Karen because she had been worried about my health, too.

Then, she asked about the studios and I told her about all the student loss. She said, "It's the same down here, people just can't afford to send their children any more. The economy has got to turn around, or we are all gonna have to close our studio doors."

She then asked me what I was going to take from the marriage. I said, "I hope I can escape with my health and the Fire Bird. That is, if he hasn't already torn it up driving like a maniac." We visited for a little longer then said, goodbye. I promised her I would let her know when Daddy, went home.

My next project was to start a list of people to be notified when Daddy, went home. Of course, at the top of the list were Yane's and

Cecil's names. I took it downstairs and placed it by my telephone so that it would be handy to add to, or to place calls.

FEELING SOMEWHAT LESS STRESSED BECAUSE SOME definite progress and positive plans had been decided upon, I did some laundry and took care of some of the household tasks I had neglected.

Some of the parents of my students, called to lend their support, others to make my life more miserable. I got so that I hated the sound of the telephone's ring. Sometimes I put my hands over my ears and prayed it would just disappear. It had become a constant dread. I started thinking of it as the enemy. That's when I knew I really needed some time out, my nerves were almost gone.

With my chores finished, I went in and sat with Daddy for awhile. He was so weak, but he looked very peaceful. Sometimes, he would open his eyes and look to his left side, as if someone else was there. He would then mumble or respond in some way. Watching him for awhile, I fantasized that he was talking to Mamma, and they were planning his trip back home.

I gave him a kiss and squeezed his hand. Asking, "How are you doing, Daddy?" He turned his head and looked at me with those soft hazel eyes. He was ready, and he wasn't afraid, I could tell. It was almost like he was telling me not to worry, now. He was okay. My bond with him never felt stronger.

LATER, I WENT BACK TO KAREN'S HOUSE AND WE SAT around for awhile talking. I said, "I am going to bed early tonight and if I feel like it tomorrow night, I might try to join the guys for awhile at the Country Dam and see if I can still sing."

"That's a good idea," Karen replied, "They would like that."

The doorbell rang and when Karen answered, it was Gary. He had stopped by for a nightcap and to get caught up on all the latest. Boy, was he really happy to hear I was not going to keep the house and would be Karen's roommate.

He left early, so that I could go to sleep, and said, "I hope to see you at the *Dam,* tomorrow night. Maybe I can take you to breakfast afterwards."

"That sounds good," I answered as I headed for my little bedroom.

Getting up early the next morning, I stopped by and picked up the supplies Monie needed and headed for home.

Daddy seemed to be a little brighter. I said, "Good morning, Brody."

He grinned and whispered, "Mornin'." That was the first word I had heard him say since his outburst.

It was nice to be able to talk to him for awhile. I'm not sure how much he really understood but he stayed awake and pretended to listen. Trying to be cheerful, I told him only positive things.

Since he seemed better, I decided to go to the Country Dam and sing a few songs with the guys tonight.

The kids had also planned to go to the *Country Dam* for awhile, too, so they were delighted to find out I was planning to go and sing.

Pam said, "Mom, I think that would be good for you because I know how much you miss singing."

"Yeah I do," I replied, "So let's do it tonight!"

I tried to relax as much as possible the remainder of the day, then I got dressed and headed for the *Country Dam*.

Cords, Rick and Donnie were all delighted to see me walk through the door, as were many of my friends. Gary was already there.

Uncle Bob was busy behind the bar. He smiled and said, "Sure good to see you back!"

"Don't count me back in yet, Uncle Bob," I replied. "I'm only going to be here for a set or two."

Everyone asked about Daddy's condition and I sadly filled them in on his status. They were all so nice and very supportive.

Leroy and Dick were there, also. and were delighted when I told him I was giving the house to the weasel, along with all the bills that go with it.

I wanted to wait till my kids arrived before I got up and sang. You never heard such hooting and hollering as when Cords said, "Let's put your hands together for. Miss Reta Lee!"

For awhile, I was able to become totally lost in my music. Of course, I sang, *They Don't Make 'Em Like My Daddy Anymore, Love Is The Foundation, Bridge Over Troubled Water*, plus many more good old country songs.

Pam yelled out, "Do, *Coal Miner's Daughter*, Mom!" That was her favorite song, whereas Kim's favorite was, *Bridge Over Troubled Water*.

I am so thankful that Loretta Lynn wrote and recorded so many beautiful songs. It was a dream of mine, that someday, I would get my chance to sing, using all that sophisticated equipment the real stars use when performing. There was no way to know if I would ever get my turn to be a real star or not. Right now, at least, I was sure a local star and I thanked God for that.

About eleven o'clock I was really exhausted. I took a rain-check for the breakfast with Gary, kissed the kids goodnight and told *Pure Gold* and all my friends goodbye.

Brad assured me he would get the girls home early so that they could get up to go to Chuck's house before noon the next day for the Albrecht Christmas. I knew they would probably whine about going home early, but knew that Brad would win out and get them there anyway.

On the way back to Karen's house, I kept thinking about what Louie had said New Year's Eve, They always seem to get better before the end. Daddy had been so bright, today, it made me wonder.

Karen was playing music with Gregg and Clarion tonight, so I didn't look for her home until late. As soon as I arrived at Karen's I called Monie to make sure Daddy was sleeping peacefully, and she assured me he was just fine. I slipped into my blue pajamas and hit the bed, I had my usual chat with God and didn't even wake up when Karen came home.

SUDDENLY, I WOKE AND SAT STRAIGHT UP IN THE bed. Looking at the clock, I saw it was 3:00 a.m. The strong feeling that Daddy needed me was almost overpowering. It was that bond again, just like I had felt before his stroke last year when I HAD to leave immediately for Texas.

Going into the bathroom, I washed my face. I couldn't shake the feeling. Hating to wake Monie up, never the less, I just HAD to call.

Monie, very sleepily, answered the telephone on the first ring. I told her about my feeling. She assured me Daddy was okay. I insisted, "Monie, will you please go over and double check him?"

She said, "Sure." In a minute, she came back and said, "I promise, he is okay."

"Did you check his toenails and fingernails?" I asked.

"Just a minute and I will," she answered. A few minutes later, "They are just fine, the color is okay. Try to get some sleep, Reta, and we'll see you in the morning."

"Okay," I answered, "I'm sorry I woke you."

"No problem," she assured me.

I went back to bed and finally slept. Suddenly, again I woke up and sat straight up in the bed. Someone had called my name. I said, "What?" No one answered and I was sure that Karen had called.

I went back to her room and she was sleeping soundly. Thinking, Reta, you're losing your mind. Go back to bed, the sun will be up soon. As I got back in bed, I looked at the clock and it said 4:30 a.m.

It took longer, but I finally drifted back to sleep, only to be awakened by someone calling my name, again.

Running to the telephone, I called Monie, again. Once again, we went through the same procedure we had gone through earlier. After she assured me Daddy was okay, I apologized, again.

Going back to my room, I looked around for someone. The voice had been familiar and I knew that it was real, or at least real to me. I decided I must be losing my mind or just overly tired. Finally, I got back to sleep.

There were no more voices but when I woke up at 7:00 a.m., I knew that I had to get home, immediately! Calling Monie, I had her check Daddy's toenails, fingernails and vital signs. Her report was the same as before, he was okay.

My senses told me that something was dreadfully wrong. I made a pot of coffee to brew while I got dressed. Karen came in with her eyes still half closed, "What the hell is going on, are you okay?"

"I don't know, Karen," I answered. Then I explained the crazy night I had, complete with the voice.

She just looked at me as if to say, You poor little thing, you're really losing it.

I gulped down the rest of my coffee, grabbed my purse and headed for the door. Turning around at the door, with tears in my eyes, I said, "Karen, I believe my Daddy is going home, today."

She put her arms around me, "If you need me, just let me know," she assured.

Driving rather fast, I drove straight out to the house, parked the car and ran inside. Pam, Kim, Brad and Monie were sitting at the table having a discussion. I said, "What's going on."

Pam said, "Monie told us about your calls last night, Mom, and if you feel that way, we're staying home today."

"I don't want you all to give up your Christmas party with your Dad. Probably, I'm just overly tired and imagining things."

"Well, we're staying home with you and Grandpa, Mom," Kim insisted.

I went straight in and checked Daddy over for myself. Monie was right, his toenails and fingernails were just fine. He opened his eyes and looked straight into mine. Squeezing his hand, I said, "Daddy, I'm here and I'm not going anywhere," I assured him.

He tried to grip my hand, but he was too weak. I could tell he was trying to tell me something, but couldn't because of his weakness. I kissed him and assured him I was okay. I paused and continued, "Daddy, if you are ready to go home, it's okay. I'll be fine."

He formed the word with his mouth, he was too weak to even whisper, "Okay." He then drifted back off to sleep.

Monie came in to feed him and give him his bed-bath. She had the little pieces of egg crate placed all around under his body so he wouldn't develop any bed sores. I was amazed at the loving way she handled him.

Daddy had been so fortunate throughout his entire illness. He never had a bed sore. Just the beginnings of one after his brief stay at the Amery hospital, and Betty had stopped it dead in it's tracks.

Going back into the kitchen, I tried to convince the girls to go to their Dad's house. Pam said, "Do you still feel like Grandpa is going home, today?"

"I could say no, but I just have this terrible feeling. I'm not leaving this house today," I replied.

"That does it," Kim quickly said, "then we're not either."

Monie finished Daddy's bed-bath and got him fed. Then she replaced the egg crate pieces under some new red spots which had developed on his skin. They looked like they might be breaking down. She came out and poured herself a cup of coffee and joined us.

"Is he asleep?" I asked.

"Like a baby," she replied.

I went up to my office and started working on bills. Suddenly, I had the same feeling that woke me up that morning. I ran downstairs and straight to Daddy's bed. I quickly checked his toenails and my heart almost stopped beating. They were turning blue! I screamed for Monie as I checked his fingernails, they also were turning blue! He was just lying there looking toward the window. I grabbed his hand, there was no response.

Within seconds, Monie, Pam, Kim and Brad came running in. I looked at them with tears streaming down my face, "Check his toenails, Monie! Maybe I'm wrong!"

She quickly uncovered his feet then slowly looked up at me and nodded her head. Pam and Kim ran out of the room and cried their little hearts out.

This was the moment that I had been praying for, but now, I knew I wasn't really ready to face it. Feeling so helpless because I knew that I couldn't call the ambulance to take him to emergency, the doctor or anyone for help.

Suddenly, I thought of Joyce Shaffer, my Home Care nursing supervisor. In the past, if I needed anything, I could always call her.

Quickly, I dialed her number. Thank, God, she was home from church, her husband was the local minister. I was crying so hard as I told her about Daddy's toenails and fingernails.

She said, "You know they took us off the case since Vernon started downhill and I'm not supposed to make any more home visits."

"I'm so scared, Joyce. What happens next after the blue? How long, what do I do?" I cried.

She paused for a moment, then said, "Would you like for me to come out, just for support?"

"Please do, Joyce, I would really appreciate that. I'm just so scared," I pleaded.

She said, "I will be there within the next thirty minutes." It was already 2:30 p.m.

I ran back to Daddy's bed. Monie had a wet cloth on his forehead and said, "He's running a temperature." She looked almost as scared as me. Pam, Kim and Brad had already taken their positions at the foot of his bed.

I went to the left side of Daddy, sat on the bed next to him and put my arms around him. Monie was standing to his right continuing to take his vital signs. I kept wiping his forehead with the wet cloth, telling him how much I loved him and assuring him we were all there. He was not alone.

Suddenly Joyce appeared at the bedroom door. None of us had heard her knock, so she just came on in. She looked like an angel to us. Immediately she walked over to the bed and took Monie's place at Daddy's right side. Monie moved to the end of the bed with Pam, Kim and Brad.

Joyce reached over and patted my hand as she asked, "Have you ever been through this before?"

"Only when my mother died, but, I was real young then," I answered.

"I'll walk you through each stage as he enters it,." she assured me.

All of us felt relieved and thankful for her presence, including Monie. She had become so close to Daddy, she was having trouble fighting the tears back too.

Joyce checked Daddy's vital signs, his toenails, and fingernails, again. She looked at me with certainty and said, "He is in his last stages, now. It won't be long."

Daddy was breathing really heavy and his eyes were still fixed on the window His eyes were still soft hazel and I knew he was at peace.

As Daddy breathed heavier and slower, Joyce explained each step of death to us. I kept wiping his forehead and telling him how much I loved him.

His breathe seemed to start leaving from his feet and climbing upward. Joyce explained his breath would slowly leave his body. I could hear the air travel to his chest and then it was like he couldn't breath anymore.

Pam and Kim kept crying, "We love you, Grandpa, don't leave."

I kept holding him tight, and the tears flowed all the while I was assuring him we were all there and how much he was loved.

All of a sudden, his last breath climbed to his throat, and I felt his spirit leave his body with that last breath. His color had changed from blue to pale white, then last, it turned a pale gray. Those hazel eyes turned to a glassy stare and his whole body just relaxed.

I quickly looked at Joyce and she nodded her head, "He's gone," she said. Then I took the wash cloth and moved it down over Daddy's eyes and closed them for the last time..

ALL OF A SUDDEN, I HAD A FLASHBACK OF MAMA'S death. I remembered how Yane and I were packing ice bags to place around her body to bring her temperature down. We were doing it because the Winters Hospital was understaffed.

Also, I remembered how Yane's friend, Betsy Aldridge, came to the door and said, "Girls, go to your Daddy." We ran out in the hallway and Daddy was standing there sobbing.

I turned around and ran back to mother's bedside just in time to see her body relax, then her head thrust back and I saw fluids come out of her nose and mouth. They had tubes in both her nostrils and down her throat.

My head hit the concrete floor when I fainted, and I woke up in Cecil's lap. For many years, I could shut my eyes and see that fluid—believe me.

Immediately, I yelled for Pam, Kim and Brad to leave the room. I didn't know if this would happen to Daddy or not, but I didn't want to take the chance of them witnessing it. That wasn't what I wanted them to remember the rest of their lives, as I had about my mother.

They quickly headed for the living room with their tears flowing. I looked at Joyce and said, "Are you sure he's gone?" She assured me he was. I almost took the washcloth off his eyes, just to see if he had returned, but I realized that was only the little girl in me not wanting to believe my Daddy was dead. I left it in place and started for the door to join the kids in the living room.

Quickly, I turned around and went back to the bed. I looked at Joyce through my tears and said, "Please take that tube out of his stomach." She assured me she would take it out, immediately.

I gave him a kiss on his forehead, squeezed his hand and said through my tears, "I love you Daddy."

Then I walked into the living room and joined the kids. Pam and Kim ran to me, put their arms around me and we all cried together. My knees turned into jelly and they moved me over to Daddy's Lazy Boy and set me down.

After a few minutes, Monie picked up the list by the telephone and said, "Reta, do you want me to make the calls?"

"Please," I cried.

Of course, the first call was to *Williamson Mortuary* in Amery where they would, in turn, contact Mike at the *Winters Funeral Home* for the final instructions. Then she called Yane and Cecil to let them know their Daddy had just passed away.

Being totally numb at the time, to this day I can't even describe the way I felt. Everything was FINAL, at last. Now, I had to get ready for the trip back to Texas, just as I had promised Daddy. It was a good thing that I had already packed his little suitcase for the final trip home.

In a few minutes, Brad got up and closed the window curtains covering the big bay window. That is how I knew the *Williamson Mortuary* hearse had arrived to take my Daddy and get him ready for the trip back to Texas.

Brad went out to meet the crew and guide them up Daddy's ramp to the patio doors going out of my bedroom. He was protecting us from seeing them take Daddy away, and I will always love him for that.

I could hear them enter through the patio doors with the stretcher and then getting Daddy ready to place him on it. Joyce was still in the room with Daddy, along with Brad.

Suddenly, I remembered his little bag with his pajamas and underclothes in it that I had packed for him to wear for his trip back to Texas.

I jumped up and ran to the bedroom door and opened it just in time to see them taking my Daddy out the patio doors on the stretcher. I just stood staring, as I noted that they had placed his body in a gray, body bag with the name of the funeral home printed on it. Daddy had lost so much weight, that the bag looked more like it contained a child rather than a grown man.

Monie was right behind me and she quickly steered me back to the lazy boy. "Monie, I have to give them Daddy's little bag that I packed for his trip back to Texas. The one with his pajamas in it. It's in the closet."

She assured me that she would take care of it as she hurried back into the room to get the bag and take it out to them.

She and Joyce came back into the living room and closed the door behind them. When Joyce came over and put her arms around me, I cried even harder. I told her, "You will never know how much I appreciate what you did today. I don't believe we could have handled this without you because we just didn't have any idea how hard it was gonna be."

She patted my back and said, "He's in God's Hands, now. It's all over but if you need me for anything else, please don't hesitate to call me."

I hugged her again and she left to go home. Always, I will remember her kindness, especially, for what she did for us that day. She went the Extra Mile. She didn't have to come over and help us, that day. As I have mentioned before, Daddy and I had made some wonderful friends throughout this past year. Friends like Joyce, Fred, Betty, Kathy and Monie, that also took that Extra Step, even when they weren't being paid for what they did.

Just then, Cheryl came running in. She had been at the *Northside Convenience Store* in Amery when she saw the hearse go by. Putting her arms around me and she sobbed, "I knew they were coming for Grandpa when I saw them. Why couldn't I have been here?"

"It's okay, Cheryl," I assured her, "Grandpa is with God, now."

Rusty, Mark and Dan from the peanut gallery arrived. The news traveled like wildfire throughout Amery. Brad came and got them. He took them out the front door, back up the ramp and into my bedroom. Within a short space of time, he opened the door and walked out.

I got up and went into my bedroom. They had totally cleared the hospital bed, wheelchair, *Geri Chair* and all other traces of Daddy from the room. Going to him I put my arms around him and said, "I love you Brad." I also gave Rusty, Mark and Dan a hug too, our little team was getting bigger and bigger.

JUST THEN, THE TELEPHONE RANG AND   MONIE answered it. She said, "Reta, it's your sister, Yane." Slowly, I walked to the telephone, praying she hadn't called just to tell me it was my fault Daddy died or insult me in some way. I got the shock of my life after I said, "Hello?"

She said in a very nice tone, "Are you okay, Reta?"

"I'm okay," I answered.

"Well," she said, "Monie said you were driving down with the kids but Dub wanted us to get you am airline ticket to fly down instead of driving."

I was totally overwhelmed by this wonderful gesture on their part. I actually felt my big sister cared about me, even though it had been Dub, her husband, who had initiated this kindness.

I said, "Thank you, but I still have room on my credit card to pay for a ticket." I didn't want her to think I was a charity case.

"That's okay, we want to do this," she replied. "I will have a ticket for you at the Minneapolis airport and call you back with the times. I have my own travel agent and she gives me deals that she gives to no one else."

The kids couldn't believe her generosity. Pam said, "Mom, take her up on it! That's the least she could do after the way she has treated you. We will all drive Grandpa's car down."

Monie said, "I would like to go, too and I can help out with the driving."

It wasn't long before Yane called back and told me my flight would leave at five o'clock in the morning. She gave me the flight numbers and times. I thanked her again and found I was still having trouble believing in her generosity.

"We'll get everything ready tonight and leave early enough in the morning to drop you off at the airport. Then we'll head straight for Texas," Pam said. Everyone went into action, and Monie and Cheryl were going, too.

Brad said, "I'm glad you got those new tires for Grandpa's car. I'll get it ready for the trip." Then he, Rusty, Mark and Danny headed for the garage to service Daddy's car.

Pam, Kim, Monie and Cheryl all started their own packing. All I needed to do was get dressed and catch the airplane. Fortunately, I already had Daddy and myself packed for the trip.

Monie came up and said, "Reta, why don't you call Karen and we'll take you to her house while we get things settled around here and pack for the trip. You should get as much rest as possible."

"Okay." I was totally exhausted and felt so empty and numb.

Karen was still working at the bar so I called her there and told her my Daddy had just died. There was a long silence, then she said, "Are you okay?"

"No, I'm really not," I cried. Then, I explained our plans for leaving and about the ticket Yane Was getting for me. Karen, too, was overwhelmed by my sister's generosity.

She quietly said, "Come on home and I'll meet you there as soon as I get off work."

"Thanks, Karen," I said, "I do need a friend, right now."

MONIE AND PAM TOOK ME INTO AMERY. PAM SAID, "We'll get everything ready for the trip, then come and pick you up later. Just try to get some rest Mom." She put her arms around me and said, "I love you." We had a few tears, then she headed back home to help Kim and Cheryl with the packing.

They were fixing sandwiches and different snacks to take with them so that they could save on food costs during the trip. My little team was still working together and planning their strategy down to the last mile.

I sat down on Karen's sofa. All of a sudden, everything was so quiet. I looked at the clock and knew Karen would be off work in fifteen minutes and then would come straight home. While I waited, I decided I had better call and see if Sissy or Mary could pick me up in Abilene.

Thank, God, Sissy was home from the boat. She tried to be so strong for me when I talked to her. She said, "Baby, I'll be there to get you at the airport. Don't you worry."

"If you don't feel like making the trip up there, Sissy, I'm sure Mary will come and get me."

Very firmly she said, "I'll be there."

Again, I thanked God, for her being home. I knew if she was with me, I wouldn't have any problems with Yane.

As I continued to wait for Karen, I tried to go over all the details Daddy had told me he wanted done for his funeral, many times in the past. It still didn't seem real, and I couldn't believe that the time was really upon me.

The little bag with his wedding ring from mother, the death insurance papers and, of course, his will, in the event Yane and Cecil wanted to read it, was already packed.   I was so glad I had packed the little bag several days ago, because the condition I was in now, I probably would not have brought all the necessary papers and clothing that were needed.

Cecil knew Daddy's and my financial situation, but I had no idea what Yane thought. All I knew was, Daddy had always said, "I don't want no fussin' or fightin' at my funeral." So I made up my mind that no matter what it took, I wasn't going to let her upset me.

Daddy also had specified, many times, that he wanted Brother Brooks to preach his funeral just as he had preached Mother's. I am sure that another reason was that Brother Brooks had not only married Mother and Daddy years ago, but had also baptized them.

The thought came to me, I just hope he is still alive. Since he had come to the Abilene Hospital to see Daddy, last year, I felt sure that he was still alive..

I LOOKED AT THE CLOCK, AGAIN.   WHERE   WAS Karen? She should have been off work thirty minutes ago. My mind kept jumping from one thing to another.

Damn, where is she?" I thought. She had now been off work over an hour. I called the bar and was told she'd had a few drinks after work, then left.

I waited impatiently a little longer, before I concluded that she wasn't coming home. Why wasn't she there? I just didn't understand because if ever I needed her, it was now. Maybe she just couldn't face another tragedy, after all, she had enough within her own family.

I sat there for a few more minutes and thought, *What am I doing? I need to be home helping the kids get ready. They are hurting and scared, too. We all need each other right now—not me here, and them there.*

I hated to call and tell Pam to come and pick me up. After all, she had just dropped me off a couple hours ago and I was supposed to be resting.

Suddenly, I remembered what Leroy Becker had told me, If you need anything, just call. I'm as near as the telephone.

I looked his number up and, thank, God, he was home. Telling him about Daddy, Karen not showing up and that I wanted to go home, I was so glad when I heard him say, "I'll be there in ten minutes." He didn't waste any time talking, just hung up the phone.

Leroy had been such a wonderful friend, to me. I knew that he would make someone a wonderful husband, but I was only interested in being his friend. He had understood how I felt, and had been perfectly happy just being friends.

In less than ten minutes, he pulled up in his four-wheel truck. I opened the door and let him in. He put his arms around me and said, "I'm so sorry, what can I do?"

I said, "Just take me home to Pam and Kim. We all need each other, right now." No wasted words or actions, he grabbed my coat, helped me put it on, and out the door we went.

On the ride home, he was puzzled about Karen deserting me at this time. But I knew she had been through a lot in her own life and maybe she didn't feel strong enough to go over this hurdle with me.

I told Leroy about the five o'clock flight in the morning I had to catch. He said, "Snow is forecast for later on tonight, why don't I take you to the airport in my truck, then I know you'll make it. The kids can wait a little later, in case the plows have to go first."

Again, I started crying as I said, "Leroy, if you would do that, it would take such a load off the kids. Brad needed to pick up a few things for the car after Bumper To Bumper opens, plus they might be able to get a little rest tonight before they start that long trip."

He smiled, "Be glad to help."

When we walked in, the kids were busy as little bees. Pam and Kim started crying, "Mom, I'm so glad you're here." We put our arms around each other and cried some more.

Leroy told Brad that he would take me to the airport and Brad said, "Boy, that would really help."

Looking at his watch, Leroy said, "It's not that long before we have to leave. In this weather it will probably take two or three hours to get to the airport, according to what the weather is south of us.

Let's make a pot of coffee and I'll just stay right here until it's time to go." With that, he sat down at the dining table while the coffee brewed.

Monie took me into my bedroom and said, "Now, lay down and try to sleep at least a couple of hours before you have to leave. Don't worry, I'll wake you."

Walking into my bedroom, I looked around. There was not a trace of Daddy, there. Brad had everything big moved out and the girls had changed my bed and cleaned everything up.

I went over to the closet and took out Daddy's black suit, his little bag I had packed and my suitcase. In a travel bag, I hung my dress and his suit, then I took everything out to the living room for Leroy to put in his truck.

Daddy's new boots with his belt pushed down inside, I gave to Pam to take in the car. Then I gave her the Stetson hat and Western shirts that Yane had sent him, to take, also.

I double checked to make sure I had everything for Daddy so that he would look spiffy for his homecoming. Tears came as I looked at his old Stetson hat in the top of my closet. He wouldn't be wearing it any more and I took it down and caressed it as I remembered how important that old hat had been to him. He never went anywhere without it. It had also played such an important part in his overall therapy throughout the year.

I almost gave it to Pam to take in the car, also, but they were going to be crowded enough without having to worry about placing two hats where they wouldn't get crushed. Anyway, Daddy wouldn't be able to wear it now. I gently placed it back in my closet.

The wristwatch he had worn for years, I placed in his little bag along with the new glasses I had bought for him. As I looked at the watch, I decided I would give it to Yane, if she wanted it. Cecil already had some of his personal things and so did I. Never was I gonna part with his hat. Even though I would have loved to keep his watch, I decided Yane needed something that was really special to him, too.

Leroy said, "Is that everything?"

"I think so," I replied.

He headed outside to put the bags in his truck and Brad followed him out. He said to Leroy, "I'll pull the old Lincoln out and you pull your truck inside the garage." The snow was already falling pretty heavily.

I took a hot bath, slipped on my blue pajamas and lay down. It didn't seem like very long when Monie shook me and said, "Reta, it's time to get up."

I opened my eyes and there she stood with a cup of coffee. For a moment, I thought I had dreamed this whole nightmare. Quickly glancing over to where Daddy's hospital bed had been, I realized it was for real. Daddy was gone.

The kids had all their bags upstairs ready for their trip. Daddy's cowboy boots were sitting on top of their suitcases, ready for the final trip home. I choked back the tears and said, "Did you guys get any sleep?"

"Not much," Kim replied.

Leroy was sitting at the table. "Did you sleep at all, Leroy?" I questioned.

"Oh, I nodded off a time or two. I'm fine, but we need to get going as soon as possible. I'm a little concerned about the weather, and everything is already loaded."

"I'll be ready in ten minutes," I answered as I hurried back into my room. I threw on a pant suit, heels, a little make up and put my hair up in the old faithful Banana Clip.

I walked out and announced, "I'm ready." We all gave each other many hugs and kisses.

Brad said, "Don't worry, I'll get the girls there okay. We'll be there tomorrow."

The tears came again, "Brad," I said, "if you get too tired, get a room. All I need is for you guys to get into an accident."

He laughed, "Don't worry about that. We've got five drivers so we won't drive too long without changing."

I gave him a hug, Leroy took my arm and aimed me for the garage.

THE SNOW WAS COMING DOWN PRETTY HEAVY AS we drove toward the Twin Cities. Leroy stopped once, in Somerset as I remember it, and got us some hot coffee. With his four-wheel truck, we made it in plenty of time before my flight was scheduled to leave.

With a concerned look on his face, he said, "Are you sure you're gonna be all right? You look a little pale."

I assured him I was okay. However, I didn't know if I was trying to convince him or myself. Actually I felt like my body didn't belong to me. I was totally numb and feeling as though I was floating instead of walking. It was a very strange feeling.

I gave Leroy a hug and thanked him again for his kindness. He said, "Just give me a call and I'll be here to pick you up and take you home when you return."

I shook my head, smiled and said, "You're one-in-a-million, buddy." I waved goodbye and took my seat in the airplane.

DURING THE WHOLE FLIGHT I KEPT THINKING about Daddy. *Williamson Mortuary* in Amery had called with information on

Daddy's flight. He would be arriving in Dallas about the same time my plane would be getting there.

I had asked them how Daddy would ride and they had explained to me the method of transporting a body. They would embalm him, that was the law, dress him in the pajamas and under clothes I had sent, then, he would be placed in a wooden crate for transporting.

Thinking of Daddy, in that cold crate in the baggage compartment of the airplane, made the tears start flowing again. It sounds absurd, but I found myself worrying about him being cold and alone down there.

Mike had promised me that he would have the hearse at the airport to pick up Daddy in Dallas, as soon as the plane landed. That way Daddy wouldn't have to wait in some gosh-awful place in the airport, all alone.

I was beginning to feel as though I had abandoned him. I remembered the many times he had come to Wisconsin to visit me and how he always worried he would get lost in that big airport terminal in Dallas when he returned..

Suddenly, I snapped myself out of this stupid thinking. Daddy was okay. I had just been taking care of him so long that it was hard to put him in the hands of someone else, even though he was gone.

I leaned my seat back and tried to relax while mulling over how long I was going to be in the air. Having made this trip many times throughout the years, I remembered that it never took more than two hours for me to get to Dallas.

Deciding to look at my ticket to verify this, I couldn't believe what I was reading. Yane had routed me from Minneapolis to Houston, with a long layover. There I changed planes and was flown back to Dallas.

I thought to myself, if her travel agent only gave HER these great deals, then she must not have liked Yane very much.

I was so angry! Why hadn't I just put the ticket on my credit card and avoid all this hassle? For a few extra dollars I could have gone nonstop to Dallas. The thought crossed my mind, Did she do this to save money or to make things a little more difficult for me. I wanted, so much, to think she did it because she truly cared, but with her past track record, now I wondered.

Before long, the pilot said, "We are now flying over Ft. Worth and Dallas..." I couldn't believe it! I was on my way to Houston! At that moment I could have gladly choked her. I had no choice, though, but to continue on with this horrible flight my sister had lined up for me.

Finally, I got back to Dallas. By then, I was so exhausted I could hardly hold my head up.

I looked at my watch and thought, Daddy is here somewhere. I'll call Mike to make sure the hearse was here. Mike assured me they were there and still waiting for Daddy's plane.

I said, "Do you think I could ride from here with Daddy?"

"Reta, that is not a good idea. You go ahead and take the plane to Abilene and we'll see you in Winters."

"Okay," I mumbled.

After hanging up the phone, I thought, He must think I'm nuts. I've got to get a hold on myself.

Looking at my watch, I realized that this long, drawn out trip had been hell and it wasn't over. My thoughts weren't pleasant, I had already been gone from my home since three o'clock this morning, it's two o'clock now, and I just got to Dallas. At this rate, the kids will be home before me.

I took the shuttle over to the little airlines that would take me to Abilene. Thank, God, within the hour I'd be with Sissy.

The pilot announced we would be landing in Abilene in about ten minutes. I was so thankful he didn't say we would be flying over Abilene, to San Angelo and then back to Abilene. This had truly been the *Flight From Hell!*

AS I WALKED INTO THE ABILENE TERMINAL, THERE stood my Sissy. She truly looked like an angel. The tears started flowing from both of us as we put our arms around each other, holding on for dear life. We regained our composure, grabbed Daddy's and my bags and headed for Winters.

As she drove, I filled her in as much as possible on the trip and Daddy's death. I said, "Sissy, I want to go straight to the funeral home, if it's okay with you. Daddy's suit needs to be given to Mike and I would like to get a casket picked out for him as soon as possible. When he arrives, I want him out of that crate!"

She said, "If that's what you want to do, Baby, then that's damn sure what we will do."

I paused for a moment then said, "Sissy, I hate to ask you, 'cause you've been through so much, but would you help me pick out the casket and get things lined up for Daddy's homecoming? I know if you are part of it, Yane won't give me any trouble by complaining about what I picked out or anything." I started to cry, "Sissy, I don't want to have any problems with her."

She looked at me with all the assurance her little body could muster up and said, "I guarantee you, Yane won't give you any problems. I'll see to that and if you want me to help you, then I damn sure will."

I felt so relieved, now. Cecil would be fine with anything I did, but Yane was another story. Sissy totally understood how I felt. Oh, was I thankful to God that she was home, and not out on the boat.

We went straight to the funeral home and it was already getting dark. Going in we then had an opportunity to thank Mike, in person, for his kindness. He told us that Daddy hadn't arrived yet, but, he was expecting him at any time.

I took out Daddy's little bag and suit. Handing the suit to him with the tie, I then unzipped the little bag and handed Mike Daddy's clean underwear, tee-shirt and socks. I told him, "My daughters will be here tomorrow with Daddy's cowboy boots and belt.

Then I gave him the insurance papers so he could contact Mr. Denim Blue, Daddy's agent, who had sold him the insurance way back when I was a little girl. I said, "I don't know how much this policy is worth, Mike, but whatever the balance is will be my responsibility, totally."

Surprised, he asked, "Aren't your brother and sister going to help you?"

"I doubt it," I answered. "Since I had power of attorney and received what little money Daddy had, plus what we got from his house, Yane probably would have a fit if I asked her for any assistance."

"Cecil can't afford to help me now, or I know he would. Anyway, if you will extend credit to me on the balance, I guarantee you, I will pay you every penny. You've got my word."

He was so kind and assured me we would work everything out.

"Mike," I repeated," don't even consult Yane about the bill. Daddy and me will handle it. He still has a few things I can sell up North like his hospital bed, wheel chair and some other things. We will get you paid." I started to cry and he patted my shoulder and assured me he would grant my wishes.

We proceeded then to go back and pick out a casket. Mike showed us several and I said, "Mike, I want my Daddy to have something really nice, but you know our situation."

He said, "I understand perfectly," as he lead us to a beautiful, baby blue casket.

"I like this one," I said, "and I know Daddy would. What do you think, Sissy?"

She said with tears in her eyes, "Baby, I think it's beautiful. Vernon would like that one."

I looked at Mike and said, "Can we afford this one?"

He smiled and said, "You sure can."

We returned to his office where he and Sissy helped me decide on flowers, and other needed details. It was decided the funeral date would be for Wednesday, January 13, at two o'clock.

Another favor, I asked of him, was, if he could contact Brother Brooks for the service.

He said, "I sure will, I have his number on file. A lot of the old timers want him to preach their last service."

Then he asked me about songs. I said, "I will leave that up to Yane. I'm sure she will want her sons to sing."

"Daddy did tell me, many times, he wanted Precious Memories sung at his funeral, just as it had been at my Mother's.

Other than that, he never told me anything else as far as his services, except for Brother Brooks to preach."

"So, Yane can choose whichever songs she wants. Her husband, Dub, is a minister so he can handle the special prayers, eulogy or anything else needed."

"What about pall bearers?" he asked.

I said, "Well, I briefly talked to Yane and Cecil about this before and suggested Daddy's grandsons be the pall bearers. If that's okay with them, I think it would be nice."

I looked at Sissy and said, "What do you think, Sissy?"

"Now, I think that would be really nice. I'm sure Vernon would like that," she answered.

He wrote down the grandson's names; Dexton and Delferd Shores and Christopher Fuller as I spelled them out to him. Then I said, "When Cecil gets here, he will know whom else Daddy might have wanted to help them."

All of a sudden Ol' Shorty's name popped into my head. I looked at Sissy and said, "Daddy talked many times about Ol' Shorty during the past year. I think he was one of Daddy's old Domino playing buddies here in town, but I'm not sure. Do you know?"

She thought for a moment then said, "I think you're right. I remember Vernon talking about Ol' Shorty playing Dominoes with him."

"I'll see if Cecil can find him. He knows most of Daddy's old buddies down here. If he can be located, I sure would like for him to be a pall bearer," I said.

Next, I ordered a spray for the casket with red and white carnations and a banner reading, Daddy.

Since Daddy's favorite color has always been red, I ordered two sprays from the grandchildren, with one banner reading, Papa and the other reading Grandpa.

Yane and Cecil's children had always called him Papa. When Pam and Kim were really little, they used to call him *Pa Pa Texas*, but as they got older, it changed to just plain Grandpa.

I was trying so hard to do everything right so that no one would get their feelings hurt or feel that their wishes had not been taken into consideration.

Mike figured it all up and said, "That looks like all we need. I will see how much the insurance will pay and then we can make the payment arrangements before you leave."

The mortuary's telephone rang, and it was his driver telling him that Daddy's flight had been late arriving due to the bad weather out of Minneapolis.

Mike said, "They will not be here for another two hours. Why don't you go home and get some rest and I promise to call you as soon as your Daddy gets here.

I said, "Mike, could you get Daddy dressed and into his casket as soon as he gets here?" The tears started flowing again, "I don't want him in that cold crate any longer than he has to be."

Sissy put her arms around me and tried to comfort me. Bless his heart, Mike assured me he would stay as late as necessary to get Daddy ready.

I asked, "Will I be able to see him tonight so that I know he's okay?"

Smiling, he said, "I will have him ready for you to view before you go to bed." I shook his hand and thanked him again.

Sissy said, "Mike, we're going to my house." Then she started to cry, "Call us when Vernon gets here. The baby is worried about him getting home."

We went back to Sissy's house and Aunt Em called to let us know that Cecil was on his way and would be there in a couple of hours.

Aunt Em had been married to Daddy's brother, Virgil, for many years before a stroke took his life a few years back. I loved her so much because she was always so sweet and such a good woman.

Yane then called Sissy and told her that they would be there by morning. My heart fell just with the thoughts of seeing her again. I just prayed that I wouldn't have any problems with her.

Sissy and I sat down at her little kitchen bar to have a cup of coffee. My mind just wouldn't stop, and it was going one hundred miles per hour on so many things that I couldn't even concentrate.

"Baby," Sissy asked, "what are you thinking about?"

"I'm trying to decide if I should open Daddy's casket at the service. He lost so much weight during the past six weeks that he doesn't look that good. I wish I knew what he would want me to do," I answered.

She paused for a moment, then said, "Well, I don't want to see Vernon. I just want to remember him the way he was, but you do whatever you think is best."

"I'll talk to Mike about it when we go back to the funeral home." Looking at the clock, I said, "Daddy should be here soon."

Linda Jones, Kathy's best friend, had moved in with Sissy after Kathy's death the previous year. She was so sweet and fixed me a sandwich, trying to get me to eat, but I wasn't hungry. My mind was totally on the telephone ringing to tell me Daddy was home.

I unpacked my suitcase and got my dress out that I was going to wear to the funeral. Then I took the little ring box, containing his wedding band from Mama, out of the bag and slipped it into my purse. I wanted to get it on his finger as soon as possible.

His watch I took downstairs and placed it on the kitchen bar, so I could give it to Yane when she arrived. Looking at his timepiece sitting there, I remembered once taking the band in for a cleaning at our local jewelry store in Amery. It was so bad, the lady had to put it through the solution two times, then let it soak. Daddy had never really had it cleaned in all those years he had worn it, and that was quite a few.

I said, "Sissy, do you think Yane will be happy to get his watch?"

"Of course she will, Baby. I'm glad you brought it for her," she replied.

Tears welled up in my eyes as I said, "You know, Sissy, I do love her and I wish we could at least be friends. I just don't know what else to do. What did I do to make her hate me so?" I cried.

She sat there for a moment, then said, "I guess you got born, baby. I just don't know."

Among all my other thoughts, I was beginning to worry about the kids on the road. The weather had been so bad when they left. All I wanted was for my entire family to get home, safely and without incident.

It wasn't long before Pam called to let me know they were about halfway there and would be home sooner than expected. Light traffic. However, she said, "One of the new tires you bought, blew out though, but Brad fixed it, and everything's fine. Don't worry about us. Is Grandpa home yet?"

I explained about the delay in his flight and assured her he would be home soon.

She paused for a moment, then said, "Mom, you won't believe this, but when we started down Highway 8, we came up behind the hearse from *Williamson Mortuary* taking Grandpa to the airport. We escorted it all the way, then waved goodbye and headed down Highway 35." She started to cry, "We all felt like Grandpa was riding down here with us."

I fought back the tears and said, "Well, I was waiting for him in Dallas when he arrived, and I'll be here when he gets home, so Grandpa never was really left alone for the trip." Somehow we both seemed to feel better.

"Gotta go, Mom. I love you, and Kim, Monie, Cheryl and Brad said to tell you they love you, too," she assured me.

The tears started again as I said, "I love you, too, honey. Give everyone a hug for me and tell them I love them, too. Drive careful, and I'll see you tomorrow."

I dried my eyes and waited awhile longer for Mike to call. Finally, I said, "Sissy, let's go back to the funeral home and see what's happened. I'm getting worried."

"Okay," she said, "but let me first call Emma back to let her know we'll be down there if Cecil and Margaret get here earlier."

"Ask her to send Cecil to the funeral home if he gets here early enough. I really would like for him to approve all we did today, before Yane gets here, that is," I pleaded.

"Now, Baby," she said, "you are worrying too much about what Yane is going to say or do. Just quit thinking about it. Everything will be okay, you'll see."

I almost believed her, or maybe, I just wanted to believe her. All I knew was, I didn't want any unnecessary problems, and any dealings I had ever had with my sister in the past had turned into disasters.

WE GOT IN HER CAR AND HEADED BACK TO THE funeral home, it was already after ten o'clock. We pulled up to the front door and my heart skipped a beat. I saw the hearse parked by the side door with the headlights still on. They must have just pulled in.

I cried out, "Sissy, Daddy's home! He's finally home, just like I promised him."

The tears were flowing as I ran into the funeral home with Sissy close behind me. The door was slightly open and I could see the wooden crate. I started running to that door, all I wanted to do was see my Daddy and make sure he was all right.

Mike and Sissy stopped me before I got through the door. He assured me Daddy had a blanket over him and was warm. Taking care of him had become such a habit, I just couldn't stop taking care of him, I wasn't ready to let go yet.

Mike said, "I'll have Vernon dressed within the hour for you to view. I know you need to see for yourself that he's okay."

I was crying so hard now, but they were mostly tears of relief. I had fulfilled my promise to Daddy, as he was finally back in big Ol' Texas, home at last.

Mike said, "I promise I'll call just as soon as Vernon's ready."

Sissy took me by the arm and said, "Let's go back to the house and wait, Baby."

I knew she was right so I reluctantly said, "Okay, but Mike please call as soon as possible." He assured me he would.

We went back to the house and continued drinking more coffee. There was no way I would go to sleep until I had seen my Daddy.

My friend, Mary, called to make sure I was there and was okay. Sissy talked to her for awhile and filled her in on the details.

Mary told her, "Well, tell Reta my home is open for her and the kids if they need a place to stay." She wanted to come over but Sissy told her it would be better to wait until morning.

We had another cup of coffee and continued to wait. About an hour later the telephone rang. I jumped up and grabbed my coat as Sissy said, "We'll be right there." We jumped in the car and headed for the funeral home again.

Mike had Daddy in the chapel where the services were to be conducted. I was so happy he hadn't been placed in the same room where Mama had been placed for viewing all those years before.

My heart was pounding as I walked toward the chapel. Mike started in with me, but I turned to him and said, "Mike, I would like to be alone with him." He understood and took Sissy into his office for a cup of coffee.

VERY SLOWLY, I WALKED UP TO THE CASKET. THERE my Daddy was, all dressed in his black suit and tie. His glasses were in place and he looked so peaceful. I was glad that I recently had put some color in his hair. It looked just perfect, no gray, but not too dark. His eyebrows still had just enough color in them that they didn't show any gray either and looked quite natural. I was pleased to see that his skin was no longer gray, but back to a pale white.

I kissed his forehead and squeezed his hand, but this time, there was no response. His soft hazel eyes were closed, now, forever.

Gazing at him, I felt better when I saw that he looked so peaceful and still. Through my tears I said, "Daddy, you look really spiffy. That long ol' trip back home is finally over."

I assured him Pam and Kim would have his boots and belt here by tomorrow. Then I checked to make sure his clothes looked just right.

When everything was arranged to my satisfaction, I reached into my purse and took out the little gold wedding band my Mother had given him so many years ago. Kissing it, I then placed it on his finger. I looked up and said, "Mama, he's finally with you, now."

I was overwhelmed by the closeness I felt to both of them at that moment. Without a doubt, I knew they were now together. He had missed her all these years so very much, I knew, and now, he was where he wanted to be. As I held his hand, I thanked God for bringing him home safe.

I walked back out to the waiting room where Mike and Sissy quickly joined me. Looking at Mike, I said, "He looks wonderful, and I'm so thankful you dressed him tonight. I really appreciate it and feel so much better now that he is out of that crate and home."

We then talked some more about the services. Mike said he would be putting the announcement over the radio in the morning so all of Daddy's friends would know he was home. He said, "I couldn't make the announcement until Vernon actually arrived.

I told him, "My daughters will be here in the morning with Daddy's boots and belt. I'll bring them down as soon as they get here." I paused, "He does have his socks on, doesn't he?" I asked.

"Yes, he does," Mike assured me. I sat there a few moments going over things in my head to be sure I had done everything Daddy wanted me to do.

Sadly, I looked at Mike and said, "The only thing missing is his Stetson hat. You know, Daddy never went anywhere without that hat. During his stay at the hospital, he had to be wearing it, even when he would go for all his tests." I smiled to myself as I remembered the nurses always reminding each other to get his hat before they took him out of his room.

Mike quickly said, "That's not a problem. Many old timers, like your Dad, hold their hats. So if you want him to hold his hat, just bring it down and I'll place it with him when I put on his boots and belt."

My heart just sank. Now I wished I had sent his old Stetson with the kids like I had started to do.

Suddenly, I remembered the Stetson that Yane had sent to him. I said, "I'll bring the Stetson my sister gave him for Christmas. My daughters are bringing it, too. It's not the one he always wore, but he did have it on. She wanted it back for a refund, but he could at least hold it for the services, right?"

"Sure," Mike said, "I'll take it out and place it on top of the casket after we close it, and then she can have it back. That's the way we always do it, if the family doesn't want to bury it with their loved one."

I was so happy to know others had done this, and that it was possible to do without a great deal of trouble. But then, others didn't have a sister like Yane. I looked at Sissy with tears in my eyes and said, "Sissy, this means Daddy will get to hold that Stetson one more time. Now I'll feel like he is totally dressed."

Mike asked, "Do you want to keep his glasses?"

Puzzled, as I had never really thought about it, I thought for a moment, then said, "No, but I'll see if my daughters or anyone else would like to keep them."

"Just let me know. If no one wants to keep them, we just take them off after the services and place them in his hand before we close the casket."

I sat there for a minute mulling it over then said, "I want to ask you one more thing before we leave, Mike." I paused for a moment, "Daddy has been through a great deal the past six weeks and has lost a lot of weight, I was concerned about letting his friends view him. He doesn't really look the way they would remember him, though I think he looks just fine, really handsome." I paused, "It's just that I saw him come back from so far, and he looked so good, then suddenly, it all went the other direction. You've known my Daddy all your life, Mike, does he look like you remember him? Do you think we should open the casket for the services?"

"Reta," Mike said, "I have never seen anyone who has gone through what your Daddy has that looks as good as he does. Quite frankly, I was amazed when I started to dress him. He has no bedsores or even a skin breakdown, his skin is flawless.

"I realize he has lost a lot of weight, and if I had prepared him, I would have done his mouth differently, but then I knew him, where the folks in Amery didn't. But I can honestly say, if he were my father, I would let his old friends say goodbye. They will be amazed, like me, at how well he looks after what he's been through. It's obvious he was well cared for. You've done a wonderful job with him."

Through my tears I said, "Thank you, Mike, but I can't take all the credit. I had some wonderful people working with him in my home. Monie, the young lady coming down with my daughters, you'll meet her in the morning, was his last nurse. She kept a vigilance over Daddy for the last six weeks." I told him about the egg crate mattress she cut up and used to place under the pressure points, plus all the tender loving care he had received.

I said, "Let me think it over and I'll see how Cecil, Yane and my daughters feel after they see Daddy. You know how particular Daddy was about the way he looked, and he never went anywhere unless he looked totally spiffy."

"Well, as an old friend of Vernon's, I think he looks wonderful, and like I said, I was totally amazed, not really expecting to see him in such excellent condition.

"I believe his friends would be more relieved to see him, than to always wonder how he looked after his long illness. Again, you and your group can be mighty proud of the care you gave your Daddy."

"I appreciate that, Mike and I'll tell Monie and the rest what you've said. I know they will appreciate it, too. I'll talk to you tomorrow, after everyone else gets here.

I looked toward the chapel, but decided not to go back in to say goodnight. I didn't think I had any more tears left. Thanking Mike, again, I gave him a hug, then Sissy and I slowly walked out, rolled into the car and drove home.

My body finally started to relax on the way home. Just knowing Daddy was home, dressed and out of that crate gave me so much comfort. Now, when my babies get here safe, I can totally relax.

I had no idea how exhausted I was. When Sissy led me up to her bedroom, I felt like a zombie. I slipped into my blue pajamas, gave her a big hug and said, "Thanks, Dit, for being here for me. I love you." I was asleep within seconds.

A few hours later, Sissy woke me up and said, "Baby, can you roll over on your side? Huh? You're snoring so loud I can't get to sleep."

"I'm sorry," I said, "I guess it's because I'm so tired and have had so much on my mind." I obliged and went right back to sleep.

Later, I woke up again and Sissy was missing. I went downstairs and found her sitting at the kitchen bar drinking coffee. "What time is it?" I asked.

She looked at her watch and said, "Six o'clock. Want some?"

"Sounds great. I could use some coffee," I replied, heading for a stool.

She laughed, then said, "Baby, I love you dearly, but we've got to make other arrangements for sleeping. I have never heard anyone snore like that. You sounded like a train highballin' it to Birmingham! I'll sleep on the sofa tonight, maybe with artillery earmuffs on!"

"I don't understand it. I never snore. You know that. We've bunked together many times over the years. It must be all the pressure and tension.

"Anyway, I'll sleep on the sofa tonight, so don't worry yourself about it another moment.

"Or I might even go over to Mary's house with the kids. Hopefully, I'll settle down by tonight."

"I hope so, too," she chuckled, "or they'll gag you!"

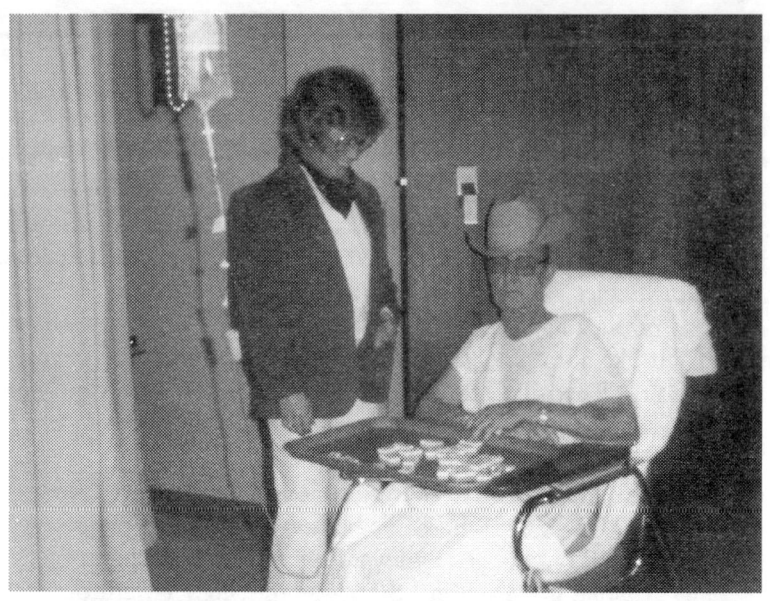

TOP: **COUNTRY SINGER, KAREN DEE & VERNON. HE'S WEARING HIS FAITHFUL STETSON HAT & CHALLENGING HER TO A GAME OF DOMINOES**

BELOW: **GREGG & CLARION LANE, "THE REX CACTUS SHOW,"**
IN HAPPIER DAYS WITH VERNON, FOUR MONTHS BEFORE HIS STROKE.
"NO," GREGG HASN'T JOINED MY BALLET CLASS. HE'S ONLY WEARING
A TUTU I GAVE HIM FOR THE COMEDY PORTION OF THEIR SHOW.

10

LINDA MADE US SOME BREAKFAST.   I WASN'T
HUNGRY but knew I had to eat something, as a big day lay ahead.

Cecil called around 7:00 in the morning and said, "We got in late
last night, and we drove by Sissy's house—but it was dark. We figured
you were all asleep, so decided not to wake you."

"I'm glad you're here Cecil," and the tears started flowing again.
"Have you seen Daddy?" I asked.

"Yeah," he said, "we went straight there after arriving."

"Are you happy with the casket Sissy and I picked out?" This was
probably the wrong thing to say straightway, but it had been on my mind.
"I just had to get Daddy out of that shipping crate, didn't want him to
spend the night in it, and I knew you and Yane wouldn't be here until this
morning."

"It's just fine," he assured me. "I'm glad you went ahead and took
care of it. Daddy really looks good, so much better than the last time I saw
him."

"Really?" I questioned. "I was concerned about the amount of
weight he had lost and wanted to see how you felt about opening the casket
for the services."

"Well, Mike told me you were worried about that, but he looks a
hell of a lot better than the last time I saw him. Don't worry about letting
his old friends see him. They'll be surprised how good he looks, too." He
choked up and said, "I felt a lot better after I saw him, Reta. What time are
you going over to the funeral home?"

"Just as soon as Pam and Kim get here with his boots and belt. I'll
call you before I leave, all right?"

"Okay, then I'll see you there. Oh, by the way, has your sister
called yet?"

I laughed and said, "No, has yours! I just hope she approves of
the casket and overall funeral arrangements. I don't want any problems
from her. Remember, Daddy always said he didn't want any fussin' or
fightin' at his funeral."

"Well," Cecil said with a drawl, "Margaret has been chewing on me
all the way down here to keep my mouth shut if Yane starts any thing, so
I'll just keep bitin' the bullet like I always do when she's around."

"Just try to be nice for Daddy's sake, and I will, too," I promised.

That was a load off my mind, and Cecil was in total harmony with the grandsons being the pallbearers.

Suddenly, Ol' Shorty came to mind, and I said, "Cecil, do you know who Ol' Shorty is and if he's still alive? Daddy spoke of him so many times throughout the last year, and I thought it would be nice if we asked him to be one of the pallbearers, too."

He thought for a moment, then said, "I know Ol' Shorty was one of Daddy's domino player buddies, but I'm sure he died a couple of years ago." A chill ran up the back of my neck. Maybe Daddy had been visiting with Ol' Shorty all those times. Cecil assured me he would think of some other friends of Daddy to make the six needed for pallbearers. I was glad Cecil was there. Even though we had our problems, like all brothers and sisters do, I knew I could always count on him to support me.

ALL THE CHURCH LADIES AND FRIENDS STARTED bringing food to Sissy's house before eight o'clock, and offering us their condolences. One of the ladies from the Southside Baptist Church, where Yane and Dub attended when they lived in Winters a few years before, said, "Reta, it was so nice of your sister to send you a round trip ticket so you didn't have to drive such a long way, wasn't it?"

I couldn't believe Yane had told them about her generosity, but then I should have known. If she had a chance to grandstand, she would. I wanted so much to say, "Yes, it was wonderful of her to send me on the flight from hell so she could brag to everyone," but I didn't. Instead, I said, "Yes, it was very generous of her, but as I understand, it was Dub's idea. He's so wonderful! She only made the flight arrangements." I was so disgusted, I turned and walked out.

As I walked back into the kitchen, I mumbled to Linda, "I wonder if she will have it printed in the Winters' paper, and the Church Bulletin how she helped her poor, degenerate little sister get home for her Daddy's funeral."

I grabbed a cup of coffee and flopped down on a kitchen stool. "She'll probably have her church people believing I sent Daddy home in a cardboard box, stashed in a box car headed for Texas, and on a train with square wheels!" I continued. Linda just laughed 'cause everyone knew how Yane loved to grandstand, and I felt it was no big news flash to anyone who really knew what was going on.

About eight-thirty, Dub appeared at the back door. I was so relieved he was alone. He walked in and gave me a hug, and I started crying again. I had been a little girl when he married Yane, and had always loved him. He had always been good to me and when Yane would be mean, he would always take up for me. He was an honest man, and one preacher who practiced what he preached.

Linda poured him a cup of coffee and he joined me at the kitchen bar. I said, "Dub, I really appreciate you sending me a ticket. That was really nice of you, but I want to assure you I did have enough space on my credit card to have paid for it myself."

"I know," he replied, "but I wanted to do something for you. I know it's been rough. How was the trip?" I didn't have the heart to tell him his wife had sent me on the flight from hell. Why? I knew he gave me the ticket because he truly cared. That made the difference.

Instead, I only said, "It was a big help being able to fly and not have to drive. Thank you so much." You see, I can be a nice person with only half an effort!

Then he looked at me very seriously and said, "I just left the funeral home, and I want you to know Vernon looks very acceptable. Mike told Yane you were worried about an open casket service when she called, but believe me, Vernon looks better now than he did when he left a year ago.

"You have to remember, we didn't see him at his peak like you did. We haven't seen him since he left, except for the video you sent from Kim's graduation, and we thought he looked wonderful then."

"Dub," I said, "he came back so much more after that video, you wouldn't believe." I opened up the album I had kept from the beginning of Daddy's stroke and showed him the miraculous improvement he had made since the video.

After studying some of the pictures quite carefully, he said, "I can see now where you had reservations, but you and your family are the only ones who saw that improvement. The rest of us only remember how he looked when he left here and on the video." He made sense, and I knew then I could open the casket for the service so his old friends could say goodbye, one last time.

Reluctantly, I said, "Has Yane seen Daddy yet?" Dub paused for a moment then offered, "She called when we got in this morning, and when Mike told her you were waiting until she and Cecil saw Vernon to decide about the open casket service, well, she wanted me to go check Vernon over first before she went to see him." I could already feel my blood pressure rising. He continued, "I am going to pick her up and take her to the funeral home as soon as I leave here. She's at brother James's house having breakfast."

That did it! My blood pressure went straight up, but like Cecil, I tried to control my feelings. However, I couldn't hide the fact I was a tad bit upset. After all, it was obvious what she wanted Dub to think, and heaven only knows who else. I'm sure she was filling the James household in on her predictions at this moment, while at the same time eating her breakfast.

Sarcastically, I said, "Dub, what did she think Daddy would look like, for heavens sake! Did she think I had abused him or something? I'm sure Mike told her it was only because of the weight loss." I shook my head. "For God's sake! That's all I need! Gossip like that to get started in this town!"

Dub quickly went to her defense. "She didn't think that. She just wanted me to check him over first." Dub always tried to soothe things over, but I knew exactly why she sent Dub first, and so did he. Without a doubt, Daddy's casket was going to be opened for visitation and for the service. I didn't want my sister to have anything to gossip about, or plant any ugly thoughts in anyone's head.

Dub and I discussed the remaining arrangements, and he assured me he would handle everything else needed for the service. I told him Sissy and I had already filled out the information on Daddy's family. As we continued talking, I heard a car drive up, and I knew it was my babies. I jumped up and ran to the door to meet them. When I saw them in Daddy's little red car, the tears started flowing. Now, everyone was home, including Daddy's little car.

After all the hugs and kisses were received and given, and the tears stopped flowing, they came in and sit down and had a cup of coffee. Then Linda fixed them something to eat. Dub greeted them, then said, "I'm going to pick up Loraine now and take her to the funeral home. We'll see you later." I gave him a hug and thanked him again for his kindness. And I meant it.

The kids greeted Sissy and filled us in on the trip coming down. The little car ran well, and the only problem had been a blowout. We then introduced Monie to Sissy and Linda. Sissy gave her a hug and said, "I've heard some awful nice things about you, Monie."

"I hope they were all good," she jokingly replied. Sissy smiled, "They sure were, I'm glad you came." She gave Brad and Cheryl a hug, too.

Pam told us again about escorting Daddy to the airport, and about how they felt like he was with them on the trip. Kim said, "Mom, at times we could smell grandpa's after shave lotion. Do you think his spirit was in the car with us?" I knew this was going to open an extensive conversation if we continued, so I said, "Honey, let's talk about all this later. Right now we need to get you guys over to Mary's house so you can unpack and get settled."

"Are you gonna stay with us over there?" Kim begged. I looked at Sissy, chuckled and said, "Well, if Sissy can handle not bunking with me."

"Oh, please take her," Sissy cried. "You'll be ready to give her back soon. Just remember," she laughed, "I've got a sofa if you decide to bring her back."

"What's the joke?" Pam asked.

"We'll talk about that later, too," I said, as I headed upstairs to get a change of clothes. When I got back downstairs, I told Sissy I would plan to spend the night at Mary's house with the kids, but would come over the next morning to dress at her house for Daddy's funeral. Linda had pressed the wrinkles out of my blazer, and I didn't want to take a chance on wrangling it all up again. I gave Sissy a hug, grinned and said, "Maybe you can get some rest while I'm gone."

"Okay," she laughed, and hollered to the kids as they headed for the car, "Good luck sleeping tonight!"

Mary, her husband, M.J., and daughters Michelle and Melinda had everything ready for our arrival. They were such good friends, and Daddy and I had always been able to count on them. Melinda and Michelle were really excited to see the kids again, and I introduced them to Monie.

Mary, M.J. and I then headed for the kitchen for more coffee while the kids unloaded the car, and I began filling them in on the details for the funeral. M.J. said, "We were down at the funeral home to see Vernon this morning, and he really looks good. I know you're glad he's finally home." Then M.J. added, "While you girls catch up on everything, I'll run down and get that hamburger meat."

I smiled and said, "Mary, are you making your famous Big Texas hamburgers for the kids?"

"Yeah," she answered, "I remember how much they like them."

"I appreciate your taking them in every time we come home. They love staying with you guys!"

"Hey, we enjoy them, too," M.J. yelled, as he hurried out the door.

The girls unpacked their clothes and hung them so the wrinkles would fall out before the funeral. Brad, of course, was busy lugging suitcases and clothes in and out. Mary poured us another cup of coffee, and by this time I was getting the caffeine jitters and thought maybe my eyes would turn *Sanka*.

Pam and Kim came out from the bedroom, and Pam was carrying Daddy's boots and belt. She started crying as she handed them to me. The tears really flowed when I told them their Grandpa could hold his Stetson one more time. "But, Mom," Pam said, "we didn't bring Grandpa's Stetson. You told me not, too."

"I know honey, but just give me the one Yane gave him for Christmas. He can hold it for the services and then we can give it to her to take back to the store," I assured her.

Pam quickly said, "I didn't know that, Mom, and I gave the hat and western shirts to Tammy while you and Sissy were upstairs getting your stuff to bring over here. I just wanted to get it out of the car and not have to be responsible for it any longer."

"That's okay, honey," I interrupted, for I could see she was about to start crying again. "I'll just take it down later this evening or even in the morning before the services. I just wanted Daddy to be able to hold his hat when his old friends see him for the last time."

With those words, she relaxed. "Yeah, Grandpa 'd like that. He always said he felt naked without his hat."

I took a shower, put on makeup, banana-clipped my hair and put on a pant suit. Then I called Aunt Emma's house to tell Cecil and Margaret I would be leaving for the funeral home by ten-thirty. Aunt Emma answered the telephone and said, "Shug, Cecil, Margaret and the kids left for the funeral home about thirty minutes ago. He said to tell you he would meet you there." She paused for a moment, in obvious reflection, then continued, "How are you and your little family doing?" then started to cry.

"We're fine, Auntie Em," I assured her, "Are you okay?"

"Oh, yeah, I'm fine," but she was so choked up she could hardly talk to me. I knew she was reliving Uncle Virgil's death. She had gone though seven years of caring for him after his stroke, and even though he had been in the Winters Nursing Home the last couple of years, she still was there from the time he opened his eyes until he closed them at night. The old folks in Winters referred to that nursing home as The Hell.

Auntie Em regained her composure and generously offered, "Shug, if you or the kids need anything, you know where I live. I love you," and her tears came again.

"I love you, too, Auntie Em, and I'll see you tomorrow at the services." I had to hang up before I started crying, too.

A few minutes later my little family came out all dressed to see their Grandpa. Pam said, "Mom, I dread this. Does Grandpa look good?"

"Yes, indeed, he does, honey. I promise you guys will feel better after you see your Grandpa. He looks really spiffy in his black suit and tie," I said as cheerfully as I could under the circumstances.

Kim started crying, "Mom, he'll be dressed like he was at my graduation, won't he?"

"Yes, honey, exactly," I answered. "And you remember how handsome your grandpa looked then," I said confidently.

"Yeah," she sniffled.

Then I took Daddy's boots and belt, climbed into Daddy's little red Pontiac and Brad, who was driving us, headed toward the Winters Funeral Home to reunite the kids with their grandpa.

On the drive over, I couldn't help from hoping Yane had already been to see Daddy and had already left. I just wasn't ready to see her yet. I was also hoping and praying that I was just being paranoid and assuming by thinking she would be hateful. Maybe she would be different this time. After all, she had just lost her Daddy, too. If this loss didn't make us closer, nothing would. I knew, in her way, she loved him, too, but Daddy had never been any different than Cecil and I in Yane's eyes. Sad but true. None of us ever quite measured up to her standards, nor did many other people. She had never been able to control any of us, and I think that's the reason she was so angry. I decided to try not to look for a problem.

My mind went back to the conversation I had earlier with Dub. Maybe I had overreacted about her sending him to check Daddy over, maybe she wasn't trying to find fault or hurt me, but after years of her verbal abuse, I had reason to feel the way I did. Anyway, I asked God to help me through the next few days, and not let me overreact to any situation I might face.

I decided, too, as far as my reaction to her sending Dub to check Daddy over, I was going to give her the benefit of the doubt. So the mental sobriety started in my corner.

We arrived at the funeral home and quietly walked in. Cecil and Margaret were visiting with some of Daddy's old friends, and Chris and Jennifer were sitting next to them, sad looks on their faces, and understandably so. They immediately got up and grabbed Pam and Kim, and the tears started. I tried to hold it back as best I could, but as my brother put his arms around me, I totally broke down, too.

Margaret was so sweet, and assured me Daddy was all right because he was now with The Heavenly Father.

I regained my composure and looked around. Cecil knew I was looking for Yane and said, "Yane and them have already left to go over to Sissy's."

"Was she satisfied with the casket and the arrangements I made?" I cried.

"Well, she didn't say anything, so I guess she was," he replied. Margaret quickly assured me how pleased she and Cecil were with everything, for she knew how concerned I was.

Quickly I looked around the room for Pam and Kim, and saw them standing over by Daddy's casket with Chris, Jennifer, Brad, Monie and Cheryl. They were all holding on to one another, patiently waiting for someone to open the casket, so they could see their Grandpa.

Mike had moved Daddy out of the chapel, and into the main room for visitation. I was still hanging on to Daddy's boots and belt. The beautiful sprays I had ordered were all in place, plus so many flowers had arrived from his friends. Mike came out to meet me, and I gave him

Daddy's boots and belt. He assured me he would put them on Daddy immediately. He asked, "Is that your family over by Vernon?"

"Yes," I replied as I motioned Pam and Kim to come over to me.

I immediately introduced them to Mike, and he shook hands with them, then said, "I was almost ready to move your grandfather back into the chapel. I know Sissy and some of the others wanted to just remember him the way he was, so I didn't want them to walk into the waiting room and see him. If you will give me a few minutes, I will move him and also put his boots and belt on."

I assured him I would have Daddy's Stetson there before the services tomorrow, as he and his attendant rolled Daddy back into the chapel.

Suddenly, I remembered the procedure we had to go through to put Daddy's boots on. I called Mike back and said, "The socks I sent with Daddy were silk, so his boots would slide on easier, and he always put a little talcum powder in his boots, too. That really helped to get them on. He just bought them and didn't have time to really break them in." Mike could see I was really concerned, smiled and assured me he would do whatever had to be done to get them on. I felt so bad as I remembered Daddy complaining about how those damn boots hurt his feet, but he would always wear them anyway, and I knew he would want them on now for his final goodbye.

My heart was full as I remembered back when, as a little girl... *I would straddle his foot, hold on to one boot with both hands while he would then place his other foot on my behind and push until the boot came off, usually sailing me across the room and holding the boot in my hand all the way. Then we would repeat the same procedure for the other boot. Daddy would sit there and laugh at me as I picked myself up and laughed back at him. He made a game out of everything we did.* During the past year, I still took his boots off the same way, but he could only push with his left foot. At times, though, he had still been strong enough to almost sail me across my living room at home. He still laughed sometimes, even at the end, as I pretended to fall and pick myself up, and I know he remembered, too.

The kids and I walked back to Cecil and his family. The kids were busy talking to Chris and catching up on what he had been doing since vacation with us the past summer.

Chris had come to see Grandpa just like he promised he would do after school was out, and Daddy had cried when he saw Chris come in. Daddy had remembered him—clearly. Chris had been so good to help with Daddy. He went with him to therapy, helped with his bath or anything else Daddy needed.

I never really knew Jennifer that well, for there had always been too many miles between us. She was a pretty little girl and very intelligent.

Unlike Chris, who was always in some kind of trouble, she was very studious and never gave her mom and dad any trouble. I hoped someday I would get to know her as well as Chris.

I joined Cecil and Margaret, and Cecil assured me he had arranged for the remaining pallbearers. As far as he could find out, Ol' Shorty had passed away. He asked me if I had called Bill Sneed. "No," I admitted, "it slipped my mind. Could you contact him? I know he would want to know Daddy was home." He assured me he would.

Then Mike walked out and announced Daddy was ready for visitation. My heart sank as the kids stood up. Pam and Kim looked at me with tears in their eyes and I asked, "Would you like to see Grandpa alone?"

"Maybe it would be best, Mom, if just the grandchildren went in the first time." I agreed, for I knew if I went with them, they might hold back their real feelings. I wanted them to cry if they felt like it, and not feel like they had to be strong in front of me.

As Daddy's grandchildren went in to visit him, I sat back down with Cecil and Margaret. Pam took Kim and Brad's hand and started for the chapel. Chris and Jennifer were right beside them. Kim turned around and said, "Monie, you and Cheryl come, too. You're his grandchildren, too, you know," and they quickly took their places beside them.

Mike came over and assured me Daddy's boots and belt were in place. Daddy was now fully ready, except for his Stetson hat. I told Cecil and Margaret about the Stetson, and they also thought it would be nice for Daddy to hold his hat for the service, and on that issue, we were in agreement.

I visited with several of Daddy's old friends who showed up to see him. Some I remembered, and some I didn't. One older gentleman walked over to me holding his hat in his hand, and said with a little smile, "Now I betcha, little lady, you don't remember me, do ya?" The tears started flowing as I hugged him and cried, "Connie Gibbs! Of course I remember you! I used to ride horses at your ranch when I was a little girl. I remember watching you rope, break horses and everything, just like Daddy. It's so good to see you again!"

As tears welled up in his eyes, he said, "Well, I'll be! I never dreamed you'd remember me."

I smiled and said, "How could I forget you?" Actually, Connie had changed very little, a few wrinkles, yes, but the twinkle in the eye and friendly demeanor would have given him away.

Before long, the kids came out of the chapel and their eyes were totally dry. They looked so content and relieved. I went to them and asked, "Are you all right?" Pam and Kim put their arms around me and walked me over to a sofa. Pam said, "Mom, I feel so much better.

Grandpa looks so peaceful and happy, I don't feel like crying anymore."
"Me, either," Kim injected. "Grandpa just looks so handsome in his black
suit, and I feel like he wouldn't want us crying. I think he would want us to
be happy he's out of the mess he was in."

The rest of the kids joined us and relayed the same feeling. We
had seen Daddy go through so much in the past few weeks, and all of us
knew Daddy would never want to go back to the way he was, even before
the set back. The kids had totally accepted Daddy's death, and now I
knew I had to.

Slowly, I got up and walked alone into the chapel. They were
right—Daddy looked so handsome and peaceful in his suit and tie. I knew
he would have been more comfortable wearing his white western shirt and
black western pants, but he was dressed exactly the way he requested. I
checked to make sure his belt was okay, and I was still concerned about the
boots. I wanted to see for myself they were on right.

I walked to the door and asked Mike to join me, then said, "Mike,
would it be possible for me to see Daddy's entire body? I've just been in
charge of dressing him for so long that I want to make sure everything is
the way he would want it."

"Of course," Mike said as he opened the lower part of the casket
to reveal Daddy's feet. Sure enough, the black boots were in place just as
Mike said. I double-checked everything, then looked at Mike and said
graciously, "Thank you. I just needed to see for myself."

"I totally understand," Mike smiled, as he closed the lower part of
the casket again, then started for the door. Halfway there, he stopped,
turned around and came back. In a low voice, he said, "Reta, I just want to
double-check with you. Cecil and Yane were in harmony for an open
casket service tomorrow and said you were, too, but I haven't really heard
that from you."

"Oh, yes, Mike, they were right. We decided for sure to let his
friends say goodbye. I was just over-concerned about the weight loss."

Mile looked reassured, and left me alone with Daddy.

Alone with Daddy, I kissed his forehead and squeezed his hand. I
didn't have any more to say, for it had all been said. I just stayed with him
for awhile and remembered what a wonderful dad he had been and how
proud I had always been of him.

Again, I squeezed his hand again and kissed him, then said,
"Daddy, you really look spiffy! I'll have your Stetson here for you to hold
during the services tomorrow." Then I slowly walked back out to the kids.

Every eye was on me as I walked over to them, and I sensed they
were wondering if I was going to fall apart. "I'm okay!" I said with a little
smile. "You're right. He is happy to be home and to finally have all this
behind him."

As we spoke, Mike came over and told me flowers had been delivered from some of my students, and a big one from Pure Gold. He showed them to us, and they were beautiful! It made me feel so good to know they all cared so much.

Cecil, Margaret and Jennifer had already left for Sissy's house, and Chris, of course, stayed with Pam and Kim. I went into Mike's office to let him know we would be leaving in a few minutes. He looked up and said, "While you're here, I'd liked to talk to you about the procedure tomorrow for the funeral."

"Sure," I answered and sat down.

"I realize that you and your family are extremely close to your dad, but during the program tomorrow, your sister and her family will be escorted into the chapel first, then your brother and his family. You and your family will be escorted and seated last. This line up will prevail during the funeral procession and at the grave site. It's just a matter of protocol used at all funerals. The recognition goes from the oldest child to the youngest. I didn't know if you and your family were aware of this procedure or not, and I wanted to make sure you knew before tomorrow."

"No, as a matter of fact I didn't know about this procedure, and I appreciate your concern, but it's okay. I've done everything now that Daddy wanted done, so where I sit or where his car and my family is placed in the services doesn't really matter to me. I will inform my children so they will understand. I appreciate your advising me of this, so I can make them aware."

"Do you have any questions regarding the services tomorrow?" he asked.

"I don't think so, Mike," I answered. "Everything seems to be done, except for the Stetson. You will make sure it is given back to my sister after the service, won't you?" I asked.

"You can count on it," he assured me.

As I started toward the door to return to the waiting room, I turned around and said, "Mike, I will take care of the payment plan on the balance of the funeral before I leave town. You will get every penny I owe you." I extended my hand, "And to quote my Daddy, 'You got my word on it.'"

Mike smiled and said, "Your Daddy's word was always his bond, just like my dad. I'm not worried. We'll cover everything later."

After leaving Mike's office, I joined the kids in the waiting room where they were talking and visiting with friends that stopped by to give their condolences. "I guess we should go to Sissy's house now. Everyone is supposed to be there for a bite to eat," I announced, and everyone piled into Daddy's little car and we headed for Sissy's. I decided not to tell the kids about the protocol until later at Mary's house when we had plenty of time to discuss it. I knew they would be upset until they understood, so I wanted to make sure we had plenty of time.

My heart was going ninety miles an hour as we pulled into Sissy's driveway. Cars were everywhere. Ladies were coming in with all kinds of food, and it looked like the entire Southside Baptist Church was there, and that meant my sister would be there, too. God give me the strength, I thought.

As if reading my thoughts, Pam said, "Mom, she better not start anything." In a firm voice, I said, "Now, I don't care what she does or says, just don't you say anything. And most of all, don't be looking for her to do something wrong, or you'll find it like the nose on your face."

"Okay," Kim said, "but she better not make you cry." Everyone promised to be on their best behavior.

Brad opened the back door for me, and I took a deep breath, thanked him and went in. The house was packed full of people, and I do mean packed. Yane was sitting at Sissy's dining-room table, busy talking to her church people. She didn't even see me come in. Cecil and his family were sitting in the living room.

Dexton and Delferd were also sitting in the living room with their families. Delferd had recently married, but of course, I never received an announcement, much less an invitation to the wedding. I had briefly met his wife at the hospital in Abilene last year. Dexton had two or three children now, but as it had been with Delferd's marriage, I never received any announcements of their births. Sissy always kept me informed as to the happenings as best she could, and I cringed to think of what their families must think of me—after all, they didn't know me personally, only what Yane had told them. Quite frankly, that thought ran a shiver up my spine, and I thought about the old axiom, You can never pick your in-laws!

The kids walked through and took a seat all together in the living room while I stopped at the sink to receive a cup of coffee little Linda handed to me. I gave her a hug and said, "In case I haven't mentioned it, you're wonderful and I do appreciate you!" She gave me a hug and said, "I'm just happy to help out."

Yane looked over at me and stopped talking, and a hush fell over the room. I said, "Hi, Yane." She returned the greeting, but neither of us knew what to do or say at that time. I wished she would have stood up, put her arms around me and told me she loved me, and would have liked to believe she was thinking the same thing. However, that never happened.

We exchanged a few *insignificant* words, then she went back talking to her ladies. However, Dexton and Delferd gave me a hug—like everyone else, but they were uncomfortable, too.

I joined my family in the living room and visited with Cecil and Margaret. Cecil told me he had planned to go back to the funeral home just as soon as he ate. He felt some of the family should be there during the next few hours to visit with Daddy's friends who would be stopping by to pay their respects. I agreed with him.

None of us really knew too many of the people at Sissy's house—they were mostly friends of Yane's family, representing the Southside Baptist Church. They all knew she was staying with brother James and his family, and I'm sure most of them knew about the airline ticket she had purchased to fly me down for the funeral.

Cecil and I visited with a few of Daddy's old friends that stopped by to give their condolences and to bring a dish of food. I had never seen so much food in my life. I had forgotten how wonderful some of these fine folks were in Texas.

Suddenly, I felt as if the switch had been turned OFF, and all my energy evaporated. I was physically and emotionally drained, and I knew the kids were ready to go over to Mary's house and visit with Chris, Michelle and Melinda. I told them to go ahead because I had a couple of things I needed to do, then would get someone to run me over to the house shortly. Pam quickly looked over at Yane and said, "Are you sure you're gonna be okay, mom?"

"I'm sure, honey. I'll be okay. You kids run along," I assured her. It didn't take them long to get in the car, closely followed by Chris, and head over to Mary's.

I waited until many of the ladies left, then went into the kitchen, sat down on one of the kitchen stools and started visiting with Sissy and Linda. Dub joined us and before long Yane came over and stood at the end of the little bar. I nicely asked, "Yane, is there anything you would like to add to the service?" She glared at me and said in a mean voice, "Well, it looks like you've already taken care of everything."

I tried to explain to her why I proceeded as quickly as I did, but I don't know if it made her feel any better. I was still glad I didn't leave Daddy in that damn crate over night, even if she did get bent out of shape. My heart was beating ninety miles per hour and I didn't want any problems. However, she didn't say any more, and I assumed she was satisfied with what I had done. I certainly wasn't going to push the issue.

Then I took out Daddy's watch I had placed in the cabinet above the bar and said, "Yane, I brought Daddy's old wrist watch he's worn all these years," and scooted it over to her. "I thought you might want to have it." She looked at it, but never picked it up or showed any emotions. She just simply said, "Thanks."

I looked at Sissy and could see how tense she was, as she so wanted to see Yane and me as friends, but in her heart she knew it was only a prayer. That wish was deteriorating more by the minute.

At this time, I wished I had never given her the watch—I really thought she would want it. Maybe she did and just didn't show it. To this day I don't know.

I then asked Yane about borrowing the Stetson hat she had given Daddy for him to hold during the service tomorrow. I assured her I would have brought Daddy's old Stetson had I known it was possible for him to hold it one last time. I told her about Mike assuring me that many families of the old timers did this. She didn't say a word, so I continued to plead. "Yane, that hat would mean a lot to him to be able to hold it just one more time while his old friends say goodbye.

Yane stood there for a moment then said, "Well, I've already taken it over to brother James's house with the shirts."

"That's okay," I answered. "You could just bring it tomorrow. I just wanted Daddy to hold it during the service, then Mike will place it on top of the casket after he closes it, and then you can have it back." She mumbled "Okay," then turned to pour herself a cup of coffee. I knew she didn't understand how important that hat had been to Daddy, or maybe she thought I was just being ridiculous. One thing I knew for sure, though, she wasn't in harmony with me, as Cecil had been.

Cecil and Margaret had already left for the funeral home before I had the discussion with Yane, but now I wished I had talked to her before he left. Maybe he could have made her feel more comfortable about the hat.

Exhausted, I asked Sissy if I could borrow her car to run over to Mary's house. She said, "Sure, baby, just keep it over night, then you can come back in the morning to get dressed for your Daddy's funeral."

"Aren't you going to have quite a few dressing here?" I said.

Dub quickly interjected, "We won't be here. We will all be getting ready at brother James' house."

"Okay," I said, as I gave her a hug. I looked at Dub and added, "I'll see you guys tomorrow."

"By the way, Reta, I know you're exhausted. Loraine is going to rest tonight, and if you want to just stay at Mary's and rest too, the boys and I will relieve Cecil and Margaret for visitation." I gave him a hug and said, "Thanks, Dub, I would appreciate that."

As I drove back to Mary's, I was so relieved. Even though it had been tense, everything had gone all right. I had to chuckle to myself as I thought of the way Yane glared at Monie when she left. I'm sure she thought I had picked up a streetwalker to care for Daddy. Monie's dark roots had grown out because she had been so busy taking care of Daddy, and over all, she didn't look like the kind of woman who would sit in the front pew at Yane's church. But if Yane could have seen the way she cared for our Daddy, she would have given her a hug, I am sure, and maybe even would have said, "Thank you."

Walking in to Mary's, I found the kids all eating hamburgers. She immediately jumped up and asked, "Are you ready for one?"

"Maybe half of one," I answered. "I've snacked too much at Sissy's." Mary's hamburgers are the best, and that one half filled me up. With a good meal in me, my last reserves of strength were gone, and I had to get to bed.

After dinner the kids made out the beds, and it was wall-to-wall beds in the trailer house. We bathed, changed into our pajamas, then we started reminiscing about grandpa. Everyone had a special memory to share. As each one of us spoke, Monie just sat there listening. Finally she spoke up softly and said, "Reta, if it is all right with you, I would like to put one red rose in Grandpa's casket from me. I'll put it off to the side, or even where it won't be seen, but I just want to give him something special from me," and started crying. I put my arms around her and so did Pam and Kim. I said, "Monie, that's a beautiful thought, and of course you can give Grandpa a rose. You can put it wherever you want to." She looked at me and smiled, then dried her eyes and said, "You know I did love him."

"I know you did, and I'll always love you for being so wonderful and caring to him," I said through my tears. She looked at Brad and asked, "Will you take me to the florist in the morning?"

"Sure," he answered with a smile.

Then I said seriously, "I have something to talk to all of you about, and I want you to try and understand. I know none of you have really been to that many funerals, thank God, but there is such a thing as protocol."

"What's that?" Kim asked.

"Well, it's the diplomatic way of doing things. For instance, tomorrow at the funeral, Yane and her family will be seated first, their car will be first behind the hearse and they will also be seated first at the grave site." I could feel the tension building. "Now let me finish before you say anything," I warned. "Cecil and his family will be next, then me and my family. All funerals are conducted this way, the first born is recognized first, then on down to the youngest child, which is me. This has nothing to do with who loved Grandpa the most, or who he loved the most. It is just the protocol used at all funerals."

"Well, I think it stinks," Brad said fiercely. "You mean you, Pam and Kim will be riding in Grandpa's car, third behind the hearse?"

"Yes," I answered, "and remember, it doesn't matter if we are last in the entire line, grandpa knows how much we loved him, and that's all that matters."

Then Chris put his two bits in. "Well, I think you and your family should be right behind Grandpa. You've always been there for him and besides, Grandpa's car should be in front!"

"Chris," I said, "Now I know you've inherited the Fuller temper, so I want you to promise me you will bite your tongue just like your dad and I are having to do. You know Grandpa didn't want any fussin' and fightin'. Besides, where someone sits or rides is not important. What's important is the fact we're all here together. That's what's important," and I started to cry.

Pam, Kim and Chris immediately put their arms around me and promised they would do what ever had to be done, and make Grandpa and me proud of them tomorrow. I gave them a hug and said, "I knew I could count on you guys to be nice."

Just then Brad mumbled, "Yeah, I'll just run her off the road with Grandpa's car!"

The other kids laughed, but I yelled, "Brad, what do you mean? You've got to be joking!" Everyone started laughing again and he said, "Well, at least I got everyone to stop the bawling!" Then he started to lecture all of us. "Grandpa wouldn't want all of you bawling, he would want you to be happy that he's finally home and doesn't have to go through any more of this hell with people poking and pulling at him!"

Then he looked at me and said, "And I promise you, Reta, everyone will be a good sport tomorrow, so don't you worry. I'll see to that," as he glanced over at Chris who slouched down into his chair and mumbled, "You won't hear nothin' outta me."

I put my arms around Brad and said, "You're right, Brad. No more bawling, and I know I can count on all of you tomorrow to understand the protocol."

"You betcha," Pam said with a smile.

We continued to tell Mary and M. J. some of the things Daddy did up north, and how many friends he had made even in his condition. Mary laughed, "Vernon always was a charmer!"

Then the telephone rang and Mary got a very sober look on her face and said, "It's for you, Reta. It's your sister," and rolled her eyes as she handed me the phone. My heart just dropped, and everyone got really quiet. I said, "Hello—"

"Reta, I've been thinking over the ones you've decided to use for Daddy's pallbearers." I quickly interrupted and said, "We talked about this some time ago, Yane, and you seemed to think it would be nice to use the grandsons."

"Well, I'm not sure, and Cecil is getting others lined up," she said.

"Yane, if you're not happy with the pallbearers, then by all means, get whomever you want. Daddy never specified who he wanted," I said, and sensed that my agreeing with her took some of the wind out of her sails.

"Well, it's a little late now," she said sarcastically.

"Oh, no, it isn't," I contradicted. "Nothing is in print. You call Mike and select anyone you want, it doesn't matter to me, and I'm sure it won't matter to Cecil, either. Chris wanted to be one, but if you have a problem with the ones selected, then change them. I don't want you to be upset. I just want us to all get through this with no fussin' or fightin', the one thing Daddy did specify he didn't want at his funeral," I said.

Yane instantly mellowed out. Now that she could change the pallbearers, she didn't seem so unhappy with the ones we had selected, and said, "Well, I'll think about it."

Amazed, I hung up the phone! I couldn't believe it! It appeared almost like she was trying to pick a fight, but I told myself I was just being paranoid again. But deep down inside, I knew it was just the fact that Yane hadn't been in control of everything that bothered her, and this was her way of trying to feel that she had some say in the matter. I was still amazed at her self-centeredness, even at Daddy's funeral.

At any rate, I was determined she wasn't going to get to me, no matter what she did or how horrible she acted. Then I told the kids what had been said, and Chris' temper started to flare.

Brad jumped in and said sternly, "Chris, just settle down. Remember what you promised Reta."

Chris mumbled, "Yeah, but it ain't gonna be easy. Everyone has to always worry about what Yane thinks. It's like my dad and Reta have no feelings. She hasn't done a damn thing for Grandpa, but thinks she can decide everything about his funeral. She didn't even care about him!"

Chris was right, but instead of responding to his comments, I picked up the conversation where we had left off, and changed the subject. The kids continued to tell me all about their trip down, and Brad said, "I just hope Grandpa's little car runs as good going back as it did coming down." I said, "I hope Karen gets in touch with all our students so they won't be screaming when we get home."

After awhile I said, "I'm ready to get in bed. I am exhausted." I was asleep by the time my head hit the pillow.

I woke up in the wee hours and looked around. I jumped as I saw ten eyeballs staring at me. Alarmed, I asked, "What's wrong?"

"Mom, we can't sleep for your snoring. Now I know what Sissy meant. We've stuck Kleenex in our ears and everything," Pam said.

"I've never heard you snore before," Kim echoed.

"Like I told Sissy, it must be the pressure and tension I'm under. I don't know what to do about it," I answered, then started to cry. I felt so bad I was keeping everyone awake.

By this time, Mary had come out. She was laughing and said, "Who are you trying to kill out here?" Everyone laughed then, and she said, "I tell you what, let's move all the beds into the other rooms, and your mom can snore as loud as she wants to."

Everyone started grabbing their bed rolls and following her to their new bedroom. Pam and Kim kissed me goodnight, and Pam laughed on her way out, "Give 'em hell, mom!" I went back to sleep, and I guess I did give 'em hell the rest of the night.

I AWOKE TO THE DELICIOUS SMELL OF FRYIN' BACON and coffee brewing. I pulled myself up off of the living room floor and staggered into the kitchen. Mary chirped, "Did you sleep okay?"

"The question is," I answered, "was everyone else able to get some sleep?"

"You didn't bother us, if that's what you mean! After we closed the doors, we just let you roar!" and Mary was still laughing as the kids drug themselves into the kitchen. They all had fun teasing me about the snoring. I just had to take it!

After I finished my breakfast, I finished my coffee, brushed my teeth, threw my hair up, jumped into my jeans and sweat shirt and got ready to head for Sissy's house. I told the kids to hurry up.

"We'll get dressed here. We'll get Monie's rose, then go by the funeral home so she can give it to Grandpa." Pam fought back the tears as she continued, "Then we'll meet you over at Sissy's."

"Sounds good," I said, as I headed out the door.

Sissy was sitting at her kitchen bar when I got there. I poured me another cup and joined her, then told her about Yane's call. Tears came to her eyes as she said, "Baby, I just hope and pray that you, Yane and Cecil can get along until your Daddy is buried." I looked her straight in the eye and said, "Sissy, I promise you I'm not going to allow anyone or anything to make me break my word to Daddy. You know I promised him there would be no fussin' or fightin', and no matter what, I am going to keep my word. As Daddy would say, 'You can take it to the bank.'"

Sissy smiled and said, "Okay. I just love all of you so much, and I wish things could be different."

"Me, too," I assured her, "but I don't know what else to do. I don't want to hurt anyone or try to take over. All I wanted was to get Daddy out of that crate," and tears began forming in my eyes.

"I know that, baby. I think you've done real good, and I think Yane and Cecil are happy with what you've done, too."

I shook my head, "I sure hope you're right, Sissy. I don't want them to ever think I was trying to take over or hurt them in any way."

Just then, a man walked up to the back door, and for a moment my tired mind lapsed back to the past and I cried, "It's Humpty!" and headed for the door. Suddenly, I realized it wasn't Humpty, but his son, Terry, whom I hadn't seen since he was a little boy. He looked just like Humpty did back then, and Sissy yelled, "Come on in, Terry!" I gave him a hug and said, "Yep, you've grown a little throughout the years." He was over six feet, and smiled at me. "It's been a long time. How are you doing?"

"Other than needing a long vacation, I'm fine," I answered with a smile. He then filled me in on his family, and I filled him in on mine. I was so impressed with him! He had really grown into a handsome man, and just a plain nice person.

Before long, visitors started stopping by, and some brought more food. I said, "I better go get dressed before any more people get here. Besides, it's not too long before we have to leave for Daddy's services." I gave Terry another hug and went upstairs.

Getting my things together, I took a shower, washed my hair and got dressed in my black double knit dress with the little black and white blazer Kim had picked out for me to wear. I slipped on my smoke-black nylons, and stepped into my black high heels. I back-combed my hair and fluffed it, then decided I would wear it down. I was amazed at how much it had grown. Since I had worn it most of the time in a pony tail, I didn't realize the growth. I stood in front of Sissy's mirror for a final look, then looked up and prayed, "Dear God, please give me the strength I need for today, and be with everyone in my family. Amen." I took a deep breath and headed downstairs.

When I got downstairs, Cecil and Margaret had arrived. I gave them a hug, and we all had another cup of coffee. Cecil asked, "Are we going to read the will?"

"If you want to, but there's nothing left but bills. If yawl want to split them three ways, I'll let you," I said, but he quickly changed the subject.

Together we went over the last minute details. Evidently, Yane hadn't called him about the pallbearers and I sure wasn't going to tell him she was having a problem. At this point, all was well, at least on the surface, and I wanted to keep it that way.

Then Yane called and told Sissy they would meet us at the funeral home. She also told Sissy she wanted to talk to her privately when she got there. I assumed it was something to do with the pallbearers. Logical, right?

When the kids came in, Monie apologized, "I'm sorry it took so long, but by the time we all got dressed and got the rose delivered to Grandpa, the time had just slipped away."

"It's fine. I have plenty of time," I reassured her. Pam and Kim told me how nice I looked, and of course I told them how proud I was of my little family. Everyone was decked out in fine fashion, and I was very proud of them all.

Then I took Monie over and introduced her to Cecil and Margaret. Cecil said, "Reta told me how great you were with Daddy, and I just wanted to say thanks for what you did for my father," then patted her on the shoulder. She smiled and said, "He was a joy." It made me feel good that she was told "thank you" by someone other than me. She had worked hard, and deserved a lot of thanks.

Before long, the clock told us it was time to go to the funeral home. The hour and minute hands of a clock do not lie. Suddenly, my heart was in my mouth. I knew this was the final chapter in Daddy's life, but now his body would be laid beside mother's, just as I had promised. Without realizing it, tears started to form in my eyes.

Sissy asked, "Baby, do you want to ride with Tammy and me?" Tammy was Kathy's only child, and Sissy's only grandchild. They had become especially close since Kathy's death. Kim was standing on one side of me, and Pam on the other, and I said, "Thanks, but I'll ride with the kids. We'll see you there."

She choked up and said, "I love you," and I went over and gave her a hug. "I love you, too, Sissy, and if at anytime you want to come home, do so, okay?"

"Okay," she sobbed as Tammy seated her in the car.

The trip to the funeral home was very quiet, and we're talkin' about no sounds for hundreds of miles, here. Cecil and his family pulled up ahead of us. Dub's car was already there, and we all walked in together.

Mike came over to me and asked, "Have you decided about the glasses?"

I said, "Just place them in Daddy's hand. No one wanted to keep them."

As I glanced around, I saw Yane was talking to Sissy. In a few minutes, Sissy came over, crying, and said, "Baby, can I talk to you privately?"

"Sure," I said as I followed her outside.

"I just talked to Yane," she said, "and..." She paused and started sobbing.

I knew immediately what the problem was, and asked, "Sissy, Yane doesn't want Daddy to hold the Stetson hat, is that the problem?"

"Yes," she sobbed, "she just doesn't want to do that. I know how much it meant to you for your Daddy to hold it one more time," and continued to sob.

I put my arms around her and said comfortingly, "It's okay, Sissy. This really doesn't surprise me. After the way she acted yesterday when I asked her about it, I guess I knew this was coming, but why didn't she just say so yesterday? Why wait until a few minutes before we go into the services?" How I hated her for such a selfish act.

I started to cry—not for me, but for Daddy's sake. I knew Sissy was scared I was going to make a scene, and maybe that's why Yane waited until now to take Daddy's hat away. Maybe she wanted me to start a scene in front of the entire gathering, but whatever her reasoning, I was not going to let her get to me.

I put my arm around Sissy, walked back into the waiting room and straight over to Yane. She and her family was standing together, and she was talking to Cecil and Margaret. I refused to cry, and in fact, my body was totally numb. She was glaring at me as I walked over to her, and I looked her straight in the eye and calmly said, "Yane, if you don't want Daddy to hold your hat, it's okay. It really was never his anyway."

She rolled her eyes and glared at me as though I was some kind of idiot. "Well, I certainly don't want it put in the casket with him," she snapped. I'm sure she had convinced Cecil I was just being ridiculous to want Daddy to hold his hat, and it would be totally out of line, no matter what Mike had said.

I turned to walk back to Pam and Kim when Cecil called after me. I turned around and, sarcastically, he said, "What do you want to do, put a saddle and spurs in there with him, too?" Margaret quickly hushed him. This comment from him really hurt me, for I had thought he understood my reasoning for the hat, but obviously Yane had changed his mind.

I turned around and walked back to both of them and said as calmly as I could, "Neither one of you have any idea how important that hat has been to Daddy, or you would feel the same as I do. I wanted to add, "If you had only seen how Daddy clung to that Stetson, you both would realize how much that hat would have meant to him to hold one last time. This was something Daddy would have wanted, and I wish you could understand!" I felt my temper climbing, but remembered Daddy wanted no fightin' or fussin', and I held my tongue instead. I just turned and walked back to my own family, shaking my head in disbelief.

I calmly filled Pam and Kim in on the conversation, and let them know Yane had put an end to their Grandpa holding his hat for the last time. I was fighting the tears back, and trying to hide the hurt I was feeling inside. I didn't want them to get upset. I knew they were hurt, too, but there was nothing we could do about it. Pam said, "I wish we had brought Grandpa's old hat with us."

"Yeah," Kim mumbled. "Well, that one wasn't Grandpa's hat anyway, and besides, the brim was too little." My whole little team was disappointed, but after all, it was her hat and her decision. Sissy breathed a sigh of relief as she took her place to enter the chapel.

Dexton was playing the organ, and all of Daddy's friends were gathered in the chapel. Mike came over and lined us up according to protocol. Yane and her family was escorted into the chapel, then Cecil and his family. There were only two chairs left in the front row as Sissy, Tammy and my little family entered the chapel. Mike started to seat Sissy and I in the last two chairs, but I pulled away and clung to Pam and Kim. "I'll sit with my daughters," I said, and he seated Sissy and Tammy in the remaining two seats.

My family took their places in the second row directly behind Yane and her family. Pam was seated next to me on my left, and Kim was seated to my right. Brad, Monie and Cheryl were close by in the pew. I looked at Daddy and thought he looked so handsome in his black suit, even if he didn't have his Stetson.

I was doing just fine until Dexton started playing *Precious Memories*. As the congregation started singing, I lost total control and sobbed openly, and the tears just wouldn't stop coming. As I looked at my Daddy in his casket, flashbacks began rushing into my mind of my mother lying in her casket. I was actually attending both their funerals in my mind. It was horrible!

Pam and Kim tried their best to comfort me, but the tears were flowing from them, too. They couldn't stand to see me cry. Yane would occasionally turn around and look at me. I don't know if she would have liked to have tried to comfort me, or if she was embarrassed and thought I was making a fool of myself. I really don't know, my big sister was a stranger to me—more so on that day than ever before.

At that moment, I lost all feeling or caring about Yane. That did it. I didn't give a damn any more what she thought. She had become a total void in my life, and I didn't have to try and please her anymore, and didn't have to try and make her love me anymore; In a sense, I had been set free.

I don't remember very much about the services. I know Dexton and Delferd sang, and Dub gave the eulogy and some of the prayers. I do know, however, Brother Brooks did preach Daddy's funeral.

The next thing I remember, Pam and Kim were helping me to stand and aiming me for Daddy's casket to tell him goodbye for the last time. We stood next to his casket with our arms around each other. I saw the little red rose off to the side that Monie had given to him this morning. And I remember thinking that I was glad she placed it pretty much out of sight, or someone might have decided it didn't belong in the casket, either. I kissed Daddy's forehead and squeezed his hand for the last time. Through my tears I whispered, "I love you, Daddy!" Pam and Kim kissed him goodbye and told him they loved him, too. We then joined Brad, Monie, Cheryl, Sissy and Tammy out in the waiting room.

All of Daddy's old friends started pouring out of the chapel. I heard someone say, "Reta." I turned around—and the tears started flowing again as I grabbed Madilene Smith, Mama's very best friend and my Sunday School teacher at Content when I was a little girl. She put her arms around me and we both shed a few tears. She and my mother had been more than just good friends; they had been more like sisters. Her husband, Claude, was right beside her. They were always such a handsome couple. Madilene had written a long letter to Pam and Kim a few years back telling them some wonderful things she remembered about their grandmother. That letter was as precious to me as it was to them, and when I hugged her, I felt close to Mama. That's just how it was.

Pam and Kim were trying to steer me toward Daddy's car to line up for the procession to the cemetery when a tall, good-looking man walked up to me and said, "Are you okay, Reta?" It was Bill Snead, President of the Coleman State Bank, and truly one of Daddy's best friends. I gave him a hug and said, "I'll be okay in time, Bill. Thank you for being here and for all you did for Daddy and me."

"I'm glad I could help," he said. "Cecil called this morning, and I wouldn't have missed saying goodbye to my ol' friend."

Next to seek me out was Georgie Derden. I had spent many nights at her home when I was a little girl, and she had bought me my first *Toni Doll.* She and her husband, Russell, had spoiled me rotten back then. She was crying as she hugged me and told me she loved me. I loved her, too. Always.

The line just went on and on. Daddy had so many friends and so many I hadn't seen since I was a little girl. They all remembered me, and like Connie Gibbs, they were surprised when I remembered them, too.

Finally, Sissy came to me and said, "Baby, we've got to get in the car. Mike is ready to take the services to the cemetery." Pam and Kim were still hanging on to me, and my knees were so weak I believe if they had let go of me, I would have collapsed. I was so thankful for my two wonderful daughters. It felt so special to have them on each side of me.

Pam and Kim helped me walk to the car, then seated me in the front seat of Daddy's little red Pontiac. Brad took the driver's seat and Pam slid in beside me as Kim, Monie and Cheryl slipped into the back seat.

Yane took her position behind the hearse, then Cecil. Brad asked, "It's our turn now, right?"

"Right," I answered as he pulled into place. I was so proud of all the kids, including Chris. Everyone had been very understanding and good sports about the protocol.

Every car that met us pulled over and stopped as we passed by. I remembered how Daddy felt about stopping for a hearse. He always pulled over, got out of the car and took his Stetson off as they passed. He would say, "If people are in such a hurry that they can't pay their respects to the dead, then it's pretty damn bad."

We were all doing just fine until Pam turned on the radio to kill the silence. The tears started flowing from all of us as we listened to Randy Travis sing, Take My Body Home In A Freight Train. Brad reached over and turned the radio off immediately.

In a few minutes, we arrived at the Lake View Cemetery were Mama was buried. As we turned into the entrance, my mind flashed back to the day we had brought my mother out here—I was having a hard time keeping the two funerals separated. I knew it was partially because I was so exhausted and all of the pressure I had been under for so long.

Brad pulled Daddy's little car right up behind Cecil's, then went around and opened the door as Pam and Kim helped me out. I felt so weak and knew my legs were going to fail, that I'd end up a clump on the ground. My body had never felt this weak before.

The chairs were set by the grave site, and Daddy's casket placed over his final resting spot next to Mama. With difficulty, Pam and Kim slowly moved me toward the chairs. Yane, Cecil and their families were already seated in the front row with one chair remaining. Mike offered that chair to me, but again, I said, "I'll sit with my daughters." We then took our places in the second row behind Yane, and I remember looking toward Madilene and Claude. It gave me such comfort to have her there. Through her, I felt so close to Mama again. She smiled at me, as if to assure me everything was all right; it meant a lot. Just about the entire town was there to pay their last respects to my Daddy. I knew Daddy had a lot of friends, and this gathering certainly proved it. Soon, Brother Brooks opened the services with a prayer, and from that point on, I don't remember much of the service.

The next thing I remember was Pam and Kim taking my arms and standing me up. We moved away from the graves. As we slowly walked, someone said, "Hi, Reta." I turned around and there stood one of my high school friends, Patricia Yost. I hadn't seen her for years, since I had been the maid of honor at her wedding to Jackie Cumby. At that time, I had been married to his brother, Tommy. Our marriage had ended in divorce, due to, most probably, the fact we were so young when we got married. Anyway, I'd like to think that was the reason.

Patricia gave me her condolences, then said, "Tommy sends his love and wanted me to tell you he would have been here if he had known sooner about your Daddy."

That started the tears flowing again, and I gave her a hug and said, "Let's get together, sometime. I would love to see Tommy and Jackie, too, one day, if that is possible." We had all been such good friends throughout our high school years. Pat and I had been in grade school together, so we had known each other practically all our lives. With another hug, Patricia left.

The cemetery was full of people, and most of them were coming over to visit with me, but I felt like I was floating. I tried to visit, but I couldn't concentrate on what they were saying. I felt like I was going to pass out, and my legs felt like jelly. Thank God my daughters were with me.

Suddenly, I looked up and Yane was heading for me with her arms outstretched. Of course, everyone was watching this display of affection to her little sister. The way she wrapped her arms around me, no one would have ever believed what had transpired earlier in the week—or throughout our lives, especially after Mama died.

My arms were hanging to my sides, and I didn't hug her back. I couldn't do it. She pulled me away from Pam and Kim, and every eye was on her as she went through the motions of consoling me. She very sweetly said, "Dub and the boys are going to give a special prayer for just the family, and I want you and the girls to join us." I looked over, and sure enough, there was her family with Cecil's family all standing together holding hands.

My body totally froze and my mind flashed back to the day Mama died. I had come running into the hospital thinking she was going home that day. I had my suitcase in the car all packed to go home with her. Daddy had met me at the door and told me she had taken a turn for the worse. I could tell by looking in his eyes she was bad. I started hurrying back to her hospital room when Yane had appeared in front of me, just like she just did today. Back then, as now, she looked at me with those same page-cold eyes which I had seen so many times growing up. She had taken my arm and pulled me into the ladies room, then made me kneel by the commode and pray with her. I didn't want to pray with her, and I certainly didn't want to hold her hand and pray. I just wanted her to leave me alone and continue her theatrics without me.

The memory caused me to sob uncontrollably, and Pam and Kim were just standing there helpless, not knowing what to do. After all, Yane had just taken their mother from them. Suddenly, I felt two strong hands on my waist that pulled me from Yane, turned me about, then pushed me into Pam's arms. The hands were authoritative, and their directing strength confusing, so much so that I stopped sobbing and looked about to see who it was. Could you believe it! The lady was Mama's best friend, Madilene

Smith. But instinctively, Pam and Kim retook their positions at my side, as if protecting me from some unforeseen evil.

After a few words, I decided we should go ahead and join Dub for the family prayer. I knew he was sincere, even if Yane wasn't, and I didn't want everyone to think I had been rude. However, everyone knew the situation.

After the prayer, I talked to Madilene some more and thanked her for what she had done. She said, "Reta, I had the strangest feeling come over me when I saw that performance of Yane's. I honestly believe it was your mother's hands, through me, that gave you to Pam. I still have the funniest feeling about what happened, and I guess I never will completely understand why I did what I did, but I couldn't stand to watch that scene any longer," and she started crying. I hugged her tightly and said, "Madilene, I felt the same way. I have felt my mother's presence all day, and I know she's watching over us."

From the cemetery, we went to Sissy's house. As we walked in, I spotted my sister immediately. She was, of course, totally in her element. All the church ladies were gathered around her as she busily took care of distributing the floral arrangements to the churches and other active groups in town who were so supportive. She was reading the sympathy cards containing donated, memorial money, and I'm sure these money gifts were donated to her church in memory of Daddy just so she could continue to impress her peers from church.

At that point, I walked over and gave Cecil and Margaret a hug. Then I sat down with the kids and visited with some friends.

After awhile, I knew the kids were ready to go back over to Mary's house, so I told them to go ahead. I felt much better after I ate something, for I had been living on coffee and that is what probably added to my being so weak. I said, "I'm going to retrieve a couple of the floral arrangements before she gives them all away." I also had a couple of places I wanted to give an arrangement to.

The kids took off for Mary's house, and I waited until I saw an opening around Yane. I walked over and said, "I would like to have two of Daddy's floral bouquets. You can do whatever you want with the rest, but I want to take one to Uncle R. A. and one to the Winter's Domino Hall to all of Daddy's ol' domino buddies." She glared at me then said, "You're taking one down there?"

"Yeah," I snapped, "I probably won't catch anything."

Yane rolled her eyes and said, "You can have the one up there on the refrigerator your students sent you," then looked around, "and that one your friends in the band sent." Then she got up and walked over and got her purse, walked back over to me where I was sitting at the kitchen bar, took an envelope out and pushed it toward me. I asked, "What's that?"

Sarcastically, she said, "That's Daddy's funeral bill. I believe it belongs to you!"

At that moment, if it hadn't been for the promise I made to Daddy and Sissy, I believe I would have physically attacked her. Instead, I said, "Yes, Yane, I made arrangements with Mike when I got here on the bill." God only knows how I wanted to punch her, but I wouldn't have given her the satisfaction. I knew at that moment there never had been, nor would there ever be a relationship between us. She was the most self-serving, mean and heartless person I had ever known, and I promised myself then and there that I would never allow myself to be hurt by her again. I would not try to please her anymore and wasn't ever going to worry about trying to measure up to her standards because, at the moment, she looked very small to me. Pity was all I could feel for her as I collected the flowers, Daddy's photo album, and the funeral bill. At that point, I walked out of there and didn't look back.

I BORROWED SISSY'S CAR AGAIN AND DROVE AWAY. I just wanted to be alone for awhile, to settle down and regain my composure. Before I realized it, I was turning into the Lake View Cemetery. Slowly, I drove back to Mama and Daddy's graves. I was so happy everyone had left and the funeral home had covered Daddy's grave. The floral sprays covered both graves, plus a few more around them.

I got out of the car and stood at the grave, looking at the foot marker Daddy had bought a couple years before. It matched mother's. He had brought me out to show it to me as soon as it was in place. Mike had promised me he would take care of filling in the death date. I remembered how many times Daddy and I had come to visit Mama's grave throughout the years.

Then I thought of my children. I knew Pam and Kim would have a fit if they knew I had come out here alone, but actually I felt much better to see that Daddy was totally laid to rest. I had a sad but warm feeling come over me as I said, "Goodbye, Daddy," and climbed back into Sissy's car and headed for the Domino Hall before all of Daddy's friends went home.

Most of his friends had attended the funeral, but I knew they would head for the Domino Hall as soon as it was over, just as Daddy always did. I knew the Domino Hall was always off limits to women, for I had found that out long ago when I inadvertently walked in on a game in progress. At the time, I got filled in real fast that women didn't belong in Domino Halls, but I figured this time, though, they might forgive me for entering their private domain. I opened the door and walked in bold as brass, and you could have heard a pin drop as all Daddy's ol' friends looked up from their domino game. I smiled and nervously said, "Hi, I'm Vernon Fuller's youngest daughter, Reta." They all had a puzzled look on their face as they eyeballed the flower I was carrying. I continued, "I brought one of Daddy's plants for you in memory of him. I know he would have wanted to share with his friends," and set it on the counter. I then walked over to one of the tables and carried along Daddy's photo album. I said, "Daddy made a lot of progress after the stroke, and he called out many of your names during his illness." I didn't mention Ol' Shorty, for I figured they were probably still missing him, too.

As I put the photo album down, everyone gathered around and looked at the pictures. They marveled at the way Daddy had bounced back, and I said, "If any of you would like to ask me anything, please do." One ol' gentleman said, "He didn't suffer, did he?"

Everyone grew quiet and turned to me. I explained as best I could about the kidney failure, and how Daddy had just gone to sleep. I visited for awhile, answered some more questions, then started for the door. I turned around and said, "Now you guys take care of that plant." Then I jokingly warned, "My friend, Mary Casey, will be stopping in occasionally to make sure you keep it watered!" and they all laughed. My heart felt good about that visit, and I knew it was something my Daddy would have wanted me to do.

From the Domino Hall I headed the car towards the Winter's Nursing Home, otherwise known as "The Hell." I walked in, and the urine smell almost took my breath away. I walked up to the nurse and said, "I'm here to visit my uncle, R.A. Long." She looked at her chart and said, "He's in the recreation room." I thanked her and turned to go find the room.

As I walked down those halls and witnessed all those lonely, sad old folks, my heart just hurt for them. I was so thankful my Daddy or Mama never had to be in this place. No wonder Aunt Emma kept a vigilance over Uncle Virgil during the time he spent there before his death. I counted two aids trying to take care of the entire place, plus the nurse up front. Hell, General Custer was better off against Sitting Bull!

I walked into the recreation room, and there at one of the tables, sitting in his wheelchair was Uncle R.A. He looked awful, but when he looked up and saw me, he smiled from ear to ear and his eyes filled with tears. I gave him a kiss on his forehead and squeezed his hand, "Are you okay, Uncle R.A.?" I asked as I set my students' plant down on the table in front of him.

He mumbled, "Yeah, I'm fine, Reta," and his eyes brightened up as he looked at the gift plant I had brought. "That sure is a perty flower," he exclaimed.

"Well, Daddy had so many and I knew he would want to share one with you." He took out his handkerchief and blew his nose and regained his composure. The nurse walked in with a tray full of pills, and she handed Uncle R.A. several to take. He looked like a chicken peckin' corn as he plopped them in his mouth.

Amazed, I asked, "What are all those pills for, Uncle R.A.? You never were on that much medication." After all, he had only been in there a little over one year. He shook his head and mumbled, "I don't know. They just say I gotta take 'em."

I had called Uncle R.A. back when Daddy was making so much progress and tried to get him to come to my house and be a companion to Daddy. They had always been very close, and Uncle R.A. could pretty much take care of himself. I also knew his biggest illness was called "loneliness," so I knew he would be able to take care of the majority of his own needs. He had been just fine until Aunt Lois, Daddy's sister and his wife, had died from a massive stroke in 1983. I had gotten really close to him during the time I lived by Daddy that year.   I was really surprised when Daddy had told me that Uncle R.A. had just come by one morning like he always did, and announced he had given his home and car to some friends of his and Aunt Lois', and was going to have them drive him down to the nursing home and check himself in.   His only illness, besides loneliness, was his hip—he had a hard time getting around and didn't want to go in for a hip replacement.

That's why I had tried to get him up north, too. I knew if I could get him in for some proper medical treatment, he would be around for a long time. But he was just like my Daddy had been all those years. Until tragedy stuck, he wouldn't leave big ol' Texas. They thought Wisconsin was a million miles away. Actually, it's still very much this way today. To a true Texan, there's Texas and that's it. Nothin' else matters, and anywhere else, in fact, is a foreign land.

Uncle R.A. took his plant and I wheeled him back to his room and placed it on his dresser. We looked at Daddy's photo album, and he, too, was amazed at the progress Daddy had made before his kidney failed. I showed him a photo of Daddy that I took one Sunday afternoon. The photo showed him sitting on my sofa and talking to me while I snapped the picture. Uncle R.A. held it close and really studied the photo. I said, "Uncle R. A., would you like to have that picture?"

"I sure would, if it's okay?" he said. I took it out of the album and placed it next to the flowers. "Well, consider it yours!" I replied. I also told him some of the fun things Daddy did up north and made him feel much better about Daddy's death. He was looking tired, so I gave him a big hug and helped him into bed and said goodbye.

On my way out, I stopped by the nurses station and questioned them about Uncle R.A.'s health. They assured me he was just fine, only tired. When I asked about the pills, they simply told me his doctor had prescribed the medication, and that obviously he needed it or it wouldn't have been prescribed.

I didn't know then, but this was to be the last visit I would ever have with my Uncle R. A. He passed away in that hell hole a few weeks later. I prayed then that someday I could build a nursing home where all of these wonderful old people who are the foundation of this country could go and be cared for with the honor and dignity they deserve. My heart just breaks for them.

After leaving Uncle R.A., I stopped by Aunt Emma's house and visited with her. She made me a glass of iced tea and we reminisced about old times. I always loved to stay with Uncle Virgil and Aunt Emma when I was a kid back on the farm in Content. She always had special food goodies around, and was always so good to me. If my prayers could be answered, she would never have to go to that hell hole.

Finally, I went back over to Sissy's house. Most everyone had gone home. Yane and her family had returned to brother James' house, and Cecil and his family were on their way back to Weatherford, and my Daddy was peacefully at rest next to Mama.

Sissy was totally exhausted. I told her to go upstairs and lie down, that I felt okay and would stay until everyone else was gone. She wasn't hard to convince, and I knew this had really been a hard day for her. She went directly to bed.

In the kitchen I joined Linda for one more cup of coffee. I told her how much the family had appreciated all she and her family had done. Of course, she was very modest and acted like she had done nothing. The more I got to know her, the more I could see why she was Kathy's best friend.

Dub stopped by again to say goodnight and let Sissy know they would be staying overnight with the James family. Yane was so exhausted, she was resting at brother James' house. Quite frankly, I was glad. I didn't want to see her anymore, or have any more confrontations with her. Dub didn't wake Sissy, for he knew how hard everything had been on her.

I visited with Dub for awhile, but I was very uncomfortable and it was obvious he was, too. We discussed how well everything went at the service and I told him how much I appreciated him making sure everything was taken care of appropriately for the service. Neither one of us mentioned what had transpired with his wife.

After a few minutes of chit-chat, he said, "Loraine and I decided you could just keep Vernon's car. That seems to be all that's left of his estate anyway, isn't it?"

"That's right, except for the bills." I couldn't believe what I was hearing, but I tried to be as diplomatic as possible. I knew Dub was only following instructions as usual. I continued, "And you can tell Yane not to concern herself. Daddy and I will handle his bills," I assured him.

He quickly said, "I know you will, and we're not worried about that."

He didn't mention anything about her wanting the will read, and I guess I should have been thankful she didn't demand her third of Daddy's 1978 Pontiac, which was worth approximately $1,500 at the time. I'm sure my family appreciated her generosity, too, since Daddy's car was their transportation back to Wisconsin.

I was exhausted—mentally and physically, so I called Mary to come and get me. Dub left to go back over to brother James' house, for they had planned to visit with his mother in Abilene the next day, then go back home. Within a few minutes, Mary was there to pick me up. I told Linda to tell Sissy I would see her the next morning, then said goodnight.

At Mary's house, everyone was in good form and spirits. M.J. said, "How about a Miller Lite?"

"Sounds great," I answered, and we sat around the living room and talked about old times. The kids decided to meet some of Michelle and Melinda's friends, and I was glad they were going out to have some fun. We had all been under such a strain. Now we were all relieved Daddy was home and at rest. The crying and worrying was over. Now came the time for healing. And I thought of the Bible, again... *A time to plant and a time to reap; A time to be born and a time to die,* from the Old Testament book, *The Preacher,* Ecclesiastes 3:11, and of course, a great song of the protest '60s, *Turn! Turn! Turn!* made so by The Byrds, with words rearranged for music by Pete Seeger.

Before the kids left, I told them how proud I was of them all, and how proud their Grandpa would have been of them. I gave Pam and Kim a kiss and said, "I could have never made it without you girls holding onto me today. I love you!" They told me they loved me, too, as they took off for the car.

I looked at Mary and said, "Maybe my family can get back to normal when we get home. This has been the tallest mountain the Lord ever gave me to climb." I laughed, "I'm not sure if I remember, though, what normal is."

Mary asked, "When do you go back?" I told her the kids planned to leave Friday morning early and I would be flying back Saturday. We needed a day to get ready to go back to work at the studios." Suddenly I remembered Leroy. "That reminds me, I need to call Leroy and give him my flight number and time of arrival." Mary teased, "Reta, who is Leroy?"

"Get that out of your mind! If I ever decide to get tangled up with another man, I hope someone takes me out and shoots me on the spot," I declared. And I meant it.

"Unless you find a good one like me," M.J. interjected with a smile. "Yeah, right," Mary scoffed, as she handed me the phone. I called Leroy and he assured me he would be there.

About an hour later, the kids got home. It didn't take long to see all the sights in Winters. Everyone was really tired, so we pulled out our bed rolls. The kids headed for the back of the trailer with Mary's family, and left me all alone in the living room so I could raise the roof again. Before I fell asleep, I thanked The Guy Upstairs for seeing to it that everything went well at the funeral. Most of all, though, I thanked Him for helping me keep my mouth shut, and not letting my sister upset me. But instead of falling asleep, I laid awake for awhile and did some serious thinking. My body was tired, but my mind wouldn't let me sleep.

As a million thoughts raced around in my head, one thought began to stand out, and I knew I would never feel the same as I once had about Yane, whatever that originally meant. It made me sad because we are both products of Mama and Daddy, and I know we were created out of love, but I knew that after the funeral, I would never care about her or feel the need for her to love me, as I had throughout my life—even though it had always been a dead end. I knew I had my daughters, and knew they loved me—and that's all that mattered.

I remembered back when I was married to Chuck—Pam and Kim's dad. Yane had been bragging about how wonderful and good Nolita and Virlie were, brother James' daughters. It hurt me so because she didn't love me like that, and I guess I was just jealous of them because they had my sister's love and I didn't. Anyway, soon I was crying like my heart would break—I so wanted my sister's approval and love. Chuck had looked at me and said, "Reta, you've got to forget trying to make her love you. That's the way she is. A cold fish." He had continued, "Just look at Pam, Kim and me. You have three people right here that love you more than anything. Just give us all your love, and let her love whomever she chooses."

Well, it's taken a long time, Chuck, but after the way our daughters cared for me today, I know you were right back then. I don't need her love or approval anymore, and I certainly don't need her verbal abuse anymore.

As I drifted off to sleep, I decided if her family or anyone else believed the ugly things she might say about me, then I couldn't help it—that's not my responsibility, in other words. I promised myself I would never allow her to upset me again, and divorced myself emotionally from my sister from that moment on.

I woke up the next morning to the smell of bacon and eggs frying and coffee brewing. I put on my housecoat and went into the kitchen. There was a beautiful plant setting on the table, and I asked in a sleepy voice, "Where did that plant come from?" Mary handed me a cup of coffee, put her hand on her hip and said, "Well, that's the plant we bought for your Daddy, and after I saw the way your sister was giving them all away yesterday, I just took it home with me. I decided to wait until today to give it to you. I wanted you to have it, not anyone else."

Tears filled her eyes and I put my arms around her and said, "I'll take it back home and set it next to the African Violet Daddy gave me when I had my surgery." I knew, however, I was going to have a problem getting it home. The kids didn't have enough room to take it in the car, and it would freeze in the trunk. And I sure as hell didn't know how I was gonna get it on the plane. But I knew I one thing—I would get it home somehow.

Before long, the entire group was up. We all looked more rested than we had in weeks, and I ate the best breakfast I had eaten in weeks. Mary was an excellent cook, and with the pressure off, we sat around the table talking and cutting up. Monie said, "Is there anywhere around here where we could go dancing tonight? I feel like having a little fun." Of course, Pam, Kim, Cheryl, Michelle, Melinda and even Brad were in harmony. I couldn't help but wonder if they had planned this outing during their tour of the big city of Winters the night before. At any rate, it sounded good to me.

Then Mary said, "Why don't we go to the Badlands?" Kim quickly chimed in, "That's were Grandpa took us the last time we were here, wasn't it?"

"Yeah," I added, "Daddy went dancing down there just about every Saturday night," and in my mind's eye, I could just visualize Daddy standing in front of that little gold mirror I gave him, twisting his behind and chirping, "Gotta shake a leg tonight. Let's get going, Piss Ant." We'd jump in his little red Pontiac and head for the Badlands. I was usually the designated driver, but didn't mind.

Back in 1983, when I lived next to Daddy, Sissy's daughter, Kathy, and her boyfriend, Jackie Danford, used to go with us, and we had so much fun. Kathy was my favorite cousin, and I really missed her. My heart hurt for Sissy, for Kathy had been her life. I was so thankful Kathy had left a beautiful daughter, Tammy, to fill part of Sissy's broken heart.

Brad warned, "Just remember, all you girls, we're leaving for home in the morning." Everyone promised faithfully they would be ready to go when he said.

Then Monie said, "Reta, I was thinking. Why don't I get a ticket and fly back with you? That flight your sister put you on has got to have seats left."

I laughed, "If it were the same going back as it was coming down, probably so, but it's a nonstop going back. We can check and see how much it would be, though."

Pam said, "Mom, I would really like that 'cause right now I worry about you flying alone again."

"I'll be all right," I assured her. "But the company would be nice," I admitted.

Kim said, "What about work, Monie?" She immediately realized what she had just said. With Daddy's death, she didn't have a job anymore.

Monie quickly said, "Yeah, I'm unemployed for the moment, so I'll just call the airlines and get me a ticket, too. I could use another day off."

She called, and sure enough, they had an available seat. She asked, "Reta, would you put it on your credit card? I have money coming in before the payment is due so I can get it back to you."

"Sure," I said, as I took the telephone to give the credit card information to the clerk. I was glad to be able to help her after all the help she had given Daddy.

After breakfast, I got dressed and went over to Sissy's. She was sitting at her little kitchen bar, drinking coffee when I walked in. "Good morning, Dit. You sure look better."

"Let me tell you, I feel a hell of a lot better, too," she assured me. She poured me another cup of coffee and we discussed how well the funeral went. I didn't say anything about Yane, and neither did she. I felt comfortable with the decision I had made last night that I didn't even feel angry at my sister anymore. In fact, I didn't feel anything toward her at all. I had asked the Lord to take the hurt and anger from me, and now I believed He had answered my prayer.

I decided to go take care of the payment arrangements with Mike. I had no idea what Yane had said to him when she picked up the bill, but I wasn't going to let that bother me. I called Mike and he told me to come on down. In fact, Mr. Denim Blue was there from Daddy's insurance company.

I drove to the funeral home, and choked backed the tears as I entered. Mike and Mr. Blue were sitting in his office, and Mr. Blue hadn't changed a bit in all these years. There had been a Mr. Blue for as long as I could remember. He would come by our home occasionally, have coffee with Daddy and Mama and make sure their insurance needs were filled. I shook hands with him and he shared some wonderful memories with me.

Then he said, "I'm afraid the death clause in the insurance policy Vernon took out all those years ago didn't increase with the cost of rising funeral costs today. I talked to him about increasing it, Reta, but he was sure it was enough. You know how your dad was."

"Yes, I do Mr. Blue, but I do know he thought an awful lot of you," I replied, then handed Mike the bill and apologized for my sister interfering.

Mike said, rather confused, "I thought you had discussed it with Yane, and asked her to pick it up—or some of it." I could tell he was confused as to what was going on.

"My sister has a way of always poking her nose in my business, as you probably figured out by now, Mike. There's not a lot of love between us, but like I assured you when I got here, I will be totally responsible for the balance on Daddy's funeral bill. I don't want her or Cecil contacted," I said firmly.

He assured me they would not be contacted in any way. Then he said delicately, "The insurance only pays $1500.00, so it still leaves about $4,000.00." He looked at me for a reaction.

"Does that cover *Williamson's* funeral home and transportation, too?" I asked, for I didn't need any unnecessary surprises.

"Yes," he answered, "I've already taken care of them. This is the total balance." I was actually relieved because I thought I was going to have to pay everyone individually. We made an agreement on $50.00 a month or whatever I could handle, and I said, "Mike, I'll whittle away at this figure as best I can until every penny is paid. You'll never know how much I appreciate what you have done for Daddy and me." I gave him and Mr. Blue a hug, took the paperwork and walked out into the sunshine. I was so thankful the weather had been good for Daddy's homecoming.

I went back to Sissy's house and we visited for awhile, then I invited her to go to *The Badlands* with us. "I'm sure people will be talking about me going dancing the day after Daddy's buried, but what the hell!"

Sissy interrupted, "But hell, baby, if people are gonna talk, they're gonna talk anyway, no matter what you do. Just don't let 'em bother you. If I wanted to go dancing and have a good time, then that's just exactly what I would do."

I smiled and said, "You always know how to make me feel better."

I told her about the plant Mary wanted me to take home, and she started laughing as she tried to visualize me on the plane with that big plant, trying to get it back to Wisconsin without freezing. She was glad Monie was going back with me, too.

Awhile later, I went back over to Mary's and rested. The kids had everything packed, ready to put in Daddy's little red car and head for Wisconsin the next morning. Brad was told they would all be up and ready for the road early, with no griping.

As the afternoon approached, we started getting ready fairly early. The hair spray was flying, and with the scent of all our perfumes mixed together, M.J. said, "Brad, why don't you and me go put air in Vernon's tires."

"Sounds good to me," Brad chirped as they went out the door.

Mary and I talked about our high school days as we put on our makeup, and back-combed our hair. I put on a pair of new jeans and a white blouse, and even wore my white heels. My eyes looked better, but the circles were still visible.

Mary said, "What the hell, we can't stop the wrinkles," as she checked herself in the mirror.

"Mary, I just want to tell you again how much I've appreciated you throughout the last few years, taking care of Daddy's laundry and for being there when he needed anything. Especially for all the times I called when I was worried about him, and you or M.J. would run over and check on him for me, and for taking care of the kids when they're down here, not to mention spoiling them rotten with your great Texas burgers. You know I do love you guys!" I said, and my eyes filled with tears.

"Now hush," she said, "before we both start blubbering and ruin our makeup. We love you guys, too, and you know we loved Vernon. Besides, your kids are like mine," and she went back to messing with her hair again. Then she started to laugh. "By the way, did Vernon ever tell you about all the gossip that got out into town about me and him?" she asked.

I shook my head and said, "Seems like he said something about that, but fill me in," I replied.

"Well, as the story goes, someone saw me coming out of his house early one morning. True enough. I went over to pick up his laundry, and the tongues started wagging. I guess we were the gossip of the town for months!" she chuckled. "And the way your sister looked at me yesterday at the funeral, I'm sure she's had her ears filled, too."

"That probably explains her actions over the plant you and M.J. sent Daddy when he was in the hospital back in 1984. She was reading off the name cards on the flowers to Daddy that were sent to him, and when she got to yours, she did her famous eye-rolling and, in her holier-than-thou voice, said, 'Oh, these are from Mary Casey.' She then quickly put the card back before she caught something. It was obvious you were not one her favorite people," I said laughing. Mary started laughing, too.

I then said, "Well, I wouldn't worry about it. Like Daddy always said, 'If they're talking about you, they're letting some other poor soul rest.'"

The girls yelled, "Are you two about ready?" "Now listen to that," Mary quipped, "Before long they will be trying to raise us." We both walked out, and the girls started whistling and telling us how young we looked. Mary said, "You're still paying for your own beer tonight, but we'll take all the compliments you guys will dish out!"

About that time, Brad and M.J. pulled up in front, and we all loaded up—M.J., Mary and I in their car, and the kids in Daddy's little red Pontiac—and headed for *The Badlands.*

It was sad to look back and see that little red car heading for the Badlands without Brody in it. I couldn't help but remember all the fun we'd had. I looked over at Mary and knew she was thinking the same thing. She and M.J. had gone with Daddy many times to the Badlands, too. Suddenly, I started laughing and asked, "Do you guys remember when Daddy got picked up on his way back from he Badlands and they took him to the Ballinger jail?"

"No," Mary laughed, "When was that?"

"It was back around 1980. This was before Daddy realized his high blood pressure pills and beer didn't mix. Anyway, he had been to the stock sale in San Angelo and decided to stop by the Badlands and have a beer before he headed back home. He still had his white pickup then. The cops pulled him over, and of course, Daddy knew all the cops in the area and they knew him, so he wasn't worried. But this time, it was a young new cop he didn't know. The young officer checked Daddy's driver's license, then said, 'Step out of your truck, Mr. Fuller.' Daddy stepped out and the young cop said, 'Mr. Fuller, will you take a breathalyzer test?' Well, Daddy was so insulted, he looked him up and down, then said, 'Well, you young stupid little sonofabitch, I damned sure won't. I've only had two beers. I just stopped on my way back from the stock sale in San Angelo and was on my way back to Winters. That's the stupidest thing I've ever heard!'"

Mary laughed and asked, "What did the cop do?"

"That's exactly the question I asked Daddy when he told me about it, and after he stopped laughing, he said, 'Well, hell, that young, stupid little sonofabitch took me to jail!' He never did take that breathalyzer test, though. You know how stubborn Daddy was. He got Uncle R.A. to bail him out, but he was on probation!"

By now, M.J. was really laughing. "That must have been when we lived in Odessa 'cause I'm sure the town was buzzing about that when the paper came out."

"Yeah," I laughed, "Daddy was pretty embarrassed, but the judge went easier on him after he found out about the high blood pressure pills he was taking, and informed Daddy they didn't mix with alcohol."

Mary chuckled, "What did your sister say about that?"

"Frankly, I don't know if she ever found out. I sure didn't tell her, and I guarantee you Daddy didn't. He didn't even tell me until he decided to come live with me in 1982," I said. "We had sold his house, furniture and even his white pickup and were getting ready to take off in a few days. He finally had to 'fess up. Boy, was he embarrassed! 'Reta," he had said, 'I got to go see the probation officer about me moving out of state.' He had then told me the entire sad story, and after I quit laughing, I said, 'Well, let's go, you teenage delinquent.'

"We went to Ballinger and got all the paperwork signed. That was the first time I signed to be responsible for him." I paused for a moment, then continued, "We then took off for Wisconsin."

"When did he come back to Winters?" Mary asked. I laughed, "Oh, about two weeks later. You know he couldn't stand to be that far from big Ol' Texas. He came back and bought that little green house, and set up housekeeping again. I wish he would have stayed with me, or I would have stayed down here in 1983. Then he would be going with us tonight," I sighed.

"How do you figure you could have prevented the stroke?" M.J. asked, downplaying her question, but I could tell she wanted to know.

"I would have made sure he took his Lopresser pills on the right schedule. That's what caused the stroke, you know. Cecil and I found bottles dated back two months that he hadn't even opened when we packed his things after the stroke. He had the prescription filled each month, but didn't remember to take the pills. That's why I was so upset when he left to come back after his last visit to Wisconsin. If I didn't remind him to take his medication, he would forget. One day, while he was there, I said, 'Daddy, what do you do when you forget to take your pills?' He just laughed and said, 'Oh, I just take two the next time.' So you see, if I had been with him, I would have made sure he took his medication on time, and that might have prevented that damned stroke."

Mary could tell I was thinking too much and getting upset, so she quickly said, "Well, Vernon was a big boy, and he was just like my dad, one of those stubborn ol' Texans. They did things the way they wanted to, and no matter what we told them, they were still gonna do what they wanted to do. Vernon wanted to stay independent. I know he never thought he would ever wind up like he did. I think he believed he would go fast like his sister, Lois, so quit punishing yourself. You did all you could do. Now let's have some fun!"

Just then M.J. said, "Well, here we are." Mary looked at her watch and said, "Great! The band will be starting any time."

We pulled in, and the kids pulled in right behind us. We all got out and went inside.

I don't know what I was expecting, but when I walked in everything looked the same as it had when I was there last with Daddy. I knew for sure Daddy would want us to have fun. Kim and Pam looked around, then grabbed a big table, and Brad pulled another one over to make it even bigger. It was obvious everyone was ready to relax and have some fun. I didn't say anything, but I knew the girls grabbed that particular table because it was the one we all had sat at the last time we had been down here with Daddy. None of us mentioned it—just our unsaid secret.

After getting our table together, I glanced around the club for familiar faces, and was surprised to see how many were looking back at me. So many of Daddy's old friends were there. One lady named "Tiny" came over. She said she remembered me singing the last time I was there with Daddy and gave me her condolences. Then she asked, "Are you gonna sing for us tonight? I know the band would love to have you sit in, but if you don't feel like it, we'll all understand." I looked around and knew Daddy's old friends would like for me to sing, so I smiled and said, "Okay, I'll do one for Daddy."

"Great! Everyone will be so happy," she said and rushed off to talk to the band about getting me up. I went around the room and visited with several of Daddy's old friends. They were all missing him, too, and many asked how he did up north. I filled them in as much as possible, and they were all surprised to hear how far he had come back, and about the rehabilitation he received. They thought when a person had a stroke, or just got old, they were sent straight to a nursing home until they died. I gave them hope for a better tomorrow.

Soon the band leader came over and introduced himself to me. He remembered my dad, too, and said, "Yeah, Vernon always requested Waltz Across Texas."

"That never changed," I replied, thinking back. "He still enjoyed that song after the stroke, and my band in Wisconsin always sang it for him, too." He said, "We'll kick things off, then call you up." I nodded back.

Before long, the band started, and we ordered a round of drinks and everyone was having a good time. I was glad we had come, no matter what anyone might say. Like Daddy always said, "If they're talking about you, then they're letting some other poor soul rest!" I was enjoying myself, and the others were, too.

After two or three songs, the band leader said, "We have a very special guest with us tonight, and all the way from Wisconsin, though she was born and raised right here in Texas! Let's give a big Texas welcome to Miss Reta Lee!" The round of applause brought tears to my eyes, and I remembered how proud Daddy was of me the last time I got up at the Badlands and sang for him and his friends. The band had recognized him that night, too, when they had called me up. They had said, "Let's welcome Vernon Fuller's daughter, Reta Lee!" Daddy had smiled from ear to ear that night.

I really didn't feel like singing, but the kids, Mary, M.J. and of course, Daddy's old friends put me in the mood. To break the ice I sang the old standard, *Jambalaya*. I paused for a moment, looked at the band and said, "Key of G," then said, "I'm gonna sing this next song in memory of my Daddy, Vernon Fuller, and for all his wonderful friends here tonight!" I fought back the tears, and with all the courage I could muster up, started singing, *They Don't Make 'Em Like My Daddy Anymore.*

When the song was over, the round of applause I received was overwhelming, especially from my table. The kids knew the entire story behind that song and how hard it was for me to sing it. I said, "Let's have a hand for this wonderful band, and thanks for sharing your stage with me!" I quickly took my seat. I didn't dare push my luck, for the tears were too close.

Pam said, "Mom, I have to give you credit. I don't know how you did it." Kim echoed, "Me either, but grandpa would really be proud." Coming from my daughters, that was the best compliment I could have received. I then got up and visited with more of Daddy's old friends and danced with a few. We all had a really good time, but Brad reminded all of us about heading home the next morning, so we left before midnight.

When we got back to Mary's house, I was really tired, but felt good that I had brought a little joy to some of Daddy's old friends. Plus Mary and M.J. hadn't heard me sing since the last time I had got up at The Badlands. I also felt good that I had given a few old folks a hope for something better than just getting old and going into a nursing home to wait to die.

MORNING CAME TOO SOON. THE GIRLS GOT UP JUST as they promised. We had breakfast, then helped Brad get everything loaded in Daddy's little red Pontiac. The kids said goodbye to Mary and her family, then Monie and I rode over to Sissy's house with them to say goodbye to Sissy and Tammy.

Pam said, "Mom, I dread telling Sissy goodbye. I just know I'm gonna start cryin' again!"

"Well, you wouldn't be a normal female in this family if you didn't cry. That's one thing we do real well," I assured her.

Brad mumbled, "Ain't that the damned truth. I've never heard so much bawling in my life. Grandpa would kick all your butts!"

"Oh, hush, Brad!" Pam barked. "What do you know about it!"

Sissy was having coffee when we got there, and she looked so much more rested. "I don't think I've done anything but sleep since the funeral, but I do feel better." We visited for a while, then Brad said, "The bus is leaving for Wisconsin. All aboard!" Then he gave Sissy a hug and headed for the door.

Meanwhile, we all lived up to our heritage and we had a tearful good bye. I said, "I'm not bawling anymore. I'll see you guys tomorrow night. Now drive carefully, Brad. You know you're carrying precious cargo."

He grinned and said, "I know! I'll get 'em home okay." I reminded him he was part of that special cargo, too.

Pam sadly said, "Mom, we are gonna stop at the cemetery and say goodbye to Grandpa and Nan Nan." I smiled through my tears and said, "That would be nice. Then you can see for yourselves he is completely at rest."

After the hugs and kisses, they drove off. I watched Daddy's little red car as long as I could see it, and asked God to watch over my little family and get them home safely. Then Sissy and I blew our noses and joined Monie and Tammy for some more of that good ol' Texas coffee.

As we drank our coffee, we visited for awhile, then Tammy said, "Well, Nan Nan, I need to head back to Fort Worth." She gave us a hug and away she went.

Monie, Sissy and I visited for a while, then I gathered my things up and started getting ready for our trip back to Wisconsin the next day. Sissy asked, "Baby, have you figured out how you're gonna take Mary's plant back?"

Monie started laughing, "I think we are going to have to buy a seat for it!"

"I'm gonna take it to the airport in the morning and hope they'll let me take it aboard," I said.

"Do you want me to take you to the airport, or is Mary taking you?" Sissy asked.

"I'll just get Mary to take me so you can get some more rest before you go back to the boat," I replied.

"Hell," she said, "I'm gonna be so lazy, they'll probably fire me!"

Mary came over later, and we all sat around Sissy's little kitchen bar and talked the rest of the day away and into the wee hours. Finally, Sissy said, "Baby, you better get some rest so you'll be ready to get everything back to normal when you get home."

"I hate to think of going back," I sighed.   "I just know my students' mothers are going to be yelling, 'Where have you been?'"

"Wasn't Karen going to call and let them know about Grandpa?" Monie asked.

"Yeah, if she saw the note I left—" I answered. "If she didn't call, there'll be hell to pay. I wish I could take the next few months off, but like you, Sissy, we've got to take care of ourselves—and that means working for a living."

"Ain't that the damned truth," Sissy sighed.

VERNON IN THERAPY AT THE APPLE RIVER HOSPITAL, AMERY, WISCONSIN. WITH PROPER REHABILITATION AND *"THE INGREDIENT CALLED LOVE"* HE HAD TOTALLY ACCEPTED THE RIGHT SIDE OF HIS BODY. OTHER THAN BEING IN A WHEEL CHAIR, THE STROKE WAS NOT TOO OBVIOUS BEFORE WE LOST HIM TO KIDNEY FAILURE.

11

WE GOT UP EARLY THE NEXT MORNING AND HAD coffee with Sissy. Mary came over, and right on time. We put our suitcases in the car, along with the monster plant that Mary had wrapped like a brand new baby. Monie gave Sissy a hug and thanked her for the generous hospitality, and Sissy assured her she was always welcome.

I put my arms around Sissy and said, "I'm gonna make this fast. I think we've cried enough tears for awhile. I love you and appreciate you beyond words—"

She choked up, gave me a big hug and said, "I love you, too, Baby."

I held back the tears until we were out of sight, and I know she did the same thing.

I asked Mary to stop by the cemetery for a few minutes. Daddy and Mama's graves still had the flowers on them, but they were wilting fast and looking a little forlorn..

While I stood by their graves and thought back, I felt total relief, for I knew in my heart Daddy was now next to Mama—where he had wanted to be after all those years apart from her. I also knew that Daddy was glad this chapter in our lives was over, as was Pam, Kim and myself. Although the past year had been the biggest mountain the Good Lord had ever given me to climb, I will never regret taking care of Daddy during his time of need. Even in his condition he had been a joy, and I had come to truly love my new Daddy. I whispered, "Goodbye, I love both of you with all my heart!" then climbed back into the car.

Without a word, Mary headed for the airport in Abilene.

MARY GOT US TO THE AIRPORT WITH PLENTY OF time to spare, and we were able to board early. We were so happy when the stewardess took the monster plant and safely placed it on board. I felt relieved that the plant would make it home with me, and Monie shared my happiness.

As the airplane was pushed back for take-off, I looked out the window and saw Mary. She stood there waving as the little passenger plane took off for Dallas.

In Dallas we caught our connecting flight with no problem, the plant was transferred and stored on board the new plane, and it seemed only a short time before the pilot announced we would be landing in Minneapolis in a few minutes. The flight was going quicker than I thought, probably because my mind was playing the events of the last several days over and over. I knew I wasn't ready to go back to the old grind, for I felt like there was no get-up-and-go left in me. Poor Monie! I'm sure I wasn't good company for her.

My mind went back to 1983 when I lived next to Daddy. I was burning the candle at both ends, as he used to say, and one day I came running into his house. Daddy had said, "Reta, you better slow down and start taking care of yourself or one day you're gonna break, just like ya' Mama did one time. Now I'm telling you, you better slow down and pay attention to your health while you still got it!"

As I sat there on the plane, I wondered if that was my problem—maybe I'd pushed myself too hard and finally bottomed out.

Our plane landed, Monie and I retrieved the monster plant and deplaned. I wondered if Leroy would be there to pick us up as we walked into the terminal.

As we entered the terminal, there was Leroy standing in the waiting section holding one red rose. He gave me a big hug and said, "Welcome home!" as he handed me the slightly frozen rose. He took the monster plant, and laughed when we told him about the adventure we had with it. Quickly, he retrieved our baggage, and before we knew it, we were in his truck and on our way back to Amery.

During the drive, I filled him in on the funeral and assured him I was all right, but inside I didn't know for sure. I had started to relax and my body was telling me I needed a long rest. Fortunately, Monie did most of the talking. I just sat and relaxed, trying to focus on what had to be done as soon as I got home. My mind just didn't want to quit!

The divorce from the weasel would be coming up the twenty-first, and I sure would be glad when that was over. I laughed to myself as I thought about the reaction he would have when he found out he was actually going to get to keep his stupid house, along with all the payments that would go with it.   I could just imagine the whining he would do to his newest girlfriend about having to make all those payments. Of course, I knew she would be making them, if they were made at all. Poor thing! I hoped she could afford him and his women. It was a relief just knowing I would soon be rid of that poor excuse for a man and out from under all those bills.

Leroy asked, "Are you girls hungry?"

"Yeah," Monie chirped, "I could eat a skunk."

Leroy laughed, "We'll try to do better than that!"

After a few minutes of silence, I thought out loud, "I wonder if the kids are home yet?" and sighed. "If I know them, they drove straight through again. They were already half way when they called early last night."

"Don't worry about them, Reta. Brad will get them home safe and sound," Leroy assured me as we pulled into Wayne's Restaurant in Amery.

As we sat at the restaurant waiting to order, I realized I was more hungry than I had thought. Everything on the menu looked good, but I decided on a sandwich and some more coffee. I said, "Drinking so much coffee is probably what's wrong with my stomach. It's been churning for the past few days."

Monie agreed, then reminded me of the ulcers Dr. Rimestad thought I had. She said, "Now I hope you start taking care of your health, and quit worrying so much."

I laughed. "Maybe I can stop breathing, too! That would be just about as easy."

When we had finished our meal, Leroy insisted on picking up the tab, saying, "It's my treat!" Monie and I both thanked him for his thoughtfulness as we all went out to the truck. Soon we were on our way home.

I was really hoping the kids would be there, because I dreaded going back into the house alone. All the past was liable to rush back and overwhelm me because there would be so many memories of Daddy, everywhere. I was glad that Brad and his friends had taken down the hospital bed in my bedroom, and the girls had packed away all the supplies. I don't think I could have handled having to see it when I went to bed.

Leroy pulled into the driveway and my heart skipped a beat when I saw the lights on. As we pulled up in front of the house, there was Daddy's little red Pontiac, and I thanked God for getting my little team home safe.

As we pulled up, the kids came running our to greet us. They had been home about thirty minutes, and after the hugs and kisses, we went inside.

The telephone was ringing off the hook, and Pam said, "Mom, I don't think Karen called any one. The answering service is full of mothers screaming, and the telephone hasn't stopped since we got here."

Great! I thought, just what I needed! Another problem the minute I hit the door. Monie brewed a pot of coffee and when I smelled it I realized that I really needed some. I swear I'd had so much coffee the last few days that if I stopped drinking it now, I would topple over.

Kim said, "The mail is on the table but it's mostly bills." I started going through it, and sure enough, that's just about all there was—more bills. I put them aside and sipped on a fresh cup of coffee.

Then, Brad said, "Reta, I hate to tell you this, but we blew two more tires on the way back. I was able to pick up some more pretty cheap..."

"But those were brand new!" I interrupted. "What made them blow?"

"Well, I had hoped they would be okay, 'cause they sold you recaps, and some times you get a bad bunch. I guess that's what happened. Don't worry though, I've got everything taken care of," he assured me.

Pam was diligently trying to take the calls and explain why we weren't at classes last week and suddenly I could have choked Karen for not calling my students—of all times for her to let me down!

Angry, I started listening to the messages on the answering service. The first calls were all the same—mothers screaming, "Where were you?"

Then Karen's voice was next, and I could tell she was practically in tears. "Babe, I know I let you down when you really needed me, but I didn't know what I was gonna say to you. Knowing how important your Dad was to you, I guess I just took the cowards way out. Call me when you get home. I promise I'll be there for you this time!"

She sounded so pitiful, I couldn't stay mad at her. I realized how much she had been through with her family, and still needed comforting herself. My anger towards her began to dissipate.

The next message was from a man, and it was the landlord from the studio in Cumberland. "Reta, I'm sorry to tell you this, but we had some water damage at the building where you are renting, and you will be unable to teach there anymore. If I can think of somewhere else for you to move your studio, I will let you know. I'm really sorry."

"Me, too," I screamed as I took off my glasses and threw them across the room. "What in the hell does everyone want from me, blood? For God sakes, can't they let me get unpacked before they start tearing at me? I've only been home fifteen minutes and look at what's happened!"

I was crying uncontrollably, and right in the middle of my outburst, the telephone started ringing, again. I grabbed the phone and yelled, "I'm sorry, but my father died last week and I took him home to Texas and buried him next to my mother! And, yes, we will make up the classes missed or refund your damn five dollars, and I'm sorry you were inconvenienced. My secretary was unable to contact everyone on such a short notice!" then slammed it down again so hard it bounced off of it's cradle and lay on the floor.

As I glanced around the room, the kids were all sitting very quiet, and so were Monie and Leroy. I guess they figured I had lost my mind, and for a moment I think I had. You could have heard a pin drop. Suddenly, I realized what I had done and started laughing hysterically. "I can't believe I just did that!" I said between fits of laughter. "I wonder who that was on the telephone," and by this time everyone was laughing with me.

Leroy said, "Well, I betcha one thing, they don't call back."

Slowly I regained my composure, and Monie handed me a Miller Lite. I grabbed one of her cigarettes and snarled, "I'll quit again later!" and glared at everyone just daring them to object. Believe me, after my outburst, no one was gonna argue with me about that cigarette!

Brad unplugged the telephone so I couldn't scream at any more callers, then popped open a Gatorade. He sat down and mumbled, "That'll take care of that damned phone!"

"Reta, why don't you let Leroy run you over to Karen's house and spend the night with her? In fact, I can't think of a better time to start being her roommate than right now," suggested Monie.

Pam and Kim echoed her. Pam said, "Mom, we will start packing in the morning to move to the blue house. You just try to relax and figure out what we're gonna do about the studios. Whatever you decide to do will be fine with us," she assured me. "I'd just soon get a day job myself."

"Me, too, but I think we should just get the hell outta' Dodge!" Kim said.

Instantly my ears perked up. That was the first thing I had heard in a long time that made any sense, and I said, "Kim, maybe you're right. Maybe we should just get the hell outta' Dodge. I would like nothing more than to just dump this house, start singing full time and never again have to teach the Shuffle Hop-step."

Kim had definitely given me some food for thought. I knew after my big outburst that I was in no condition to continue with the studios or be pulled at anymore. I also knew I had to make some major changes in my life, or wind up in a mental institution.

I told the kids they were right, I did need to get out of there and try to get myself together. I gave them a hug and again told them how much I appreciated them. Then I turned to Leroy and asked if he would mind driving me to Karen's.

"Sure," he answered, then put me in his truck and we headed for Amery.

On the way to Karen's, I thanked Leroy for picking us up at the airport and driving me around. I kind of felt sorry for him, and didn't want to scare him with my outrageous behavior.

He just smiled and said, "I understand, Reta. I don't know how you've done it all this time. Remember, if you need anything, just let me know." He turned and smiled at me again, and I felt a lot better.

KAREN'S LIGHTS WERE ON WHEN WE GOT   THERE.
She was so embarrassed about what had happened, and through big tears
said, "I'm so sorry! I'm such a coward!"

"It's okay, Karen, I understand. I know what you've been through,
so let's not even discuss it," I said, and consoled her with a hug.

Karen invited us into the kitchen and fixed Leroy and me a Bacardi
Coke. It was so peaceful at her little trailer. The telephone was quiet, and I
knew I was safe from complaining mothers until I returned home. Then I
started feeling like a coward for leaving the kids to face all those memories
in the house, especially with all of Daddy's clothes and things still
downstairs. Waves of panic swept over me, and I knew I was either having
a nervous breakdown, or was losing my mind.   All I wanted was for
everyone to leave me alone!

Karen interrupted my brief reverie and asked, "When is your
divorce date with that little f---er?"

"Oh, my gosh! I had put that out of my mind, or maybe there isn't
any room in my mind for it," I laughed, "but it's coming up in four days, as
a matter of fact."

"Are you still giving him everything?" she asked.

"For sure," I said. "He can have it all and the bills that go with it.
The kids are going to start packing in the morning because they've rented
that farmhouse I told you about," then laughed. "They've already named it
the blue house and can't wait to get out of the present house, too. There's
too many bad memories there!"

Leroy agreed. "I think you've made the right decision, Reta. Just
lick your wounds and consider that house a nice place you provided for
your Daddy to spend his last days."

"You're right, Leroy," I said. "At least I had a nice place to bring
my Daddy to die." Then I said sarcastically, "Anyway, it'll be a couple of
years yet before the foundation completely crumbles under that house the
weasel built."

Karen gave out one of her robust laughs, "I hope the little f---er is
in there when it goes!" and we all laughed together.

After we had finished our drinks, Leroy said, "I'm gonna take off
so you can get some rest."

I got up and put my arms around him. "How can I thank you for
all you've done?" I asked softly.

He just smiled and answered, "Just stay my friend."

"Forever," I promised.

After he had left, Karen said, "Reta, he wants to be more than just
your friend."

"Oh, no!" I assured her, "I've already told him I would never be more than just a good friend." I paused, "I just hope he will remember that. Why can't men just be happy being a friend?" I asked.

"Because of what hangs between their legs, that's why," she laughed. "Besides, all women are just a conquest to them. So if you become a bitch like me, they'll leave you alone! Personally, I wouldn't give you two cents for all of 'em."

"Well, after I go through this last round with the weasel, I might feel the same way," I said with a laugh. Then the beer and the Bacardi Coke caught up with me, and I told Karen I had to go to bed. She showed me my bed and said "Good-night!" and as soon as I laid down, I fell into a deep sleep.

THE NEXT MORNING OVER COFFEE, I TOLD KAREN all about the trip, the funeral, all the hell that broke loose after I got home and about Kim's idea to get outta' Dodge!

"I think Kim's right. You should just close some of those damn studios and go back singing full-time. Quite frankly, I don't see how you put up with all those little f----ers anyway!" Karen said.

"That reminds me," I said. "Did you find the note I left asking you to call my students about classes being canceled last week?"

She paused for a moment then said, "Yeah, but it was too late to call them after I got back and found it. I stayed down in the city with my daughter for two days. Damn, I'm sorry for letting you down like I did."

"That's okay," I assured her, "you might have done me a favor, because I'm seriously thinking about gettin' outta' Dodge! Some of my parents have been really supportive and understanding, but it only takes a few bad apples to spoil the entire barrel. Pam and Kim have tried so hard to keep them happy, and have done such a great job teaching. None of them really have anything to complain about, and if they can't understand about last week, then I don't want to be associated with them! You know, there's always got to be those few that ruin it for everyone," I concluded.

After a bit, I called Don Novitzke and told him of my plan to give the house to Steve along with all the bills that go with it. I made it perfectly clear that I didn't want to be stuck with any bills since he would be getting all the assets. "All I want is my Pontiac Firebird back, free and clear, and he can have everything else. Of course, he's already taken everything he could carry out that's worth anything, since you never stopped him!" I said accusingly.

Of course he gave me some legal mumbo-jumbo as to why he never enforced the restraining order, but assured me he would handle everything as I asked and promised I would get the Firebird.

However, I didn't really have a lot of faith in him—after all, he hadn't done a thing throughout the past eight months to keep Steve from taking things out of the garage. The weasel even took a new electric drill out of the pump house I had bought for Brad to work with. Brad had to put everything away when he left, because we never knew when the weasel would slither out to the house and rip-off something else.

Finished with the attorney, I got dressed and went out to the house. I felt like a total zombie, and my mind felt completely shut down. I just wanted to get the divorce over with, see the kids moved into their new place, then runaway for awhile.

The kids were busy as little bees when I got to the house. Brad, Rusty and Danny were already loading boxes to take to the blue house, and Pam, Kim, Cheryl and Monie were packing so fast I was scared I was going to wind up in a box! I was glad I had already moved most of my personal things to Karen's house during Daddy's illness, or they might never have surfaced again.

Pam said as she came up the stairs carrying another box, "Well, Mom, have you decided what we're gonna do with the studios?"

"If you guys will take a few minutes and sit down, I will tell you what I would like to do," I answered. Everyone stopped, opened a pop and gathered around the sofa where I had already collapsed. Every eye was on me as I began, "I feel so bad that I have dumped so much on you guys, I don't feel right leaving all of this packing to you."

"You'd just be in our way," Monie laughed and interrupted. "We're actually having fun! It's like we're all starting a new life, and although everyone loves you, Pam and Kim are looking forward to having their own place."

"You don't feel bad about that do you, Mom?" Pam asked nervously, no doubt not wanting to hurt my feelings.

"Of course not," I answered, "I haven't always been a mom. I was once just like you, and I remember how much I wanted to have my own place, too! Actually, it makes my decision much easier," I confessed.

"Why?" Kim asked.

"Well, honey, you really got me to thinking last night when you said let's get outta' Dodge. You were right! That's exactly what I need to do, but there's just one problem."

"What's that?" Pam asked anxiously.

"The studios," I replied. "I don't want to teach right now, and in fact I don't even want to go back singing right now. I just want, more than anything in this world, to get in Daddy's little car and go away somewhere for awhile, by myself, to think and try to get my body to function like it used to. I know I'm physically and mentally falling apart, and after that outburst last night, I'm sure you agree!"

Monie chuckled, "I'll drink to that, but it had to feel good to tell one of them off."

"Yeah," I agreed, "providing it was one of them on the telephone."

"This is true," she replied.

By this time, I had everyone's full attention. "Where do you want to go, Mom?" Kim asked.

"Anywhere! I just want to be alone to try and find myself again. It's time for me to take another step forward in my life, too, just like it is for you. The only way I can do this, though, is..." and I paused and looked straight at Pam and Kim.

"What, Mom?" Pam asked.

I repeated, "The only way I can do this is for you and Kim to take over the studios. You need jobs, and you would be able to keep all the income." They sat there for a moment as though they were in shock.

"Mom, do you think we can do it?" Pam asked slowly.

I laughed. "Pam, you and Kim have been the backbone of the studios ever since Daddy had the stroke. Of course you can do it, but now you'd be getting a good paycheck you could cash."

"What would you live on?" Kim asked in a concerned voice.

"Don't worry about me! I'll join another band or take a secretarial job. I would be fine if I knew you girls would be all right," I said. I could tell their minds were running one hundred miles per hour.

Finally, Pam said, "Could we just keep Ladysmith and Clear Lake Studios? The other ones have just about all folded anyway, and if some of those mothers continue to badmouth the studios like they have been, they'll make life a living hell for us."

"I know," I replied. "The sad part of it is, there's only five or six that have really been terrible. But believe me, I understand. They've ruined it for me, too!"

Anyway, to answer your question, yes, I'll close all of the studios except for Ladysmith and Clear Lake, if that's what you want. The Cumberland Studio is already closed due to no fault of ours, and the Spooner and Luck Studios lost so many students over the holidays, they wouldn't be that big of a loss, either. I just hate to abandon those students who have been so understanding and loyal, but I have to think of us now."

I took a deep breath, then continued. "My health is going down really fast. If I don't make some major changes in my lifestyle immediately, I'm going to wind up in the hospital and wouldn't be able to teach anyway." We hashed it over until we all three agreed on our plan of attack.

"I'll make up a letter and we will send it out to everyone and just hope they will understand," Monie said. "If not, it will be their problem, not ours."

"I don't care what they think! Right now my Mom is the most important one," Pam assured everyone as she put her arms around me, quickly followed by Kim.

After a few hugs and kisses I said, "I'll turn the business checkbook over to you girls. It will totally be all yours. You will have to make refunds to those students who have prepaid for their recital costumes in the studios we're closing, but I'll try to help with those funds once I am productive again," I assured them.

"Don't worry about it, Mom. We'll make it. Monie assured us she would handle all the books and telephone work," Kim said.

In other words, Monie was going to be an extension of me, and I will always love her for volunteering her help and support to both me and the girls. I had really leveled with her about the way I felt, both physically and emotionally, during our flight back from Texas, so she knew how sick I really was and how desperately I needed to get away from all the pressures.

After we discussed many more aspects of the business, Pam and Kim were beginning to like the idea of running their own business. After all, they knew the kind of money I had always made teaching, and in fact, I had raised them with my baton, ballet and tap shoes, and if I say so myself, "I didn't do half bad!" My singing career had always been supplemental money, plus something I did for myself as a person. I guess that little girl's dream of singing at the Grand Old Opry had never really died, just faded some through the years. The studios, though, had always been my bread-and-butter job.

When I finally left, Pam and Kim were busy making new plans for their studios. This was not the way I had planned for things to happen after they graduated, but I was so happy to see them excited about something for a change. The pressures I was feeling had also touched them more than they had let me know. Monie was already taking notes so they wouldn't forget any of their great ideas.

As I drove back to Amery, I felt tons of pressure off my back. Just to be done with the studio gave me great relief, and to know Pam and Kim were actually excited about taking them over gave me even greater relief.

We had planned to open dance studios all over the upper Midwest when they were growing up, but now it looked as though the Good Lord had made other plans for us. I prayed for Him to watch over my little girls and let their studios flourish. I also thanked Him for taking the responsibility off my back.

As walked into my new roommate's house, I felt great! Of course, I didn't know what the hell I was going to do, but whatever it was would be better than to continue the way I was.

Karen was busy making herself a new winter coat. She could sew just about anything she wanted to. She looked up at me and said, "Damn, it's good to see you smiling! What happened, did you talk to that Bob fellow?"

"No, but you know what? I'm glad you brought him up. I'm gonna give that some serious thought, and maybe I'll have time to take that hot air balloon ride now."

Karen laid her work aside, ready for gossip and said, "Okay, what the hell is going on?"

I poured us a cup of coffee and filled her in on all the plans. I told her how excited the girls were and how relieved I felt about the decision.

Her reaction was that she was happy for me, but like me she asked, "What the hell are you gonna do?"

For the first time in my life I felt only responsible for myself. It was the strangest feeling. Pam and Kim had just given me the most wonderful gift I had ever received—the freedom and chance to find Reta Lee and see who she really was and what she really wanted to be. I only wished I had the energy to pull myself up again, as I had done so many times in the past.

Karen and I finished our coffee and she went back to her sewing. I decided to call Cords and see if I still had a band. I was a little concerned about them because I hadn't heard a word since the flowers at the funeral home had arrived.

It was a good thing I called Cords. We ended up having a long talk and I told him of my plans. He was in total agreement with me, and as a matter of fact, he, Rick and Donnie were wanting to take some time out of the entertainment business to just be home with their families. "I have two kids I hardly ever see and my wife is ready to divorce me," he said.

This was just another sign to me that I had made the right decision to leave the area and start new somewhere else. I promised him I would stay in touch and thanked him for the beautiful bouquet sent to Daddy's funeral.

I then called Rick and Donnie to say "goodbye" and thank them for the flowers, too. They had both asked me the same question, "Where are you going?" and I had given them the same answer as I had given Karen and Cords—"Damned if I know, but wherever it is, I'm looking forward to getting there!"

After making the calls, I went back to my bedroom and unpacked the boxes I had brought back from the house, then laid down and tried to make some decisions about my future. My stomach was churning, so I got up and took some Maalox.

Karen yelled, "Is your stomach still bothering you?"

"Nosey!" I yelled back.

"You better call Dr. Rimestad and go in again. I know you've got ulcers!" she said as she walked into my bedroom.

"Maybe you're right. It seems like now that I have my life planned, my entire body is falling apart!" I complained.

"Your entire body has been falling apart for a long time," she laughed. "You just now have had the time to start listening to it," she explained.

I appreciated her concern, and to make her happy I called Dr. Rimestad to make an appointment. The nurse told me to come right in, and I looked at Karen and said accusingly, "Now see what you got me in to?"

I dressed and arrived at the doctor's office right on time. After Dr. Rimestad gave me his condolences, he started nagging at me again. He had nagged at me for nine years because I didn't take care of myself, and my answer had always been the same, "If I did what you told me to do, then I would never get you paid or any other bills paid! I would have to be rich to just take off and lay in a bed." I told him that again.

He just frowned at me and said, "Well, that's what you need, about a year off on total rest."

After he checked me over and I had told him about my stomach problems, he said, "Like I told you awhile back, I want to put you in the hospital and run some tests. I really believe you have a stomach full of ulcers."

This time I listened. "Okay," I surrendered, "I'll check into the hospital after my divorce, but until then could you go ahead as though the tests had been run, and you had found a stomach full of ulcers?"

He shook his head. "Will you ever take time out for your health."

"Yes," I replied, "when I can get the time. You know I have to get this divorce over with."

The doctor agreed I could wait as he wrote out some prescriptions for me. Then he said, "Call me next week and I'll make arrangements for you to check into the hospital. Now, you better call me," he warned.

I stopped by Chet's Pharmacy and filled my prescriptions, then went back to my new home. I called the kids and they were just about ready to take the last things over to their new home. Monie told me they had everything taken care of with the studios. The letter had been typed and sent to the ones they were going to close, and another letter was sent to Ladysmith and Clear Lake advising them I had health problems and was going to take an extended leave, but in the mean time, Pam and Kim would be teaching the lessons.

I was so proud of them—they had already taken over in great style. I knew they were going to be okay, so I laid down and started thinking about where I was going to start my new life.

All of a sudden I thought of my friends, Jeanie and Wendy Howell. They had always been after me to come visit with them in Sarasota, Florida, and I knew then where I was going. I quickly grabbed the telephone and called Jeanie. She was delighted to hear from me and wanted me to come down right away. "We'll help you open a studio, or if you want to start a band, we can help you with bookings or anything!" She really made me feel welcome.

After I hung up, I quickly yelled at Karen, "Well, I know where I'm going now!"

She fixed us a drink, then said, "Okay, I'm ready. Lay it on me."

I explained to her about my impulsive call to Jeanie, and about my decision to go to Florida. "It just popped into my head, and it seems so right!" I exclaimed.

Karen was in total harmony with me. "I just hate to lose you!" she said sadly.

"Don't worry," I assured her. "With Pam and Kim here, I'll be back real often."

"Yeah, Pam and Kim will join you wherever you go. You know the three of you won't be separated very long."

I paused for a moment, thinking how much I was going to miss my girls. We had never been separated very long, and I said, "I hope you're right, but we'll have to cross that bridge later."

THE NEXT DAY I WENT OVER TO THE KID'S HOUSE to visit with them. They were busy putting everything away. For some reason, I felt really strange. My things were there, but it was not my home. I told them how wonderful everything looked. Pam and Monie were working on the studio changeover and studio closings, while Kim and Cheryl were busy organizing their new house. Brad was busy in the garage trying to make room for the garage sale they had planned.

"Mom, wanna a *Miller Lite?*" Pam asked.

"Sure," I answered as I sat down and became a guest.

"Mom, I've got a really big favor to ask of you," Pam said as she handed me a beer.

"What's that," I asked curiously.

"Well, some of the Cumberland mothers are really mad because we are not going to find another building and continue classes. They also found out we were going to teach the last class in Luck. We decided to teach that one instead of refunding the money, but I'm not worried about the Luck mothers. Most of them have really been nice and understanding.

"Anyway, a couple of the mothers from Cumberland are planning to come over to Luck when I teach the last class. I know they are only coming over to rant and rave, and I don't want to deal with them. Can you help us?" Pam asked seriously.

My blood started to boil, for I knew the two women she was talking about. Actually, they were the main reason I didn't care to look for another studio location and continue to teach in Cumberland. With the exception of them, though, the other parents had been wonderful.

I just wasn't physically or emotionally able to try and relocate, plus try to deal with their attitudes. They had called repeatedly, with no regard for me or my family.

"Sure, honey, I'll take that class. No problem," I said quickly and she threw her arms around my neck and said, "Oh, thank you, Mom."

Actually, I kind of hoped those women would come over to Luck and start ranting and raving, because I couldn't think of anyone else more deserving to receive the wrath of one of my outbursts. The thought of such a confrontation made me smile.

As I enjoyed my beer, I marveled at the way Pam and Monie were handling the books. Monie was figuring up all the accounts and Pam was writing the refund checks. Together they had quite a system going. She and Kim had decided to refund the January classroom payments instead of teach them, with the exception of Luck.

Finally I told them about my plans to go to Sarasota. They were glad I was going to see Jeanie and Wendy, but sad I was leaving. Kim put her arms around my neck and started crying, "Mom, I'm gonna miss you so much!"

Pam quickly said, "Kim, shape up! You know Mom has to do this. Besides, maybe we'll go to Sarasota, too, if she gets studios going down there."

Brad, apparently only hearing part of the conversation, yelled from the kitchen, "Say what?"

Pam looked at him and barked, "Brad, you might as well get used to it. Where my Mom goes is where I'll probably wind up!"

"That goes for me, too," Kim yelled.

Brad opened a Gatorade and said, "Will you two girls ever cut the umbilical cord?"

"No!" they yelled in unison back at him as he went into the garage.

To smooth things over, I went out to the garage to talk with Brad. He said, "Well, if Pam goes, then I'll go, too. I don't have anything around here to stay for!"

I gave him a hug and again took the opportunity to tell him how much I appreciated all he had done. He just smiled and said, "Ain't that much, and by the way, before you go I'll put a CB radio in your car. They've got 'um on sale at Hardware Hanks this week."

"I'll pick one up," I assured him and went back into the house to be with the girls. I visited for a while, and they assured me everything was out of the weasel's house. He could have it back Friday after the divorce hearing.

My mothering instincts were in a turmoil. On one hand I was glad to see them adapt to life on their own so readily, but the other side felt hurt that they didn't need their Mom around anymore. I guess I was beginning to feel the empty nest syndrome, except I was the one leaving the nest.

Pam sensed the loss I was feeling first and said, "Mom, you know you can always come home!"

"Something seems wrong with that picture," I said laughing, "but I love it! I'm so proud of you guys. At least I don't have to worry about you getting along without me. It just shocks me at how fast you went into action."

"Well, we're like our Mom," Kim teased.

Just then the phone rang, and it was Karen calling to ask me to join her and some of our friends at *T.J.'s*. I agreed, then called my long time friend, Yvonne, and asked her to meet me there.

Then I told the kids good bye and headed for the door. As I took a second look at the rooms of the house, I said, "I hadn't noticed before, but I wonder why all the rooms are blue?" I laughed, "Now I see why you call it the blue house!"

As I drove out to *T.J.'s*, I felt so much more relaxed, but, it seemed the more relaxed I got, the more pain I felt. Maybe Karen was right—I had been falling apart and didn't take the time to recognize it. This new feeling of independence was starting to feel good, but physically and mentally I was very sick. All of a sudden the tears started and I couldn't stop them. I pulled over and cried for a while, then fixed my face and continued on to TJ's. After crying, I did feel better.

When I got to TJ's, everyone was there, including Yvonne. Leroy gave me a hug and said, "You sure look more rested!"

"Yeah, that's what happens when you retire," I laughed. "My only problem is, I don't have the money to retire."

"So when did that ever stop us?" Karen said, and everybody laughed.

I soon found out Karen had already filled everyone in on my leaving. Gary was looking pretty sad, and finally said, "You know, I'm really gonna miss you!"

I gave him a kiss and said, "I'll be back. I just need some time-out right now."

Yvonne gave me her 800 number and said, "You call everyday and let me know where you are, then I will call and let everyone else know. That would save on telephone calls."

"That's great thinking, Yvonne," I praised, "cause you know Pam and Kim will want to talk to me everyday." She got everyone's telephone number so she could keep them all informed of my whereabouts.

Unfortunately, we broke up fairly early. Everyone had to work but me. Karen said, "It's strange watching Reta relax. She used to make me so tired just watching her run, I would have to go home and take a nap!" We all had a good laugh, then everyone said goodbye and good luck, and we left.

I felt really loved as I drove back to Karen's trailer. Everyone was so supportive, and they honestly cared about me. I thanked God once again for the great friends He had given me.

Back at Karen's, I went to bed but not to sleep. I laid there and began to plan my trip to Florida. I figured I would have just enough money left on my credit card to get me to Sarasota, but then I would have to go to work immediately. The thought of work didn't bother me because I realized I would become bored if I didn't do anything while there.

Then my thoughts turned to the divorce. I was dreading it in some ways, but at the same time couldn't wait to get it over with and be done with that little bastard. Just two more days! I had planned to leave Daddy's car with Pam and Kim and take my Firebird to Sarasota. I had to laugh as I thought of that lazy, good-for-nothing Steve facing all those bills. I figured he would lose everything within three months, unless his new woman could afford to make the payments, finance his womanizing, plus take care of him and all his child support.

Karen drove up, for she had been bartending and had to close the bar, but I was too tired to get up. As I lay there, I started thinking about Bob. He had made me promise to call him if something should happen to my dad, or if I needed anything. After mulling it over, I decided I needed him, and promised myself I would call him the next morning. Maybe he would invite me to go on that hot air balloon ride again, and by golly, this time I would take it!

My thoughts started running wild, and I wondered if it was too late for him and I to have a relationship, or if he was still single. Maybe he wouldn't want to have anything to do with me. All these questions were running through my mind as I drifted off to sleep...

WHEN I WOKE UP THE NEXT MORNING, I WAS STILL thinking about Bob and asked Karen what she thought about me calling him.

"You've been hung up on him for a long time, so I think you should call him and see what happens. Besides, I still haven't met him!" Trust Karen for logical reasons!

"I don't think he'll be coming this way for awhile," I said, "and I'll be gone by then."

"Think positive!" she scolded. "Maybe he'll send you an airline ticket and you can join him for that rest and relaxation you need."

I had to laugh. "That does sound nice!" and got up to pour myself another cup of coffee. Then I looked up his number and nervously dialed it.

Bob's secretary answered and said, "Mr. Marcum is not in. May I take a message?" I gave her my name and Karen's number and asked her to have him call. Then I waited and wondered if he'd call.

Within fifteen minutes the telephone rang. Karen said, "It's for you, Reta, and he sounds nice!"

"Hello," I said.

"Hi, there," Bob said sweetly, "are you okay?"

When I heard his voice, I started to cry, and I told him about Daddy. He could tell I was falling apart, and quickly said, "There is no way I can come to you now, I've got business appointments I just can't cancel."

"That's all right," I assured him, "I didn't expect you to come to me, although I could use some strong arms right now, but you did ask me to call you if anything happened."

I regained my composure and talked with him for about thirty minutes, telling him what had all happened. Also, I told him about Pam and Kim taking over the studios and how I was wanting to relocate.

Secretly, I was wishing he would interrupt and asked me to join him, but no such luck. I guess he still didn't know what to do with me. After we hung up, I felt blue. I guess I had my hopes up that he would invite me to be with him.

Karen and I went about getting the house cleaned up and taking care of some business I needed to get done before the divorce hearing in the morning. We turned on the television and a big blizzard was forecast for later on that evening. I was sure glad the kids were all moved and I was safe and sound at Karen's.

About thirty minutes later the telephone rang again and Karen answered. A huge smile threatened to crack her face and she said in a loud stage whisper, "It's him again!" My heart jumped into my throat.

"Hello?" I said tentatively, not wanting to get my hopes up again.

"I've got a ticket and I'll be in Minneapolis tonight. Can you come and get me at the airport?"

I was so excited I could hardly speak! "Yes I can, but a big blizzard is coming our way and I may not be able to get out."

"Well, my truck is in storage clear across town, and I'd have to take a taxi over to get it, so try to come and get me if you can," Bob said wistfully. "I can only stay through tomorrow, then I have to fly back to

Chicago." Eagerly I took down his airline, flight number and time of arrival, and promised I would be there if I could.

After I hung up, I felt as light as air. I jumped up and hugged Karen and started crying. I was so happy that he would drop everything and come to my side!

Karen and I really started cleaning the house now, for I would be having company that night, plus I was trying to figure out what I was going to wear.

Suddenly I said, "Crap, that damn divorce is in the morning at ten!" I was just sick. The divorce had been postponed at least three times because Steve had given his attorney hot checks or couldn't come up with the funds. Why couldn't it be over with? Then maybe Bob would take me back with him.

Later on that afternoon snow starting to fall, and the weatherman warned everyone to stay home unless they had an emergency. "What am I going to do, Karen?" I cried. "He's already on the airplane!"

About an hour later the telephone rang again. This time I answered and Bob said, "Are you gonna make it?"

"Are you there already?" I asked in a panicked voice.

He laughed, "No, I'm still a few thousand miles away in the air, but I'm on my way. We are going to be late, due to the weather, but I'll keep you posted."

My legs felt weak and I plopped down on the couch after we had hung up. I was sick and said, "It doesn't look like it's meant for him and me to ever have our turn! I started to cry. "Why can't anything ever go right for me?" Karen tried to comfort me, but she wasn't succeeding.

Bless his heart, Bob called every fifteen minutes for the next three hours, and that alone helped me keep my sanity, at least temporarily. I couldn't imagine the bill he was running up, but each call made me appreciate him more, and I wanted to see him so bad. But the snow kept falling, and so did my tears. Karen finally said, "If you don't stop that bawling, you're gonna look like hell when he gets here!"

I knew she was right, but I also knew I wouldn't be able to go to the airport. I couldn't even get out of the driveway!

Bob finally called again, and this time I could tell he was about smashed. He was in first class and they were trying to keep the passengers all happy. At least he certainly sounded happy. "Hi there, I'm in Kansas," he said cheerfully.

"You're where?" I screamed in frustration.

"Yeah, this damn weather is so bad they've re-routed us three times, and we had to come here to fuel again. I don't know how long we'll be here. Some of my new friends and I broke into one of the airport bars that were closed, but we are mixing our own drinks and having a good time. Wish you were here!" he said.

"Me, too," I replied sadly, "because I'm not going to be able to get to the airport."

"Well, I guess I'll just have to break into storage and retrieve my truck, 'cause I'm coming to you no matter what!" Bob announced solemnly.

Then in the background I heard someone yell, "Are you talking to that dynamite little lady you've been bragging about all night?"

"Yeah!" he said, "I sure am. You wanna talk to her?"

Suddenly a strange voice said, "Hi! I just wanna know if you're as smart and pretty and wonderful as Bob's been telling us you are."

I laughed and said, "Well, I don't know about that, but I am a survivor!"

The voice continued, "Well, all he's done for the last two hours is brag about his woman, Reta Lee. He told us how you run a big home, cared for your ailing father, took care of your daughters, ran six dance studios, sang like an angel, but was unhappy because you didn't have time for him."

Again I laughed. "Well, that's nice to know, but now I have all the time in the world for him!"

The voice said, "Well, I'll give you back to your man, but I sure hope I get to meet you someday."

"I would like to meet you, too," I said, then Bob took the phone back. It was obvious they were feeling no pain. Bob and I talked some more then he said abruptly, "Gotta go! They're calling our flight to board. See you soon, honey," and hung up.

I was laughing so hard, Karen thought I had lost my mind. I told her what he had said and she laughed, "Hell, maybe you've found a real man this time that will appreciate you and take care of you for a change!"

"That would be nice, wouldn't it?" I sighed. I looked at the clock and it was already getting late. I called Pam and Kim to tell them about Bob coming, and what he was going through to see me.

They were delighted, for all of the kids liked Bob. I could tell they were halfway hoping he would take me with him, too. They knew he would take care of me until I could heal.

Pam assured me they had everything taken care of for the studios that needed to be done, and the only thing left was the one class in Luck. Also she told me the telephone calls had stopped since they moved to their new home. They had put the new telephone in Brad's name and only gave it to the Ladysmith and Clear Lake studios. "Mom, it is so nice not to have that thing ringing day and night. The parents calling now are really supportive and concerned about your welfare and wanted us to let you know they cared," Pam said.

They also had all the refund checks sent out for the January classes, and only a few left for the recital costumes. "I don't think we're gonna have enough to pay back the costumes until next month, but don't worry, we'll take it out of the tuition in February," she assured me.

I was so relieved everything was finally on track again, but most of all, I was proud of my daughters for taking over when I really needed them to, without whining. They did what they knew had to be done, and probably saved my life. I don't believe I could have ever held up under the stress that I would have had to endure.

Karen finally said, "I'm going to bed, and I think you should get some rest, too. He probably won't be here until the wee hours, and don't forget you have a date with that little f----er in the morning."

"Yeah, and I certainly don't want to miss that. I'll finally be done with him! I just hope Bob can stay until I get back," I said, then told her good night and thanked her for all her support.

When Karen went to her bedroom, I went back and soaked in the tub for about thirty minutes. My mind was running wild. If only I didn't have that divorce hearing in the morning, I would have more time with Bob and maybe we could make some temporary plans for my get away. I knew he cared a great deal for me or he wouldn't be going through all this trouble to get to me. It made me feel so good to know someone cared about me that much.

Getting out of the tub, I looked in my closet and there staring back at me was my new little black teddy I had bought last year, but never had a chance to wear. I took it out and put it on, looked in the mirror and decided I better put it back in the closet until I knew he was taking me with him. Reta, get a grip! The man may be just coming to be your friend, I told myself and slowly took off the little teddy and hung it back on the hanger. I then slipped into some lingerie that was a little more conventional. Then I blow-combed my hair, almost put it in the banana clip, then decided to let it hang down. I sprayed on some perfume, walked back into the living room and continued to wait.

I must have dozed off, because the telephone startled me awake about one o'clock in the morning. I quickly answered it and Bob announced wearily, "I'm finally in Minneapolis. This has been one hell of a trip, but are you okay?" His concern for me touched me deeply. It was just what I needed to hear.

"I'm fine, Bob, but the roads are terrible, and there was no way I could get down there," I explained.

"Well, you stay right where you are. I don't want you out in this. I'll get my truck out of storage and I'll be there in about three hours." I then gave him directions to Karen's trailer and before I hung up, I pleaded with him to be careful. "I don't want to lose you now," I told him boldly.

As we hung up, my heart was beating so fast I thought it would blow up. Then I realized I would only have a few hours with him before I had to leave for court. It just didn't seem fair! Why didn't I wait to call him after the divorce was over? Of course, I had no idea he would come to me like this, even though I had secretly hoped he would. How romantic for him to go through all this just to get to me! He made me feel real important and loved.

Karen came in and asked sleepily, "Was that him?" I gave her an update on our status, then she went back to bed. Going back to my room, I tried to get some sleep, but I was so worried about him driving up in the blizzard I couldn't sleep.

I prayed to God that He would bring Bob to me safely. Then I looked out my window and saw that the snow was really piling up. What if he wouldn't be able to see Daddy's little red Pontiac under all of the snow and wouldn't be able to find me.

I must have dozed off again, for suddenly my entire bedroom lit up by a vehicles headlights. I jumped up because I thought someone was coming right through my room. Quickly I looked out my window, and there was Bob's truck! I ran to the door like a child to the Christmas Tree on Christmas morning. My heart was racing and I hadn't felt like that since my first date.

I opened the door and there was Bob! He grabbed me, picked me up and gave me a kiss like I had never experienced before, and I moaned in pleasure. We still hadn't said a word, but just clung to each other like drowning people to a board. He was still holding me when Karen came running in. The commotion out front had awakened her, along with the rest of the trailer court, I'm sure.

Bob put me down and I introduced him to Karen. She said, "What the hell are you driving, a *Peterbilt?*"

With a laugh he said, "No, but with this weather, that's what I needed."

Then he looked at me and said softly, "Damn! It's good to hold you again!"

"It's good to be held again," I cooed.

He gave me another kiss and said, "I'm glad you didn't try to come and get me. It's terrible out there!"

Karen started brewing a pot of coffee, and I looked at the clock and saw it was already five o'clock in the morning.

As I looked at him, I couldn't believe he had come all that way for me. He looked so handsome and was still wearing a black business suit, white shirt, tie and a black trench coat. His black hair still had snow flakes in it, and I could tell by the way Karen looked at him she approved totally.

Reluctantly I told him about the divorce hearing later that morning and he said, "Damn! I have to catch a plane back to Chicago tomorrow afternoon. That doesn't give us much time."

In my mind I figured it would be plenty of time for me to go to court, pack my bags and run a way with him, but of course I didn't tell him what I was thinking. I just hoped he was thinking the same thing.

After making coffee, Karen considerately went back to bed so we could have some privacy. Bob took his suit coat and tie off, and we sat down on the sofa and he took me in his arms and said, "Well, it's been one hell of a trip, but here are those strong arms you wanted." I started to cry I was so happy, and he gently kissed me on the forehead.

We both needed sleep, so we went back to my little bedroom and he held and comforted me until my alarm went off. Right then I could have killed Steve for all the delays of our divorce hearing. The timing couldn't have been any worse!

I DECIDED TO LET BOB SLEEP LONGER, FOR HE WAS exhausted from the trip. I got up, took a shower, got dressed and joined Karen in the kitchen. She was already sitting at the table dressed for work and sipping on her coffee. She looked a me and smiled. "He's a hunk!" she said. "He's even more gorgeous than you told me!"

"Yeah, I know!" I said as I sat down with a cup of coffee.

"Well, you sure look more relaxed!" she teased.

I smiled and said, "Yeah, I sure hope he waits for me this morning. I think I'm in love!"

"Hell, after being married to that little f----er, you're probably just in lust!"

"Karen!" I protested and we both started laughing.

We heard my shower start and knew Bob would be joining us momentarily. Then he yelled out, "Reta, would you please bring me my suitcase?"

"Sure will!" I yelled back. Karen grabbed her purse and headed for the door. She said over her shoulder, "Come over to *T.J.'s* and I'll whip up some breakfast for you guys before you go to court, then I'll do my best to keep him there until you get back!"

"Can you get out?" I asked, now worried about the snow. She assured me the snow plow had already been there and would have no problem getting out. I felt better.

I then took Bob his suitcase, and got all my papers together for court. He walked out dressed in his casual clothes. He still was handsome, but I would never forget the way he looked last night. He held me for a few minutes and kissed me. Then I told him about Karen's plan for breakfast. He glanced at his watch and said, "We better take off then. I could use some breakfast."

Bob went out and started Daddy's little red Pontiac and his truck so they could warm up. I felt so secure and safe with him, and wished I could feel like that always.

Before long we were on our way to T.J.'s to meet Karen. It was nice to look in my rear view mirror and see his truck again!

Karen made us a good breakfast while we continued to talk. Finally he said sadly, "I won't be able to stay until you get back. I had to cancel a very important business appointment to come, and it is rescheduled for this evening." He kissed me gently again and sighed, "Why can't things ever be normal for you and me?"

"I don't know, Bob. Maybe it's still not our turn, but I have to leave now or I'll be late for court," I replied. "Thank you so much for coming to me," I said sincerely and he took me in his arms and kissed me like I had never been kissed before. I didn't know if it was a kiss "goodbye" or a kiss "hello," but the tears were flowing as I ran out the door. God, how I hated Steve for all the delays!

I tried to put Bob out of my mind and concentrate on the divorce, but it was a futile attempt.

I arrived at the Balsam Lake Courthouse in plenty of time, and took the elevator up to the floor Don had told me to meet him on. When I stepped out of the elevator, there sat the weasel, along with Andy and his new woman. I could have thrown up when I looked at him. He looked like something the cats drug in and the dogs fought over. Andy smiled and said, "Hello, Reta, I'm so sorry about your dad."

Very quietly I said, "Thanks, Andy," then looked away. I couldn't believe I had married that little weasel! I must have really had low self-esteem at the time.

Then Steve said, "Me, too."

I spun around and glared at him for a few seconds, then snapped, "Don't you even talk to me after what you've done to me and my family!" The nerve of that idiot! He didn't say any more, and his woman just sat there with her head down. She definitely looked like she belonged to him.

Don finally got there and motioned for me to follow him into a little conference room. We went over everything again and he said, "I just met with Steve's attorney and they don't want to give you the Firebird."

"What!" I yelled. "My God, that's all I'm asking for!"

"What about the medical problem you had that took the money you borrowed from the finance company?" he asked.

"What the hell are you talking about?" I yelled, getting angrier by the second.

"Well, they want you to pay that bill since you got all the money."

"That's a damn lie, Don," I yelled. "He knows as well as I do that money went to pay off more bills incurred with building that damned house! I put my medical bills on my credit card."

"Well, we can fight them on that, but it might drag it out another month or so," he said, and I knew he was pressing me to just settle.

"No!" I screamed. "I want to be free of that bastard today!" I was so furious. I was paying him to get what I asked and just now he was talking with the other attorney.

"Well, do you want to give him the car and take the responsibility for that one bill?" he asked.

"If that's the only way I can get rid of him, okay. Doesn't the money I've pumped into that house for the past four years account for anything? This means I come out of that courtroom today with absolutely nothing. Is that right?" I asked.

He didn't say anything as he handed me the paperwork to sign. "Are the payments all up to date?"

"Yes," I cried, "the little son of a bitch can walk in there with his sweat hogs and take over. I can't believe this is happening and I can't believe you are letting this happen!" I yelled, letting all of my anger and frustration out. "What good are you? I could have lost everything without you, but now I lose everything and have to pay you, too!"

"Well, if you want to fight it, we will," he said lamely as he looked at his watch. "What do you want to do?"

"Just get it over," I hissed. "You've allowed him to screw me over from the very beginning, it's a little late now for any changes. Just give him all of it!"

Steve put on the biggest performance of his life before the judge. All divorces in Wisconsin are considered "No Fault," which essentially means they don't care if Steve had slept with his cousin, a cow or stole everything. So much for justice.

I wasn't allowed to say anything about what Steve had done to me or my family. I tried to tell the judge about his cheating, about stealing the money from the winch refund, about stealing all the things out of the garage, including the one thousand dollar air compressor, and when I tried to tell him about the speed I had found in Steve's night-stand at the time I packed his things, the judge quickly informed me again that what he had done was not pertinent. Steve whined, "That speed belonged to her daughters!" The dirty little bastard knew my daughters never took any kind of drugs, just like he knew where the loan money went, but it was obvious no one in the courtroom gave a tinker's damn.

I couldn't believe it! They wouldn't let me finish one sentence, and my renowned attorney just sat there like a bump on a pickle. I never had felt so railroaded in my life by anyone, including my attorney. I realized then the true meaning of the country song, *She Got The Mine And I Got The Shaft.* All I had to do was change "she" to "he," and it would define the gross example of injustice to which I was subjected.

When I walked out of that court room, I had lost everything I had worked for in the last four years. In fact, I not only lost everything, but was five thousand dollars in debt. I guess I should be thankful though, my attorney was able to stop them from taking Daddy's little red Pontiac. Of course I would have killed Steve before he got Daddy's car. It was hard to believe his attorney even brought Daddy's car up in the proceeding, but he used it to justify the fact I had a car and would leave the poor little bastard car-less if I took the Firebird. Nobody seemed to care that my daughters and I were homeless now. I felt violated.

Then, as I walked out to my Daddy's car, Don came running after me. He quietly handed me his bill for services rendered. I didn't say a word, although I wanted to say, "You're charging me for giving away everything I had? What did you do to earn any money? You should get it from Steve. After all, you might as well have represented him! You're just as worthless as he is!" Instead I just took it and climbed in my car and prayed Bob would be waiting on me. Those strong arms sounded awfully good right now.

As I drove off, I looked at the bill and laughed at Don's audacity. Even after the $350.00 retainer I had given him, he still had a balance owing of $850.00. He actually wanted me to pay him another $850.00 for what he had done, or in reality, not done!

After I saw that, my opinion of attorneys dropped to something below cow-pies, and hasn't changed since.

I did as Leroy had told me to do, licked my wounds and thanked God I had been able to provide a nice place for my Daddy's last days. I headed toward *T.J.'s* and had to laugh to keep from crying as I drove Daddy's little car down the road. My Daddy was taking better care of me from the grave than that sorry ex-husband of mine ever did.

Suddenly, I dwelled on the word "ex-husband." Damn, it sounded good! Thank, God, it was all over, and even if I only had Daddy's car left, I still had my sanity, my life and my children. I wondered, though, about the sanity. I hoped I still had it.

Glancing down at my gas gauge, I saw it was getting low. In this weather, they warn never to let the gas tank get much lower than one half full, so I turned around and went back to the gas station and filled up. I looked at my watch and saw it was already afternoon. I knew Bob would already be gone, and all I could do was hope he would send for me.

I got to *T.J.'s* and Karen yelled, "Where have you been? He just left about ten minutes ago! That poor man has been going through hell, and he must have made a hundred telephone calls. He just couldn't wait any longer!" she said as she handed me a Bacardi Coke as I flopped down on the bar stool and started sobbing.

"Why did I stop to get that damned gas? I would have been here before he left," I cried.

"I really felt sorry for him. He really cares about you and kept telling me, I just don't know what to do with her. Then he would shake his head, order another drink, make another telephone call and repeat the same thing. Maybe he'll come back," Karen said hopefully.

"No," I sobbed, "he won't be back, and I really don't think I will ever see him again! He's just too scared of my situations, and I can't blame him. I'm not your normal everyday woman!"

Karen laughed, "Well, thank God, for that. Probably that's what attracted him to you. He kept saying how much he admired your strength."

"Yeah," I snapped, "I'm so damned strong, why can't I find someone who will allow me to be weak once in awhile?" I looked at Karen and asked pitifully, "Do you think he'll send for me?"

"The way he was acting, I don't think he's out of your life yet," she said comfortingly.

I went back home and cried some more, then decided to get my clothes packed and be ready if he did send for me. Busily getting my things ready, I realized that he hadn't really given me any indication he was going to send for me. Maybe I was just being a big fool, and I felt a little silly, but I still wanted to be ready if he did call.

Pam and Kim stopped by to see how the divorce went. They couldn't believe what had happened, but like me they were glad that sorry person was out of our lives for good, and I was out from under all those bills. I assured Pam I would take that last class in Luck on Tuesday night, and if Bob didn't call, I wanted to leave for Sarasota by the weekend.

Kim started to cry. "Mom, are you sure you have to go?" Tears started to form in Pam's eyes, too, and I put my arms around both my girls and cried with them. We all knew I was doing the right thing by leaving, and also knew it would only be for awhile.

TWO DAYS PASSED WITHOUT A WORD FROM BOB, SO I assumed he had truly given up on me. It was too bad, for he had hung in so long, and just when it was our turn, he gave up. I was so depressed for the next few days all I did was cry. Mostly I was angry at myself for being such an idiot and believing in another man. I was beginning to feel about men like Karen and Sissy did. Finally, I'd had enough and vowed that no man would ever get a chance to hurt me again.

After accepting the fact that Bob was no more, I started packing my little car for the trip to Sarasota. I put Daddy's little pearl-handled .22 in the glove compartment, and Brad put the CB radio in as he had promised.

Pam and Kim were trying to be really strong for me. They had planned a Going-Away party for Friday night because I was going to try and leave Saturday morning. The forecast had been clear for the entire weekend, and I figured I could be out of snow country by Sunday night.

One more class to teach, then I would be free to leave. I got up that morning, got dressed and went out to the blue house to pick up the equipment. I hated changing into my leotards. I just had no enthusiasm left for teaching—the joy had totally been taken away by all the turmoil. Cheryl said, "Reta, do you want me to go with you?"

I quickly said, "Sure, if you want to," and she ran upstairs to get dressed.

Pam and Kim loaded the equipment into her car and said, "Good luck." Then Cheryl and I headed for the Luck High School where Pam had been teaching.

My nerves were shot before I got there, and I kept telling myself, it's only two classes, you'll be okay.

When we got there, we took out the equipment and got set up. Soon the little students started coming in and I was actually happy to see them. They were so sweet and understanding. One little girl asked, "Reta, did your Daddy really die?"

I smiled at her and said, "Yes, honey, my Daddy is in heaven now."

"Do you miss him?"

"Very much so, but he's with God now," I said, ready to change that subject. I could feel the tears about to start.

Then the Luck parents came in, and the majority of them were extremely understanding. Although they hated to see the studio fold, they realized we didn't have enough students left. I explained to them that we would try again next year, if at all possible.

I went through both classes with flying colors, and actually it had been good for me to be back in the classroom with my little students. They were all so sweet and refreshing.

After the last class ended, Cheryl and I started packing up. When I turned around, I saw a pack of mothers lead by the two trouble-makers from Cumberland. They looked like a pack of wolves headed for me.

I guess I just went totally nuts. I yelled, "Come on! Come on! Just try to take what little is left of me! You're nothing but a pack of dogs looking for a kill!" and I started moving toward them continuing to yell. They didn't say a word, just started backing up and then running out of the room.

Cheryl started laughing hysterically. "Well, you got rid of those bitches, didn't you?"

I regained my composure and said, "My, God, Cheryl, have I lost my mind or what? I really wanted to tear them apart! Do you think I would have taken on all of them if they hadn't turned around?"

"Yeah," she laughed, "and I think you could have kicked all their butts." I started laughing with her and we got the car packed and headed back to the blue house.

Pam and Kim were cracking up as Cheryl told them of my outburst. She said, "Boy, would you've been proud of your Mom! She really let 'em have it."

Actually, I was quite embarrassed over the way I had acted. It only proved to me I had done the right thing by giving up the studios. After that outburst, I knew for sure I wouldn't have been able to hold up under all those pressures.

On my way back to Karen's, I had to laugh a little to myself about the way I had acted. It was so unlike me to blow-up like that in a classroom, but since I did, I was glad it was to those couple of mothers.

The next day I continued to get Daddy's little car packed. Before I realized it, it was the day before I planned to leave. I put the last things into the car and went out to the blue house. I had planned to spend the night with Pam and Kim before I left the next morning. The kids were really sad as we got dressed for my Going-Away party. I was glad, though, they were trying to be strong for me.

We arrived for the party, which was at *T.J.'s Club*, and they had it all decorated. Immediately I was overwhelmed, and tears filled my eyes, for I looked around the room and saw all my friends were there—even the band and their wives. It was the whole gang!

They handed me a drink, then gave me all kinds of good luck and farewell cards. Gary gave me a little coffee cup with a little mouse on it surrounded by big cats. It read, "I need a hug!" and I laughed and gave him a big hug and kiss. I said, "That little mouse looks like I feel."

"Yeah, it reminded me of you when I saw it," he laughed. I knew I was gonna really miss him as much as anyone, for he had been such a good friend to me.

Leroy gave me a hug and said, "If you need anything, just let me know. If you need money to get home or anything, just call." I hugged him and told him again how much I appreciated all he had done for me and my family.

The party didn't last too late, and we all went home fairly early so I could get some rest for the long trip to Sarasota. I was truly blessed to have so many dear friends, and it was so hard to say goodbye to Karen, Ma,

Lee and Yvonne. It certainly was not without tears, but at last I had said good bye to everyone and gone home with the girls.

AS PLANNED, THE NEXT MORNING I GOT UP EARLY because Bob Nelson, my insurance agent, was to stop by so I could sign my life insurance forms. I had made a will and took out one hundred thousand dollars worth of life insurance in the event something should happen to me. That way Pam and Kim would be financially secure.

They almost had a fit when they found out what he was there for, until he explained to them how smart I was to do this. I signed and completed all the paperwork, then he shook my hand and wished me luck.

I gave the paperwork to Pam to keep in a safe place. Also, I had made Chuck their trustee, for I knew if anything should happen, he would make sure they would get everything coming to them.

Busily I began packing and re-packing the car. It seemed I was taking more than I had planned. Then Monie came out with her little microwave and said, "Reta, I want you to have this because I don't know when I will be able to pay you back for the airline ticket we put on your credit card in Texas."

The money she had counted on never came. It was to be a settlement from her ex-husband.

"Monie, are you sure you want me to take it?"

"Yeah," she answered, "We have one, and besides it's just the right size for you!"

I checked over the car and finally found just the spot for it.

Just then Pam yelled, "Mom, you're wanted on the telephone. It's Jeanie Howell."

A little surprised, I ran inside to see what she wanted, probably to see what time I was planning to leave. Jeanie said apologetically, "Reta, do you think you could wait until the end of the month to come? Some unexpected guests came in and we are going to be so busy with them, I just don't think we'll have the time to help you get settled." She went on to assure me they would be gone by the end of February and would have all the time in the world to help me.

Inside I was devastated, but held back the tears and assured her that it would be all right. However, I knew I wouldn't be staying in Wisconsin waiting on their company to leave, even though I had my heart set on going to Sarasota. I knew I had to make plans to go elsewhere now.

I hung up the telephone and started to sob, "Why can't something turn out right for me?"

"Now, what are you going to do, Mom?" Pam asked.

"Well, I don't know where I'm going, but I know I'm going there today." I said. My mind was going ninety miles per hour, and suddenly I remembered a couple of fans I had talked to a few weeks back. They had told me they were planning to leave this same weekend for Scottsdale, Arizona, and had tried to convince me to follow them out there. They had even offered to help me start a dance studio or introduce me to a band they knew who was losing their female vocalist.

I quickly looked up their number and called them. They, like me, were getting ready to head out and were delighted I wanted to travel along with them. They also had room in their van to take some of my band equipment, and assured me they would be over shortly to load up and hit the road.

We repacked everything again—with them taking the equipment, I would have more room for other things. I was all ready to go by twelve o'clock.

By one o'clock they still hadn't shown up, so I called to see what happened. Ben said, "I was about to call you. We are having some problems with the van and have decided to wait until in the morning to leave. Will that be okay with you?"

"No," I cried, "I have been held up long enough. I will just meet you in Scottsdale. I am leaving as planned." He gave me their number in Scottsdale and made me promise to look them up the following week.

I was so upset! It seemed like nothing was ever going to work out. Pam and Kim didn't know what I was going to do, and neither did I. I sat down at the kitchen table and had another cup of coffee and tried to figure it all out.

Finally I said, "I'm gonna re-pack the car, just like it was before, and head down Highway 35 south. I'll have it all figured out by the time I get out of snow country. I've just got to get out of here!" My mind felt as though it were going to explode.

Again we re-packed the car like it had been before. Pam suggested shipping some of my things by UPS after I had got situated. Within one hour, I was ready to leave. Poor little Pam and Kim didn't know what to do, they were so worried about me. They knew I had to get away, but for their Mother just to leave with no destination in mind, they were really scared.

Ma called just as I was about to walk out the door and said, "Please come by and say goodbye."

"Ma," I pleaded, "please just give me some time. I just want to leave, now," and started crying because I didn't want to talk to anyone, see anyone or anything. Space between me and everybody was what I needed. I assured her I would be okay and that I would call her when I got to wherever I was going.

"Aren't you going to Sarasota?" she asked surprised.

"Ma," I pleaded again, "please just let me go! I love you and I will call you, but I want to go now."

Hanging up the telephone, I looked at my two little girls with tears streaming down their face. I embraced both of them and assured them I would be okay, and that I would call Yvonne every night and report in. She had already promised them she would call, immediately. Then Brad assured me he would take care of my girls, and Monie and Cheryl promised they would do all they could to help with the studios.

"I would like to ask one thing," I said, and everyone was listening with open ears. "Please don't tell me anything negative when I call. I can't do anything when I'm gone, and I just don't think I could handle it. If the mothers are bad, please don't tell me, it would only upset me. The studios are now yours. Do whatever you want with them. If something happens with any of you, I want to know. I'm just talking about the everyday complaints. Those I don't want to hear about, okay?"

"Mom, don't worry, we'll handle it all," Pam said. The tears were streaming down all our faces as I got into Daddy's little red car and headed toward St. Paul. I'll never forget my two little girls standing in their big front window waving goodbye and trying to be brave for me. God, how I loved them! I knew I was abandoning them, but also knew I had to go. I really didn't have a choice.

As I drove toward St. Paul, the tears were flowing. Sometimes it was hard to see the road. I had no road map or no real destination. Thank, God, the weather was clear. I kept seeing Pam and Kim's little faces in that big old window, and several times I almost turned around and went back. I was so glad I had taken out the life insurance, because in my frame of mind, I didn't know if I was safe on the road.

I got through St. Paul and headed toward Iowa. I had cried so much my eyes hurt. I saw a roadside park and pulled in. I made sure my doors were locked and I sat there for about thirty minutes trying to regain my composure and figure out where I was really going.

Suddenly, I remembered my Best Friend. It was so quiet in the car—no telephones, no one asking anything from me. It was just me and sweet silence. I looked up and said, "Dear God, please help me! I don't know why my life has fallen apart like this. All I wanted to do was give my Daddy a safe place to live out his life, and a good home for Pam and Kim. I know I'm a good mother, and You've blessed me with the sweetest and most precious daughters a mother could ever pray for, but why are things in my life such a mess? I know I would be a good wife, but everyone seems to screw around on me or hurt me. I don't understand why Bob came all that way, then never called or returned. Please don't let me ever get tangled up with another man unless he is the right one. I've been hurt enough, Lord. I know I'm a good person, but why do I have to always be hurt like this?" By then, the tears were flowing like a river.

I regained my composure, blew my nose and said "I'm sorry, God, but You're my only hope right now. You know I'm both physically and emotionally drained, and I need some time-out to gain strength. You also know why I took out that insurance policy. I was hoping I could leave Pam and Kim financially secure, 'cause God, I don't want to live like this and be this unhappy! So if you want to just run me off a cliff or crunch me between two trucks or something, I want You to know it's okay with me. You also know I promised Pam and Kim I would never do anything stupid, but Dear, God, if my life is going to just be more of the same, then please take me home to my Mama and Daddy!"

A few minutes later my tears stopped falling and I felt warm all over. If I ever felt the arms of God embrace me, it was at that moment. I knew he had heard my cry, and I knew, somehow, He was going to guide me on my journey. I took a deep breath and said, "Thank you for hearing me. Please guide me into a new life for me and my little girls."

Then out of nowhere my favorite poem, Footsteps, kept running through my mind as I started my car and headed on down Highway 35. I truly felt the presence of my guardian angel sitting on the passenger side and pretended it was my Mama or Daddy, or even my first cousin, Kathy, whom I loved so much. I did know, though, I wasn't alone.

Turning on my CB radio, I started listening to the chatter of the truck drivers. Finally I broke in and said, "Is anyone out there heading south on thirty-five?"

"Yeah," a voice came back, "what's your handle?"

I thought for a moment, then answered, "Runaway."

"Well, where ya' running to, Runaway?"

"Somewhere out of this snow country," I answered.

"Are you alone?" he came back.

I smiled and said, "No, I have a passenger with me." Between him and another truck driver, they made me the rocking chair and escorted me safely into Des Moines, Iowa, where I said goodbye, thanked them and got a room at the Best Western Motel.

After I had checked in and got my things into the room, I called Yvonne and reported in as I had promised I would do. I knew Pam and Kim would be worried to death about me, and I assured her I was all right.

"I'll call Pam and Kim as soon as we hang up," she said, and I was so thankful she could help, because we couldn't afford a big telephone bill.

I only had a little over one thousand dollars to my name, plus enough left on my credit card to get me to wherever I was going.

After calling, I flopped down on the bed ready to spend my first night on the road, alone. I still had no idea where I was going!

BEFORE DAWN, I GOT UP AND CHECKED OUT.   I bought a newspaper and read the forecast. It didn't sound good, and I wanted to get out of snow country before I got into a blizzard. Before I hit the road, again, I ate a bite of breakfast.

The truckers picked me up and escorted me all the way to Kansas where again I pulled off to spend the night. Thank, God, the threat of snow was over.

While looking for a place to stay, I saw a *Grandy's Chicken Restaurant,* and remembered how much I loved their fried gizzards and gravy. I bought a bucket full, with a big portion of white gravy and checked into a motel.

Locking the door, I then turned on the television to see what the weather was doing, and called Yvonne to report in. Then I sat in the middle of the bed with my bucket of gizzards, and for the first time, since Daddy's funeral, I think my mind was totally relaxed.

I stayed in that room for two days, just enjoying the silence. Thank, God, I had a bucket of gizzards! I cried, ate gizzards and talked to God for those two days.

Sometimes, I wondered if I had totally lost my mind. I kept telling myself that no one could find me, or pull at me. I would laugh, then cry uncontrollably, then laugh some more. Looking back, I believe I had a total emotional breakdown, and through the grace of God, I came though.

WHEN I FINALLY CAME OUT OF THAT MOTEL, I FELT like a new woman. My mind was more rested and I felt much stronger. I loaded my suitcase back into the car, then looked at the telephone and decided to call Pam and Kim.

When they answered, they were so happy to hear from me and to know I was safe! I didn't tell them about the breakdown I had experienced over the past two days, but only told them positive things. If you could have heard that conversation, you would have thought we were all the happiest people in the world! Each one of us was trying to be brave for the other, and I assured them I would be fine, now. Also, I assured them that I loved them more than anything in this entire world. In turn, they assured me the studios were fine and they were all getting along great. Relieved, I said goodbye, climbed into Daddy's little red Pontiac and headed down Highway 35 again.

I still didn't have a road map, but then I really hadn't needed one. Why do you need one if you don't know where you are going?

As I drove, more truckers picked me up and I chattered with them all the way to Oklahoma City. There, I pulled into a truck stop for a bite to eat and a cup of coffee. Amazingly, I had not thought about any of the problems behind me. My mind was totally focused on the future. Now, I knew through the grace of God, my mind was starting to heal.

When I got back into the car, I had to decide to go either east or west because if I kept going south, I'd wind up in Texas, and I knew I didn't want to go back there at this time.

Instead, I headed my car west, went on some of the worst roads, and somehow I got off the main freeway. I did, however, see some interesting places.

I ended up spending the night at some little town near New Mexico. The next morning, the truckers gave me the directions I needed to go toward Scottsdale.

Driving all day and into the evening, I made it to Tucumcarie, New Mexico, and got a room at the local Best Western.

After I had checked in, I walked into the lounge and to my delight, a country band was playing. It didn't take long before I was on the bandstand singing with them.

They were a road group and told me of another band that was looking for a female vocalist who could travel. I said, "Well, I'm sure free to travel," and they gave me the name of the club the band was playing at in Albuquerque, New Mexico.

Thanking them, I left and went to my room. I was excited about the possibility of joining a road band. If it worked out, I would be able to make good money, then I could send some back to Pam and Kim to help with the refunds.

The next day I headed for Albuquerque where I had truly planned to stop and spend the night and to listen to the band I had been told about. When I came into the city limits, I just kept going because I had an overwhelming urge to not stop. Something told me it was not what I wanted. I didn't even stop for gas, and it seemed as though I couldn't get through that town fast enough. I listened to my feelings and kept on driving.

As I headed for Arizona, I remembered a dear friend, Sue Gregorson, who had moved to Flagstaff a few years back. I decided I would try to find her.

Once in Flagstaff, I rented a motel room and went to one of the local real estate offices. Sue had been a broker, so I figured if she was in the area they would know where to find her. I asked everywhere possible, but no one knew who she was.

Disappointed, I washed the car as it was a mess from all the slush I had gone trough up north. When I had finished, it shone brightly in the sun.

Next, I took the remaining traveler checks I had and stuffed them into my winter boots which I had worn from home. Then changed into my jeans, sweatshirt, tennies and, of course, the famous banana clipped pony tail.

It felt so good to breath all that fresh air. I filled my lungs up again and again and realized that I was starting to really feel good. In my shiny, clean car, I hit the road again, heading to my final destination, Scottsdale, Arizona.

As I was driving down the road, I suddenly thought of Dr. Rimestad. If I ever saw him again, he would probably choke me for not checking into the hospital, but then I realized what I had done was much better than any hospital.

Then I saw a sign that had arrows pointing one way to Arizona and straight ahead to Las Vegas. I couldn't believe I was almost to Las Vegas, Nevada. A few years back, when the band I was working with had played the lounge at the Golden Nugget was the first time I had been there. I had been there again with some friends of mine who were high rollers, and that time we had stayed at the Flamingo. I remembered how much I enjoyed that trip and thought what a shame it would be to be so close to Las Vegas but not take an extra couple of days to go there.

Quickly I pulled the car over and had another little talk with my Navigator as to what I should do. I knew without a doubt He hadn't wanted me to join that road band, but at this point I really was feeling inspired to go to Las Vegas. While I sat there for a few minutes, the feeling kept getting stronger to go straight ahead. I put Daddy's little car into gear, smiled from ear to ear and headed for Las Vegas, Nevada.

Soon I had again become the rocking chair between two big trucks. The lead truck was carrying a load of cars, which scared me to death. I could just see one come flying off and crushing me. Then I marveled at the safe trip I had had so far. I hadn't had as much as a flat tire, so I knew the Good Lord wasn't gonna take me home yet. He had something planned for me, I could just tell.

When I drove across Hoover Dam, I was never so scared. I finally got to the other side and my entire body was trembling. Soon I calmed down and a few minutes later I saw all the lights and knew I had arrived in Las Vegas. After thanking the truckers, I pulled off into the heart of Las Vegas.

I parked my car out front of a hotel and went inside. I asked where the Flamingo was located, but was quickly informed that I had just gotten to Nevada and Las Vegas was a few more miles down the road. I felt like an idiot. With that many lights, I had just assumed I was on the strip when, in fact, I was only at the *Gold Strike Casino*. Quickly, I got back into my car and headed in the direction they had told me.

Finally, I saw the lights in the distance. It was the most beautiful sight I had ever seen. It had always been daylight when I had flown in before, and I had never driven. My heart was going ninety miles per hour.

Before long I was on the Boulder Highway. Again I thought I had to be on the strip and started looking for the *Flamingo*. Before I knew it, I was downtown on Fremont street. I was so tired I could hardly hold my eyes open, and I started talking on the CB trying to find someone who could direct me to the *Flamingo*. Finally a man came on and told me how to get to the strip.

I finally found the *Flamingo* and parked my car and walked inside. It was just like I remembered from before, years past. I went to check in, but almost died when they gave me the price of seventy-five dollars for one night. I smiled and said, "I'll have to think it over."

I quickly got back into my car and headed down the strip. I knew I couldn't afford that kind of money, for I would be broke in four days at that rate. Finally, I stopped at a Mexican restaurant on Paradise Road. I ordered a taco salad and asked where I could find a motel at a reasonable rate. They recommended a little motel up the street called *The Granada*. Since I was so tired, I asked them to put my taco salad in a carry-out.

Following their directions, I found *The Granada* and sure enough, they had rates I could afford at twenty-five dollars a night. I immediately checked in, took a hot bath and slept like a baby. I never did eat that taco salad.

MY FIRST DAY IN LAS VEGAS I DIDN'T GET UP UNTIL almost noon. I immediately called the front desk and reserved my room for another night, then got dressed and decided to see the big town.

What surprised me most was that it looked so different during the day, not near as exciting as the night before. It was just a regular town, and I couldn't get over how cheap the food was. I went straight to the *Flamingo* again. Somehow, even though I couldn't afford to be their guest, they seemed like an old friend.

Then I walked across to the *Dunes* and ordered a big hot dog for a few cents. I thought, at this rate, my money will last forever! I heard a band playing, and walked into the lounge to eat. Everything seemed really laid back, not like I had remembered Las Vegas. I felt more like I was attending a jam session at *The Foxhole*. After listening to the entertainer, Dusty Barren, I realized why the mood was like it was—he had the ability to make everyone feel so welcome. It didn't take long for him to find out I was from Wisconsin and also a country singer. He said, "Don't go away, I'll talk to you on my break. Maybe I can give you some leads." I just smiled and enjoyed the show.

Sure enough, on his break Dusty told me about a few more musicians who would be coming in. "Just hang around and I'll introduce you," he promised. I really wasn't there looking for work, and I tried to remember I was on my way to Scottsdale, but I decided to check it out. After all, my Navigator had brought me here.

True to his word, before I left, Dusty had introduced me to several musicians in town. I was advised to go to the *Silver Dollar* on Sunday afternoon for a jam session, and was assured I would meet many country musicians there.

After thanking everyone for their help, I took the usual scenic tour of the strip and went back to *The Granada.* I had dinner in their little casino, then sat down at the piano bar and listened to a fantastic entertainer named Peer. Before long he was encouraging me to stay in Vegas, too!

That night I went back to my room feeling pretty good. I thanked the Lord, again for all of his help, then fell asleep feeling at peace with myself.

The next day was about the same, and I kept meeting more and more entertainers. I had met the lead player and his wife, Johnny and Linda, from the *Class Act Band* playing at the *Holiday,* and they invited me to sit in with them, too. Everyone was so supportive, I really felt at home.

Again that night I slept like a baby.

However, the next morning the front desk advised me the room rent would double for the Valentine weekend. I couldn't believe it! I decided right then I should head on down to Scottsdale before I ran out of money. I dug out my friend's phone number in Scottsdale and called. They were all set to help me upon my arrival.

On my way out, I went over to say goodbye to Peer. "You can't leave Las Vegas! I know you'll be working within the week," he said.

"Well, I can't take a chance when I'm this low on money and I can't afford to pay twice as much for a room," I explained. Not to be ignored, he talked to the bartender about a place to stay for less. He told me to go over to the *Tropicana Inn,* a little weekly rental motel (not to be confused with the big casino hotel!) that had studio apartments. I figured what-the-heck, it wouldn't hurt to check it out.

When I got there, the man on the front desk smiled and said, "You are a mighty lucky young lady! A room just became available this morning." He laughed and explained, "We're always booked full."

The only problem was I had to rent the room by the week to get the good rate and had to move fast in order to lock it in or lose it. I felt like this was the right thing to do, so I quickly said, "I'll take it!"

The little room was so nice. There was a little table, refrigerator and everything else I needed. I unpacked and put my new little home in order. It felt so good to have my own little private place. Quickly, I called

Pam and Kim to let them know what I was doing. They were so excited when I told them what had happened.

"Mom, try to get started there! I want to live in Las Vegas, too!" Kim said excitedly. She was quickly echoed by Pam, and they both wanted to join me as soon as I got something going.

After I had talked to the girls, I felt really good. I didn't know why, but I felt like this was the place I should stay for a while. I decided if I got a job at that jam session, then this was where God wanted me to stay for awhile.

With everything put away, I was so happy Monie had given me the little microwave. It looked so cute in my miniature kitchen and then I sat down to just enjoy my little place.

Suddenly, Bob's face ran through my mind and I decided to call and let him know where I was, just in case he wanted to find me. I called his office and left my number with his secretary. Unlike before, he didn't call back for two days, and I knew then that the last kiss was obviously a goodbye kiss. I couldn't blame him, for my life would scare the hell out of most men.

When he did call, I had already made up my mind that it was over, too. We chatted for awhile, and I could tell he still didn't know what to do with me. Of course, the answer to that question was simple, and it was obvious he couldn't understand. All he needed to do was love me! We said goodbye and until this day, I've never seen or heard from Bob again, nor have I called.

I still don't know why our relationship went the way it did. Maybe he was there in my life for just those occasions when the Lord knew I needed to feel someone loved me. But whatever the reason, I thank the Lord for the time we had and like to think that it was part of His plan for me.

SUNDAY CAME, AND I GOT DRESSED UP IN ONE OF my stage outfits and headed for the Silver Dollar. What a great bunch of people I met there! I was so impressed with the female singers there in Vegas. Not only could they sing, but they welcomed me with open arms. A young blond named Mary Huron instantly became one of my best friends. We just hit it off right away. She got up and sang, followed by Janie Stark. They were so good I felt intimidated to get up and deliver my two songs, but I did anyway. Everyone really applauded and made me feel good.

After I got off stage, a bass player named Barry came up to me and politely asked, "Are you working anywhere?"

"No," I admitted, "I just got into town."

"Well," he said slowly, "our female vocalist is quittin', and if you would like to work with my band, you gotta job," he offered.

I couldn't believe it! I had only been in town for a week and here I was with a job and my own little private place to live. I quickly said, "Sure, when do I start?"

He smiled and said, "We'll practice this week on your songs and you can start Friday night."

"Thank you!" I said excitedly, and he told me about the pay. The money wasn't any better than at home, and in fact it wasn't as good, but it was enough to pay my rent, feed me and make Daddy's funeral payment.

THAT FIRST WEEK TURNED INTO A MONTH, AND soon I was jobbing with other bands and making enough money to survive, but I knew I had to start a studio in order to get Pam and Kim here. In my spare time, I located a studio on Tropicana sub-renting from a ballroom dance studio. I got fliers out and ran some ads in the Nifty Nickel, a local bargain paper. By the time I got all the advertising paid for, I was down to $300.00 in my boot. I was beginning to get a little nervous, for I knew Las Vegas was no town in which to be broke.

As I said before, Mary Huron became my best friend. She would stop by every morning for coffee with me at my little apartment, and we had a lot of fun together. She decided to work for me part-time at the studio like Karen had done in Wisconsin. She had a little girl, so we were going to barter her lessons for Mary's help.

One morning she said, "I want to come out and listen to your show. I have been in this town six months and haven't been able to find a full time job, yet you come in and start working within a week." She laughed, "I gotta come see what you do and maybe take some pointers."

"Mary," I said honestly, "as far as I'm concerned, you're a better singer than me. Maybe I'm just fuller of *el toro poo poo!*" and we both cracked up. We really had fun together! We went to all the show-cases on the strip, and I just kept making more and more friends. It seemed for certain that I would never get to Scottsdale, so I called my friends and thanked them for their concern and assured them I was all right.

Pam and Kim wanted to come for the grand opening, but I didn't know how I could afford it. The garage sale hadn't made enough money to pay back the refunds and, what was left, Brad had taken to the auction house in Dressor. I knew I couldn't expect more than a couple of thousand dollars from it. However, that would be enough to keep things rolling for us and take care of the refunds. The only problem was the next auction was a month away.

"Mom, I sent all your mail today, plus the equipment we will need for the studio," Kim said. They had decided that she would stay in Vegas and teach with me when they came for the grand opening, and Pam would go back and finish the year, then join us after recitals.

I was still worried. The money was really low and I didn't know how I was going to tell Pam and Kim I didn't have the money for their tickets. I started going through the mail, which was mostly bills. Steve wasn't paying anything, which didn't surprise me. Then I opened up a letter from a credit card company, and to my surprise it was a card with a two thousand dollar limit. The tears came as I thanked God for that credit card, for this was His answer to my prayers. Now Pam and Kim could come and we would have the money to really get things rolling with the studio! I was ecstatic.

But that wasn't all the good news, though. Before I got done opening the mail, I had a second credit card worth twenty-five hundred dollars. I knew then, for sure, that God was still watching over me! I had forgotten about applying for either one of them, but they couldn't have come at a better time.

The next day I took a cash draw from one of the cards and opened a business account. Then I called and got Pam and Kim a ticket to fly down for the grand opening. Everything was going my way for a change. However, the thought of opening another studio made me sick, for I still hadn't recovered from before. I just wasn't strong enough to face all those problems again.

THE DAY PAM AND KIM WERE TO ARRIVE, I WAS SO nervous I could hardly stand myself. I went to the airport to meet them, and thought they would never get off the plane. Finally I saw my two little girls wagging the purple suitcase containing all the albums used for the studios. Pam had transferred all the music from the albums on to cassettes to finish out the year up north.

I don't believe there has been, or ever will be, a happier reunion in this entire world than that one. We were all hugging and talking excitedly, but finally, we had to stop and get our breaths. Then we began again, only talking slower and not interrupting. We all had so much to say!

I took them on a tour of the strip, and we stopped at the Dunes and they met Dusty. It didn't take long before they decided I had definitely picked the right place to relocate. We went back to my little apartment and they couldn't get over how cute it was. We didn't stop talking for two days straight.

The day of the grand opening arrived, but none of our hearts were into opening another dance studio. We were all burned out, and Kim said,

"Mom, I would rather just get a regular job." Her idea was quickly echoed by Pam.

"Well, let's see what happens today." I knew I hadn't really made a great big effort of advertising and deep down I guess I was hoping it would flop.

We met Mary at the studio location, and I had cookies and punch ready for the new students and their moms. We spent the entire afternoon there, but only had twenty-five students enroll. I think Mary was the only one truly disappointed.

Pam had to go home the next day, and it was so hard to say good bye to her at the airport. I said, "If you decide you want to come back sooner, I will call Ginger, another dance teacher I know in the Amery area, and I'm sure she would take over the last two studios up there." Pam felt better just knowing she had a way out if she and Brad decided to take it.

With Pam gone, Kim and I started looking for an apartment. We found the one we wanted at the Tropicana Apartments on Harmon street. It was two bedroom with two bathes, affording us each our own privacy which I never wanted to lose again. With the new credit cards, I was able to pay the down payment and first month's rent. We moved in immediately.

Of course we had no furniture, so for the first few nights we slept on the floor. We checked the *Nifty Nickel* regularly to find bargains, and finally got what we needed.

The studio was obviously not going to make it. Not only was it a bad time of year to start, but I think Las Vegas already had enough dance studios. I hadn't cashed any of the checks given for enrollment, so I called and told them we would not be able to open at this time and mailed their enrollment money back. Actually, I was totally relieved I didn't have to start teaching again.

Kim and I decided we had better both get a job. She went to work immediately as a pool attendant at the *Lady Luck*. Meanwhile, the band I was working with went on the road, but now with Kim there, I had to stay. I really didn't want to go with them anyway.

The Lord was looking out for me again, and I found out the apartment complex was looking for a leasing agent with secretarial experience. The corporation hired me and I went to work immediately. The manager I worked for was an overweight, bleached blond, insecure woman who was married to a musician. She gave me a lot of problems because her husband would come into the office and talk music with me. He even volunteered to pick up some furniture for me and she almost had a fit. I told her I would get someone else if she didn't want him to help me, for I certainly didn't have any desire to steal her husband. She assured me it would be all right, but she continued to make trouble for me.

The final blow came when she made a fifty dollar mistake in her deposit and tried to blame it on me. The mistake was finally found, but if it had not been it would have looked bad for me. I decided right then and there I was not going to continue working for this company as long as they hired managers of her caliber. I could have done her job easily and she knew it, and that, too, was a another reason for her trying to sabotage me.

I started looking at the *Nifty Nickel* postings for work available. It had been many years since I was in the work force, but my eyes zeroed in on an ad that read, "Help, mother had a stroke." My heart just sank. I remembered how hard it was for me to find decent help with Daddy, and knew I was certainly qualified to care for someone with a stroke, so I called and made an appointment for an interview.

When I knocked on the door, I was greeted by a gentleman with silver hair. He was so nice, and invited me in and called his wife. Their names were Jack and Pat Dearen, and I instantly could tell they were the sweetest couple. She was a beautiful woman with blond hair who had worked as a cocktail waitress at the Union Plaza. Jack was retired, but did work at home with some type of crafts with mirrors.

Pat explained to me about her mother, Grandma Flo, who'd had the stroke. Pat said, "My daughter has totally taken over and we do not get along at all, but Flo is my mother." I could immediately detect a problem within the family and of course it was all too familiar to me.

They took me next door to their daughter's house, and she was a snooty person. In fact, I almost called her Yane. She was rude to her mother and barked orders like she was some kind of goddess. After she looked me up and down, she took me in to meet her grandmother. My heart sank as I said hello to this poor little woman. I asked which side of the brain had been affected, and the daughter said, "They told us the left, but it's her right side that doesn't work."

I explained to them how it is always the side of the body affected is opposite of the side of the brain the stroke occurred in. Then I took Grandma Flo's right arm, just like I remembered Monie doing on her interview, and tried to bend it. Grandma Flo screeched with pain and started swearing at me. The granddaughter, Dawn, yelled, "What are you doing? Stop that, you're hurting her!"

"She needs range of motion badly," I explained. "If you don't do that, she will be in more pain." I tried to explain the procedure to her, but she would not listen. She was just as hateful and overbearing as my sister, and I knew I could not work under that strain. I also realized quickly that I wasn't emotionally ready for such a job.

I followed Pat back over to her house, and she apologized for her daughter's behavior. "Believe me," I said sympathetically, "I know how you feel!" I told her about my experiences with Daddy, and after a pot of coffee and a couple of hours later, I really felt sorry for this wonderful couple.

I couldn't believe they had been sent home with her mother and not given any instructions. They knew nothing about range of motion, rehabilitation or anything else which I had taken for granted. I told them about Sister Kenny and about all the support I had received from them.

"They never told me anything like that," Pat exclaimed, "We are just on our own."

"Pat, emotionally I am not ready to work with your mother, but I will teach you what I know so you can take better care of her." I got up and asked Jack for his belt. I placed it around Pat and sat her in a chair. Then I taught her how to use it to transfer her mom into the wheel chair, etc. I told her about the bath bench, demonstrated the way to perform range of motion on her bad side and continued to inform her of as many things as I possibly could.

Finally, I gave her my telephone number and told her not to hesitate to call me if she needed anything or had any questions.

As I drove back to the apartment, I thanked God for all the support I had had with Daddy. I felt so sorry for these wonderful people. All they wanted to do was care for her mother. My heart just hurt for them.

I APPLIED FOR A FEW JOBS, BUT WAS OVER-qualified for most of them. When I put down my previous income and profession, they would assume I would only work until I could go back to singing or dancing. I learned fast how to play the game and began putting down only what they wanted to hear. I would put down that I was a cocktail waitress or food waitress at the *Country Dam* instead of a singer, and lowered my previous salary. It worked, too, and I got a job as a food waitress in a gourmet room at the *Royal Las Vegas Hotel.*

When I went in for the job, I was a little worried since I had never been a waitress in my life, but they had assured me they would have a girl train me. I told myself that I had better learn fast, or I would get into trouble of my own making. It sure would have been great if I could have imported Sissy to train me. She had worked with food most of her life.

That night Kim and I called Pam to tell her all our good news. She laughed when I told her I was going to be a food waitress.

"Mom, what are you going to do?" she asked.

"Probably get fired the first day," I laughed.

Then in a serious voice she said, "Mom, Brad and I want to come out there now and get a job, too. Could you talk to Ginger and see if she wants to take over the studios now and handle the recitals. I am scared to death about the recitals anyway."

I could tell she was really wanting to come to us, so I assured her I would call Ginger and see what I could work out.

After we had hung up, I called Ginger immediately. She was a sister to my dear friend Leroy Becker, so she knew our situation. She gladly took the studios without hesitation and assured me she would take care of the remainder of the year. I thanked her profoundly, but she just said she was glad to help. The Lord was looking after me again.

I called Pam right back and told her the good news. After all the squealing was over, they decided they would be there as soon as possible, probably within a week. I told them to totally liquidate my things and raise every penny they could. Brad decided he would buy a trailer and bring enough household goods with them to get us all set up. We had everything planned by the time we hung up.

Just before we hung up, I remembered Grandma Flo and asked Pam to pack all the supplies and equipment we had left from Grandpa so I could give them to Pat for her mother. She assured me she would, and that they would be here within the week. Everything was moving fast.

I called Pat and told her I would be bringing all of Daddy's supplies I had left over to her as soon as my daughter arrived with them, including all the manuals and instructions I had been given by Sister Kenny regarding range of motion and therapy.

She was so grateful, and I felt sorry for her. I had lived all the hurt I heard in her voice, including the pain she was feeling about her daughter's actions. They had not been able to find anyone to help that her daughter approved of.

The week went really fast. Kim loved her job and I was really nervous about starting my new one the next week. Pam called and told me they had everything done up north and would be there in two or three days. She hesitated, then said, "Mom, Cheryl and Danny are coming with us. They want to move to Vegas, too."

I totally blew my stack. "What in the hell do you mean Cheryl and Danny are coming with you? Pam, I'm not going to start taking care of other people's kids again. You don't know how hard it has been just getting settled out here!" I yelled and started to cry. Suddenly, I remembered all the hell I had gone through up north and the expense incurred by trying to be nice. It made me cry even harder.

"Mom, I'm sorry, but they said they will get a job and take care of themselves." I knew she didn't understand the way things were out here, but what could I do? I knew Cheryl would get work and take care of herself, but I couldn't have that many people living in one apartment. As far as Danny was concerned, I didn't know that much about him, but I really had a bad feeling about him taking care of himself. I just vowed that I would only take care of me and my girls, and not get an ulcer over the others. That was all I could do.

THE DAY THE KIDS WERE TO ARRIVE, KIM AND I were so excited we could hardly stand it. We had the apartment all cleaned up and ready, and I knew the manager I had worked for would try to find anything she could to bitch about, so I knew I would have to start looking for another place with the extra two passengers coming. If only Pam had just said "no" to Cheryl and Danny, then we would have had plenty of room, but she didn't know the situation out here. All she knew was, Mom had always had room for one more during her growing up years, and didn't understand how things had changed.

I was waiting for the telephone to ring so I could guide them to the apartment, when suddenly I heard Brad's truck pull in. I should have known Brad would find us without a guide. God, was it good to see my kids again, including Cheryl and Danny.

Immediately Brad and Danny started unloading the trailer. It was so good to see my sewing machine and a few other items I thought I would never see again. Pam and Kim were hugging and kissing and talking about all the things they were going to do in Vegas. I was just praying we could all find work and survive.

Pam gave me the box of Grandpa's supplies she had packed for Pat. I praised her and Brad for a job well done in taking care of the liquidations.

Pam said, "Mom, I know you really lost a lot of money, but we did the best we could," and she handed me a check for eight hundred dollars. "That's all we got from the auction barn," she sighed.

I couldn't believe what little they had cashed out at the auction for all my beautiful furniture. Daddy's Lazy Boy only brought $200.00. I was just sick, but knew the kids had done the best they could and had willingly taken all the responsibility on their little shoulders to help me. I put my arms around them and told them again how proud I was of them.

Then Pam said eagerly, "I want to take Brad and them on the strip and show them all the sights."

I looked at Kim and suggested, "Why don't you go with them and I'll start getting things put away here. I'll go with you tomorrow night." I really didn't want to stay out all night seeing the same things I had looked at for two months.

The kids all got dressed and hit the strip. While they were gone, my friend, Joe Martin, who was also my hairdresser, came over to visit. He said, "They are having a wine and cheese party at The Shark Club tomorrow afternoon. Do you want to go with me?"

I said, "Sure, that sounds like fun, but I have to go out with my daughters tomorrow night."

"Great," he said, "we can meet them somewhere."

The kids had a blast and slept in the next morning. When they finally got up, I told them about Joe and I going to a wine and cheese party.

Then I had remembered a friend of mine asking me to bring the kids to the Continental Hotel where his band was opening. He wanted them to help cheer them on that night. I told the kids how to get to the Continental and that Joe and I would meet them over there after we had gone to the party. They were excited and I left to meet Joe.

Everything went as planned, and Joe and I joined the kids at the Continental right before the band started. My friends were from Canada and delighted I had remembered to come. We started partying big time, really celebrating our reunion.

About eleven o'clock everyone was ready to go home. The kids were all still tired from the night before, and Joe, as well as Kim, had to be at work early the next morning.

Pam and I were not ready to go at all, and those Bacardi Cokes had been tasting mighty good. Besides, we had a lot to catch up on. I knew how Pam felt to be out from under all those responsibilities with the studios, plus getting everything ready for the move. We told everyone to go on home and we'd be see them later. Since the apartment was only a couple of blocks from the Continental, I knew we wouldn't get lost. I was starting my new waitress job the next afternoon, but right then I just wanted to visit and have some fun with my daughter.

We ordered us another round, and the band wanted me to sing a song, but I declined due to the fact I was celebrating a little too much. Pam was busy talking to me when she stopped and said, "For heaven sakes!"

"What are you talking about?" I asked.

"Mom, there he is!"

"There is who?" I asked, totally confused.

"There's that man you told us about!"

"Pam, what in the world are you talking about?"

"Don't you remember when you told us that the next time you got involved with a man he was gonna be tall, over fifty, wearing a white Stetson hat and preferably from Texas?"

"Yeah, so what?" I slurred.

"Mom, there he is," she whispered. I turned around to see who she was talking about, then said, "Mmmmmm, not too bad!" as I took another sip of my drink. He did look like the man I had fantasized about, but I was in no way going to get involved with anyone. Bob had hurt me enough.

But Pam kept nagging at me to ask him to dance. "Mom, he keeps looking over here! Just ask him to dance or give him the eye or something."

"Pam," I snapped, "will you shut up! I don't want to dance with him or anyone!"

"Okay," she mumbled, "but I think he's cute and you should get to know him." I gave her the, That's enough! look, and she hushed immediately.

Before long, the tall, good looking gentleman went to the bathroom or to make a telephone call or something. Pam was quickly giving me blow-by-blow bulletins of his whereabouts. Then he walked back in and stood by our table for a moment. Pam kicked me and looked at him. To make her happy, I turned around and the alcohol said, "Do you want to ask me to dance or are you chicken?"

His face turned bright red as he stuttered, "I think I'll ask you to dance." I was feeling no pain as I walked out onto the dance floor with him, and as we danced, I found out his name was Paul. He had come to audition the band that was going on after my friend's. He had never been to the *Continental* before and neither had I. When he told me he was from Texas, I almost fainted.

We danced just about every set, and he was nervous as he could be. He told me his wife had passed away five years ago after a thirty-three year marriage. I couldn't believe it when he said he had never cheated on her. I thought how lucky she had been, because as far as I was concerned, all men were bastards. But he seemed so unlike anyone I had ever met and I figured it was just the Bacardi Cokes doing the thinking.

Paul joined Pam and I at our table, and of course Pam was feeling like little *Miss Cupid.* Paul continued to talk about what a wonderful wife he had had, and I continued to talk about what a bastard I had had. He then told me what a wonderful life he had had, and I told him what a miserable life I had had.

I started bending his ear about all the men who had hurt me during my life, and I assured him I would never allow anyone else to hurt me again. He just sat there and listened with an open ear, and actually I think he was totally in shock.

Many feelings started surfacing that I had thought were hidden away forever. Why did I feel so comfortable talking to this man?

Paul asked me to dance again, and as he held me close on the dance floor, I had this overpowering urge to kiss him, which I did. He sort of staggered backwards in shock. It definitely felt like a kiss "hello" instead of a kiss "goodbye."

I couldn't believe what I had just done. Now, I knew it was time for me to make an exit before I gave him the total wrong impression—if I hadn't already.

I collected Pam and told Paul goodnight. He walked me out to my car and asked if he could take me out to dinner some night. I told him I was starting a new job tomorrow at the *Royal Las Vegas* and invited him to come over for a Caesar salad. Why I did that, I will never know, especially since I had no idea how to even start making a Caesar salad. Anyway, I guess I figured he was some tourist and wouldn't even know where the *Royal Las Vegas* was located.

Still thinking he was from Texas, I gave him my telephone number and he gave me his. I never expected to see or hear from him again. After all, I really didn't think I was what he was looking for. I was sure I had given him a terrible impression, after all, I had drank a few Bacardi Cokes and smoked at least a pack of cigarettes. He didn't drink or smoke, and after I thought about it, he never swore, either.

Paul closed my door and walked around to her side. Pam was so excited. She teased, "Mom, he really likes you."

"Pam, I will never hear from that man again," I assured her.

"Betcha do," she laughed. As we drove away, she spotted Paul getting into his Lincoln and she squealed, "Look, Mom, he even has his own car. I'll betcha he pays for your dinner, too! At least you won't have to support him."

"Pam," I said, "my supporting days are over, even for you and Kim. We're all on our own now."

The biggest headache I had ever had greeted me the first thing next morning besides my breath smelled like a human ashtray. Pam and I both headed for the Tylenol. Then she began telling Brad all about the man at the *Continental.*

"After the way I acted, I probably scared the hell out of him and I hope I did! I've got to concentrate totally on this new job." I was starting to get really nervous and besides, I had a hangover.

I was scheduled for the early evening shift. The gourmet room closed at ten o'clock, and I got dressed in my little white blouse, short black skirt, black high heels and headed for my new job.

The girl I was replacing, Torey, was really nice. She started training me for my new job and realized rather quickly that I didn't know beans from peas about being a waitress. She said, "Well, you're gonna learn fast cause I want to get out of here." She had plans to meet her friend in three days.

The girls who worked in the coffee shop were really nice, too. They were sisters, and I got to be really good friends with the one sister, Debbie. She helped me get my orders ready in the back and Torey took over when I got to the front. Believe me, after working that job, I have a lot more respect for waitresses now than I ever did before. They really have a hard job and deserve every tip they get, if they do a good job.

Fortunately, everything was really going well. The biggest mistake I had made was not having a customer sign his credit card receipt for $125.00. I was the luckiest girl on this earth, though, for he happened to be staying at the hotel and came right down and signed it after I had called in a panic. Otherwise, my first check would have paid for him and his party's dinner. I was learning fast.

I just about had my first day licked, as well as my headache, and it hadn't been easy. But I was pleased with myself. Suddenly I looked up and couldn't believe my eyes! There stood the tall man in the white Stetson, grinning from ear to ear. Paul! I was so embarrassed because now I was totally sober and felt really bad about the way I had acted the night before. Nervously I said, "Hi! I see you found the place."

"Yeah," he replied with a smile as he sat down at a table. Then he introduced me to one of his business associates who had joined him for, of all things, that damned Caesar salad!

Why couldn't someone have ordered a Caesar salad before now so I would have some indication of how to make it? My face turned red and I excused myself to find Torey to rescue me. She came over and put me through the paces on how to mix a Caesar salad at the table, and Paul could see just how little I knew about my new job.

The only good thing was they were the only customers at this time, and I was able to visit with them. His friend said, "I understand you woke Paul up last night with a kiss!"

I don't know whose face was the reddest, mine or Paul's. It was obvious he didn't want him to mention the kiss, and I quickly said with a laugh, "Well, I had a lot to drink, and believe me, I'm paying the fiddler today!"

They finished their salad, and I gave them the bill. Paul asked if I would join him at the Continental, after I got off, for a night cap. I smiled and said, "I might join you for a Coke, but I don't want any Bacardi for a very long time. And I'm done with cigarettes again!"

"I'll see you in a little bit over there, then," he said with a smile. I reminded him again that I needed to get home early because my job demanded my mind to be totally rested. He agreed it would only be for a short time.

My heart was pounding as he walked out of the room, and Torey teased, "Who was that? He sure seemed to have the eyes for you." I explained to her about the night before and she said, "Well, he looks like somebody very distinguished!" I thought, *Yeah, he does look just like my dream man!*

As soon as the shift was over, I hurriedly got out the door. I redid my hair, fixed my face and walked into the little lounge at the *Continental* where I had been feeling so good the night before. This time I was very reserved and a total lady. Paul stood up and scooted my chair out when I went to his table, and it was nice to see chivalry wasn't dead.

"I can only stay for a while because I've got to get home," I reminded him. Paul could see how tired I was and was very understanding. After one Coke, he walked me to my car and asked, "Would you like to go with me to Mount Charleston, on Sunday and have dinner at the lodge?"

I was so excited, but didn't want him to know just how much. I calmly said, "That sounds nice, but where is Mount Charleston?" He told me about this wonderful getaway he enjoyed going to located in the mountains about thirty-five miles away. I asked, "You are planning on coming back after dinner, aren't you?"

He could tell I was a little concerned about leaving town with him, and smiled reassuringly. "I'll have you back whenever you want," he promised.

Needless to say, the kids were all excited about my date with Paul. After all, Pam had their curiosity going about this man, and she grinned at me and said, "I told ya' so!"

Sunday came before I knew it. By then I was much more comfortable with my job and ready for my date with Paul. I had been so busy, though, I hadn't dropped the supplies off to Pat for Grandma Flo. I decided to ask Paul if he would mind taking me over to her house before we left for Mt. Charleston.

I called him and he was very accommodating. "I'll get there a few minutes early so we will have plenty of time," he promised me. I had never been around anyone that nice and caring before. He was blowing my mind!

Paul arrived right on time, and of course, he had to meet the entire package and receive the once over. I could tell he had won everyone's approval, even Brad's. After Steve, I had been told by the kids, Gregg, Clarion, Karen and everyone else that cared about me, "We're gonna check out the next one before you get yourself into another mess!"
So far, Paul was approved.

"Is this the box you're taking to your friend?" he asked politely.

"Yes," I said, and he picked it up. We said good bye and headed for his Lincoln. He put the box inside the trunk, then opened my door for me. I was so impressed! He really knew how to treat a woman. His Mama certainly had raised him right. I thought, Daddy sure would like this man, just like my little package did.

We arrived at Pat and Jack's house, and Paul took the little box out and followed me to their door. They both gave me a big hug and welcomed me with open arms. I introduced them to Paul, then we went next door to see Grandma Flo. Pat's daughter, Dawn, was a little nicer to me this time. I guess she might have assumed I knew what I was doing after Pat and Jack informed her about my experience with Daddy.

I visited with Grandma Flo again and checked her over for bed sores. She would swear at me for moving her, but I knew that was only a result of the stroke. I showed them how to move her with Daddy's transfer-belt, and went through as many techniques as I could in demonstrating some variations.

They were really shocked when Grandma Flo started yelling at me, and I very firmly said, "Now, listen, Flo, you know how to do this as well as I do! You're just bull shittin' your family to get your own way, aren't you? You know exactly what you're doing."

She gave me one of those you-got-me-figured-out grins I had seen so many times with Daddy. I tried to explain how important it was to keep her muscles working, and how they shouldn't let her manipulate them into not performing the range of motion exercises. "It's called tough love, and it has to be done for her sake.

"You also have to keep moving her around to avoid bed sores." I told them about the pressurized mattress and everything else I could think of that mattered.

Then I went though Daddy's supplies which contained the transfer-belt, blood pressure cuff, blue pads, brace I had purchased to strap Daddy's hand in place during transportation in the wheelchair, his arm slings, plus many more things I prayed I'd never need again. I patiently explained what each was and how it worked, and how best to overcome the hardships.

Pat was deeply grateful, especially for the Sister Kenny manuals on form, function, and use, which would, as it did me right from the beginning, help her understand what she was undertaking and how to properly care for her mother. She said, "What do I owe you for the supplies?"

I just smiled and said, "Not a thing, Pat, I'm just glad I could help!"

The whole time, Paul had just stood there observing me in total shock. We said goodbye, and again I told Pat not to hesitate to call if she needed me for anything. We got back in the car and Paul headed for Mt. Charleston.

As we drove, Paul was quiet for a while, then he laughed. "You are just full of surprises! You are certainly different than the woman I met that first night."

"I hope so!" I replied. "I really never expected you to call me after that night. Why did you?"

He thought for a moment, then said, "Well, Reta, I could sense a really special little spirit inside you. I didn't think the woman I met that night was the real one, and after what I just witnessed, I was right. But to tell you the truth, I never thought I would ever go out with a woman that drank or smoked, but somehow I was drawn to you, like it was meant to be."

I quickly let him know I wasn't smoking anymore and that night was just an anomaly. He was really happy to hear that.

Then I got a little nervous as I remembered my prayer when I had asked God to lead me to the right man if I ever got involved again. I began thinking about how strange everything had been, the way things had turned out for me since I had turned my problems and life over to God that Saturday morning in Minnesota. A chill ran up my spine as I thought, "Dear God, is he the one?"

Paul and I never stopped talking all the way up the mountain. I told him all about Daddy, and everything else I ever did in my life. I couldn't believe how comfortable I felt with him. It was like I had known him forever. I continued to tell him the story about taking Daddy out of Texas in the van, all we had gone through in Minnesota and Wisconsin, to when we had taken him home to Mama. He said looked at me in awe and said, "You should write a book about this. It would be a best seller, and probably an academy award movie!"

"You think so?" I asked with a laugh.

"I know so," he answered enthusiastically.

"Well, maybe someday I'll give that some serious thought," then told him about Ma wanting to write my life story.

"Sounds like you have a lot to write about," he said laughing.

"She thinks so," I replied, "She keeps saying the Lord is just testing me, and if that's true, I will be glad when He's done."

I never had any one ask me so many questions in my entire life, and I felt like I was being interrogated.

After a pleasant drive, we arrived at Mt. Charleston and I loved it up there. I could readily see why Paul loved this place for a getaway. We sat by the open fireplace and I drank Mt. Charleston coffee, while he drank hot chocolate. We had a beautiful dinner and listened to a tremendous band called *The Dumkopff's.*

I finally asked Paul about himself, and he told me he had been a Navy pilot all through the Korean War, and after he was discharged worked for his father in the lumber business. In fact, he showed me some of the artifacts from his father's lumber mill on display at the *Mt. Charleston Hotel.* He then worked as a banker to put himself through college.

After graduating with a Master's Degree in Fine Arts, he had substituted for the professor of Fine Arts at the University of Alabama.

Since then, he had been a real estate broker, architectural draftsman, and artist for the Mardi Gras in Mobile, Alabama, where Mardi Gras first began in the United States.

By this time my head was spinning. "What did you do after that," I asked. He thought for a moment then told me he had moved back to Las Vegas where he worked as a portrait artist for approximately one year. He had then graduated at the top of his class from the Las Vegas Police Academy, then worked in the Crime Scene Investigations Department as a police artist for the next three years.

After that, Paul went into the District Attorney's office for six-and-a-half years where he was promoted to chief investigator. From there, he was hired by Howard Hughes to be his Director of Intelligence, which he did until Hughes' death. Then he became an adviser for the Howard Hughes Estate for the next four years. During that same four year period he had also worked secretly on unsolved murder cases for the City of Las Vegas Police Department.

By this time he totally had my attention. I sat there with my mouth wide open for the next few minutes, and for the first time since I had met him, nothing came out. I was in total shock! Now I could also understand why he had asked me so many questions coming up the mountain. He had actually been interrogating me to see what kind of a person I was. Evidently, I had passed his test—he hadn't run yet!

When I finally got home that night, we knew each other's pasts, plus our hopes and dreams for the future. He kissed me goodnight and made a date to meet me after work the next night. As I went to sleep that night, I thought it was he who should write a book!

TWO MONTHS LATER, I WAS STILL MEETING PAUL after work each night and spending every waking hour with him. The kids were all working and we had moved to larger quarters. Kim was still a swimming pool attendant at *Lady Luck,* and Pam was working in the little coffee shop at *Royal Las Vegas* as a food waitress where I worked. Brad was busing trays at the *Golden Nugget,* Cheryl was housekeeping at the *Hilton* and Danny had long gone back to Wisconsin...still owing me money!

One night Paul picked me up after work and we went to the *Continental* for a drink. He was acting rather mysterious that night, and finally said, "Let's go somewhere private. I want to talk to you." He took me over to the *Alexis Park Hotel.* I had no idea what he was up to. We had such a good friendship going, and I couldn't imagine him messing it up by trying to bed me. We walked around for awhile and continued to talk, but he was different in some way.

Finally, we went into the lounge and ordered a drink. He took my hand and said, "I want to ask you a question and I want you to really think about the answer before you say anything." Now he really had me wondering. "If you had all the money you needed, what would you do?"

I laughed then said immediately, "Well, I would pay off my Daddy's funeral bill and all the other bills I owe."

"No," he replied, "let's say you had all your bills paid, all your personal needs met and you had a large sum left to buy or do anything you wanted to. What would it be?"

I thought for a moment, then said, "I guess I would go to Winters, Texas, buy that hell hole they call a nursing home and give the old people a decent place to live out their last days, complete with honor and dignity!"

I continued to tell him all the wonderful things I would do for my children, my aunt Sissy, my Uncle Humpty, my brother Cecil, my adopted mom, Louise, and all the people I loved. "Why are you asking me this?" I asked suddenly.

"Well, I want to tell you something about me. I have multi-millions in assets, but not much liquid. I guaranteed a building company for some friends, and when they didn't meet their obligations, I was held responsible for the entire project. Then my wife's five-year illness cost over three hundred thousand in medical bills, so between the two, my liquid cash was pretty well eaten up." He now had my full attention. I had just been happy he could afford to take me out and supply his own vehicle. I couldn't believe what I was hearing.

Paul continued, "My brother, Frank, and my nephew, Brady, and I are about ready to close some financing which will have the liquid flowing again. I want you to be part of this, and I would like to say I am so impressed with what you would do if you had money. It's obvious you're not a greedy person. You never once mentioned anything you would do for yourself, only what you would do for everyone else. I knew that was the kind of person you are. You're definitely a giver, but now it's your turn to be a receiver!"

He went on and told me their financing should close within the month, and I would be able to pay off all my bills, especially Daddy's funeral bill. We talked some more about the future and he told me he had never dreamed of falling in love again, but he had started to really care a great deal about me. He also told me how much he liked my daughters. I confessed I was feeling the same way about him.

That night I couldn't sleep and sat out in the living room. Somehow, I knew Paul was the answer to my prayers, the reason my Navigator had directed me to Las Vegas and why I couldn't leave. I had a really long talk with God that night, and by the time the sun came up I felt as though I had made it to where He wanted me to be.

I was still sitting in the living room chair when the kids got up. I told them what Paul had told me, and they, too, were shocked.

Paul called me that morning to see how I was feeling. "Well, considering you just blew my mind last night, I guess I'm fine," I answered.

"I got something else I want to talk to you about," he said with a laugh. "I didn't sleep much last night either. Let's go get some breakfast," he suggested.

I agreed and quickly got dressed, unable to imagine what else he was going to tell me. Pam and Kim were going nuts with curiosity as they went off to work. I said, "I'll fill you in later."

Paul picked me up within a few minutes, and again we went to Alexis Park. He said, "I didn't sleep much last night, just couldn't get you off my mind."

"That makes two of us," I replied.

Paul put his arms around me and said, "I now know I'm in love with you. I know we haven't known each other that long, but I do love you and want to marry you!"

I almost fell out of my chair. After I regained my composure, I said, "Paul, I love you as much as I'm capable of loving anyone at this time, but I don't understand why you want to get married so soon!"

He explained his religion to me, and told me that marriage was the only way he could have a close relationship with me and feel right with God.

My mind was trying to figure everything out, but in the process only jumbling my thoughts. I did know that everything was moving too fast, and also realized I was not emotionally ready for such a big decision at this time. Lord knows I had been too fast to say, "I do!" in the past, and I didn't want to blow it again.

Paul was persistent and explained how we could go through the motions of getting married on Catalina Island by a ship's captain three miles out into international waters, have a short honeymoon on the island, return to land, but never really have to file the marriage.

I couldn't believe what I was hearing! I looked at him and snapped, "What kind of a marriage are you proposing? It sounds to me like you just want a nice romp in the hay with a gal, make it legal enough so you will feel peace with God, then go back to land and say thanks for the relief."

If he had only known how much abuse I had suffered in my lifetime in the name of love, he would have never made such a selfish proposal. I was so angry and humiliated! I just couldn't believe my ears.

I realized Paul was really confused by now and didn't know why his idea had not made a big hit. Worried, he again assured me how much he cared for me and that he meant no insult by his proposal. He explained he was just under a tremendous strain with losing his wife of thirty-three years and frustrated at not being allowed to have any type of a relationship without feeling a strong guilt. He had always walked close to God, and assured me that, until he met me, he had not met anyone he cared to be with. With the mood broken, I told him I had to think it over.

Paul took me back to my apartment, and I gave him a kiss goodbye and felt rather sorry for him because I knew he cared for me, but even though I also cared for him, the bizarre proposal had just about blown me away!

Again, I didn't sleep much. I remembered my prayer at the wayside park before I left Minnesota when I had asked God not to let me get tied up with another man unless he was the right one.

Paul was a gentle man and I knew he would be good to me and my family. By morning, I had decided to go with him to Catalina. After all, if his religion was that important to him, then he had to be a very special person!

When I got up the next morning, Pam and Kim where wide-eyed and all ears to find out what had happened the night before. They almost flipped when I told them the news. Of course, I didn't tell them about not filing the marriage. I was still trying to digest the entire thing myself.

"Mom, are you sure he's the right one?" Kim asked seriously.

I laughed, "With my track record, who can tell? I've always heard you have to kiss a lot of frogs before you find the prince, and Lord knows, I hope he's the prince and not another frog!"

I refilled my coffee cup and dialed Paul's number. He was delighted when I told him of my decision then confided to me, "You know, I didn't sleep much last night either. I did a lot of praying and God revealed to me that you and I would have a future together, so when we get back from Catalina, we will keep the marriage certificate and decide later if we want to make this marriage forever. If we do, then we will have another wedding, after the financing comes through, where everyone can attend!" I agreed and we planned our trip for the following weekend.

After I hung up the telephone, I told Pam and Kim of our plans. Pam pouted, "Can we go, too?"

"Not this time, honey. Later after the financing comes through, we are going to repeat our vows and have a nice wedding where everyone can be there," I explained.

"When will that be, Mom?" Kim asked.

"Well, if the bank Paul is dealing with comes through like he thinks they will, it will be really soon."

Paul called back within a few minutes and told me I could give notice at work if I wanted to because he would take care of my needs. I couldn't believe my ears! No one had ever taken care of my needs since Daddy. I quickly called my boss and he was able to replace me right away.

Paul came over, and true to his words, gave me the funds to take care of my pending bills. I had to pinch myself to see if this was really happening. I then called Mike at the Winters Funeral Home and told him I would be able to pay Daddy's funeral bill off within the next couple of months. He said, "I think you are more worried about it than I am."

"I will either send the full payment or hopefully I will be able to pay you in person. I plan to come to Winters soon."

He assured me everything would be all right until I could pay the bill in full, and because of our conversation, I didn't send him the $50.00 due that month. I was completely sure I would be able to pay it in full.

THE WEEKEND FINALLY CAME, AND I WAS SO nervous I could hardly stand it. When Paul picked me up, the kids gave him a big hug and their total approval, including Brad, and off we went to the airport.

The trip on the ship out to Catalina was really fun. I had never been on a ship before, and Paul was really enjoying watching me have fun. We met with Tom Sturdivant, the ship's captain. He was a retired fireman and was really a bubbly man. He took us three miles out into the waters on his big ship and married us. It was just Paul, myself, the captain and a couple of witnesses. It was a beautiful ceremony, held under the stars with just the rushing of the water around us. We sealed it with a kiss and somehow I felt truly married to Paul, even though I knew better. We honeymooned on the island for three wondrous days, then reluctantly returned to Las Vegas.

Everyone was so excited when we got back. I couldn't believe how fast everything moved, but I felt like this was what God had chosen for me, and I felt like Paul was the man he had picked for me to spend my life with. I had never felt so safe and secure in my entire life. He handled the bills and all the responsibilities, just like I always had heard a husband should do. For the first time in my life, I had someone to work with me instead of against me.

I moved into Paul's apartment at Harbor Island and the kids decided to go back to Wisconsin and wait for the financing to come through. They had lost their enthusiasm for Las Vegas.

Paul continued to try and close the financing he was working on. For a wedding gift, he told me he was going to build a new facility in Winters, Texas for my nursing home. I had decided I wanted to call it *Fuller-Merck Care Center*, and the facility would be a memorial to my mother and father. It would be a modern facility, staffed by professionals, just like the ones who cared for my Daddy. I wanted to hire a big team who demonstrated the same love and caring as had my little team up north.

Unfortunately, Paul was having some problems with the financing, but told me to go on to Winters and locate the property where I wanted to build my nursing home. He said he would join me in a couple of weeks. Apparently the Savings and Loan scams had really created some problems within the finance world, and it seemed no one wanted to make a decision by himself anymore. No one seemed to trust anyone, especially within his own company. Of course, the learned attorneys, otherwise known as cloacas, were always on hand to kill the deals unless they personally could find a way to work themselves into a deal. That's what Paul was dealing with each and every day.

I began making plans to go to Winters, and Paul told me I would be able to pay Daddy's funeral bill off by the end of the month. However, before I left I received a call from my brother, Cecil. He said, "Reta, I just got a call from Yane and she is madder than hell." That in it's self didn't really surprise me, for she was always looking for something to complain about. He continued, "We both got a bill from the funeral home advising us you hadn't paid last month's payment. I knew what was going on, since you had called me about your new husband and told me he was going to pay the funeral bill off. But she was really going crazy!"

"What did she say," I cried.

"Well, I don't think you want to know, but she said she was going to get an attorney and find out just what you did with all of Daddy's money, and that if you hadn't squandered it all away, you could have paid Daddy's funeral off in full. She then said you were ruining her Daddy's good name in Winters," Cecil finished.

"Cecil," I cried, "did she even ask if I was okay, alive or anything?"

"No, she just wanted to sue you." He then assured me he hadn't been concerned when he got his notice, for he knew I had everything taken care of.

I was sure glad I had mentally divorced myself from Yane and made her a mere void in my life or that would have hurt me more than it did. I cried, though, and Paul held me. I said, "I thought when Daddy died I would never let her hurt me again, but she just keeps coming back, like a bad dream!" I sobbed. "I wonder if she ever thought I might be dead or sick. Obviously, she doesn't care. In fact, I think she will rejoice when I am gone. She only cares about her good name and Daddy's money, at least the money she thought he had in her sick mind!"

After I had stopped crying, I called Mike and asked him what happened. He was unaware a billing had been sent to Yane and Cecil. Evidently, his office had sent one out not knowing about the conversation

I had had with him. Mike felt really bad and assured me something like that would never happen again.

I said, "Well, I should have made those last two payments, then none of this would have happened, but since I had discussed it with you, I didn't think it would be necessary!"

Again, he reassured me not to worry about it. Of course, he didn't know that it had only given my hateful sister more fuel for her fires.

Paul put me on a plane to Texas. I was so excited! My Uncle Humpty, Elton Merck, his wife, Betty Ruth and their son, Elby, had moved in with Sissy for a while following his open heart surgery. I hadn't seen them for a very long time, and was really excited when I arrived and they were at the airport to pick me up. I happily told them all about Paul and our whirlwind romance and marriage. I filled them in on my plans for the nursing home and assured them their life would be better soon.

Sissy returned from the boat and was just as excited as the rest of us. We were looking for the property to build my nursing home when Paul called one evening, completely devastated. He told me the financing he had been working on was killed off by the cloaca representing the bank he was dealing with. This attorney, with all his wonderful knowledge, had advised his clients, the bank, not to give any commercial loans at this time.

I was devastated, too. After I told Sissy and Humpty the bad news, I called the kids and told them, too. I also advised them to go ahead and find jobs to keep them going because Paul was going to have to start all over again with another bank. I then called Mike and told him I wouldn't be able to pay Daddy's funeral off after all, but he could rest assured the payments would always be on time. He assured me, again, I would never have any more problems with a bill being sent to my sister.

While I waited in Winters for Paul, I visited the nursing home known as The Hell. I felt so bad when I met Janie Richey, one of Daddy and Mama's neighbors from Content. She told me Earl, her husband, was in the nursing home. She, like Aunt Emma had done with Uncle Virgil, was there from the time he opened his eyes until the time he closed them at night. Being there was the only way a family could be sure their loved ones were being cared for properly.

I went in to say "hello" to Earl. I'm not sure if he really knew who I was, but I sure knew him. It broke my heart when I tried to perform range of motion on his legs. They were permanently bent from sitting so many hours in a wheelchair and not being exercised. I was shocked when Janie told me he had walked in there on his own. He was only suffering from Altzeimer's disease. But now, through neglect, he was totally bedridden. When he laid down, his legs remained in the sitting position.

To this day, I still have nightmares from what I witnessed that day. I accompanied Earl and Janie to the cafeteria. There were five little old women sitting at a round table with an aid in the circle. The aid was shoveling a spoonful of food to one little mouth and then to the other. They looked like little birds being fed. If they didn't have their food swallowed by the time they were to received the next spoon full, it was just poked into their mouth. They would pull away and gag, but the food kept coming. After witnessing this for awhile, I couldn't stand it another moment. I stood up and yelled, "My God, are you trying to choke them or what? Let them swallow!"

The aid yelled back, "I'm doing the best I can, lady, there are only two of us to handle all of these patients!" I looked around and there were at least forty or fifty patients in this hospital on total care and only two aids, plus one nurse up front to take care of them all.

After checking into the matter further, I found out the state was trying to close them down due to the conditions found there. I had seen animals treated better than that. I talked to the young aid later and apologized. She admitted, "It's horrible around here! We do the best we can, but we need help desperately."

I started back to Earl's room and saw an old man sitting in his wheelchair in the hallway. He begged, "Please, little girl, will you give me a glass of cold water?" I ran as fast as I could to get him some cold water. When the others saw him getting cold water, they started begging for the same. I knew now how this place had earned its name.

For the rest of the day I worked with the patients. One old man was begging for his bed so I said, "Do you know which one is your room?" He pointed to a room, and by gosh, I pushed him toward it. I asked, "Which bed is yours?" and he pointed to the one by the window. I pushed his wheelchair over to the bed, took the filled urinal out of the bed, grabbed one of his belts out of the closet, put it around his waist and transferred that poor old soul into bed.

The little aid stopped by and said, "That's not his bed, his is the other one." I said, "Well, he's got this one now. You can change him later!" The old man was already fast asleep. He was still in his street clothes, and I realized most of the patients slept in the same clothes they wore during the day.

At the end of the day, I promised the little aid I would be back everyday to help them for as long as I was there. She and the other girl were so appreciative. They were both excellent and caring people, but there is only so much one person could do.

The horrors I witnessed during the next few weeks will never leave my memory. I got to bed at night, but could still see some of those pitiful little faces. My heart broke as I thought of my Uncle R.A. dying there. I was so thankful Aunt Emma and Janie were there to care for Uncle Virgil and Earl.

Sissy and I would ride our bicycles over to Aunt Emma's house just about every evening when I got home from The Hell. The horrors I told her about did not surprise her. She would cry and say, "Shug, I witnessed that for seven years. Now you understand why the old folks here call it what they do. I tried to help back then, but I had all I could do to take care of Virgil," and she started to cry as she told me the things she witnessed back then.

Every night I called Paul and told him of the horrors I had witnessed that day, and how I prayed we could build my nursing home as soon as possible. "Paul, I will never allow my Auntie Em or Sissy to be put in The Hell Hole!" Paul was so sweet, and I could tell he was as frustrated as I was. If I could have gotten my hands around those cloaca's necks, I would have choked them to death.

The financing Paul was trying to put together was going to be spent on projects to better humanity. He said, "Sweetie, the old devil knows we are only going to do good things with this money, and you know he's in charge of this world for the moment."

"God's stronger than the devil," I cried, "Why doesn't he stop him? Paul, these people are awful! I've got to get that nursing home built immediately."

Paul felt as bad as I did, but his hands were tied. The economy had gone to hell and the banks and other lending institutions were not loaning any moneys at all. He had finally been able to find a firm willing to take some of his properties for a three-to-one dollar back program, that is, if their attorneys didn't find a way to kill the deal. He was really hopeful this program would produce the moneys we needed to kick off all our programs.

Meanwhile, Sissy, Humpty and I had found the exact property where I wanted my nursing home, the Fuller-Merck Care Center, built.

I had also gotten together with a friend, Kyle Mansell, who I hadn't seen since our school days. He and his family had run on to some hard times, too, and he was like Paul, asset rich and liquid poor. He had been trying for the past two years to save their dying John Deere business which had been in his family as long as I could remember. He had been unable to shake any money loose from his bank or any other lending institute, either. They just didn't want to talk to him. "Well, you gotta prove you don't need the money to get it," he said dryly.

We rekindled our friendship, and Kyle was anxious to meet Paul and possibly work with him in the future.

I had everything worked out for the projects I wanted to do in Texas, but Paul just kept running into problems. Real estate was at an all-time low, and it was definitely a buyer's market. However, the banks and lending institutions were all hanging on to their money for dear life.

Absolutely no one was getting commercial loans, thanks to the cloacas who had scammed the Savings and Loans.

Pam and Kim had gone to work at Constant Care, a nursing home in Amery, Wisconsin. They couldn't believe the horrors I was telling them about the Winters nursing home. Pam said, "Mom, our patients are spoiled rotten up here, like Grandpa was treated. Mr. Dixon runs a tight ship."

Kim added, "Yeah, Mom, it's so good here, I wouldn't have worried about Grandpa being in here at all!" They just couldn't comprehend the horrors I was telling them. They understood now why I had fought so hard to keep Daddy at home. As far as I was concerned, all nursing homes were like *The Hell.*

Each night I called and talked to Pam and Kim when I got home from *The Hell* so they could assure me all nursing homes were not like this one.

Then one night Paul called and told me everything was on hold, but he was coming to Winters to get me and also to get out from under all the strain for a few days. I was so happy, for I wanted everyone to meet him. I had to laugh when Sissy said, "Well, I can't wait to meet him 'cause he's either the most generous man I've ever known or he's crazy as hell."

Humpty laughed, "Hell, I ain't never met a millionaire before!"

"Well, at least he's still a millionaire in assets," I sighed, a little discouraged.

Paul flew to Winters, but only got to stay for three days before one of his finance people called and assured him they would be able to close on one of his projects.

Everyone fell in love with Paul during his short visit, and he felt the same about them. Sissy decided he was, indeed, the most generous man she had ever met, and Humpty realized Paul put his pants on the same way he did and really liked him. Even my Auntie Em thought he was the nicest little ole ' boy she had ever met.

When we were alone, Paul told me he was really proud to be part of my family. "Your people have really nice spirits living in them. They're definitely choice.

When I introduced them, Kyle and Paul got along like they had known each other forever. Paul assured him he would be part of our group whenever things started rolling our way.

Finally we said goodbye to everyone and flew immediately to Phoenix, Arizona. We hoped to find good news there.

WHEN WE GOT TO PHOENIX, WE FOUND THE lender's attorney had killed that deal, too. Absolutely no one could make a decision, and the government was closing banks daily. All of the little big men were scared to death of losing their jobs.

Discouraged, we flew back to Las Vegas where we stayed for the next few months, trying to get a bank to back us. Everything was on hold again, but Paul was always trying other avenues. I knew he would someday get the financing through and I would have my nursing home, but I also knew the economy had to turn around first. Together we prayed God's will would be done. After all, it was His plan.

Through all of this, I was getting mentally stronger by the day and my mind and body started to heal from the turmoil I had been through the past few years. Paul was wonderful to me, and I had never been with anyone that treated me as good as he did. When he heard me sing with some of my friends at the *El Dorado Rodeo,* he exclaimed excitedly, "You can't give up singing! All you need is a few doors opened and you could do an album!"

He also encouraged me to write, and day-by-day I was getting to know who Reta Lee really was—and she wasn't such a bad person! I thought, *How sad her big sister never really knew her.*

Auntie Em or Sissy would call and let me know when one of my old friends would pass away in that Hell Hole they called a nursing home. Earl Richey passed away not too long after I left, and each time one of my old friends died, I would thank, God, for taking them home and out of that place. I would then ask God to please help Paul get the financing through so I could build them a safe place to retire. But I knew it was to be on His schedule.

FOR THE NEXT FOUR YEARS PAUL AND I TRAVELED extensively. We visited New Orleans, Key West, Texas, Mississippi, California, plus many other interesting places. For me, it was like being on a perpetual vacation. Everyday, we kept hoping things would turn around in the financial world, but to no avail.

Sometimes Paul would withdraw into depression, as he did in the past, and I felt like I was living with two different men. I missed Pam and Kim so much, at times I could hardly stand it. I questioned myself many times as to whether I had made the right decision to stay with Paul. Should I have just got on with my life and given him the freedom he seemed to want so that he could get back into his religion. If I talked to him about my feelings, he would deny how he felt.

Many times, he would decide, and all of a sudden, that we should just be friends and business associates. Our relationship had become more of a friendship than a marriage. I knew Paul was still not feeling good about the mock marriage, for he had planned to have a real wedding after he got the financing through. But the financing just didn't seem to happen, and he wasn't interested in trying to just live a somewhat normal life. He was hell-bent on the big financing coming through before we did anything.

After awhile, I realized my life was going nowhere and I got more unhappy by the day. Paul seemed to keep withdrawing with every financial upset. His health was deteriorating and I knew we had to make some drastic changes immediately. I sure didn't want to wind up miles away from home with no money and Paul into a deep depression.

Each time Paul arranged for more money, he would return to normal and start talking about our future again—together. I felt like I was on a roller coaster and the ride would never end. I couldn't go forward and I couldn't go backwards. I was not progressing at all and neither was Paul.

I had met a lot of cloacas throughout our travels. However, most of them wanted Paul to do something for them, instead of helping to get our financing through. The worst ones I met were the brokers, which usually turned into a daisy chain of brokers. These cloacas were always trying to get in the middle of our deals.

Paul taught me more about financing than I ever dreamed was possible. The only financing I had ever done was simply conventional. I had never worked with ten figures in my life, or ever dreamed of such, but there I was in the middle of it all, and absorbing knowledge like a sponge.

I have heard every excuse in the book, and then some, but Paul had the patience for the job. Patience is something I never had or probably ever will have. I got so sick of hearing the same excuses! For instance, "It's in the mail!" or "It will be ready tomorrow!" or "We're playing catch up from the holiday!" or "So-and-so's out of town!" or "You know nothing happens on Mondays!" or "We're just so busy!" plus all the other everyday excuses why they didn't move their butts.

We were in Baton Rouge when our money started to run out again, and I finally convinced Paul to work on the financing in Minnesota and Wisconsin. I wanted to be with Pam and Kim, plus back home in my element where I could make some money on my own and feel more secure. He agreed, and I introduced Paul to Wisconsin in October when the leaves were starting to turn. I knew, he being an artist and all, that he would love the area and maybe decide to make our home there. I hoped his health would start to improve so he would start feeling better about life.

One of the first things I did was try to locate my old band, *Pure Gold,* but they were all scattered. The economy was still so bad the lounges were only hiring single piece bands or duets.

Brad taught me how to use an electronic band and I started working alone to keep my voice in training until the financing came through for me to record my first album. The money wasn't all that great, but sometimes it was all we had.

Paul started having a rough time trying to raise going money through investors. He helped me with my equipment, moving from club to club. He cheered me on and kept my hopes up that someday I would get my chance at the big time in country music, but after a few months my hopes started to die and my mind was more geared to survival.

Then Paul made a deal to rent, with an option to buy, a white cedar, three-story log home on eighty acres with a private lake in Wisconsin. He knew how important it was to me to have some roots, and I was so tired of traveling. All I wanted was a safe place for Pam and Kim. He knew how much I had missed having a home to take my children to during hard times in the past. Only God knows how much I had missed my Mama and a home to return to during those years. I wanted Pam and Kim to always have a safe place to go if they needed it. It was so good to have my entire family back together.

Paul truly believed the money would come through and he would be able to purchase the home, but to no avail. He kept slipping further into depression and his health continued to worsen. I tried to get him to check himself into the Veteran's Hospital, but he refused. He would always say, "I can't do anything until the financing comes through." I prayed that God hadn't forgotten us.

DURING THE NEXT YEAR, PAM AND BRAD DECIDED to go their separate ways, but to remain friends. Actually, friends were about all they really ever were.

Pam began dating a nice young man named Bryan Aubert, a junior at the University of Minnesota. Not to be outdone, Kim was dating another nice young man named Blain Martin, a fire-fighter who dreamed of being on one of the big fire departments one day. I really liked both Bryan and Blain, and so did Paul.

Brad had become engaged to a young lady named Sue Cook. Everyone was happy with their new partners, and I was happy that everyone was happy.

Pam and Kim started to go to school in New Richmond at WITC taking accounting and computers. Brad also started school in Rice Lake at WITC to become an engineer. Cheryl had a good job and was living on her own. I was impressed with how the kids were progressing. They each had a goal in life, but were still praying Paul's financing would eventually come through.

They received a lot of flack from some of their friends and family, but I assured them the people that teased and made fun of their dreams were very shallow and had no vision. However, sometimes I had second thoughts myself and wondered if the financing would ever come though.

Unfortunately, the economy got worse, and a new presidential election set the financing world into a tailspin. Everything came to a screeching halt for the next year, and Paul had one disappointment after another, but he never gave up his dream. I tried to keep Sissy, Humpty, and all my loved one's hopes up, but each day it got harder to do.

Finally, I decided to start teaching dancing again, against Paul's advice. We were behind on our bills, including the rent. Our landlord, Joyce, was a wonderful lady. She had helped me tremendously with my singing engagements, and had even helped carry in equipment and pack up with each show. She was middle-aged and the house was all her husband had left her after he had died of cancer. She was hanging in waiting on Paul's financing to come through, too. It seemed like all of our lives revolved around the damn financing.

I selected studio locations for the following year and commenced getting business in order. Paul kept assuring me the financing would come through, but after six years, I couldn't take that chance. I was not going through another year like the last one, and I didn't know from day-to-day what Paul was going to do. His health got worse and the depression continued. Sometimes he only got dressed to go help me on the weekends.

I was so unhappy, but I wouldn't abandon him. I received notice that Daddy's funeral bill was paid in full, and was pleasantly surprised when Mike told me someone had paid the remaining one thousand dollars, but wanted to remain anonymous. That was a great relief not to have it hanging over my head.

FINALLY IN THE WINTER OF 1994, PAUL GOT HIS FIRST real break in the financing arena. He was into six figures instead of ten, but it was the break we needed to make it all happen and be able to kick off all our projects—including the *Fuller-Merck Care Center* and my singing career. Pam and Kim took care of our home in Wisconsin and we packed my little Escort, which had become well known in the area as, Reta's Little Limo, with all my equipment, then packed what we could into the old Lincoln and headed for Las Vegas in the dead of winter. I truly believed this time we were finally going to get our chance.

Paul had designed some customized cars throughout the years and believed he had the backing needed to kick off that program. He wanted to work immediately on that project as soon as we got to Las Vegas.

Late one Sunday afternoon we arrived, and it was only through the grace of God that those old cars made it. We immediately rented an apartment by the week and barely had the money to cover that, but by the end of the first week, one of Paul's business associates told us we could stay at one of his houses he was trying to sell. It was empty and we had no furniture, but at least we had a roof over our head. We slept on the floor and I got enough things out of storage to halfway set up house keeping. I set up my equipment in the front room and immediately started rehearsing.

Another of Paul's business associates had assured me he would have me booked into one of the hotels immediately, but like the financing, that never happened, either.

After two months, I decided to find a club to rehearse in with real live people. I needed someone to sing to. I also needed a place to get exposure so I could try and make some going money. Jobs in Las Vegas are few and far between, but I did find a little club on the south end of Las Vegas Boulevard. It not only had a real stage, but it even had stage lights.

Eager to be singing again, I set up on a Friday night. The place was packed with construction workers, but they were very respondent to country music and made me feel really welcomed.

Later on in the evening, a man walked into the bar and sat down. He was about fifty-five years old, tall with a full head of salt-and-peppered hair. He ordered a drink, but never took his eyes off me. He seemed to really enjoy my singing and made several requests. He also tipped me after each song, and those tips were the only money I received for the evening. I could sense he was different from most of the bar crowds and I couldn't take my eyes off him, either. He really made me feel like a star.

At break time, which I rarely took, I went over to him, smile and said, "Hello, I'm Reta Lee, and I really appreciate your support."

He smiled broadly and said, "I'm John Milam, and I really enjoy your singing. But what is someone who sings like you doing here?"

"Well, I'm still waiting on my big break," I said with a laugh.

"Could I buy you a drink?" he asked politely.

"After I get done tonight you can, that is, if you're still here. I don't drink when I'm performing. I stick to my hot water and honey. That way I can be sure of pushing the right buttons," I explained.

"Smart girl," he replied with a warm smile. From the conversation, I assumed he was a truck driver and this was his local hang out. He made me feel really comfortable in the club, and somehow I knew he would always watch over me if he was there. I played that little club four nights a week, and each night Johnnie was there to cheer me on.

Finally, Paul was able to get some substantial going money, and we were able to rent a nice apartment. With the credit I had established, I was able to get furniture and other items needed to furnish it. Then we made arrangements for the kids to come for a visit. I was so excited, for I hadn't seen them in four months. Paul made arrangements with one of the hotels for complimentary tickets for the girls.

Paul was so sure this time that the financing would come through that he called Little Richie Johnson, a well known producer and promoter he had known many years ago and made arrangements to fly to New Mexico to talk to him regarding his producing and promoting an album for me. Needless to say, I was really excited. After all this time, it was finally going to be my turn!

I went to the club that night and sang my heart out. I could hardly wait for my truck driving buddy, Johnnie, to show up so I could tell him all about my forthcoming album.

Johnnie was late getting to the club, but as soon as he walked in, I took a break. He smiled at me and said, "What are you so happy about?"

I quickly told him all my good news, but instead of pleasing him, his smile slowly faded. He swallowed hard and asked sadly, "Will I ever see you again?"

I gave him a hug and said, "Of course you will! I will be back just like a bad penny!" At that moment, I knew he cared a great deal for me, and I also knew I had grown very fond of him, too.

THE KIDS ALL CAME FOR A VISIT, AND KIM DECIDED to stay in Las Vegas with us, but Bammer went back to Wisconsin with Pam and Bryan. I knew she really was going to miss him.

The trip to New Mexico was overwhelming for me. Little Richie agreed to take me as a client and produce my album. Kim and I started immediately screening new songs from various song writers submitted to me by Little Richie. Paul had given him an overwhelming budget to work with, but of course, all this was contingent to the financing coming though.

Then Paul introduced me to his long time friend, Jack Kogan, who had his own talk show being broadcast out of Debbie Reynolds' hotel. Jack was instrumental in introducing me to some very interesting and influential people in the entertainment world.

Jack is a kind-spoken man with a lot of energy. He enjoys helping young people get started, and I might add, he knows just about everyone who is anyone in the entertainment world.

His co-hostess is Ginger Williams, a beautiful lady with silver hair. She had been an actress on the silver screen during her younger days, and was still a beauty. She has become one of my dearest friends and confidant.

Ginger came to see me perform at my little club several times, and one night coming home from the club, we were discussing the book I was writing, *The Ingredient Called Love*. She was extremely interested in Daddy's story, and I said, "My mother always told me God had a reason for everything he did. Sometimes we may have to wait to see that reason, but He always had one." I looked at Ginger and continued, "But until this day,

Ginger, I still haven't figured out the reason why God took her from me when I was so young."

Ginger looked at me very calmly with her beautiful blue eyes and said, "Reta, through your mother's death you gained the strength you needed to get through the tragedies you've had to face in life. My heart tells me that's one of the reasons your mother was taken at that time," she said softly.

All of a sudden, after all these years, what Ginger said made sense. I did have to face the world on my own at a very young age, and yes, it did make me strong.

Somehow, with incredible insight, this wonderful lady had helped me to deal with Mama's death after all these years. From then on, I could understand why God had taken Mama from me when I was so young.

Paul and I still got away to Mt. Charleston whenever we could, and on one of our trips up the mountain, we went to the hotel. I heard a fantastic country voice coming from the lounge, and we immediately went in to see who was singing. We met John Windsor, an Englishman, who had been in America a little over a year but was singing country music like he was an American. We invited John to Jack's radio show and was really happy when Jack had a spot to interview him.

Since then, John and I have done a few local shows together in Vegas.

Before we knew it, summer was over and we were still waiting on someone in the finance world to move their butt. Kim had started modeling and was starting to do quite well. She was selected as one of the featured extras in the movie, *Casino*, starring Robert Deniro, Joe Pesci and Sharon Stone. It wasn't a big part, but it was a part. Kimberly, like her mother, dared to dream, and now those dreams were coming true.

In September, Paul told me the financing would be through by the middle of October, and told Kim and I to fly to Wisconsin and see Pam, then he would met us in Nashville to start working on my album. The first week of October, Kim and I flew to Wisconsin to visit Pam, and Paul was sure he would have everything wrapped up in two weeks.

Well, one month passed and the financing still hadn't happened. I told Paul I would give it until November first, then we were coming back to Vegas so we could go to work. In the mean time, we enjoyed visiting with Pam and Bryan.

Before we knew it, November arrived and we were still waiting on the financing. I made arrangements with Joyce for her son to move back into the log home, and we moved our belongings over to Pam and Bryan's apartment. The majority of the stuff, though, we shipped back to Las Vegas. I knew in my heart that home would never be mine, and I also knew Joyce couldn't keep hanging on. Her children were really giving her a lot of problems regarding her waiting for Paul's financing to come through, and I knew giving it back would take a load off her shoulders.

Unfortunately, Kim and Bammer decided to go their separate ways and try to just remain friends. Pam reluctantly took us to the airport and Kim and I returned to Las Vegas with our tails tucked between our legs like sad puppies.

BACK IN LAS VEGAS AGAIN, I IMMEDIATELY CALLED A small club on Boulder Highway which had told me to call if I ever needed work in Las Vegas. I went to work immediately four nights a week, and Kim notified her agencies she was back and started working again.

Meanwhile, Paul went further into depression and his health started worsening. Our relationship had been over for some time and all he talked about was the financing and his religion. Many times, I wished we could just go our separate ways. I had not been happy with Paul for a very long time and I knew I was standing in the way of him and his religion, and he was standing in the way of me progressing in life.

As far as a relationship, we had not had one for so long I couldn't remember. He pursued his financing and I tried to keep singing. I was extremely unhappy.

I called my following in Las Vegas to let them know I was back and where I was singing. I wanted so much to see my friend, Johnnie. I called his house, but could never catch him home. I even called Bob Mikes who I thought was Johnnie's boss. He assured me he would let Johnnie know where I was and that they would all come out to see me. I really needed to see my friends!

Paul's health got worse and so did his depression. We decided he should check himself into the Veterans Hospital and try to get himself straightened out. They admitted him immediately. The depression had worsened to the point where he couldn't keep his food down. All he talked about was getting back right with God. I told him to do whatever he had to do and I would try to pull things together for Kim and myself.

We were left in a total mess. I needed two hundred more dollars to cover rent, the Escort was running on one cylinder and I needed three thousand dollars a month just to pay all the bills. I knew my album was down the toilet and so was my credit unless a miracle from God happened, and quick.

Kim and I sat down and tried to figure out some way we could make it. In desperation, I called John Windsor and told him about Paul's admission to the hospital and about the sad condition Kim and I were left in. He helped me get my car running, for it was in bad need of a tune up.

He also sold the old Lincoln for enough money to finish paying our rent. He helped us as much as he could, and I thanked him profusely.

I booked into another club where I could make a little more money, but it was impossible for me to make the kind of money I needed. Deciding to trade the Escort in on a new car while it was still running was planning because I knew we would have to go back to Wisconsin if we couldn't get enough work in Vegas. I knew we damn sure couldn't make that trip in the Escort. Our living expenses in Las Vegas would force us to relocate, and I knew I could make pretty good money at a ski resort in southern Minnesota. I made all of these plans in my mind, but didn't want to tell Kim until I saw no way out.

After a few weeks at the Boulder Highway Club, I knew I had to find another club that would pay more money. I was working myself to death four nights a week and not making enough to make it worth my while. So, I contacted another little club on Boulder Highway and worked there for awhile, in fact, until it closed. Then I started singing at another little lounge on Tropicana. The owner knew my situation and gave me three nights.

Wisconsin was getting closer, and I knew this would be the last club in Las Vegas I would try. I would have to go home.

I was so embarrassed to write my friends and tell them I was back in Las Vegas and my album was on hold. I really had egg on my face, but I had to face them and tell them my dream of recording an album was still just a dream. At least the club owner gave me the postage I needed to let them all know were I was. I only could call a few when I started on Boulder Highway.

What I really was hoping was my friend, Johnnie Milam, would show up for my opening. He had always been such a strength for me, and I really missed him. I called him to see if he had gotten my invitation, but he was not home. I figured he was driving a truck over the road. I knew Bob and Lee Mikes would give him the message as they had before.

In frustration, I called and talked to Lee. She was so sweet and assured me that Johnnie would get the message.

The following weekend I opened. I looked for Johnnie, Bob and Lee, but to no avail. This new club was clear across town from where they were used to seeing me, so I thought I might not ever see them again unless I moved back to their area.

I didn't have a stage at this new club, in fact, they moved two big trash cans and that spot became my stage. I was co-starring with a pool table, and my following was not happy with the tiny little room he had put me in. I still had some faithful followers who supported me regardless of the circumstances.

Kim was getting some modeling jobs, but nothing steady. My pay was awful, and I didn't know what I was going to do, but I knew I had to do something within the next couple of weeks. I said a prayer and hoped He heard.

One Sunday afternoon I went to work and the owner asked to talk to me. I knew his crowds were not doing what he expected, but with the conditions he had me playing under, I didn't know what he expected me to do about the situation. I had to turn my volume up to get over the pool players and I was practically playing for tips. He told me he was either going to cut my pay or cut back to two nights.

Totally devastated, I knew my hands were tied. He was in no way going to put that damned pool table in my room and bring my show out front. I began my first set with tears in my eyes. Thank God for Sue, Rick and Marlene, three wonderful people who were always there for me. They were the only ones in my back room, and I prayed that God would help me through the night. As usual, the pool players started cracking pool balls, and the bar crowd increased their volume—and so did I in my little back room.

While I sang, I decided I would leave for Minnesota or Wisconsin within the week. I knew there was no hope here and the money would not be any better anywhere else in town.

About nine o'clock I looked to my right and couldn't believe my eyes. There stood two of the sweetest faces I had ever looked at—it was Bob and Lee Mikes grinning at me from ear-to-ear! I quickly gave them a hug and asked excitedly, "Is Johnnie coming, too?" If Bob and Lee had come to see me, I knew Johnnie would more than likely meet them.

Lee smiled and said, "He'll be here later." My heart began to pound and I didn't want to be disappointed if he didn't show up.

They took a seat at one of the little tables and ordered a drink. I knew God had heard my prayer. I so needed to see some more of my dear friends. I sang some Patsy Cline songs for Lee and Bob, their favorite requests, and as I sang, I kept watching the door for Johnnie. Apparently he was late. Lee kept assuring me he would be there. I didn't know until then how much I missed him!

About eleven o'clock that night, the door opened and Johnnie walked in. My heart jumped right into my throat. To this day, I still don't know what I was singing at that moment. He was wearing a tan sport coat and looked like a million bucks. He slowly walked toward me, smiling that wonderful smile I had missed so much. As soon as he got close enough to where I could reach him, he got the biggest hug he ever got from anyone! He put his arms around me and suddenly I felt like I would be okay.

Johnnie ordered a drink and joined Lee and Bob. Immediately, I began to sing his favorite songs. After singing to him all those nights in the past, I knew exactly the ones he wanted to hear. For the first time in a very long time I felt like singing.

Before I knew it, the old clock on the wall said it was time to go. I sang my closing song, said goodnight to everyone, then started putting my equipment away. Rick, Marlene and Sue assisted me as usual. They had been such a support to me, I will always love them.

I looked up and saw Lee, Bob and Johnnie heading for the door. Frantically, I ran up to them to say good night. Lee said they had to get on home because of work the next day. Even at that time, I still thought Bob was Johnnie's boss. I thanked them for coming to see me, then looked at Johnnie and asked, "Can you stay for one drink with me?"

He smiled and answered, "Sure!" and I gave Bob and Lee a hug and thanked them for coming.

Together, Johnnie and I walked over to the bar. He ordered us a drink as he always did after I finished my show. He knew I never drank when I was working, but I would always have two drinks when I got off the bandstand. He sat down on the bar stool and I stood next to him. When the drinks came, he asked softly, "Are you okay?"

"Not really," I answered. "I've got a few personal problems and it looks as though I might have to go back to Wisconsin so I can make a living."

He looked totally confused and asked, "Where's Paul?"

I quickly told him about Paul's condition and how he wanted to get back to his church and how Kim and I were left on our own.

"How much do you need to see you through so you don't have to go back to Wisconsin?" he asked quickly.

I outlined our needs and he told me he would help. I knew he made good money driving trucks or whatever, but I didn't want to put him in a financial bind just because I had a problems. He assured me he could handle the loan and told me to meet him the next day and he would loan me what I needed. I was so relieved, this was the first time in months I felt the stress lifted.

Then Johnnie asked me about the backing on my album. I said, "Well, I guess that is just a thing in the past. The money just never came through to complete that project."

He smiled his incredible smile and casually asked, "How much do you need?"

I told him and he very nonchalantly said, "I'll back you. You've come too far to give up your dream. I know all you need is a break and you could make it. You're a damned good singer and I believe in you."

At that moment, tears came to my eyes, and I said, "Johnnie, I really appreciate you, but I don't want you to get yourself into a bind for me."

He just smiled and said, "Don't worry. I can handle it!"

I went straight home that night and woke up Kim and told her the good news. We both prayed that Johnnie was for real. After seven years of disappointments, it was hard not to be pessimistic. I said, "Well, I'm going to meet him tomorrow, and just maybe he means what he says."

I went to bed shortly after talking with Kim and asked God to please let Johnnie be for real and truly in a position to help me with my career without jeopardizing his own well-being.

The remainder of the night was a restless adventure, and I dozed off intermittently feeling nervous and insecure. Finally, towards sunrise, I fell asleep.

The next day he gave me the loan he promised, and said, "Now, when do you want to meet with Little Richie in Albuquerque?" What?#!/! You gotta be kiddin' me!

Needless to say, I was totally overwhelmed. I couldn't believe he was really going to try and make my dreams come true, with the album as well as taking all the financial stress off me, too.

He said, "Baby, you've been waiting on the 'If come' (that's Las Vegas jargon, by the way) for so long, you don't know a real promise when you get one! You'll soon find out something about me, sure 'nough. When I tell you I'll do something, you can count on it."

I can truly say that from that day forward, Johnnie has done everything he said he would do—even more. He took me to New Mexico to meet with Little Richie, and two months later I was in the Alta Vista Studio recording my first album. I named it *Dare To Dream,* in honor of people like my Johnnie who gave me such hope. And by the way, Johnnie didn't work for Bob! Bob actually worked for him, along with many other employees. He wasn't a truck driver but owned a fleet of trucks along with a lot more investments, even including race horses. To this day, I still don't know if he can drive an eighteen-wheeler or not! But quite frankly, I really don't care! Between the two of us, we'll be driving my bus until we decide to hire a driver, which will probably be after the *Hey Baby... Tour* is long over. Johnnie Milam is quite the business man and I know he will make wise investments for me; that is, as soon as I have any money to invest!

Daddy always told me, "Piss Ant, always give a 150 per cent performance, even if you have only one person in the audience." He was certainly right, as one never knows what truck driver, share cropper, school teacher, or corporate CEO may one day be sitting in the audience and who might be that one special person to make your dreams come true and provide the opportunity for you to *Dare To Dream* even more.

12

Hey Baby...Que Paso? was picked by Little Richie Johnson (Albuquerque, New Mexico) as the single from my first album to be released internationally. He has 58 number one hits to his credit, and he believed *Hey Baby...* would make it to the hallowed ground of number one on the independent chart. He was right! **It hit number one!**

Johnnie Milam (Manager and Executive Producer) and I formed Reta Lee Enterprises, Inc., and opened an office in Las Vegas, Nevada, which Kim manages along with her modeling career. She is also engaged to a young man from Las Vegas, Jerry Swope. Jerry is a baseball pitcher and hopes one day to be drafted by a major league team; he is a good pitcher, but most of all, he is a wonderful young man. Currently, Jerry is also modeling, and finds that particular new career path very exciting. Pam opened my office in Wisconsin, which she manages along with her dance studios. She is engaged to another super guy, Bryan Aubert, and they've been together for two years now. Bryan is in college and studying to be a chiropractor. I couldn't be happier about the young men my daughters have picked to marry. They both have my total blessing.

I recorded my second album, *Dreams Come True*, and it's doing well. In fact, *Ship of Fools* on that album, *Dreams Come True*, hit #1 on the Airplay International Chart in early 1996; already *Hey Baby...* hit #1 on the Airplay International Chart in 1995 on the *Dare To Dream* album! I was selected the C.M.A.A. King Eagle Female Rising Star for 1994-95, and my *Dare To Dream* album was picked as the King Eagle Rising Star Album for 1994-95. I have also signed with Foxfire Records in Nashville, Tennessee, located in the United Artist Tower. God has certainly blessed!

My very successful *Hey Baby... Tour* took us through the southwest and into Winters, Texas, where I saw my Auntie Em again, and checked on Daddy and Mama's graves. From there we went to Louisiana to see Humpty and Betty Ruth. Sissy met us at Humpty's house. Oh yes, we went to Weatherferd, Texas, and visited my brother, Cecil. No, we didn't have any plans to visit my big sister, Yane, as that will have to be put off until the next lifetime in the cosmos, off in a remote corner somewhere in God's country, somehow, with His help. She is still a void in my life, and since my decision regarding the matter, I am a much happier person. I don't have to worry about her criticizing my singing, my albums, my band members, or anything else, not anymore. Funny how that works—

The *Hey Baby... Tour* wound up in Nashville where I performed at the American Eagle Awards, and had a marvelous time and met so many wonderful people. From there, we traveled through the upper midwest, then made our way back to Las Vegas. We visited many radio stations along the way and held autograph sessions in each town. Johnnie said I would never again have to work anywhere I didn't want to, and certainly not have to work three jobs at the same time! What a blessing! I can truly say that I have never been so happy in my entire life. God has looked down on me and truly smiled. Maybe Louise was right: God was testing me all those years to make me truly appreciate the good things that have happened to me in the past few years.

Johnnie Milam is not only my best friend, he is also my business manager and confidant. How we met was, in a sense, a sort of destiny for me. Thank God! He came to the place where I was singing and continued to come back, time and again.

I thank God for my life, my daughters, my friends, and for having given me the most wonderful father and mother a daughter could ever have. In writing *The Ingredient Called Love,* I learned a great deal about myself. This book has been better therapy for me than any doctor I could have ever gone to. It has made me truly appreciate those very special persons in my life who truly care and love me. I am so thankful my parents allowed me to *Dare To Dream* and encouraged me to be the best person I could be, just as I have, in turn, done the very best I can to instill those same virtues in my daughters, Pam and Kim. I thank God for answering my prayers. I thank Him also for the lesson I learned from my favorite poem, Footsteps. I know he was truly carrying me during those times when I thought he might have abandoned me, but instead, He delivered me safely to where I am today.

MY ADVICE TO EVERYONE WHO READS MY WORDS, DARE TO DREAM: DON'T BE AFRAID TO FOLLOW THOSE DREAMS. SET YOUR GOALS HIGH, SO HIGH YOU HAVE TO PUSH HARD EVERY DAY TO REACH THEM. HAVE A VISION AND FOLLOW IT. LIVE UP TO YOUR OWN STANDARDS NOT SOMEONE ELSE'S, AND NEVER ALLOW ANYONE TO PUT YOU DOWN. ABOVE ALL, BE TRUE TO YOURSELF. GOD LOVES YOU AND SO DO I.

I would like to close with two poems I wrote in memory of my wonderful parents.

"Mother"

She was gentle and sweet, so loving and kind;
She taught me so much in just a short time;
She was a loving mother and a faithful wife;
A friend to all throughout her life.
The values she gave me were sent from above;
Caressed in her heart and told with much love;
She was here on this earth only forty-one years;
And to lose her so young, I shed many tears.

I was so blessed to have her, even for a short time;
You see, God had a plan for her brilliant mind;
I'll see her again in that mansion someday;
But until then, I'll just have to pray,
that God will guide me and so many others,
to walk in like footsteps...and be more like my mother.

"Father"

He was so full of life, so gentle and warm;
He always loved me and kept me from harm;
He was a giant among men until that dreadful day;
When a stroke took his mind and half his body away.

Now I cared for his life so gentle and warm;
For now it was my turn to keep him from harm;
My love for my Daddy extended his life;
And with help from above, we dealt with frustrations and strife.

But God had a plan, so he was not healed;
Through the death of my Daddy, it meant others might live;
A much closer life with the ones that they love;
Then God will smile down from his throne up above.

THIS IS FOR YOU, DADDY...

An Ode To Brody

You betcha—

TO ORDER ADDITIONAL COPIES OF:

"THE INGREDIENT CALLED LOVE."

Ship to: (please print)
Name:

_____

Address:_____

City-State-
Zip:_____

Telephone No:_(____)_____

"THE INGREDIENT CALLED LOVE"
            ____copies @ **\$14.99 EACH** $_____
POSTAGE AND HANDLING:

UNITED STATE ADD **\$2.00** EA BOOK $_____
OR ADD $ 3.00 *PRIORITY MAIL* $_____

CANADA ADD **\$2.00** *EA BOOK SURFACE MAIL* $_____
OR **\$5.00** EA AIR MAIL $_____

OVERSEAS ADD **\$3.00** *EA BOOK* SURFACE MAIL $_____
OR **\$12.00** *EA AIR MAIL*

TOTAL AMOUNT ENCLOSED $_____

MAKE CHECKS PAYABLE TO *"RETA LEE ENTERPRISES, INC."*

ALL CREDIT CARDS ACCEPTED: CARD:_____ NO:_____

EXP:_____ CARD HOLDER'S SIGNATURE:_____ _____

MAIL TO: 3957 SOUTH EUCLID AVE. LAS VEGAS, NEVADA
89121 U.S.A.   TEL: 702-734-7406   FAX: 702-734-7393